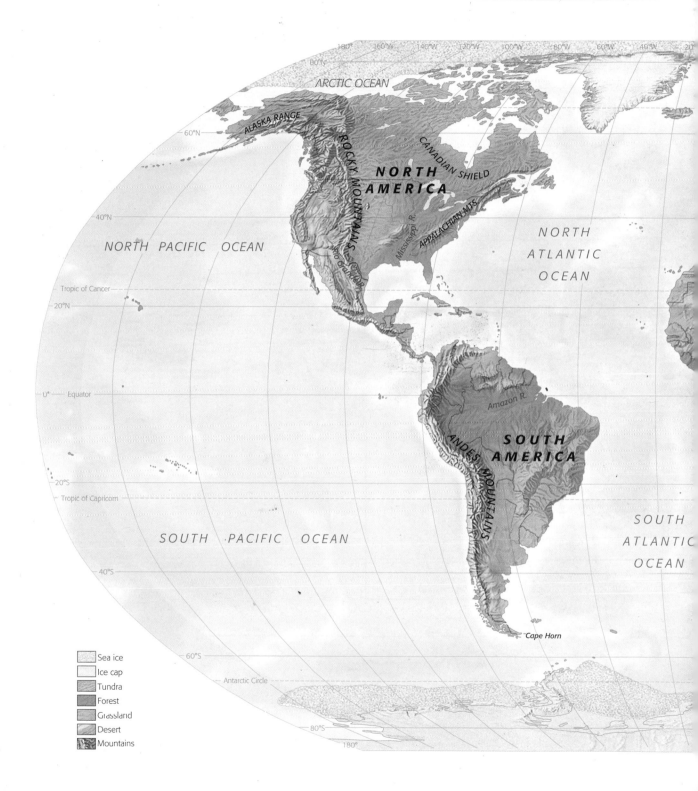

ARCTIC OCEAN

ALASKA RANGE

NORTH AMERICA

ROCKY MOUNTAINS

CANADIAN SHIELD

APPALACHIAN MTS.

Mississippi R.

Rio Grande

NORTH PACIFIC OCEAN

NORTH ATLANTIC OCEAN

Tropic of Cancer

Equator

Amazon R.

SOUTH AMERICA

ANDES MOUNTAINS

SOUTH PACIFIC OCEAN

SOUTH ATLANTIC OCEAN

Tropic of Capricorn

Cape Horn

Antarctic Circle

Sea ice
Ice cap
Tundra
Forest
Grassland
Desert
Mountains

ARCTIC OCEAN

EUROPE

ALPS

URAL MTS.

Volga R.

Ob R.

ASIA

GOBI

HINDU KUSH

HIMALAYA MTS.

SYRIAN DESERT

SAHARA

Nile R.

Indus R.

Ganges R.

DECCAN PLATEAU

AFRICA

80°N

60°N

40°N

Tropic of Cancer

20°N

PACIFIC OCEAN

Arctic Circle

0°

INDIAN OCEAN

NAMIB DESERT

KALAHARI DESERT

Cape of Good Hope

AUSTRALIA

GREAT SANDY DESERT

20°S

Tropic of Capricorn

N

0   1,000   2,000 Km.

0   1,000   2,000 Mi.

60°S

Antarctic Circle

ANTARCTICA

80°S

180°

Voyages in
World History

Voyages in World History

VOLUME 1: To 1600

Valerie Hansen

YALE UNIVERSITY

Kenneth R. Curtis

CALIFORNIA STATE UNIVERSITY LONG BEACH

WADSWORTH
CENGAGE Learning™

Australia • Brazil • Japan • Korea • Mexico • Singapore • Spain • United Kingdom • United States

WADSWORTH
CENGAGE Learning™

Voyages in World History
Valerie Hansen and Kenneth R. Curtis

Senior Publisher: Suzanne Jeans

Senior Acquisitions Editor: Nancy Blaine

Senior Development Editor: Jennifer E. Sutherland

Consultant Development Editor: Jean L. Woy

Associate Editor: Adrienne Zicht

Senior Marketing Manager: Katherine Bates

Marketing Coordinator: Loreen Pelletier

Marketing Communications Manager: Christine Dobberpuhl

Senior Content Project Manager: Christina M. Horn

Senior Media Editor: Lisa Ciccolo

Art Director: Jill Haber

Print Buyer: Arethea Thomas

Permissions Editor: Terri Hampton

Text Designer: Henry Rachlin

Art Editor: Charlotte Miller/Janet Theurer

Photo Researcher: Linda Sykes

Copyeditor: Susan Zorn

Cover Designer: Faith Brosnan

Cover Image: Caravan crossing the Silk Road, detail of the map of Asia, from the *Catalan Atlas,* Spain, Majorica, 14th century. Photo: Kunstbibliothek, Staatliche Museum, Berlin/Bildarchiv Preussischer Kulturbesitz/Art Resource, NY.

Title Page Photo: *Universale descrittione di tutta la terra conoscivta fin qui,* by Paolo Forlani, 1565. From the Rosenwald Collection, Library of Congress, no. 1304.

Compositor: NK Graphics

For product information and technology assistance, contact us at **Cengage Learning Customer & Sales Support, 1-800-354-9706.**

For permission to use material from this text or product, submit all requests online at **www.cengage.com/permissions.** Further permissions questions can be e-mailed to **permissionrequest@cengage.com.**

Library of Congress Control Number: 2008938670

ISBN-13: 978-0-618-07723-6

ISBN-10: 0-618-07723-5

Wadsworth
25 Thomson Place
Boston, MA 02110-1202
USA

Cengage Learning products are represented in Canada by Nelson Education, Ltd.

For your course and learning solutions, visit **www.cengage.com.**

Purchase any of our products at your local college store or at our preferred online store **www.ichapters.com.**

Printed in the United States of America
1 2 3 4 5 6 7 12 11 10 09 08

BRIEF CONTENTS

CONTENTS

CHAPTER 1 **The Peopling of the World, to 4000 B.C.E.** 2

TRAVELER: Kennewick Man

CHAPTER 2 **The First Complex Societies in the Eastern Mediterranean, ca. 4000–550 B.C.E.** 28

TRAVELER: Gilgamesh

Note: All images are copyrighted. For full photo credit information, please see each chapter opener page.

CHAPTER **3**

Ancient India and the Rise of Buddhism, 2600 B.C.E.–100 C.E.
60

TRAVELER: Ashoka

CHAPTER **4**

Blueprint for Empire: China, 1200 B.C.E.–220 C.E.
88

TRAVELER: First Emperor of the Qin Dynasty

CHAPTER **5**

The Americas and the Islands of the Pacific, to 1200 C.E.

114

TRAVELER: Yax K'uk Mo'

CHAPTER **6**

New Empires in Iran and Greece, 2000 B.C.E.–651 C.E.

144

TRAVELER: Herodotus

CHAPTER **7**

The Roman Empire and the Rise of Christianity, 509 B.C.E.–476 C.E.

174

TRAVELER: **Polybius**

CHAPTER **8**

Hindu and Buddhist States and Societies in Asia, 100–1000

208

TRAVELER: **Xuanzang**

CHAPTER **9** **Islamic Empires of Western Asia and Africa, 600–1258**   238

TRAVELER: Khaizuran

CHAPTER **10** **The Multiple Centers of Europe, 500–1000**   268

TRAVELERS: Gudrid and Thorfinn Karlsefni

CHAPTER **11**   Expanding Trade Networks in
Africa and India, 1000–1500   300

TRAVELER: Ibn Battuta

CHAPTER **12**   China's Commercial Revolution,
ca. 900–1276   328

TRAVELER: Li Qingzhao

CHAPTER **13**

Europe's Commercial Revolution, 1000–1400

356

TRAVELERS: Peter Abelard and Heloise

CHAPTER **16**

Maritime Expansion in Afro-Eurasia, 1500–1700

450

TRAVELER: **Matteo Ricci**

MAPS

Visual Evidence

Movement of Ideas

WORLD HISTORY IN TODAY'S WORLD

PREFACE

What makes this book different from other world history textbooks?

- Each chapter opens with a narrative about a traveler that grabs the reader's attention.
- Shorter than most world history textbooks, this survey still covers all of the major topics required in a world history course.
- The book's theme of "movement" highlights cultural contact.
- A single authorial voice makes many comparisons among different societies, reinforcing what students have learned in previous chapters.
- Innovative, reader-friendly maps show the travelers' routes while inviting students to think analytically about geography and its role in world history.
- A beautiful, open, student-friendly design—with chapter outlines, bold key terms, and an on-page glossary and pronunciation guide—helps students learn better.
- Chapter-opening focus questions and chapter summaries (which can be downloaded to an MP3) help students grasp the main ideas of the chapters.

This world history textbook will, we hope, be enjoyable for students to read and for instructors to teach. We have focused on thirty-two different people and the journeys they took, starting ten thousand years ago with Kennewick Man (Chapter 1) and concluding in the twenty-first century with the film director Mira Nair. Each of the thirty-two chapters (one for each week of the school year) introduces multiple themes. First, the travelers' narratives introduce the home society and the new civilizations they visited. This demonstrates the movement of people, ideas, trade goods, and artistic motifs. We introduce other evidence, often drawn from primary sources, to help students reason like historians. Each chapter also covers the effects of increasing contact and trade among civilizations, changes in political structure, spread of world religions, and finally, the prevailing social structure and gender.

These chapter-opening narratives enhance the scope and depth of the topics covered. The travelers take us to Mesopotamia with Gilgamesh, to Africa with the hajj pilgrim Ibn Battuta, to Peru with the cross-dressing soldier and adventurer Catalina de Erauso, to the Americas with the African Olaudah Equiano, and to Britain during the Industrial Revolution with the Russian socialist Alexander Herzen. They wrote vivid accounts, often important sources about these long ago events that shaped our world.

Chapter 12, for example, tells the story of the Chinese poet Li Qingzhao. She lived during the Song dynasty (960–1275) and experienced firsthand China's commercial revolution and calamitous warfare. Her eyewitness account of her husband's death brings this pivotal period in Chinese history to life. Students also learn about the contacts between China and Japan, Korea, and Vietnam during this time of economic growth. In Chapter 24, the focus is on the great Japanese reformer Fukuzawa Yûkichi, an influential participant in the revolutionary changes that accompanied his country's Meiji Restoration (1868).

Students new to world history, or to history in general, will find it easier, we hope, to focus on the experience of thirty-two individuals before focusing on the broader themes of a new society each week. Instead of a canned list of dates, each chapter covers the important topics at a sensible and careful pace, without compromising coverage or historical rigor. Students compare the traveler's perceptions with alternative sources, and so awaken their interest in the larger developments. Our goal was to select the most compelling topics and engaging illustrations from the entire record of human civilization, presented in a clear spatial and temporal framework, to counter the view of history as an interminable compendium of geographical place names and facts.

We have chosen a range of travelers, both male and female, from all over the world. Many travelers were well-born and well-educated, and many were not. The Scandinavian explorers Thorfinn and Gudrid

Karlsefni (Chapter 10) and the blind Chinese sailor Xie Qinggao (Chapter 20) were born into ordinary families. These individuals help cast our world history in a truly global format, avoiding the Eurocentrism that prompted the introduction of world history courses in the first place.

The book originated at a meeting in 1998 that reviewed twenty or so of the most important world history textbooks on the market. Most of the books seemed similar and all felt encyclopedic. They were crammed with facts, big as phone books, and hard to read. Everything about these books was sacrificed for the sake of comprehensiveness. Few of these texts conveyed the excitement—or pleasure—of studying history.

When we asked Ken Curtis to join the project, he responded very cautiously to the idea of co-authoring a traditional world history textbook. But eventually the chance to write a different type of book, one focusing on the experience of individual travelers, one that worked toward making students enthusiastic about world history, won him over.

Achieving the right balance between the traveler's experience and the course material has certainly been a challenge. After circulating draft chapters to over 120 instructors of the course, we have found that most agree on the basic topics to be covered. The long process of revision resulted in our giving less space to the traveler and more to the basic themes of the book. We realized that we had achieved the right balance when the reviewers asked for more information about the travelers.

In this way, our book is self-contained but open-ended, should instructors or their students wish to do more reading. Some instructors may decide to devote some time in their lectures to the travelers, who are indeed fascinating; students, we hope, will naturally be inclined to write term papers about them. Almost all of these travel accounts are available in English translation, listed in the suggested readings at the end of each chapter. If instructors assign readings in addition to the textbook, they can assign those travel accounts from the world area with which they are most familiar. Where a Europeanist might assign additional readings from Herodotus, for example, an Asianist might prefer to assign the narratives of the Buddhist pilgrim Xuanzang.

We aspire to answer many of the unmet needs of professors and students in world history. Because our book is not encyclopedic, and because each chapter begins with a narrative of a trip, our book is more readable than its competitors, which strain for all-inclusive coverage. They pack so many names and facts into their text that they leave little time to introduce beginning students to historical method. Because our book gives students a chance to read primary sources in depth, particularly in the Movement of Ideas feature (described below), instructors can spend class time teaching students how to reason historically—not just imparting the details of a given national history. Each chapter includes discussion questions that make it easier for instructors new to world history to facilitate interactive learning. Each chapter closes with answers to those questions: a feature in response to student views as expressed in focus groups.

Our approach particularly suits the needs of young professors who have been trained in only one geographic area of history. Our book does not presuppose that instructors already have broad familiarity with the history of each important world civilization.

Volume 1, which covers material from the first hominids to 1500, introduces students to the important regions and societies of the world: ancient Africa and the Americas (Chapter 1), Mesopotamia and Egypt (Chapter 2), India (Chapter 3), China (Chapter 4), and the Americas again (Chapter 5). The next section of the book emphasizes the rise of world religions: Zoroastrianism in the Persian empire (Chapter 6); Rome's adoption of Christianity (Chapter 7); the spread of Buddhism and Hinduism in East, South, and Southeast Asia (Chapter 8); and the rise of Islam (Chapter 9). The final third of Volume 1 focuses on the parallel commercial revolutions in Europe and China (Chapters 12 and 13) and the gradual increase in knowledge about other societies resulting from the Vikings' voyages to Iceland, Greenland, and Newfoundland (Chapter 10); Ibn Battuta's trips in North, Central, and East Africa (Chapter 11); the Mongol conquest (Chapter 14); and the Spanish and Portuguese voyages to the Americas (Chapter 15). Because many of the people who traveled long distances in the premodern world did so for religious reasons, many of the travelers in Volume 1 were pilgrims. Their experiences help to reinforce student's understanding of the traditions of different world religions.

Volume 2 explores the development of the increasingly interconnected modern world, with the rise and fall of empires a persistent theme. We explore the new maritime trade routes that connected Europe to Asia

(Chapter 16) and the relationship between religion and politics in both the Christian and Muslim empires of western Eurasia (Chapter 17). The analysis of the colonial Americas (Chapter 18) is expanded by Chapter 19's discussion of Africa and the Atlantic slave trade. The expansion of Asian empires (Chapter 20) is complemented by an analysis of the relationship between science and empire in the Pacific Ocean and around the world (Chapter 21). The role of revolutions in modern history is addressed in Chapters 22 and 23. Chapters 24 through 26 address the global impact of the Industrial Revolution in Asia, the Americas, Africa, and Southeast Asia. The twentieth century is explored (Chapters 27–31) with an emphasis on the common experiences of globalized humanity through world wars, economic upheavals, and the bitter divisions of the Cold War. Though we cannot properly assess twenty-first century conditions using the historian's tools, Chapter 32 attempts to lay out some of the main challenges and opportunities we face today.

Themes

Our book has four themes: (1) increasing contact; (2) changing political structures of empire; (3) religion; (4) and social structure. The first is linked to our overall theme of movement, but the other three—the changing political structures of empire, religion, and social structure—form the backbone of all world history classes. The book develops these themes in each chapter.

Movement is the key theme of world history because world historians focus on connections among the different societies of the past. The movement of people, whether in voluntary migrations or forced slavery, has been of the most fruitful topics for world historians, as are the experience of individual travelers like Ibn Battuta or Simón Bolívar. Their reactions to the people they met on their long journeys reveal much about their home societies as well as about the societies they visited.

Theme 1: The Effects of Increasing Contact

Our focus on individual travelers leads naturally to the first major theme of the book: the increasing ease of contact among different civilizations with the passage of time. This theme highlights the developments that resulted from improved communications, travel among different places, the movement of trade goods, and the mixing of peoples: the movement of world religions, mass migrations, and the spread of diseases like the plague. The book shows how travel has changed over time—how the distance covered by travelers has increased at the same time that the duration of trips has decreased. As a result, more and more people have been able to go to societies distant from their own.

The book examines the different reasons for travel over the centuries. While some people were captured in battle and forced to go to new places, others visited different societies to teach or to learn the beliefs of a new religion like Buddhism, Christianity, and Islam. This theme, of necessity, treats questions about the environment: how far and over what terrain did early man travel? How did sailors learn to use monsoon winds to their advantage? What were the effects of technological breakthroughs like steamships, trains, and airplanes—and the use of fossil fuels to power them? Because students can link the experience of individual travelers to this theme, movement provides a memorable organizing principle for the book.

Theme 2: Changing Political Structures of Empire

Our second theme, the changing structure of empire, introduces students to political history. This theme permits students to compare the different empires under consideration and to understand that empires became increasingly complex over time, especially as central governments took advantage of new technologies to register and to control their subjects. Students need not commit long lists of rulers' names to memory: instead they focus on those leaders who created innovative political structures. After an opening chapter on the peopling of the world, the book begins with the very ancient empires (like Mesopotamia and Egypt) that did not control large swathes of territory and progress to those that did—like Qin dynasty China, Achaemenid Persia, and ancient Rome. It examines the political structures of empire: What was the relationship of the central government to the provinces? How were taxes collected and spent? How were officials recruited? Such questions remained remarkably persistent into the modern period, when societies around the world had to contend with rising Western empires.

The focus on the structure of empire helps students to remember the different civilizations they have studied, to explore the borrowing that occurred among various empires, and to understand how the empires were structured differently. This theme fits well with travel because the different travelers were able to make certain journeys because of the political situation at the time. For example, William of Rubruck was able to travel across all of Eurasia because of the unification brought by the Mongol empire, while Jean de Chardin's tavels from France to Iran were facilitated by the size and strength of the Ottoman Empire.

Theme 3: Religion

Our third theme, religion, follows naturally from the second because many rulers patronized religions to increase their control over the people they ruled. Students of world history must grasp the teachings of the major world religions, and, more important, they must have some understanding of how originally regional or national religions moved across political borders to become world religions. Volume 1 introduces the religions of Judaism (Chapter 2), Buddhism (Chapters 3 and 9), Confucianism (Chapter 4), Christianity (Chapters 6 and 10), Hinduism (Chapter 8), and Islam (Chapter 9). Volume 2 provides context for today's complex interplay of religion and politics (Chapter 17) and the complex cultural outcomes that occurred when such religions expanded into new world regions (Chapters 16 and 18). The renewed contemporary focus on religion, as seen in the rise of fundamentalist movements in various parts of the world, is analyzed in the two final chapters.

The theme of religion fits well with our focus on travelers. Some chapters examine the experience of religious travelers—such as the Chinese monk Xuanzang who journeyed to India and Matteo Ricci who hoped to convert the Chinese emperor to Christianity. Other travelers did not travel for religious reasons, but they had their own religious beliefs, encountered the religious traditions of the peoples they conquered, and sparked religious exchanges. Because the different chapters of the book pay close attention to the religious traditions of diverse societies, students gain a familiarity with the primary religious traditions of the world.

Theme 4: Social Structure

Our final theme is social structure. Students of world history need to understand how societies have been structured and how these ways of organizing society have changed over the past five thousand years. Abandoning the egalitarian structures of the distant past, Sumerian and Egyptian civilizations and their successors developed more hierarchical societies. Between 500 and 1500 both Europe and China moved from land-based aristocracies toward bureaucracy, but European and Chinese governments conceived of bureaucracy very differently. Some societies had extensive slavery; others did not.

Because the travelers were acutely aware of the differences between their own societies and those they visited, they provide crucial comparisons, although their observations were not always correct. For example, in the early seventh century the Chinese pilgrim Xuanzang described the Indian caste system as though it were rigidly structured, but he was not aware of groups who had changed the status of their caste.

The topic of gender falls under social structure, and each chapter devotes extensive space to the experience of women. Because in many societies literacy among women was severely limited, especially in the premodern era, we have included as many women travelers as possible: the slave girl and eventual wife of the caliph, Khaizuran (Chapter 9), Leif Eriksson's sister-in-law Gudrid (Chapter 10), the Chinese poet Li Qingzhao (Chapter 12), Heloise (Chapter 13), Catalina de Erauso (Chapter 18), Pauline Johnson-Tekahionwake (Chapter 25), Louise Bryant (Chapter 27), Halide Edib (Chapter 28), Nancy Wake (Chapter 29), and Mira Nair (Chapter 32). In addition, each chapter provides extensive coverage of gender so that students can grasp the experience of ordinary women.

Features

We see the features of this book as an opportunity to help students to understand the main text better. Each chapter opens with a map feature about the route of the chapter's traveler and then presents—not always in the same order—World History in Today's World, Movement of Ideas, and Visual Evidence.

Chapter Opening Map

At the beginning of each chapter is a map illustrating the route of the traveler. With their imaginative graphics, these chapter-opening maps look more like the maps in a travel book than the usual textbook maps. This section provides a biographical sketch for each traveler, a portrait, and extended passage from his or her writings (or, if not available, an extended passage about the individual). The goal of this feature is to capture the student's attention at the outset of each chapter. Although many students do not bother to read the beginning of each chapter, we hope that shifting smoothly from the traveler to the focus questions encourages them to do so.

World History in Today's World

This brief feature (no longer than 400 words, more often around 250) picks one element of modern life that originated in the period under study. We have made every effort to find things interesting to students ("The World's First Beer," "Japanese Baseball," and "The Coffeehouse in World History") and to highlight their relationship to the past. This feature should provide material to trigger discussion and help instructors explain why world history matters since so often students simply have no sense that the past has anything to do with their own lives.

Movement of Ideas

This feature offers an introduction, an extensive excerpt from one or more primary sources, and discussion questions. The chosen passages emphasize the movement of ideas, usually by contrasting two different explanations of the same idea. This feature aims to develop the core historical skill of analyzing original sources. Topics include "Doing What Is Right in *The Avesta* and the Bible" and "Fascism and Youth."

Visual Evidence

The goal of this feature is to train students to examine either an artifact, a work of art, or a photograph and to glean historical information from them. These features are illustrated with pictures or photographs to explain the importance of the find or the artwork. A close-up photograph of the Chinese terracotta warriors, for example, shows students how the figurines were mass-produced yet have individual features. Portraits of George Washington and Napoleon Bonaparte lead students to analyze the symbolism they contain to view the portraits as *representations* of political power. Discussion questions help students analyze the information presented.

Ancillaries

A wide array of supplements accompany this text to help students better master the material and to help instructors teach from the book:

- *Student Website*
- *Instructor Website*
- *CL Testing CD-ROM (powered by Diploma)*
- *Online Instructor's Resource Manual*

- *PowerPoint maps, images, and lecture outlines*
- *PowerPoint questions for personal response systems*
- *Blackboard™ and WebCT™ course cartridges*
- *Interactive ebook*
- *HistoryFinder*

The Student Website is a companion website for students, which features a wide array of resources to help students master the subject matter. The website, prepared by Mark Seidl, includes material such as learning objectives, chapter outlines, and pre-class quizzes for a student to consult before going to class; review material like interactive flashcards, chronological ordering exercises, primary sources, and interactive map exercises; and our successful ACE brand of practice tests as well as other self-testing materials. Students can also find additional text resources such as an online glossary, audio MP3 files of chapter summaries, and material on how to study more effectively in the "General Resources" section. Throughout the text, icons direct students to relevant exercises and self-testing material located on the Student Website.

The Instructor Website is a companion website for instructors. It features all of the material on the Student Website plus additional password-protected resources that help instructors teach the course, such as an electronic version of the *Instructor's Resource Manual* and *PowerPoint* slides. Access both the Student and Instructor Websites for this text by visiting **www.cengage.com/history/hansen/voyages1e.**

The *Instructor's Resource Manual,* prepared by Candace Gregory-Abbott of California State University, Sacramento, contains instructional objectives, chapter outlines, lecture topics and suggestions for discussion, classroom activities and writing assignments, analyzing primary sources, activities for the traveler feature, map activities, geography questions, audiovisual bibliographies, suggested readings, and Internet resources.

CL Testing (powered by *Diploma*) offers instructors a flexible and powerful tool for test generation and test management. Now supported by the Brownstone Research Group's market-leading *Diploma* software, this new version of *CL Testing* significantly improves on functionality and ease of use by offering all the tools needed to create, author, deliver, and customize multiple types of tests. Diploma is currently in use at thousands of college and university campuses throughout the United States and Canada. The *CL Testing* content for this text was developed by Dolores Grapsas of New River Community College and offers multiple-choice questions (with page references to the correct response), key term identification, geography questions (with blank outline maps provided), and essay questions (with guidelines for how to effectively write the essay).

We are pleased to offer a collection of World Civilization *PowerPoint* lecture outlines, maps, and images for use in classroom presentations. Detailed lecture outlines correspond to the book's chapters and make it easier for instructors to cover the major topics in class. The art collection includes all of the photos and maps in the text. *PowerPoint* questions and answers for use with personal response system software are also offered to adopters free of charge.

A variety of assignable homework and testing material has been developed to work with the *Blackboard™* and *WebCT™* course management systems. *Blackboard™* and *WebCT™* are web-based online learning environments that provide instructors with a gradebook and communication capabilities, such as synchronous and asynchronous chats and announcement postings. They offer access to assignments such as more than 650 gradable homework exercises, writing assignments, interactive maps with questions, primary sources, discussion questions for online discussion boards, and tests, which all come ready-to-use. Instructors can choose to use the content as is, modify it, or even add their own. They even contain an interactive ebook, which contains in-text links to interactive maps, primary sources, and audio pronunciation files, as well as review and self-testing material for students.

HistoryFinder, a new Cengage Learning technology initiative, helps instructors create rich and exciting classroom presentations. This online tool offers thousands of online resources, including art, photographs, maps, primary sources, multimedia content, Associated Press interactive modules, and ready-made *PowerPoint* slides. *HistoryFinder'*s assets can easily be searched by keyword or browsed from pull-down menus by topic, media type, or by textbook. Instructors can then browse, preview, and download resources straight from the website.

Acknowledgments

It is a pleasure to thank the many instructors who read and critiqued the manuscript through its development:

Wayne Ackerson, Salisbury University; Sanjam Ahluwalia, Northern Arizona University; Mark A. Allee, Loyola University, Chicago; Michael Thad Allen, Georgia Institute of Technology; Patricia Ali, Morris College; Ali Al-Taie, Shaw University; Melanie A. Bailey, South Dakota State University; William P. Bakken, Rochester Community and Technical College; Brett A. Berliner, Morgan State University; Corinne Blake, Rowan University; Stanley E. Blake, Ohio State University; Wayne Bowen, Ouachita Baptist University; Connie Brand, Meridian Community College; Michael Burger, Mississippi University for Women; Suzanne E. Cahill, University of California, San Diego; Michael Cassella-Blackburn, Peninsula College; Leslie G. Cecil, Baylor University; Robert Chisholm, Columbia Basin College; William Clay Poe, Sonoma State University; Paul R. Clementi, Immaculata University; Robert Cliver, Humboldt State University; Christine A. Colin, Mercyhurst College; Theron Corse, Tennessee State University; Scott Cotton, University of Texas, Dallas; Eric Cunningham, Gonzaga University; Jennifer Kolpacoff Deane, University of Minnesota, Morris; Hilde De Weerdt, University of Tennessee, Knoxville; Timothy C. Dowling, Virginia Military Institute; Mark Dupuy, Edith Cowan University; Elizabeth Endicott, Middlebury College; Krista Feinberg, Lakeland College; Kyle Fingerson, UW Rock County; Eve Fisher, South Dakota State University; David Flaten, Tompkins Cortland Community College; Monica Fleming, Edgecombe Community College; Hal Friedman, Henry Ford Community College; Erik Gilbert, Arkansas State University; Dolores Grapsas, New River Community College; Robert Greene, University of Montana; Candace Gregory-Abbott, California State University, Sacramento; Sumit Guha, Brown University; Jim Halverson, Judson University; Jason Hardgrave, University of Southern Indiana; David Head, Jon Tyler Community College; James Heitzman, University of California, Davis; Henry Heller, University of Manitoba; Craig Hendricks, Long Beach City College; Gerald Herman, Northeastern University; Lisa R. Holliday, Appalachian State University; Tamara L. Hunt, University of Southern Indiana; Raymond P. Hylton, Virginia Union University; Matthew Jacobs, University of Florida; Effie Jones, Crichton College; David M. Kalivas, Middlesex Community College; Joy Kammerling, Eastern Illinois University; Frank Karpiel, College of Charleston; Robert L. Kelly, University of Wyoming; Steven King, Valley City State University; Michael Krenn, Appalachian State University; Michael Kulikowski, University of Tennessee; Scott Levi, University of Louisville; Marilyn Levine, Lewis-Clark State College; Michael Lewis, Salisbury University; Ann Livschiz, IPFW; Christine E. Lovasz-Kaiser, University of Southern Indiana; Norman D. Love, El Paso Community College; Lynn MacKay, Brandon University; Moira Maguire, University of Arkansas, Little Rock; Fred McDonald, Cecil College; Patrick F. McDevitt, University at Buffalo SUNY; Mark McLeod, University of Delaware; Brendan McManus, Bemidji State University; John T. McNay, University of Cincinnati, RWC campus; Eben Miller, Southern Maine Community College; Garold Mills; Tim Myers, Butler Community College; Ken Orosz, University of Maine at Farmington; Donald Ostrowski, Harvard University Extension School; John Pinheiro, Aquinas College; Margaret Power, Illinois Institute of Technology; Richard Reiman, South Georgia College; Robert Reinert, Our Lady of the Lake University; Len Rose, Myers University; Ivancica Schrunk, University of St. Thomas; Jane Scimeca, Brookdale Community College; Bruce Scott, Northeastern Junior College; Jonathan Seitz, Drexel University; Courtney Shah, Lower Columbia University; Colonel Rose Mary Sheldon, Virginia Military Institute; David Simonelli, Youngstown State University; Paul D. Steeves, Stetson University; Forrest Studebaker, Clinton Community College; Steve Tamari, Southern Illinois University, Edwardsville; Loyd Uglow, Southwestern Assemblies of God University; David J. Ulbrich, Ball State University; Michael G. Vann, California State University, Sacramento; Dr. Maria Vecchio, Felician College; Tommy Walter, Jacksonville University; Charles Wheeler, University of California, Irvine; Gregory R. Witkowski, Ball State University; William Wood, Point Loma Nazarene University; Aharon Zorea, University of Wisconsin; and Alex Zukas, National University, San Diego.

Valerie Hansen would also like to thank the following for their guidance on specific chapters: Benjamin Foster, Yale University; Karen Foster, Yale University; Stephen Colvin, London University; Phyllis Granoff,

Yale University; Stanley Insler, Yale University; Mridu Rai, Yale University; Thomas R. H. Havens, Northeastern University; Charles Wheeler, University of California, Irvine; Haydon Cherry, Yale University; Marcello A. Canuto, Yale University; William Fash, Harvard University; Stephen Houston, Brown University; Mary Miller, Yale University; Stephen Colvin, University of London; Frank Turner, Yale University; Kevin van Bladel, University of Southern California; Anders Winroth, Yale University; Paul Freedman, Yale University; Frederick S. Paxton, Connecticut College; Francesca Trivellato, Yale University; Stuart Schwartz, Yale University; and Koichi Shinohara, Yale University.

The study of world history is indeed a voyage, and Kenneth Curtis would like to thank the following for helping identify guideposts along the way. First, thanks to colleagues in the World History Association and the Advanced Placement World History program, especially Ross Dunn, San Diego State University; Patrick Manning, University of Pittsburgh; Peter Stearns, George Mason University; Jerry Bentley, University of Hawai'i; Merry Wiesner-Hanks, University of Wisconsin–Milwaukee; Alan Karras, University of California, Berkeley; Omar Ali, Vanderbilt University; Heather Streets, Washington State University; Laura Mitchell, University of California, Irvine; Anand Yang, University of Washington; Heidi Roupp, Ane Lintvedt, Sharon Cohen, Jay Harmon, Anton Striegl, Michelle Foreman, Chris Wolf, Saroja Ringo, Esther Adams, Linda Black, and Bill Ziegler. He would also like to acknowledge the support of his colleagues in the history department at California State University Long Beach, especially those who aided with sources, translations, or interpretive guidance: Houri Berberian, Timothy Keirn, Craig Hendricks, Margaret Kuo, Andrew Jenks, Ali Igmen, Sharlene Sayegh, and Donald Schwartz. He also benefited from the feedback of the students who read early drafts of the modern history chapters and gave valuable feedback, with a special nod to those graduate students—Charlie Dodson, Patrick Giloogly, Daniel Lynch—who brought their passion for world history teaching in the public schools to the seminar table, and to Colin Rutherford for his help with the pedagogy.

The authors would also like to thank the many publishing professionals at Houghton Mifflin and Wadsworth/Cengage Learning who facilitated the publication of this book, in particular: Nancy Blaine, for guiding us through the entire process from proposal to finished textbook; Jean Woy, for her extraordinary historical judgment; Jennifer Sutherland, for paying attention to everything from the smallest detail to the largest conceptual questions; Jan Fitter, for elegant and perceptive readings of many chapters; Adrienne Zicht, for an excellent ancillary package to accompany the text; Linda Sykes, for her extraordinary photo research that has made this book so beautiful to look at; and Christina Horn, for shepherding the book through the final, chaotic pre-publication process.

In closing, Valerie would like to thank Brian Vivier for doing so much work on Volume 1; the title of "research assistant" does not convey even a fraction of what he did, always punctually and cheerfully. She dedicates this book to her children, Lydia, Claire, and Bret Hansen Stepanek, and their future educations.

Kenneth Curtis would like to thank Francine Curtis for her frontline editing skills and belief in the project, and his mother Elizabeth J. Curtis and siblings Jane, Sara, Margaret, Jim, Steve, and Ron for their love and support. In recognition of his father's precious gift of curiosity, Ken dedicates this book to the memory of James Gavin Curtis.

ABOUT THE AUTHORS

Valerie Hansen

Since her graduate work in premodern Chinese history at the University of Pennsylvania, Valerie Hansen has used nontraditional sources to capture the experience of ordinary people. Professor of History at Yale, she teaches the history of premodern China, the Silk Road, and the world. *Changing Gods in Medieval China* drew on temple inscriptions and ghost stories to shed light on popular religious practice in the Song dynasty (1127–1276), while *Negotiating Daily Life in Traditional China* used contracts to probe Chinese understandings of the law both in this world and the next. Her textbook *The Open Empire: China to 1600* draws on archaeological finds, literature, and art to explore Chinese interactions with the outside world. With grants from the National Endowment for the Humanities and the Fulbright Association, she has traveled to China to collect materials for her current research project: a new history of the Silk Road.

Kenneth R. Curtis

Kenneth R. Curtis received his Ph.D. from the University of Wisconsin–Madison in African and Comparative World History. His research focuses on colonial to post-colonial transitions in East Africa, with a particular focus on the coffee economy of Tanzania. He is Professor of History and Liberal Studies at California State University Long Beach, where he has taught world history at the introductory level, in special courses designed for future middle and high school teachers, and in graduate seminars. He has worked to advance the teaching of world history at the collegiate and secondary levels in collaboration with the World History Association, the California History/Social Science Project, and the College Board's Advanced Placement World History course.

NOTE ON SPELLING

Students taking world history will encounter many new names of people, terms, and places. We have retained only the most important of these. The most difficult, of course, are those from languages that use either different alphabets or no alphabet at all (like Chinese) and that have multiple variant spellings in English. As a rule, we have opted to give names in the native language of whom we are writing, not in other languages. In addition, we have kept accents and diacritic marks to a minimum, using them only when absolutely necessary. For example, we give the name of the world's first city (in Turkey) as Catalhoyuk, not Çatalhüyük.

In sum, our goal has been to avoid confusing the reader, even if specific decisions may not make sense to expert readers. To help readers, we provide a pronunciation guide on the first appearance of any term or name whose pronunciation is not obvious from the spelling. There is also an audio pronunciation guide on the text's accompanying website. A few explanations for specific regions follow.

The Americas

The peoples living in the Americas before 1492 had no common language and no shared identity. Only after 1492 with the arrival of Columbus and his men did outsiders label the original residents of the Americas as a single group. For this reason, any word for the inhabitants of North and South America is inaccurate. We try to refer to individual peoples whenever possible. When speaking in general terms, we use the word "Amerindian" because it has no pejorative overtones and is not confusing.

Many place names in Spanish-speaking regions have a form in both Spanish and in the language of the indigenous peoples; whenever possible we have opted for the indigenous word. For example, we write about the Tiwanaku culture in the Andes, not Tiahuanaco. In some cases, we choose the more familiar term, such as Inca and Cuzco, rather than the less-familiar spellings Inka and Cusco. We retain the accents for modern place names.

East Asia

For Chinese, we have used the pinyin system of Romanization, not the older Wade-Giles version. Students and instructors may wish to consult an online pinyin/Wade-Giles conversion program if they want to check a spelling. We use the pinyin throughout but, on the first appearance of a name, alert readers to nonstandard spellings, such as Chiang Kai-shek and Sun Yat-sen, that have already entered English.

For other Asian languages, we have used the most common romanization systems (McCune-Reischauer for Korean, Hepburn for Japanese) and have dropped diacritical marks. Because we prefer to use the names that people called themselves, we use Chinggis Khan, for the ruler of the Mongols (not Genghis Khan, which is Persian) and the Turkish Timur the Lame (rather than Tamerlane, his English name).

West Asia and North Africa

Many romanization systems for Arabic and related languages like Ottoman Turkish or Persian use an apostrophe to indicate specific consonants (*ain* and *hamza*). Because it is difficult for a native speaker of English to hear these differences, we have omitted these apostrophes. For this reason, we use Quran (not Qur'an).

Voyages in
World History

CHAPTER 1

The Peopling of the World, to 4000 B.C.E.

From the earliest moments of human history our ancestors were on the move. Archaeologists continue to debate when and how our earliest forebears moved out of Africa, where humankind originated millions of years ago, and how it populated the rest of the world. One of the last places people reached—probably around 16,000 years ago—was the Americas. For this reason, archaeologists are particularly interested in any human remains that date from this early period.

On Saturday, July 28, 1996, two college students found this skull in the riverbed of the Columbia River, near the town of Kennewick in Washington State. The students called the police, who the next day contacted Chatters to determine if the bones were those of a murder victim. At the find-spot, Chatters collected an additional 350 bones and determined that the man had lived between 7580 and 7330 B.C.E. (As is common among world historians, this book uses B.C.E. [Before Common Era] and C.E. [Common Era] rather than B.C. [Before Christ] and A.D. [Anno Domini, In the Year of Our Lord].) Here James C. Chatters, a forensic anthropologist, describes what he learned by examining the skull of the skeleton now known as **Kennewick Man**:

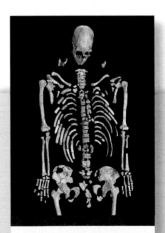

KENNEWICK MAN

(Chip Clark, Museum of Natural History, Smithsonian Institution)

I looked down at the first piece, the braincase, viewing it from the top. Removing it from the bag, I was immediately struck by its long, narrow shape and the marked constriction of the forehead behind a well-developed brow ridge. The bridge of the nose was very high and prominent. My first thought was that this skull belonged to someone of European descent. . . .

I turned the bone to inspect the underside, and what I saw seemed at first to be at odds with the rest of the picture. The teeth were worn flat, and worn severely. This is a characteristic of American Indian skeletons, especially in the interior Pacific Northwest, where the people ate stone-ground fish, roots,

 This icon will direct you to interactive activities and study materials on the *Voyages* website: **www.cengage.com/history/hansen/voyages1e**

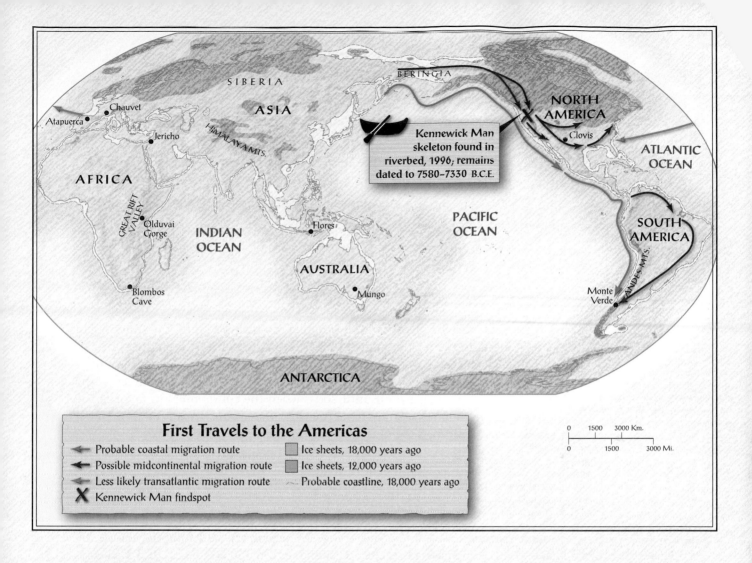

First Travels to the Americas

← Probable coastal migration route
← Possible midcontinental migration route
← Less likely transatlantic migration route
✕ Kennewick Man findspot

◻ Ice sheets, 18,000 years ago
◻ Ice sheets, 12,000 years ago
⌇ Probable coastline, 18,000 years ago

Kennewick Man skeleton found in riverbed, 1996; remains dated to 7580–7330 B.C.E.

0   1500   3000 Km.
0   1500   3000 Mi.

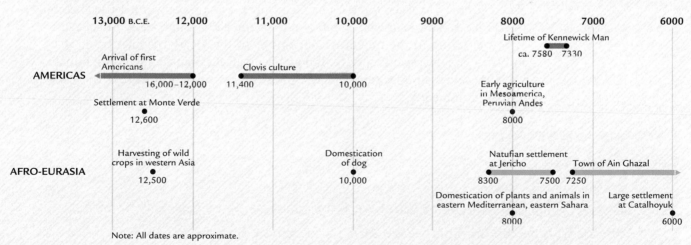

| 13,000 B.C.E. | 12,000 | 11,000 | 10,000 | 9000 | 8000 | 7000 | 6000 |

AMERICAS

Arrival of first Americans
16,000–12,000

Clovis culture
11,400   10,000

Lifetime of Kennewick Man
ca. 7580   7330

Settlement at Monte Verde
12,600

Early agriculture in Mesoamerica, Peruvian Andes
8000

AFRO-EURASIA

Harvesting of wild crops in western Asia
12,500

Domestication of dog
10,000

Natufian settlement at Jericho
8300   7500

Town of Ain Ghazal
7250

Domestication of plants and animals in eastern Mediterranean, eastern Sahara
8000

Large settlement at Catalhoyuk
6000

Note: All dates are approximate.

and berries and lived almost constantly with blowing sand. My mind jumped to something I'd seen when I was fourteen years old, working at an ancient site on the Snake River in Washington. . . . "Paleo-Indian?" came the involuntary thought. "Paleo-Indian" is the label given to the very earliest American immigrants, traditionally presumed to be early versions of today's Native Americans.

No, I thought, that can't be. The inhabitants of the Americas had broad faces, round heads, and presumably brown skin and straight black hair. They had come over from Siberia no more than 13,000 years ago across the Bering Land Bridge and therefore resembled their modern-day Siberian relatives. This was no Paleo-Indian—was it?[1]

• **Kennewick Man**
Remains of a male found near Kennewick, Washington, dated to between 7580 and 7330 B.C.E.

• **hominids** Term referring to all humans and their ancestors.

• ***Homo sapiens sapiens*** Biological term for modern human beings belonging to the genus *Homo,* species *sapiens,* and subspecies *sapiens.*

The day after the discovery, the Umatilla (oo-mah-TILL-uh), the Amerindian people living in the region, argued that Kennewick Man was their ancestor and the remains should be given to them for reburial. A group of scientists counter-sued, arguing that the remains were so ancient that they could not be linked to the Umatilla. The case dragged on until 2004, when the courts ruled in favor of the scientists, who hope that studying Kennewick Man's remains can help them determine how and when the Americas were first settled.

The peopling of the Americas was a late phase in the history of humankind. As early as seven million years ago, the earliest **hominids** (HAH-moh-nids), a term referring to all humans and their ancestors, branched off from gorillas and chimpanzees. These early hominids had moved out of Africa by 1.8 million years ago. By 150,000 B.C.E., anatomically modern people, the species ***Homo sapiens sapiens*** (HO-mo SAY-pee-uhnz SAY-pee-uhnz), had fully developed. By 60,000 B.C.E. people had reached Australia, and by 50,000 B.C.E. they had populated Eurasia. However, the Western Hemisphere was probably not settled before 14,000 B.C.E., and Kennewick Man is one of the earliest and most intact skeletons ever found in the Americas. Since none of these early peoples could read and write, no documents survive. But archaeological evidence, including human remains, cave paintings, and ancient tools, allows us to reconstruct the early history of humanity.

Focus Questions

🛶 **Who were the first hominids? What were the main stages in their development?**

🛶 **When and how did hominids leave Africa and settle Eurasia?**

🛶 **When did ancient hominids become recognizably human?**

🛶 **How and when did the first people move to the Americas? What was their way of life?**

🛶 **How and where did agriculture first arise? How did its impact vary around the world?**

🌍The Origins of Humankind

Paleontologists (pay-lee-on-TAHL-oh-gists), scientists who study ancient life in the distant past, agree that humans and chimpanzees are descended from a species that no longer exists. About seven million years ago in central Africa that lost species gave rise to two separate species. One branch developed into chimpanzees, the other, into hominids. After leaving their homeland in Africa around 1.8 million years ago, hominids continued to develop until anatomically modern people, or *Homo sapiens sapiens,* appeared 150,000 years ago.

The First Hominids: Australopithecines

Biologists use four different subcategories when classifying animals: family, genus (JEAN-uhs) (the Latin word for group or class), species, and subspecies. Modern humans are members of the Primate family, the genus *Homo* ("person" in Latin), the species *sapiens* ("wise" or "intelligent" in Latin), and the subspecies *sapiens,* so the correct term for modern people is *Homo sapiens sapiens.* Members of the same species can reproduce, while members of two different species cannot. The species closest to modern human beings today is the chimpanzee, whose cells contain nuclei with genetic material called deoxyribonucleic acid (DNA) that overlaps with that of humans by 98.4 percent.

Scientists use the concept of **evolution** to explain how all life forms, including modern humans, have come into being. In the nineteenth century Charles Darwin proposed that natural selection is the mechanism underlying evolutionary change. He realized that variations exist within a species (we now know that genetic mutations cause them) and that certain variations increase an individual's chances of survival. All variations, beneficial or not, are passed along to offspring. Because those individuals with beneficial traits—perhaps a bigger brain or more upright posture—are more likely to survive, they will have more offspring. And, because traits are inherited, these offspring will also possess the beneficial traits. Individuals lacking those traits will have few or no offspring. As new mutations occur within a population, its characteristics will change and a new species can develop from an earlier one, typically over many thousands or even millions of years.

The process of natural selection caused the early hominids to diverge from other primates, especially in their manner of walking. Our very earliest ancestors did not belong to the genus *Homo* but to the genus **Australopithecus** ("southern ape"), whose habitat was also Africa. The defining characteristic of australopithecines (au-stral-oh-PITH-uh-seens) was bipedalism (buy-PEH-dahl-izm), the ability to walk on two feet, whereas chimpanzees and gorillas knuckle-walked on all four limbs.

● **evolution** Model proposed by Charles Darwin to explain the development of new species. In each generation, genetic mutations cause variation among members of a species, eventually changing the characteristics of that population into new, distinct species.

● *Australopithecus* Hominid species, dating to 3.5 million years ago, who walked on two feet (adjectival form: australopithecine).

Paleontologists have found australopithecine remains in different regions of Africa, including Malawi, Chad, South Africa, and most importantly northern Tanzania in the Olduvai (OHL-doo-vaye) Gorge, which lies in the Great Rift Valley. Located along a crack in the earth's crust where two giant tectonic plates are slowly moving apart, the Great Rift Valley runs for 2,000 miles (3,600 km) from the Red Sea to Tanzania. Now 25 to 50 miles (40–80 km) wide, it exposes many earlier layers of human occupation. In the 1960s and 1970s, Richard and Mary Leakey found in this valley australopithecine skulls, jawbones, teeth, and even footprints, the first tangible evidence of the australopithecine ability to walk.

Since early hominids could walk, they were able to leave the cover of forests and hunt in the open grasslands. Scientists believe that millions of years ago grasslands began to replace forests. At that time the African continent, then much wetter than it is today, began to dry up. As grassy savannah replaced rainforest, walking upright conferred an important advantage over those species that walked on four limbs. Upright walking also used fewer calories than knuckle-walking.

One of the most complete sets of australopithecine remains comes from a female known as Lucy. She was named for "Lucy in the Sky with Diamonds," a Beatles song playing on a tape recorder when, in 1974, archaeologists found her remains in Ethiopia. She stood 39 inches (1 m) tall and lived 3.5 million years ago. Her face was shaped like an ape, with a small brain like a chimpanzee, and she made no tools of her own. But the remains of Lucy's knee showed that she walked upright.

Homo Erectus and the First Migrations Outside of Africa, 2.5–1.8 Million Years Ago

One can easily get the impression that our ancestors evolved in a logical progression, with ancient tiny hominids growing taller and more human-like, but the reality was more complex. Fossil evidence suggests that a number of species came into existence, flourished for a time, and then died out. Some of these had more human characteristics, while others had more in common with chimpanzees and gorillas.

Recent finds suggest that four different groups of human ancestors coexisted 2.5 million years ago, or one million years after Lucy was alive. These different human ancestors all shared two important characteristics that set them apart from the australopithecines: they had bigger brains and made tools of their own by chipping off stone flakes from cores. This innovation marked the beginning of the **Paleolithic** (pay-lee-oh-LITH-uhk) period, or Old Stone Age (2.5 million years ago–8000 B.C.E.). The earliest tools were sharp enough to cut through animal hides and to scrape meat off bones. Over the long course of the Paleolithic period, protohumans made tools of increasing complexity.

• **Paleolithic** The "Old Stone Age" period, from 2.5 million years ago to 8000 B.C.E.

These early hominids belonged to the same genus, but not the same species, as modern people: they are called *Homo habilis* (HO-mo hah-BEEL-uhs) ("handy human"). Standing erect, *Homo habilis* weighed less than 100 pounds and measured under 5 feet tall. They ate whatever fruits and vegetables grew wild and competed with other scavengers, such as hyenas, to get scraps of meat left behind by lions and tigers.

• ***Homo erectus*** Hominid species, appearing 1.9 million years ago, who left Africa and populated Eurasia.

The species that evolved into modern humans—***Homo erectus*** (HO-mo-ee-RECT-oos) ("upright human")—appeared about 1.9 million years ago. *Homo erectus* had a brain double the size of earlier hominid brains, about the same size as that of modern humans, as well as far greater mobility than any earlier human ancestor. Armed with hand axes, and perhaps even simple boats (evidence of which does not survive), *Homo erectus* left Africa and migrated to Asia.

Two main routes connect Africa with Eurasia: one leads across the Strait of Gibraltar into Spain, and the other crosses the Sinai Peninsula into western Asia. The earliest hominid remains found outside of Africa date to 1.8 million years ago in Dmanisi, Georgia (in the Caucasus Mountains) and in Ubeidiya, Israel, from 1.4 million years ago. The distribution of the few *Homo erectus* finds in Eurasia shows that the route into western Asia was more heavily traveled than the route across the Mediterranean at the Strait of Gibraltar.

These early species did not move quickly from western Asia to Europe, perhaps because the cold climate there was not inviting. They entered Europe by crossing the Bosporus strait in modern Turkey and then walking along the northern shore of the Mediterranean. The earliest evidence that our ancestors lived in Europe, from Atapuerca (ah-TAH-poo-air-kah), Spain, dates to 1.1 million years ago.

It seems likely that *Homo erectus* learned how to control fire at this time. One early find, dating to 1.4 million years ago, at the site of Chesowanja (chuh-SOH-wahn-juh), Kenya, included lumps of burnt clay alongside animal bones and stone tools, but many think a natural fire might have occurred. A more convincing find, from northern Israel, dates to 790,000 years ago. There archaeologists found fragments of flint next to charred remains of wood in different layers of earth, an indication that the site's occupants passed the knowledge of fire making to their descendants. To keep a fire going requires planning far ahead, an ability that earlier hominids lacked.

Following the discovery of fire, our ancestors began to eat more meat, which resulted in a larger brain size. By 500,000 years ago, they had settled many sites throughout Europe and Asia. At this time, *Homo erectus* began to evolve into archaic *Homo sapiens*.

The Emergence of *Homo Sapiens Sapiens*, 2 Million–150,000 Years Ago

One of the fiercest debates currently raging among paleontologists concerns the development of humankind between about 1.9 million years ago, when *Homo erectus* was alive, and the appearance of *Homo sapiens sapiens*, or anatomically modern people, about 150,000 years ago. The "regional continuity" school holds that, after *Homo erectus* settled the Eastern Hemisphere about two million years ago, different hominids from different regions gradually merged to form modern people. The "single origin" school posits a very different history for humankind. It agrees with the regional continuity school that *Homo erectus* settled the Eastern Hemisphere starting 1.9 million years ago, but it suggests that a second wave of migration out of Africa—of *Homo sapiens sapiens* between 100,000 and 50,000 years ago—supplanted all pre-existing human species.

The "single origin" school cites DNA evidence in support of its position. The DNA in the nucleus of every cell in our bodies contains about 100,000 genes, an inherited mix of one's father's and mother's DNA. In addition, all of our cells contain structures outside the nucleus called mitochondria (my-toe-CON-dree-uh). Each of these mitochondria contains a single DNA strand that is inherited only from the egg cell of the mother. If one examines mitochondrial DNA from different populations around the world, statistical analysis of minute differences points toward an ancestral female population that lived somewhere in Africa about 100,000 years ago, an indication that the descendants of an "African Eve" replaced all other human populations after a second migration out of Africa.

The "regional continuity" scholars argue that different regional populations could have mixed with the second wave of migrants from Africa and that they did not necessarily die out. Everyone agrees, though, that the earliest hominids originated in Africa and that *Homo erectus* left Africa about 1.9 million years ago.

How Modern Humans Populated Eurasia and Australia

When anatomically modern humans (*Homo sapiens sapiens*) first appeared in central and southern Africa some 150,000 years ago, their bodies and braincases were about the same size as ours. They lived side by side with other animals and other hominid species. But in important respects they were totally different from their neighbors, for they had learned to change their environment with radically new tools and skills. Carrying their supplies themselves since they had no domesticated animals, they moved out of Africa into Eurasia after 150,000 B.C.E. By 60,000 B.C.E. they were using simple rafts or boats to travel over water to Australia.

The First Anatomically Modern Humans Leave Africa

Paleontologists have found very few human remains dating to the time when *Homo sapiens sapiens* first arose in Africa, but in 2003 they were extremely pleased to find three skulls (from two adults and one child) dating to 160,000 B.C.E. in Ethiopia. Of the same shape and dimensions as modern human skulls, these skulls show that the *Homo sapiens sapiens* species arose first in Africa. Concluding that all modern people are descended from this group, one of the excavating archaeologists commented: "In this sense, we are all African."[2]

Starting in 150,000 B.C.E., *Homo sapiens sapiens* began to migrate out of Africa to populate Eurasia. By 100,000 B.C.E. they had reached North Africa and crossed the Sinai Peninsula into modern-day Israel in western Asia. As they migrated, they encountered groups of pre-modern humans called **Neanderthals** (knee-AHN-dehr-thalls) in Israel and then western Europe. Named for the site in West Germany where their remains were first found, Neanderthals were shaped differently from modern humans: their skulls were longer and lower, their faces protruded, and their bones were bigger and heavier. Neanderthal tools included longer stone flakes, which they chipped off larger stone cores. They painted themselves, their dwellings, and their graves with clumps of pigment such as ocher (OH-kerh), a naturally occurring mineral that can be mixed with water to make a red paint. The Neanderthals used fire to cook large animals that they had caught.

To be able to migrate out of Africa and displace existing populations in Asia and Europe, modern humans had to behave differently from their forebears. They showed a capacity for symbolic thinking, evident in the creation of the world's

• **Neanderthals**
Group of pre-modern humans who lived between 100,000 and 25,000 B.C.E. in western Asia and Europe, eventually replaced by *Homo sapiens sapiens.*

first art, as well as an ability to plan far ahead. (See the feature "Visual Evidence: The First Art Objects in the World.") Archaeologists believe that these characteristics indicate a new stage in human development, when humans became recognizably human.

The earliest evidence of religion comes from sites dating to 100,000 B.C.E. The defining characteristic of **religion** is the belief in a divine power or powers that control or influence the environment and people's lives. The most reliable evidence is a written text demonstrating religious beliefs, but early humans did not write. They did, however, bury their dead. In 100,000 B.C.E., anatomically modern humans who had migrated to western Asia interred three people in the Qafseh (KAHF-seh) cave near Nazareth, Israel, most likely because they believed in an afterlife, a major component of many religious belief systems.

Modern humans had larynxes starting around 150,000 B.C.E., but many suspect that they did not begin to speak until sometime between 100,000 and 50,000 B.C.E. We cannot know exactly because the act of speaking produces no lasting evidence in the archaeological record.

● **religion** Belief system that holds that divine powers control the environment and people's futures.

The Settling of Australia, ca. 60,000 B.C.E.

Homo sapiens sapiens of the Upper Paleolithic Era were sufficiently versatile that they could adjust to new, even cold, habitats far removed from their original home in central Africa, and their improved hunting skills allowed them to move to new places. The farthest they traveled was to Australia. One of the most isolated places on earth, this continent provides a rich environment for animals, such as kangaroos, that are found nowhere else in the world. No animals from Eurasia, except for rodents and modern humans, managed to reach Australia.

How *Homo sapiens sapiens* traveled to Australia is still a mystery. Oceans then lay about 250 feet (76 m) below modern levels, and the body of water dividing Australia from the Asian landmass was at least 40 miles (65 km) across, suggesting that this species knew how to cover short distances by raft. Yet no watercraft from this time have been found, possibly because any remains would have disintegrated.

Once they reached Australia, the early settlers did not stay on the coast but moved inland rapidly, reaching the site of Mungo (muhn-GO), in southeast Australia, by 60,000 years ago. There archaeologists found a burial in which a male skeleton (known as Mungo Man) was placed in the ground and sprinkled with red ocher powder. Nearby was a woman (Mungo Woman), whose burnt remains constitute the earliest known example of human cremation. Since many later peoples cremated the dead in the hope that their souls could proceed safely to the next world, the human settlers of Australia may have had similar beliefs.

The Settling of Eurasia, 50,000–30,000 B.C.E.

The settlers of Europe continued to refine the advanced hunting technologies of their African forbears, who had formed large, organized hunting parties that killed big game with sharp-pointed spears. In addition to hunting, the migrants also gathered wild plants. Starting around 50,000 B.C.E. the humans living in Europe began to organize hunts of migrating animals in the fall to provide meat during the winter. The Paleolithic period entered its final phase, the Upper Paleolithic, or the late Stone Age, around 38,000 B.C.E. The rise of agriculture around 10,000 B.C.E. (see page 21) marks the end of this period.

THE FIRST ART OBJECTS IN THE WORLD

One site in Africa—Blombos Cave in South Africa—has produced some of the earliest art objects in the world. The Blombos Cave site, near Stilbai about 186 miles (300 km) from Cape Town, dates to 75,000 B.C.E. The surface of this chunk of ocher (opposite) bears a geometric design of triangles between three parallel lines. This pure design, with no functional purpose, points to the capacity for abstract thinking.

The occupants of Blombos Cave fished and hunted and made sets of fine bone tools, all of the same size. First they cut bone with stone tools and then polished it with leather and abrasive powder. The excavating archaeologist explains the significance of these tools: "Why so finely polished? It's actually unnecessary for projectile points to be so carefully made. It suggests to us that this is an expression of symbolic thinking. The people said 'Let's make a really beautiful object.'"*

At Blombos archaeologists found nineteen snail shells, about the size of a kernel of corn, each with a hole through it (see opposite, bottom). Traces of wear at the ends of the shell indicate that they were originally strung together to make a strand of beads, worn perhaps on the wrist or at the neck. The beads also show traces of ocher. The beads, archaeologists speculate, may have functioned at Blombos as they

do among the Ju/'hoansi people who live in the Kalahari Desert in Botswana and who are sometimes called Bushmen. Speakers of a language with many click sounds, the Ju/'hoansi present ostrich shell beads to other groups with whom they hope to form alliances.

The scientist who discovered these shells argued convincingly that these are very early signs of human creativity. A recent discovery suggests that they may be more. In 2007, archaeologists excavating the Pigeon Cave site in Morocco have found similar shells dated between 91,000 and 74,000 years ago. These beads also have holes, abrasion marks at the ends where they were strung together, and traces of ocher. They are not from exactly the same species of snail as those from Blombos Cave, but the two species of snail look identical to the naked eye (one can see the differences between them only with a microscope). Other undated finds of similar shells in Israel and Algeria suggest that a trading network that spanned Africa and Israel may have existed as early as 82,000 years ago.

The chunk of ocher, the bone tools, and the beads from Blombos reveal that their makers were able to produce beautiful objects because they had the time and energy left over after meeting basic subsistence needs. These early objects clearly display the artistic impulses of their makers and suggest that *Homo sapiens sapiens* engaged in the recognizably human activity of making art objects as early as 75,000 B.C.E. and possibly even before.

---

*Interview with Christopher Henshilwood in "When Humans Became Human," *New York Times*, February 26, 2002, p. F5.

QUESTIONS FOR ANALYSIS

 Which evidence from the archaeological record (including, but not limited to, the objects discussed above) do you find most convincing as the earliest indication of people becoming recognizably human? Why?

This is a block of red ocher, a pigment made from iron oxide. Now the color of rust, the surface would have originally been a vivid blood red. This block, 2.5 inches (6 cm) long, formed a small crayon that was used, perhaps, to decorate the body.

These abstract triangle markings may be purely decorative or may represent a way to count something, perhaps the passage of days.

This object was found in Blombos Cave, some 186 miles (300 km) from Cape Town, where the cave's occupants hunted and fished around 75,000 B.C.E.

The humans living in Europe during the Upper Paleolithic period are called Cro Magnon (CROW MAG-nahn), after the site where their remains were first found. Their methods of food acquisition show that they were better able to think about the future, not just the present. Cro Magnon bands traveled to rivers and coasts to catch fish. As they moved in search of more game and fish, they built new types of houses and developed better clothes.

These humans also produced the extraordinary cave paintings of Chauvet (SHOW-vay) in southern France (dated to 30,000 B.C.E.), which show the different animals hunted by the local peoples: mammoths (various types of extinct elephants), lions, and rhinoceroses. Some are decorated with patterns of dots or human handprints. Other cave sites, such as the well-known Lascaux (las-KOH) (15,000 B.C.E.) site in southwestern France, show horses, bison, and ibex, suggesting that ancient hunters targeted different animals during different seasons. (See the feature "Movement of Ideas: The Worship of Goddesses?")

Most experts thought that by 25,000 B.C.E. *Homo sapiens sapiens* was the only human species on earth, since all other species, including the Neanderthals, had died out. But a discovery announced in October 2004 has forced everyone to reconsider this view. Archaeologists working on the island of Flores in western Indonesia announced that they had discovered bones from a previously unknown

■ **An Ancient Artist at the Chauvet Caves of France**   Traces of charcoal from the battling woolly rhinoceros (*lower right*) have been dated to about 30,000 B.C.E., making this one of the earliest cave paintings found anywhere in the world. The panel also portrays the same horse in four different poses, rare sketches done by an individual artist. Many of the paintings in the Chauvet caves display this artist's distinctive style.   (AP/Wide World Photos)

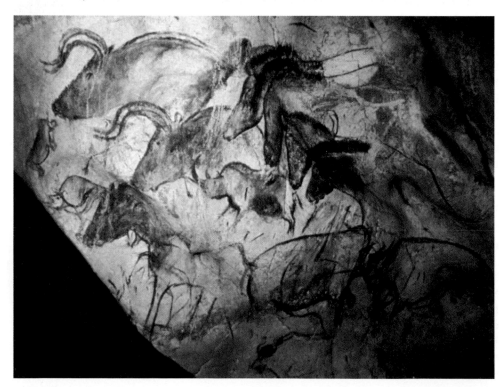

human species they called *Homo floresiensis* (HO-mo flor-ehs-ee-EHN-suhs) ("Human from Flores"). The remains date from 95,000 to 13,000 B.C.E. The most complete skeleton, intact except for missing arms, came from a female who stood only 3 feet (.9 m) tall and whose brain was as small as the australopithecine Lucy's. The excavating archaeologists propose that the new species was a descendant of either the australopithecines or *Homo erectus*. Because other pygmy animals, such as pygmy elephants, developed on the island, these scientists suggest that the process of island-dwarfing could also have produced smaller-than-usual *Homo erectus*. The island is currently home to a group of human pygmies, who could be the descendants of the earlier population.[3]

Yet some scientists have loudly voiced their skepticism, largely because the stone tools found at the site are much more sophisticated than any associated with australopithecines or *Homo erectus*. They suggest, instead, that the skeleton may be that of a small *Homo sapiens sapiens* afflicted with a disorder called microcephaly (my-cro-SEPH-uh-lee) that results in a shrunken brain and other deformities. This controversial find shows how a single discovery can prompt radical revision of the scientific consensus on human evolution.

The Settling of the Americas

*H*omo sapiens sapiens reached the Americas much later than they did any other landmass. The earliest confirmed human occupation in the Western Hemisphere dates to about 10,500 B.C.E., some forty thousand years after the settling of the Eurasian landmass and Australia. Accordingly, all human remains found so far in the Americas belong to the *Homo sapiens* species.

We know, however, much less about the settlement of the Americas than we do about the other continents. Scholars are not certain which routes the early settlers took, when they came, or if they traveled over land or by water. Far fewer human burials have been found in the Americas, and the few that have been found were excavated with much less scientific care than in Eurasia and Africa. Many sites had been disturbed so that the original layers of earth, so valuable to archaeologists, are no longer intact. Many early sites contain no human remains at all. For this reason, even skeletons like Kennewick Man are of great interest to those studying early migration to the Americas.

Beringia: The Land Bridge from Siberia to the Americas

One theory is that humans reached America on a land bridge from Siberia. **Beringia** (bear-in-JEE-uh) is the landmass, now below water, that connected the tip of Siberia in Russia with the northeastern corner of Alaska. Today Beringia is covered by a 50-mile-wide (80-km-wide) stretch of the Bering Sea. The water in this part of the Bering Sea is shallow, consistently less than 600 feet deep (182 m). As the earth experienced different periods of extended coldness, called Ice Ages, ocean water froze and covered such northern landmasses with ice. During these periods the ocean level declined and the ancient Beringia landmass emerged to form a land bridge between Russia and America. It was a large land bridge, measuring over 600 miles (1000 km) from north to south.

• **Beringia** Landmass now submerged below water that connected the tip of Siberia with the northeastern corner of Alaska.

The Worship of Goddesses?

What were the religious beliefs of the residents of Europe between 26,000 and 23,000 B.C.E.? Over twenty female figurines have been found at sites in Austria, Italy, Ukraine, Malta, the Czech Republic, and most often France. Made from mammoth ivory tusk, soapstone, and clay, the figurines range in size from 2 inches (5 cm) to a foot (30 cm) tall. The wide distribution of the figurines poses an interesting problem: Did different groups learn independently to make similar objects, or did one group first craft a model, which was then diffused to other places? Modern archaeologists require striking similarities before they can be persuaded of diffusion. It seems likely in this case that people in different places crafted women according to their own conceptions and that diffusion did not necessarily take place.

Some of the women are shown with extremely wide hips and pendulous breasts. Almost none have feet. They may have been placed upright in dirt or on a post. Their facial features remain vague, a suggestion that they are not portraits of particular individuals. Some appear to be pregnant, others not. Some have pubic hair, and one, from Monpazier, France, has an explicitly rendered vulva.

Some have suggested that the figurines are fertility icons made by men or women who hoped to have children. Others propose that the images are self-portraits because no mirrors existed at this early time. If women portrayed their own bodies as they looked to themselves, they would have shown themselves with pendulous breasts and wide hips. Still other archaeologists take these figurines as a sign of a matriarchal society, in which women served as leaders, or a matrilineal society, in which people traced descent through their mother (as opposed to a patriarchal society, in which descent is traced through the father). Since most of these figurines were found in the nineteenth century and were taken to museums or private collections, we do not know their original context and cannot conclude more about their function.

The one exception is a cave site at Laussel in the Dordogne region of France, where five different two-dimensional pictures were carved onto the cave walls and could not be easily removed. One picture, Woman with a Horn, was carved into the face of a block of stone. This two-dimensional rendering has the large breasts and wide hips of the smaller freestanding figurines, but her right hand is unusual in that it holds a horn, perhaps from a bison.

The Laussel cave had other pictures of a similar woman, a younger man in profile, a deer, and a horse. One design showing a woman on top and another figure below has been interpreted alternatively as two people copulating or a woman giving birth to a child. Several vulvas and phalluses were shown in the same cave. The conjunction of these different images strongly suggests that the Woman with a Horn was worshiped, along with the other images and sexual body parts, probably to facilitate conception or easy childbirth.

QUESTIONS FOR ANALYSIS

▶ How do archaeologists determine if an idea or motif diffused from one place to another or developed independently?

▶ What constitutes evidence of religious belief among preliterate peoples?

▶ How have scholars interpreted female figurines found across Europe between 26,000 and 23,000 B.C.E.?

Woman with a Horn, Laussel Cave, Dordogne River Valley, France. An Ancient Pregnancy? Standing 17.5 inches (44 cm) high, this block of stone, along with five others, came from a rock shelter occupied by people between 25,000 and 21,000 B.C.E. Similar carvings of women with wide hips and pendulous breasts have been found throughout the Dordogne River Valley region in France, but only this woman holds a bison horn. Interpreting the markings on the horn as calendrical records (perhaps of moon sightings), some analysts propose that her hand on her stomach indicates that she may be pregnant. (Musée d'Aquitaine, Bordeaux, France/Erich Lessing/Art Resource, NY)

Being covered with ice, sometimes very deep, Beringia would not have been an easy route for humans to cross. Yet we know that people had already migrated as far south as the site of Monte Verde (MAHN-tay VEHR-day), Chile, in South America at a time when Beringia was covered with ice. So how did humans get there?

Core samples of the ocean floor, drilled into what used to be Beringia, have yielded the remains of animal, insect, and plant life that reveal the extent of glaciation. The most intense phase of the late Wisconsin Ice Age was in 16,000 B.C.E., a time when the sea level fell 650 feet, exposing Beringia to its largest extent. The islands of the Bering Sea then stood as giant peaks on the Beringia landmass.

Less ice formed on the Alaskan and Canadian side of Beringia. In fact, cores reveal that small, low shrubs, many of them dwarf birches, shaped a tundra environment.

The first migrations to the New World may have occurred in 14,000 B.C.E. or even earlier, and certainly took place by about 10,500 B.C.E., when ice still covered much of Beringia. Much of North America was covered by sheets of ice over 10,000 feet (3,000 m) thick. Some scientists believe that an ice-free corridor between ice masses allowed movement through today's Canada. Others hypothesize that the ancient settlers hugged the coast, traveling in boats covered by animal skins stretched tight over a wooden pole frame. Boats would have allowed the settlers to proceed down the coast from Beringia to modern Chile, going from ice patch to ice patch. Where no ice had formed, the early settlers could have disembarked to pitch temporary camp.

Monte Verde, Chile: How the First Americans Lived, 10,500 B.C.E.

• **Monte Verde, Chile**
Earliest site in the Americas, dating to 12,500 B.C.E., where evidence of human occupation has been found.

• **stratigraphy**
Archaeological principle that, at an undisturbed site, material from upper layers must be more recent than that from lower layers.

• **carbon-14**
Isotope of carbon whose presence in organic material can be used to determine the approximate age of archaeological samples.

The best evidence for this first wave of migration comes from far down the west coast of the Americas, from a settlement called **Monte Verde, Chile,** which lies only 9 miles (14 km) away from the Pacific coast, south of the 40th parallel. Monte Verde is the most important ancient site in the Americas for several reasons. First, without a doubt it contains very early remains. Lying under a layer of peat, it also preserves organic materials like wood, skin, and plants that almost never survive. Finally, and most important, professional archaeologists have scrupulously recorded which items were found at each level following the key principle of **stratigraphy.** This is the idea that, at an undisturbed site, materials from lower levels predate those found above them. Using this principle, we can conclude that, at an undisturbed site, any remains found under one layer are earlier than anything from above that layer.

Monte Verde's undisturbed state made it an excellent place from which to collect samples for carbon-14 testing. **Carbon-14** is an isotope of carbon with a known half-life of 5,700 years. A fixed percentage of the carbon atoms in a living organism consists of this isotope, but this percentage declines after death because new carbon no longer enters the organism. Accordingly, one can determine the approximate age of an archaeological sample by analyzing the percentage of carbon-14 in it. Carbon-14 dates always include a plus/minus range because they are not completely accurate: the farther back in time one goes, the less accurate the dating is. (This book gives only one date for ease of presentation.) Carbon-14 analysis of evidence from Monte Verde gave an approximate date of 10,500 B.C.E. for the lowest level definitely occupied by humans.

Forming a bony spine running along the western edge of the Americas, the Rocky Mountains and the Andes Mountains formed a barrier that kept the first settlers in the coastal zones west of the mountain chain. Latin America's climate in this early period, like Africa's, is still the subject of intense study. Climatologists concur that the climate was extremely variable: periods of heavy glaciation were much cooler than those when glaciers retreated. In comparison to North America, there was much less ice, except in the southernmost reaches of the continent. Major rivers and lakes had not yet formed.

Although no human remains have been found at Monte Verde so far, the footprints of a child or a young teenager were preserved on the top of a level dated to 10,500 B.C.E. This finding provides indisputable evidence of human occupation. The twenty to thirty residents of Monte Verde lived in a structure about 20 yards (18 m) long that was covered with animal skins; the floor was also covered with skins. The residents used poles to divide the structure into smaller sections, probably for family groups, and heated these sections with fires in clay hearths. There they prepared food that they had gathered: wild berries, fruits, and wild potato tubers. An even lower layer with stone tools has been dated to approximately 31,000 B.C.E., but the evidence for human occupation is less convincing than the human footprints from the higher level.[4] If people lived at the site at this time, then the Americas may have been settled much earlier than the 14,000 B.C.E. date that is widely accepted today.

A separate building, shaped like a wishbone, stood about 100 feet away from the large structure. The residents hardened the floor of this building by mixing sand, gravel, and animal fat to make a place where they could clean bones, produce tools, and finish animal hides. Healers may have treated the ill in this building, too, since the floor contained traces of eighteen different plants, some chewed and then spit out, as though they had been used as medicine.

The unusual preservation of wood at Monte Verde means that we know exactly which tools the first Americans used. The site's residents mounted stone flakes onto wooden sticks, called hafts. They also had a small number of more finely worked spear points. Interestingly, Monte Verde's residents used many round stones, which they could have easily gathered on the beach, for slings or bolos. A bolo consists of a long string made of hide with stones or round beach pebbles tied at both ends. Holding one end, early humans swung the other end around their heads at high speed and then released the string. If on target, the spinning bolo wrapped itself around the neck of a bird or other animal and killed it.

The residents of Monte Verde hunted mastodon, a relative of the modern elephant that became extinct about 9000 B.C.E. They also foraged along the coast for shellfish, which could be eaten raw. In the initial stages of migration, the settlers found a coastal environment much more hospitable than an inland one because they could forage for many different types of food at the beach. Hunting parties could leave for long periods to pursue mastodon and other large game, confident that those left behind had ample food supplies.

The main weapon used to kill large game at Monte Verde and other early sites was the atlatl (AHT-latt-uhl) a word from the Nahuatl (NAH-waht) language spoken in central Mexico. The atlatl was a powerful weapon, capable of piercing thick animal hide, and was used for thousands of years (see the illustration on the next page).

◼ A Powerful Ancient Weapon: The Atlatl   The residents of the Monte Verde site used the atlatl spear-thrower to kill game. The atlatl had two parts, a long handle with a cup or hook at the end, and a spear tipped with a sharp stone point. The handle served as an extension of the human arm, so that the spear could be thrown farther with much greater force.   (Illustration by Eric Parrish from James E. Dixon, *Bones, Boats and Bisons: Archaeology and the First Colonization of Western North America* [Albuquerque, N.M.: University of New Mexico Press, 1999], p. 153, Figure 6-1.)

The Rise of Clovis and Other Regional Traditions, 11,400–10,900 B.C.E.

By 11,000 B.C.E., small bands of people had settled all of the Americas. They used a new weapon in addition to the atlatl: wooden sticks with sharp slivers of rock, called microblades, attached to the shaft. Studies of different sites have determined that while the people in these regions shared many traits in common, different technological traditions also existed in different North American regions. Each left behind distinct artifacts (usually a spear point of a certain type). In contrast, South American sites do not show the same clear signs of regional difference because the residents of different sites mixed and matched different types of tools and spear points.

Like the residents of Monte Verde, these later peoples combined hunting with the gathering of wild fruits and seeds. They lived in an area stretching from Oregon to Texas, with heavy concentration in the Great Plains, and hunted a wide variety of game using atlatl tipped with stone spear points. Archaeologists call these characteristic spear points the **Clovis technological complex.** It takes its name from Clovis, New Mexico, where the first such spear points were found. It is difficult to estimate the number of residents at a given location, but some of the Clovis sites are larger than earlier sites, suggesting that as many as sixty people may have lived together in a single band. The Clovis people ate small animals such as rabbit, ground sloth, and turtle as well as larger animals like deer and bison. They also used tools to grind vegetables, but the types of vegetables have left few traces in the archaeological record.

The Clovis spear points impress all viewers with their beauty: their makers chose glassy rocks of striking colors to craft finely worked stone points. Foraging bands covered large stretches of territory, collecting different types of stone and carrying them far from their areas of origin. The Clovis peoples buried some of these collections in earth colored by ocher, the same mineral element used by the

• **Clovis technological complex** The characteristic stone spear points that were in use ca. 11,000 B.C.E. across much of modern-day America.

ancient peoples of South Africa and Australia. Archaeologists working at later Clovis sites throughout the Great Plains have also found a different type of stone blade lodged in bison bones. It seems that, as mammoth and mastodon became extinct, the residents shifted to hunting bison.

The Oldest Americans?   Who lived at sites like Monte Verde in the Americas in 10,500 B.C.E. or at the different Clovis sites in 9000 B.C.E.? This question would be much easier to answer if archaeologists had found multiple human remains at Monte Verde or at the Clovis sites in the Western Hemisphere. In both North and South America, thirty-six sites predate 9500 B.C.E., but only thirty-eight skeletons older than 9000 B.C.E. have been found.[5] Unfortunately, almost all of these early skeletons were removed from their original location. As a result, archaeologists must study bones divorced from their original context as they reconstruct the patterns of ancient migration to the Americas.

Some scholars of early migration to the Americas have conducted statistical analysis of these early remains in the hope of identifying the ancestors of today's Amerindians. Although we use the concept of race in casual conversation every time that we say someone is white or black, it is impossible to classify people by race scientifically. Many of the world's peoples do not fall into the widely used categories of black, white, or yellow; Australian aborigines have dark skin but light hair color, and Polynesians do not fit any of these categories. Rather than use the problematic category of race, scientists today focus on determining the geographic origin of a given population.

Physical anthropologists use one basic technique for identifying the characteristics of a given population in modern times. They collect measurements of the skull and other body parts for many different people from one place and input all the values into a computer database. Because skulls give the most information, anthropologists measure their shape, eye sockets, and teeth carefully. All provide clues about a given skeleton's background. Skulls and bones from a single place, however, tend to vary widely. A bone or skull may look like those normally associated with one place but may actually belong to an atypical individual from another place.

Once they have finished measuring a skeleton, physical anthropologists use databases containing thousands of data points to assign, however tentatively, a certain skeleton to a given population. The thirty-eight skeletons found in the Americas divide into two groups: individuals with longer heads and those with rounder heads. Those with rounder heads have wider, flatter faces. Their teeth share certain characteristics with modern-day Chinese, Japanese, Siberians, Russians, and Amerindians. They could well be the ancestors of today's Amerindians, who also have rounder, flatter faces and teeth like those of people living in Asia.

Those with the longer heads have small faces that tend to be narrow and noses that jut out. Their teeth have the characteristics of one group whose modern members live in Indonesia and Southeast Asia. Kennewick Man belongs to the group with the longer heads. Examination of his remains showed that he had sustained several injuries, the most obvious being a projectile point lodged in his pelvis. The growth of bone around the wound showed that the injury had occurred long before his death in his 40s. He had broken ribs, a dent on his forehead (perhaps from a wound), and arthritis in his elbows and knees, and he probably did not have full use of his left arm, which was fully grown but less developed than his right arm.

Kennewick Man in Court

For over a century Amerindian skeletons, unlike European skeletons, were kept in storage bins and displayed in museums. In 1990 the U.S. Congress passed the Native American Graves Protection and Repatriation Act, or NAGPRA, which required that all Amerindian skeletal remains that demonstrated cultural affiliation to an existing, federally recognized Amerindian people be offered for repatriation.

The case of Kennewick Man is different from most because of the skeleton's great age. Kennewick Man lived nearly ten thousand years ago, and his bone structure does not resemble that of the Umatilla people living near the Columbia River. One Umatilla leader insisted that they had lived in the region for ten thousand years: "Our oral history goes back 10,000 years. We know how time began and how Indian people were created."* Bruce Babbitt, Secretary of the Interior at the time of the discovery, agreed and ordered the remains of Kennewick Man repatriated to a consortium of five tribes living in the Northwest, including the Umatilla.

A group of scientists led by Robson Bonnichsen, a professor of anthropology at Texas A & M University, sued the government for return of the remains.

The scientists focused on the language of NAGPRA: "Native American means of, or relating to, a tribe, people, or culture that is indigenous to the United States." The act, they contended, required a relationship first to be established between the Umatilla and Kennewick Man before the Umatilla could claim him.

If Kennewick Man belonged to a group that had died out, they argued, then the Umatilla did not have the right to claim his remains. The scientists and their legal team hoped to show that Congress had not considered an exceptional example like Kennewick Man when drafting NAGPRA.

In 2002 a federal magistrate decided that Kennewick Man could not be "related to any identifiable group or culture, and the culture to which he belonged may have died out thousands of years ago."† In 2004 the Ninth Circuit Court of Appeals upheld his ruling, and scientists examined the remains in the summer of 2005.

---

*New York Times, September 30, 1996, Section A, p. 12.
†New York Times, July 19, 2005, Section F; Column 2; Science Desk; p. 4.

Like the other members of the longer-head group, Kennewick Man's head and body measurements did not seem to correspond to those of any Amerindians living in the region today. In fact, those in the long-headed group do not closely resemble *any* modern population. This lack of correspondence suggests that the long-headed group may have become extinct in the past, leaving no descendants today.

Scientists are still grappling with the implications of these finds, and many refuse to speculate further, since the data are so sparse and inconclusive. However, a small number of scientists have proposed a provocative, but tentative, model for the peopling of the Americas: they suggest that, as early as 14,000 B.C.E. and certainly by 10,500 B.C.E., the long-headed peoples came first, perhaps from northeast Asia, and lived along the west coast of the Americas. These settlers may have lived in Monte Verde and other early sites. Several thousand years later, these scientists suggest, a second wave of round-headed settlers came to the Americas, replaced the original settlers, and moved inland. Others dispute this hypothesis vigorously. (See the feature "World History in Today's World: Kennewick Man in Court.")

In sum, many scholars agree that people migrated to the Americas but not on when or in how many waves. Everyone concurs that the age of migrations ended when the world's climate warmed quickly at the end of the Wisconsin Ice Age. Between 8300 and 7000 B.C.E., the sea level (as measured near British Columbia, Canada) rose 400 feet (122 m), from 350 feet (107 m) below today's level to 50 feet (15 m) above it.[6] By 7000 B.C.E., the Bering Strait had filled with water and most of Beringia lay under water once again. The only regions of the world that had not yet been settled were the islands of the Pacific (see Chapter 5). After 7000 B.C.E., the ancestors of modern Amerindians dispersed over North and South America, where they lived in almost total isolation from the rest of the world until 1492.

The Emergence of Agriculture, 12,500–3000 B.C.E.

The development of **agriculture,** when people planted the first seeds and harvested the resulting crops using domesticated animals, marked a crucial breakthrough in the history of humankind. Before it, all ancient peoples were hunters and gatherers and never established permanent settlements. They were constantly in motion, whether following herds of wild animals or gathering wild berries and plants. Over thousands of years, early peoples in different parts of the globe experimented first by gathering certain plants and hunting selected animals. Eventually they began to plant seeds in specific locations and to raise tame animals that could help them harvest their crops. The cultivation of crops facilitated settled life first in small farming villages and then in towns.

• **agriculture** The planting of seeds and harvesting of crops using domesticated animals.

The Domestication of Plants and Animals, ca. 12,500–7000 B.C.E.

The first people in western Asia, and possibly the world, who learned how to plant seeds, domesticate animals, and cultivate crops were the Natufians (NAH-too-fee-uhnz), who lived in Palestine and southern Syria in 12,500 B.C.E. (see Map 1.1). Hunters and gatherers, they harvested fields of grain, particularly wild barley and emmer wheat, which flourished because the region's climate was warmer and wetter than today. They also picked fruits and nuts and hunted wild cattle, goats, pigs, and deer.

The Natufians used small flint blades mounted on wooden handles to cut down the stands of wild barley and emmer wheat, and they ground the harvested grain in stone mortars with pestles. Because they knew how to make advanced stone tools, archaeologists class them as **Neolithic,** literally "New Stone Age." Unlike Paleolithic peoples, the Natufians and other Neolithic peoples practiced agriculture. Gradually the Natufians began to modify their way of life, possibly to support a growing population.

• **Neolithic** "New Stone Age," the archaeological term for societies that used stone tools and practiced agriculture.

The Natufians at first gathered wild grain where it grew naturally. But wild grains had two flaws: their stems were so weak that their seeds easily fell to the ground, and their thick husks made it difficult to remove the kernels of grain from inside the seeds. The Natufians gradually started to weed these naturally occurring stands of grain and to plant extra seeds in them. The Natufians picked seeds from tall plants, a practice that eventually fostered the growth of wheat with stronger stems. Similarly, as they favored plants whose kernels had thinner husks, the wheat and barley they planted began to diverge from their wild prototypes.

People took thousands of years to master the two major components of farming: taming animals and planting crops. The first step to domesticating wild animals was simply to stop killing young female animals. Then people began to watch over wild herds and kill only those animals that could no longer breed. Eventually,

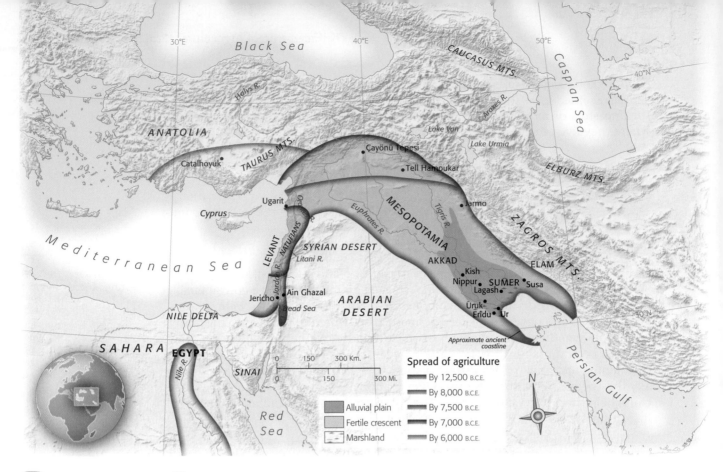

🌐 MAP 1.1

Ancient Southwestern Asia   The Natufians, who lived in Palestine and southern Syria, began to practice agriculture around 12,500 B.C.E. and gradually learned how to raise animals and plant crops over the next several thousand years. Agriculture eventually spread beyond the Levant and Mesopotamia to southern Anatolia, where agriculturalists built the world's earliest city at Catalhoyuk.

the Natufians began to feed the herds in their care. The dog was the first animal to be tamed, around 10,000 B.C.E., and its function was to help hunters locate their prey. After several thousand years, villagers had domesticated goats, sheep, and cattle. All these animals produced meat, and sheep produced wool that was woven into cloth.

The size of excavated Natufian sites suggests that groups as large as 150 or 250 people—far larger than the typical hunting and gathering band of 30 or 40—lived together in settlements as large as 10,800 square feet (1000 sq m). Although some analysts have idealized life in ancient society and imagined early peoples sharing their food and clothing with each other, archaeological evidence shows just the opposite: some people, presumably the higher-ranking members of the group, gained control of more resources than others. Burials reveal the greatest differences: some Natufian tombs contain the unadorned corpses of the lower ranked, while corpses decorated with shell, bone, or stone ornaments are clearly those of the more powerful members of the society.

After 8300 B.C.E., possibly because of a sustained period of dryer weather, it became increasingly difficult for the Natufians to continue gathering wild grain as before. Some Natufians returned to a life of hunting undomesticated crops and gathering wild plants, a possible indication that they found the cultivation of crops too difficult. Still others intensified their planting and gathering of wheat and barley.

By 8000 B.C.E. many peoples throughout the eastern Mediterranean, particularly near the Zagros Mountains in modern Turkey, had begun to cultivate wheat and barley (see Map 1.2). Unlike the Natufians, these peoples did not live near pre-existing stands of wild wheat and barley but rather in more difficult living conditions that forced them to experiment with planting seeds and raising crops. Archaeologists have noticed that peoples living in marginal areas, not the most fertile areas with the heaviest rainfall, tended to plant crops because they had to innovate. Once they had begun to cultivate crops, the larger size of their villages forced them to continue farming because agriculture could support a larger population than hunting and gathering.

The First Larger Settlements, 7000–3000 B.C.E.

Between 8300 and 7500 B.C.E., the largest Natufian settlement was Jericho (JEHR-ih-koh), near the Jordan River in the present-day occupied West Bank, where as many as one thousand people may have lived in an area of 8 to 10 acres (.03–.04 sq km).[7] Residing in mud-brick dwellings with stone foundation bases, the residents of Jericho planted barley and wheat, possibly along with figs and lentils, at the same time they continued to hunt wild animals. The more grains they ate, the more their bodies needed salt, which they collected by evaporating water from the Dead Sea.

The residents of Jericho dug a wide ditch and built a wall at least 8 feet (2.5 m) high around their settlement to protect their accumulated resources from wild animals, human enemies, or possibly both. They also built a 28-foot (8.5-m) tower inside the wall that may have served as a lookout post. The ditches, the wall, and the tower all show the ruler's ability to mobilize laborers and supplies for large-scale construction.

Around 7250 B.C.E., more than one thousand people lived at the site of Ain Ghazal (AYN GUH-zahl) near Amman, Jordan, which also covered 10 acres (.04 sq km).

The Earliest Depictions of People? The Plaster Statues of Ain Ghazal, Jordan Dating to 6500 B.C.E., these figures were probably used in rituals and commemorated the dead. Their makers fashioned a core of reeds and grass, covered it with plaster, and then painted clothes and facial features on it. The eyes, made from inlaid shells with painted dots, are particularly haunting. (Photo by John Tsantesi, courtesy Dr. Gary O. Rollefson, Whitman College, Walla Walla, Washington)

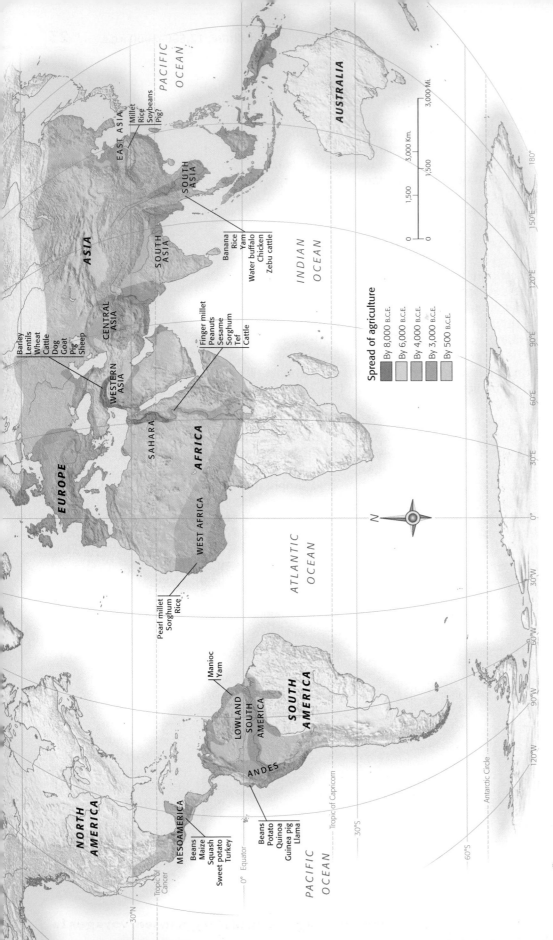

MAP 1.2

Early Agriculture Agriculture developed independently at different times in the different regions of the world. In some places, like western Asia, residents gradually shifted to full-time cultivation of crops and raising domesticated animals, while in others, like New Guinea, they continued to hunt and gather.

 Interactive Map

Spread of agriculture

- By 8,000 B.C.E.
- By 6,000 B.C.E.
- By 4,000 B.C.E.
- By 3,000 B.C.E.
- By 500 B.C.E.

EAST ASIA
Millet
Rice
Soybeans
Pig?

SOUTH ASIA
Banana
Rice
Yam
Water buffalo
Chicken
Zebu cattle

WESTERN ASIA
Barley
Lentils
Wheat
Cattle
Dog
Goat
Pig
Sheep

Finger millet
Peanuts
Sesame
Sorghum
Tef
Cattle

WEST AFRICA
Pearl millet
Sorghum
Rice

LOWLAND SOUTH AMERICA
Manioc
Yam

MESOAMERICA
Beans
Maize
Squash
Sweet potato
Turkey

ANDES
Beans
Potato
Quinoa
Guinea pig
Llama

In 6500 B.C.E., the site had become twice as large, and by 6000 B.C.E. it was three times as large. Like the residents of Jericho, the people of Ain Ghazal planted wheat, barley, and lentils, even as they continued to hunt for wild animals and gather wild plants. They also raised their own domesticated goats. The site is most famous for producing quantities of unusual human figurines, some as tall as 3 feet (.9 m), with distinctive shell eyes.

By 7000 B.C.E. early farmers were living in villages in western Turkey and the region of the Levant (the eastern shore of the Mediterranean in today's Lebanon and Israel). Their residents could depend on rainfall to support their crops, and they continued to hunt and gather as they raised their own herds. By far the largest settlement in the region was at Catalhoyuk (CHAH-tal Her-yerk) in south central Anatolia, where some five thousand people were living in 6000 B.C.E.

Catalhoyuk did not resemble earlier settlements. Unlike Jericho, it had no external wall or surrounding moats. The residents lived in mud-brick dwellings touching each other, and the exteriors of the houses on the perimeter of the village formed a continuous protective wall.

Frequently white-washed, the walls of the Catalhoyuk dwellings depicted animals, hunters, gods, and even the earliest known landscape painting of a volcano exploding. Of the more than one hundred rooms that have been excavated, forty had plaster models of bull or ram heads mounted on the walls or paintings showing women giving birth to rams or bulls. Some archaeologists believe that these rooms served as shrines where residents worshiped bulls and rams; others see them simply as the homes of the wealthy, who worshiped ram and bull deities.

The different types of houses at Catalhoyuk indicate that some residents had more wealth than others. The wealthy buried their dead with jewelry and tools, while the poor interred only their dead bodies. At the same time that they worked in the fields, some families worked bone tools, wove cloth, or made clay pots, which they could trade for other goods, especially obsidian, a naturally occurring volcanic glass. Ancient peoples treasured obsidian because they could use it to make sharp knives and beautiful jewelry.

Archaeologists have found evidence of the independent development of agriculture in a number of regions around the world: in western Asia around 12,500 B.C.E., as we have seen in this chapter (see Map 1.2); in Mesoamerica around 8000 B.C.E.; in the Yangzi Valley of China around 7000 B.C.E.; in the Indus River Valley in today's Pakistan between 6500 and 5000 B.C.E.; in the Peruvian Andes around 8000 B.C.E.; in New Guinea around 5000 B.C.E.; in eastern Sahara around 8000 B.C.E.; and in sub-Saharan Africa around 2000 B.C.E. Many peoples of the world continued to hunt and gather as the major source of their food supply. In the spring hunter-gatherers in New Guinea planted the seeds of a particularly desirable crop, such as bananas, and then returned in the fall to harvest the ripened fruit. Only in a few places in the world did the development of agriculture lead to the rise of a complex society, as we will see in Chapters 2 through 5.

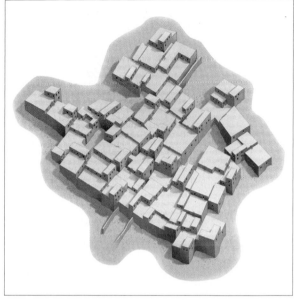

The World's Earliest City: Catalhoyuk, Turkey This artist's reconstruction shows what Catalhoyuk looked like in 6000 B.C.E., when it had a population of around five thousand people. The settlement had no streets, and the houses had no doors at ground level. Instead, residents walked on top of the roofs to get from one place to another. Entering houses through a hole in the roof, they climbed down a ladder to get inside. (From *Vanished Civilization: The Hidden Secrets of Lost Cities and Forgotten People*. Reader's Digest Association, Ltd., London, 2002.)

Chapter Review

CL Download the MP3 audio file of the Chapter Review and listen to it on the go.

The remains of Kennewick Man shed light on the settlement of the Americas, one of the last phases in the peopling of the world. The movement of peoples from Africa to almost every corner of the globe was a long one, requiring six or seven million years. This complex migration involved many different human ancestors, some closely related to modern people, some less so. One theme is constant: from the very beginning ancient hominids were constantly moving. They followed herds, crossed rivers, traveled by boat, and ultimately covered enormous distances at a time when their most powerful weapon was a stone hand ax and the fastest means of locomotion was running. From their beginnings, early humans were voyagers who traveled the world.

Who were the first hominids? What were the main stages in their development?

The history of humankind began some seven million years ago in Africa, when the first hominids probably broke off from chimpanzees and other primates. By 3.5 million years ago, australopithecines like Lucy stood upright. Around 2.5 million years ago, Homo habilis made the first tools by breaking flakes off stone cores.

When and how did hominids leave Africa and settle Eurasia?

The first human ancestor to move outside of Africa, *Homo erectus,* crossed the Sinai Peninsula and reached modern-day Georgia in the Caucasus Mountains by 1.8 million years ago and Ubeidiya, Israel, 1.4 million years ago. *Homo erectus* could probably control fire but did not settle in northern Eurasia because it was too cold.

When did ancient hominids become recognizably human?

Homo sapiens sapiens, or anatomically modern humans, first arose in central Africa around 150,000 B.C.E. In 100,000 B.C.E. they buried their dead in Israel, a sign that they believed in the afterlife, a major element of most religious systems. In 75,000 B.C.E. they created the world's first art objects, such as the chunk of ocher from Blombos Cave. By 50,000 B.C.E. these humans were planning hunting expeditions in the fall so that they had meat over the winter, and they probably used speech to do so. Their ability to hunt, to build boats and rafts, and to adjust to new environments allowed them to settle Australia by 60,000 B.C.E. and Europe by 50,000 B.C.E.

How and when did the first people move to the Americas? What was their way of life?

The final phase of the expansion occurred when *Homo sapiens sapiens* moved from Siberia across the Beringian land bridge to the Western Hemisphere about 14,000 B.C.E. The earliest confirmed site with human habitation in the Americas is Monte Verde, Chile, where humans lived in 10,500 B.C.E. Almost all of the residents of the Americas were hunter-gatherers who lived in small bands of about forty members.

 How and where did agriculture first arise? How did its impact vary around the world?

Agriculture arose first in western Asia around 12,500 B.C.E. There, the Natufians and other Neolithic peoples used stone tools to gather wild barley and emmer wheat. By 8,000 B.C.E. different peoples in western Asia had domesticated dogs, goats, sheep, and cattle, and they were planting and harvesting strains of barley and wheat. In some parts people continued to hunt wild animals and gather plants at the same time they cultivated certain crops, while in other parts of the world, including western Asia, agriculture resulted in the rise of complex societies, as we will learn in the next chapter.

 WEB RESOURCES

Pronunciation Guide

Interactive Maps

MAP 1.1 Ancient Southwestern Asia

MAP 1.2 Early Agriculture

Chapter Objectives

ACE Multiple-Choice Quiz

Flashcards

For Further Reference

Benedict, Jeff. *No Bone Unturned: The Adventures of a Top Smithsonian Forensic Scientist and the Legal Battle for America's Oldest Skeletons.* New York: HarperCollins, 2003.

Chatters, James. *Ancient Encounters: Kennewick Man and the First Americans.* New York: Simon and Schuster, 2001.

Dillehay, Thomas D. *The Settlement of the Americas: A New Prehistory.* New York: Basic Books, 2000.

Dixon, E. James. *Bones, Boats, and Bison.* Albuquerque: University of New Mexico Press, 1999.

Fagan, Brian M. *The Great Journey: The Peopling of Ancient America.* London: Thames and Hudson, 1987.

Fagan, Brian M., ed., *The Oxford Companion to Archaeology.* New York: Oxford University Press, 1996.

Klein, Richard, with Blake Edgar. *The Dawn of Human Culture.* New York: John Wiley, 2002.

Koppel, Tom. *Lost World: Rewriting Prehistory—How New Science Is Tracing America's Ice Age Mariners.* New York: Atria Books, 2003.

Stiebing, William H. *Ancient Near Eastern History and Culture.* New York: Longman, 2003.

Stringer, Chris, and Peter Andrews. *The Complete World of Human Evolution.* London: Thames & Hudson, 2006.

Wells, Spencer. *The Journey of Man: A Genetic Odyssey.* Princeton: Princeton University Press, 2002.

White, Randall. *Dark Caves, Bright Visions: Life in Ice Age Europe.* New York: American Museum of Natural History in association with W. W. Norton, 1986.

Websites

American Museum of Natural History, History of Human Evolution (http://www.amnh.org/exhibitions/permanent/humanorigins/history/humans5.php).   Virtual, interactive tour of the Museum's Hall of Human Origins.

Northern Clans, Northern Traces (http://www.mnh.si.edu/arctic/html/kennewick_man.html).   James Chatters provides his explanation of the Kennewick man discovery.

Scientific American (http://www.sciam.com).   Excellent source for latest discoveries in human history and archaeology.

The Smithsonian Institution: Human Origins Program (http://anthropology.si.edu/humanorigins/). Comprehensive introduction to the history of all human species.

Films

"Nova: Mystery of the First Americans."

CHAPTER 2

The First Complex Societies in the Eastern Mediterranean, ca. 4000–550 B.C.E.

⬤ **The Emergence of Complex Society in Mesopotamia, ca. 3100–1590 B.C.E.** (p. 31)

⬤ **Egypt During the Old and Middle Kingdoms, ca. 3100–1500 B.C.E.** (p. 38)

⬤ **The International System, 1500–1150 B.C.E.** (p. 46)

⬤ **Syria-Palestine and New Empires in Western Asia, 1200–500 B.C.E.** (p. 51)

The epic *Gilgamesh* (GIL-ga-mesh), one of the earliest recorded works of literature, captures the experience of the people of Mesopotamia (mess-oh-poh-TAME-ee-ah), who established one of the first complex societies in the world. **Mesopotamia** (Greek for "between the rivers") is the region between the Tigris (TIE-gris) and Euphrates (you-FRAY-teez) Rivers in today's Iraq and eastern Syria. The epic *Gilgamesh* indicates that the people in this region remembered what life was like before the rise of cities. It describes the unlikely friendship between two men: Enkidu (EN-kee-doo), who lives in the wild like an animal, and **Gilgamesh,** the king of the ancient city Uruk (OO-rook), located in modern-day Warka in southern Iraq. Ruler of the walled city between 2700 and 2500 B.C.E., Gilgamesh enjoys the benefits of a complex society: wearing clothing, drinking beer, and eating bread. Early in the epic, when a hunter complains to Gilgamesh that Enkidu is freeing the animals caught in his traps, Gilgamesh sends the woman Shamhat, a priestess at the main temple of Uruk, to introduce Enkidu to the pleasures of complex societies:

> Enkidu, born in the uplands,
> Who feeds on grass with gazelles,
> Who drinks at the water hole with beasts, . . .
> Shamhat looked upon him, a human-man,
> A barbarous fellow from the midst of the steppe:
> Shamhat loosened her garments,

GILGAMESH KILLING A BULL

Courtesy Schoyen Collection

 This icon will direct you to interactive activities and study materials on the *Voyages* website: www.cengage.com/history/hansen/voyages1e

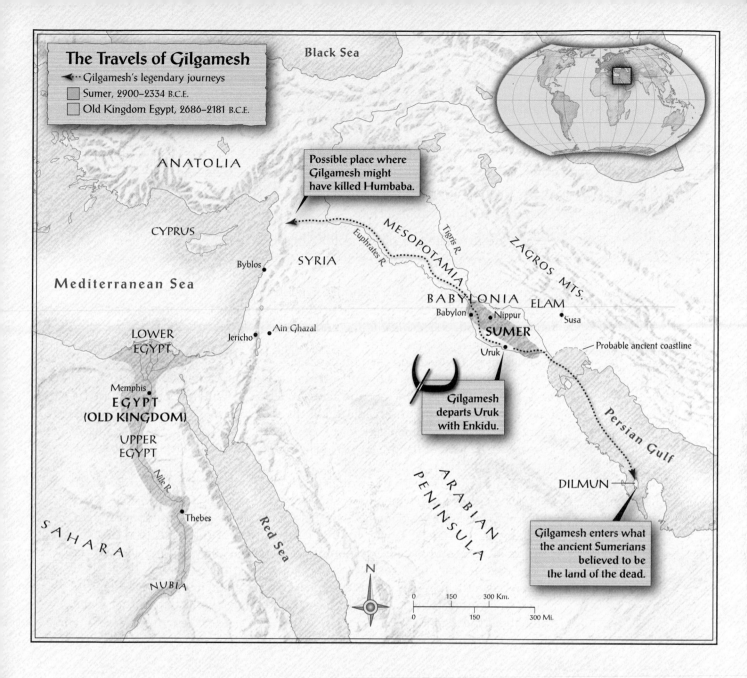

The Travels of Gilgamesh

- ◄····· Gilgamesh's legendary journeys
- Sumer, 2900–2334 B.C.E.
- Old Kingdom Egypt, 2686–2181 B.C.E.

Black Sea

ANATOLIA

CYPRUS

Mediterranean Sea

Possible place where Gilgamesh might have killed Humbaba.

MESOPOTAMIA

Tigris R.

Euphrates R.

ZAGROS MTS.

SYRIA

Byblos

BABYLONIA

ELAM

Babylon

Nippur

Susa

SUMER

LOWER EGYPT

Jericho

Ain Ghazal

Uruk

Probable ancient coastline

Gilgamesh departs Uruk with Enkidu.

Memphis

EGYPT (OLD KINGDOM)

UPPER EGYPT

Nile R.

ARABIAN PENINSULA

Persian Gulf

SAHARA

Thebes

Red Sea

DILMUN

Gilgamesh enters what the ancient Sumerians believed to be the land of the dead.

NUBIA

N

| 0 | 150 | 300 Km. |
| 0 | 150 | 300 Mi. |

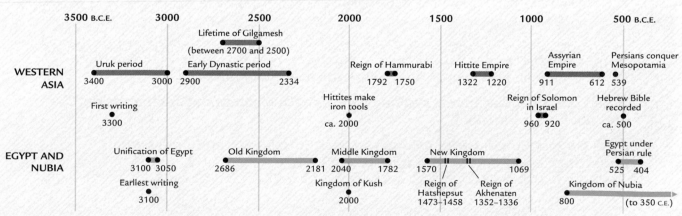

	3500 B.C.E.	3000	2500	2000	1500	1000	500 B.C.E.

Lifetime of Gilgamesh
(between 2700 and 2500)

WESTERN ASIA

Uruk period
3400   3000

Early Dynastic period
2900   2334

Reign of Hammurabi
1792 1750

Hittite Empire
1322 1220

Assyrian Empire
911   612

Persians conquer Mesopotamia
539

First writing
3300

Hittites make iron tools
ca. 2000

Reign of Solomon in Israel
960 920

Hebrew Bible recorded
ca. 500

EGYPT AND NUBIA

Unification of Egypt
3100 3050

Old Kingdom
2686   2181

Middle Kingdom
2040   1782

New Kingdom
1570   1069

Egypt under Persian rule
525   404

Earliest writing
3100

Kingdom of Kush
2000

Reign of Hatshepsut
1473–1458

Reign of Akhenaten
1352–1336

Kingdom of Nubia
800   (to 350 C.E.)

She exposed her loins, he took her charms, . . .
After he had his fill of her delights,
He set off towards his beasts.
When they saw him, Enkidu, the gazelles shied off,
The wild beasts of the steppe shunned his person. . . .
Enkidu was too slow, he could not run as before,
But he had gained reason and expanded his understanding.[1]

CL Primary Source:
The Epic of Gilgamesh
Find out how Gilgamesh's friend Enkidu propels him on a quest for immortality, and whether that quest is successful.

After his encounter with Shamhat, Enkidu immediately adopts the ways of those living in complex societies and becomes Gilgamesh's close friend. First written around 2100 B.C.E., *Gilgamesh* is not a strict chronicle of the historic king's life but the romanticized version of a legendary king's life, complete with appearances by different gods who controlled human fate.

The hero of the epic is constantly in motion. Gilgamesh makes two long journeys, traveling overland by foot and across water on a small boat he guides with a pole. First, he travels with Enkidu to kill the ferocious monster Humbaba, who guards a cedar forest somewhere to the west. Then, after Enkidu dies, Gilgamesh voyages to the land of the dead, where he learns about a flood surprisingly like that described in the Hebrew Bible.

The story of Gilgamesh was written by people living in one of the world's first complex societies. This chapter traces the rise of the first cities, then city-states, then kingdoms, and finally regional powers that interacted in an international system spanning Mesopotamia, Egypt, and the eastern coast of the Mediterranean, including Anatolia (the western section of present-day Turkey), Crete, and Greece in the Aegean Sea. These societies were significantly more complex than those that preceded them. As the centuries passed, an international system developed in which envoys traveled from one ruler to another and merchants transported goods throughout the region.

Focus Questions

⚲ **What were the similarities in political structures, religion, and social structure in Mesopotamia and Egypt? What were the main differences?**

⚲ **When did the international system of the eastern Mediterranean take shape, and how did it function?**

⚲ **How did monotheism arise among the ancient Hebrews, and under what circumstances did they record their beliefs?**

●The Emergence of Complex Society in Mesopotamia, ca. 3100–1590 B.C.E.

As we have seen in the previous chapter, the settlements of the eastern Mediterranean increased in size gradually, reaching some five thousand people living in Catalhoyuk by 6000 B.C.E. Eventually some villages became larger than the surrounding villages and thus became centers. In time these centers grew to become cities of twenty thousand inhabitants or more. By 3100 B.C.E. even larger urban centers had formed in southern Mesopotamia, where the first city of forty or fifty thousand people was located at Uruk. Here complex society took shape for the first time.

Scholars define a **complex society** as a large urban center with a population in the tens of thousands whose residents pursue different occupations, the mark of specialized labor. Some have higher social positions than others, an indication of social stratification. Some earlier definitions of complex society required the presence of a writing system, but today the term also covers urban societies without writing systems. In recent years, analysts have stressed that, unlike Neolithic societies, early complex societies had much larger surpluses—of both material goods and labor—and believed that their rulers, their gods, and their human representatives, the priests, were entitled to a large share of these surpluses.

The shift from a simpler society to a complex one took thousands of years. Complex societies interest historians because they had larger populations than simple societies and their residents often left behind written records that allow historians to study how they changed over time, the major topic of historical writing. The world's first complex societies appeared in Mesopotamia and Egypt at about the same time, before 3000 B.C.E.; this chapter first considers Mesopotamia.

● **Mesopotamia** Greek "between the rivers": the region between the Tigris and Euphrates Rivers in today's Iraq and eastern Syria.

● **Gilgamesh** Name of a historic king of Uruk (modern-day Warka, Iraq) who ruled between 2700 and 2500 B.C.E. Also, the name of an epic about him.

● **complex society** Societies characterized by large urban centers with specialized labor and social stratification, as well as the belief that rulers and deities were entitled to the surpluses these societies produced.

City Life in Ancient Mesopotamia

The first settlers came to southern Mesopotamia from the eastern Mediterranean and western Turkey. They found the environment harsh. Each year not enough rain fell to support farming, and no wild grain grew naturally in the marshlands. In addition, the Tigris and Euphrates Rivers tended to flood in the late summer, when crops were ripening, and the floodwaters often washed away the settlers' homes.

The settlers responded by developing techniques for draining the water. They settled along the shore of the Euphrates, which flowed less rapidly than the Tigris, and dug channels for the floodwater from the Euphrates. They discovered that they could use these channels to move the water to fields far from the river. Using irrigation, these early farmers permanently settled the lower Mesopotamian plain between 6000 and 5000 B.C.E.

Their first villages were small, but by 4000 B.C.E. some villages had grown into walled urban centers of over ten thousand people. The farmland within the walls could not produce enough food for the growing population, so the urban centers came to depend on surplus food grown by the residents of the surrounding villages. The food was stored in temples. Excavations reveal that temples had a main chamber surrounded by multiple rooms for the storage of grain. In turn, the cities provided the villages with military protection from raids by neighboring cities.

• **city-state** A city whose ruler governs both the city center and the surrounding countryside.

Historians use the term **city-state** for a city whose ruler governs both the city center and the surrounding countryside. Kings descended from prominent families, like Gilgamesh, ruled these city-states, often with the support of temple priests and in consultation with other prominent families (see page 36). The first kings were probably successful military leaders who continued to rule in peacetime.

The epic describes Gilgamesh's city of Uruk as the leading city of its time, and ancient texts simply call Uruk "the city," because no other city rivaled Uruk in size or importance between 3400 and 3000 B.C.E., the dates of the Uruk period. One of the most ancient cities to be excavated by archaeologists, Uruk meets the definition of a complex society: its population numbered between forty and fifty thousand, and its inhabitants had specialized occupations and were divided by social level. The surrounding countryside provided a large surplus of grain that the ruler and temple leadership distributed to the residents of the city.

The opening section of *Gilgamesh* provides a vivid description of the region's greatest city:

> Go up, pace out the walls of Uruk,
> Study the foundation terrace and examine the brickwork.
> Is not its masonry of kiln-fired brick?
> And did not seven masters lay its foundations?
> One square mile of city, one square mile of gardens,
> One square mile of clay pits, a half square mile of Ishtar's dwelling,
> Three and a half square miles is the measure of Uruk!

Uruk, then, contained one square mile each of land occupied by residences, farmland, and clay pits, with the remaining half square mile taken by the temple of Ishtar, the city's guardian deity. (The Sumerian mile does not correspond exactly to the modern English mile.)

Dating to 700 B.C.E., the most complete version of the Gilgamesh epic is a retelling of the original story, and historians must use archaeological data to supplement the information it provides about early Uruk. Although the epic claims that the walls were made from fired bricks, the actual walls were made from sun-dried mud brick. In roughly 3000 B.C.E., the city had a wall 5 miles (9.5 km) long. Enclosing approximately 1,000 acres (400 hectares), it was by far the largest city in the world at the time. Much of it consisted of open farmland.

Farming required year-round labor and constant vigilance. Unlike Neolithic farmers, whose tools were made from bone, wood, or stone, Mesopotamian farmers had much more durable tools made of **bronze,** an alloy of copper and tin. In addition to axes used to cut down trees and clear fields, they used bronze plow blades to dig the furrows and bronze sickles to harvest the grain. Other workers also had bronze tools. Those who smelted metal used hammers and tongs, while carpenters had saws and drills.

• **bronze** An alloy of copper and tin used to make the earliest metal tools.

Archaeologists are not certain where the wheel was first invented. One of the most important tools used by the Mesopotamians, it first appeared sometime around 3500 B.C.E. in a wide area extending from Mesopotamia to the modern European countries of Switzerland, Slovenia, Poland, and Russia. The earliest wheeled vehicles were flat wooden platforms that moved on two logs pulled by laborers. By 3000 B.C.E. the Mesopotamians were using narrow carts, usually with four solid wooden wheels, to move loads, both within city-states and over greater distances. By 2500 B.C.E., they had begun to add spokes to wheels, which moved much faster.

Built in the flood plain of the Euphrates, Uruk had no tall trees suitable for lumber, little stone, and almost no mineral deposits. The epic tells of Gilgamesh and Enkidu's overland journey to the wooded home of the monster Humbaba to obtain lumber, and the real-life inhabitants of Uruk shipped wood in carts or by boat first from the highlands of northern Mesopotamia, near the Zagros (ZAH-groes) Mountains, and later from the forests of Lebanon.

At Uruk, archaeologists have found extensive evidence of occupational diversity and social stratification, both important markers of a complex society. Large quantities of broken pottery found in the same area suggest that potters lived and worked together, as did other craftworkers like weavers and metalsmiths. Because people received more or less compensation for different tasks, some became rich while others stayed poor. Poorer people lived in small houses made of unfired mud bricks and mud plaster, while richer people lived in fired-brick houses of many rooms with kitchens. They hosted guests in large reception rooms in which they served lavish meals washed down with generous quantities of beer. (See the feature "World History in Today's World: The World's First Beer.")

The Beginnings of Writing, 3300 B.C.E.

People living in southern Mesopotamia developed their writing system sometime around 3300 B.C.E., making it the earliest in the world. Scholars call the language of the first documents Sumerian, after **Sumer,** a geographical term referring broadly to the ancient region of southern Mesopotamia. It is not always easy to determine whether a given sign constitutes writing in ancient script. Markings on pottery, for example, look like writing but may be only the sign of the person who made the pot. A sign becomes writing only when someone other than the writer associates a specific word or sound with it.

•**Sumer** A geographical term from Akkadian meaning the ancient region of southern Mesopotamia.

We can track the invention of writing in Mesopotamia because the residents used clay, a material that once baked was virtually indestructible. At first, sometime between 4000 and 3000 B.C.E., the ancient Sumerians used small clay objects of different shapes to keep track of merchandise, probably animals being traded or donated to a temple. Eventually they began to incise lines in these objects to stand for a certain number of items. Later, they placed these small objects in a bag made from a clay sheet and incised these bags, while still soft, on the outside to indicate their contents. These markings did not yet constitute written language because they could be understood in different ways; one had to cut open the clay bag, after it had hardened, to find out what was inside.

The transition to written language came when people drew a picture on a flat writing tablet that represented a specific animal and could not be mistaken for anything else. The first documents in human history, from a level dating to 3300 B.C.E., depict the item being counted with a tally next to it to showing the number of items. Temple accountants needed writing to record increasingly sophisticated transactions, like the number and type of animal or the amount of grain donated on successive days.

By 3300 B.C.E., a full-blown writing system of more than seven hundred different signs had emerged. Some symbols, like an ox-head representing an ox, are clearly pictorial, but many others are not. The word *sheep,* for example, was a circle with an *X* inside it (see Figure 2.1).

Over time, the marks lost their original shapes, and by 700 B.C.E. each symbol represented a certain sound; that is, it had become phonetic. We call this later

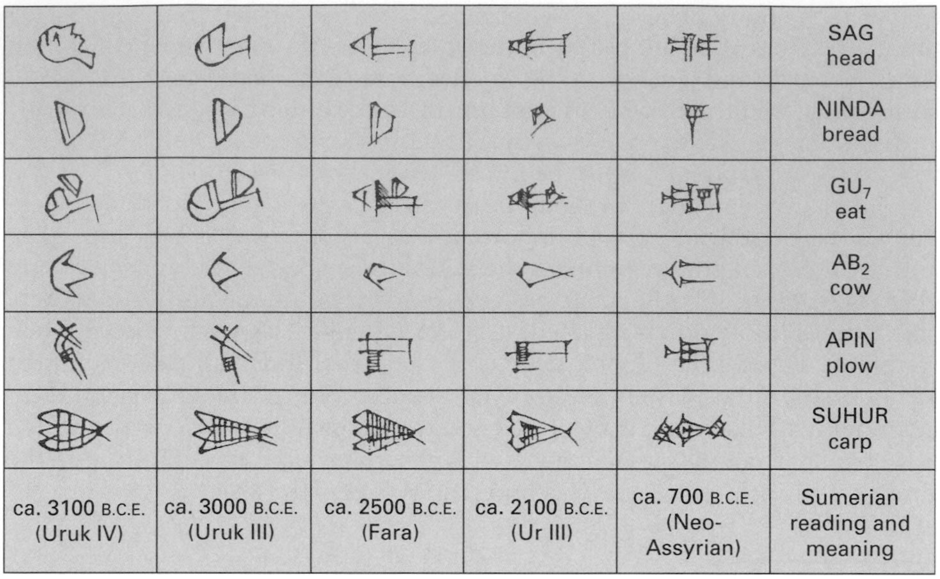

ca. 3100 B.C.E. (Uruk IV)	ca. 3000 B.C.E. (Uruk III)	ca. 2500 B.C.E. (Fara)	ca. 2100 B.C.E. (Ur III)	ca. 700 B.C.E. (Neo-Assyrian)	Sumerian reading and meaning
					SAG head
					NINDA bread
					GU₇ eat
					AB₂ cow
					APIN plow
					SUHUR carp

FIGURE 2.1

Cuneiform   The Mesopotamians first made small pictures, or pictographs, to write, but these symbols gradually evolved into combinations of lines that scribes made by pressing a wedge-shaped implement into wet clay. The cuneiform forms from 700 B.C.E. hardly resemble their original pictographic shapes from 3100 B.C.E. (From J. N. Postgate, *Early Mesopotamia: Society and Economy at the Dawn of History* [New York: Routledge, 1992], p. 63. Reprinted with permission of Taylor and Francis Books Ltd.)

• **cuneiform**
The term, meaning "wedge-shaped," for the writing system of Sumer in its late stages, when the script became completely phonetic.

writing **cuneiform** (cue-NAY-i-form), meaning "wedge-shaped," because it was made by a writing implement pressed into clay. These early records, most of them temple accounts, allow us to understand early Sumerian religion and how the ancient Sumerians distributed their surplus wealth.

Sumerian Religion

The people of ancient Sumer believed that various gods managed different aspects of their hostile environment. The most powerful god, the storm-god, could control storms and flooding. Like human beings, the Sumerian gods had families who sometimes lived together in harmony and sometimes did not.

The largest building in Uruk was the temple to Ishtar, the protective deity of Uruk and the storm-god's daughter. Sumerian temple complexes sometimes housed a thousand priests, priestesses, and supporting laborers. The largest structure inside each temple was a ziggurat, a stepped platform made from bricks. Throughout the year both rich and poor participated in different festivals and ceremonies presided over by priests and priestesses. The Warka Vase from Uruk (Warka is the modern name for Uruk) shows the residents of the city-state bringing different offerings to Ishtar (see the illustration on page 36).

The human king played an important role in Sumerian religion because he was believed to be the intermediary between the gods and human beings. The epic describes Gilgamesh as two-thirds divine, one-third human. He was sufficiently attractive that Ishtar proposed marriage to him. He brusquely turned her down, pointing out that each of her previous lovers had come to a bad end.

The World's First Beer

"Enkidu did not know how to eat bread, / Nor had he ever learned to drink beer!"* the author of *Gilgamesh* exclaims. Having grown up in the wild, Enkidu had never tasted the two basic foodstuffs of the Sumerians—bread and beer—both made from barley and wheat.

The usual way to make malt is to add water, allow barley or wheat to germinate partially in a sealed container, and then remove the water before the grain sprouts. Partial germination creates enzymes that produce the malty flavor. The Sumerians used large clay jars with lids for this process. We do not know exactly how they learned to make malt, but perhaps someone tasted a piece of discarded bread that had become wet and then fermented. The Sumerians were the first people in the world to make beer.

Gilgamesh vividly describes Enkidu's first taste:

Enkidu drank seven juglets of the beer.
His mood became relaxed, he was singing
   joyously,
He felt light-hearted and his features
   glowed.

The Sumerians drank beer constantly. The rations provided by the king to royal messengers included beer, bread, and onions. Temple-goers offered clay jars full of beer to their gods, and Sumerians regularly gave wedding presents ranging from 5 to 10 gallons (20–40 liters), or one-third or two-thirds of a modern keg of beer.

By the year 2000 B.C.E., the Babylonians had learned to make at least twenty types of beer, some from emmer wheat, some from barley, and some from a mixture of the two. The art of brewing spread throughout the region, and people throughout Egypt and Mesopotamia learned how to make beer.

The main ingredient in beer, even today, is malt extract, which is made from grain that has been allowed to ferment. Home brewers make beer by boiling water mixed with malt extract, adding sugar, combining it with still water, and adding yeast. After one to two weeks, the mixture is drinkable but tastes quite different from commercial beers.

*Quotes from Benjamin R. Foster, *The Epic of Gilgamesh: A Norton Critical Edition* (New York: W. W. Norton, 2001), p. 14.

Ishtar persuaded her father to retaliate by sending the Bull of Heaven to punish Gilgamesh and destroy Uruk. Gilgamesh's friend Enkidu killed the bull, to the delight of Uruk's residents but to the dismay of the gods, who then convened in council. The storm-god decided that Enkidu must die.

Before he died, Enkidu dreamed of the world of the dead:

To the house whence none who enters comes forth,
On the road from which there is no way back,
To the house whose dwellers are deprived of light,
Where dust is their fare and their food is clay.
They are dressed like birds in feather garments,
Yea, they shall see no daylight for they abide in darkness.

This description provides certain evidence—not available for earlier, preliterate societies—that the Sumerians believed in an afterworld.

After Enkidu dies, the heartbroken Gilgamesh resolves to escape death himself and travels a great distance over mountains and desert to reach the entrance to the underworld, believed to be near modern-day Bahrain. At the end of his journey, Gilgamesh meets Utanapishtim (OO-tah-nah-pish-teem), who tells him that a great flood occurred because the storm-god became angry with humankind and that Utanapishtim escaped when another divinity secretly informed him in time to build a boat. Utanapishtim, a human being to whom the gods granted

The Warka Vase: The Earliest Example of Narrative Art in the World? Found at Uruk, this limestone vase dates to 3200 B.C.E. and stands over 3 feet (1 m) tall. Like a comic book, it tells a story in different panels; the bottom shows crops and sheep on their way to the temple where they will be presented to the gods; the middle, nude priests carrying more offerings; and the top, the deities, who stand on the back of a ram, receiving all the offerings. (Iraq Museum, Baghdad/Art Resource, NY)

immortality, tells Gilgamesh the story of the flood, and Gilgamesh realizes that he, like all human beings, must die, and returns to Uruk to rule the city-state.

Sumerian Government

The ruler of each city-state claimed to rule with the support of the local guardian deity, but an early version of *Gilgamesh* makes clear that he actually ruled in consultation with one or more assemblies. Faced with a demand from a neighboring kingdom to surrender, Gilgamesh consults with two separate assemblies, one of elders, one of younger men. While the elders oppose Gilgamesh's decision to go to war, the younger men support him.

During the Early Dynastic period, between 2900 and 2334 B.C.E., settlers moved out of Uruk to build new city-states closer to supplies of lumber and precious metals. Because transportation was slow and communication difficult, these satellite cities had their own rulers but maintained trade ties with the mother cities. Thirty-five different city-states, each with a temple and its own guardian deity, traded and increasingly warred with one another. Higher city walls, increasing numbers of bronze weapons, and more artistic depictions of battle victories indicate regular warfare among these different city-states.

The first ruler to conquer all the city-states and unify the region was **Sargon of Akkad** (r. 2334–2279 B.C.E.). Sargon (SAHR-gone) and the Akkadians ruled the world's first **empire,** defined as a large territory with subject peoples of different languages and different religious traditions. He and his descendents ruled over southern Mesopotamia for slightly over one hundred years until their empire broke apart. As surviving inscriptions show, Sargon changed the language of administration from Sumerian to Akkadian (uh-KAY-dee-uhn), named for his home city of Akkad (AHK-cad). Akkadian was a Semitic language related to modern Arabic and Hebrew. Sumerian, which was not related to any other language, continued to be used as a religious language, but Akkadian replaced it as the language of daily life in the Mesopotamian region. *Gilgamesh,* like many other literary works originally in Sumerian, was retold and embellished in the Akkadian version.

The Babylonian Empire, 1894–1595 B.C.E.

After the fall of the Akkadian empire, Mesopotamia again broke into several different kingdoms. Sometime around 2200 B.C.E., a new city, Babylon, located north of Uruk on the Euphrates, gained prominence. Babylon was a small city-state ruled by a succession of kings until the great military and legal leader Hammurabi

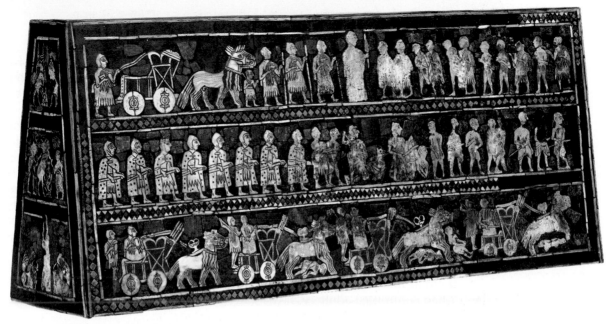

Documenting the Violence of War: The Standard of Ur Like the Warka vase (opposite), this object tells a story of war in different panels read from bottom to top. Notice the trampled bodies of the enemy under the feet of the donkeys on the bottom frame. The battle continues in the middle, and, on the top, officials present prisoners to a larger-than-lifesize king. (© British Museum, London/Art Resource, NY)

(ham-u-ROB-ee) (r. 1792–1750 B.C.E.) unified much of Mesopotamia. Surviving lists give the king's name and how long he ruled, enabling historians to count backwards to determine the exact dates of a given ruler's reign.

Hammurabi is famous, even today, for the laws that he issued. Many people have heard of a single provision in Hammurabi's law—"an eye for an eye"—but few realize that the original document contained nearly three hundred articles on a host of topics, including the treatment of slaves, divorce, criminal punishments, and interest rates on loans.

Hammurabi's laws were inscribed onto stone tablets over 7 feet (2 m) tall. Although they are often called a "code," the texts of many surviving decisions indicate that judges did not actually consult them. The king carved different legal cases in stone as proof of his divine rule and as model cases for future kings to study.

The laws recognized three different social groups, who received different punishments for the same crime. The most privileged group included the royal family, priests, merchants, and other free men and women who owned land. In the middle were commoners and peasants, and at the bottom were slaves.

The original wording of the famous eye-for-an-eye clause says, "If an awālu [freeman] should blind the eye of another awālu [freeman], they shall blind his eye."[2] At the most basic level this is the law of exact retaliation: if you bring harm to someone else, the identical wound shall be your punishment. It operated only among social equals, however. If a freeman destroyed the eye of a commoner, he paid only a moderate fine. If he destroyed the eye of a slave or broke one of his bones, then he had to pay the owner half of the slave's value, an even lesser amount. The laws stipulated the payment of fines in fixed amounts of silver or grain because coins did not yet exist.

As trade increased in the years after 2000 B.C.E., the Babylonian law codes on regulations governing commerce became more detailed. The main trading partners

• **Sargon of Akkad** (r. 2334–2279 B.C.E.) The first ruler to unify Mesopotamia. Changed the language of administration to Akkadian.

• **empire** A large territory in which one people rule over other subject peoples with different languages and different religious traditions.

CL Primary Source: The State Regulates Healthcare: Hammurabi's Code and Surgeons *Consider the various rewards and punishments for surgeons who either succeed or fail at their job in 1800 B.C.E.*

of the Babylonians lay to the southeast and included communities in the Persian Gulf and modern-day Afghanistan, who exported copper, the blue semiprecious mineral lapis lazuli, and other metals and precious stones in exchange for Mesopotamian textiles.

Hammurabi's laws also provide insight into marriage and the roles and status of women. Marriage had to be recorded in a written contract to be legally valid. Women were entitled to a share of their father's and/or mother's property, either as a gift when they married or as a share of the father's wealth upon his death. Punishment for adultery was severe: if a wife was found "lying with" someone other than her husband, she and her lover were tied together and thrown into water to drown; she was permitted to live if her husband allowed it.

At the same time, the law afforded women certain legal rights: if a woman was accused of adultery and denied it (and was not found with a lover), she could take an oath of innocence before a god and return to her husband's house unpunished. A wife could initiate divorce on the grounds that her husband failed to support her or had committed adultery. If the judge found that her husband had taken a lover but she had not, the divorce would be granted.

The tablets reveal only how the king hoped his laws would operate, not how they actually did. One case, recorded shortly before Hammurabi's reign on a clay tablet found at Nippur, shows how the legal system actually functioned. Three men—a barber, a gardener, and a third person whose occupation is not mentioned—killed a temple official named Lu-Inanna. They confessed to the victim's wife, but she, for unstated reasons, failed to report the crime.

Eventually the murderers were apprehended and the case came before the assembly of Nippur. A group of about ten men, including a bird-hunter, a porter, and a gardener, argued against the murderers: "They who have killed a man are not worthy of life. Those three males and that woman [the widow] should be killed in front of the chair of Lu-Inanna." An official and a gardener, whose different social ranks show the mixed composition of the assembly, spoke on the wife's behalf: "Granted that the husband . . . had been killed, but what had the woman done that she should be killed?"[3] The assembly decided that the murderers should be punished but that the wife was innocent.

Hammurabi's dynasty left a permanent imprint on southern Mesopotamia, which came to be known as Babylonia. Yet his dynasty was short-lived. Babylonia reverted to a city-state after his death, and the dynasty officially ended in 1595 B.C.E., when the Hittites (see page 50) sacked the city. Although the pace and extent of trade continued to increase, between 3300 and 1500 B.C.E. Mesopotamia remained politically apart from the other kingdoms of the eastern Mediterranean, as well as from Egypt, its neighbor to the west.

Egypt During the Old and Middle Kingdoms, ca. 3100–1500 B.C.E.

Complex society arose in Egypt at about the same time as in Mesopotamia— 3100 B.C.E.—but under much different circumstances. The people of Egypt never lived in city-states but rather in a unified kingdom made possible by the natural geography of the Nile River Valley. Their god-king was called the **pharaoh.** Although Egypt did not have the large cities so characteristic of early complex societies, its society was highly stratified, with great differences between the poor and the rich. Large construction projects, like the building of the pyramids, required the same kind of occupational specialization so visible in Mesopotamian cities. The less tangible aspects of complex societies—the belief that the ruler governed with the support of the gods and that his subjects owed him their surplus—were also present in ancient Egypt.

In certain periods Egypt was unified under strong rulers, while in others someone with the title of pharaoh presided over Egypt but did not actually govern the entire region. Historians call the periods with strong governments "kingdoms" and those with weak governments "intermediate periods." The pharaohs of the Old Kingdom, between 2686 and 2181 B.C.E., ruled the Nile Valley from the Delta to the first impassable rapids; those who ruled during the Middle Kingdom, between 2040 and 1782 B.C.E., controlled an even larger area.

• **pharaoh** The god-king who ruled the unified kingdom of Egypt since at least 3100 B.C.E.

The Central Role of the Nile

The Egyptian climate is mild, and the country is protected by natural barriers: deserts on three sides and the Mediterranean Sea on the fourth. Fed by headwaters coming from Lake Victoria and the Ethiopian highlands, the Nile flows north, and its large delta opens onto the Mediterranean. Along the river are six steep, perilous, unnavigable rapids called cataracts (see Map 2.1). Lying 620 miles (1,000 km) upstream, the First Cataract formed a natural barrier between Egypt and **Nubia,** an ancient kingdom that straddled modern Egypt and Sudan (see page 48). Egypt was divided into three parts: Lower Egypt (the Delta region north of present-day Cairo), Upper Egypt (which ran from the First Cataract to the Delta), and Nubia (sometimes called Kush), south of the First Cataract.

• **Nubia** Region south of the First Cataract on the Nile, in modern-day Egypt and Sudan; was an important trading partner of Egypt.

Because almost no rain falls anywhere along the Nile, farmers must tap the river to irrigate their wheat and barley fields; thus the Nile Valley waters almost all the arable land in Egypt. Two types of soil filled the banks of the Nile: averaging one-quarter mile (.65 sq km) on both sides, "the black land" consisted of very fertile soil, each year renewed by the river's deposits of silt; beyond the black land lay the red land, which was less fertile. Beyond the red land lay uncultivable desert.

The Nile, with its annual summer floods, was a much more reliable source of water than the Tigris and Euphrates in Mesopotamia; thus the Egyptians had no equivalent of the vengeful Mesopotamian storm-god who ordered the flood in *Gilgamesh.* The Egyptians began to cultivate the flood plain of the Nile between 4400 and 4000 B.C.E. Their calendar had three seasons, each 120 days long: "Inundation," "Emergence of the Fields from Waters," and "Drought." During "Emergence," farmers used irrigation to move the Nile waters to their fields and planted seeds, which they harvested during the "Drought" season.

Egyptian Government and Society

Scholars have wondered if the Sumerian invention of writing prompted the Egyptians to develop their own writing system. But the **hieroglyphs** (pictorial and phonetic symbols) of written Egyptian are so different from Sumerian writing that the two societies probably developed writing independently. The Egyptians were writing by 3100 B.C.E., but the surviving record does not explain how writing

• **hieroglyphs** The writing system of ancient Egypt, which consisted of different symbols, some pictorial, some phonetic, used on official inscriptions.

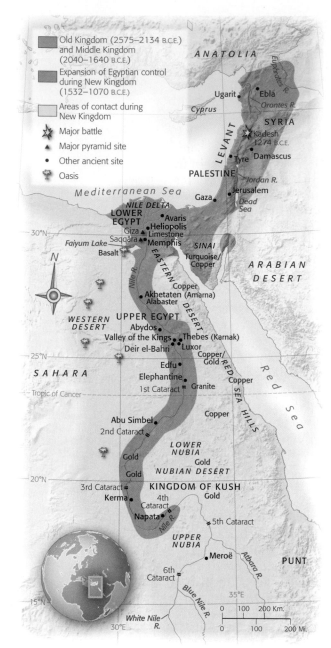

Legend:
- Old Kingdom (2575–2134 B.C.E.) and Middle Kingdom (2040–1640 B.C.E.)
- Expansion of Egyptian control during New Kingdom (1532–1070 B.C.E.)
- Areas of contact during New Kingdom
- ★ Major battle
- ▲ Major pyramid site
- • Other ancient site
- Oasis

🌐 **MAP 2.1**

Ancient Egypt and Nubia   The Nile River lay at the heart of ancient Egypt, but one could not sail all the way from its headwaters in Lake Victoria and the Ethiopian highlands to the delta at the Mediterranean. Because no boat could cross the sheer vertical rapids called cataracts, the First Cataract formed a natural barrier between Egypt and the Nubia, the region to the south where many gold fields were.

CL Interactive Map

developed in Egypt because the Egyptians used a perishable writing material, **papyrus.**

Papyrus (pah-PIE-rus) was a reed that grew along the banks of the Nile. After removing the outer stem, the Egyptians layered strips of the inner stem horizontally and vertically. When they placed a weight on the reeds and left them to dry, the fibers bonded to form a lightweight, convenient writing material that was far more fragile than the clay tablets of Mesopotamia. Most of the surviving sources for Egyptian history were carved into stone, which was much more durable than papyrus.

Ancient historians credited the legendary founder of the First Dynasty (3200–3000 B.C.E.), Narmer, with consolidating the entire Nile Valley into a single kingdom, but many scholars today think that Egypt may have been unified as early as 3500–3200 B.C.E. It seems likely that Upper Egypt and Lower Egypt originally formed two separate regions. Over time various rulers of Upper Egypt gradually conquered more of the Delta until they unified Egypt.

The lack of certainty about these basic events shows that important gaps persist in our knowledge of Egypt. In the third century B.C.E., the Egyptian historian Manetho listed thirty separate dynasties without explaining what caused one dynasty to end and another to begin. Even today, after comparing Manetho's list with others, historians do not agree about the dates of individual dynasties. Thus the dates given in this book, although accepted by many, are only approximate.[4]

One of the earliest records, possibly recording the unification of Lower and Upper Egypt, is a piece of slate. At the top is a horizontal catfish (pronounced "nar") suspended above a chisel ("mer"). These hieroglyphs indicate the king's name, Narmer (NAR-mer), and the piece is called the Narmer Palette. (See the feature "Visual Evidence: The Narmer Palette.") In other contexts these hieroglyphs could be used to mean catfish or chisel; one can determine their use only from the context, which makes deciphering hieroglyphs difficult. By 2500 B.C.E., Egyptians were using two writing systems: a pictorial script, called hieroglyphs, and a cursive form, called hieratic ("priestly"). Hieroglyphs were reserved for public writing on monuments and plaques.

Certainly after 3050 B.C.E., and possibly even before then, Egypt was united under the rule of one man, the pharaoh. As a god-king, the pharaoh presided over rituals to the Egyptian gods. In theory, the pharaoh removed the gods' statues from their shrines in each temple, dressed them, fed them, and prayed to them. In the evening he fed them again before returning them to their shrines. In practice, the pharaoh performed these rites in the capital and delegated his duties to priests throughout Egypt.

Egypt was one of the few cultures that did not observe the incest taboo. Since the pharaoh's family members shared his semidivine status, pharaohs often married their closest kin, including their sisters and mothers. They also took multiple wives. The frequency of intermarriage meant that a single woman could simultaneously be the wife of the serving pharaoh, the mother of the future pharaoh, and the daughter of the previous one. For example, the wife of King Tutankhamen (too-tunk-AH-muhn), Ankhesenamen (ON-kays-ah-muhn), was also his half-sister.

The pharaoh's chief adviser, the vizier, was the only person permitted to meet with the pharaoh alone. Since the pharaoh was often occupied with ritual duties, the vizier handled all matters of state. He was assisted by a variety of higher- and lower-ranking officials, many of whom came from the same small group of families.

Egypt was divided into some forty smaller districts, each ruled by a governor with his own smaller establishment of subordinate officials and scribes. Scribes were among the few Egyptians who could read and write. Legendary for its record keeping, the Egyptian government employed a large number of scribes to keep detailed papyrus records of every conceivable item. The demand for scribes was so great that the government often hired people from nonofficial families, and some of these managed to be promoted to higher office, a rare chance for social mobility in Egyptian society.

Craftspeople and farmers formed the illiterate majority of Egyptian society. Slavery was not widespread. Those who worked the land gave a share of their crop to the pharaoh, the owner of all the land in Egypt, and also owed him labor, which they performed at fixed intervals on roads and royal buildings.

• **papyrus** A convenient but perishable writing material made from a reed that grew naturally along the Nile.

The Old Kingdom and Egyptian Belief in the Afterlife, 2686–2181 B.C.E.

The five hundred years of the Old Kingdom, between 2686 and 2181 B.C.E., marked a period of prosperity and political stability for Egypt. No invasions occurred during this time. The Old Kingdom is also called the Pyramid Age because government officials organized the construction of Egypt's most impressive monuments at this time, an indication of how complex Egyptian society had become.

Egyptians believed that each person had a life-force (*ka*) that survived on energy from the body. When the body died, Egyptians preserved it and surrounded it with food so that the life-force could continue. The Great Pyramid was built between 2589 and 2566 B.C.E. to house the life-force of the pharaoh Khufu (KOO-fu), also called Cheops (KEY-ops).

Covering an area of 571,211 square feet (53,067 sq m), the Great Pyramid stands 480 feet (147 m) tall. It contains an estimated four million stone blocks ranging from 9.3 tons (8,445 kg) to 48.9 pounds (22.2 kg) in weight.[5] By pouring water into channels forming a grid, Egyptian architects managed to construct a base that was perfectly level. They also used a system of ramps and poles to move the large blocks, since they had no system of levers. An estimated fifteen to twenty thousand laborers, both male and female, worked on the pyramids at any single time. None of these laborers were slaves. About five thousand skilled workers and craftsmen worked full-time, while the remaining fifteen thousand unskilled workers

THE NARMER PALETTE

Found buried in a temple in southern Egypt, the Narmer Palette portrays the conquest of Lower and Upper Egypt by the ruler Narmer (ca. 3200–3000 B.C.E.) on a 25-inch-long (63.5-cm-long) piece of slate only half an inch (1.27 cm) thick. The slate is shaped like an ordinary *palette,* the word archaeologists apply to stone dishes that were used to mix ground minerals such as malachite for make-up or medicinal purposes. Palettes were usually about 6 inches (15 cm) long. This palette has a place for mixing minerals on the front face and is much larger than ordinary palettes, an indication that it was used as a ceremonial object.

Although very early, the Narmer Palette employs many artistic conventions familiar to us from later Egyptian art. Narmer, the pharaoh, stands larger than either his servant or his defeated enemies. The artist presents Narmer in a classic pose with his chest facing forward but with his head and legs sideways.

The palette documents the early use of hieroglyphs. Scholars can decipher Narmer's name because they know that *catfish* was pronounced "nar" and *chisel* "mer," but they do not know what the hieroglyph label reading "Wash" on the defeated enemies means. Various proposals have been put forward

This framed box, which resembles a walled palace, holds two hieroglyphs: a catfish (*nar*) and a chisel (*mer*) that together form Narmer's name.

The top frame of the palette, which appears on both the front and back faces, contains two bull's heads with human facial features; these bulls represent Narmer.

Narmer, identifiable by the catfish-and-chisel hieroglyphs to the right of his face, wears the chair-shaped crown used by the ruler of Lower Egypt. Behind him stands a servant; in front of him is an officer leading shorter soldiers. On the right lie ten fallen enemy soldiers in two horizontal rows, with their cut-off heads between their feet.

Two servants hold back the reins connected to the long, serpentine necks of two felines. The circular space between their entwined necks provides the area for the mixing of minerals, indicating that this is the front of the oversized palette.

Here a bull, representing Narmer, knocks down fortified walls and tramples on an enemy.

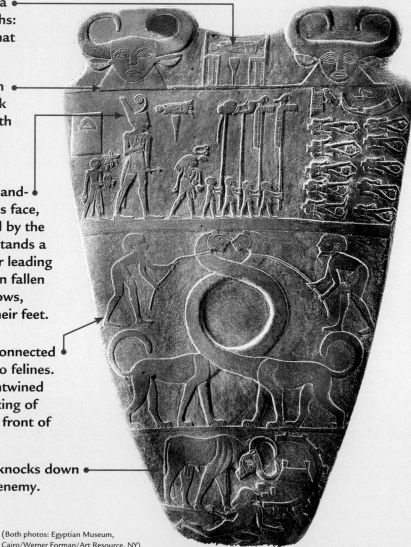

(Both photos: Egyptian Museum, Cairo/Werner Forman/Art Resource, NY)

about their identity, but no one is certain: Were they the residents of a certain region? Could they have lived outside Egypt?

However, scholars concur on the basic meaning of the palette: Narmer is claiming victory over his enemies. On one face of the palette, he wears the conical crown of Upper Egypt, and on the reverse, the chair-shaped crown of Lower Egypt. Because the palette dates to around 3100 B.C.E. and because historians believe that Egypt was unified at that time, they accept Narmer's claim as put forward by the palette's artist.

The themes of Narmer's palette are exactly those we would expect of a society in the early stages of becoming a complex society. Narmer rules with the support of the deities, including the sky-god, who appears as a falcon. His subjects owe him labor, as represented by his servants and soldiers, and goods, such as papyrus, because he, like a powerful bull, defends them by clubbing, decapitating, castrating, and trampling enemy troops. The ruler's task is exactly that of the two servants who rein in the felines in the central image on the face of the palette: to restrain the forces of disorder.

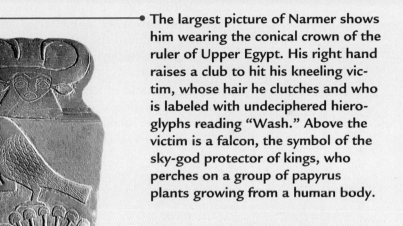

The largest picture of Narmer shows him wearing the conical crown of the ruler of Upper Egypt. His right hand raises a club to hit his kneeling victim, whose hair he clutches and who is labeled with undeciphered hieroglyphs reading "Wash." Above the victim is a falcon, the symbol of the sky-god protector of kings, who perches on a group of papyrus plants growing from a human body.

These two soldiers beneath Narmer's feet have been defeated. The penis of the figure on the right is visible, while that of the left figure is not, suggesting that he has been castrated. Both men are probably dead.

QUESTION FOR ANALYSIS

How did Egyptian and Mesopotamian artists who made the Narmer Palette and the Warka Vase portray their different understandings of what the ruler owes his subjects and what they owe him in return?

came to the site during the Inundation season to perform their labor service and then returned home, to be replaced by a new group of workers the following year.[6]

The size of his funerary monument provides a tangible measure of each ruler's power. The government had to organize the labor of all the workers and coordinate the shipment of large stones to the site of the pharaoh's tomb. Projects like the building of the Great Pyramid required a level of social organization and occupational specialization characteristic of early complex societies; at the same time, they also contributed to the growing complexity of these ancient societies.

During the Old Kingdom, only the pharaoh and his family could afford to preserve his corpse for eternity, but in later centuries, everyone in Egypt, whether rich or poor, hoped to travel to the next world with his or her body intact. The earliest surviving examples of Egyptian mummification date to 2400 B.C.E., just after the time of the Great Pyramid, yet detailed descriptions date from much later, around 450 B.C.E., when the Greek traveler Herodotus (he-ROD-uh-tuhs) visited Egypt (see Chapter 6).

Embalmers offered their customers three options, Herodotus explained, depending on how much money they could spend. In the most expensive process, embalmers removed the brain through the nose with a hook and pulled out the internal organs through an incision in the abdomen. Then they rinsed the body

Great Pyramid of Khufu (Cheops): How did the Egyptians Do It?   The Great Pyramid contains some four million stone blocks, which the builders moved by means of a system of ramps and poles. They managed to construct a perfectly level base by pouring water into a grid of channels, some still visible here.   (Photos.com/Jupiter Images)

and covered it with natron (NAY-tron), a crystallized form of potassium carbonate that kept the corpse dry. After forty days, bandagers spent two weeks wrapping the body in linen before placing it in a coffin. The earliest surviving mummy, from 2400 B.C.E., happens to be one of the best preserved, with his facial features and even a callus on his foot still visible.

In the less expensive option, the embalmers simply injected the body with cedar oil, which caused the internal organs to decay and to be expelled through the anus. Bandaging and burial followed. The poorest Egyptians could only afford to have the unbandaged corpse prepared and buried.

Egyptians believed that the dead had to appear before Osiris (oh-SIGH-ruhs), the god of the underworld, who determined who could enter the realm of eternal happiness. Compiled in the sixteenth century B.C.E. yet drawing on materials dating back to 2400 B.C.E., the *Book of the Dead* contained detailed instructions for what the deceased should say on meeting Osiris. At the moment of judgment, the deceased should deny having committed any crime:

CL Primary Source:
The Egyptian Book of the Dead's Declaration of Innocence
Read the number of potential sins that would likely tarnish a journeying spirit and prevent entrance into the realm of the blessed.

> I have not committed evil against men.
> I have not mistreated cattle.
> I have not committed sin in the place of truth [that is, a temple
>   or burial ground]
> I have not blasphemed a god. . . .
> I have not made (anyone) sick.
> I have not made (anyone) weep.
> I have not killed. . . .
> I have not held up water in its season [that is, denied floodwaters to others].
> I have not built a dam against running water. . . .[7]

The list reveals the offenses thought most outrageous by the Egyptians: diverting water from the irrigation channels belonging to one's neighbor constituted a major infraction.

During the First Intermediate Period (2180–2040 B.C.E.), Old Kingdom Egypt broke apart into semi-independent regions ruled by rival dynasties. The pharaoh was unable to appoint regional governors because certain families refused to give up government posts they had retained for multiple generations. Nor could the pharaoh collect as much revenue as his predecessors, possibly because sustained drought reduced agricultural yields.

Egyptian Expansion During the Middle Kingdom, 2040–1782 B.C.E.

In 2040 B.C.E. the ruler based in Thebes (modern-day Luxor) reunited Egypt and established what became known as the Middle Kingdom (2040–1782 B.C.E.), the second long period of centralized rule. Egypt's trade with other regions increased dramatically. Like Mesopotamia, Egypt had few natural resources and was forced to trade with distant lands to obtain wood, copper, gold, silver, and semiprecious stones. Its main trading partners were modern-day Syria and Lebanon to the north and Nubia to the south. At the height of the Middle Kingdom, the pharaoh sent his armies beyond Egypt for the first time, conquering territory in Palestine and Nubia. Various Middle Kingdom rulers conquered and governed the regions south of the First and Second Cataracts.

Sometime around 2000 B.C.E., Egyptian sources begin to mention the kingdom of Kush, another name for Nubia, whose capital lay south of the Third Cataract.

Since the cataracts of the Nile could not be crossed in a ship, merchants hired bearers to unload goods and carry them to the next stage of the river. During the Middle Kingdom, trade goods coming from sub-Saharan Africa, including panther and other rare animal skins, gold, ivory from elephant tusks, and slaves, traveled through Nubia, overland around the cataracts, and down the Nile to Egypt.

By 1720 B.C.E., the Middle Kingdom had weakened, most likely because a group of immigrants from Syria and Palestine, whom the Egyptians called Hyksos (HICK-sos) (literally "chieftains of foreign lands"), settled in the Delta. Historians call the years between 1782 and 1570 B.C.E. the Second Intermediate Period. The Hyksos had horse-drawn chariots with spoked wheels as well as strong bows made of wood and bone, while the Egyptians had no carts and only wooden bows. The Hyksos formed an alliance with the Nubians and ruled Egypt from 1650 to 1570 B.C.E.

⬤ The International System, 1500–1150 B.C.E.

Around 1500 B.C.E., western Asia entered a new stage of increasingly sophisticated material cultures and extensive trade. During the third period of centralized rule in Egypt, the New Kingdom (1570–1069 B.C.E.), Egypt had more dealings with the other kingdoms of the eastern Mediterranean than in previous periods. Pharaohs of the Eighteenth Dynasty (1570–1293 B.C.E.) exchanged diplomatic envoys with rulers in Crete, Cyprus, and Anatolia and brought captured foreigners from the Mediterranean and Nubia to serve in the Egyptian army and to work as slaves.

Egypt's main rivals in the region were the Hittites (see page 50), who were based in Anatolia, Turkey, and Syria (see Map 2.2). Smaller kingdoms also arose in southern and northern Mesopotamia, eastern Iran, the Aegean islands, and Syria and Palestine. Egypt reached its greatest extent at this time, governing a swath of territory that included Palestine, Lebanon, Syria, and Nubia. For five hundred years, the states of the eastern Mediterranean enjoyed a period of relative tranquility as they intensified their trade and diplomatic contacts to form what has been called the first international system.

New Kingdom Egypt and Nubia, 1570–1069 B.C.E.

During the New Kingdom period, Egypt continued to expand into Nubia. After eliminating the kingdom of Kush as a rival, Egypt destroyed its capital and extended control all the way to the Fourth Cataract. Nubia's most valuable natural resource was gold, which the pharaohs required in large amounts.

The pharaohs of the Eighteenth Dynasty venerated the sun-god Amun-Ra (AH-muhn–RAH) above all other deities because they believed that he had enabled them to expel the Hyksos from Egypt and establish their dynasty. They built an enormous temple at Karnak to house the image of Amun-Ra. Every day the temple's priests carried the bathed image around the temple, and once a year they sent the main image of Amun-Ra in an elaborate barge along the Nile to the capital at Thebes.

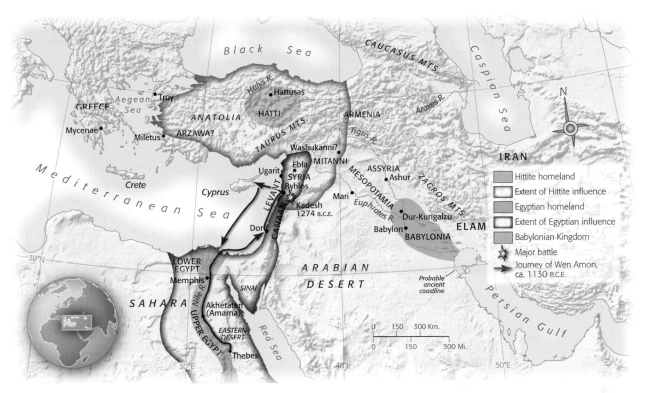

🌐 **MAP 2.2**

The International System, ca. 1500–1250 B.C.E. Wen-Amun's journey from Egypt to Lebanon and Cyprus in around 1130 B.C.E. shows the ease with which individuals moved in the region of the eastern Mediterranean. International credit networks made it possible for Egyptian merchants to send gold, silver, linen, and papyrus to Lebanon, meaning that Wen-Amun did not have to return to Egypt to collect them.

🔍 **Interactive Map**

The Egyptians believed that the most appropriate offerings to Amun-Ra were made from gold because gold was the color of the sun. Being indestructible, gold also represented immortality. Living people who wore gold became like gods, and the Egyptians buried the dead with multiple gold ornaments in the hope that they would live forever. While Egypt had some gold mines (see Map 2.1), Nubia had many more, and New Kingdom pharaohs were able to exploit these mines to the fullest extent.

After conquering Nubia, the pharaohs of the Eighteenth Dynasty worked to transform Nubia into an Egyptian society: they brought the sons of Nubian chiefs to Egypt, where they studied the Egyptian language, wore Egyptian linen clothing made from the flax plant, received Egyptian names, and worshiped Egyptian deities like Amun-Ra. When they returned home, they served the Egyptians as administrators.

Egypt continued to trade with Nubia and other regions during the reign of Hatshepsut (hat-SHEP-soot) (r. 1473–1458 B.C.E.), the only woman pharaoh of the Eighteenth Dynasty. Older women, whether mothers and aunts, occasionally served as regents when the pharaoh was too young to rule on his own, but Hatshepsut ruled for a full fifteen years as pharaoh. She imported gold, ebony, and cedar to add new rooms at Amun-Ra's temple at Karnak and build a spectacular new temple in the Valley of the Kings, where the New Kingdom pharaohs were buried. She was particularly proud of an expedition that she dispatched to Punt (in modern-day Ethiopia), which brought back to Egypt exotic goods such as monkeys and myrrh trees.

One ruler near the end of the Eighteenth Dynasty, Akhenaten (Ah-ken-AHT-n) (r. 1352–1336 B.C.E.), introduced an important change to Egyptian religion. Rather than accepting Amun-Ra as the supreme deity, he worshiped a different form of the sun-god, whom he called the "living sun-disk," "Aten" (AHT-n) in Egyptian. Artists of his reign portrayed Aten as a circular disk whose rays ended with small human hands extending downward to the pharaoh and his wife. The art of Akhenaten's reign was also new: realistic portraits showed him frontally, with stomach protruding, rather than in profile. In the past analysts erroneously thought Akhenaten worshiped Aten as the only god. In fact, he continued to worship other gods as well, even though Aten clearly ranked highest among them. After Akhenaten's death, Egyptians restored Amun-Ra to his position as the most important deity.

During the New Kingdom period, Egypt established a series of alliances with the various powers in the region and occasionally went to war with them. An extraordinary find of 350 letters concerning diplomatic matters at Amarna, where the pharaoh Akhenaten (see above) established his capital, makes it possible to reconstruct the international system of the time. Akhenaten addressed the rulers of Babylonia, Assyria, and Anatolia, who governed kingdoms as powerful as Egypt, as "brother," an indication that he saw them as his equals, while he reserved the term "servant" for smaller, weaker kingdoms in Syria and Palestine.

Many of the letters concern marriage. Akhenaten tried to persuade other rulers to send their daughters to marry Egyptian men, but he did not ask for their sons because Egyptians would not allow Egyptian women to marry non-Egyptians. Even though the arrangement was unequal, the rulers usually sent their daughters because they wanted gold, and only Egypt had gold (obtained from Nubia).

The Kingdom of Nubia, 800 B.C.E.–350 C.E.

Much weaker after 1293 B.C.E., when the Eighteenth Dynasty ended, Egypt eventually lost control of Nubia. For several centuries no centralized power emerged in Nubia, but around 800 B.C.E. a political center formed at Napata, the administrative center from which the Egyptians had governed Nubia during the New Kingdom.

Seeing themselves as the rightful successors to the pharaohs of the Eighteenth Dynasty, the rulers of Nubia conquered Egypt under King Piye (r. 747–716 B.C.E.). King Taharqo (690–664 B.C.E.) ruled over Nubia at its peak. The builder of an elaborate cult center to Amun-Ra, King Taharqo also revived the building of pyramids, a practice that had long since died out in Egypt. His pyramid was the largest ever built by the Nubians, standing 160 feet (49 m) tall (see the photo opposite).

The Nubians continued to erect pyramids even after 300 B.C.E., when they shifted their capital from Napata to Meroë. Initially the Nubians, like the Egyptians, used hieroglyphs for monuments and hieratic script for less important matters, but by 300 B.C.E. they had developed their own writing system, called Meroitic

■ **Nubia, Land of Pyramids** Modern Sudan has more pyramids—a total of 223—
than Egypt. Modeled on those of Old Kingdom Egypt, the Nubian tombs are steeper
and originally had a layer of white plaster on their exterior. Starting in the mid-700s
B.C.E. and continuing to 370 C.E., the Nubian rulers of Kush built pyramids over their
tombs, which were in the ground—unlike the Egyptian tombs, which were constructed
above ground and inside the pyramids (contrast with Cheops' tomb shown on
page 44). (Photograph courtesy of SacredSites.com)

(mer-oh-IT-ick), which combined hieroglyphs with hieratic script. Scholars know
how to pronounce the Meroitic script because it is phonetic, but they cannot understand it because it is not related to any living language.

The royal cemetery at Meroë contains the pyramids of thirty kings and eight
queens. As was common throughout sub-Saharan Africa, the Nubian dynasties
practiced matrilineal succession in which the king was succeeded by his sister's
son. (In a patrilineal system, the son succeeds the father.) If the designated successor was too young to rule, the king's sister often ruled in his place. Nubian queens
did everything the male kings did, including patronizing temples, engaging in
diplomacy, and fighting in battle.

The kingdom of Meroë thrived because it was able to tax the profitable trade
between sub-Saharan Africa and the Mediterranean, but it broke apart in the fourth
century C.E., possibly because the trade was diverted to other sea routes it did
not control. Located south of Egypt, Nubia had little contact with the different
states of the eastern Mediterranean to the north of Egypt. Accordingly, it did not

actively participate in the system of international alliances that had begun to take shape as early as 1500 B.C.E.

The Hittites, 2000–1200 B.C.E.

• **Hittites** A people based in Anatolia, Turkey, and Syria who spoke the Indo-European language of Hittite and learned to work iron around 2000 B.C.E. The Hittite Empire reached its greatest extent between 1322 and 1220 B.C.E. and ended around 1200 B.C.E.

During the New Kingdom period, Egypt's rulers frequently wrote to the rulers of a powerful new kingdom based in Anatolia and Syria, the **Hittites.** The language of the Hittites belonged to the Indo-European language family, meaning that its structure resembled that of Latin, Greek, and Sanskrit (see Chapter 3). The Hittites were the first speakers of an Indo-European language to establish a complex society in western Asia.

The Hittites were able to do so because, sometime around 2000 B.C.E., they learned how to work iron, which had a much higher melting point (2,786 degrees Fahrenheit, 1,530 degrees Celsius) than other metals, including bronze. The high melting point meant that iron could not be melted and then poured into molds like bronze. Metalsmiths heated iron and hammered it into the shape of the tool or weapon needed, a process that removed impurities in the metal. Much stronger than bronze weapons, the iron weapons of the Hittites were much prized.

The Hittite Empire reached its greatest extent between 1322 and 1220 B.C.E., when the Hittites controlled all of Anatolia and Syria. In the thirteenth century B.C.E. the Hittite ruler wrote to the ruler of the Assyrians to apologize for not sending any unworked iron. Instead he sent a single blade, an indication of iron's value at the time.

The Hittites had another advantage over their enemies: they had mastered the art of chariot warfare. Two horses pulled a chariot that carried three men (a driver and two warriors). While consolidating their rule in Anatolia, the Hittites sent only a small number of chariots into battle. Thus in 1750 B.C.E., the Hittite king commanded only 40 chariots. But by the Battle of Kadesh in 1285 B.C.E., when the Hittites faced the Egyptians, the ruler commanded 2,500 chariots.[8] Egyptian documents claim that the pharaoh Ramesses II (r. 1290–1224 B.C.E.) had triumphed, but Egypt gained no territory, an indication that the Hittite and Egyptian forces were probably evenly matched. After the Battle of Kadesh, Egypt signed a treaty with the Hittites, who sent a Hittite princess to marry Ramesses II.

The Hittite kingdom came to an end in 1200 B.C.E. when their capital fell to outsiders. Historians are not certain who the invaders were, but they note a period around 1200–1150 B.C.E. of prolonged instability throughout western Asia. Egyptian sources mention attacks by "sea peoples," and Egypt lost control of both Syria-Palestine to the north and Nubia to the south.

Wen-Amun's Voyage to Lebanon and Cyprus, 1130 B.C.E.

In the centuries after 1200, Egypt continued to enjoy extensive trade relations with the Mediterranean, as we can see in the earliest detailed account of an actual voyage, recorded on a torn papyrus dating to 1130 B.C.E.[9] In that year, an Egyptian priest named Wen-Amun (one–Ah-muhn) traveled first to Cairo, where he caught a ship across the Mediterranean to Lebanon to buy cedar for the Amun-Ra temple at Karnak, which had so much money and land that it was independent of the pharaoh's authority.

On arriving at a port in modern-day Lebanon, Wen-Amun realized that a shipmate had stolen almost 9 pounds (4 kg) of gold and silver—all the money Wen-

Amun had with him to buy the lumber for the ceremonial boat. Desperate, he sailed to the next port, where he stole some silver. When the victims reported the theft to their king, he refused to allow Wen-Amun to land.

Then something unusual happened. A young boy at court was suddenly afflicted by seizures, and the king's advisers concluded that Amun-Ra was responsible. Their explanation reveals that the Egyptian deity's reputation had spread far beyond Egypt. The local ruler made a proposal: if Wen-Amun sent to his home temple for funds, he would be allowed to depart. The credit network of the local merchants was sufficiently sophisticated that Wen-Amun was able to write home to request that another ship bring him gold, silver, ten linen garments, and five hundred rolls of papyrus to cover the cost of the lumber.

When Wen-Amun set off for home, his ship was blown off course to the island of Cyprus. There he met an Egyptian interpreter, who explained his predicament to the ruler, and Wen-Amun managed somehow to make his way back. Thus even during this time of instability, the international system of the time functioned smoothly enough that people could obtain credit and travel in the eastern Mediterranean.

● Syria-Palestine and New Empires in Western Asia, 1200–500 B.C.E.

Several kingdoms occupied the land along the eastern shore of the Mediterranean where modern-day Palestine, Israel, Lebanon, and Syria are located. They participated in the international system, but always as minor players in a world dominated by kings of larger powers such as Egypt, Assyria, Babylonia, and Anatolia. Around 1000 B.C.E. a smaller complex society arose in the eastern Mediterranean that was notable for its innovation in religion.

This lightly populated and politically weak region was important because it was the homeland of the ancient Hebrews or Israelites. The Hebrews were the first people in the eastern Mediterranean to practice **monotheism,** or belief in only one god, whom they called Yahweh (YAH-way) in Hebrew (God in English). Belief in a single god underlay the religious teachings recorded in the Hebrew Bible (called the Old Testament by Christians). Hebrew monotheism would profoundly shape both Christian and Islamic teachings (see Chapters 7 and 10).

● **monotheism** Belief in only one god.

The History of the Ancient Hebrews According to the Hebrew Bible

Geographers call the region bordering the eastern Mediterranean the Levant (see Map 2.3). The most populated section of the Levant was the strip of land between 30 and 70 miles (50–110 km) wide along the Mediterranean coast. The northern section, between the Orontes River and the Mediterranean, formed Lebanon, while the land west of the Jordan River formed Israel and Palestine. Israel and Palestine stretched only 250 miles (400 km) from north to south, with the southern half consisting almost entirely of desert. Its population around 1000 B.C.E. has been estimated at 150,000, and its largest city, Jerusalem, reached its maximum population of 5,000 in 700 B.C.E.[10]

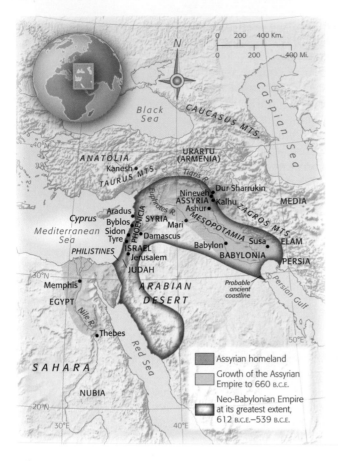

🌐 **Map 2.3**

The Assyrian and Neo-Babylonian Empires at Their Greatest Extent   The rulers of the Assyrian empire were the first in the eastern Mediterranean to resettle subject populations. Their successors, the Neo-Babylonians, continued the practice and resettled many subject peoples, including the Hebrews, in their capital at Babylon.

Ⓒ Ⓛ Interactive Map

Historians and archaeologists of Israel and Palestine disagree sharply about the value of the Bible as a historical source. Some view everything in the Bible as true, while others do not credit the accounts of the Bible unless they are confirmed by other documentary or archaeological evidence. World historians rarely have as much material for a given society as they have for ancient Israel and Palestine, and they often rely on orally transmitted sources far more recent than the Hebrew Bible, which was written sometime around 700 B.C.E. and whose current text dates to around 500 B.C.E.[11]

The first book of the Hebrew Bible, Genesis, traces the history of the ancient Hebrews from the earth's creation. The Hebrew Bible contains a later version of the flood story that closely resembles that in *Gilgamesh*. After the flood, Yahweh makes a promise, called a covenant, to Noah that he will not bring another flood. The ancient Hebrews, like many of the other peoples of the eastern Mediterranean, believed that certain individuals, whom they respected as prophets, could speak directly with God and also speak for him. Archaeologists have not found evidence of a single flood as described in either *Gilgamesh* or the Hebrew Bible; most think the flood narrative collapses repeated floods in the Tigris and Euphrates into a one-time calamity. (See the feature "Movement of Ideas: The Flood Narrative in the *Epic of Gilgamesh* and the Hebrew Bible.")

The most important event in their history, the ancient Hebrews believed, was God's choice of Abraham to be the leader of his people. Abraham, like his direct ancestor Noah, spoke directly to God and agreed to be the leader of his people. Abraham's father had brought the ancient Hebrews from the city-state of Ur to Haran, Genesis reports, and Abraham then brought them from Haran to Canaan, or modern-day Israel. God, in turn, made Abraham promise that all his descendants would be circumcised.

Although God designated Abraham as the leader of his community, the Hebrew Bible teaches, he and his wife Sarah had no children. God promised that Sarah would give birth to a son, even though Abraham was 100 years old and Sarah 90. When their son Isaac was born, she was overjoyed. Abraham had one son, Ishmael, with Sarah's maid Hagar, but Sarah sent Hagar away after the birth of Isaac.

God then subjected Abraham to the most severe test of all: he asked him to sacrifice his son Isaac as an offering. Abraham led his young son up into the mountains and prepared the sacrificial altar. At the moment when he was about to kill

Isaac, the Bible records, God, speaking through an angel, commanded: "Do not lay your hand on the boy or do anything to him; for now I know that you fear God, since you have not withheld your son, your only son, from me" (Genesis 22:12). Abraham untied Isaac and allowed him to go free.

The Bible's dramatic account of Isaac's rescue reflects a crucial change in Israelite religious observance. In an earlier time, the ancient Hebrews sacrificed animals and perhaps even children to their gods. An inscription dating to the eighth century B.C.E. from modern-day Lebanon records that during a plague the priests advised the local ruler to sacrifice a son or a grandson, in addition to an animal offering, to end the disease.[12] In later times, when the Isaac story was recorded, the Hebrews abandoned child sacrifice. The Bible gives no dates for the events it describes.

After the ancient Hebrews came to Israel, the book of Exodus claims that they went to Egypt and then returned to Israel under the leadership of the patriarch Moses. Since no archaeological evidence confirms that a single migration out of Egypt occurred, many scholars suggest that the Exodus may have been a series of migrations.

The History of the Ancient Hebrews According to Archaeological Evidence

The earliest archaeological evidence of the ancient Hebrews dates to between 1300 and 1100 B.C.E. In 1300 B.C.E. approximately twelve to fifteen thousand people lived in three hundred small villages on previously unoccupied hillsides in the southern Levant; by 1100 B.C.E. the population had mushroomed to seventy-five to eighty thousand.[13] No urban centers existed. Most of the residents had tools made of bronze, flint, and occasionally iron. Archaeologists have analyzed the bones they deposited in refuse pits and found no more than 1 percent are pig, an indication that the taboo on eating pork that is recorded in the Hebrew Bible may already have been in effect.

The few inscriptions found so far reveal that the residents wrote ancient Hebrew, a Semitic language. An Egyptian inscription dated 1210 B.C.E. lists several different defeated peoples living in modern-day Lebanon, one of whom it calls "Israel peoples,"[14] most likely the residents of the hill country.

Although the Bible portrays the ancient Hebrews as practitioners of monotheism from ancient times on, archaeological evidence indicates that they, like all the other peoples of the eastern Mediterranean, worshiped several different deities. The most important were the storm-god, called El or Ba'al (BAIIL), and his wife, a fertility goddess. In this early period, some of the Israelites also worshiped a storm-god named Yahweh.

The Bible describes the ancient Hebrews as living under a united monarchy that linked both the north and the south. King David built a shrine to Yahweh in Jerusalem, which his successor Solomon (r. 960–920 B.C.E.) rebuilt and expanded. After Solomon's death the kingdom broke into two parts: Judah in the south with its capital at Jerusalem, and Israel in the north.

Archaeologists have not found evidence of a united kingdom under the rule of either David or Solomon. But a significant change did occur sometime between 1000 and 900 B.C.E., when complex society first took shape in the region. The main evidence, as in Mesopotamia, is the formation of large urban centers with massive walls and impressive gates. At this time what had been a loose tribal confederacy

The Flood Narrative in the *Epic of Gilgamesh* and the Hebrew Bible

The striking similarities in the two versions of the flood story demonstrate that the Hebrew Bible drew on oral traditions circulating throughout Mesopotamia. The most complete version of the *Epic of Gilgamesh* was written in 700 B.C.E., but it drew on written versions dating to at least 2100 B.C.E. and even earlier oral traditions. Like the *Epic of Gilgamesh*, the Bible had a long history of oral transmission before being recorded in its current version around 500 B.C.E. Some of its oldest content may have circulated orally as early as 1200 B.C.E., when the ancient Hebrews first settled what is now modern Israel.

The two accounts of the flood differ most notably in their depiction of the divine. In the *Epic of Gilgamesh*, multiple gods squabble and the god Enki warns Utanapishtim that the storm-god Enlil is sending the flood to destroy his home city of Shuruppak. In the Bible, one god decides to punish all of humanity except for Noah and his family.

Sources: Benjamin R. Foster, *The Epic of Gilgamesh: A Norton Critical Edition* (New York: W. W. Norton, 2001), pp. 85–89; Genesis 6:11–19, Genesis 7:17–18, Genesis 8:1–3, Genesis 8:6–12 (New Revised Standard Version).

The Flood Story in Gilgamesh

Instructions to Utanapishtim for Building the Ark

O Man of Shuruppak, son of Ubar-Tutu,
Wreck house, build boat,
Forsake possessions and seek life,
Belongings reject and life save!
Take aboard the boat seed of all living things.
The boat you shall build,
Let her dimensions be measured out:
Let her width and length be equal,
Roof her over like the watery depths.

The Length of the Flood

Six days and seven nights
The wind continued, the deluge and windstorm
   leveled the land. . . .
The sea grew calm, the tempest stilled, the
   deluge ceased.

The End of the Flood

When the seventh day arrived,
I [Utanapishtim] brought out a dove and set it
   free.

The dove went off and returned,
No landing place came to its view so it turned
   back.
I bought out a swallow and set it free,
The swallow went off and returned,
No landing place came to its view, so it turned
   back.
I brought out a raven and set it free,
The raven went off and saw the ebbing of the
   waters.
It ate, preened, left droppings, did not turn back.
I released all to the four directions,
I brought out an offering and offered it to the
   four directions.
I set up an incense offering on the summit of the
   mountain,
I arranged seven and seven cult vessels,
I heaped reeds, cedar, and myrtle in their bowls.

The Flood Story in the Bible

Instructions to Noah for Building the Ark

Now the earth was corrupt in God's sight, and the earth was filled with violence. And God saw that the earth was corrupt; for all flesh had corrupted its ways upon the earth. And God said to Noah, "I have determined to make an end of all flesh, for the earth is filled with violence because of them; now I am going to destroy them along with the earth. Make yourself an ark of cypress wood; make rooms in the ark, and cover it inside and out with pitch. This is how you are to make it: the length of the ark three hundred cubits, its width fifty cubits, and its height thirty cubits•. Make a roof for the ark, and finish it to a cubit above; and put the door of the ark in its side; make it with lower, second, and third decks. For my part, I am going to bring a flood of waters upon the earth, to destroy from under heaven all flesh in which is the breath of life; everything that is on the earth shall die. But I will establish my covenant with you; and you shall come into the ark, you, your sons, your wife, and your sons' wives with you. And of every living thing, of all flesh, you shall bring two of every kind into the ark, to keep them alive with you; they shall be male and female."

The Length of the Flood

The flood continued forty days on the earth; and the waters increased, and bore up the ark, and it rose high above the earth. The waters swelled and increased greatly on the earth; and the ark floated on the face of the waters. . . .

But God remembered Noah and all the wild animals and all the domestic animals that were with him in the ark. And God made a wind blow over the earth, and the waters subsided; the fountains of the deep and the windows of the heavens were closed, the rain from the heavens was restrained, and the waters gradually receded from the earth. At the end of a hundred fifty days the waters had abated.

The End of the Flood

At the end of forty days Noah opened the window of the ark that he had made and sent out the raven; and it went to and fro until the waters were dried up from the earth. Then he sent out the dove from him, to see if the waters had subsided from the face of the ground; but the dove found no place to set its foot, and it returned to him to the ark, for the waters were still on the face of the whole earth. So he put out his hand and took it and brought it into the ark with him. He waited another seven days, and again he sent out the dove from the ark; and the dove came back to him in the evening, and there in its beak was a freshly plucked olive leaf; so Noah knew that the waters had subsided from the earth. Then he waited another seven days, and sent out the dove; and it did not return to him any more.

* **cubit**   Approximately 450 feet (137 m) long, 75 feet (23 m) wide, 45 feet (14 m) tall.

QUESTIONS FOR ANALYSIS

▶ What are the similarities between the two versions of the flood story? What are the differences? Explain why the later version diverges from the original.

became a small kingdom, complete with a bureaucracy and intermediate-level cities.

The residents of both Judah and Israel worshiped Yahweh, but in the ninth century two distinct groups formed. One, consisting of the rulers and probably most of their subjects, continued to worship Yahweh as one of many gods. The other, called the prophetic school, strongly believed that Yahweh was the most important god.

The Assyrian Empire, 911–612 B.C.E.

The two kingdoms of Israel and Judah remained separate and independent until 721 B.C.E., when the Assyrians, whose homeland was in northern Mesopotamia, conquered southern Mesopotamia, Egypt, and the kingdoms of Israel and Judah. Like the Hittites, the Assyrians had iron weapons. In addition, their cavalry was particularly powerful because it was the first true army on horseback. The cavalry soldiers rode bareback since neither saddles nor stirrups had been invented.

Unlike the various conquerors of the eastern Mediterranean before them, the Assyrians did not simply send in armies and subjugate enemy territory. Because the Assyrian ruler saw himself as the representative of the gods, he asked the rulers of foreign territories to submit voluntarily to him and his deities. Those who surrendered he treated gently, but his troops were infamous for their cruel treatment of those who resisted. Soldiers skinned captives alive, removed their eyes or cut off their hands and feet, and impaled others on stakes. These atrocities served as a warning to those who had not yet been conquered: if they surrendered quickly, they could avoid such barbarities. Such treatment was justified, the Assyrians believed, because the subject populations were resisting the gods, not just a human king.

Once the Assyrians had conquered a given region, they forcibly resettled the conquered rulers and skilled craftsmen to another part of the empire. The original intent in the ninth century was to fill up the lightly populated sections of the empire; later, resettlement was simply a demonstration of the ruler's power. Several hundred thousand people were resettled in this way, including many people from Israel and Judah who were sent to Assyria.

The last Assyrian king, Asshurbanipal (as-shur-BAH-nee-pahl) (r. 668–627 B.C.E.), built one of the world's earliest libraries, which consisted of over 1,500 texts for his own private use. In the 1850s, British excavators found the most complete set of clay tablets of the Gilgamesh epic, and the basis of all modern translations, in the ruins of Asshurbanipal's palace.

The Babylonian Captivity and the Recording of the Bible, 612–539 B.C.E.

The Neo-Babylonians conquered the Assyrians and established their capital at Babylon. Their most powerful ruler was Nebuchadnezzar II (r. 605–562 B.C.E.), who rebuilt the city of Babylon, repaired its temples, and constructed magnificent hanging gardens. They were so beautiful that the second-century B.C.E. compilers of the Seven Wonders of the World included them with the Great Pyramids (the only wonder still standing). Nebuchadnezzar II (nab-oo-kuhd-NEZ-uhr) extended his empire all the way to Syria, Palestine, and Lebanon. He sacked Jerusalem twice, in 597 and 586 B.C.E., and destroyed much of the city. He leveled Solomon's Temple and, like the Assyrians, deported thousands of Hebrews to Babylon, in what is known today as the Babylonian Exile or Babylonian Captivity.

The exiled Hebrews living in Babylon were not allowed to return to Israel, but otherwise they had some freedom of movement, and some seem to have prospered as merchants or farmers. The exiled community reached a new understanding of their past. Many of the tales they told, including those about Noah and Abraham, included episodes in which God punished the ancient Hebrews for failing to follow his instructions, and they interpreted the Assyrian and Neo-Babylonian conquests in the same light. The Israelite community, the prophets explained, had strayed from righteousness, which they defined as ethical behavior.

The Hebrew Bible took shape during these years. Some parts, such as the book of Deuteronomy, already existed in written form, but the exiles recorded the core of the modern Hebrew Bible, from Genesis to 2 Kings. The first five books of the Bible, known either as the Torah in Hebrew or the Pentateuch in Greek, stress that God is the only god and that he will not tolerate the worship of any other gods. This pure monotheism was the product of specific historical circumstances culminating in the Babylonian Exile and the recording of the Bible.

The Neo-Babylonians were the last dynasty to rule from Babylon. In 539 B.C.E. Cyrus the Great, the leader of the Persians, conquered Mesopotamia, and the entire Neo-Babylonian empire came under Persian rule (see Chapter 6). In 538 B.C.E. Cyrus allowed the Hebrews to return to Judah, bringing the Babylonian Captivity to an end, and he ordered the rebuilding of the Temple in Jerusalem. The word "**Jew**," derived from the Hebrew *Yehudhi*, literally means a member of the nation of Judah. After 538 B.C.E., it came to refer to all Hebrews.

• **Jew** A term (derived from Hebrew) that originally meant a member of the nation of Judah and later came to refer to all Hebrews.

The Mesopotamians, along with the Egyptians, were the first people to use writing to record the past. A gulf of several thousand years separates the people of the Mesopotamian city-states and Egypt from the present, yet their literature and documents vividly capture the experience of the world's first peoples in complex societies. The next chapter will contrast their complex society with that of India.

Chapter Review

KEY TERMS

Mesopotamia (28)
Gilgamesh (28)
complex society (31)
city-state (32)
bronze (32)
Sumer (33)
cuneiform (34)
Sargon of Akkad (36)
empire (36)
pharaoh (39)
Nubia (39)
hieroglyphs (39)
papyrus (40)
Hittites (50)
monotheism (51)
Jew (57)

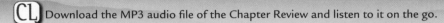 Download the MP3 audio file of the Chapter Review and listen to it on the go.

Complex society arose in the eastern Mediterranean. Gilgamesh prided himself on the splendors of the city of Uruk. Society at Uruk fulfilled the definition of a complex society: living in a large city, the residents specialized in different types of labor and were socially stratified.

What were the similarities in political structures, religion, and social structure in Mesopotamia and Egypt? What were the main differences?

In both Mesopotamia and Egypt human kings ruled with the assistance of officials and bureaucrats. Both societies worshiped many different deities and believed a few gods were more powerful than all the others. Both societies had distinct social classes: the ruler and his or her relatives at the top, officials and priests below, and the vast majority of ordinary people at the bottom.

Mesopotamia and Egypt also differed in important ways. The Mesopotamian kings were believed to be intermediaries between their subjects and the gods; the Egyptian pharaohs were thought to be living gods. The Mesopotamians lived first in city-states and then in regional empires after Sargon first unified the region around 2300 B.C.E. Egypt never had city-states, since the first pharaohs ruled both Lower and Upper Egypt.

When did the international system of the eastern Mediterranean take shape, and how did it function?

Starting around 1500 B.C.E. an international system took shape throughout the eastern Mediterranean that included the New Kingdom in Egypt, the Assyrians in northern Mesopotamia, and the Hittites in Anatolia. The rulers of these kingdoms corresponded with each other frequently, usually to arrange marriages among the different royal families, and also traded goods with one another.

How did monotheism arise among the ancient Hebrews, and under what circumstances did they record their beliefs?

The ancient Hebrews had worshiped Yahweh as one of many deities since at least 2000 B.C.E. After 1000 B.C.E., one group of ancient Hebrews came to believe that they should worship Yahweh as the most important god. In the sixth century B.C.E. they recorded their monotheistic beliefs in the core of the Hebrew Bible, which took shape in Babylon during the Babylonian Exile and was written down in about 500 B.C.E.

For Further Reference

Andrews, Carol. *Egyptian Mummies*. Cambridge, Mass.: Harvard University Press, 1984.

Brewer, Douglas J., and Emily Teeter. *Egypt and the Egyptians*. New York: Cambridge University Press, 1999.

Casson, Lionel. *Travel in the Ancient World*. Baltimore: Johns Hopkins University Press, 1994.

Dever, William G. *What Did the Biblical Writers Know and When Did They Know It? What Archaeology Can Tell Us About the Reality of Ancient Israel*. Grand Rapids, Mich.: William B. Eerdmans, 2001.

Foster, Benjamin R. *The Epic of Gilgamesh: A Norton Critical Edition*. New York: W. W. Norton, 2001.

Kramer, Samuel Noah. *History Begins at Sumer: Thirty-nine Firsts in Recorded History*. Philadelphia: University of Pennsylvania Press, 1981.

Manzanilla, Linda, ed. *Emergence and Change in Early Urban Societies*. New York: Plenum Press, 1997.

Postgate, J. N. *Early Mesopotamia: Society and Economy at the Dawn of History*. New York: Routledge, 1992.

Richards, Janet, and Mary Van Buren, eds. *Order, Legitimacy, and Wealth in Ancient States*. New York: Cambridge University Press, 2000.

Shaw, Ian. *The Oxford History of Ancient Egypt*. New York: Oxford University Press, 2000.

van de Mieroop, Marc. *A History of the Ancient Near East, ca. 3000–323 B.C.* Malden, Mass.: Blackwell Publishing, 2004.

 WEB RESOURCES

Pronunciation Guide

Interactive Maps

MAP 2.1 Ancient Egypt and Nubia

MAP 2.2 The International System, ca. 1500–1250 B.C.E.

MAP 2.3 The Assyrian and Neo-Babylonian Empires at Their Greatest Extent

Primary Sources

Chapter Objectives

ACE Multiple-Choice Quiz

Flashcards

Websites

The Metropolitan Museum of Art (http://www.metmuseum.org/).   Important collections of Egyptian, Nubian, and Mesopotamian art.

Museum of Fine Arts, Boston (www.mfa.org).   Important collections of Egyptian, Nubian, and Mesopotamian art.

The Nubian Museum in Aswan (http://www.touregypt.net/nubiamuseum.htm). Introduction to the museum with photographs of artifacts.

CHAPTER 3

Ancient India and the Rise of Buddhism, 2600 B.C.E.–100 C.E.

For the first eight years he was king, **Ashoka** (r. 268–232 B.C.E.) led his armies on a series of campaigns in north and central India that culminated in a ferocious struggle in Kalinga (kuh-LING-uh) in modern-day Orissa on India's eastern coast. Victorious at last but appalled by the losses on both sides, Ashoka (uh-SHO-kuh) made a decision that would affect world history long after his Mauryan (MORE-ee-ahn) dynasty (ca. 320–185 B.C.E.) came to an end: he decided to embrace the teachings of Buddhism.

Because the ancient Indians used perishable materials like palm leaves as writing material, we have no written documents before the third century B.C.E. from South Asia (including the modern countries of India, Pakistan, Bangladesh, Nepal, Sri Lanka, Bhutan, and the Maldives). However, throughout his reign, Ashoka had his ideas carved on both large and small stones, called rock edicts, and later on stone pillars. Thus Ashoka's inscriptions provide the fullest record of a single individual's thoughts and movements in South Asia before the modern era. Ashoka explained why in an inscription carved in 260 B.C.E., shortly after conquering Kalinga:

(Vidya Dehejia, *Unseen Presence: The Buddha and Sanchi* (Mumbai: Marg Publications, 1996)

ASHOKA AND HIS WIFE DISMOUNTING FROM ELEPHANT

When he had been consecrated eight years the Beloved of the Gods, the king Ashoka, conquered Kalinga. A hundred and fifty thousand people were deported, a hundred thousand were killed and many times that number perished. Afterwards, now that Kalinga was annexed, the Beloved of the Gods very earnestly practiced dharma, desired dharma, and taught dharma. On conquering Kalinga the Beloved of the Gods felt remorse, for, when an independent country is conquered the

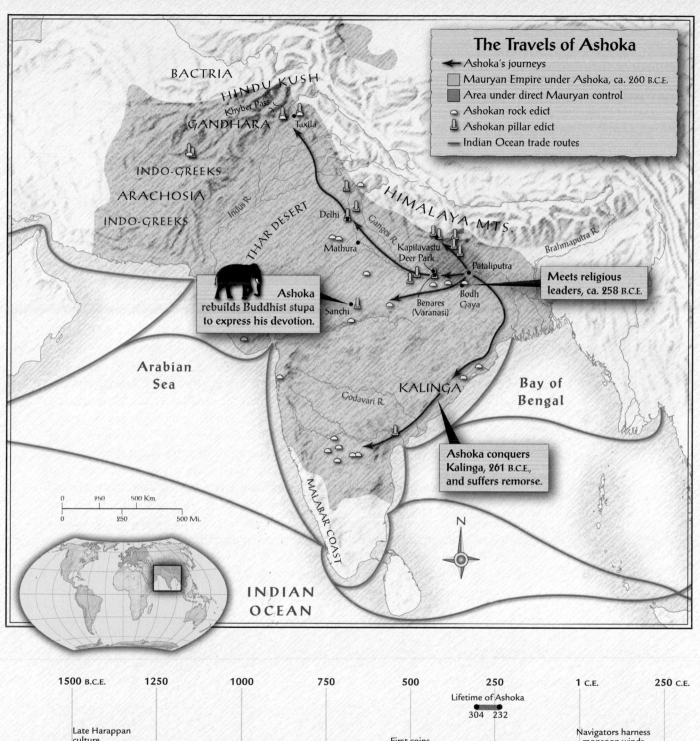

The Travels of Ashoka

← Ashoka's journeys
▢ Mauryan Empire under Ashoka, ca. 260 B.C.E.
▦ Area under direct Mauryan control
⌒ Ashokan rock edict
⌷ Ashokan pillar edict
— Indian Ocean trade routes

BACTRIA
HINDU KUSH
Khyber Pass
GANDHARA
Taxila
INDO-GREEKS
ARACHOSIA
INDO-GREEKS
Indus R.
THAR DESERT
Delhi
Ganges R.
HIMALAYA MTS.
Brahmaputra R.
Mathura
Kapilavastu
Deer Park
Pataliputra
Benares
(Varanasi)
Bodh
Gaya

Ashoka
rebuilds Buddhist stupa
to express his devotion.

Sanchi

Meets religious
leaders, ca. 258 B.C.E.

Arabian
Sea

Godavari R.
KALINGA
Bay of
Bengal

Ashoka conquers
Kalinga, 261 B.C.E.,
and suffers remorse.

MALABAR COAST

0   250   500 Km.
0   250   500 Mi.

N

INDIAN
OCEAN

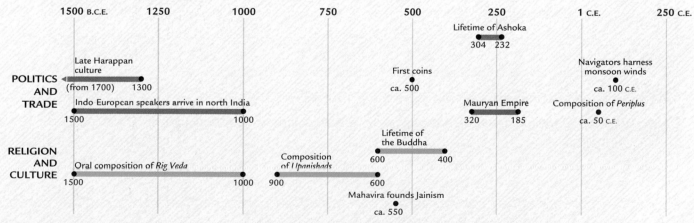

	1500 B.C.E.	1250	1000	750	500	250	1 C.E.	250 C.E.

Lifetime of Ashoka
304 232

**POLITICS
AND
TRADE**

Late Harappan
culture
(from 1700) 1300

First coins
ca. 500

Navigators harness
monsoon winds
ca. 100 C.E.

Indo-European speakers arrive in north India
1500   1000

Mauryan Empire
320   185

Composition of *Periplus*
ca. 50 C.E.

**RELIGION
AND
CULTURE**

Lifetime of
the Buddha
600   400

Oral composition of *Rig Veda*
1500   1000

Composition
of *Upanishads*
900   600

Mahavira founds Jainism
ca. 550

slaughter, death, and deportation of the people is extremely grievous to the Beloved of the Gods, and weighs heavily on his mind. Today if a hundredth or a thousandth part of those people who were killed or died or were deported when Kalinga was annexed were to suffer similarly, it would weigh heavily on the mind of the Beloved of the Gods.[1]

●**Ashoka** (r. 268–232 B.C.E.)   The third king of the Mauryan dynasty (ca. 320–185 B.C.E.), the first Indian ruler to support Buddhism.

●**dharma**   A Sanskrit term meaning correct conduct according to law or custom; Buddhists, including Ashoka, used this concept to refer to the teachings of the Buddha.

The concept of dharma occurs repeatedly in Ashoka's inscriptions. The word **dharma** here means the teachings of the Buddha, but more broadly it means correct conduct according to law or custom, which is how many people in South Asia would have understood it. Dharma was also an important concept in Hinduism, the major religion that arose in India after Buddhism declined (see Chapter 8).

Ashoka governed an unusually large area. Riding on an elephant, he traveled along the trunk roads that radiated out like spokes on a bicycle wheel from his capital at Pataliputra (puh-TAH-lee-poo-truh). For much of its history South Asia was divided into separate regions governed by various rulers; only a few dynasties, like the Mauryan, succeeded in uniting the region for brief periods. Although not politically unified, Indians shared a common cultural heritage: living in highly developed cities, many spoke Sanskrit or related languages, used religious texts in those languages, and conceived of society in terms of distinct social ranks.

In contrast to rulers of the city-states of ancient Mesopotamia, the kingdom of ancient Egypt, and the Neo-Assyrian and Neo-Babylonian empires, South Asian rulers exercised much less direct control over their subjects. Instead, leaders like Ashoka ruled by example, often patronizing religion to show what good monarchs they were. Indeed, religion provided one of the major unifying forces in the often-disunited South Asia. This chapter first discusses the ancient Vedic religion of India and then the exciting alternatives that appeared around the fifth century: Buddhism and Jainism (JINE-is-uhm). It concludes by discussing the Indian Ocean trade network.

Focus Questions

What evidence survives of social stratification at the Indus Valley sites? How did the Indo-Aryans describe the social stratification in their society?

What were the main teachings of the Buddha?

Why did Ashoka believe that supporting Buddhism would strengthen the Mauryan state?

Who were the main actors in the Indian Ocean trade? What types of ships did they use? Along which routes? To trade which commodities?

The Origins of Complex Society in South Asia, 2600–500 B.C.E.

We can glimpse the origins of South Asian social structures and religious traditions from archaeological evidence in the Indus River Valley dating between 2600 and 1700 B.C.E. One of the most important urban sites lies near the modern Pakistan village of Harappa (ha-RAHP-pa). The Harappan culture, with its brick cities, elaborate water systems, fertility deities, and extensive trade, extended over a wide area that included parts of present-day Pakistan, India, and Afghanistan (see Map 3.1). The people of the Indus Valley society used the same script, but, because archaeologists have not deciphered their writing system, we do not know what cultural forces bound them together. We learn more about ancient Indian society from evidence dating to 1500 B.C.E., when people in India, though never politically unified, came to share certain religious beliefs and conceptions of society. The pattern they established at that time held for much of Indian history.

● **monsoon** A term referring both to seasonal winds in South Asia blowing northeast in spring and early summer and southwest in fall and winter, and to the heavy seasonal rains they bring.

Complex Society in the Indus River Valley, 2600–1700 B.C.E.

Long before the continents assumed their current configuration, India was a separate, diamond-shaped island located south of what would become the Eurasian landmass. Over time, the tectonic plate carrying India shifted north until it collided with the Eurasian landmass, forming a massive chain of mountains, the Himalayas. Mount Everest, at 29,028 feet (8,848 m), is the highest mountain in this chain. The South Asian landmass, often called a subcontinent, can be divided into three geographical regions: the high and largely uninhabited mountains to the north, the heavily populated plains of the Indus and Ganga (GUN-ga) Rivers, and the southern peninsula, which is not as densely settled.

The Indian subcontinent has two great rivers: the Indus to the west and the Ganga to the east. The headwaters of both rivers start in the high mountain chain of the Himalayas and drain into the sea, with the Indus flowing into the Arabian Sea and the Ganga into the Bay of Bengal. The earliest farmers planted wheat and barley on the hillsides of what is now western Pakistan. The domestication of plants and animals, sometime between 6500 and 5000 B.C.E., made it possible for the people to create larger settlements in the valley of the Indus River.

India's pattern of rainfall differed from that in Mesopotamia and Egypt. Much of the annual rainfall came in several months in late summer or fall, called the **monsoon** season, and a second period came in the winter months. Indus Valley farmers had to build water storage tanks and measure out the water

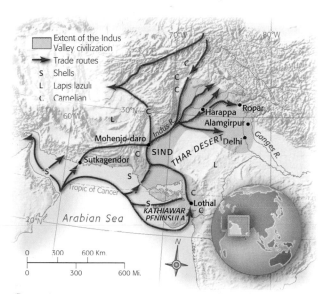

🌐 **MAP 3.1**

Indus River Valley Society   Between 2600 and 1700 B.C.E., the Indus River Valley society covered a large area in modern-day India and Pakistan. The most important sites were at Mohenjo-daro and Harappa. The region exported carnelian and lapis lazuli to Mesopotamia, to the northeast, and imported shells in return.

🆑 Interactive Map

carefully until the next monsoon came. Like the Mesopotamians and the Egyptians, the Indus Valley residents learned to make pottery and to work metal, usually copper and bronze.

In the 1920s British and Indian archaeologists began to excavate huge mounds of brick and debris near the town of Harappa in the **Indus River Valley.** They uncovered the remains of a large urban settlement built from mud brick, complete with walls, drainage systems, open plazas, and avenues several yards (meters) across. Subsequent excavations have revealed that at its height Harappa had an area of over 380 acres (150 hectares) and a population between forty and eighty thousand.[2] Archaeologists have found over fifteen hundred settlements belonging to the Indus River Valley society, the largest complex society of its time on the Indian subcontinent.[3]

Mohenjo-daro (mo-HEN-juh DAH-ro), the second-largest site of the Harappan settlements, was perhaps the most impressive. The city's great bath measured 40 feet (12 m) high and 23 feet (7 m) wide and was "without doubt the earliest public water tank in the ancient world." Although it resembles a swimming pool, complete with staircases at either end, it was actually the source of water for eight bathing rooms in an adjacent building. Unlike other cities of the ancient world, the cities of the Indus River Valley provided drinking water, bathing facilities, and sewer drains to all their residents, not just a privileged few.

We know frustratingly little about the people who occupied the Harappan sites because their script has yet to be deciphered. Seals with the same signs have been found at different sites throughout the Indus River Valley, suggesting that the region shared a common writing system. Archaeologists have identified 400 to 450 signs. But this number is puzzling; 400 signs is more than an alphabet (most alphabets contain fewer than 50 letters) yet fewer than a pictorial writing system (the earliest, simplest phase of Sumerian writing had 700 signs). Scholars wonder whether these mysterious signs stood for an individual word, syllable, or sound.

• **Indus River Valley**
Site of the earliest complex society on the Indian subcontinent (2600–1700 B.C.E.), characterized by brick cities, drainage systems, open plazas, and broad avenues.

■ **The "Great Bath" at Mohenjo-daro, Pakistan**   One of the most impressive ruins from the Harappan period (2600–1700 B.C.E.), the Great Bath is misnamed. It was a water tank—not a pool or a bathing area. It held water for the ritual use of the city's residents, who bathed in a nearby building.   (Borromeo/Art Resource, NY)

Can You Decipher the Harappan Seals of Mohenjo-daro, Pakistan?
These five seals have Indus Valley writing above several figures (*from top left to right, clockwise*): a unicorn, a rhinoceros, an elephant, a water buffalo, and a short-horned bull. A water fountain, possibly with a square sieve on top, stands below the unicorn's mouth; other animals eat from feeding troughs on the ground. No one has yet deciphered the symbols of the Indus Valley writing system.   (Copyright J. M. Kenoyer. Courtesy Department of Museum and Archaeology, Government of Pakistan)

Since no key giving their meaning in another language has yet been found, they are almost impossible to decipher.

A seal made in the Indus River Valley was found at the Mesopotamian city-state of Ur from a level occupied in 2600 B.C.E. The ancient peoples of the Indus River Valley were heavily involved in trade, and the people of Mesopotamia were among their most important trading partners. The residents of ancient Mesopotamia imported carnelian and lapis lazuli from the Indus Valley (see Chapter 2), and shells traveled in the opposite direction (see Map 3.1).

The absence of written documents makes it difficult to reconstruct either the social structure or the religious practices of the residents of the Indus River Valley. As in Mesopotamia, craftsmen who made similar goods seem to have lived in the same residential quarter. There is clear archaeological evidence of social stratification, one of the hallmarks of cities and complex societies. The people who had more possessions than others lived in bigger houses and were buried in graves with more goods.

Beginning in 1900 B.C.E., the large urban sites of the Harappan society become smaller. Archaeologists have different explanations: one possibility is that a slight environmental change adversely affected farmers, who were no longer able to supply urban dwellers with foodstuffs. The characteristic Indus River pottery vessel types give way to new shapes and decorative patterns. Some of the pots have graffiti markings in Indus Valley script, indicating that the script remained in use.

We know too little about the Indus Valley peoples to identify any particular practices that continued in later periods. With incontrovertible evidence of social stratification, occupational specialization, and large urban centers, the Indus River Valley sites certainly meet our definition of a complex society, including a writing system. Although the people were probably not united under a single ruler, they shared a common system of weights and measures, standardized brick size, and urban planning. Shared cultural practices in the absence of political unification characterized later South Asian societies as well.

The Spread of Indo-European Languages

● **Sanskrit**
A language, such as Latin, Greek, and English, belonging to the Indo-European language family and spoken by Indo-Aryan migrants to north India around 1500–1000 b.c.e.

Our understanding of the South Asian past becomes much clearer with the first textual materials in the Indo-European language of **Sanskrit.** Linguists place languages whose vocabulary and grammatical structures are most closely related into the same language family. If you have studied French or Spanish, you know that many words are related to their English counterparts. English, French, and Spanish all belong to the Indo-European language family, as do ancient Greek, Latin, Hittite, and Sanskrit. The Indo-European languages contain many core vocabulary words related to English, such as the words for mother, father, and brother (see Table 3.1). If you study a non-Indo-European language, like Chinese or Arabic, few words will resemble any word in English, and word order may be different.

Sometime in the distant past, thousands of years ago, a group of herding peoples who spoke Indo-European languages began to leave their homeland. The migrations took place long before the introduction of writing, so even today we cannot be certain where the homeland of the Indo-European speakers was or when they left. Horse-drawn carts gave these peoples a technological edge because they could cover far more ground than most of their contemporaries, who did not know how to breed horses or drive wheeled carts.

The distribution of Indo-European languages over Eurasia shows how far these peoples went: Russia, most of Europe, Iran, and north India, but not southern India or East Asia (see Map 3.2). By at least 2000 b.c.e., those going west reached Anatolia, where they spoke Hittite (see Chapter 2); they reached the island of Crete in the Mediterranean Sea at about the same time (see Chapter 6). Those going east passed through Iran and arrived in north India sometime between 1500 and 1000 b.c.e., where they spoke Sanskrit. The modern inhabitants of the region speak a range of Indo-European languages descended from Sanskrit, including Hindi (HIN-dee), while those in south India speak Dravidian (druh-VID-ee-uhn) languages, which belong to a different language family.

Most people living in the northern regions of modern South Asia speak Indo-European languages, including Hindi and Urdu, while those living in the south speak Dravidian languages like Tamil and Telegu. The dominance of Indo-European languages in much of today's Eurasia is the result of migrations occurring over three thousand years ago.

When linguists first discovered the similarities among Latin, Greek, and Sanskrit in the early nineteenth century, they assumed that the speakers of Indo-European languages invaded and wiped out the indigenous peoples. Modern scholars have since proposed variations on the original conquer-and-destroy model. Perhaps, when the Indo-European speakers migrated into a new region, their superior technology convinced the local peoples to adopt the newcomers' language.

Table 3.1 **Related Words in Various Indo-European Languages**

English	Latin	Greek	Sanskrit
mother	mater	meter	matar
father	pater	pater	pitar
brother	frater	phrater	bhratar
sister	soror	(unrelated)	svasar
me	me	me	ma
two	duo	duo	duva
six	sex	hex	shat
seven	septem	hepta	sapta

The Indo-European Migrations and Vedic Culture, 1500–1000 b.c.e.

The Indo-European migrants left us the **Rig Veda** (RIG-VAY-duh), a collection of 1,028 hymns that were preserved because the priests who sang them passed them down orally from one generation to the next. They date to around 1500 to 1000 b.c.e., the

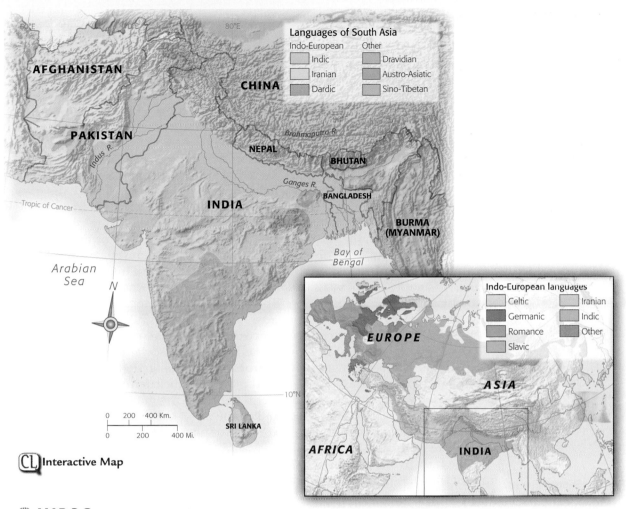

Languages of South Asia

Indo-European
- Indic
- Iranian
- Dardic

Other
- Dravidian
- Austro-Asiatic
- Sino-Tibetan

Indo-European languages
- Celtic
- Germanic
- Romance
- Slavic
- Iranian
- Indic
- Other

Interactive Map

🌐 **MAP 3.2**

Distribution of Languages in Modern South Asia   Most people living in the northern regions of modern South Asia speak Indo-European languages, including Hindi and Urdu, while those living in the south speak Dravidian languages like Tamil and Telegu. The dominance of Indo-European languages in much of today's Eurasia is the result of migrations occurring over three thousand years ago.

probable time of the Indo-European migrations to South Asia, yet they were not written down until more than two thousand years later, perhaps in 1000 C.E.[4] The word *hymn* is slightly misleading, since hymns touch on many everyday activities, including sex and gambling. Accordingly, they reveal much about ancient society.

Linguists have concluded that the Sanskrit of the older hymns varies slightly from the later hymns, making it possible to determine the order of their composition. The earlier hymns mention many place names to the west of those included in the later hymns, an indication that the migrants came first to northwest India and later to all of north India.

These migrants sometimes called themselves "Aryan," a Sanskrit word whose meaning is "noble" or "host." While modern researchers think that many and varied peoples spoke Indo-European languages, the propagandists of Nazi Germany wrongly imputed a racial unity to what was a linguistic group. Always mindful that we know nothing of their appearance, it is best to refer to these migrants as Indo-Aryans because their language belonged to the Indo-Aryan branch of the Indo-European language family.

> **● *Rig Veda***
> A collection of 1,028 Sanskrit hymns, composed around 1500 to 1000 B.C.E. yet written down around 1000 C.E. One of the most revealing sources about Indo-Europeans who settled in north India.

• Vedic religion Religious belief system of Indo-European migrants to north India; involved animal sacrifice and elaborate ceremonies to ensure that all transitions in the natural world—day to night, or one season to the next—proceeded smoothly.

• nomads A term for people who migrate seasonally from place to place to find grass for their herds. They do not usually farm but tend their herds full-time.

Primary Source: The Rig Veda
Read how Indra, "the thunder-wielder," slew Vritra, "firstborn of dragons," and how Purusha created the universe through an act of ritual sacrifice.

• varna From the Sanskrit word for "color": the four major social groups of ancient Indian society, ranked in order of purity (not wealth or power): Brahmin priests at the top, then warriors, then farmers and merchants, and finally dependent laborers.

Scholars have named the religion of the Indo-Aryans Vedic (VAY-dick), from the *Rig Veda*. The roots of Hinduism, a major religion in modern South Asia, lie in **Vedic religion,** but the religious practices of the early Indo-Aryans differed from later Hinduism, which will be discussed in Chapter 8. Many scholars of South Asian religion date the rise of Hinduism to the seventh century C.E., after the decline of Buddhism.[5]

Many Vedic rituals focused on the transition between day and night or between seasons. A priest had to make the correct offering to the appropriate deity to ensure that the sun would rise each day or that at the winter solstice the days would begin to grow longer. The deities mentioned in the *Rig Veda* include the war-god, Indra (IN-druh), who carried a thunderbolt and led large conquering armies, the god of fire, the sun-god, and the god of death, as well as many minor deities. Often the rituals involved fire, thought to be the purest of the elements. Rituals honoring these gods could last several days and involve intricate sequences of steps, including animal sacrifice, and the ritual specialists who performed them, the Brahmin (BRAH-min) priests, were paid handsomely by local rulers. There was no single ruler in Vedic society. Instead a number of kings ruled small territories by collecting taxes from farmers to finance these lavish ceremonies.

The *Rig Veda* provides a few valuable hints about social organization. The original Indo-European migrants were **nomads** who migrated seasonally from place to place to find grass for their herds. Carrying their tents with them, they usually did not farm but tended their herds full-time. The most important animal in their society was the horse, which pulled the carts that transported their families and possessions across Eurasia. According to some hymns, some people began to cultivate grain after settling in India.

One early hymn, addressed to Indra, gives a clear sense of the diverse occupations of the Indo-European speakers:

> Our thoughts bring us to diverse callings, setting people apart: the carpenter seeks what is broken, the physician a fracture, and the Brahmin priest seeks one who presses Soma.[6]

Soma was an intoxicating beverage, possibly made from ephedra (AY-fay-druh) leaves, that was drunk at ceremonies. This poem shows that Vedic society included carpenters, doctors, Brahmin priests, and people who prepared the ritual drink.

The position of women in Vedic society was probably not much lower than that of men. Girls could go out unsupervised in public. Both girls and boys received an education in which they memorized hymns and studied their meaning, yet only male specialists recited hymns in public ceremonies. One hymn instructs educated girls to marry educated husbands. Girls could sometimes even choose their own husbands, provided they had obtained permission from their mother and father. Women could inherit property, and widows could remarry.

Changes After 1000 B.C.E.

The later hymns, composed perhaps around 1000 B.C.E., indicate that social roles in Vedic society became more fixed, and women's freedom declined, as the former nomads settled down to a life of agriculture. Eventually people came to be classed into four different social groups, called **varna** (VAR-nuh), that were determined by birth. The literal meaning of *varna* is "color," reflected in the modern English word *varnish*. One hymn, "The Hymn of the Primeval Man," explains that when the gods dismembered a cosmic giant, they created each varna from a different part of his body:

> When they divided the man, into how many parts did they apportion him?
> What do they call his mouth, his two arms and thighs and feet?
>
> His mouth became the Brahmin; his arms were made into the Warrior, his
> thighs the People, and from his feet the Servants were born.

This passage sets out the major social groups of late Vedic society, ranked in order of purity (not wealth or power): Brahmin priests at the top, then warriors, then farmers and merchants ("the People"), and finally dependent laborers. Brahmins were the purest because they conducted Vedic rituals; the warrior category included the kings who sponsored the rituals. The farmers and merchants were supposed to farm the land and tend the herds. The fourth varna of dependent laborers, many of whom were the region's original residents, served all the varna above them. Like all documents, however, this hymn has a distinct point of view: a Brahmin priest composed it, and it is not surprising that he placed Brahmins at the top of the social hierarchy.

India's caste system has changed greatly over the last three thousand years. There is no exact equivalent in Indian languages of the English word *caste,* which comes from the sixteenth- to seventeenth-century Portuguese word *castas,* meaning breed or type of animal or plant. Most Indians would say that the word **jati** (JAH-ti), sometimes translated as "subcaste," comes closest. People in a jati sometimes specialize in a certain occupation, but many jati have members with many different occupations, and some jati have completely given up their traditional occupations in favor of something new. (See the feature "World History in Today's World: The Modern Caste System and Its Ancient Antecedents.")

● **jati** A term, sometimes translated as "subcaste," for groups of 5,000 to 15,000 people in modern India. Many, but not all, Indians marry someone from the same jati and share meals on equal footing only with people of the same jati.

Different changes took place in the centuries after circa 1000 B.C.E., when the later poems in the *Rig Veda* were composed. Iron came into widespread use, and iron tools proved much more effective at clearing land than bronze or copper ones. Between 1000 and 500 B.C.E. the residents of the lower Ganga Valley cleared much of the forest cover so that they could intensively pursue agriculture there. The sedentary peoples, armed with horses and iron weapons, continuously extended the area of cultivated land. Higher agricultural yields prompted an increase in population and a boom in trade, as shown by the appearance of the first coins around 500 B.C.E., at the same time as in China (see Chapter 4) and the Persian Empire (see Chapter 6).

This time period also saw other challenges to the old order. Composed between 900 and 600 B.C.E., the *Upanishad* (oo-PAHN-ih-shahd) texts claim to be linked to the Vedic tradition but introduce entirely new ideas. These texts turn inward, away from costly sacrificial rituals. One new and exciting idea was that souls transmigrated: according to the doctrine of karma, people's acts in this life determined how they would be reborn in the next. New gods appeared and are still worshiped by Hindus today. Unlike the gods of the *Rig Veda,* these gods intervene actively in human affairs and sometimes assume human form.

The *Mahabharata* (muh-HAH-bah-ruh-tuh) and the *Ramayana* (ruh-MAH-yuh-nuh), the two great Sanskrit epics, began to be composed at this time, although they were recorded only in the fourth century C.E. The *Mahabharata,* over 100,000 verses in length, describes a long-running feud between two clans. Its major theme is dharma, or right conduct. The epic vividly enacts some of the most basic conflicts in the human psyche as the characters struggle to understand what it means to be good and what the consequences of evil actions might be. We see men and women struggling with the question of whether it even matters if a person is

The Modern Caste System and Its Ancient Antecedents

If asked to identify their own caste, most South Asians would name their jati first and then perhaps add the varna to which they think they belong. Varna is the general term describing the same four groups as in Vedic times: Brahmin, warrior, farmer or merchant, and dependent laborer. People often disagree about the varna ranking of a given jati; for example, one person may think a given jati belongs to the warrior category, while another may place it within the merchant and farmer varna. These disagreements can result in actual disputes between members of different jati.

Not all jati fit neatly into the four-varna classification. Approximately 15 percent of modern Indians belong to government-listed castes and 7.5 percent to government-listed tribes (two groups previously considered untouchables). Although India's constitution, adopted in 1949, abolishes untouchability and forbids discrimination against untouchables, both groups continue to suffer widespread discrimination. However, today government quotas ensure them a certain number of university places and civil service positions in proportion to their size.

Most outside observers tend to exaggerate the rigidity of caste in modern India. The caste system is most powerful in small communities, such as villages, in which everyone recognizes everyone and people marry people from families they know well. Politicians frequently invoke jati identity to get votes. Of course, as soon as someone enters a large city, no one can tell simply from that person's appearance to which jati or varna he or she belongs. Still, it is possible to make an educated guess because members of lower-ranked jati often continue to practice their traditional occupations, like sweeping, by force of circumstance.

Jati usually range in size from five thousand to fifteen thousand people. Many, but not all, people in modern South Asia find their spouse through arranged marriages with people from the same jati. Because each generation tends to marry within its own jati, the jati have developed into social groups with strong identities. People socialize within their own jati and share meals together. They naturally turn to others in their jati to ask for jobs, loans, and assistance with their problems. Castelike groups exist within other modern societies, too, although we do not realize how many people in non-Indian societies, including the United States, also tend to marry spouses from similar social and economic backgrounds.

actively trying to change the world, or whether perhaps everything is simply fated to be the way it is.

One part of the *Mahabharata,* the *Bhagavad Gita* (bug-GAH-vud GEEH-tuh), was often read as an independent work. Composed around 200 C.E., it tells the story of a battle between two armies. One leader hesitates before the battle: his dharma is to fight, but he will not be able to escape from the cycle of death and rebirth if he kills any of his relatives fighting on the other side. The deity Krishna, in human form as a chariot driver, argues that each person should fulfill his dharma, or his given role, in life. Then Krishna appears as a deity and urges the warrior to devote himself fully to worshiping him. Krishna's teaching later become a key tenet in Hinduism.

The much-shorter *Ramayana* tells of a great king, Rama (RAH-muh), whose wife is abducted by a demon king. Rama fights to get Sita (SEE-tuh) back, but when he defeats the demon king he greets her coldly and explains that he cannot take her back because, although a married woman, she has lived alone with her captors. After ordering a pyre of wood to be built, she jumps into the flames, but the fire-god lifts her from the flames and presents her to Rama. Only then does he accept that she has remained loyal to him. Some have seen this as evidence that widows committed suicide by immolating themselves at their husbands' cremations. (The first detailed evidence of widow immolation, from the early nineteenth century, indicates that the practice was limited to specific regions and small social groups.) In the centuries after their initial composition, both the *Mahabharata* and the *Ramayana* spawned many versions throughout South Asia and even Southeast Asia, and today's television versions captivate millions of viewers.

Different teachers continued to debate new religious concepts in succeeding centuries. Between the sixth and fourth centuries B.C.E., Jainism, an Indian religion with some two million followers today, took shape. Mahavira, the founder of the Jains (JINES), went from place to place for twelve years, testing himself and debating ideas with other ascetics. After thirteen months he stopped wearing even a single garment and wandered naked for eleven years before reaching liberation from the bondage of human life. He died, it is thought, in his seventies after voluntarily renouncing food and water. Jains believe in right faith, right knowledge, and right conduct, and they emphasize the obligation to harm no living beings. They abstain from eating and drinking at night, when it is dark, so that they will not kill any insects by mistake.

The Rise of Buddhism

Also living in this time of religious ferment was the founder of the Buddhist religion, Siddhartha Gautama (sid-DAR-tuh gow-TA-muh), or the Buddha. The word **Buddha** literally means "the enlightened or awakened one." The religion that he founded became one of the most influential in the world, and Ashoka's decision to support Buddhism marked a crucial turning point in the religion's history. Buddhism spread to Sri Lanka, Central Asia, Southeast Asia, and eventually to China and Japan, where it continued to thrive after it declined in its Indian homeland. Today Japan, Tibet, and Thailand have significant Buddhist populations, and growing Buddhist communities live in Europe and North America.

We know many details about the Buddha's life but cannot be sure which are facts and which are myths because all our sources date to several centuries after his death and were recorded by Buddhist monks and nuns. Born at a time when India was not politically unified, the Buddha did not intend to found a religion that would bind Indian society together. His stated goal was to teach people how to break out of the endless cycle of birth, death, and rebirth.

● **Buddha**
The founder of the Buddhist religion, Siddhartha Gautama (ca. 600–400 B.C.E.); also called the Buddha, or the enlightened one.

The Life of the Buddha   Even the dates of the Buddha's life are uncertain. Born along the southern edge of the Himalaya Mountains in today's Nepal, the Buddha lived to almost eighty. Sri Lankan Buddhist sources point to a death date of 543 B.C.E., while Chinese and Tibetan Buddhist sources suggest either 486 B.C.E. or 370 B.C.E. Scholarly consensus now puts the death of the Buddha closer to 400 B.C.E. than to 500 B.C.E.

The legend of his life, known to all practicing Buddhists, recounts that his mother dreamed of a white elephant with a lotus flower in his trunk. The wise men she consulted explained that she was going to give birth to either a great monarch or a great teacher. One seer predicted that, if he learned about human problems, he would become a teacher, prompting his parents to raise him inside a walled palace precinct so that he would never see any signs of suffering or illness. He grew up, married, and fathered a child.

One day when he was driving inside the palace park with his charioteer, he noticed an extremely elderly man. Later he glimpsed a feverish man who was so ill that his skin was covered with growths. His third encounter with human suffering came when he saw a corpse being taken away to be cremated. The fourth encounter, with a wandering ascetic who wore a simple robe but who looked happy, gave him hope, and he resolved to follow his example. For six years he subjected himself to all kinds of self-mortification. Then he decided to stop starving himself and meditated under a tree, later known as the Tree of Wisdom (also called a bodhi tree), for forty-nine days. He gained enlightenment and explained how he had done so.

The Teachings of the Buddha

According to much later Buddhist tradition, the Buddha preached his first sermon in the Deer Park near Benares (buh-NAR-us) in the Ganga Valley to five followers, who, like him, were seeking enlightenment. First he identified two incorrect routes to knowledge: extreme self-denial and complete self-gratification. The Buddha preached that his listeners should leave family life behind and follow him, and they should live simple lives, avoiding the strenuous fasts and self-mortification advocated by other ascetic groups.

He explained that one could escape from the endless cycle of birth, death, and rebirth by following a clear series of steps, called the Noble Eightfold Path. Like a doctor, the Buddha diagnosed suffering in the First Noble Truth, analyzed its origins in the Second Noble Truth, stated that a cure exists in the Third Truth, and explained that cure in the Fourth Noble Truth: to follow the Noble Eightfold Path. This path consists of right understanding, right resolve, right speech, right action, right livelihood, right effort, right mindfulness, and right meditation. When people follow the Noble Eightfold Path, their suffering will end because they will have escaped from the cycle of life and rebirth by attaining nirvana. The word **nirvana** literally means "extinction," as when the flame on a candle goes out, but in the Buddha's teachings it took on a much broader meaning: those who followed the Eightfold Path and understood the Four Noble Truths would gain true understanding.

Buddhism shared with Jainism much that was new. Both challenged Brahminic authority, denied the authority of the Vedic hymns, and banned animal sacrifices. Vedic religious practice did not address the question of individual liberation; the goal of Vedic ritual was to make sure that the cosmos continued to function in an orderly way. In contrast, the Buddha preached that salvation was entirely the product of an individual's actions. He focused on the individual, outside of his or her family unit and any social group and without regard to his or her varna ranking.

The people who heard the Buddha preach naturally wanted to know how they could attain nirvana. He urged them to leave their families behind so that they could join him as monks in the Buddhist order. Those who followed him went from place to place, begging for their daily food from those who did not join the

[CL] **Primary Source: Setting in Motion the Wheel of Law**
Siddhartha's first sermon contains the core teaching of Buddhism: to escape, by following the Middle Path, the suffering caused by desire.

• **nirvana** A Sanskrit word that literally means "extinction," as when the flame on a candle goes out. In Buddhism the term took on broader meaning: those who followed the Eightfold Path and understood the Four Noble Truths would gain true understanding.

order. They lived nowhere permanently except during the monsoon months, when it was not practical to live by begging. The early monastic orders reached decisions by consensus. When the members of the Buddhist order did not agree, they voted, and the leader of the group implemented the decision.

Only those monks who joined the Buddhist order could attain nirvana, the Buddha taught. His first followers were all men, but Buddhist sources record that the Buddha's aunt asked to join the Buddhist order. The Buddha refused her until his star disciple Ananda (uh-NAN-duh) intervened and persuaded him to change his mind. Women did become Buddhist nuns, but they were always subordinate to men.

The Buddha assumed that the people who could not become monks and nuns would donate food and money instead. Those outside the order could not attain nirvana, but they could gain merit by making such donations, the Buddha taught, and many kings and merchants gave large gifts in the hope of improving their lives, either in this world or in future rebirths.

This teaching marked a major departure from the pre-existing Vedic religion. According to the *Rig Veda*, Brahmins stood at the top of the ritual hierarchy, and those who ranked below them could do nothing to change their position. The Buddhists took a radically different view: a merchant, a farmer, or even a laborer who made a donation to the Buddhist order could enhance his or her standing. From its very earliest years, Buddhists attracted merchant support, and communities of Buddhists often lived near cities, where merchants had gathered.

The Buddha forbade his followers from worshiping statues or portraits of him. Instead, they worshiped at the four sites that had been most important during the Buddha's life: where he was born, where he gained enlightenment, where he preached the first sermon, and where he died. Before his death the Buddha had instructed his followers to cremate him and bury his ashes under a bell-shaped monument built over a burial mound, called a stupa (STEW-pah). The first generation of Buddhists divided the Buddha's remains under many different stupas, where they honored him by circling them in a clockwise direction, in a practice called circumambulation (pradaksina) (pra-DUCKSH-ee-nah). To gain merit, they walked with their right arm, thought to be more pure than the left, facing the stupa for a fixed number of times. They also left flowers, incense, and clothing on the stupas, where they lit lamps and played music as an expression of their devotion. (See the feature "Visual Evidence: The Buddhist Stupa at Sanchi.")

The depictions of the Buddha changed in later centuries. Beginning in the first and second centuries C.E., sculptors began to make images of the Buddha himself. One group in north India portrayed the Buddha as a young man, while another, active in the Gandhara (gahn-DAHR-ah) region of modern Pakistan and Afghanistan, was influenced by later copies of Greek statues brought by Alexander the Great and his armies in the fourth century B.C.E. They made statues of the Buddha, often in a sitting position, with noticeably Greek-looking facial features (see photo).

A Mix of Sculptural Traditions from Gandhara, Afghanistan
This Gandharan statue's posture is classically Buddhist: his legs are crossed so that both feet face up, the left hand grasps his robe, and the right makes a gesture meaning to dispel fear. But the facial expression, hair, and overall posture are drawn from Greco-Roman models already familiar to Gandharan sculptors for several centuries. Neither Buddhist nor Greco-Roman, the spokes in the halo behind the Buddha's head probably represent the sun's rays. (The Metropolitan Museum of Art. Gift of Moneichi Nitta, 2003)

THE BUDDHIST STUPA AT SANCHI

The oldest and best-preserved stupa in India is at Sanchi (SAN-chee), near Bhopal, India. The Buddha never visited Sanchi during his lifetime, but Ashoka chose it as the site of a new stupa because it lay on the main route between Pataliputra and the western coastal ports and had frequent visitors. Ashoka ordered the remains of the Buddha removed from their original resting place and placed in a new burial mound. He covered the mound with a layer of sandstone and erected a wooden railing around it. He also placed a pillar edict on the site.

The site today looks the way it did after extensive renovations done during the first century B.C.E. A square stone wall with a central gate on each side surrounds the main burial mound; beautifully carved stone pillars decorate each of the gates (see opposite). In addition to the main stupa, Sanchi contains two other large stupas and hundreds of smaller ones, where monks seeking to share the Buddha's merit were buried. Buddhists believe that visiting a stupa holding someone's remains brings them closer to the deceased.

Built in the first century B.C.E., the Eastern Gate at Sanchi contains three horizontal sections held up by the two main vertical posts. The carvings of people and animals worshiping the Buddha are wonderfully lifelike. The artists carved scenes from the Buddha's life but never the Buddha himself. In his dying instructions, the Buddha forbade his followers to worship representations of him.

The top horizontal scene shows Buddhists standing with hands folded in a position of reverence facing a series of stupas, each of which represented the Buddha. In the middle horizontal scene depicting the Great Departure, when the Buddha left his father's palace, the Sanchi artists showed five riderless horses at increasing distances from the palace, each scene portraying a moment in continuous action. At the right end of the frame, the artists carved a pair of footprints under a parasol, a convention the viewers would have understood to represent the Buddha.

The beautifully carved frieze on the lowest horizontal section depicts an Indian monarch, most likely Ashoka, at a royal procession. Ashoka and his wife have dismounted from a crouching elephant, and they pause to observe musicians. At the center of the scene is a depiction of the Tree of Wisdom under which the Buddha gained enlightenment. A structure protects the base of the tree, where people are praying and making offerings.

After looking at the friezes on the front and back of the gate, worshipers followed the path leading them through an outer wall to the stupa itself, climbing a flight of steps to reach a railed walkway that led all the way around the stupa. The pillars and gates at Sanchi contain hundreds of inscriptions from Ashoka's time and later, recording the names of those making a donation to pay for part of a railing or a frieze in the hope of gaining merit. All those who circumambulated the stupa shared the same goal.

QUESTION FOR ANALYSIS

 How did people of different social ranks—Ashoka, monks, nuns, and ordinary people—express their devotion to Buddhism at different places—the friezes of the gates, the pillars, the walkways, and the stupa itself—at the site of Sanchi?

(Dinodia Photo Library)

The Eastern Gate was built in the first century B.C.E. The high quality of the carvings makes this one of the greatest surviving monuments of Buddhist art in India, as well as one of the earliest.

This buxom woman beneath a mango tree is a local female deity, credited with the ability to help women conceive and undergo easier childbirth. Buddhist monuments often incorporated local deities in subordinate positions.

This railing surrounds the interior walkway on which worshipers circumambulated the stupa. Individual stones bear the names of contributors—including monks, nuns, and merchants—who made donations to finance the building of the walkway.

The stupa mound was first built over the remains of the Buddha in the third century B.C.E. and attained its current size—120 feet (36.5 m) in diameter and 54 feet (16.5 m) high—one hundred years later.

●The Mauryan Empire, ca. 320–185 B.C.E.

During the Buddha's lifetime, Buddhism was but one of many different teachings circulating in India. The support of Ashoka, the third ruler of the **Mauryan dynasty,** founded by Ashoka's grandfather, transformed Buddhism into the most influential religion of its day. Ashoka's adoption of Buddhism as the state religion promoted cultural unity as well as strengthened his political control. The Mauryans came to power at a time when trade was increasing throughout the region, and Buddhism was able to succeed because it appealed to merchants. The Mauryans created the first large state in India, extending over all of north India (see the map on page 61).

Surprisingly few materials about the Mauryans survive. As a result, historians continue to debate the amount of control the Mauryan Empire exercised over the regions it conquered. Local rulers may have retained considerable power. In addition to archaeological excavations, our major sources are the partial report of a Greek ambassador named Megasthenes (ME-gas-thuh-nees), written after 288 B.C.E., and Ashoka's rock edicts.

Life and Society in the Mauryan Dynasty, ca. 300 B.C.E.

In 320 B.C.E. the grandfather of Ashoka, a general named Chandragupta (chuhn-druh-GOOP-tuh) Maurya (r. ca. 320–297 B.C.E.), defeated another general and gained control of his territory and his capital Pataliputra (modern-day Patna [PUTT-nuh]), located on the Ganga. After Chandragupta Maurya took power, his forces fought those of Seleucus I (321–281 B.C.E.), a general who succeeded Alexander the Great (see Chapter 6) in Mesopotamia. After making peace, Seleucus (seh-LOO-kuhs) sent an ambassador named Megasthenes to the Mauryan court at Pataliputra in 302 B.C.E., where he stayed for fourteen years.

Megasthenes wrote a work entitled *Indika* (IN-dick-uh), which provides a detailed description of Pataliputra in approximately 300 B.C.E., some thirty years before Ashoka ascended to the throne. Unfortunately, Megasthenes's original work does not survive; we know it only from passages quoted by later Greek and Roman writers.[7]

Pataliputra's size impressed Megasthenes deeply.

> This city stretched in the inhabited quarters to an extreme length on each side of eighty stadia [nearly 10 miles or 16 kilometers], and that its breadth was fifteen stadia [nearly 2 miles or 3.2 kilometers], and that a ditch encompassed it all round, which was six hundred feet in breadth and thirty cubits [45 feet or 14 meters] in depth, and that the wall was crowned with 570 towers and had four-and-sixty gates.

This description of the city's size is plausible. Archaeological excavations early in the twentieth century around Patna revealed clear evidence of large fortification walls, including large reinforcing wooden trusses.

The Mauryans exercised considerable control within the capital. Most of their officials supervised trade and commerce, the major source of Mauryan revenue. Market officials regulated weights and measures to ensure that no one was cheated.

They encouraged merchants to sell only one type of good by charging them twice as much tax as if they sold more, and they levied fines on those merchants who passed off old goods as newly made. The Mauryans concentrated their officials at marketplaces in the capital, where they could regulate measures and prices at the same time that they collected taxes.

The passages that have come down to us take a detached tone: Megasthenes includes no personal anecdotes. His account of the officials who watched over the foreigners comes closest to describing his own life in Pataliputra:

> Those of the second branch attend to the entertainment of foreigners. To these they assign lodgings, and they keep watch over their modes of life by means of those persons whom they give to them for assistants. They escort them on the way when they leave the country, or, in the event of their dying, forward their property to their relatives. They take care of them when they are sick, and if they die bury them.

We may surmise that city officials gave Megasthenes a servant.

According to Megasthenes, the military section of the government was the same size as the urban section: thirty men, divided into six branches, each with its own area of responsibility—navy, supplies, infantry, cavalry, war chariots, and elephants. Elephants fascinated Megasthenes, who devoted many lines to their capture, training, loyalty to their masters, and general care; when on active duty, he reports, they consumed rice wine and large quantities of flowers.

Megasthenes's descriptions of Indian society have long puzzled analysts. He identifies seven ranks within Indian society: (1) philosophers, (2) farmers, (3) herdsmen, (4) artisans, (5) soldiers, (6) spies, and (7) councillors. This overlaps only slightly with the varna scheme described in the *Rig Veda* some seven hundred years earlier (discussed above), with its four ranks of Brahmin, warriors, merchants and farmers, and dependent servants. Three of Megasthenes's groups (herdsmen, artisans, and spies) do not even appear in the varna ranking.

The top-ranking group, according to Megasthenes, was the smallest: the king's advisers, military generals, and treasury officials, who were "the most respected on account of the high character and wisdom of [their] members." Megasthenes's ranking suggests that this was the group he probably encountered directly.

Ranking second were the "philosophers," or religious practitioners. They performed sacrifices and funerals, and Megasthenes explains that the Brahmins among them married and had children but lived simply. Another group of religious practitioners underwent various privations, such as abstaining from sexual intercourse or sitting in one position all day. The Jains would have belonged to this group. Finally, a third group followed the Buddha, "whom they honor as a god on account of his extraordinary sanctity." Although the Buddha had taught his followers not to worship him as a god, Buddhist devotees began to credit him with divine capabilities soon after his death, as we can see from Megasthenes's report. Megasthenes devotes only a few sentences to the Buddhists, an indication that the Buddhists had only a small following in 300 B.C.E.

Conceptions of caste, Megasthenes suggests, were much more fluid than many of our surviving sources, which almost always place Brahmins at the top, would indicate. Megasthenes lists five other groups (farmers, herdsmen, artisans, soldiers, and spies) without ranking them in any way. The farmers, the largest group, were exempt from military service but paid a land tax to the king as well as one-quarter of all their crops. The military was the second-largest group. Megasthenes concludes his list by saying, "No one is allowed to marry out of his own caste, or to exercise any calling or art except his own."

Mauryan Control Outside the Capital

The Mauryans exercised close supervision over the rural areas in the immediate vicinity of the capital, but not over all of north India. Megasthenes reports that the kingdom contained three different types of territory: those ruled directly by the Mauryan king, those territories where the local king was allowed to remain in place with reduced powers, and local republics. This description of the Mauryans suggests an empire quite different from that of the Assyrians (see Chapter 2). Whereas the Mauryans exercised direct rule in only a limited area, the Assyrians sometimes forcibly resettled large groups of people throughout their empire.

The Ashokan inscriptions, written after Megasthenes left India (most likely between 260 and 232 B.C.E.), provide more information about the extent of Mauryan control outside the capital. Some of the inscriptions were written on tall pillars, while others were carved on boulders (shown on the map on page 61). They were placed in the capital, in northwest India in the Punjab (PUHN-juhb) region, on the east and west coasts, and in central India.

Earlier analysts have often assumed that one could connect the different monuments with a line, with the territory inside the line being that of the Mauryan Empire. Recently, however, historians have realized that since not all empires were able to exercise a uniform control over a large area, the Mauryan Empire should be mapped differently. The region about Pataliputra should have the darkest shade to indicate where Mauryan control was greatest. The trade routes linking the capital with outlying trade centers should also be shaded dark because the Mauryans could have dispatched officials to markets to collect sales taxes. But the regions lying in between the trade routes should remain lightly shaded, if at all.

◼ **An Ashokan Column from Vaishali, Bihar, India** This pillar, made of polished red sandstone, stands 60 feet (18.3 m) high. Capped with a lion, it was visible in all four directions. This and the other stone columns Ashoka commissioned are the first monuments worked in stone anywhere in ancient India. Some scholars have wondered if Ashoka knew of other stone monuments in neighboring regions like Iran. (Dinodia Photo Library)

The Mauryan Empire remained a decentralized one in which local people continued to speak their own languages. Ashoka drafted the texts of his inscriptions in his native language of Magadhi (muh-GUH-dee), a language related to Sanskrit. They were then translated into the different Prakrit (PRAH-krit) vernaculars used in north India, which are all descended from Sanskrit. Some in the northwest were translated into Greek, a European language, and Aramaic, a western Asian language, because the local population spoke both languages.

Ashoka drafted short, medium, and lengthy versions of each edict so that his local officials could decide which one to use. Officials sometimes left out passages from the original to save space, Ashoka realized, and the officials at Kalinga did not even put up the text cited at the beginning of this chapter about Ashoka's bloody conquest of the region, possibly because they did not want to antagonize the local population.

The inscriptions report that Ashoka sent officials to inspect outlying regions every three to five years. He claims to have built new roads, along which his men planted trees and dug wells, and he encouraged his officials to discover new medicinal herbs and plant them where they had not previously been cultivated. Ashoka and the other Mauryan rulers did not mint their own coins; rulers in each locality did.

Ruling by Example: The Ceremonial State

Ashoka was the first major Indian ruler to support Buddhism. The ideal ruler followed Buddhist teachings and made donations to the Buddhist order, which he did not join. Nor did he renounce his family. The Buddhists called such a ruler a *chakravartin* (chuh-kruh-VAR-tin), literally "turner of the wheel," a broad term indicating that the sovereign ruled over a wide territory. Although Ashoka does not use the word, his inscriptions fully express his ideal of ruling by example. Every measure he took had the same goal: to encourage his subjects to follow dharma, which he described in this way:

> There is no gift comparable to the gift of dharma, the praise of dharma, the sharing of dharma, fellowship in dharma. And this is—good behavior towards slaves and servants, obedience to mother and father, generosity towards friends, acquaintances, and relatives and towards shramanas [shrah-MUH-nuhz; Buddhists and other renunciants] and Brahmins, and abstention from killing living beings.[8]

Many subsequent rulers, particularly in South and Southeast Asia, followed Ashoka's example.

Historians call this type of rule a **"ceremonial state"** to contrast it with empires in which rulers exercised more direct control. The ruler of a ceremonial state sponsored religious observances and contributed money for the construction of religious edifices in the hope that his subjects would recognize his generosity and willingly acknowledge him as their leader.

Ashoka's inscriptions permit us to see how his devotion to Buddhism increased over time. Before the battle of Kalinga (discussed at the beginning of the chapter) in 260 B.C.E., he was not yet a Buddhist, and so he was able to lead his armies into battle and kill thousands of enemy soldiers. At the end of the battle the huge number of deaths filled him with remorse and he made a decision to follow the teachings of the Buddha. In the following year he promised to uphold the five most important precepts—not to kill, steal, commit adultery, lie, and drink alcohol—

• ceremonial state States whose rulers sponsored religious observances and construction of religious edifices in the hope that their subjects would willingly acknowledge them as rulers. Usually contrasted with rulers who depended on sheer force to govern.

The First Sermon of the Buddha and Ashoka's Fourth Major Rock Edict

After gaining enlightenment under the Tree of Wisdom at Bodh Gaya, the Buddha preached his first sermon at the Deer Park at Benares. The Buddha's sermon presented the main teachings of Buddhism in a capsule form that could be translated into other languages when Buddhism spread beyond India to East and Southeast Asia. Because the language is easy to understand, this would have worked well as a spoken sermon, with repetition of important concepts to ensure the comprehension of his five followers, or bhikkhus (BEAK-kooz), whom he addressed. This text was transmitted orally by Buddhists in north India. Hundreds of monks met, first following the Buddha's death and then one hundred years later, to make sure that they were reciting the standard version of the sermon. The text was committed to writing only in the first century B.C.E. by

monks in modern-day Sri Lanka, evidence that Buddhism had spread to south India and beyond by that time.

The Fourth Major Rock Edict provides a summary of Ashoka's beliefs. Some overlap with the Buddha's teachings in the First Sermon, while others differ. Although Ashoka himself embraced Buddhism, he reached out to both Buddhist and non-Buddhist subjects by erecting pillar and rock throughout India (see page 78). The location of his edicts provides a rough indication of how far Buddhist teachings reached during his reign.

Sources: Walpola Sri Rahula, *What the Buddha Taught* (New York: Grove Press, 1974), pp. 92–94; Romila Thapar, *Aśoka and the Decline of the Mauryas* (Delhi: Oxford University Press, 1973), pp. 251–252. (Some changes in spelling and capitalization made for the sake of consistency.)

The First Sermon of the Buddha

Thus I have heard. The Blessed One was once living in the Deer Park at Isipatana (the Resort of Seers) near Varanasi (Benares). There he addressed the group of five bhikkhus:

Bhikkhus, these two extremes ought not to be practiced by one who has gone forth from the household life. What are the two? There is devotion to the indulgence of sense-pleasures, which is low, common, the way of ordinary people, unworthy and unprofitable; and there is devotion to self-mortification, which is painful, unworthy and unprofitable.

Avoiding both these extremes, the Tathagatha [the Buddha] has realized the Middle Path: it gives vision, it gives knowledge, and it leads to calm, to insight, to enlightenment, to nirvana. And what is that Middle Path . . . ? It is simply the Noble Eightfold Path, namely, right view, right thought, right speech, right action, right livelihood, right effort, right mindfulness, right concentration. . . .

The Noble Truth of suffering (*dukkha*) is this: Birth is suffering; aging is suffering; sickness is suffering; death is suffering; sorrow and lamenta-

tion, pain, grief and despair are suffering; association with the unpleasant is suffering; dissociation from the pleasant is suffering; not to get what one wants is suffering—in brief, the five aggregates of attachment are suffering.

The Noble Truth of the origin of suffering is this: It is this thirst (craving) which produces re-existence and re-becoming, bound up with passionate greed. It finds fresh delight now here and now there, namely, thirst for sense-pleasures; thirst for existence and becoming; and thirst for non-existence (self-annihilation).

The Noble Truth of the cessation of suffering is this: It is the complete cessation of that very thirst, giving it up, renouncing it, emancipating oneself from it, detaching oneself from it.

The Noble Truth of the path leading to the cessation of suffering is this: It is simply the Noble Eightfold Path, namely right view; right thought; right speech, right action; right livelihood; right effort; right mindfulness; right concentration.

"This is the Noble Truth of Suffering (*dukkha)*"; such was the vision, the knowledge, the wisdom, the science, the light, that arose in me with regard to things not heard before. "This suffering, as a noble truth, should be fully understood"; such was the vision, the knowledge, the wisdom, the science, the light, that arose in me with regard to things not heard before. "This suffering, as a noble truth, has been fully understood"; such was the vision, the knowledge, the wisdom, the science, the light, that arose in me with regard to things not heard before. . . .

As long as my vision of true knowledge was not fully clear . . . regarding the Four Noble Truths, I did not claim to have realized the per-

fect Enlightenment that is supreme in the world. . . . But when my vision of true knowledge was fully clear . . . regarding the Four Noble Truths, then I claimed to have the perfect Enlightenment that is supreme in the world. . . . And a vision of true knowledge arose in me thus: My heart's deliverance is unassailable. This is the last birth. Now there is no more re-becoming (rebirth).

This the Blessed One said. The group of five bhikkhus was glad, and they rejoiced at his words.

The Fourth Major Rock Edict

In the past, the killing and injuring of living beings, lack of respect towards relatives, Brahmins and shramanas had increased. But today, thanks to the practice of dharma on the part of the Beloved of the Gods, the king Ashoka, the sound of the drum has become the sound of dharma, showing the people displays of heavenly chariots, elephants, balls of fire, and other divine forms. Through his instruction in dharma abstention from killing and non-injury to living beings, deference to relatives, Brahmins and shramanas, obedience to mother and father, and obedience to elders have all increased as never before for many centuries. These and many other forms of the practice of dharma have increased and will increase.

The Beloved of the Gods, the king Ashoka, his sons, his grandsons and his great grandsons will advance the practice of dharma, until the end of the world and will instruct in the law, standing firm in dharma. For this, the instruction in the law, is the most valuable activity. But there is no practice of dharma without goodness, and in these matters it is good to progress and not to fall back. For this purpose, the inscription has been engraved—that men should make progress in this matter, and not be satisfied with their shortcomings. This was engraved here when the Beloved of the Gods, the king Ashoka, had been consecrated twelve years.

QUESTIONS FOR ANALYSIS

▶ What are the Four Noble Truths taught by the Buddha, and what is the relationship among them?

▶ What are the signs that the First Sermon was transmitted orally?

▶ Which Buddhist teachings did Ashoka think most important? What did he mean by dharma?

and became a lay Buddhist (*upasaka*). Anyone could become a lay Buddhist; one simply had to vow to uphold the five precepts and then continue in one's normal profession while living with one's family. Four distinct groups formed the early Buddhist order: monks and nuns were ordained, while male and female lay Buddhists were not.

In the tenth year of his reign, around 258 B.C.E., Ashoka visited the site at Bodh Gaya where the Buddha had gained enlightenment and decided to increase his devotion to Buddhism even further. Presumably along with learned Buddhists, he conducted a series of meetings with non-Buddhist "ascetics" engaged in different austerities, as well as with Brahmin priests, who continued to sacrifice animals. Ashoka discussed the teachings of the Buddha and gave them gifts to encourage them to convert to Buddhism. He used the same combination of persuasion and gift giving with elderly people and with ordinary people in the countryside. (See the feature "Movement of Ideas: The First Sermon of the Buddha and Ashoka's Fourth Major Rock Edict.")

Ashoka visited the Deer Park in Benares as well as the site of the Buddha's birth in present-day Nepal, where he built a stone fence and erected a stone pillar in memory of the Buddha. Another legend records that, as a sign of his devotion to Buddhism, Ashoka paid for the construction of 84,000 stupas, none of which survive, and later Buddhist rulers often emulated him by building monuments to express their devotion to Buddhism.

Ashoka's style of governing was very personal. One inscription describes how seriously he took the business of ruling and explains that his officials were free to interrupt him with public business no matter what he was doing. "And whatever I may order by word of mouth, whether it concerns a donation or a proclamation, or whatever urgent matter is entrusted to my officers, if there is any dispute or deliberation about it in the Council, it is to be reported to me immediately, at all places and all times." We learn that some officers could speak directly to the king and that there was a council, but not how it functioned.

Ashoka claimed to exercise influence over lands far from north India because of his support for dharma:

> The Beloved of the Gods considers victory by dharma to be the foremost victory. And moreover the Beloved of the Gods has gained this victory on all his frontiers to a distance of six hundred yojanas [about 1,500 miles, or 2400 km], where reigns the Greek king Antiochus [in Syria], and beyond the realm of that Antiochus in the lands of four kings named Ptolemy [in Egypt], Antigonus [in Macedonia], Magas [of Cyrene], and Alexander [of Epirus]; and in the south over the Colas and the Pandyas as far as Ceylon.

This inscription, composed between 256 and 254 B.C.E., claims that Ashoka had brought about "victory by dharma" far beyond his frontiers, as far west as the realms of Greek rulers in Egypt and Greece, and as far south as the island of Ceylon, modern Sri Lanka. Modern scholars concur that he may have sent missionaries, particularly to Sri Lanka, where oral accounts record their names. Otherwise, there is no independent evidence of Buddhism spreading outside the Indian subcontinent in Ashoka's reign.

We must keep in mind that Ashoka wrote his inscriptions and had them carved into huge, dramatic monuments to remind his subjects that he had the right to rule over them. The only external confirmation of their veracity comes from later Buddhist sources, which mention Ashoka's devotion to Buddhism. If

Ashoka had violated his Buddhist vows, or if a certain region had risen up in rebellion during his reign, we can be sure that the inscriptions would not mention it. One recent analysis suggests that the inscriptions not be seen "as solid blocks of historical fact, but as flightier pieces of political propaganda, as the campaign speeches of an incumbent politician who seeks not so much to record events as to present an image of himself and his administration to the world."[9]

After Ashoka's death in 232 B.C.E., the Mauryan Empire began to break apart; the Mauryans lost control of the last remaining section, the Ganga Valley, around 185 B.C.E. Few documents survive from this time. Historians wonder if the central government was unable to raise the funds it needed to support its sizable army, without which it could not control the massive territory that Chandragupta and Ashoka had conquered. A series of regional kingdoms gained control, as was the usual pattern for much of South Asian history.

South Asia's External Trade

India's geographic proximity to western Asia meant that outsiders came to South Asia in very early times, and, conversely, Indian culture, particularly Buddhist teachings, traveled out from India on the same paths. In ancient times travelers seeking to enter South Asia had a choice of routes. Although the Himalaya Mountains in the north and extensive mountains in the northeast prevented large-scale overland trade, regular cultural contacts and the movement of valuable goods always remained possible. Land routes through the Hindu Kush (HIHN-doo KOOSH) in the northwest, including the Khyber (KAI-ber) Pass, allowed more extensive contacts between South Asia and Central Asia through what is today Afghanistan. These are the routes that allowed the expansion of Indo-European languages and that Megasthenes used when he came to India.

However, the most important mode of communication between South Asia and the rest of the world was by sea. By 100 C.E., if not earlier, mariners from South and Southeast Asia had learned to capture the monsoon winds blowing northeast in the spring and early summer, and southwest in the fall and winter, to carry on regular commerce and cultural interaction with Southwest Asia and Africa. Finds of Harappan artifacts in the archaeological assemblages of early Sumer testify to the importance and age of these ancient sea routes.

Because no written descriptions of the ancient trade exist, archaeologists must reconstruct the trade on the basis of excavated commodities. Natural reserves of the semiprecious blue stone lapis lazuli exist only in the Badakhshan (BAH-duck-shan) region of northern Afghanistan, so we know that, by 2600 B.C.E., if not earlier, trade routes linked Badakhshan with ancient Sumer, where much lapis lazuli has been found. Similarly, the red-orange semiprecious stone carnelian traveled from mines in Gujarat (GOO-juh-ruht), India, to Mesopotamian sites. The presence of Harappan seals and clay pots at Sumer reveals that the trade included manufactured goods as well as minerals. These goods traveled overland or by boat down the Indus River to the Arabian Sea, where they hugged the coast as they traveled west to the Persian Gulf. Ancient sea routes across the Indian Ocean connected India with Mesopotamia, the Arabian Peninsula, and East Africa (see the map on page 61).

The monsoon winds changed direction two times a year, so if one caught them going west on a summer departure, one could return in the following winter as they blew east. They varied enormously in their intensity. Merchants traveling in the Indian Ocean usually sailed in small boats called **dhows.** Dhows (DOWZ) were made from teak planks laid edge to edge, fastened together with coconut fiber twine, and then caulked to prevent leaking. This method of construction gave them greater flexibility during storms than boats made from nailed wooden planks.

● **dhows** Small sailboats used in the Indian Ocean made from teak planks laid edge to edge, fastened together with coconut fiber twine, and caulked to prevent leaking.

We learn much about the Indian Ocean trade during the first century C.E. from an unusual work called the *Periplus* (PAY-rih-plus) (literally "around the globe"), written in colloquial Greek not by a scholar but by an anonymous merchant living in Egypt around 50 C.E. By the first century C.E., navigators from Egypt had learned how to harness the monsoon winds and travel by boat to India. The *Periplus* describes the routes sailors took and the goods they traded at Indian ports.

Written explicitly for merchants, the *Periplus* is organized as a guidebook: port by port, down the East African coast, around the Arabian Peninsula, and then to India. One-quarter of the book describes the trade with East Africa, one-quarter with Arabia, and one-half with India, the most important trading destination. In African and Arabian ports sailors could purchase ivory or gum resins like frankincense and myrrh, which were prized for their fragrance, but India offered far more goods than either Arabia or Africa. The author says almost nothing about social structure and little about government, other than the names of local rulers; he is much more interested in which commodities were for sale.

Analyzed carefully, however, the descriptions in the *Periplus* have much to tell us. For example, it summarizes the import trade on India's southwestern Malabar (MAH-lah-bar) coast. At the markets one could buy a yellow gem called peridot (PAY-ree-doh), clothing and textiles, coral, raw glass, copper, tin, lead, and wine. The author instructs his readers to bring money, and lots of it, to the southwestern coast because there were few opportunities for barter. Thousands of Roman silver and gold coins have been found on the south coast but not farther north, suggesting that the traders could barter in the north but had to pay Roman coins in the south (see Chapter 7, "The Roman Empire and the Rise of Christianity"). The author continues his discussion of the southwest coast by explaining the goods the region exported. Most of the items on the list, like pepper, pearls, ivory, and precious stones, are valuable even today, and nard and malabathron (MAH-la-bath-ruhn) were two indigenous plants used for their fragrance or as ingredients in drugs.

Aimed at non-Indian readers, the *Periplus* gives the misleading impression that the Indian Ocean trade was controlled by foreigners, possibly because its author was a Greek living in Egypt who used Roman coins to purchase Indian goods. In fact, though, Indian merchants played an active role in the Indian Ocean trade.

The author offers much briefer descriptions of the ports on the east coast of South Asia because foreign ships were too big to travel through the shallow channels separating India from Sri Lanka. Greek and Roman geographers exaggerated the size of Sri Lanka for centuries because no one had actually sailed around the island. At the end of the *Periplus,* the author describes one final destination:

> Beyond this region, by now at the northernmost point, where the sea ends somewhere on the outer fringe, there is a very great inland city called Thina from which silk floss, yarn, and cloth are shipped by land . . . and via the

Ganga River. . . . It is not easy to get to this Thina; for rarely do people come from it, and only a few.[10]

Thina? The spelling makes sense when one realizes that ancient Greek had no letter for the sound "ch," so the author had to choose either a "th" or an "s" for the first letter of the place whose name he heard from Indian traders. He opted for Thina. We cannot be sure how the word was pronounced in local ports, but *China* was pronounced "CHEE-na" in Sanskrit (and is the source of our English word *China*).

The author thought Thina was a city, not a country, but he knew that silk was made there and exported in three forms: yarn, floss, and woven cloth. The *Periplus* closes with the admission that China lay at the extreme edge of the world known to the Greeks: "What lies beyond this area, because of extremes of storm, bitter cold, and difficult terrain and also because of some divine power of the gods, has not been explored." The India described in the *Periplus,* then, was a major trade center linking the familiar Roman Empire with the dimly understood China.

Chapter Review

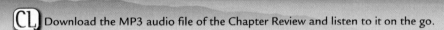

 Download the MP3 audio file of the Chapter Review and listen to it on the go.

KEY TERMS

Ashoka (60)

dharma (60)

monsoon (63)

Indus River Valley (64)

Sanskrit (66)

Rig Veda (66)

Vedic religion (68)

nomads (68)

varna (68)

jati (69)

Buddha (71)

nirvana (72)

Mauryan dynasty (76)

ceremonial state (79)

dhows (84)

Between 2600 B.C.E. and 100 C.E. South Asia was seldom unified, and, even during the rare intervals when a ruler like Ashoka managed to conquer a large amount of territory, their rule was decentralized, granting much authority to local rulers. Yet political disunity did not result in cultural disunity. Different cultural elements, particularly Vedic religion and Buddhism, bound together the people living under various rulers in different regions.

What evidence survives of social stratification at the Indus Valley sites? How did the Indo-Aryans describe the social stratification in their society?

At the time of the Indus Valley society (2600–1700 B.C.E.), people lived in enormous cities with clear evidence of social stratification. The wealthy occupied bigger houses than the poor, and when dead, graves with more goods. Because the Indus Valley writing system is still undeciphered, we do not know exactly how the people conceived of these social differences.

Written evidence survives from one of the great mass migrations of antiquity, sometime between 1500 and 1000, when the Indo-Aryans entered north India. The Indo-Aryans created a forerunner of the modern caste system, ranking different occupational groups. The late hymns of the *Rig Veda*, dating perhaps to 1000 B.C.E., equate four social groups, called varna, with parts of a mythic body: at the top, Brahmins form the mouth; warriors, the arms; farmers and merchants, the

www.cengage.com/history/hansen/voyages1e

thighs; and servants, the feet. Today, we may not understand all the details of the ancient caste system, but we know that different people, even within South Asia, understood it in various ways and that it evolved over time.

thighs; and servants, the feet. Today, we may not understand all the details of the ancient caste system, but we know that different people, even within South Asia, understood it in various ways and that it evolved over time.

 ## What were the main teachings of the Buddha?

The Buddha founded a religion that challenged the caste system and the primacy of Brahmin priests, who had been so influential in Vedic times. He taught that one could escape the sufferings of this life by adhering to the Four Noble Truths. His new religion welcomed members of all social groups, and merchants found the religion particularly appealing because they could improve their social position by making large donations to the Buddhist order.

 ## Why did Ashoka believe that supporting Buddhism would strengthen the Mauryan state?

Ashoka made extensive donations to the Buddhist order because he wanted to fulfill the Buddhist ideal of the chakravartin ruler. As the ruler of a ceremonial state, Ashoka led by example: he sponsored religious observances and contributed money to build Buddhist structures in the hope that his subjects would support his Mauryan Dynasty. This style of ruling influenced later dynasties.

Ashoka, unlike any South Asian ruler before or since, erected stone pillars bearing his inscriptions through his empire. Uncannily, some forty years later, the founder of the Qin dynasty (r. 221–210 B.C.E.) in China also carved royal pronouncements on gigantic rocks throughout his empire, as we shall see in the next chapter.

 ## Who were the main actors in the Indian Ocean trade? What types of ships did they use? Along which routes? To trade which commodities?

Though separated from the rest of Eurasia by high mountains, India in ancient times traded goods and ideas with people far to the west. Carnelian and lapis lazuli from South Asia have been found all over Mesopotamia and Egypt, evidence of active trade networks linking South Asia to the outside world in at least 2600 B.C.E., and the trade continued long after the collapse of the Mauryans at the end of the second century B.C.E. Traders, both foreign and Indian, sailed to the ports of the Indian Ocean in dhows and purchased semiprecious stones, metals, spices, and textiles. Few traveled beyond India to China.

For Further Reference

Basham, A. L. *The Wonder That Was India: Survey of the Culture of the Indian Sub-continent Before the Coming of the Muslims.* New York: Grove Press, 1959.

Casson, Lionel. *The Periplus Maris Erythraei Text with Introduction, Translation, and Commentary.* Princeton: Princeton University Press, 1989.

Elder, Joe. "India's Caste System." *Education About Asia* 1, no. 2 (1996): 20–22.

Fussman, Gerard. "Central and Provincial Administration in Ancient India: The Problem of the Mauryan Empire." *Indian Historical Review* 14 (1987–1988): 43–72.

Kenoyer, Mark. *Ancient Cities of the Indus Valley Civilization.* Karachi: Oxford University Press, 1998.

Liu, Xinru. *Ancient India and Ancient China: Trade and Religious Exchanges, A.D. 1–600.* Delhi: Oxford University Press, 1988.

O'Flaherty, Wendy Doniger. *The Rig Veda: An Anthology.* New York: Penguin Books, 1981.

Pearson, Michael. *The Indian Ocean.* New York: Routledge, 2003.

Thapar, Romila. *Aśoka and the Decline of the Mauryas.* Delhi: Oxford University Press, 1973.

Thapar, Romila. *Early India: From the Origins to AD 1300.* Berkeley: University of California Press, 2003.

Websites

Homepage of the Wales Professor of Sanskrit, Harvard: Michael Witzel (http://www.people.fas.harvard.edu/~witzel/mwpage.htm). Information on various topics in ancient Indian history, including Harappan society.

An Introduction to Buddhism (http://webspace.ship.edu/cgboer/buddhaintro.html). Detailed information on Buddhism and Buddha from a faculty member at Shippensburg University, Pennsylvania.

Sanchi (Madhya Pradesh) Berger Foundation (http://www.bergerfoundation.ch/wat4/museum1?museum=Sanchi&col=pays&country=Inde&genre=%&cd=7256-3191-2328:7256-3191-2325:7256-3191-2326&cdindex=1). Excellent collection of sharp, clear photographs from Sanchi.

Films

The Little Buddha.

WEB RESOURCES

Pronunciation Guide

Interactive Maps

MAP 3.1 Indus River Valley Society

MAP 3.2 Distribution of Languages in Modern South Asia

Primary Sources

Chapter Objectives

ACE Multiple-Choice Quiz

Flashcards

Blueprint for Empire: China, 1200 B.C.E.– 220 C.E.

In 221 B.C.E., the **First Emperor of the Qin dynasty** (259–210 B.C.E.) united China for the first time and implemented a blueprint for empire that helped to keep China united for much of the following two thousand years. Born in the Qin (CHIN) territory in the town of Xianyang (SHYEN-yahng) in Shaanxi (SHAHN-shee) province, western China, the future emperor was named Zheng (JUHNG). Prince Zheng's father, one of more than twenty sons of a regional ruler in west China, lived as a hostage in the eastern city of Handan (HAHN-dahn) because it was customary for younger sons to be sent to the courts of allied rulers. Two years after Zheng's birth, during an attack on Handan, his father escaped home, and his mother and the young prince went into hiding. Six years later they returned to Xianyang, and in 246 B.C.E., on the death of his father, Prince Zheng ascended to the Qin throne at the age of 13. For the first nine years he governed with the help of adult advisers until he became ruler in his own right at the age of 22.

During his reign he went on five different expeditions. At the top of each mountain he climbed, he erected a stone tablet describing his many accomplishments and asserting widespread support for his dynasty. One of these tablets read as follows:

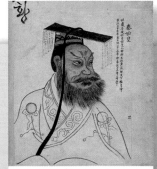

FIRST EMPEROR OF THE QIN DYNASTY

(British Library, London/HIP/Art Resource, NY)

In His twenty-sixth year [221 B.C.E.]
He first unified All under Heaven—
There was none who was not respectful and submissive.
He personally tours the distant multitudes,
Ascends this Grand Mountain
And all round surveys the world at the eastern extremity. . . .
May later ages respect and follow the decrees He bequeaths
And forever accept His solemn warnings.[1]

This icon will direct you to interactive activities and study materials on the *Voyages* website: www.cengage.com/history/hansen/voyages1e

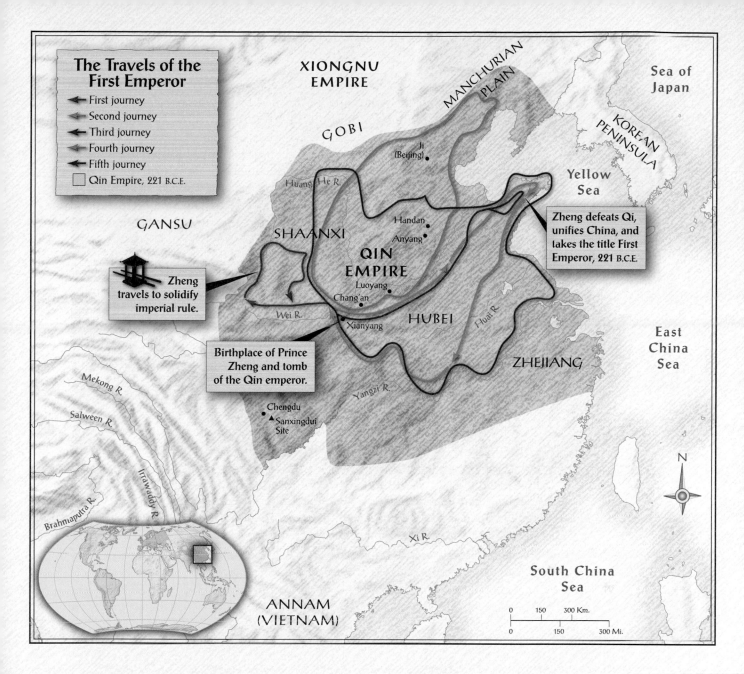

The Travels of the First Emperor

← First journey
← Second journey
← Third journey
← Fourth journey
← Fifth journey
☐ Qin Empire, 221 B.C.E.

XIONGNU EMPIRE

Sea of Japan

GOBI

MANCHURIAN PLAIN

KOREAN PENINSULA

Huang He R.

Ji (Beijing)

Yellow Sea

GANSU

SHAANXI

Handan

Anyang

QIN EMPIRE

Zheng defeats Qi, unifies China, and takes the title First Emperor, 221 B.C.E.

Zheng travels to solidify imperial rule.

Luoyang

Chang'an

Wei R.

Xianyang

HUBEI

Huai R.

East China Sea

Birthplace of Prince Zheng and tomb of the Qin emperor.

ZHEJIANG

Mekong R.

Salween R.

Yangzi R.

Chengdu
▲ Sanxingdui Site

Irrawaddy R.

Brahmaputra R.

Xi R.

South China Sea

N

0   150   300 Km.
0   150   300 Mi.

ANNAM (VIETNAM)

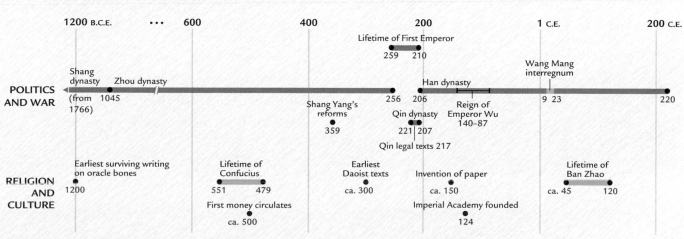

	1200 B.C.E.	•••	600	400	200	1 C.E.	200 C.E.

Lifetime of First Emperor
259 210

POLITICS AND WAR

Shang dynasty (from 1766)

Zhou dynasty
1045

Shang Yang's reforms
359

256

Han dynasty
206

Qin dynasty
221 207

Qin legal texts 217

Reign of Emperor Wu
140–87

Wang Mang interregnum
9 23

220

RELIGION AND CULTURE

Earliest surviving writing on oracle bones
1200

Lifetime of Confucius
551   479

First money circulates
ca. 500

Earliest Daoist texts
ca. 300

Invention of paper
ca. 150

Imperial Academy founded
124

Lifetime of Ban Zhao
ca. 45   120

● **First Emperor of the Qin dynasty** Founder of the Qin dynasty (221–207 B.C.E.) and the first ruler to unify ancient China. Eliminated regional differences by creating a single body of law and standardizing weights and measures.

The new emperor traveled overland in a sedan-chair carried by his servants and along rivers by boat. By the time he finished his last journey, he had criss-crossed much of the territory north of the Yangzi (YAHNG-zuh) River in modern-day China.

His unusual childhood must have affected Prince Zheng, but surviving sources convey little about his personality except to document his single-minded ambition. For the next fifteen years, he led the Qin armies on a series of brilliant military campaigns. They fought with the same weapons as their enemies—crossbows, bronze armor, shields, and daggers—but their army was organized as a meritocracy. A skilled soldier, no matter how low-ranking his parents, could rise to become a general, while the son of a noble family, if not a good fighter, would remain a common foot soldier for life.

The Qin was the first dynasty to vanquish all of its rivals, including six independent kingdoms, and unite China under a single person's rule. The First Emperor eliminated regional differences by creating a single body of law for all his subjects, standardizing all weights and measures, and even mandating a standard axle width for the ox- and horse-drawn carts. He coined a new title, *First Emperor* (*Shi Huangdi*), because he felt that the word *king* did not accurately convey his august position. The First Emperor intentionally stayed remote from his subjects so that they would respect and obey him.

On his deathbed, the First Emperor urged that his descendants rule forever, or "ten thousand years" in Chinese phrasing. Instead, peasant uprisings brought his dynasty to an end in three years. The succeeding dynasty, the Han dynasty (see below), denounced the Qin but used Qin governance to rule for four centuries. Subsequent Chinese rulers who aspired to reunify the empire always looked to the Han as their model. Unlike India, which remained politically disunited for most of its history, the Chinese empire endured for over two thousand years. Whenever it fell apart, a new emperor put it back together.

Focus Questions

What different elements of Chinese civilization took shape between 1200 and 221 B.C.E.?

What were the most important measures in the Qin blueprint for empire?

How did the Han rulers modify the Qin blueprint, particularly regarding administrative structure and the recruitment and promotion of officials?

Which neighboring peoples in Central, East, and Southeast Asia did the Han dynasty conquer? Why was the impact of Chinese rule limited?

The Origins of Chinese Civilization, 1200–221 B.C.E.

Agriculture developed independently in several different regions in China circa 7000 B.C.E. In each region, as was true elsewhere in the world (see Chapters 2 and 3), people began to harvest seeds on an occasional basis before progressing to full-time agriculture. By 1200 B.C.E., several independent cultural centers had emerged. One, the Shang (SHAHNG) kingdom based in the Yellow River Valley, developed the Chinese writing system. Many elements of Chinese civilization— the writing system, the worship of ancestors, and the Confucian and Daoist systems of belief—developed in the years before China was united in 221 B.C.E.

The First Agriculture, 7000–1200 B.C.E.

North China was particularly suited for early agriculture because a fine layer of yellow dirt, called loess (less), covers the entire Yellow River Valley, and few trees grow there. The Yellow River carries large quantities of loess from the west and deposits new layers each year in the last 500 miles (900 km) before the Pacific Ocean. As a result, the riverbed is constantly rising, often to a level higher than the surrounding fields. Sometimes called "China's River of Sorrow," the Yellow River has exhibited a dangerous tendency to flood throughout recorded history.

Three major climatic zones extend east and west across China (see the map on page 89). Less than 20 inches (50 cm) of rainfall each year falls on the region north of the Huai (HWHY) River; about 40 inches (1 m) per year drops on the middle band along the Yangzi River; and over 80 inches (2 m) a year pours on the southernmost band of China, including Guangzhou (GWAHNG-joe) and Hong Kong. This differential pattern of rainfall is due to the monsoon winds off the ocean: the water-laden winds first cross south China, where they drop much of their water; by the time they reach the north, they are carrying much less water. The climate of the Yellow River was probably hotter and wetter than it is today. Elephants and rhinoceros both lived there as late as 1000 B.C.E.

Agriculture was not limited to the Yellow River Valley. Wheat and millet cultivation extended as far north as Manchuria and as far south as Zhejiang (JEH-jeeahng), near the mouth of China's other great river, the Yangzi. The peoples living farther south raised rice; some hunted and gathered while others depended on agriculture. The different implements found in various regions suggest great cultural diversity within China between 7000 and 2000 B.C.E.

These different peoples evolved from small, egalitarian tribal groups who farmed intermittently to larger settled groups with clearly demarcated social levels living in large urban settlements, demonstrating all the elements of civilization described in Chapter 2. A given people can be identified as Chinese when they use Chinese characters, because only then can archaeologists be certain that they spoke Chinese. Some pots dating to circa 2000 B.C.E. are illustrated with different pictures, but these were probably potters' marks and not written characters (see Chapter 2 about first writing).

Early Chinese Writing in the Shang Dynasty, ca. 1200 B.C.E.

•**Shang dynasty**
China's first historic dynasty. The earliest surviving records date to 1200 B.C.E., during the Shang. The Shang king ruled a small area in the vicinity of modern Anyang, in Henan province, and granted lands to allies in noble families.

The first identifiable Chinese characters appeared on bones dating to around 1200 B.C.E. The discovery and deciphering of these bones mark one of the great intellectual breakthroughs in twentieth-century China. In 1899 the city of Beijing experienced an outbreak of malaria for which there was no known cure. In desperation the city's residents turned to an untried remedy: so-called dragon bones. When a scholar examined one of these bones, he realized that the scratchy lines on it were not magical symbols but vestiges of writing. The bones came from near the modern city of Anyang (AHN-yahng) in the central Chinese province of Henan (HUH-nahn), the core region of China's first historic dynasty, the **Shang dynasty** (1766–1045 B.C.E.).

Scholars call the excavated bones **"oracle bones"** because the Shang ruler used them to forecast the future. Like many ancient peoples around the world

■ The Earliest Records of Chinese Writing

Starting around 1200 B.C.E., ancient Chinese kings used the clavicle bones of cattle (as shown here) and the bottom of turtle shells to ask their ancestors to advise them on the outcomes of future events, including battles, sacrifices, their wives' pregnancies, and even their own toothaches. After applying heat, the fortunetellers interpreted the resulting cracks and wrote their predictions—in the most ancient form of Chinese characters—directly on the bones and turtle shells. (Lowell Georgia/Corbis)

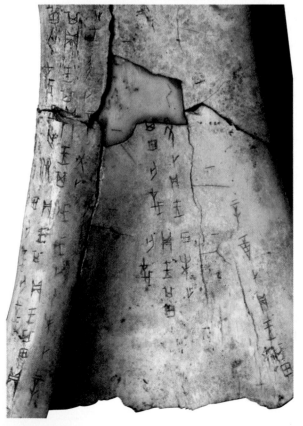

who used oracles to consult higher powers, the Shang placed a heated poker on cattle shoulder blades and turtle shell bottoms, or plastrons, and interpreted the resulting cracks. They then recorded on the bone the name of the ancestor they had consulted, the topic of inquiry, and the outcome. It was an extremely difficult feat, and we still do not know how the ancient Chinese incised characters on these bones with the bronze tools available to them.

Since 1900 over 200,000 oracle bones, both whole and fragmented, have been excavated in China. The quantities are immense, with 1,300 oracle bones concerning rainfall in a single king's reign, and their language is grammatically complex, suggesting that the Shang scribes had been writing for some time, possibly on perishable materials like wood. Scholars have deciphered the bones by comparing the texts with one another and with the earliest known characters. Shang dynasty characters, like their modern equivalents, have two elements: a radical, which suggests the broad field of meaning, and a phonetic symbol, which indicates sound. Like Arabic numerals, Chinese characters retain the same meaning even if pronounced differently: 3 means the number "three" even if some readers say "trois" or "drei."

During the Shang dynasty only the king and his scribes could read and write characters. Presenting the world from the king's vantage point, some oracle bones treat affairs of state, like the outcomes of battles, but many more touch on individual matters, such as his wife's pregnancy or his own aching teeth. The major religion of the time was **ancestor worship.** The Shang kings believed that their recently dead ancestors could intercede with the more powerful long-dead on behalf of the living. They conducted frequent rituals in which they offered food and drink to the ancestors in the hope of receiving help.

The Use of Component Parts in Chinese Food

Have you ever wondered how even a small Chinese food stand staffed by a single person quickly turns out so many distinctive dishes? Using a technique developed in at least 1200 B.C.E., if not before, chefs in today's Chinese restaurants combine component parts in various ways to produce a slightly different product each time. They start with a variety of precut meats and vegetables. When a customer gives the order for chicken in peanut sauce, the chef tosses chicken cubes and peppers into a wok, stir-fries them, and adds sauce as the final touch. The chef modifies the same technique to cook precut meat and vegetables in an array of sauces to make a large number of dishes, each with a different name and recognizable taste.

Chinese people eat these dishes with an accompanying starch, usually white rice in south China and noodles, dumplings, or wheat gruel in the north. Since the beginnings of agriculture, people in north China have eaten millet and wheat as their main starches, while those living in south China have almost always eaten rice.

This division between dishes and starch gave Chinese cuisine great flexibility. The poor could eat a single vegetable dish with whatever starch was cheapest, and the Chinese even developed labor-intensive recipes, like boiled almond shells, for normally inedible foods that could be prepared during famines. The rich could eat many dishes made from expensive delicacies with only a small amount of starch. However, even today, the most lavish banquets end with a bowl of plain white rice.

Shang dynasty cooks used many of the same tools as today's cooks—knives, stirring utensils, and bronze cooking pots. However, rather than stir-frying, they steamed and braised food. Those who presided over Shang rituals used chopsticks, one of the hallmarks of East Asian culture, to move food from large serving vessels to smaller plates. People then ate the food with their hands. Ordinary diners began to use chopsticks as eating utensils sometime around 200 B.C.E., the time of the first stir-fried food.

The peoples living in China used two types of vessels: flat bronze vessels for grain (usually wheat or millet) and baskets and wooden and pottery vessels for meat and vegetables. The division between starch and dishes made from cut-up meat and vegetables continues to the present day: Chinese chefs always prepare the starch separately from the meat and vegetable dishes. (See the feature "World History in Today's World: The Use of Component Parts in Chinese Food.")

Historians of China have ingeniously combined the information in oracle bones with careful analysis of Shang archaeological sites to piece together the outlines of early Chinese history. Like the Mesopotamians, the early Chinese lived inside walled cities. They mastered the exacting technology of mixing copper, tin, and lead in differing ratios to cast impressive bronze vessels. The earliest bronze vessels, from circa 2000 B.C.E., predate the first writing, but bronze-casting techniques reached full maturity around 1200 B.C.E. Ancient Chinese bronze casters made ritual vessels, farm implements, mirrors, chariot fittings, and daggers.

• oracle bones The earliest surviving written records in China, scratched onto cattle shoulder blades and turtle shell bottoms, or plastrons. These record the diviners' interpretations of the future.

• ancestor worship The belief in China that dead ancestors could intercede in human affairs on behalf of the living. Marked by frequent rituals in which the living offered food and drink to the ancestors in the hope of receiving help.

Shang Dynasty Relations with Other Peoples

Oracle bones have allowed scholars to understand how Shang government and society functioned between 1200 and 1000 B.C.E. Until then, the main source for early Chinese history was a book entitled *Records of the Grand Historian*, written by **Sima Qian** (SUH-mah CHEE-EN) (145– ca. 90 B.C.E.) in the first century B.C.E. Combining information drawn from several extant chronicles, Sima Qian wrote a history of China from its legendary founding sage emperors through to his lifetime. He gave the founding date of the Shang dynasty as 1766 B.C.E. and listed the names of the Shang kings but provided little detail about them. Setting a pattern for all future historians, Sima Qian believed that there could be only one legitimate ruler of China at any time and omitted any discussion of regional rulers who coexisted with the Shang and other dynasties.

In fact, though, the Shang exercised direct control over a relatively small area, some 125 miles (200 km) from east to west, and the Shang king sometimes traveled as far as 400 miles (650 km) away to fight enemy peoples. Beyond the small area under direct Shang control lived many different non-Shang peoples whose names appear on the oracle bones but about whom little is known. Shang kings did not have a fixed capital but simply moved camp from one place to another to conduct military campaigns against these other peoples.

■ **Early Chinese Bronze-working** The ancient Chinese combined copper, tin, and lead to make intricate bronze vessels like this wine container, which dates to circa 1050 B.C.E. and was found buried in the hills of Hunan, in southern China. Analysts are not sure of the relationship between the tiger-like beast and the man it embraces. The man's serene face suggests that the beast is communicating some kind of teaching—not devouring him. (Musée Cernuschi, Paris/Scala/Art Resource, NY)

Many oracle bones describe battles between the Shang and their enemies. When the Shang defeated an enemy, they took thousands of captives. The fortunate worked as laborers, and the less fortunate were killed as an offering. One oracle bone asks the ancestors' opinion about the number of human sacrifices necessary—ten? twenty? thirty?—and gives the name of the conquered people.

Shang subjects interred their kings in large tombs with hundreds of sacrificed corpses. Even in death they observed a hierarchy. Placed near the Shang king were those who accompanied him in death, with their own entourages of corpses and lavish grave goods. Royal guards were also buried intact, but the lowest-ranking corpses, most likely prisoners of war, had their heads and limbs severed.

The Shang were but one of many peoples living in China around 1200 B.C.E. Yet, since only the Shang left written records, we know much less about the other peoples. Fortunately an extraordinary archaeological find at the Sanxingdui (SAHN-shing-dway) site near Chengdu (CHUHNG-dew), in Sichuan (SUH-chwan) province, offers a glimpse of one of the peoples contemporary with the Shang. Inside the ancient city walls, archaeologists found two grave pits filled with bronze statues, bronze masks, and elephant tusks that had been burnt and cut into sections. Like the Shang, the people at the Sanxingdui site lived in small walled settlements and cast various bronze tools.

The people of Sanxingdui also made bronze masks more than a yard across with huge protruding eyes, whose significance no one can explain satisfactorily.

■ **Early Bronze-working Outside the Core of Ancient China**   Found in Sanxingdui, Sichuan, over 1,000 miles (1600 km) west of the Shang dynasty heartland, this statue looks completely different from anything made at Anyang, in the Yellow River Valley. This priest (or king or deity?) stands over 6 feet (1.8 m) tall. His enlarged hands originally held some type of round object—an elephant tusk?—and he stands on a base made from four elephant heads. Scholars now recognize that many distinct regional cultures coexisted in China at the same time as the Shang dynasty, in about 1200 B.C.E.   (Sanxingdui Museum, Guanghan, Sichuan Province/Cultural Relics Publishing, Beijing)

Whereas the Shang made no human statues, the most impressive artifact from Sanxingdui is a statue of a man. Unlike the Shang, the people at Sanxingdui do not seem to have practiced human sacrifice, nor do they appear to have had a writing system, although some archaeologists hope in the future to find samples of their writing.

The Zhou Dynasty, 1045–256 B.C.E.

The oracle bones are most plentiful during the period from 1200 to 1000 B.C.E. and diminish in quantity soon after. In 1045 B.C.E. a new dynasty, the **Zhou dynasty,** overthrew the Shang. The Grand Historian Sima Qian wrote the earliest detailed account of the Zhou (JOE) conquest in the first century B.C.E., long after the fact, and historians question his account. Claiming that 48,000 Zhou troops were able to defeat 700,000 Shang troops because the Shang ruler was corrupt and decadent, Sima Qian alleged that the last Shang ruler killed his enemies and roasted them on a rack or cut them into mincemeat before eating them.

Sima Qian's description set a pattern followed by all subsequent historians: vilifying the last emperor of the fallen dynasty and glorifying the founder of the next. According to Sima Qian, the Zhou king was able to overthrow the Shang because he had obtained the **Mandate of Heaven.** A new god, worshiped by the Zhou ruling house but not previously worshiped by the Shang, Heaven represented the generalized forces of the cosmos, rather than the abode of the dead. China's rulers believed that Heaven would send signs—terrible storms, unusual astronomical events, famines, even peasant rebellions—before withdrawing its mandate. But because the recipient of the Mandate of Heaven could only be known after the fact, it often served as a retrospective justification for overthrowing a dynasty by force.

Many other states coexisted with the Zhou dynasty (1045–256 B.C.E.), the most important being the Qin, who first unified China. The long period of Chinese history known as the Zhou dynasty is usually divided into the Western Zhou, 1045–771 B.C.E., when the capital was located in the Wei (WAY) River Valley, and the Eastern Zhou, 771–256 B.C.E., when, after defeat in battle, the Zhou rulers were forced to move east.

Throughout the long years of Zhou rule, the people writing Chinese characters gradually settled more and more territory at the expense of other peoples. Because the final centuries of the Zhou were particularly violent, the period from 481 to 221 B.C.E. is commonly called the Warring States Period. Yet constant warfare brought benefits, such as the diffusion of new technology. Iron tools spread throughout China, and people were able to use iron farm implements to plow the

● **Zhou dynasty** The successor dynasty to the Shang that gained the Mandate of Heaven and the right to rule, Chinese historians later recorded. Although depicted by later generations as an ideal age, the Zhou witnessed considerable conflict.

● **Mandate of Heaven** The Chinese belief that Heaven, the generalized forces of the cosmos (not the abode of the dead), chose the rightful ruler. China's rulers believed that Heaven would send signs before withdrawing its mandate.

land more deeply. Agricultural productivity increased, and the first money—in the shape of knives and spades but not round coins—circulated around 500 B.C.E., at roughly the same time as in India.

Changes in warfare brought massive social change. Since the time of the Shang, battles had been fought with chariots, and only boys who grew up in wealthy households had the time and the resources to learn how to guide a galloping horse pulling a chariot with three men into battle. But in the sixth and fifth centuries B.C.E., as they went farther south, armies began to fight battles in muddy terrain where chariots could not go. Instead, generals began to use large armies of foot soldiers. Some of the most successful generals were not necessarily the sons of powerful families, but those, regardless of family background, who could lead armies of ten thousand soldiers into battle. At this time ambitious young men studied strategy and general comportment with tutors, one of whom became China's most famous teacher, **Confucius** (551–479 B.C.E.).

Confucianism

Confucius was born in 551 B.C.E. in Shandong (SHAHN-dohng) province. His family name was Kong (KOHNG); his given name, Qiu (CHEE-OH). (*Confucius* is the English translation of *Kong Fuzi* [FOO-zuh], or Master Kong, but most Chinese refer to him as Kongzi [KOHNG-zuh], which also means Master Kong.) Acutely aware of living in a politically unstable era, Confucius was a professional teacher who lived off fees from his students. They have left us the only record of his thinking, a series of conversations he had with them, which are called *The Analects,* meaning "discussions and conversations." Recently scholars have begun to question the authenticity of the later *Analects* (especially chapters 10–20), but they agree that the first nine chapters probably date to an earlier time, perhaps just after Confucius's death in 479 B.C.E.

Confucianism is the term used for the main tenets of Confucius's thought. The optimistic tone of *The Analects* will strike any reader. Teaching students in one of the most chaotic periods in Chinese history, Confucius did not advocate violence. Instead, he emphasized the need to perform ritual correctly. Ritual is central because it allows the gentleman, the frequent recipient of Confucius's teachings, to express his inner humanity (a quality sometimes translated as "benevolence," "goodness," or "man at his best"). Since Confucius is speaking to his disciples, he rarely explains what kind of rituals he means, but he mentions sacrificing animals, playing music, and performing dances.

Confucius's teachings do not resemble a religion so much as an ethical system. Filial piety, or respect for one's parents, is its cornerstone. If children obey their parents and the ruler follows Confucian teachings, the country will right itself because an inspiring example will lead people toward the good. (See the feature "Movement of Ideas: *The Analects* and Sima Qian's Letter to Ren An.")

Confucius was also famous for his refusal to comment on either the supernatural or the afterlife:

> Zilu [ZUH-lu; a disciple] asked how to serve the spirits and gods. The Master [Confucius] said: "You are not yet able to serve men, how could you serve the spirits?"
> Zilu said: "May I ask you about death?"
> The Master said: "You do not yet know life, how could you know death?"[2]

If we define religion as the belief in the supernatural, then Confucianism does not seem to qualify. But if we consider religion as the offering of rituals at different

●Confucius (551–479 B.C.E.) The founder of Confucianism, a teacher who made his living by tutoring students. Known only through *The Analects,* the record of conversations with his students that they recorded after his death.

●Confucianism The term for the main tenets of the thought of Confucius (551–479 B.C.E.), which emphasized the role of ritual in bringing out people's inner humanity (a quality translated variously as "benevolence," "goodness," or "man at his best").

Primary Source: The Book of Documents *Read this Confucian classic to discover how rulers gain or lose the right to rule, an authority known as the Mandate of Heaven.*

turning points in one's life—birth, marriage, and death—then Confucianism can be considered a religion. Confucius's immediate followers made offerings to their ancestors and other gods.

Daoism   Many of Confucius's followers were also familiar with the teachings of **Daoism** (DOW-is-uhm) (alternate spelling Taoism), the other major belief system of China before unification in 221 B.C.E. The earliest Daoist texts excavated so far, dated to 300 B.C.E., were found in tombs alongside Confucian texts, an indication that the deceased did not necessarily think of Daoism and Confucianism as separate religions. Both Confucius and the leading Daoist teachers spoke about the "Way," a concept for which they used the same word, *dao* (DOW).

For Confucius, the Way denoted using ritual to bring out one's inner humanity. In contrast, the Way of the early Daoist teachers included meditation, breathing techniques, and special eating regimes. They believed that, if one learned to control one's breath or the life-force present in each person, one could attain superhuman powers and possibly immortality. Some said that immortals shed their human bodies much as butterflies cast off pupas. Such people were called Perfect Men. One early Daoist text, *Zhuangzi* (JUAHNG-zuh), named for the author of its teachings, Master Zhuang (JUAHNG), describes such people: "The Perfect Man is godlike. Though the great swamps blaze, they cannot burn him; though the great rivers freeze, they cannot chill him."[3]

Zhuangzi is one of the funniest and most ironic books ever written in China. It describes many paradoxes, including this well-known anecdote:

> Once Zhuang Zhou [Zhuangzi] dreamt he was a butterfly, a butterfly flitting and fluttering around, happy with himself and doing as he pleased. He didn't know he was Zhuang Zhou. Suddenly he woke up and there he was, solid and unmistakable Zhuang Zhou. But he didn't know if he was Zhuang Zhou who had dreamt he was a butterfly, or a butterfly dreaming he was Zhuang Zhou.

The question of knowledge—of how we know what we think we know—permeates *Zhuangzi*.

Zhuangzi often mocks those who fear death because they cannot know what death is actually like; he dreams that a talking skull asks him, "Why would I throw away more happiness than that of a king on a throne and take on the troubles of a human being again?" *Zhuangzi*'s amusing tales underline how profoundly gloomy was the Daoist view of death, which pictured it as a series of underground prisons from which no one could escape.

The other well-known Daoist classic, *The Way and Integrity Classic*, or *Daodejing* (DOW-deh-jing), combines the teachings of several different masters into one volume. It urges rulers to allow things to follow their natural course, or *wuwei* (WOO-way), often misleadingly translated as "nonaction": "Nothing under heaven is softer or weaker than water, and yet nothing is better for attacking what is hard and strong, because of its immutability."[4] In the centuries leading up to 221 B.C.E., no Daoist church had a recognized leader, but many Daoist masters had disciples, and *Zhuangzi* and *The Way and Integrity Classic* offer a glimpse of the wide variety of teachings circulating alongside Confucian teachings in China at that time.

• **Daoism** A Chinese belief system dating back to at least 300 B.C.E. that emphasized the "Way," a concept expressed in Chinese as "dao." The Way of the early Daoist teachers included meditation, breathing techniques, and special eating regimes.

The Analects and Sima Qian's Letter to Ren An

Unlike the first sermon of the Buddha (see Chapter 3), Confucianism has no short text that summarizes its main teachings. Throughout history students read and memorized *The Analects* because it was thought to be the only text that quoted Confucius directly. Each chapter contains ten to twenty short passages, often dialogues between Confucius and a student, and each passage is numbered. The first chapter introduces the most important Confucian teachings, including respect for one's parents, or filial piety.

Living more than three hundred years after Confucius's death, the Grand Historian Sima Qian wrestled with the issue of how to best observe the tenets of filial piety. Convicted of treason because he defended a general who had surrendered to the Xiongnu, he was offered a choice: he could commit suicide or he could undergo castration. In the excerpts from this letter to his friend Ren An, whom he called Shaoqing, he explains why he chose castration even though it brought shame to his ancestors. According to Confucian teachings, one's body was a gift from one's parents, and each person was obliged to protect his body from any mutilation. But Sima Qian's father had begun *The Records of the Grand Historian,* and he chose physical punishment so that he could complete his father's project.

Sources: The Analects, trans. Simon Leys (New York: W. W. Norton, 1997); Sima Qian, *Records of the Grand Historian: Qin Dynasty,* trans. Burton Watson (New York: A *Renditions*-Columbia University Press Book, 1993), Appendix II: Sima Qian's letter to Ren An, pp. 233, 235.

Chapter One of *The Analects*

1.1. The Master said: "To learn something and then to put it into practice at the right time: is this not a joy? To have friends coming from afar: is this not a delight? Not to be upset when one's merits are ignored: is this not the mark of a gentleman?"

1.2. Master You said: "A man who respects his parents and his elders would hardly be inclined to defy his superiors. A man who is not inclined to defy his superiors will never foment a rebellion. A gentleman works at the root. Once the root is secured, the Way unfolds. To respect parents and elders is the root of humanity."

1.3. The Master said: "Clever talk and affected manners are seldom signs of goodness."

1.4. Master Zeng said: "I examine myself three times a day. When dealing on behalf of others, have I been trustworthy? In intercourse with my friends, have I been faithful? Have I practiced what I was taught?"

1.5. The Master said: "To govern a state of middle size, one must dispatch business with dignity and good faith; be thrifty and love all men; mobilize the people only at the right times."

1.6. The Master said: "At home, a young man must respect his parents; abroad, he must respect his elders. He should talk little, but with good faith; love all people, but associate with the virtuous. Having done this, if he still has energy to spare, let him study literature."

1.7. Zixia said: "A man who values virtue more than good looks, who devotes all his energy to serving his father and mother, who is willing to give his life for his sovereign, who in intercourse with friends is true to his word—even though some may call him uneducated, I still maintain he is an educated man."

1.8. The Master said: "A gentleman who lacks gravity has no authority and his learning will remain shallow. A gentleman puts loyalty and faithfulness foremost; he does not befriend his moral inferiors. When he commits a fault, he is not afraid to amend his ways."

1.9. Master Zeng said: "When the dead are honored and the memory of remote ancestors is kept alive, a people's virtue is at its fullest."

1.10. Ziqing asked Zigong: "When the Master arrives in another country, he always becomes informed about its politics. Does he ask for such information, or is it given him?"

Zigong replied: "The Master obtains it by being cordial, kind, courteous, temperate, and deferential. The Master has a way of enquiring which is quite different from other people's, is it not?"

1.11. The Master said: "When the father is alive, watch the son's aspirations. When the father is dead, watch the son's actions. If three years later, the son has not veered from the father's way, he may be called a dutiful son indeed."

1.12. Master You said: "When practicing the ritual, what matters most is harmony. This is what made the beauty of the way of the ancient kings; it inspired their every move, great or small. Yet they knew where to stop: harmony cannot be sought for its own sake, it must always be subordinated to the ritual; otherwise it would not do."

1.13. Master You said: "If your promises conform to what is right, you will be able to keep your word. If your manners conform to the ritual, you will be able to keep shame and disgrace at bay. The best support is provided by one's own kinsmen."

1.14. The Master said: "A gentleman eats without stuffing his belly; chooses a dwelling without demanding comfort; is diligent in his office and prudent in his speech; seeks the company of the virtuous in order to straighten his own ways. Of such a man, one may truly say that he is fond of learning."

1.15 Zigong said: "'Poor without servility; rich without arrogance.' How is that?"

The Master said: "Not bad, but better still: 'Poor, yet cheerful; rich, yet considerate.'"

Zigong said: "In the *Poems*, it is said: 'Like carving horn, like sculpting ivory, like cutting jade, like polishing stone.' Is this not the same idea?"

The Master said: "Ah, one can really begin to discuss the *Poems* with you! I tell you one thing, and you can figure out the rest."

1.16. The Master said: "Don't worry if people don't recognize your merits; worry that you may not recognize theirs."

Sima Qian's Letter to Ren An

A man has only one death. That death may be as weighty as Mount Tai, or it may be as light as a goose feather. It all depends on the way he uses it. Above all, a man must bring no shame to his forebears. Next he must not shame his person, or be shameful in his countenance, or in his words. Below such a one is he who suffers the shame of being bound, and next he who bears the shame of prison clothing. . . . Lowest of all is the dire penalty of castration, the "punishment of rottenness"! . . .

It is the nature of every man to love life and hate death, to think of his parents and look after his wife and children. Only when he is moved by higher principles is this not so. Then there are things that he must do. Now I have been most unfortunate, for I lost my parents very early. With no brothers or sisters, I have been left alone and orphaned. And you yourself, Shaoqing, have seen me with my wife and child and know I would not let thoughts of them deter me. Yet the brave man does not necessarily die for honor, while even the coward may fulfill his duty. Each takes a different way to exert himself. Though I might be weak and cowardly and seek shamelessly to prolong my life, I know full well the difference between what ought to be followed and what rejected. . . . But the reason I have not refused to bear these ills and have continued to live, dwelling in vileness and disgrace without taking leave, is that I grieve that I have things in my heart that I have not been able to express fully, and I am ashamed to think that after I am gone my writings will not be known to posterity.

QUESTIONS FOR ANALYSIS

▶ According to *The Analects,* how should a gentleman conduct himself? How should a son treat his parents?

▶ According to Sima Qian, how should a virtuous person live? Why does he choose castration over suicide?

● Qin Rulers Unify China, 359–207 B.C.E.

While Confucian and Daoist thinkers were proposing abstract solutions to end the endemic warfare, a third school, the Legalists, took an entirely different approach based on their experience governing the Qin homeland in western China. In 359 B.C.E., the statesman Shang Yang (SHAHNG yahng), the major adviser to the Qin ruler, implemented a series of reforms reorganizing the army and redefining the tax obligations of all citizens. Those reforms made the Qin more powerful than any of the other regional states in China, and it gradually began to conquer its neighbors. The First Emperor implemented Shang Yang's blueprint for rule both as the regional ruler of the Qin and as emperor after the unification of China in 221 B.C.E.

Prime Minister Shang Yang's Reforms, 359–221 B.C.E.

In 359 B.C.E., Prime Minister Shang Yang focused on the territory under direct Qin rule. The government sent officials to register every household in the Qin realm, creating a direct link between each subject and the ruler. Once a boy resident in the Qin region reached the age of 16 or 17 and a height of 5 feet (1.5 m), he had to serve in the military, pay land taxes (a fixed share of the crop), and perform labor service, usually building roads, each year. To encourage people to inform on each other, Shang Yang divided the population into mutual responsibility groups of five and ten: if someone committed a crime but was not apprehended, everyone in the group was punished.

Most people in ancient China took it for granted that the son of a noble was destined to rule and the son of a peasant was not, but the Legalists disagreed. Rejecting the Confucian values of ritual and benevolence and renouncing a special status for "gentlemen," they believed that the ruler should recruit the best men to staff his army and his government. Qin officials recognized no hereditary titles, not even for members of the ruler's family.

Instead the Qin officials introduced a strict meritocracy, which made their army the strongest in China. A newly recruited soldier might start at the lowest rank, but if he succeeded in battle, he could rise in rank and thereby raise the stature of his household. Because Qin rules tolerated no value judgments, which could be biased, a soldier had to present the heads of all those enemy soldiers he had killed before he could advance. The more heads he presented, the higher he rose in the army. This reorganization succeeded brilliantly because each soldier had a strong incentive to fight. Starting in 316 B.C.E., the Qin polity began to conquer neighboring lands and implement Shang Yang's measures in each new region.

Legalist philosophers valued the contributions of the farmer-soldiers most highly because they paid taxes and were the backbone of the army. Accordingly, Legalist thinkers ranked peasants just under government officials, or scholars, who could read and write. Because artisans made objects peasants needed, like baskets and tools, they ranked third, and merchants, who neither worked the land nor manufactured the goods they traded, ranked at the bottom of society.

This ranking reflected how Legalist thinkers thought society should be, not how it actually was. Any Chinese peasant would gladly have changed places with a merchant because merchants did not perform arduous physical labor and could afford better clothes and food. Although the Legalist ranking, like the explanation of varna in the Indian "Hymn of Primeval Man," did not reflect reality, it persisted throughout Chinese history.

The Policies of the First Emperor, 221–210 B.C.E.

In 246 B.C.E., Prince Zheng, the future First Emperor, ascended to the Qin throne and launched a series of military conquests that culminated with the defeat of his final rival, the ruler of Qi (modern-day Shandong) in 221 B.C.E. He then named himself First Emperor. Determining what happened during the Qin founder's eleven-year reign (221–210 B.C.E.) poses great challenges because immediately after his death Sima Qian portrayed him as one of the worst tyrants in Chinese history who murdered his opponents, suppressed all learning, and adamantly opposed Confucian virtues. This view of the First Emperor prevails today, but the evidence *from* his reign (as opposed to that composed *after* it) suggests that the First Emperor conceived of himself as a virtuous ruler.

After 221 B.C.E., the emperor placed stone tablets on high mountaintops that recorded his view of his reign:

> The way of good rule is advanced and enacted;
> The various professions achieve their proper place,
> And all find rule and model.
> His great principle is superb and shining.[5]

Each line invoked Confucian learning. "Superb and shining" is a title used by the first ruler of the Zhou, and the First Emperor adopted it because he, too, hoped to be perceived as the virtuous founder of a new dynasty.

To compose the stone inscriptions, the Qin emperor commissioned a team of scholars who drew on all the classical learning of China's different regions that had taken shape in the previous millennium, including Confucius's teachings. One of their inscriptions claims, "The way of filial piety is brilliantly manifest and shining!" According to Confucian teachings, the ruler's main role was to lead his subjects in ritual, and the Qin emperor assumed this role each time he put up a stone tablet.

The Qin emperor placed these monuments in the far corners of his realm to demonstrate that he directed all of his subjects, both those in the Qin homeland and those recently conquered, in correct ritual observance. Unlike the Ashokan inscriptions in different languages, all the Qin inscriptions were written in Chinese because the Qin enforced linguistic standardization throughout their empire. And whereas Ashoka's inscriptions were phrased colloquially, the Qin inscriptions were rigidly formal, consisting of thirty-six or seventy-two lines, each with exactly four characters. Although Ashoka's inscriptions were completed within the Qin emperor's lifetime, northern India lay some 1,000 miles (1,600 km) from the western edge of the Qin emperor's realm, and no evidence of direct contact between the Mauryan and Qin Empires survives.

The inscriptions use the characteristic Chinese technique of manufacture: their authors placed component parts, or characters, in various combinations to produce a slightly different text for each inscription. Each Qin stone text runs exactly the same length and covers the usual themes, but no two inscriptions are identical.

Qin dynasty sources demonstrate clearly that the First Emperor exercised far more control over his subjects than had his predecessors. Using government registers listing all able-bodied men, the First Emperor initiated several enormous public works projects. Hundreds of thousands of conscripts built 4,000 miles (6,400 km) of roads, roughly as many as the Romans did,[6] as well as long walls of pounded earth, the most readily available building material. (The Great Wall that one sees today was built of stone in the fifteenth through seventeenth centuries C.E. along the foundations of the Qin dirt walls.) The Qin emperor also used conscript labor to build his tomb, where he was buried in 210 B.C.E. (See the feature "Visual Evidence: The Terracotta Warriors of the Qin Founder's Tomb.")

Many Qin subjects left their homes either to perform labor service on these different projects or to serve in the army, which had several hundred thousand conscripts and which traveled as far north to modern-day Mongolia or south to Vietnam (see below). The central government sent supplies overland to its armies on the roads it built, but when the armies traveled too far, it became difficult to sustain their supply lines, and many died far from home in unsuccessful military campaigns.

■ **The Great Wall Then and Now** Few people realize that the Great Wall that we see today (*right*) was built during the Ming dynasty (1368–1644), not during the Qin dynasty (221–207 B.C.E.). The Qin emperor ordered the construction of the Great Wall by linking together many preexisting dirt walls. The remains of the Qin wall, which was made largely from pounded earth, survive in only a few places in China (*left*). (left: © Zhao Guangtian/Panorama Media (Beijing) Ltd./Alamy; right: © Graham French/Masterfile)

Legalism and the Laws of the Qin Dynasty

The Qin ruler viewed the establishment of laws as one of his most important accomplishments. According to one inscription, he "created the regulations and illuminated the laws" as soon as he became emperor. Viewing law as a tool for strengthening the realm, the Legalists advocated treating all men identically, regardless of birth, because they believed that only the systematic application of one set of laws could control man's inherently evil nature. Subjects could not use law to challenge their ruler's authority because the only law for Legalists was the law of the ruler. They did not acknowledge the existence of a higher, divine law.

In place for only fourteen years, the **Qin dynasty** (221–207 B.C.E.) did not have time to develop a governmental system for all of China, but it did create a basic framework. The First Emperor appointed a prime minister as the top official in his government. Different departments in the capital administered the emperor's staff, the military, and revenue. The Qin divided the empire into over forty military districts called commanderies, each headed by a governor and a military commander. They in turn were divided into districts, the smallest unit of the Qin government, which were governed by magistrates with the help of clerks. All these officials were charged with carrying out the new laws of the Qin.

● **Qin dynasty** (221–207 B.C.E.) The first dynasty to rule over a unified China; heavily influenced by Legalist teachings that promoted soldiers and officials strictly on the basis of accomplishment, not birth.

Later historians described Qin laws as arbitrary and overly harsh; they were also surprisingly detailed, clearly the product of a government deeply concerned with following legal procedures carefully. Archaeologists working in Shuihudi (SHWAY-who-dee) town, in Hubei (WHO-bay) province, found a partial set of Qin dynasty laws dating to 217 B.C.E. in the tomb of a low-ranking clerk. We know only his last name, Xi.

Clerk Xi was buried with a set of model cases illustrating legal procedures. All were written on bamboo slips preserved in stagnant water, with holes punched into them. They were then sewn together to form sheets that could be rolled up, similar to a modern placemat made from cord and reeds. Some writers used silk, but most used bamboo because silk was ruined if one's brush slipped.

Each model case described in the Shuihudi materials is equally complex, pointing to the existence of established procedures for officials to follow before reaching a judgment. One text begins as follows:

> Report. A, the wife of a commoner of X village, made a denunciation, saying, "I, A, had been pregnant for six months. Yesterday, in the daytime, I fought with the adult woman C of the same village. I, A, and C grabbed each other by the hair. C threw me, A, over and drove me back. A fellow-villager, D, came to the rescue and separated C and me, A. As soon as I, A, had reached my house, I felt ill and my belly hurt; yesterday evening the child miscarried."[7]

The text provides detailed instructions for investigating such a case. The legal clerk, someone like Clerk Xi, had to examine the fetus and consult with the local midwife; he also had to interrogate A and the members of her household to determine her condition.

The Shuihudi tomb also contained sections of the Qin legal code that make fine distinctions: the penalties for manslaughter (inadvertently killing someone) were lighter than those for deliberate murder. Officials had to examine the murder weapon: a determination of manslaughter hinged on whether the assailant had used an object lying at hand or had concealed his weapon, which indicated intent to murder. The fine legal distinctions among different types of murder resemble

THE TERRACOTTA WARRIORS OF THE QIN FOUNDER'S TOMB

The Qin emperor's tomb, sometimes called the eighth wonder of the world, was discovered in 1973 by a farmer digging a well. The enormous tomb is so big that archaeologists have to dig test pits to probe its dimensions. Test pit #1, shown to the right, contains over seven thousand soldiers of four types—foot soldiers, archers, charioteers, and soldiers riding on horseback—who staffed the emperor's terracotta army. Because the Qin emperor expected the afterlife to be exactly the same as his life, his tomb formed a miniaturized world in which he could pursue his usual activities, including commanding his troops in battle.

The terracotta warriors do not resemble the figurines placed in any Chinese tomb before or since, prompting much speculation about the identity of their creators. One intriguing possibility, recently proposed, is that the emperor used his plumbers, because the soldiers' legs greatly resemble clay water pipes found in the ruins of the Qin palace.

Over one thousand soldiers bear labels stamped into the clay by eighty-five foremen, who were presumably responsible for supervising their construction. One estimate suggests that it took eleven years for these foremen, each supervising some ten men, to make the entire army of over seven thousand figures.*

How did the Qin craftsmen make so many different soldiers in such a short time? Like chefs in today's Chinese restaurants, they arranged thousands of prefabricated parts in various combinations to make a slightly different product each time. Archaeologists have identified two types of feet, three types of shoes and four types of boots, two types of legs, eight types of torso, and two types of armor used to make the mass-produced soldiers, whose bodies range from 5 feet 11 inches to 6 feet 5 inches (180 to 195 cm) tall.

Once a soldier's body was completed, a craftsman used clay to make his facial features. All the soldiers have individual faces, as if the craftsmen worked from living models. Yet the faces are idealized: no soldier has any wounds or scars. When the soldiers were completed, craftsmen painted them with bright colors, most of which has flaked off on the surrounding dirt.

The core of the tomb, where the Qin emperor himself was buried, has yet to be excavated, but writing one hundred years later, Sima Qian described it: "Artisans were ordered to install mechanically triggered crossbows set to shoot any intruder. With mercury the various waterways of the empire, the Yangzi and Yellow Rivers, and even the great ocean itself were created and made to flow and circulate mechanically."† Sima Qian also claimed that the son of the Qin founder ordered that the craftsmen who worked on the tomb be buried alive so that the tomb's exact location would remain secret. Archaeologists have not found human remains, but they continue to announce new discoveries, most recently of clay wrestlers and tumblers who performed for the emperor's pleasure in the next world.

---

*Lothar Ledderose, *Ten Thousand Things: Module and Mass Production in Chinese Art* (Princeton: Princeton University Press, 2000), pp. 69–70.

†Maxwell K. Hearn, "The Terracotta Army of the First Emperor of Qin," in *The Great Bronze Age of China: An Exhibition from the People's Republic of China,* ed. Wen Fong (New York: Metropolitan Museum of Art, 1980), p. 357.

QUESTION FOR ANALYSIS

 How do the terracotta warriors illustrate the Chinese technique of using prefabricated component parts to mass-produce multiple objects that differ from each other?

This ordinary soldier's head was made by combining molded forms of the front and the back and smoothing them together. Like all Chinese, he did not cut his hair, considered to be a gift from his parents, but bound it in intricate patterns on the back and top of his head.

A roof of wooden beams was originally built over the entire army and then covered with mats, a layer of sand and chalk, and finally a layer of dirt.

His headdress indicates that this figure is an officer. This group of nine statues includes at least three officers who stand at the front of their unit so that they can lead their subordinates into battle.

This missing head reveals how the hollow statues were made. The armor, lower skirt, and legs were made from sheets of clay in a construction technique originally used by palace plumbers for water pipes.

(© Alfo Garozzo/Cuboimages srl/Alamy)

Each Qin soldier wore a uniform consisting of a gown to the knees, leather armor on the upper torso, short pants, leg guards, and a headdress (never a helmet).

This officer's hands originally held weapons, most likely wooden spears or staffs, which have since disintegrated.

those in Hammurabi's laws (see Chapter 2). However, whereas in Babylon an assembly decided whether the murder victim's wife was guilty of killing her husband, in China the presiding official or clerk determined an individual's guilt.

Qin punishments were grisly. One could have one's foot cut off or one's nose severed for various offenses, and many of those sentenced to hard labor were not "complete," meaning that they were missing a limb. But if we consider the punishments in use elsewhere in the world at the time, such as Roman crucifixion, the Qin punishments do not seem unusual.

The Han Empire, 206 B.C.E.–220 C.E.

The Qin dynasty came to a sudden end in 207 B.C.E. with the suicide of the First Emperor's son. The following year, in 206 B.C.E., the new emperor founded the **Han dynasty.** Although the Han founder always depicted the Qin as a brutal dynasty, he drew on many Legalist precedents to create a blueprint that allowed him and his descendants to rule for four hundred years. The Han modified the Qin structure of central and local government, developed a mechanism for recruiting officials, and linked education with bureaucratic advancement for the first time in Chinese history. Starting in 140 B.C.E. and continuing throughout the dynasty, Han emperors encouraged students and future officials to study the Confucian classics. The dynasty's support of learning encouraged the spread of Confucianism throughout the empire. The Confucian emphasis on education was so strong that the Chinese of that era schooled not only their sons but also, when they could, their daughters. Yet because the Han continued many policies of the Qin, we should recognize the Han as a Legalist dynasty with a Confucian exterior, not a genuinely Confucian dynasty.

● **Han dynasty** (206 B.C.E.–220 C.E.) The immediate successor to the Qin dynasty. Han rulers denounced Legalist governance but adopted much of the Qin blueprint for empire. Because of its long rule, the Han dynasty was a model for all subsequent dynasties.

Han Government and the Imperial Bureaucracy

The Qin forces had conquered an enormous swath of territory, but some regions, sensing weakness at the center, rebelled against the unpopular second Qin emperor and asserted their independence. Gradually one man, formerly a low-ranking official under the Qin named Liu Bang (LEO bahng) (r. 206–195 B.C.E.), emerged as leader of the rebels and founded the Han dynasty in 206 B.C.E. Liu Bang was one of only two emperors (the other founded the Ming dynasty in 1368) to be born as a commoner. When he and his forces entered the Qin capital, he assured the capital's residents:

> You elders have long suffered under the harsh laws of Qin. . . . I make an agreement with you that the law shall consist of only three sections: He who kills others shall die; he who harms others or steals from them shall incur appropriate punishment. For the rest, all other Qin laws shall be abolished.[8]

Like a modern politician's campaign promise, this statement does not provide an accurate description of Han law, which actually retained many provisions of Qin law.

When the Han forces took power, they faced the immediate problem of staffing a government large enough to govern the empire. They adopted the Legalist structure of a central government with the emperor at the head and a prime minister (sometimes called a chancellor) as the top official. Underneath the prime minister were the different sections of the central government, which had three main divisions: collection of taxes, supervision of the military, and recruitment of personnel.

The Han dynasty ruled for four hundred years, with only one interruption by a relative of the empress, named Wang Mang (WAHNG mahng), who founded his own short-lived Xin (SHIN) ("new") dynasty (9–23 C.E.). During the first two hundred years of the Han, the capital was in Chang'an (CHAHNG-ahn); historians refer to this period as the Former Han or the Western Han (206 B.C.E.–9 C.E.). After Wang Mang was deposed, the original ruling family of the Han dynasty continued to govern, but in the new capital of Luoyang (LWAW-yahng). The Later Han (25–220 C.E.) is also called the Eastern Han because Luoyang was some 300 miles (500 km) east of Chang'an.

The Han Empire exercised varying amounts of control over the sixty million people under its rule. The emperor managed to regain control of distant regions through a combination of military conquest and administrative flexibility. Immediately after taking over, the Han founder ceded about half of Qin territory to independent kings. He divided the remaining territory into one hundred commanderies and subdivided them into fifteen hundred prefectures. Each prefecture was headed by a magistrate whose task was to register the population, collect revenues, judge legal disputes, and maintain irrigation works.

To get a government position during the Han dynasty, the first step was to get a referral. Men already serving in the government suggested younger men of good reputation, usually from wealthy families with large landholdings, to staff lower positions in prefectural offices. There they could learn how government functioned.

Not content to recruit men who could read and write and knew how to draft documents, the Han was the first Chinese dynasty to require that officials study classical writings on ritual, history, and poetry, as well as *The Analects*. Although these texts did not teach the nuts-and-bolts workings of local government, which remained Legalist in all but name, officials embraced the Confucian view that knowledge of these classic texts would produce more virtuous, and thus better, officials.

In 124 B.C.E., one of the most powerful Han emperors, Emperor Wu (also known as Han Wudi) (r. 140–87 B.C.E.), established the **Imperial Academy** to encourage the study of Confucian texts. At first the Academy consisted of five scholars, called Academicians, who specialized in the study of a given text, and the fifty students who studied with them. Within one hundred years the number of students at the Academy ballooned to several thousand. Ambitious young men already in the government realized that knowledge of Confucian texts, demonstrated by success in examinations conducted by the Imperial Academy, could advance their careers.

The study of Confucian texts was aided by the invention of paper. The earliest examples of Chinese paper found by archaeologists date to the second century B.C.E. Ragpickers who washed and recycled old fabric left fibers on a screen to dry and accidentally discovered how to make paper. Initially, the Chinese used paper for wrapping fragile items, not as a writing material. But by 200 C.E. paper production had increased so much that people used paper, not bamboo slips, for letter writing and books.

With the adoption of paper as the primary writing material, the culture of learning in China shifted from an oral to a written one. In the early years, Han

● Imperial Academy Established in 124 B.C.E. by the Han emperor, Emperor Wu (r. 140–87 B.C.E.), to encourage the study of Confucian texts. Initially consisted of five scholars, called Academicians, specializing in the study of a given text.

dynasty teachers taught students to memorize texts and recite them orally, but by the end of the dynasty they were reading books. When one poet in the first century B.C.E. submitted a written poem to the court as a gift, the emperor could not imagine that someone would commit a poem to writing without first reciting it in person. By the end of the dynasty, though, writing literary works on paper without reciting them had become commonplace. Paper was one of China's most important inventions; it spread from China to the Islamic world in the eighth century C.E. and finally to Europe only in the eleventh century.

Ban Zhao's *Lessons for Women*

During the first century C.E., the Later Han capital of Luoyang became an important literary center where young men came to study. One of the most famous literary families was that of the poet and historian Ban Biao (BAHN-beeow) (d. 54 C.E.), who had three children: twin boys and a daughter. One of the boys followed in his father's footsteps, while his twin became a successful general. Their sister, **Ban Zhao** (BAHN jow) (ca. 45–120 C.E.), was the most famous woman writer of her day. She is best known for her work *Lessons for Women,* which Chinese girls continued to read for centuries after her death.

> • **Ban Zhao** (45–120 C.E.) A historian and the author of *Lessons for Women,* a book that counseled women to serve men and advocated education for girls starting at the age of 8.

Ban Zhao wrote *Lessons for Women* when in her mid-50s. It contained everything she would like to have known when she married at age 14. Ban Zhao's main theme is clear: women exist to serve their husbands and their in-laws, whom they should always obey and with whom they should never quarrel. Yet Ban Zhao's ideal woman was also literate. She began her book by advising her readers to copy down her instructions, sure evidence that they could read and write. She also criticized men who taught only their sons to read:

CL **Primary Source:** Lessons for Women *Discover what Ban Zhao, the foremost female writer in Han China, had to say about the proper behavior of women.*

> Yet only to teach men and not to teach women—is that not ignoring the essential relation between them? . . . It is the rule to begin to teach children to read at the age of eight years. . . . Only why should it not be that girls' education as well as boys' be according to this principle?[9]

This is an eloquent call to teach girls to read at the same age as boys at the age of 7 (8 in Chinese reckoning includes the time in the womb).

We must remember that Ban Zhao differed from her contemporaries in several ways. For one, she had studied with her father the historian and was sufficiently skilled that she completed his manuscript after he died. When married, she bore children, but she was widowed at a young age and became a tutor to the women at the imperial court. When an infant emperor ascended the throne in 106 C.E., his 25-year-old wife became regent, and Ban Zhao advised her on matters of state. A year later, the infant died, but the female regent retained power over the new emperor.

These two women did not have typical careers. Still, their unusual lives show that it was possible for women to take on male roles under certain circumstances. The literacy rate during the first century could not have exceeded 10 percent among men, but *Lessons for Women* was read, and Ban Zhao's ideal of literate women stayed alive in subsequent centuries. Well-off families made every effort to educate their daughters, if only to allow them to study a few years with their brothers' tutors; of course, few laboring people could afford to do so.

Extending Han Rule

As the Qin and Han dynasties left their successors with a blueprint of how to govern the empire, the territories they conquered established boundaries that would define the geographical idea of China for centuries to come. After conquering six independent kingdoms to form their empire (see the map on page 89), the Qin controlled most of the land watered by the Yellow and Yangzi Rivers. If one compares Qin dynasty China with Han dynasty China, the most visible difference is that the Han rulers controlled a narrow stretch of territory in the northwest, now Gansu (GAHN-sue) province and the Xinjiang (SHIN-jyahng) Autonomous Region. Han armies also extended the empire's borders northeast to control much of the Korean peninsula and south to modern-day Vietnam (see Map 4.1).

Han Dynasty Conflict with the Xiongnu Nomads, 201–60 B.C.E.

The Han dynasty gained much of this territory during its wars between 201 and 60 B.C.E. with the **Xiongnu** (SHEE-AWNG-new), a northern nomadic people who moved across modern-day Mongolia in search of grass to feed their sheep and horses. Only the Xiongnu had an army sufficiently powerful to threaten the Han, and they tried to conquer Chinese territory for the first century and a half of Han rule. Their military strength derived from their quick-footed horses and brilliant horsemanship, which enabled them to defeat the Chinese in battle after battle.

The Xiongnu language is completely lost. The Chinese word *Xiongnu* may be a translation of the same word as the Latin word *Hun*. If *Xiongnu* and *Hun* are different forms of the same word (scholars disagree sharply on this point), then the Xiongnu were an earlier, eastern branch of the nomadic peoples who invaded western Europe in the fifth century C.E.

Having formed a confederation of the different tribal peoples living in Mongolia in Qin times, the Xiongnu fought their first battle with the Han soon after the founding of the dynasty. The Xiongnu won. The treaty settling this conflict brought only a temporary peace because the Xiongnu continued to launch military campaigns into China.

In 139 B.C.E. Emperor Wu dispatched an envoy named Zhang Qian (JAHNG chee-en) to Central Asia to persuade the Yuezhi (YOU-EH-juh) people to enter into an alliance against the Xiongnu. Zhang Qian reached the Yuezhi only after being held hostage by the Xiongnu for ten years. When he returned to China, he explained to the emperor that he had been unable to secure an alliance against the Xiongnu, but he had visited local markets. There, to his surprise, he had seen Chinese goods for sale, certain evidence that merchants carrying Chinese goods had preceded him. Today most Chinese regard Zhang Qian as the person who discovered the Silk Road (see Chapter 8).

The Xiongnu supplied the Chinese with animals, hides, and semiprecious gems, particularly jade; in return the Chinese traded silk. The Chinese never succeeded, at least within the Chinese heartland, in breeding horses as strong as those the Xiongnu bred in the Mongolian steppe, probably because they did not have comparable grasslands.

The Xiongnu threat came to a sudden end in 60 B.C.E., not because of any military victory by the Han, but because the huge Xiongnu confederation broke apart

Xiongnu Northern nomadic people who moved across modern-day Mongolia in search of grass for their sheep and horses. Their military strength derived from brilliant horsemanship. Defeated the Han dynasty in battle until 60 B.C.E., when their federation broke apart.

into five warring groups. Much to the relief of the Han emperors, the Xiongnu never again posed a serious threat to their dynasty, but other nomadic peoples living in the grasslands to the north, like the Mongols, intermittently threatened later dynasties.

Han Expansion to the North, Northwest, and South

The Han dynasty ruled China for over four hundred years. In certain periods, it was too weak to conquer new territories, but in other periods, particularly during the long reign of Emperor Wu, the army was so strong that the emperor launched military campaigns into border areas. Once the Han army had conquered a certain region, it established garrisons in the major towns. Chinese officials and merchants in these towns led Chinese-style lives, eating Chinese food and speaking Chinese, while the indigenous peoples largely continued to live as they had before. The officials living in the garrison towns exercised

MAP 4.1

The Han Empire at Its Greatest Extent, ca. 50 B.C.E.   The Han dynasty inherited all the territory of its predecessor, the Qin dynasty, and its powerful armies conquered new territory to the north in the Korean peninsula, to the west in the Taklamakan Desert, and to the south in modern-day Vietnam.

Interactive Map

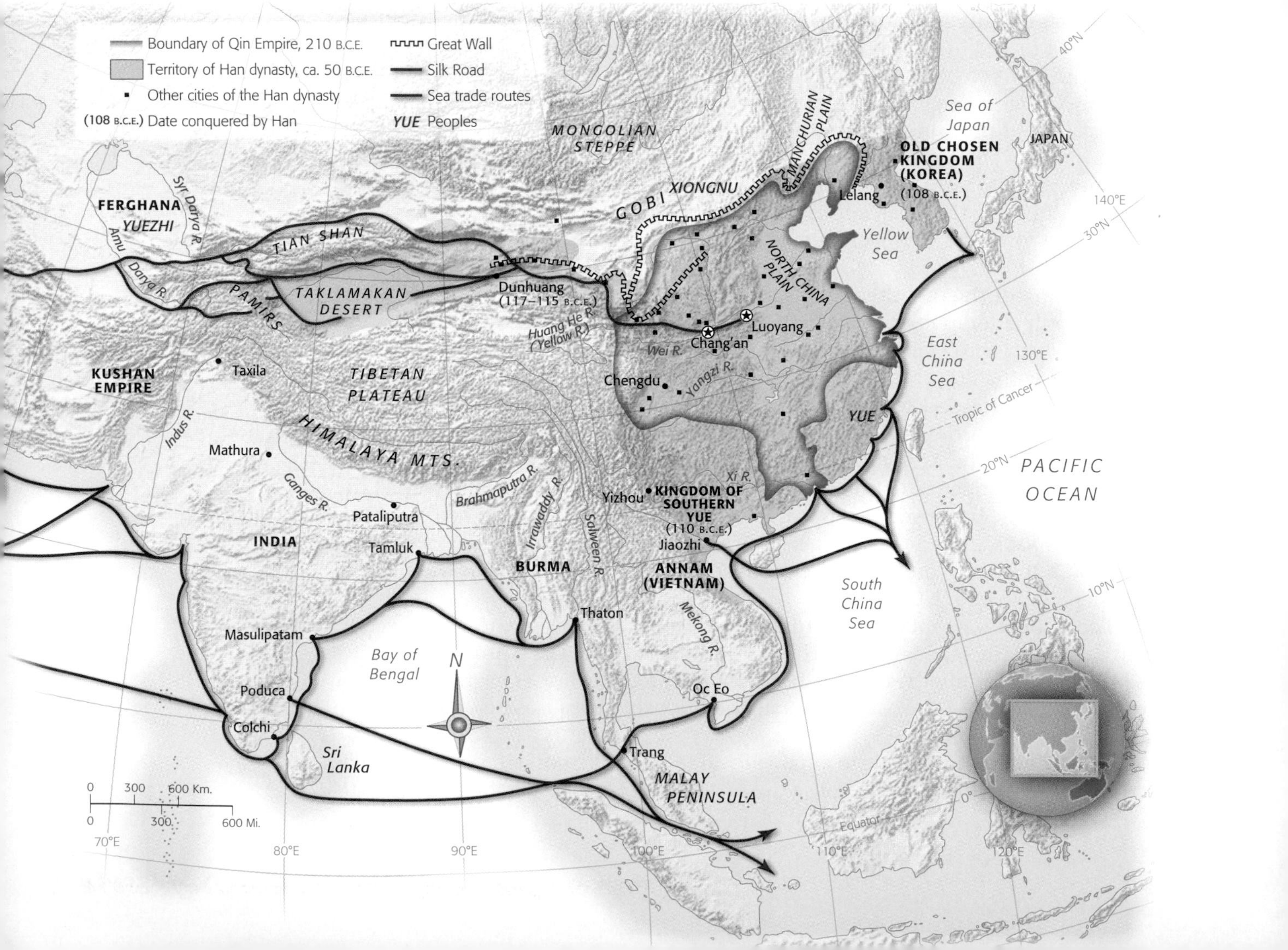

only tenuous control over the indigenous peoples, and, if a local army retook a city, Chinese control could end suddenly. Han armies managed to take parts of the Taklamakan Desert, Korea, and Vietnam, but they ruled these borderlands only briefly.

When the Xiongnu confederation collapsed in 60 B.C.E., the Han dynasty briefly took control of its headquarters and established garrisons in some of the oasis kingdoms ringing the Taklamakan Desert. After 127 C.E., Chinese supply lines were unable to reach troops in the northwest, and the Chinese ceded control to a succession of local kingdoms. But a Han garrison remained at the city of Dunhuang (DUHN-hwahng), the staging point for going farther west and the outermost point of Chinese control.

The region south of China, extending from modern-day Fujian (FOO-jee-en) province to Vietnam, differed from the northwest because one could reach it overland or, more easily, by sea. Much like camel caravans visited oases in their voyage west across the Taklamakan Desert, small boats, many propelled by oars, visited ports on the South China Sea, which offered a chance to rest, trade, and buy provisions for the next leg of the journey. Like all the rivers in Vietnam, the most important river, the Red River, drained from the mountains in the west to the South China Sea. High mountain chains separated the different river valleys, making overland transport much more difficult than sea travel.

The Vietnamese language belongs to the Austroasiatic language family, a different family from Chinese. The modern Chinese provinces of Guangdong (GWAHNG-dohng), Guangxi (GWAHNG-shee), and Yunnan (YUHN-nahn) were home to a regional people that the Chinese called Yue (YOU-EH), the ancestors of the Vietnamese. The Yue people had early (about 8000 B.C.E.) developed the cultivation of rice and were also avid sailors.

Yue cultural practices differed significantly from the Chinese. For example, they traced their descent through both their mothers and their fathers (see Chapter 8). Chinese historians writing before the Qin unification called them the people with "tattooed foreheads," a label that later Vietnamese historians thought pejorative because tattooing clearly violated the Confucian teaching that one should not physically alter one's body, a gift from one's parents. The sparse population in these southern regions also prompted Chinese historians to call the region the "Empty Land."

When the Qin armies conquered Vietnam before 207 B.C.E., they established centers of Chinese control in garrison towns. After 207 B.C.E., an independent kingdom also ruled by a Chinese leader, called the Southern Kingdom of Yue (Nam Viet), took over from the Qin. The kingdom was home to fishermen and traders who specialized in unusual goods like ivory tusks, pearls, tortoise shells, and slaves. After several attempts, the Han armies defeated this ruler and established garrison towns in 110 B.C.E., which they retained throughout the Han dynasty.

While Vietnam marked the southern extent of Han territory, Korea marked the northern extent. Korea did not receive as much rainfall as Vietnam, and its climate was much cooler. Large, dense forests covered the region, and most early settlements were along rivers or on the coast, where residents could easily fish. Before 300 B.C.E., the region was home to several tribal confederations; then, during the third century B.C.E., the Old Choson (JOE-sohn) kingdom united much of the Korean peninsula north of the Han River, in what is today's North Korea. Qin armies defeated the Old Choson kingdom, and Han armies again conquered the region in 108 B.C.E., soon after gaining control of China.

Although officially under Han rule, the local people exercised considerable independence. Many local men held positions of authority in the Chinese administration. Officials and merchants lived in a garrison city located in modern-day Pyongyang (BYOHNG-yahng), but the people outside the garrison were much less affected by the Chinese presence. Since no written documents from this period survive, archaeologists must study burials to reconstruct religious practices. Large, wealthy graves suggest that the people living on the Korean peninsula believed that the dead would travel to another realm. In one region they were buried with large bird wings so that they could fly to the next world.

In later periods (see Chapter 8), these three regions—northwest China, Vietnam, and Korea—would all join the Chinese cultural sphere and adopt the Chinese writing system. But during the Qin and Han dynasties Chinese influence was limited because the Chinese presence consisted only of military garrisons.

The most obvious signs of the Qin and the Han legacy are the words used today for "China" and "Chinese." *China* entered English via the Sanskrit word *Chee-na,* the Indian pronunciation of *Qin.* Ask your classmates studying Chinese what the modern Chinese word for the Chinese language is. The answer should not surprise you: *Hanyu,* literally, "the language of the Han." Almost all Chinese say that they are *Han-ren,* "people of the Han." In a sense they are. If the Han dynasty had not modified the First Emperor's blueprint for empire, there might not be a China today.

Chapter Review

KEY TERMS

First Emperor of the Qin dynasty (88)

Shang dynasty (92)

oracle bones (92)

ancestor worship (92)

Sima Qian (93)

Zhou dynasty (95)

Mandate of Heaven (95)

Confucius (96)

Confucianism (96)

Daoism (97)

Qin dynasty (103)

Han dynasty (106)

Imperial Academy (107)

Ban Zhao (108)

Xiongnu (109)

CL Download the MP3 audio file of the Chapter Review and listen to it on the go.

Following the lead of the First Emperor, the Qin and Han dynasties created a blueprint for imperial rule that lasted for two thousand years. In the centuries after the fall of the Han, China was not always unified. But subsequent Chinese rulers always aspired to reunify the empire and conceived of China's physical borders as largely those of the Han dynasty at its largest extent.

What different elements of Chinese civilization took shape between 1200 and 221 B.C.E.?

The culture tying the people of China together had deep roots. Their shared diet, with its division of starch and meat-and-vegetable dishes, dated to at least 1200 B.C.E. That was also the time of the first written characters, whose descendants are still in use today. Around 500 B.C.E., Confucius taught the importance of obeying both one's parents and the ruler, yet since Confucius refused to say anything about the other world, many Chinese turned to Daoist teachings, which offered immortality to a rare few and eternal detention in underground jails to everyone else.

What were the most important measures in the Qin blueprint for empire?

The Qin dynasty introduced a blueprint for empire that tied their subjects to local officials far more tightly than anywhere else in the world. Qin officials recorded the names of all their subjects and assigned them to mutual responsibility groups. They implemented a single law code for their entire empire and standardized the writing system and all weights and measures. They also created a strict meritocracy in both the army and the government that promoted only those who demonstrated success, not those born to powerful families.

 ### How did the Han rulers modify the Qin blueprint, particularly regarding administrative structure and the recruitment and promotion of officials?

The successors to the First Emperor, including the Han rulers, did not acknowledge the path-breaking role of the Qin dynasty. Yet even as succeeding rulers maligned the First Emperor, they all adopted the Qin title *emperor*. Han emperors created different administrative districts from those in use under the Qin and also recruited officials in a different way, appointing new officials to the lowest ranks on the recommendation of those already in office. After 140 B.C.E., officials could be promoted only after demonstrating knowledge of Confucian texts in written examinations.

 ### Which neighboring peoples in Central, East, and Southeast Asia did the Han dynasty conquer? Why was the impact of Chinese rule limited?

Han dynasty armies conquered and briefly controlled parts of northwest China, Vietnam, and Korea, but their influence was limited because the Chinese military rarely ventured beyond their garrison towns.

WEB RESOURCES

Pronunciation Guide

Interactive Maps

MAP 4.1 The Han Empire at Its Greatest Extent, ca. 50 B.C.E.

Primary Sources

Chapter Objectives

ACE Multiple-Choice Quiz

Flashcards

For Further Reference

The Analects of Confucius. Translated by Simon Leys. New York: W. W. Norton, 1997.

Eckert, Carter, et al. *Korea Old and New: A History.* Cambridge, Mass.: Harvard University Press, 1990.

Hansen, Valerie. *The Open Empire: A History of China to 1600.* New York: W. W. Norton, 2000.

Keightley, David N. *Sources of Shang History: The Oracle Bone Inscriptions of Bronze Age China.* Berkeley: University of California Press, 1978.

Kern, Martin. *The Stele Inscriptions of Ch'in Shih-huang: Text and Ritual in Early Chinese Imperial Representation.* New Haven: American Oriental Society, 2000.

Ledderose, Lothar. *Ten Thousand Things: Module and Mass Production in Chinese Art.* Princeton: Princeton University Press, 2000.

Schwartz, Benjamin. *The World of Thought in Ancient China.* Cambridge, Mass.: Harvard University Press, 1985.

Swann, Nancy Lee. *Pan Chao: Foremost Woman Scholar of China.* New York: American Historical Association, 1932.

Tao Te Ching: The Classic Book of Integrity and the Way. Translated by Victor Mair. New York: Bantam Books, 1990.

Tarling, Nicholas, ed. *The Cambridge History of Southeast Asia.* Cambridge: Cambridge University Press, 1999.

Twitchett, Denis, and Michael Loewe, eds. *The Cambridge History of China.* Vol. 1, *The Ch'in and Han Empires 221 B.C.–A.D. 220.* New York: Cambridge University Press, 1986.

Websites

Asian Art Museum, San Francisco (http://www.asianart.org/collection.htm). An introduction to one of America's most important collections of Asian art.

The First Emperor: China's Terracotta Warriors (http://www.britishmuseum.org/whats_on/all_current_exhibitions/the_first_emperor/exhibition_overview.aspx). A short history of the terracotta warriors including downloadable images.

Metropolitan Museum of Art (http://www.mctmuseum.org/TOAH/hd/cgrk/hd_cgrk.htm). Detailed description of Chinese gardens and collector's rocks. See the museum website for other Asian art.

Films

The First Emperor of China from the Canadian Film Board. USA orders: 800-542-2164.

The Americas and the Islands of the Pacific, to 1200 C.E.

A vast area of the globe—North and South America and the islands of the Pacific—developed in almost total isolation from Eurasia because, after approximately 7000 B.C.E., much of the ice covering the world's surface melted and submerged the Beringia ice bridge linking Alaska to Siberia (see Chapter 1). Since few of the peoples living in this area have left written records, archaeologists and historians have exercised great ingenuity in reconstructing the different paths they took to complex society, each very different from those of Eurasian peoples. Scholars know more about the Maya (MY-ah), a Central American people whose writing system was translated only in the 1970s. Yet because the deciphering of Mayan is ongoing, experts continue to debate the exact meaning of surviving texts, rarely translating word for word. Here one professor paraphrases an inscription describing a 152-day trip a ruler named **Yax K'uk Mo'** (YASH cook moh) took to Copán in what is now Honduras:

The top of Altar Q here tells the story of Yax K'uk Mo' really. It begins up here with a date, and it's a date that comes around the early fifth century. And it says that on that particular day in that time, he took the emblems of office, he took the kingship. The place where he took that kingship is recorded in the next glyph, and we've known for a long time that this glyph has some sort of connection to Central Mexico. . . . Then we have his name here, and then the date's three days later. And three days later he leaves that location.

YAX K'UK MO' FROM ALTAR Q

(© Kenneth Garrett)

CL This icon will direct you to interactive activities and study materials on the *Voyages* website: www.cengage.com/history/hansen/voyages1e

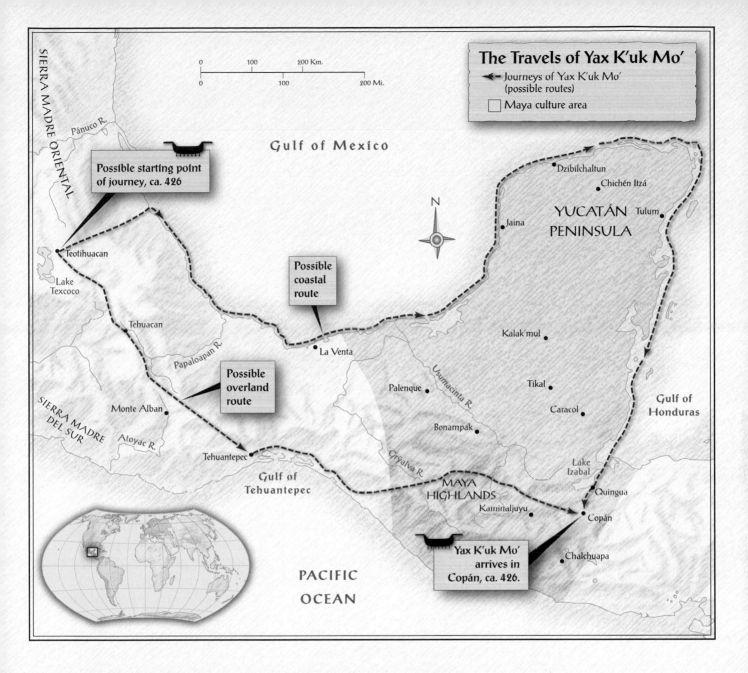

The Travels of Yax K'uk Mo'

- ← Journeys of Yax K'uk Mo' (possible routes)
- ☐ Maya culture area

0 100 200 Km.
0 100 200 Mi.

SIERRA MADRE ORIENTAL

Pánuco R.

Gulf of Mexico

Possible starting point of journey, ca. 426

Teotihuacan

Lake Texcoco

Tehuacan

Papaloapan R.

Possible coastal route

La Venta

Possible overland route

SIERRA MADRE DEL SUR

Monte Alban

Atoyac R.

Tehuantepec

Gulf of Tehuantepec

PACIFIC OCEAN

N

YUCATÁN PENINSULA

Dzibilchaltun

Chichén Itzá

Jaina

Tulum

Kalak'mul

Usumacinta R.

Palenque

Tikal

Caracol

Bonampak

Gulf of Honduras

Grijalva R.

MAYA HIGHLANDS

Kaminaljuyu

Lake Izabal

Quingua

Copán

Yax K'uk Mo' arrives in Copán, ca. 426.

Chalchuapa

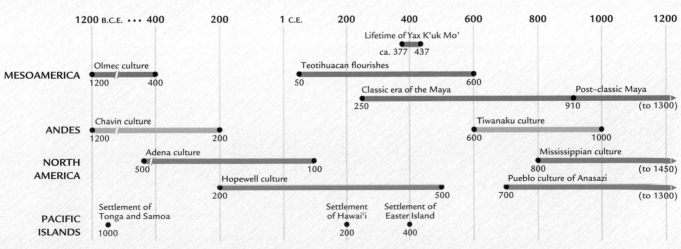

	1200 B.C.E. ··· 400	200	1 C.E.	200	400	600	800	1000	1200
					Lifetime of Yax K'uk Mo' ca. 377 437				
MESOAMERICA	Olmec culture 1200 400			Teotihuacan flourishes 50		600		Post-classic Maya	
				Classic era of the Maya 250				910	(to 1300)
ANDES	Chavin culture 1200 200					Tiwanaku culture 600		1000	
NORTH AMERICA	Adena culture 500		100				Mississippian culture 800		(to 1450)
		Hopewell culture 200			500	Pueblo culture of Anasazi 700			(to 1300)
PACIFIC ISLANDS	Settlement of Tonga and Samoa 1000		Settlement of Hawai'i 200	Settlement of Easter Island 400					

The inscription goes on to say something really remarkable. A hundred and fifty-three days after he leaves this place where he's become a king, then, on this day, he "rests his legs," or "rests his feet," and "he is the West Lord." It's a title that Yax K'uk Mo' has throughout his references at Copán. And then finally it says "he arrived" at Copán. So, I think the conclusion from this is that Yax K'uk Mo' came a long way before he arrived at Copán.[1]

● **Yax K'uk Mo'** The king of Copán during the classic period of the Maya (250–910 C.E.). Founded a dynasty that lasted at least sixteen generations, until 776 C.E.

Yax K'uk Mo' must have walked or was carried, since the Maya, like all the peoples of Americas and unlike the peoples of Eurasia, did not use the wheel or ride animals. Maya scholars are not certain where Yax K'uk Mo' began his journey. Some feel that he set out from somewhere near modern-day Mexico City, while others contend that he stayed within the territory of the Maya (see the map on page 115)—in the region known as Mesoamerica, which includes much of Mexico and Central America.

Because the Maya developed one of the few writing systems used in the Americas before 1500, they differed from almost every other people of the Americas and the islands of the Pacific. Some earlier peoples living in modern-day Mexico developed notational systems; much later, the Mexica (MAY-shee-kah) people, or the Aztecs, of Mexico used a combination of pictures and visual puns to record events, but their writing system was not fully developed (see Chapter 15).

Complex societies arose in Mexico, the Andes, and the modern-day United States at different times and in different ways than in Eurasia. Because hundreds, sometimes thousands, of years elapsed between agriculture and the rise of cities, archaeologists pay close attention to the American peoples who built large earthworks or stone monuments. Their rulers had the ability to command their subjects to work on large projects. Similarly, although the peoples of the Pacific never built large cities, they crossed the Pacific Ocean, possibly all the way to Chile. The lack of navigational instruments did not prevent them from conducting some of the world's longest ocean voyages. By 1350 they had reached New Zealand, the final place on the globe to be settled by humans.

Since the Maya had a writing system, archaeologists know more about them than any other society in the Americas or the Pacific Islands. Accordingly, this chapter begins with the precursors of the Maya in modern-day Mexico and then proceeds to the Maya themselves.

Focus Questions

How did the development of agriculture and the building of early cities in Mesoamerica differ from that in Mesopotamia, India, and China?

- What has the decipherment of the Maya script revealed about Maya governance, society, religion, and warfare?

- What were the similarities between the complex societies of the northern peoples and those of Mesoamerica? What do they suggest about contact?

- How did the history of complex society in the Andes differ from that in Mesoamerica?

- Where did the early settlers of the Pacific Islands come from, and where did they go? What vessels did they use, and how did they navigate?

The First Complex Societies of Mesoamerica, 8000 B.C.E.–500 C.E.

Unlike in Mesopotamia, Egypt, India, and China, agriculture in the Americas arose not in river valleys but in a plateau region, the highlands of Mexico. The first planting occurred around 8000 B.C.E., two thousand years after it had in western Asia. The residents of Mexico continued to hunt and gather for thousands of years as they slowly began to cultivate corn, potatoes, cocoa beans, and other crops that grew nowhere else in the world. Large urban centers, one of the markers of complex society, appeared in Mexico around 1200 B.C.E.

The Development of Agriculture, 8000–1500 B.C.E.

The people of Tehuacán (tay-WAH-káhn) in the modern state of Puebla (PWAY-bla), Mexico, initially harvested wild grasses with tiny ears of seeds. Their grinding stones, the first evidence of cultivation in the Americas, date to 8000 B.C.E. Just as the Natufians of western Asia had gradually domesticated wheat by harvesting certain wild plants with desirable characteristics (see Chapter 1), the residents of Tehuacán selected different grasses with more rows of seeds until they eventually developed a domesticated variety of maize sometime around 7000 B.C.E. (Specialists prefer the term *maize* to *corn* because it is more specific.) Unlike the early farmers of western Asia, the people of Tehuacán used no draft animals.

Maize spread from the Tehuacán Valley throughout the region of **Mesoamerica,** which includes the southern two-thirds of modern Mexico, Guatemala, Belize, El Salvador, Honduras, Nicaragua, and Costa Rica. Located between the Atlantic and Pacific Oceans, Mesoamerica is bounded by barren desert north of modern Mexico. More rain falls in the east than in the west; because of the uneven rainfall, residents used irrigation channels to move the water. Maize later spread north to Canada and south to the tip of South America.

Once planted, maize required little tending until the harvest, when the hard husk on each kernel made it very difficult to eat. The dried kernels were ground or boiled and mixed with ground limestone to make a paste, called nixtamal (NISH-ta-mal), that was used to make unleavened cakes. As the proportion of cultivated

● **Mesoamerica** The region that includes the southern two-thirds of modern Mexico, Guatemala, Belize, El Salvador, Honduras, Nicaragua, and Costa Rica.

crops in the diet increased, the Mesoamericans gradually abandoned hunting and gathering. Eating little meat because they raised no animals, they cultivated squash and beans along with maize, three foods that together offered the same nutritional benefits (amino acids and vitamin B12) as meat. The systematized cultivation of maize made it possible to support larger populations. By 2500 B.C.E., the population of Mesoamerica had increased by perhaps twenty-five times; the largest settlements had several hundred residents who both farmed and continued to hunt.

Most of the peoples living in Mesoamerica had given up hunting and gathering and adopted full-time agriculture by 1500 B.C.E., the date of the earliest agricultural villages in the region. If an ancient farmer from anywhere in Mesopotamia, China, or India had visited at this time, he or she would have been amazed to see that no one in Mesoamerica employed the basic tools of farming so familiar to them—the plow, the wheel, or draft animals. Instead of the plow, the Mesoamericans used different types of digging sticks, and they dragged or carried things themselves because they did not have draft animals or the wheel. (The only wheels in the Americas appear on children's toys around 500 C.E.)

●Olmec   A complex society (1200–400 B.C.E.) that arose on the Gulf of Mexico coast from modern-day Veracruz to Tabasco. Known particularly for the massive colossal heads hewn from basalt.

The Olmecs and Their Successors, 1200–400 B.C.E.

The **Olmec** peoples (1200–400 B.C.E.) built the first larger settlements along a 100-mile (160-km) stretch on the coast of the Gulf of Mexico from Veracruz to Tabasco (see Map 5.1) Raising two maize crops a year, the Olmec produced a large agricultural surplus, and the population may also have increased because of the nutritional benefits of the nixtamel diet.

Surviving colossal heads testify to the Olmec rulers' ability to mobilize their subjects for large labor projects. The Olmecs used stone hammers to hew these heads from basalt. They are 5 to 10 feet (1.5–3 m) tall, and the largest weighs over 40 tons (36 metric tons). The nearest source of basalt lay more than 50 miles (80 km) to the northwest, and archaeologists surmise that Olmec laborers carried the rock overland (they did not have the wheel) and built rafts to transport it along local rivers.

The peoples of Mesoamerica used two methods to count days: one cycle ran 365 days for the solar year, while the ritual cycle lasted 260 days. The solar year had 18 months of 20 days each with 5 extra days at the end of the year; the 260-day ritual cycle had 13 weeks of 20 days each. This complex calendrical system developed after the Olmec urban centers had already begun to decline around 400 B.C.E.

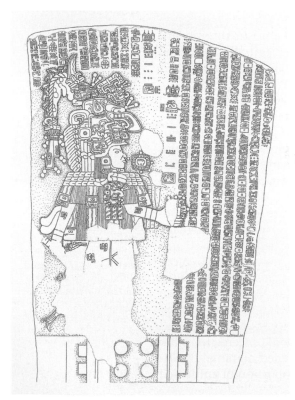

🔹 **Drawing of La Mojarra Stele**   This monument shows a warrior-king who ruled along the coast of Mexico in the second century C.E. He wears an elaborate headdress showing a bird deity. The glyphs, not all of which have yet been deciphered, describe how he became king with the assistance of a ritual specialist. The middle of the inscription uses the telltale bars and dots of the Long Count to give the date of 159 C.E.   (Drawing by George Stuart, from the Boundary End Archaeology Research Center)

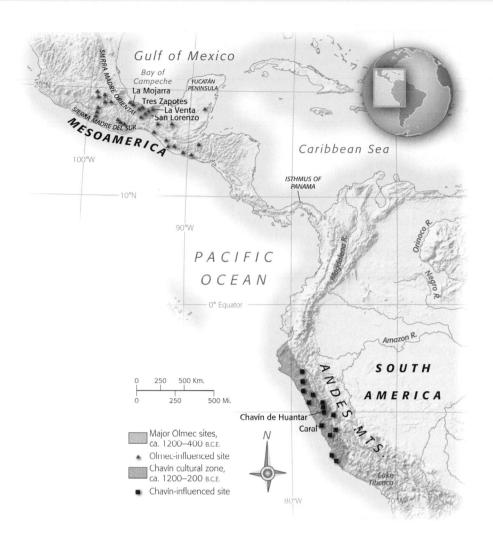

🌐 **MAP 5.1**
Complex Societies in the Americas, ca. 1200 B.C.E. Starting around 1200 B.C.E., complex societies arose in two widely separated regions in the Americas. In modern-day Mexico the Olmec hewed giant heads from basalt; in modern-day Peru, the Chavín built large temples decorated with statues combining human and animal body parts.

CL Interactive Map

If one combined the two ways of counting time so that both cycles started on the same day and ran their full course, 18,980 days, or 52 years, would pass before the two cycles converged again. The 52-year cycle had one major drawback: one could not record events occurring more than 52 years earlier without confusion. Accordingly, the peoples of Mesoamerica developed the **Long Count,** a calendar that ran cumulatively, starting from a day far in the mythical past (whose equivalent is August 13, 3114 B.C.E.) and continuing to the present. The Long Count came into use in the fifth and fourth centuries B.C.E., when the successors to the Olmecs built several monuments bearing Long Count dates. The inscriptions use a mix of bars and dots to show the different units of the calendar: 400 years, 200 years, 1 year, 20 days, and 1 day.

These monuments contain texts written in at least three different languages used in Mexico after 400 B.C.E.: one near Oaxaca (WAH-ha-kah), another on the coast in the core Olmec areas, and Mayan in the Yucatán. These difficult texts have been partially deciphered because the local Amerindians speak languages descended from those used in the inscription and because some of the words are the same as in Mayan (see page 121).

● **Long Count** A calendar that ran cumulatively, starting from a day equivalent to August 13, 3114 B.C.E. and continuing to the present. Came into use in the fifth and fourth centuries B.C.E., when inscriptions of bars and dots showed different calendar units.

Teotihuacan, ca. 200 B.C.E.–600 C.E.

At the same time that the peoples along the coast were developing the Long Count and using glyphs, a huge metropolis, covering an area of 8 square miles (20 sq km) arose at **Teotihuacan** (tay-oh-tee-WAH-kahn), some 30 miles (50 km) northeast of modern-day Mexico City. Founded around 200 B.C.E., the city continued to grow until the year 650 C.E. Estimates of its population range between 40,000 and 200,000, certainly enough to qualify as a complex society. Teotihuacan's population made it the largest city in the Americas before 1500 but smaller than contemporary Rome's one million (see Chapter 7) or Luoyang's 500,000 during the Han dynasty (see Chapter 4). (See the feature "Visual Evidence: The Imposing Capital of Teotihuacan.")

On Teotihuacan's neatly gridded streets, ordinary people lived in one-story apartment compounds whose painted white exteriors had no windows and whose interiors were covered with colorful frescoes. Divided among several families, the largest compounds housed over a hundred people; the smallest, about twenty. A plumbing system drained wastewater into underground channels along the street, eventually converging in aboveground canals. The compounds show evidence of craft specializations: for example, one was a pottery workshop.

One residential district in the city has atypical rounded houses instead of the more common apartment compounds and contains pottery similar to that in the Veracruz region. Since this type of dwelling has been found in many sites along the Gulf of Mexico, archaeologists surmise that this was a community of migrant workers from the Veracruz region that continued to make the characteristic pottery of their homeland.

Some monuments in Teotihuacan have glyphs similar to those found elsewhere in Mexico, but scholars have not succeeded in deciphering them. Accordingly, we do not know whether Teotihuacan served as the capital of an empire, but it was definitely a large city-state. Sometime around 600 C.E. a fire, apparently caused by an internal revolt, leveled sections of the city, causing the residents to gradually move away.

The Classic Age of the Maya, 250–910 C.E.

The **Maya,** like the other peoples of the Americas, differed from the Eurasian empires in that they created a remarkable complex society unaided by the wheel, plow, draft animals, or metal tools. But did the residents of Teotihuacan, the successors to the Olmecs, and the Maya people influence each other or develop separately? Scholars sharply disagree. Some see the Olmecs as a mother culture that gave both the Teotihuacan and Maya peoples their calendar, their writing system, and even their enormous flat-topped stepped pyramids—perhaps temples, perhaps palaces—of limestone and plaster packed with earth fill. These scholars believe that Yax K'uk Mo' traveled to Copán from Teotihuacan and introduced Teotihuacan's ways to the Maya. Others argue that the Olmecs, Teotihuacan, and Maya were neighboring cultures that did not directly influence each other. They think it more likely that Yax K'uk Mo' traveled only within Maya territory. Maya studies is a lively field, made even more exciting by the stream of new discoveries and new decipherments that may some day resolve these ongoing debates.

Some scholars also thought the Maya were a peace-loving people governed by a religious elite, until inscriptions dating between 250 and 910 c.e. were deciphered in the 1970s. The Maya today are seen rather as unrelentingly violent but no different from the Assyrian Empire and Shang dynasty China. Maya victors removed the fingernails of war captives, cut their chests open to remove their hearts, and publicly beheaded them as sacrifices to their deities.

The Deciphering of Maya Writing

One of the great intellectual breakthroughs of the twentieth century was the decipherment of the Mayan script. (Scholars today use the word *Maya* to refer to the people and *Mayan* for the language they spoke.) Mayan glyphs did not look like any of the world's other writing systems. They were so pictorial that many doubted they could represent sounds. In 1952, Yuri Knorosov, a Russian linguist, suggested that the Maya combined phonetic elements in different combinations to form words. Using dictionaries of various dialects spoken in the Maya heartland, he deciphered a few words that resembled their modern forms. His breakthrough meant that scholars were trying to decipher a living language, or at least the ancestor tongue of living languages, and not a dead language. Linguists suddenly wanted to do fieldwork among the 7.5 million living native speakers of Mayan dialects in Mexico and Guatemala.

For twenty years, a group of scholars and devoted amateurs—mostly Americans, but also Russians, Canadians, and Australians—pored over all known Maya ruins, making rubbings and sketching the glyphs they saw, and studying modern Mayan dialects. In 1973 they met at an academic conference held in Mexico, where for ten days they collectively deciphered the Mayan script.

The conference participants realized that one could write a single Mayan word several different ways: entirely phonetically, entirely pictorially, or using a combination of both phonetic sounds and pictures. For example, the artists who made Altar Q wrote the name of Yax K'uk Mo' by using both pictures of the quetzal (KATE-zahl) (*k'uk*) and macaw (*mo'*) birds and syllables representing the sounds "yax" and "k'inich" (*k-ih-niche*). Combined, they spell the name K'inich Yax K'uk Mo', or Great Sun Lord Quetzal Macaw (see the photo on page 114). It is as if one could write *hat* in English by drawing a picture of a hat 🎩, or writing h + a + t, h + @ + t, or simply h + @.

Scholars specializing in Maya studies refer to the period from 250 to 910 as the classic age, because there are written inscriptions on monuments, and the period before 250 as the pre-classic age. Recent discoveries of Mayan inscriptions with earlier dates are forcing scholars to reconsider these labels. In the early classic period, between 250 and 550, Teotihuacan may have exerted political influence on various Maya kingdoms, including that of Yax K'uk Mo', before Teotihuacan's prosperity came to a sudden end. In some Maya cities, such as Tikal (TEE-kal), but not in others, such as Copán, construction of monuments and inscriptions stopped between 550 and 600, possibly because of a political or ecological crisis. This half century marks the division between the early classic period (250–550) and late classic period (600–800), when the building of monuments resumed. The latest Maya monument with an inscription is dated 910, marking the end of the terminal classic period (800–910).

THE IMPOSING CAPITAL OF TEOTIHUACAN

The three magnificent pyramids of Teotihuacan, 30 miles (50 km) northeast of Mexico City, impress visitors even today. Lined with smaller pyramids, the broad Avenue of the Dead runs from the Pyramid of the Moon past the Pyramid of the Sun to the Feathered Serpent Pyramid. All of these names, including *Teotihuacan,* which means "the abode of the gods," were given by Nahuatl-speaking settlers from the north after their arrival sometime in the twelfth century (see Chapter 15).

Since we do not know what the original residents of the city called these structures and since no one has deciphered the few glyphs that appear on scattered stones, archaeologists have exercised great ingenuity in trying to understand the city's layout. Teotihuacan is unusual in that none of the city's rulers built monuments to themselves. Because deities of later peoples, like the Maya (see below), were often associated with stars and planets, most concur that the city's orientation must have been astronomical, based on the different phases of Venus, the Morning Star honored by so many peoples in the Americas.

The discovery of more than two hundred skeletons under the Feathered Serpent Pyramid has shed new light on the building's purpose. The group with the most valuable jewelry appears to have the highest social status; another group that wears less valuable shell beads seems to rank lower. A third group of women had even less jewelry, while a fourth group consisted of uniformed men buried with large quantities of projectile points, most likely an army. The people in these groups assume different postures, some with their hands tied behind their backs, as if they had been killed before burial, possibly with the accompanying obsidian knives, blades, and piercing implements. Because looters dug two large trenches in the center of the Feathered Serpent Pyramid, archaeologists cannot be certain who was originally buried there, but the mass burials and valuable grave goods make it likely that this was the ruler's tomb. The dead buried at Teotihuacan, like the terracotta warriors of the Qin founder (see Chapter 4), appear to have served as a sacrificial army for the deceased ruler, who was buried circa 200 C.E. at the time of the pyramid's completion.

The World's Largest Pyramids

Name	Site	Date	Material	Height
Great Pyramid	Giza, Egypt	2580 B.C.E.	stone	480 ft (146 m)
Pyramid of the Sun	Teotihuacan	200 C.E.	volcanic rubble and earth	216 feet (66 m)
Tarharqa's Pyramid	Nuri, Nubia	664 B.C.E.	stone	160 ft (49 m)
Pyramid of the Moon	Teotihuacan	200 C.E.	volcanic rubble and earth	140 feet (43 m)
Pirámide Mayor	Caral	2600 B.C.E.	brick and earth	60 ft (18 m)

QUESTION FOR ANALYSIS

Compare and contrast the site of Teotihuacan with the urban centers of other early complex societies in the Americas (Caral, Olmec, Maya) and in Eurasia (Sumer, Indus River Valley, Shang dynasty).

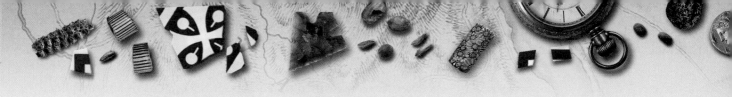

With sides over 700 feet (213 m) long at the base, and over twenty stories high, the Pyramid of the Sun is the largest structure in the Americas made before 1500.

The Feathered Serpent Pyramid, also called the Quetzalcoatl Temple, has staircases up the side of the monument with stone facades and elaborate serpent heads dividing the different terraces.

The Citadel, facing the Feathered Serpent Pyramid, was the political center of the city.

(Georg Gerster/Photo Researchers, Inc.)

The Avenue of the Dead, 50 yards (50 m) wide, extends for more than 3 miles (5.2 km) and connects the different pyramids of Teotihuacan.

Laborers made the Pyramid of the Moon in the same way that they made the Pyramid of the Sun: they piled up earth and rubble to form a pyramid shape, leveled off horizontal terraces, and then faced the surface with adobe and stone.

This modern ring road, the Periférico, was built in the 1960s to steer traffic away from the monuments.

Since 1973 Mayanists have learned to read about 85 percent of all surviving glyphs. Since inscriptions follow a set format, beginning with the rise of a particular ruler, it is possible to understand inscriptions at ruins throughout the Maya region. So far the focus on the history of royal dynasties unfortunately reveals little about ordinary people. Analysts are trying to bridge that immense information gap by ingeniously combining inscriptions and paintings from the classic period with information from European observers in the sixteenth century (see Chapter 15) and even ethnographic data on Maya peoples alive today.

Maya Government and Society

• **Copán** A typical Maya city-state. At its peak in the eighth century, Copán had a population of eighteen to twenty thousand divided into sharply demarcated groups: the ruling family, the nobility, ordinary people, and slaves.

Copán, where Yax K'uk Mo' founded his dynasty, provides a good example of a typical Maya city-state. At its peak in the eighth century, when the sixteenth king commissioned Altar Q to commemorate his sixteen dynastic predecessors, Copán had a population of eighteen to twenty thousand. The population was divided into sharply demarcated groups: the ruling family, the nobility, ordinary people, and slaves.

As the ruler of Copán and commander of the army, Yax K'uk Mo' ranked higher than everyone else. He decided when to ally with other city-states and when to fight them, as well as how to allocate the different crops and taxes received from the populace. When a ruler died, a council of nobles met to verify that his son or his younger brother was fit to rule. If a ruler died without an heir, the council appointed someone from one of the highest-ranking noble families to succeed him.

We can understand something of Yax K'uk Mo's status from his tomb. (See the feature "World History in Today's World: The World's First Chocolate.") Lying on a stone platform, the body of Yax K'uk Mo' had a jade chest ornament like that shown in his portrait on Altar Q (see page 114). In his Altar Q portrait he wears a shield on his right arm; the shattered right arm of the corpse indicates that he badly wounded this arm, perhaps in battle. Archaeologists have compared the levels of certain unusual isotopes of strontium in his bones with soil samples from different regions and have found that he was a native of neither Teotihuacan nor Copán. He most likely spent time in other Maya cities and Teotihuacan before coming to Copán in 426 near the age of 50.

Archaeologists working at Copán found an even more lavish grave near that of Yax K'uk Mo' that held a tripod vessel painted with a picture of a Teotihuacan-style pyramid and over ten thousand jade beads. They initially assumed that it was another king's tomb, yet analysis of the pelvis indicated that the person was a 50-year-old woman who had given birth to at least one child. Since her tomb contains no glyphs, archaeologists are not certain of her identity, but the grave's central location suggests that she was the wife of Yax K'uk Mo'.

Ranking just below the members of the ruling family, the nobles of Maya society lived in large, spacious houses such as those found in the section of Copán known as the House of the Officials. One typical compound there contains between forty and fifty buildings surrounding eleven courtyards. In judging a man's prominence, the Maya considered all of his relatives on both his father's and mother's side. The Mayan word for "nobles" means "he whose descent is known on both sides."[2]

Literate in a society where few could read or write, scribes came from the highest ranks of the nobility. When the king's armies did well in battle, the scribes

The World's First Chocolate

When scientists tested the residue found on a deer-shaped vessel from Yax K'uk Mo's tomb, they discovered traces of theobromine, a caffeine-like molecule found only in chocolate. They guess that Mesoamericans started preparing drinks made from pounded seeds from the cacao (*ka-ka-wa* in Mayan) tree, perhaps as early as 600 B.C.E. and certainly by the early fifth century, when Yax K'uk Mo' was buried at Copán. The origins of the English word *chocolate* are much disputed; the word probably comes from the combination of the Mayan word for "hot" (*chocol*) with "water" (*atl*) used by the Nahuatl peoples of Mexico.

The Maya did not sweeten the cacao drink but added spices and crushed chile peppers to make a variety of drinks they prized for their foam. When Spaniards introduced chocolate to Europeans in the sixteenth century, they added sugar to the cacao paste and heated it to make it more palatable. The addition of sugar made chocolate irresistible. The annual consumption of chocolate in the United States averages 11.3 pounds (5.13 kg) per person, or 1.5 million tons (1.33 million metric tons).

The Maya believed that cacao could cure a variety of ills, including hemorrhoids and nervous tension. Some Amerindian tribes in Panama have surprisingly low blood pressure, possibly because they consume cacao with every meal. Fresh cacao contains flavonol, a naturally occurring chemical that lowers blood pressure and possibly LDL ("bad cholesterol"). In the past few years, the Mars chocolate bar company and the U.S. National Institutes of Health have cosponsored research to see if they can make either a chocolate beverage or a candy bar that lowers blood pressure. Unfortunately, it is difficult to manufacture a chocolate product with as much flavonol as fresh cacao beans. Some skeptics think the potential benefits in lowered blood pressure or cholesterol, which have yet to be demonstrated conclusively, may be more than offset by the likely weight gain. Although Americans name chocolate as their favorite snack, demand has been flat for the past five years in weight-conscious America.

Sources: *New York Times*, June 10, 2003, first Science page, p. 2; *New York Times*, February 17, 2004, pp. F5, F10; Sophie D. Coe and Michael D. Coe, *The True History of Chocolate* (New York: Thames and Hudson, 1996).

enjoyed the best treatment that the king could give them. When the king's armies lost, they were often taken prisoner.

Only those scribes with mathematical skills could maintain the elaborate calendar. Having developed the concept of zero, Maya ritual specialists devised an extraordinarily sophisticated numerical system. Astronomers observed the stars and planets so closely that they could predict eclipses. They were particularly skilled in tracking the movements of Venus, which during some seasons appeared first in the evening before any stars, and in others was the last to disappear in the morning. The Maya used their knowledge of celestial bodies to determine auspicious days for inaugurating rulers, conducting elaborate religious ceremonies, or starting wars.

The most prosperous ordinary people became merchants specializing in long-distance trade. Salt was the one necessity the Maya had to import because their diet did not provide enough sodium to prevent a deficiency. They collected salt from the Yucatán beaches and shipped it in canoes along the ocean's shore and on interior rivers until it had to be carried by hand. Some of the items traded were luxury goods like jade, shells, and quetzal bird feathers, which flickered blue, gold, or green in the light.

The craft specialists who transformed these raw materials into finely worked goods lived in the small houses of ordinary people. The Maya first encountered gold around the year 800 and learned to work it, yet they made few items from it. They preferred green jade, which they carved and smoothed with saws made of coated string and different types of sandpaper.

The most important trade good in the Maya world was **obsidian,** a naturally occurring volcanic glass. The best material available to the Maya for making tools, obsidian could be worked into fine art objects, dart tips, and knife blades sharper than modern scalpels. Obsidian shattered easily though, and so the Maya also made tools from chert, a flintlike rock that was more durable.

Outside the city lived the farmers who provided Copán's residents with their food supply, since the urban inhabitants could not raise enough food to feed themselves. Their diet consisted of large amounts of maize and smaller amounts of beans, squash, and chili peppers. City dwellers had fruit gardens and were able occasionally to hunt wild game.

Since the Maya had no draft animals, most cultivators worked land within a day or two's walk from the urban center. Their fields probably marked the limit of each city-state's direct political control. The Maya practiced swidden agriculture (sometimes called slash-and-burn farming), meaning they farmed the same place for only one or two seasons. Once the fertility of a given plot gave out, cultivators moved to a new site, where they cleared fields by cutting down trees. They waited for the felled trees and plants to dry, set fire to the brush, and then planted maize in the fertile ashes. Recently, aerial photographs of the Yucatán, Mexico, and Belize have revealed raised fields dating back to the time of the Maya, which were farmed season after season.

The lowest-ranking people in Maya society were the slaves, who were forced to work in the fields after being taken as prisoners of war. Higher-ranking prisoners of war, drawn from the nobles, were almost always killed in public displays.

The Religious Beliefs of the Maya

Many Maya rituals featured the spilling of royal blood, which the Maya considered sacred. Surviving paintings from throughout the Maya region depict women pulling thorny vines through their tongues and kings sticking either a stingray spine or a pointed bone tool through the tips of their penises. No surviving text explains exactly why the Maya thought blood sacred, but blood offerings clearly played a key role in their belief system.

One of the few Mayan sources that survives, an oral epic named **_Popul Vuh_** (POPE-uhl voo), or "The Council Book," features a series of games in which players on two teams moved the ball by hitting it with their hips and tried to get it past their opponents' end line. The Maya believed that the earth was recreated each time the hip ballgame was played, and the side seen as being tested by the gods, usually prisoners of war, always lost, after which their blood was spilled in an elaborate ceremony. (See the feature "Movement of Ideas: The Ballgame in _Popul Vuh_.")

Recorded nearly one thousand years after the decline of the Maya, the _Popul Vuh_ preserves only a part of their rich legends, but scholars have used it in conjunction with surviving texts to piece together the key elements of the Maya belief system. All Maya gods, the _Popul Vuh_ explains, are descended from a divine pair. The Lizard House, the father, invented the Mayan script and supported all learning, while his wife, Lady Rainbow, was a deity of weaving and medicine who also helped women endure the pain of childbirth. Their descendants, the Maya believed, each

• **obsidian** A naturally occurring volcanic glass used by different peoples in the Americas to make fine art objects, dart tips, and knife blades sharper than modern scalpels. The most important good traded by the Maya.

• **_Popul Vuh_** One of the few surviving sources in the Mayan language, this oral epic features a series of hip ballgames between the gods and humans. Originally written in Mayan glyphs, it was recorded in the Roman alphabet in the 1500s.

presided over a different realm: separate gods existed for merchants, hunters, fishermen, soldiers, and the ruling families. Maya rulers sacrificed their prisoners of war as offerings to these deities.

The Maya communicated with the dead using various techniques. Caves served as portals between the world of the living and the Xibalba (SHE-bal-ba) Underworld described in *Popul Vuh*. One cave is 2,790 feet (850 m) long; its walls are decorated with drawings of the Hero Twins, the ballgame, and sexual acts. The Maya who visited this and other caves employed enemas to intoxicate themselves so they could see the dead. They performed these enemas by attaching bone tubes, found in large quantities at Maya sites, to leather or rubber bags filled with different liquids. Surviving drawings make it impossible to identify the liquids, but anthropologists speculate that the enema bags were filled with wine, chocolate, or hallucinogens made from the peyote cactus.

Watching a Ballgame Seven contestants play the ballgame in front of an attentive audience seated on all four sides. Spectators lean forward with great interest; mothers watch with their arms draped over their children's shoulders. This clay model was found in a tomb in Nayarit, in western Mexico, and dates to between 100 B.C.E. and 250 C.E., making it one of the earliest representations of the game ever found. (Yale University Art Gallery)

War, Politics, and the Decline of the Maya

In the past few decades, scholars have devoted considerable energy and ingenuity to sorting out the relationships among the sixty or so Maya city-states. Much hinges on the interpretation of a few key phrases that appear in inscriptions: some rulers are said to be someone else's king, an indication that they accepted another king as their overlord or ruler. It is not clear what ties bound a subordinate ruler to his superior: marriage ties, loyalty oaths, military alliances, or perhaps a mixture of all three.

Because various rulers vied continuously to increase their territory and become each other's lord, the different Maya city-states devoted considerable resources to war. Armies consisted of foot soldiers, commoners who wore light protection made from either animal skins or padded cotton. Their weapons included spears with obsidian points, slingshots, and darts propelled by a spear-thrower. The Maya did not have the bow and arrow, which appeared among the Mississippian peoples to the north around 900 C.E. On the most informal level of conflict, a group of soldiers might steal into enemy territory to take captives, while in formal battles, two opposing armies of infantry faced off and showered each other with darts or stones from slingshots. Traps and ambushes were common, and the fighters used both daggers and spears in hand-to-hand combat.

The goal of all Maya warfare was to obtain captives. Low-born captives were assigned to work in the maize fields of nobles, while prisoners of higher status, particularly those from noble families, were held in captivity for long periods of time, sometimes as much as twenty years. In inscriptions rulers brag about how many captives they held at any one time because they wanted to appear more powerful. Rulers also staged public spectacles in which they tore out the hearts of the defeated prisoners or publicly beheaded them.

The Ballgame in *Popul Vuh*

The detailed narrative of the Maya epic *Popul Vuh* describes the destruction of multiple previous worlds and the creation of a new one. The complicated plot involves two sets of ball-playing twins: after disturbing the gods with their play, one pair go to the Xibalba Underworld (derived from the Mayan word for "fear," "trembling"), where they die at the hands of One and Seven Death, the head lords of Xibalba. The severed head of one of these twins hangs on a tree from which its spittle magically impregnates Lady Blood, who gives birth to the second set of twins, Hunahpu (HOO-nah-pooh) and Xbalanque (sh-bal-on-kay). These Hero Twins, far more skillful than their father and uncle, at first trick the gods of the Underworld repeatedly and then defeat them in the ballgame described in the episode below. Eventually they also die, but because the gods grant them another life, they rise at the end of the narrative to become the sun and the moon, creating the upper world or cosmos.

The earliest archaeological evidence of the game comes from the Olmec site of El Manatí, located 6 miles (10 km) east of San Lorenzo, where a dozen rubber balls dating to around 500 B.C.E. were found. Almost every Maya city-state had a ball court, usually in the shape of L, with walls around it, located near a major temple. The Maya played this soccer-like game with heavy rubber balls measuring 12 or 18 inches (33 or 50 cm) across. The Maya cooked liquid rubber from latex trees and allowed it to cool and solidify into a heavy mass.

Sometimes the ball-makers used a human skull to make a hollow, less lethal, ball. The game spread throughout the Maya core region and as far north as Snaketown near Phoenix, Arizona, the home of an early Anasazi people who had two ball courts and rubber balls.

Since ball courts and balls do not provide enough information to understand how the game was played, anthropologists are closely studying the modern hip ballgames in the few villages near Mazatlán (ma-zát-LAN), Sinaloa (sin-A-loh-a) State in northwestern Mexico, where the game is still played. Two opposing teams of three to five players try to get the ball past the other team's end line. After serving with their hands, they propel the heavy rubber balls with their hips. Although players covered their hips with padding, called a "yoke" below, the hips of modern players develop calluses and often become permanently bruised a deep-black color. We cannot be sure that everyone who played the game knew the story of the Hero Twins, but many players probably understood the game as a contest between two teams, one representing good, life, or the hero twins, and the other evil, death, or Xibalba, which was always victorious.

This passage from the *Popul Vuh* describes the first test the twins must endure.

Source: Popul Vuh: The Definitive Edition of the Mayan Book of the Dawn of Life and the Glories of Gods and Kings, trans. Dennis Tedlock (New York: Simon and Schuster, 1996), pp. 119–122.

First they entered Dark House.

And after that, the messenger of One Death brought their torch, burning when it arrived, along with one cigar apiece.

"'Here is their torch,' says the lord. 'They must return the torch in the morning, along with the cigars. They must return them intact,' say the lords," the messenger said when he arrived.

"Very well," they said, but they didn't burn the torch—instead, something that looked like fire was substituted. This was the tail of the macaw, which looked like a torch to the sentries.

And as for the cigars, they just put fireflies at the tips of those cigars, which they kept lit all night.

"We've defeated them," said the sentries, but the torch was not consumed—it just looked that way. And as for the cigars, there wasn't anything burning there—it just looked that way. When these things were taken back to the lords:

"What's happening? Where did they come from? Who begot them and bore them? Our hearts are really hurting, because what they're doing to us is no good. They're different in looks and different in their very being," they said among themselves. And when they had summoned all the lords:

"Let's play ball, boys," the boys were told. And then they were asked by One and Seven Death:

"Where might you have come from? Please name it," Xibalba said to them.

"Well, wherever did we come from? We don't know," was all they said. They didn't name it.

"Very well then, we'll just go play ball, boys," Xibalba told them.

"Good," they said.

"Well, this is the one we should put in play, here's our rubber ball," said the Xibalbans.

"No thanks. This is the one to put in, here's ours," said the boys.

"No it's not. This is the one we should put in," the Xibalbans said again.

"Very well," said the boys.

"After all, it's just a decorated one," said the Xibalbans.

"Oh no it's not. It's just a skull, we say in return," said the boys.

"No it's not," said the Xibalbans.

"Very well," said Hunahpu. When it was sent off by Xibalba, the ball was stopped by Hunahpu's yoke [hip-pad].

And then, while Xibalba watched, the White Dagger came out from inside the ball. It went clattering, twisting all over the floor of the court.

"What's that!" said Hunahpu and Xbalanque. "Death is the only thing you want for us! Wasn't it *you* who sent a summons to us, and wasn't it *your* messenger who went? Truly, take pity on us, or else we'll just leave," the boys told them.

And this is what had been ordained for the boys: that they should have died right away, right there, defeated by that knife. But it wasn't like that. Instead, Xibalba was again defeated by the boys.

"Well, don't go, boys. We can still play ball, but we'll put yours into play," the boys were told.

"Very well," they said, and this was time for their rubber ball, so the ball was dropped in.

And after that, they specified the prize:

"What should our prize be?" asked the Xibalbans.

"It's yours for the asking," was all the boys said.

"We'll just win four bowls of flowers," said the Xibalbans.

"Very well. What kinds of flowers?" the boys asked Xibalba.

"One bowl of red petals, one bowl of white petals, one bowl of yellow petals, and one bowl of whole ones," said the Xibalbans.

"Very well," said the boys, and then their ball was dropped in. The boys were their equals in strength and made many plays, since they only had very good thoughts. Then the boys gave themselves up in defeat, and the Xibalbans were glad when they were defeated:

"We've done well. We've beaten them on the first try," said the Xibalbans. "Where will they go to get the flowers?" they said in their hearts.

"Truly, before the night is over, you must hand over our flowers and our prize," the boys, Hunahpu and Xbalanque, were told by Xibalba.

"Very well. So we're also playing ball at night," they said when they accepted their charge.

And after that, the boys entered Razor House, the second test of Xibalba.

QUESTIONS FOR ANALYSIS

▶ What tricks do the hero twins play on the lords of the Xibalba underworld? How do the Xibalba lords retaliate?

▶ What happens that is unexpected? Why do the twins lose?

■ **Celebrating a Maya Victory in Battle**   This colorful fresco in a Maya tomb in Bonampak, Mexico, commemorates the victory of the ruler, who wears an elaborate headdress and a jacket made from jaguar skin. He relentlessly thrusts his spear downwards and grasps the hair of a prisoner whose outstretched hand implores his captor. These murals, which reveal so much about the lives of the Maya, were suddenly abandoned around 800, a time when work on many other monuments stopped abruptly, marking the end of the classic era.   (© Charles and Josette Lenars/Corbis)

At the peak of Maya power in 750, the population reached eight to ten million. Sometime around the year 800, the Maya city-states entered an era of decline, evident because site after site has produced unfinished monuments abruptly abandoned by stoneworkers. So sudden was the decline that workers at some sites seem to have stopped carving after completing a single face of a square monument.

Archaeologists have different explanations for the Maya decline. In the seventh and eighth centuries, two city-states, Tikal in northern Guatemala and Kalak'mul (KA-lack-muhl) 60 miles (100 km) to the north, formed blocs of allied city-states that engaged in unending warfare. The drain on resources may have depopulated the Maya cities. The fragile agricultural base, with its heavy use of slash-and-burn farming, depleted the nutrients in the fields close to the political centers. In some places, a sustained drought between 800 and 1050 may have dealt the final blow to the ecosystem. Some residents of the different Maya city-states may have relocated to defensible locations in the northern Yucatán after 910.

Maya culture revived during the post-classic period (910–1300), and the city of Chichen Itza (CHEE-chen It-za) in the northern Yucatán, which flourished between 1000 and 1200, combined classic elements of Maya and central Mexican architecture and city planning. The ball court at Chichen Itza measures 545 feet (166 m) by 223 feet (68 m), making it the largest ball court in the Americas. The Maya continued to create monuments, but instead of carving them in stone, they used paint, which has since worn off. Although Maya culture did not die out after 1200, the Maya never again matched the social stratification, specialized occupations, and large urban centers of the classic period.

● The Northern Peoples, 500 B.C.E.–1200 C.E.

Complex society arose north of the Rio Grande, in the area occupied by the modern United States and Canada, relatively late—after the decline of the Maya—and possibly because of contact with Mesoamerica. The North Americans planted maize as the Mesoamericans did, and their cities resembled their Maya counterparts. The first complex societies in North America, both dating to after 700 C.E., were the Mississippian culture in the central United States and the Anasazi (AH-nah-sah-zee) culture in the southwest United States.

Until about 500 B.C.E., the peoples living to the north continued to hunt and gather in small bands of around sixty people, much like the residents of Monte Verde, Chile (see Chapter 1), and, as a result, their communities remained small. A major change occurred when the Adena (uh-DEE-nuh) (500 B.C.E.–100 C.E.) created earthworks along the Ohio River Valley in Ohio and Illinois. Their settlements were not large urban centers, but these earthworks demonstrate that their leaders could organize large-scale labor projects.

The Adena peoples built mounds containing rich burials, most likely of their leaders, a sign of increasing social stratification. Some mounds form perfect circles, while others are in the shape of animals, like the famous 1,300-foot (400-m) Serpent Mound of Ohio that portrays a snake eating an egg. Living in circular houses constructed from tree trunks and bark, the Adena ate a diet of wild animals, fish, and plants they gathered in the forest. They did not farm.

The successors to the Adena, the Hopewell peoples (200 B.C.E.–500 C.E.), built larger earthworks in the valleys of the Ohio, Illinois, and Mississippi Rivers. They occupied a wide region extending from western New York to Kansas and from the Gulf of Mexico to the Great Lakes. Unlike the Adena, the Hopewell peoples cultivated maize, beans, and squash. Taller and more elaborate than the Adena mounds, the Hopewell earthworks formed clusters of circles, rectangles, and polygons linked by dirt causeways. These earthworks also contained graves of their leaders, who were buried with various goods.

Archaeologists have reconstructed the Hopewell trade routes by locating the sources of unusual items, such as alligator teeth and skulls from Florida, mapping the sites where those items appear, and then inferring the trade routes by linking the source with its various destinations. The Hopewell trading networks, more extensive than those of the Adena, extended from the Rocky Mountains to the Atlantic Ocean; with their neighbors to the south in modern-day Mexico, they traded conch shells, shark teeth, and obsidian.

The Mississippian peoples (800–1450) were the first northern people to build the large urban centers that characterize complex society. They occupied over a hundred different sites concentrated in the Mississippi River Valley. Mississippian towns followed a Maya plan, with temples or palaces on earthen mounds around a central plaza. The Mississippian peoples were the first in the Americas to develop the bow and arrow, sometime around 900 C.E.

The largest surviving mound, in the Cahokia (kuh-HOKE-ee-uh) Mounds of Collinsville, Illinois (just east of Saint Louis), is 100 feet (30 m) high and 1,000 feet (300 m) long and was built in fourteen stages. The sheer magnitude of this earthwork testifies to the power the leaders had over their subjects. Cahokia, with a population of thirty thousand, held eighty-four other mounds, some for temples, some for mass burials. One mound contained the corpses of 110 young women, evidence of a sacrificial cult to either a leader or a deity.

The other major complex society of the north appeared in modern-day Colorado, Arizona, Utah, and New Mexico: the Anasazi. Their centers also show signs of contact with the Maya, most notably in the presence of ball courts. During the Pueblo period (700–1300), the Anasazi built two kinds of houses: pit houses carved out of the ground and pueblos made from bricks, mortar, and log roofs. One pueblo structure in Chaco, New Mexico, had eight hundred rooms in five stories, home to one thousand residents. After 1150 the Anasazi began to build their pueblos next to cliff faces, as at Mesa Verde, Colorado. They used irrigation to farm, and their craftspeople made distinctive pottery, cotton and feather clothing, and turquoise jewelry.

These two North American complex societies postdate the Maya, and their many similarities to the Maya suggest extensive contact with them. Like so many other urban centers in the Americas, Cahokia Mounds and Mesa Verde declined suddenly after 1200 C.E., when their populations dispersed, and archaeologists do not know why.

The Peoples of the Andes, 3100 B.C.E.–1000 C.E.

Several complex societies arose, flourished, and collapsed between 3100 B.C.E. and 1000 C.E. in the Andean region, which includes modern-day Peru, Bolivia, Ecuador, Argentina, and Chile in South America. These complex societies predated the first Mesoamerican complex society of the Olmecs by nearly two thousand years, indicating that the two regions developed independently of each other.

All the Andean complex societies built city-states with large urban centers, though never on the scale of Teotihuacan. Archaeologists have identified the largest urban centers and know when they reached their greatest population, but, since there are no documents, they know less about the cities and their relationships to the surrounding villages.

The Andean mountain chain runs up the center of the Andean region, which extends east to the edge of the dense Amazon rainforest and west to the Pacific coast. Although at a higher altitude than Mesoamerica, this region has a similarly uneven distribution of rainfall. In the east, rain falls heavily, while to the west, almost none falls. When agriculture spread from Mexico to these dryer regions, the residents collected rainwater and brought it to their fields by a system of channels.

The main staple of the diet was potatoes, supplemented by squash, chili peppers, beans, and sometimes maize, which could grow only at lower altitudes. The earliest strains of domesticated squash date to about 8000 B.C.E. Sometime around 5000 B.C.E., the Andeans domesticated the llama and the alpaca. Both animals could carry loads of approximately 100 pounds (50 kg) over distances of 10 to 12 miles (16–20 km) a day. The Andeans never rode these animals or raised them to eat. Their main source of animal protein was the domesticated guinea pig.

The earliest large urban settlement in the Americas, at the site of **Caral** (KA-ral) in the Andes, lies some 100 miles (160 km) north of Lima, the capital of modern Peru, and only 14 miles (22 km) from the Pacific coast. People have known about the site since the early twentieth century because its structures are prominent and so clearly visible from the air, but only in 2001 did archaeologists realize that it dated to 3100 B.C.E. Since then they have found more than twenty satellite communities around Caral.

•**Caral** The earliest complex society (3100–1800 B.C.E.) in the Americas, whose main urban center was located at Caral, in modern-day Peru, in the Andes Mountains.

Latin America's First Civilization at Caral, Peru   Since 1900 people have known about the Caral site, with its five smaller pyramids and one large central structure, but only recently were archaeologists able to date the site to 3100 B.C.E. Caral was a large city-state, with some twenty smaller communities in the immediate neighborhood. Archaeologists have found clear signs of social stratification: the wealthiest residents lived on the tops of the pyramids while the poorer lived on lower levels or on the outskirts of the town.   (© George Steinmetz)

The Caral site contains five small pyramid-shaped structures and one large one: the Pirámide Mayor (PI-ra-me-day my-your), which stands 60 feet (18 m) tall and covers 5 acres (.02 km) (see the table "The World's Largest Pyramids," included in the feature "Visual Evidence: The Imposing Capital of Teotihuacan"). Inside the pyramid, archaeologists found a set of thirty-two carved flutes made from condor and pelican bone with decorations showing birds and monkeys, possibly deities. The three thousand or so people at the site included wealthy residents living in large dwellings on top of the pyramids, craftsmen in smaller houses at their base, and unskilled laborers in much simpler dwellings located around the perimeters of the town. Caral, like Uruk in Mesopotamia or Harappa in India, showed clear signs of social stratification. It was probably a city-state, not an early empire.

The history of the site reflects the rise-and-fall pattern so common to the early cities of the Americas and also to the Indus Valley (see Chapter 3). Agricultural improvements led to dramatic urban growth, followed by sudden decline. Usually no direct evidence reveals why a given city was abandoned, but drought and over-farming may have caused agricultural productivity to decline and food to run out. Caral was abandoned in 1800 B.C.E.

In 1200 B.C.E., more than one thousand years after Caral was occupied, a major urban center arose at **Chavin** (cha-VEEN), about 60 miles (100 km) north of Caral (see Map 5.1). Chavin cities have large temples, some in the shape of a U, and impressive stone sculptures. The statues at the temple in Chavin combine elements of different animals such as jaguars, snakes, and eagles with human body parts to create composite human-animal sculptures, possibly of deities.

• **Chavin** Andean complex society (1200–200 B.C.E.) in modern-day Peru. Best known for its temples and large stone sculptures of animals.

In 350 B.C.E., during the last years of the Chavin culture, several distinct regional cultures arose on the south coast of Peru that are most famous for the Nazca (NAZ-ka) lines, a series of earthworks near the modern town of Nazca. The Nazca people scraped away the dark surface layer of the desert to reveal a lighter-colored soil beneath; they then used the dark earth to build embankments along the trenches. No one knows how people working on the ground created these designs, which are still visible from the air today. Some of the Nazca lines run 6 miles (10 km) in a straight line through the desert; others form elaborate designs of spiders, whales, and monkeys, which may have been offerings to or depictions of their gods. No large cities of the Nazca people have been found, but the Nazca lines, like the earthworks of the Adena and Hopewell peoples, show that their rulers were able to mobilize large numbers of laborers.

Occupied between 600 and 1000 C.E., the biggest Andean political center was at Tiwanaku (TEE-wan-a-koo), 12 miles (20 km) south of Lake Titicaca (tit-tee-ka-ka), southern Bolivia, at the high altitude of 11,800 feet (3,600 m) above sea level. The rulers of the Tiwanaku city-state, archaeologists surmise, exercised some kind of political control over a large area extending through modern-day Bolivia, Argentina, northern Chile, and southern Peru. At its peak, Tiwanaku was home to some forty thousand people. Its farmers could support such a large population because they used a raised-field system: the irrigation channels they dug around their fields helped to keep the crops from freezing on chilly nights.

Sometime around 700 to 800 C.E., the Andean peoples, alone among the peoples living in the Americas, learned how to work metal intensively. Unlike the Maya, the Andeans discovered how to extract metallic ore from rocks and heat different metals to form alloys. They made bronze both by combining copper with tin, as was common in Eurasia, and also by combining copper with arsenic.

One site in Peru, in continuous use after 700, had draft furnaces in which families melted fuel and metal ore together, producing slag with copper in it, which they extracted and worked into ingots, small sheets, or "ax money"—ax-shaped pieces of metal tied together in bundles and placed in tombs as an offering for the dead.

Andean graves have produced the only metal tools found so far in the Americas. Some are oversized, some unfinished, yet all were clearly designed for display. Most Andean metal was used to make decorations worn by people or was placed on buildings, not for tools or weapons.

The Andean use of metal challenges yet another preconception prompted by the complex societies of Eurasia. In Mesopotamia, Egypt, India, and China, people switched to metal tools—first bronze, then iron—as soon as they learned to mine metal ore and make alloys. But the Andean peoples continued to use their traditional tools of wood and stone and used their new discovery of metal quite differently: for ceremonial and decorative purposes.

The Polynesian Voyages of Exploration, 1000 B.C.E.–1350 C.E.

Almost all the societies of the Americas discussed above, including the Maya, were land-based. Their residents used canoes for trips on inland waterways and for occasional voyages hugging the ocean shore, but they focused their energies on farming and building cities. In contrast, the peoples of the Pacific, who lived on the islands inside the Polynesian Triangle, spent much of their lives on the sea. Like the residents of the Americas, they developed in isolation from Eurasia, and like them, they developed quite differently from the Eurasians. Although their urban centers never became the large cities of complex societies, their societies were stratified and their leaders mobilized large numbers of their subjects for labor projects, often the construction of stone monuments.

Humans had reached Australia in about 60,000 B.C.E. (see Chapter 1), and they ventured into the Pacific sometime after that. Starting around 1000 B.C.E., when the Fiji islands of Tonga and Samoa were first settled, early voyagers crossed the Pacific Ocean using only the stars to navigate and populated most of the islands of the Pacific. Their voyages resulted in one of the longest yet least-documented seaborne migrations in human history. How and why did these ancient voyagers travel so far? These questions have excited a century of lively debate and are far from settled.

The Settlement of the Polynesian Triangle

The islands of the Pacific fall into two groups: those lying off Australia and Indonesia—Micronesia (mike-ro-NEE-zhuh), Melanesia (mel-uh-NEE-zhuh), and New Guinea—and those within the **Polynesian Triangle,** an imaginary triangle with sides 4,000 miles (6,500 km) long linking Hawai'i, Easter Island, and New Zealand (see Map 5.2). With seventy times more water than islands, the Polynesian Triangle contains several thousand islands ranging in size from tiny

• **Polynesian Triangle** An imaginary triangle with sides 4,000 miles (6,500 km) long linking Hawai'i, Easter Island, and New Zealand and containing several thousand islands.

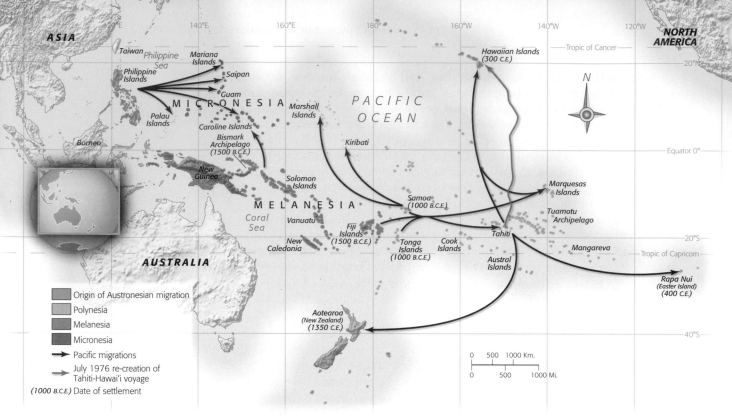

🌐 **MAP 5.2**

Pacific Migration Routes Before 1500 Starting around 1000 B.C.E., the peoples living in Micronesia and Melanesia began to go to islands lying to the east in the Pacific Ocean. At first, they took canoes to the islands they could see with the naked eye. But later they traveled thousands of miles without navigational instruments, reaching Hawai'i before 300 C.E., Easter Island by 400 C.E., and New Zealand in 1350 C.E.

uninhabited atolls to the largest, New Zealand, with an area of 103,695 square miles (268,570 sq km). The triangle's vast area can hold the continental United States twice over with room to spare.

The islands lying close to Indonesia and Australia were settled first. As the discovery of Mungo Man in Australia, which dates to circa 60,000 B.C.E., showed (see Chapter 1), ancient peoples could go from one island to the next in small crafts. Since the islands of Micronesia and Melanesia were located close together, the next island was always within sight. But as these ancient settlers ventured farther east, the islands became farther apart: between Easter Island and Peru lie 2,250 miles (3,600 km) of open ocean. Sometime before 300 C.E. the first settlers reached Hawai'i, and after the year 400 C.E. they had reached Easter Island, or Rapa Nui (RA-pah nwee). Their final destination, in 1350 C.E., was New Zealand.

All the spoken languages within the Polynesian Triangle belong to the Oceanic language family, a subset of the Eastern Austronesian family. (Western Austronesian languages, including Vietnamese [see Chapter 4], are spoken in Southeast Asia.) Languages within the Oceanic family differ only slightly among themselves; while the Tahitians say, "tabu," meaning "forbidden" or "prohibited," the Hawaiian pronunciation is "kabu." (This word has entered English as *taboo*.)

The most distinctive artifact that reveals the direction of migration in the Pacific is low-fired brown pottery with lines and geometric decorations made with a pointed instrument. This **Lapita pottery** is named for a site in Melanesia. The oldest examples found so far were unearthed on sites in the Bismarck Archipelago, northeast of New Guinea. Since pottery with Lapita (la-PEE-tuh) designs appear first on Melanesia in 1500 B.C.E. and then 500 years later on Tonga and Samoa, archaeologists have reconstructed the ancient route of migration starting from Asia's Pacific coast and traveling east.

Polynesian Seafaring Societies

While historians concur on the overall direction of travel, they disagree about almost everything else. Did the settlers intentionally explore the distant islands of the Pacific? Or were these mariners simply blown off course in the easterly direction of the prevailing winds? Since they had no nautical instruments, how did they know where they were going?

Most observers agree that the original settlers must have traveled by canoe. Unlike in a rowboat, rowers in a canoe can face forward and see where they are going. It is not known when canoes first were developed, but once their shape was perfected, it continued to be used for hundreds of years with no major modifications. Different peoples have used various coverings stretched over a light wooden frame: bark in heavily wooded areas like the temperate United States, and skins farther north, where trees were scarce. Today's fiberglass canoes have the same basic design. However, in rough water canoes are not stable and can easily capsize.

Sometime in the first century C.E., the peoples of the Pacific developed a **double canoe,** which consisted of two canoes connected by a wooden frame lashed together with rope. Much more stable than single canoes, double canoes could also carry more cargo on the platform between the two boats. A modern double canoe 50 feet (15 m) long can carry a load weighing 18,000 pounds (8,165 kg). Double canoes were propelled by a sail, an essential requirement for long ocean voyages, and could reach speeds of 100 to 150 miles (160–240 km) per day. Double canoes, however, had drawbacks. Since they had no roofs, mariners would get wet during rainstorms. If one canoe sprang a leak and began to fill with water, it would sink, pushing the other canoe higher and the sinking canoe even lower. In storms the two canoes could easily break apart, resulting in the loss of all the baggage on the platform.

The people of Tahiti and Hawai'i were using this type of vessel in the eighteenth century when the Europeans first sketched them. Many historians assume that Polynesian life in earlier centuries resembled that in the early European descriptions of the villages of Tahiti and Hawai'i. The predominantly male chiefs and their kin lived lives of leisure, supported by gifts of food from the lower-ranking populace. Ordinary people tended crops in fields, which were often irrigated, and also hunted wildlife, mostly small birds.

Although some earlier scholars wondered if the settlement of the Pacific was the purely accidental result of boats being blown off course, many modern analysts think it resulted from both deliberate settlement and accidental exploration. They know that the early settlers of both sexes were traveling in boats, because if no women had traveled, the settlers could not have reproduced and the different islands would not have been populated. They also know that the settlers carried dogs and small rats because these animals became the main sources of protein for the settlers on the islands.

• **Lapita pottery** Named for a site in Melanesia, a low-fired brown pottery with lines and geometric decorations made with a pointed instrument. In use between 1500 and 1000 B.C.E., it reveals the direction of migration into the Pacific.

• **double canoe** A sailing vessel made by connecting two canoes with rope to a wooden frame. Used by the ancestors of modern Polynesians for ocean voyages. Capable of speeds of 100 to 150 miles (160–240 km) per day.

◼ **A Double Canoe on the Pacific** This painting of masked rowers in the Sandwich Islands is one of the earliest Western paintings of a double canoe, the primary mode of transportation throughout the Pacific. Notice that a wooden frame connected two canoes of identical size. The sail gave the canoes additional speed. (National Library of Australia)

The voyagers also carried plants, most likely in pots, to all the islands they reached. The staple crops of the Polynesian diet, breadfruit and taro, dispersed throughout the Pacific. Breadfruit, a seedless fruit with the texture of bread when baked, can be quite filling; taro is an edible starchy root plant that is pounded before being eaten. The distribution of two other plants points to early contacts between the Polynesian islands and South America: the sweet potato and the co-conut. It seems most likely that the sweet potato originated in South America and later spread throughout the Pacific; the coconut, in contrast, appears first in Asia and later in Latin America.

A recent archaeological find provides further evidence that the voyagers traveled all the way to Chile. Bones found at the site of El Arenal (ell AH-ray-nahl) in Chile show that chickens occupied the site between approximately 1304 and 1424. Chickens did not originally live in the Americas. Prior to this find, many scholars believed that European settlers introduced chickens to the Americas in the 1500s (see Chapter 15), but the similarities between the Chilean and Polynesian chickens suggest that American chickens originally came from Polynesia.

The Polynesians may have followed large sea mammals, possibly orca or bottle-nose dolphins, as they migrated for long periods of time over great distances. The first European observers were struck by the Polynesians' ability to travel long distances—sometimes up to several hundreds of miles or kilometers—to go deep-sea fishing.

Most puzzling to modern observers is how the Polynesians were able to travel such large distances using only the stars for navigation. In 1976, an anthropologist at the University of Hawai'i and several others decided to see if it was possible to sail, without navigational aids, the full distance of 2,400 miles (3,800 km) from Hawai'i to Tahiti. They built a facsimile of a traditional double canoe out of modern materials like fiberglass.

Because no one in Hawai'i knew the traditional method of navigation by the stars, the Polynesian Voyaging Society sought the help of a skilled sailor who lived in Micronesia, "Mau" Pius Piailug (MOW pee-US PEE-eye-luke). Identifying the prevailing winds through careful study of the waves, he used the changing position of the stars each day to determine the boat's position. He guided the boat all the way to Tahiti on a voyage that took thirty-three days to complete and that many Pacific peoples celebrated as evidence of their ancestors' accomplishments. Piailug did not make the return trip home, but in 1980 the Polynesian Voyaging Society sponsored a second voyage, this time piloted by a Hawaiian native, that made the round trip from Hawai'i to Tahiti.

Once navigation by the stars brought boats close to land, observant navigators used other means to pinpoint the exact location of the islands. They became skilled at following the flight routes of migratory birds. Certain birds nest on land and then fly far out to sea each day to look for fish before returning to their nests in the evening. Boobies fly 30 to 50 miles (50–80 km) each day; terns and noddies, 18 to 25 miles (30–40 km). When sighting these birds, ancient sailors knew whether land was nearby and how close it was.

Although the history of the Eastern Hemisphere may suggest that long ocean voyages required large boats and navigational instruments like a compass, the Polynesian Voyaging Society sailings showed that the ancestors of the Polynesians could cross the Pacific in double canoes. They used nonmechanical means of navigation, like observing the movements of birds, ocean currents, and the position of stars. Like the peoples of the Americas who farmed without the wheel, the plow, or draft animals, the Polynesians remind us that the peoples of the Western Hemisphere developed different ways of adapting to their environments than those living in the Eastern Hemisphere, from whom they remained isolated.

The Mystery of Easter Island

These techniques may have sufficed to reach the island chains of Hawai'i and Tahiti, but no one has a good explanation for how the ancestors of the Polynesians reached Easter Island. The easternmost inhabited island in the Pacific, Easter Island lies 1,300 miles (2,100 km) southeast of its nearest neighbor, Pitcairn Island, and 2,250 miles (3,600 km) off the coast of Chile. These distances are less than the 2,400 miles (3,800 km) between Hawai'i and Tahiti, but since Easter Island is a single island only 14 miles (23 km) across at its widest point, not part of an island chain, it would have been extremely difficult for ancient navigators to locate. It was probably settled in 300 C.E. by a small party of Polynesians blown far off their original course. Since linguists believe that the Easter Island language retains many more archaic features than that of its neighbors, the early settlers probably had little contact with the other peoples of Oceania after they arrived on Easter Island.

Easter Island has two names, neither of which is original. Most English speakers refer to it as Easter Island because a Dutch navigator first glimpsed the island on Easter Day, 1722. In the nineteenth century Polynesian sailors named the island Rapa Nui after the Polynesian island Rapa, 2,400 mi (3,850 km) to the west, the name currently in use by Polynesian speakers.

The people of Easter Island, like those elsewhere in the Pacific, subsisted on a diet of sweet potatoes, taro, and sugarcane supplemented by chicken, their only domesticated animal. Their garbage pits contain bones of dolphin, porpoise, and

• **moai**   The name for the 887 statues, probably of ancestral leaders, made from tufa volcanic rock and erected on Easter Island around 1000 C.E. The largest are more than 70 feet (21 m) high and weigh more than 270 tons.

tuna, an indication that they also engaged in deep-sea fishing. With no metal, they had tools of stone, wood, and bone.

All early European visitors to Easter Island noticed the huge statues of volcanic tufa stone, called **moai** (MOH-ai), that dot the island, some taller than 70 feet (21 m). The islanders began to construct the statues during the island's most prosperous period, starting in 1000 C.E., when the population reached some fifteen thousand. The most recent count of the moai statues is 887.[3] Some stand on platforms that hold up to fifteen statues. The average weight is around 10 tons (9 metric tons), but the heaviest weighs a massive 270 tons (245 metric tons) (it was never moved from its quarry). No two statues are identical. Some have designs showing tattoos and loincloths.

■ **Moai Figures, Easter Island**   The giant stone figures, or moai, of Easter Island portray ancestral leaders. When alive, the leaders commissioned a statue of themselves that remained horizontal. After they died, the statues were placed in an upright position, and eye inlays of coral and other rock were inserted into the eye sockets. The chunk of red stone on the top of this moai represents a headdress.
(Andreas M. Gross/Westend 61/Alamy)

Local oral traditions hold that the statues portray ancestral leaders. When alive, the leaders commissioned a statue of themselves that remained horizontal; after they died, the statues were placed in an upright position and inlays of coral and other rock were inserted into the eye sockets. Many of these faces were topped with a chunk of red stone to represent a headdress or a hat with red feathers. The island was divided into small bands, whose leaders built the monuments as an expression of their power. Competition would account for the variation in height of the monuments; as leaders sought to outbuild one another, they erected ever-higher statues.

How could a Stone Age people with no metal tools make statues of such size and transport them? Earlier analysts proposed that the statues must have been brought by outsiders from South America or even outer space, but modern scholars concur that these statues were built and erected by indigenous peoples with no outside assistance. Sculptors used stone choppers and water to hew each statue's basic shape from the soft volcanic rock.

In 1998, Jo Anne Van Tilburg designed an experiment as innovative as the Polynesian Voyaging Society's sailing from Hawai'i to Tahiti. She found that between fifty and seventy people working five hours a day for a week could move a 12-ton (11-metric-ton) statue 9 miles (14.4 km). Some think that once the stone was at its destination, the Easter Islanders made a series of ramps from dirt, each steeper than the next, to move the statues into a standing position; others think they must have used ropes to hoist the statues into place. Tilburg's findings suggest that the islanders used a wooden frame, giant logs that functioned as rollers, or both to pull the statues from the quarry to their destinations. Although the island has no trees now, it did in the past. One of the largest was a palm tree that grew over 65 feet tall (20 m).

Sometime around 1600 the Easter Islanders stopped making moai. In the end, the different chiefs made war against each other so intensively and for so long, pausing only to create these monuments, that they used up their resources. The activities of the Easter Islanders resulted in the total degradation of their environment: no trees or large animals remained in the eighteenth century. The only large bones available on the island were those of humans, which the islanders worked into fishhooks, and they used human hair to make ropes, textiles, and fishnets, a chilling demonstration of survival with few natural resources.

The Impact of Humans on New Zealand

New Zealand was the final island in the Pacific to be settled by humans. The first artifacts made by humans appear in a layer of volcanic ash dating to circa 1350. Studies of mitochondrial DNA (see Chapter 1) show that the indigenous Maori people of New Zealand were descended from some seventy different female ancestors, indicating a founding population of more than one hundred settlers.

These settlers had a profound effect on the New Zealand environment. Like the Easter Islanders, they demonstrated that environmental damage is not simply a modern development. Within a century after their arrival, twenty different species of birds had died out, and hunters had killed more than 160,000 giant moa birds. Surviving skeletal remains indicate that some twenty different species of moa once flourished on the island; the tallest stood over 10 feet (3 m) tall. After the residents had eliminated the large birds, they preyed on large mammals like seals and sea lions until those populations were also depleted. The hunters then targeted smaller animals. As the supply of wild animals dwindled, the residents became more dependent on slash-and-burn agriculture for their food supply, destroying an estimated 40 percent of the island's forest cover.[4]

We do not know about the social structure of the original settlers because, like all other Polynesian peoples, they had no writing system. When the first Europeans arrived in the seventeenth and eighteenth centuries, they found many small warring bands leading an arduous existence that was the unintended result of their ancestors' overhunting and overfishing.

Chapter Review

Download the MP3 audio file of the Chapter Review and listen to it on the go.

The experience of the peoples living in the Americas, including Yax K'uk Mo', and the islands of the Pacific repeatedly demonstrates that the path taken to complex society by peoples of the Eastern Hemisphere was not the only possible one. After 7000 B.C.E. the peoples of the Americas and the Pacific Islands lived in almost total isolation from Eurasia. During the long period of separation, they developed very different techniques of adapting to their environments.

KEY TERMS

Yax K'uk Mo' (114)

Mesoamerica (117)

Olmec (118)

Long Count (119)

Teotihuacan (120)

Maya (120)

Copán (124)

obsidian (126)

Popul Vuh (126)

Caral (133)

Chavin (134)

Polynesian Triangle (135)

Lapita pottery (137)

double canoe (137)

moai (140)

How did the development of agriculture and the building of early cities in Mesoamerica differ from that in Mesopotamia, India, and China?

The first agriculture in Mesoamerica arose on the high plateau of Mexico, not in river valleys. The first farmers used digging sticks instead of the plow or the wheel so common in Eurasia, and they had no domesticated animals. Even so, they built imposing cities like Teotihuacan and the unusual colossal heads of the Olmecs.

What has the decipherment of the Mayan script revealed about Maya governance, society, religion, and warfare?

The decipherment of the Mayan writing system in the 1970s brought new understanding of the period between 250 and 910 C.E. Rulers like Yax K'uk Mo' stood at the top of social hierarchy; below them were their royal kin, then nobles, ordinary people, and, most pitiable of all, war captives who became either slaves or sacrificial victims. The many Maya rulers were locked in constant warfare, hoping to capture their enemies and dreading capture themselves. Capture might mean having to play the ballgame in an unequal contest: when the captive finally admitted defeat, the triumphant captors would hold a ceremony and spill his blood. The Maya gods played this game as well; the creation of the world, the Popul Vuh narrative reveals, resulted from the defeat of human twins in a cosmic ballgame by the gods of the underworld.

What were the similarities between the complex societies of the northern peoples and those of Mesoamerica? What do they suggest about contact?

Like the Mesoamericans, the northern peoples at Cahokia Mounds and Mesa Verde planted maize, beans, and squash, and their cities contain characteristically Mesoamerican architectural elements, such as a central plaza and ball courts. Later than the Maya, both complex societies may have developed as a result of contacts with Mesoamerica.

How did the history of complex society in the Andes differ from that in Mesoamerica?

Certain striking differences distinguished the Andean complex societies from those in Mesoamerica. The Andean diet was potato-based, and the residents only occasionally ate maize, the Mesoamerican staple, which they grew at lower altitudes. Also unlike the Mesoamericans, the Andeans domesticated animals—the llama and the alpaca—and they knew how to mine metal and make alloys. These differences all suggest that there was little contact between the Andean peoples and those living in Mesoamerica.

Where did the early settlers of the Pacific Islands come from, and where did they go? What vessels did they use, and how did they navigate?

Starting sometime before 1000 B.C.E., the ancestors of the Polynesians departed from mainland Southeast Asia and moved from one island in the Pacific to the next. Traveling in double canoes, navigating by the stars, and observing ocean currents and bird flight patterns, they landed first in Hawai'i and then in Easter Island. The final place in the world to be settled, circa 1350 C.E., was New Zealand, which lay far from any continental landmass. The early settlers of both Easter Island and New Zealand overfished the nearby waters and exterminated many of the large animals on the islands, leaving themselves with seriously depleted food supplies.

The settlement of New Zealand marked the close of the first long chapter in world history: the settlement of all habitable regions of the globe that had begun over a million years earlier with the departure of the earliest hominids from Africa. After 1350, no unoccupied land was left other than Antarctica, where humans can survive only with the help of modern technology. After that date, people migrating from their homeland to anywhere else in the world always encountered indigenous peoples, with conflict almost always being the result.

For Further Reference

Coe, Michael D. *The Maya.* 6th ed. New York: Thames and Hudson, 1999.

Coe, Michael D. *Mexico: From the Olmecs to the Aztecs.* New York: Thames and Hudson, 1984.

Flenley, John, and Paul Bahn. *The Enigmas of Easter Island: Island on the Edge.* New York: Oxford University Press, 2002.

Howe, K. R. *The Quest for Origins: Who First Discovered and Settled the Pacific Islands?* Honolulu: University of Hawai'i Press, 2003.

Jennings, Jesse D., ed. *The Prehistory of Polynesia.* Cambridge, Mass.: Harvard University Press. 1979.

Martin, Simon, and Nikolai Grube. *Chronicle of the Maya Kings and Queens: Deciphering the Dynasties of the Ancient Maya.* New York: Thames and Hudson, 2000.

Oliphant, Margaret. *The Atlas of the Ancient World: Charting the Civilizations of the Past.* New York: Barnes and Noble Books, 1998.

Popol Vuh: The Definitive Edition of the Mayan Book of the Dawn of Life and the Glories of Gods and Kings. Translated by Denis Tedlock. New York: Simon and Schuster, 1996.

Schele, Linda, and Mary Ellen Miller. *The Blood of Kings: Dynasty and Ritual in Maya Art.* Fort Worth: Kimball Art Museum, 1986.

Stuart, George E. "The Timeless Vision of Teotihuacan." *National Geographic* 188, no. 6 (December 1995): 3–38.

Sugiyama, Saburo. *Human Sacrifice, Militarism, and Rulership: Materialization of State Ideology at the Feathered Serpent Pyramid, Teotihuacan.* New York: Cambridge University Press, 2005.

Websites

Foundation for the Advancement of Mesoamerican Studies, Inc. (http://www.famsi.org/research/pohl/pohl_aztec6.html). A description of the daily life of the Aztecs.

Polynesian Voyage Society (http://pvs.kcc.hawaii.edu/welcome.html). Introduction to attempts to reconstruct Polynesian sea travel in modern times.

The Sport of Life and Death: The Mesoamerican Ballgame (www.ballgame.org). Interactive and educational introduction to the Maya ballgame.

Teotihuacan: The City of the Gods (http://archaeology.la.asu.edu/teo/). Introduction to the site of Teotihuacan.

Films

Nova movie about Easter Island in "Secrets of Lost Empires" series.

"Nova: Lost King of the Maya" (the source of the chapter-opening quote).

New Empires in Iran and Greece, 2000 B.C.E.–651 C.E.

O n September 29, 522 B.C.E., **Darius** (r. 522–486 B.C.E.) led six conspirators in a plot to kill the pretender to the throne of Iran, who ruled ancient Persia. Writing nearly one hundred years later, the Greek historian **Herodotus** (ca. 485–425 B.C.E.) recounted a lively discussion among the seven about the best form of government. While one suggested the democracy of the Greek city-state of Athens, another spoke up for rule by a few, or oligarchy (OLL-ih-gahr-key), the governing system of the city-state of Sparta. Darius (duh-RYE-uhs), the future king, vigorously defended rule by one man, or monarchy:

HERODOTUS

T ake the three forms of government we are considering—democracy, oligarchy, and monarchy—and suppose each of them to be the best of its kind; I maintain that the third is greatly preferable to the other two. One ruler: it is impossible to improve upon that—provided he is the best. His judgment will be in keeping with his character; his control of the people will be beyond reproach; his measures against enemies and traitors will be kept secret more easily than under other forms of government. . . .

   To sum up: where did we get our freedom from, and who gave it us? Is it the result of democracy, or oligarchy, or of monarchy? We were set free by one man, and therefore I propose that we should preserve that form of government, and, further, that we should refrain from changing ancient ways, which have served us well in the past.[1]

(Antikensammlung Staatische Museen zu Berlin, Berlin, Germany/ Bildarchiv Preussischer Kulturbesitz/Art Resource, NY)

CL This icon will direct you to interactive activities and study materials on the *Voyages* website: www.cengage.com/history/hansen/voyages1e

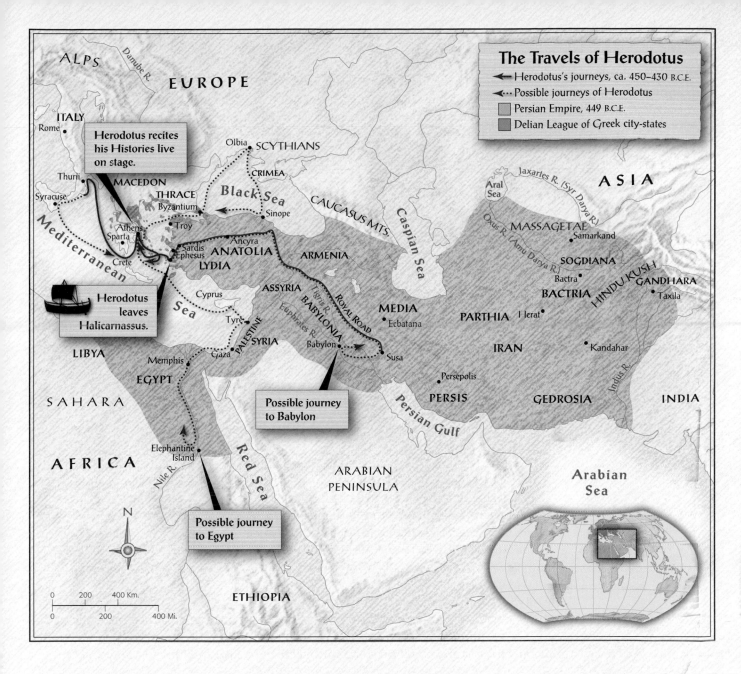

The Travels of Herodotus

← Herodotus's journeys, ca. 450–430 B.C.E.
◄⋯ Possible journeys of Herodotus
▢ Persian Empire, 449 B.C.E.
▢ Delian League of Greek city-states

EUROPE

ALPS
Danube R.

ITALY
Rome
Thurii
Syracuse

Herodotus recites his Histories live on stage.

MACEDON
Athens
Sparta
Crete

Mediterranean

Herodotus leaves Halicarnassus.

Black Sea
SCYTHIANS
Olbia
CRIMEA
Byzantium
Troy
Sardis
Ephesus
ANATOLIA
LYDIA
Sinope

Sea
Cyprus
Tyre
PALESTINE
Gaza
SYRIA
Memphis

LIBYA

SAHARA

EGYPT

AFRICA

Elephantine Island

Nile R.

Red Sea

ARMENIA

ASSYRIA
Tigris R.
BABYLONIA
Euphrates R.
Babylon

Royal Road

Possible journey to Babylon

CAUCASUS MTS.

Caspian Sea

MEDIA
Ecbatana

Susa

PERSIS
Persepolis

Persian Gulf

Possible journey to Egypt

ARABIAN PENINSULA

ETHIOPIA

N

ASIA

Aral Sea
Jaxartes R. (Syr Darya R.)
MASSAGETAE
Samarkand
Oxus R. (Amu Darya R.)
SOGDIANA
Bactra
BACTRIA
HINDU KUSH
GANDHARA
Taxila

PARTHIA
Herat

IRAN
Kandahar

GEDROSIA
Indus R.
INDIA

Arabian Sea

0   200   400 Km.
0   200   400 Mi.

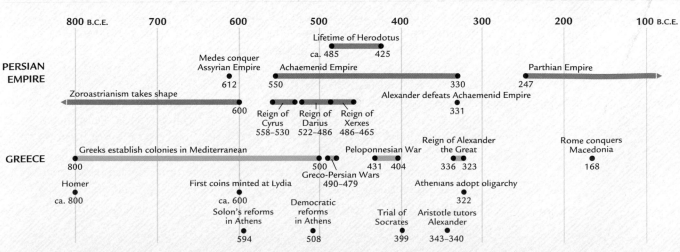

	800 B.C.E.	700	600	500	400	300	200	100 B.C.E.

Lifetime of Herodotus ca. 485 – 425

PERSIAN EMPIRE

Medes conquer Assyrian Empire 612

Achaemenid Empire 550 – 330

Parthian Empire 247

Zoroastrianism takes shape 600

Reign of Cyrus 558–530
Reign of Darius 522–486
Reign of Xerxes 486–465

Alexander defeats Achaemenid Empire 331

GREECE

Greeks establish colonies in Mediterranean 800

Peloponnesian War 431 – 404

Reign of Alexander the Great 336 – 323

Rome conquers Macedonia 168

Homer ca. 800

First coins minted at Lydia ca. 600

Greco-Persian Wars 490–479

Athenians adopt oligarchy 322

Solon's reforms in Athens 594

Democratic reforms in Athens 508

Trial of Socrates 399

Aristotle tutors Alexander 343–340

●**Darius** (r. 522–486 B.C.E.) The third Achaemenid ruler, who succeeded to the throne by coup. Conquered much territory in Eurasia but was unable to defeat the Scythians south of the Black Sea or the Greeks. Reformed the empire's administrative structure.

●**Herodotus** (ca. 485–425 B.C.E.) A Greek-speaking historian born in Halicarnassus. Author of *The Histories,* an investigation of the history, folklore, geography, plants, and customs of the known world. Known as the "father of history."

●**Achaemenids** The ruling dynasty in Iran between 550 and 330 B.C.E. At its height in the fifth century B.C.E. it governed a population estimated at thirty to thirty-five million people.

Many have wondered how Herodotus (heh-ROD-uh-tuhs) could have possibly known what was said in a secret conversation that occurred long before his birth in Persian, a language that he did not speak. Herodotus must, they conclude, have created this dialogue to enliven his narrative. No one doubts, though, that he articulated a question of great interest to his contemporaries and of equal importance to anyone studying history today: what was the most effective form of government for an empire?

Herodotus, a native speaker of Greek, was born to a well-to-do literate family in Halicarnassus (modern Bodrum), a city on the southwest coast of modern-day Turkey. Part of the Persian Empire, Halicarnassus (HAH-lee-kar-nuh-suhs) was home to a large Greek-speaking community that had settled there several centuries earlier. As a young man, Herodotus received a traditional education, and he wrote his life's great work, *The Histories,* in Greek.

The title Herodotus chose, *Historia* (hiss-TOR-ee-uh), means "inquiry" or "investigation," not necessarily about the past; it is the root of the English word *history.* Unlike other historians of his time, Herodotus makes it clear when he is including a hearsay account rather than his own observations and openly expresses doubt about some of the taller tales he presents. For this reason, the Roman orator Cicero (SIS-erh-oh) (106–43 B.C.E.) called Herodotus the father of history, a label he retains to this day.

Not a first-person travel account, *The Histories* presents the history, folklore, geography, plants, and customs of the known world in Herodotus's day. Herodotus went to Athens, where he recited sections of the book before live audiences, who loved to hear poetry, stories, and plays performed aloud. He must have traveled as well along the Aegean coast of Turkey and to Italy, if not as far as Egypt, the Crimean peninsula on the Black Sea, Sicily, Babylon, and North Africa, all places *The Histories* claims that he visited in person (see the map on page 145). Herodotus recorded his book on long rolls of papyrus sometime after 431 B.C.E. and died soon after, most likely around 425 B.C.E.

Herodotus devoted his life to explaining the success of the Persian Empire, easily the largest and certainly the most powerful empire of its time. From 550 to 330 B.C.E. the **Achaemenid** (a-KEY-muh-nid) dynasty of Iran governed the entire region extending from modern-day Egypt and Turkey through Iran and Iraq and as far east as Samarkand. Between thirty and thirty-five million people lived in the Achaemenid Empire.[2] Up to around 500 B.C.E., the greatest western Asian empires—the Akkadians, the Babylonians, the Assyrians—had been based in the Tigris and Euphrates River valleys (see Chapter 2); for more than a thousand years after 500 B.C.E., some of the largest empires were in Iran.

The Greeks were among the few who managed to defeat the powerful Persian army and resist conquest. In Athens, during the sixth and fifth centuries B.C.E., a new political system emerged, a system the Athenians called *democracy,* or rule by the people. Some 30,000 men, but no slaves and no women, made decisions affecting the estimated 300,000 people living in Athens, 1 percent or less of the total population of the Persian Empire.

The Achaemenid rulers developed a flexible type of empire that allowed them to conquer and rule the many different peoples of western Asia for more than two centuries until their defeat in 331 B.C.E. by the Macedonian king Alexander the

Great. When Alexander came to power, democracy in Athens had already failed, and he took over Persian conceptions and structures of kingship intact. Unable to match the Achaemenid feat of governing for two centuries, his empire broke apart after only thirteen years. Many different governments rose and fell in western Asia, but those that ruled the most territory for the longest periods of time—the successor states to Alexander, the Parthians, and the Sasanians—were all monarchies that drew much from the Achaemenid Empire.

Note that many of the answers this chapter proposes must be based on the work of Greek writers, including Herodotus, because so few sources in Persian survive.

Focus Questions

 What military and administrative innovations enabled the Achaemenid dynasty to conquer and rule such a vast empire?

 What were the important accomplishments of the Greek city-states? Consider innovations in politics, intellectual life, fine arts, and science.

 Who was Alexander, and what was his legacy?

 How did the Parthians and the Sasanians modify the Achaemenid model of empire?

The Rise of the Achaemenids in Iran, 1000–330 B.C.E.

After departing from their homeland somewhere in southern Russia (see Chapter 3), the Indo-European migrants broke into different branches, one of which arrived in the region of modern-day Iran in approximately 1000 B.C.E. These tribal people were largely nomads who did not plant crops but moved their sheep and camel flocks from pasture to pasture seeking fresh grass. Their language, Indo-Iranian, belonged to the same language family as Sanskrit, and their caste system resembled that of Vedic India (see Chapter 3) but had only three ranks: priests, rulers or warriors, and ordinary herders or farmers. Their herding way of life took maximum advantage of the high plateau environment of Iran, which had no major river valley comparable to the Nile, the Indus, or the Yellow Rivers. The tall mountains of Iran contain streams that drain into the high plateaus; many end in either salt lakes or trickle out into the desert.

Farming was only possible if farmers dug irrigation channels to collect water, and the first people who did so lived in the region of Persis (the origin of the English word *Persian*) in southwestern Iran. (*Iran* is the name of the larger geographic unit, while *Persia* refers to the smaller region, the heartland, of Persis.)

Starting in 550 B.C.E. the Achaemenids created an empire far larger than any the world had seen before. Their realm contained some of the world's most advanced cities, such as Babylon and Susa, and some of its most barren stretches, like the deserts of Central Asia. The key innovation in Achaemenid rule was the use of **satraps:** after conquering a region, they appointed a local governor, or satrap (SAH-trap), who was responsible for collecting taxes from the defeated and forwarding them to the capital at Susa. This flexible system suited the many different peoples of western Asia far better than the system used by the Qin and Han Empires, which had identical districts all over China (see Chapter 4).

Zoroastrianism

Our best source for understanding the early migrants to Iran is **The Avesta** (uh-VEST-uh), a book that contains the core teachings of their religion, **Zoroastrianism** (zo-roe-ASS-tree-uhn-iz-uhm). Zoroastrianism, like Vedic religion, featured hymn singing and the performance of elaborate rituals but also held that the world was governed by two opposing forces: good and evil. Describing pastoral nomads active in eastern Iran, *The Avesta* portrays ancient Iran as having no cities or any political unit larger than a tribe.

Zoroastrianism is named for its founding prophet Zarathustra (za-ra-THOO-stra) (in Persian; Zoroaster in Greek), who lived in the region of Herat, a city in the Iranian highland plateau now located in modern Afghanistan. With only *The Avesta* as their guide, scholars have no way to determine when Zarathustra lived, and informed estimates diverge widely, from 1500 to 700 B.C.E. Sometime around 1000 B.C.E. seems a reasonable compromise. Three thousand years old, Zoroastrianism is one of the world's most ancient religions still practiced today.

Written in an extremely ancient form of Indo-Iranian, *The Avesta,* which means "The Injunction of Zarathustra," contains a group of hymns attributed to the prophet Zarathustra himself, so its earliest contents probably date to circa 1000 B.C.E. The written version was first recorded sometime around 600 C.E., and the earliest surviving manuscript copies date to the thirteenth century C.E. These hymns provide our best guide to Zarathustra's original thought.

Zarathustra believed in a supreme deity, **Ahura Mazda** (ah-HURR-uh MAZZ-duh), the Lord of Truth, who created heaven and earth, day and night, and darkness and light. But Ahura Mazda was not the only spiritual force. He gave birth to twin entities, the good spirit and the evil spirit. Zoroastrianism is dualistic because it posits two equal, opposing entities: a host of good deities and evil demons, all in perpetual conflict.

Each person, whether male or female, Zarathustra taught, had to prepare for the day of judgment when everyone would appear before Ahura Mazda. Zarathustra firmly believed in the ability of human beings to shape their world by choosing between the good and the bad. People who chose the good had to think good thoughts, do good deeds, and tell the truth. Herodotus remarked that young boys were taught to "speak the truth," the fundamental Zoroastrian virtue. Whenever anyone lied or did a bad deed, the evil spirit gained ground.

Much of Zoroastrian ritual involved the worship of fire. The Zoroastrians built three permanent fire altars, each dedicated to a different caste group. At each site, male hereditary priests called Magi (MAH-jai) tended the fire to make sure that it never went out. If it did, an elaborate ritual was performed to relight the fire. Towns had fire altars, as did individual households, and worshipers fed fires five times a day, when they recited prayers.

●**satrap** The third Achaemenid ruler, Darius, divided his empire into provinces called *satrapies*, each administered by a governor, or satrap. The officials under the satrap were recruited locally, a hallmark of the Persian system.

●*The Avesta* A book, probably dating to circa 1000 B.C.E. and first recorded in writing around 600 C.E., whose title means "The Injunction of Zarathustra." Contains hymns attributed to Zarathustra himself, which provide our best guide to his original thought.

●**Zoroastrianism** Iranian religion named for its founding prophet Zarathustra (in Persian; Zoroaster in Greek), who may have lived around 1000 B.C.E. He taught that a host of good deities and evil demons, all in perpetual conflict, populate the spiritual world.

●**Ahura Mazda** The name of the supreme deity of Zoroastrianism, the Lord of Truth, who created heaven and earth, day and night, and darkness and light. On the day of judgment, Zoroastrians believe, Ahura Mazda will judge each person's good and bad deeds.

Zoroastrians also recited prayers at the daily preparation of the intoxicating, sacred potion made from the desert plant ephedra, which was called *haoma* (HOW-muh) in Persian and *soma* in Sanskrit (see Chapter 3). The potion was thought to bring various desired outcomes—victory in battle, wealth, or children, and even immortality. This practice of reciting prayers ensured the transmission of the original wording of the sacred hymns for a full two thousand years before they were written down. (See the feature "Movement of Ideas: Doing What Is Right in *The Avesta* and the Bible.")

The funerary practices of the Zoroastrians differed from those of almost all other ancient peoples. Whereas most peoples buried their dead, Zoroastrians, believing that dead flesh polluted the ground, left corpses outside so that scavenging birds and dogs could eat the flesh; then they collected the cleaned bones and buried them.

The Military Success of the Achaemenid Empire, 550–486 B.C.E.

In the centuries after Zarathustra formulated his teachings, Iran remained a tribal society that had little contact with the neighboring empires of western Asia. In 612 B.C.E., an Iranian tribe called the Medes captured the Assyrian capital and brought Assyrian rule to an end. The Medes began to expand beyond Iran's borders into western Asia. In 550 B.C.E. the leader of a different tribe, **Cyrus** (r. 558–530 B.C.E.), defeated the Medes and founded the Achaemenid dynasty, named for his ancestor Achaemenes. Since Cyrus was from Persis and natives of Persis staffed many of the important positions in the empire, the Achaemenid Empire is often called the Persian Empire. Cyrus employed many Medes in high positions as well.

When Cyrus founded his dynasty, his soldiers from Persis were obliged to serve in the king's army and to provide their own equipment. They served as foot soldiers, cavalrymen, archers, or engineers. They were not paid but were entitled to a share of the spoils from the cities they conquered.

As Cyrus's army conquered new territory, the structure of the military changed. The army of citizen-soldiers became a paid full-time army staffed by Persians and other Iranians, the conquered peoples, and large contingents of Greek mercenaries. The most prestigious unit, the king's bodyguard, was called the "Immortals, because it was invariably kept up to strength," Herodotus explains. "If a man was killed or fell sick, the vacancy he left was at once filled, so that its strength was never more nor less than 10,000." No records of the size of the army survive in Persian; Greek observers, prone to exaggerate, give figures as high as 2.5 million men, but the army certainly numbered in the hundreds of thousands, if not millions.

To bind their empire together physically, the Persians built an extensive network of roads that allowed them to supply the army no matter how far it traveled. The military stored food in designated warehouses where horse-drawn supply carts could be replenished. The Persians were fortunate to inherit a system of roads from earlier dynasties in the region: some were simple caravan tracks through the desert, while others, usually in or just outside the main cities like Babylon, were paved with bricks or rock. The main road, the Royal Road, linked the cities near the Aegean coast with the capital at Susa.

Cyrus (r. 558–530 B.C.E.) Founder of the Achaemenid dynasty in Iran. A native of Persis, Cyrus staffed his administration with many Persians as well as Medes, the tribe he defeated when he took power.

Doing What Is Right in *The Avesta* and the Bible

The ancient core texts of Zoroastrianism are still recited by one of the most active communities of Zoroastrian believers today, the Parsis of modern Bombay, India. The Parsis (also spelled Parsees, which means Persian) left Iran after the Islamic conquest and moved to India sometime between the eighth and tenth centuries C.E. Ever since then they have recited the two prayers of the first selection in the ancient Indo-Iranian language and continued to sing a small group of ancient hymns as they maintain the Zoroastrian tradition of fire worship and truth-telling.

The first prayer stresses that both the Lord of Truth, Ahura Mazda, and his true judgment should be chosen by mankind for the good of the world. These choices result in establishing a worldly sovereignty founded on good thinking that will benefit both "the Wise One" (Ahura Mazda) and "the pastor for the needy dependents" (Zarathustra) in this world. The second prayer focuses on the truth. It simply says that truth is the highest good and that everyone has the ability to follow and promote the truth.

The second selection is a prayer in *The Book of Tobit,* from the Apocrypha. All the Apocryphal texts originally circulated as part of the Hebrew Bible but were not included in certain later versions. Composed in the third or fourth centuries B.C.E., this book tells the story of an ordinary man named Tobit, a Jew who lived in exile in the Assyrian capital of Nineveh. Tobit continued to perform the ritual observances required of Jews, but the Hebrew God subjected him to various trials, including blindness, to test his devotion. Scholars think it likely that the text was written by a Jew in exile who had some knowledge of Zoroastrianism. After going blind, Tobit remembers that he deposited a large sum of money in the town of Rages in Iran, near modern-day Teheran, and sends his son there to retrieve the money. The advice he gives his son clearly reflects the influence of Zoroastrianism.

Source: The translation from *The Avesta* of the prayers in selection 1 is courtesy of Stanley Insler, Edward E. Salisbury Professor of Sanskrit and Comparative Philology at Yale University (email dated September 4, 2002). Second selection from Tobit 4:5–21 (New Revised Standard Version).

The Avesta

(1) Just as the lord in accord with truth must be chosen, so also the judgment in accord with truth. Establish a rule of actions stemming from an existence of good thinking for the sake of the Wise One and for the lord whom they established as pastor for the needy dependents.

(2) Truth exists as the very best good thing. It exists under your will.

Desire the truth for what is the very best truth.

The Book of Tobit

Revere the Lord all your days, my son, and refuse to sin or to transgress his commandments. Live uprightly all the days of your life, and do not walk in the ways of wrongdoing; for those who act in accordance with truth will prosper in all their activities. To all those who practice righteousness, give alms from your possessions, and do not let your eye begrudge the gift when you make it. Do not turn your face away from anyone who is poor, and the face of God will not be turned away from you. If you have many possessions, make your gift from them in proportion; if few, do not be afraid to give according to the little you have. So you will be laying up a good treasure for yourself against the day of necessity. For almsgiving delivers from death and keeps you from going into the Darkness. Indeed, almsgiving, for all who practice it, is an excellent offering in the presence of the Most High.

. . . For in pride there is ruin and great confusion. And in idleness there is loss and dire poverty, because idleness is the mother of famine.

Do not keep over until the next day the wages of those who work for you, but pay them at once. If you serve God you will receive payment. Watch yourself, my son, in everything you do, and discipline yourself in all your conduct. And what you hate, do not do to anyone. Do not drink wine to excess or let drunkenness go with you on your way. Give some of your food to the hungry, and some of your clothing to the naked. Give all your surplus as alms, and do not let your eye begrudge your giving of alms. Place your bread on the grave of the righteous, but give none to sinners. Seek advice from every wise person and do not despise any useful counsel. At all times bless the Lord God, and ask him that your ways may be made straight and that all your paths and plans may prosper. For none of the nations has understanding, but the Lord himself will give them good counsel; but if he chooses otherwise, he casts down to the deepest Hades. So now, my child, remember these commandments, and do not let them be erased from your heart.

And, now my son, let me explain to you that I left ten talents of silver in trust with Gabael son of Gabrias, at Rages in Media. Do not be afraid, my son, because we have become poor. You have great wealth if you fear God and flee from every sin and do what is good in the sight of the Lord your God.

QUESTIONS FOR ANALYSIS

▶ What is the single most important value of the Zoroastrians?

▶ What does Tobit tell his son to do? Which of Tobit's instructions show the influence of Zoroastrianism?

A system of government couriers made excellent use of these roads, as Herodotus remarks:

> There is nothing on earth faster than these couriers. The service is a Persian invention, and it goes like this, according to what I was told. Men and horses are stationed a day's travel apart, a man and a horse for each of the days needed to cover the journey. These men neither snow nor rain nor heat nor gloom of night stay from the swiftest possible completion of their appointed stage.

Traveling at a breathtaking 90 miles (145 km) each day, government couriers could cover the 1,600 miles (2,575 km) of the Royal Road in less than twenty days, and ordinary travelers, also allowed to use the road, could do so in three months.[3] The couriers were crucial to the army's success because generals could communicate easily with one another across large expanses of territory.

The Persian army was responsible for a long string of military conquests. Cyrus began from his base in Persis and headed north to Ecbatana (ek-buh-TAH-nuh) (modern-day Hamadan) in central Iran. In 547–546 B.C.E., his troops then moved north and west into Anatolia (modern-day Turkey), a region called Lydia in ancient times whose capital was Sardis. A busy commercial center in an enormously wealthy region, Sardis became the most important city in the western part of the empire. The riverbeds near Sardis had large deposits of electrum, a naturally occurring alloy of gold and silver. Around 600 B.C.E., the local people gathered the electrum and used it to mint **Lydian coins,** the first metal coins made anywhere in the world.

After a series of successful military campaigns, Cyrus conquered the various Ionian ports on the eastern Aegean, Syria, Palestine, and Babylon. He did not attempt to change their cultures but made offerings to local gods and allowed his subjects to continue to worship as they had before. He allowed the Jews, who had been forcibly deported to Babylon, to return home, ending the sixty-year-long Babylonian Captivity (see Chapter 2). Modern scholarship indicates that the Hebrew concepts of the afterlife and of the Devil arose after the Babylonian Captivity, and some attribute these new ideas to the influence of Zoroastrianism.

The Persian army was not invincible. In 530 B.C.E. it entered the unfamiliar terrain of Central Asia and attacked the Massagetae (mass-uh-GET-aye) peoples east of the Amu Darya River. The Persians, Herodotus reports, were able initially to gain the advantage by offering the Massagetae tribes wine so that they fell drunk, but the fierce Massagetae recovered and defeated the Persians in hand-to-hand combat. Cyrus died while campaigning in Massagetae territory.

• **Lydian coins** The first metal coins in the world, dating to ca. 600 B.C.E. Made from electrum, a naturally occurring alloy of gold and silver collected from the riverbeds in Lydia, a region on the Aegean coast of modern-day Turkey.

Darius's Coup, 522 B.C.E.

Cyrus's son Cambyses (kam-BEE-zuhs) resumed the conquests and conquered Egypt and Ethiopia before dying in 522 B.C.E. A group of Zoroastrian priests kept his death secret, placed a Magi priest named Gaumata (GOW-mah-tah) on the throne, and ruled briefly in Cambyses's name. In the same year Darius I led a group of conspirators who killed the pretender. At the time of the murder the conspirators had not yet agreed on the political system they would implement. Persuaded by Darius that monarchy was the best system (see chapter opener), they agreed to choose the future king by seeing whose horse neighed first after the sun came up. Darius's wily groom made sure that his master's horse did so first, and Darius became *king of kings,* the Persian term for the ruler of the empire.

Darius commemorated his accession to power in an extraordinary inscription at Behistun, the site of a steep cliff. Stone steps led 300 feet (100 m) from the road to the cliff face, but they were removed after the inscription was completed.

🔲 **Darius's Victory: The Stone Relief at Behistun, Iran**   In 522 B.C.E., Darius ordered this stone relief commemorating his victory over his rivals to be carved over 300 feet (100 m) above the road below. In it, Darius triumphantly places his left foot on the deposed Magi priest Gaumata, who lies dead on his back with his arms pointing vertically upward. The eight tribal leaders that Darius defeated are shown on the right; the larger figure with the pointed hat was added later. Above the human figures floats the winged Ahura Mazda, who looks on approvingly.   (Henry Rawlinson, *The Persian Cuneiform Inscription at Behistun,* 1846)

This large rock relief was 18 feet (5.5 m) long and 10 feet (3 m) tall, with blocks of text in different languages around it bragging of the murder of the imposter-king. At the simplest level, Darius's message was obvious: if you oppose me, this is what will happen to you. Darius justified Gaumata's murder by appealing to a higher authority:

> There was not a man, neither a Persian nor a Mede nor anyone of our family, who could have taken the kingdom from Gaumata the Magian. The people feared him greatly.... There was no one who dared say anything about Gaumata the Magian until I came. Then I prayed to Ahura Mazda. Ahura Mazda bore me aid.... Then I with a few men slew that Gaumata the Magian.... Ahura Mazda bestowed the kingdom upon me.[1]

Darius's inscription differs from those of Ashoka (see Chapter 3) and the Qin founder (Chapter 4), both of whom had inherited the throne from their fathers. Darius, however, had killed the reigning king, and his distant family ties to Cyrus did not entitle him to the throne. He married Artystone (AR-tih-stoe-nay), daughter of Cyrus and half-sister of Cambyses, to bolster his claim to the Achaemenid throne.

Darius's use of languages also differed from that of Ashoka and the Qin founder. The text framing the Behistun relief appears in three languages: Elamite (EE-luhm-ite), the original language of administration of the Achaemenids; Babylonian, the language they adopted as their administrative language; and Old Persian, which

THE PARADE OF NATIONS AT DARIUS'S PALACE AT PERSEPOLIS

To document his accomplishments, Darius built an enormous audience hall in Persepolis in modern-day Iran. The hall held 10,000 people and was 62,500 square feet (5,800 sq m), with a roof supported by columns more than 60 feet (20 m) high. Although the original wooden buildings, which were lavishly decorated with curtains, tiles, and paintings, no longer stand, the surviving stone reliefs show the many different peoples of the Achaemenid Empire coming to pay homage to their ruler.

The stairways leading to the audience hall have been called "perhaps the most perfect flight of stairs ever built."[*] Alongside the staircases, stone masons carved reliefs of twenty-three distinct peoples bringing gifts to the king to celebrate the coming of spring, one of the most important ritual occasions in the Zoroastrian calendar. On one side of the staircase the masons depicted the peoples of the empire as seen from the left, and on the facing side, as seen from the right. Each view of the procession occupies three tiers stretching 300 feet (92 m) long, making the frieze the largest mirror image in the world.

The top register, now partially destroyed, shows different regiments in the Achaemenid army: the Persians and the Medes have different headdresses. The soldiers lead the king's horse, two empty chariots, a tent, and the throne for the king. The king himself is not shown.

On the lower tiers, trees divide the friezes into frames that show a small group of men from each place, wearing their native dress and led by a Persian or Median envoy. They carry local products as gifts for the king and guide a native animal. The animals reflect the great reach of the empire: horses from Syria, a humped bull and a wild donkey from Pakistan, a two-humped camel from Central Asia, and an antelope and a giraffe from Ethiopia. The animals are more detailed than the people, whose faces are the same and can be distinguished only by their clothing and different hairstyles.

The portraits capture the essence of the Achaemenid Empire. Each subject people occupies the same amount of space in the tableau; tall animals like giraffes are scaled down so that they take as much space as smaller animals like sheep and horses. Each group wears its national dress and offers its own distinctive gifts, while participating in a single procession designed to honor the Persian ruler.

The timing of the monument reveals something important about the Achaemenid concept of empire. Darius began construction in 515 B.C.E., soon after he came to power, and the complex provided vivid testimony of his conquests of many different peoples. Xerxes completed the monument after the 480 B.C.E. defeat at Salamis, but the Achaemenid vision of empire remained unchanged. The omission of certain Greek peoples is the only indication that the expansion of the Persian Empire had come to an end.

The facing page shows a small section of the frieze taken from the left side of the staircase.

QUESTION FOR ANALYSIS

 How did the Persians and the Greeks illustrate their differing concepts of empire at Persepolis and the Acropolis?

---

[*]R. Ghirshman and E. Herzfeld, *Persepolis: The Achaemenian Capital* (Tehran: Mirdashti Farhangsara, 1999), p. 33.

These Scythians, from the region north of the Black Sea, wear their characteristic pointed hoods and offer a fine horse.

This magnificent two-humped Bactrian camel follows Central Asians bearing cups and other gifts from the region east of the Caspian Sea.

These seven men from the impoverished Assyrian empire, defeated in 612 B.C.E., offer low-cost objects: a pair of rams, animal skins, and bowls.

(© Corbis)

The Ionians, from the Aegean coast of modern-day Turkey, offer folded bolts of cloth, and bowls, most likely of gold.

These trees, like vertical lines in a comic strip, divide the different delegations in the Parade of Nations from one another. Each delegation is led by either a fully robed Mede, as in the bottom panel, or a bare-chested Persian guide, as directly above.

This Armenian groom keeps a close watch on this fine steed, while the countrymen behind him carry bolts of cloth.

the royal family spoke at home. All three were written in cuneiform script. The Qin founder used a single language, confident that he could communicate with his subjects in Chinese; Ashoka had the same text translated into the different languages spoken in the various parts of the Mauryan Empire. But Darius ruled a multilingual empire in which people living in the same place spoke different languages. For this reason, Darius had rubbings of the inscription made and distributed translations of it throughout the empire; fragments of an Aramaic translation on papyrus have even been found in Egypt. Most of Darius's subjects were illiterate; even the king had to have the Old Persian text read aloud to him.

When Darius commissioned the Behistun inscription, he had no way of knowing that his dynasty would last. His account largely matches Herodotus's except for a few details (they agree on the names of six of the conspirators, but not the seventh), but Herodotus has the advantage of hindsight: he knew that Darius became one of the most important Achaemenid rulers. During his reign, the empire expanded to include Thrace in northern Greece and the Indus Valley in present-day Pakistan, but not the Scythian peoples living south of the Black Sea or the Greeks in Athens (see page 162).

| Achaemenid Administration | Fully aware of the challenges of governing his large empire, Darius instituted a series of far-reaching administrative reforms that held the Persian Empire together for the better part |

of two centuries. He established a flexible administrative and taxation system and implemented a uniform law code for all his subjects.

Seeing himself as transmitting Ahura Mazda's laws to all his subjects, Darius appointed judges for life to administer those laws in his name. Just as on the day of judgment Ahura Mazda would judge each person's good and bad deeds, Persian judges were supposed to examine lawsuits carefully. They were to inquire deeply into the facts of a dispute and to reach a judgment that took into account the previous conduct. Accordingly, a man who had adhered to Zoroastrian teachings and told the truth his entire life was treated more leniently than one who had not.

As they reformed the courts, the Achaemenids also changed the system of taxation. Herodotus explains:

> During the reign of Cyrus and Cambyses there was no fixed tribute at all, the revenue coming from gifts only; and because of his imposition of regular taxes, and other similar measures, the Persians called Darius a huckster, Cambyses a master, and Cyrus a father; the first being out for profit wherever he could get it, the second harsh and arrogant, and the third, merciful and ever working for their well-being.[5]

We must remember that Cyrus had died nearly a century before Herodotus was writing and that Cambyses was reputed to be insane, a judgment with which Herodotus enthusiastically concurred. The view of Darius as a huckster, though, contains an important element of truth: in seeking to put his empire on sound financial footing, Darius revolutionized the way the Persians collected taxes.

Darius divided his empire into provinces called satrapies, each administered by a governor, or satrap. The officials under the satrap were recruited locally, a hallmark of the Persian system. Darius required each satrap to submit a fixed amount of revenue each year, and the taxes due from many of the different regions were assessed in silver. Silver was more convenient because government administrators could use a single system to calculate the empire's revenue and expenses. Darius allowed several regions to pay some of their taxes in other items: Egypt, the empire's breadbasket, was required to forward 120,000 bushels of grain each year. The Indians, Herodotus explains, paid in gold dust, which they collected from riverbeds, while the Ethiopians submitted an annual quota of "two quarts of unrefined gold, two hundred logs of ebony, and twenty elephant tusks."

Archaeologists have found over three thousand baked clay tablets giving the day-to-day accounts of the empire in the ruins of Persepolis (per-SEH-poe-lis), the site of the royal ritual center some 200 miles (360 km) west of Susa. Darius had several wives, but his favorite was Artystone, who possessed her own palace and wielded genuine authority within her own estate. The tablets record her orders to organize banquets and trips, and sometimes the king would even take her with him on military campaigns. Darius frequently gave his wives gifts of food or wine. One such order reads: "King Darius has instructed me: 100 sheep from my property are to be delivered to Queen Artystone."

The friezes at Persepolis illustrate beautifully how Darius ruled over such a diverse empire (see the feature "Visual Evidence: The Parade of Nations at Darius's Palace at Persepolis"). After Darius died in 486 B.C.E., his son Xerxes (ZERK-sees) succeeded him, ruled for twenty years, and completed the complex at Persepolis. But in 465, Xerxes' younger son killed both his father and his elder brother, the designated heir, so that he could succeed to the throne. Royal assassinations occurred frequently over the next one hundred years, and the Achaemenids conquered no new territory, but the administrative structure they originated allowed them to hold on to their empire until 331 B.C.E., when Alexander defeated them (see below).

Ancient Greece and the Mediterranean World, 2000–334 B.C.E.

A branch of the Indo-European speakers reached the Greek peninsula around 2000 B.C.E., earlier than they arrived in either India (see Chapter 3) or Iran (see above) but the same time as the Hittites reached Anatolia. The Greek speakers, as well as the Phoenicians (FOE-knee-shuns) (see page 158), were active traders in the Mediterranean. Although historians sometimes speak of the Phoenician and Greek "empires," neither people had a centralized administration governing many different peoples. Instead, both lived in scattered city-states, whose residents sailed across the seas to establish new outposts that retained their ties to the mother city-state.

Although we tend to think of Greece as a single Greek-speaking entity, whether in earlier times or today, there was no unified nation called "Greece" in the ancient world. Greek speakers thought of themselves as citizens of Athens, Sparta, or the city-state where they lived. By the year 500 B.C.E. Athens emerged as the largest of over one hundred different Greek city-states, and only Athens had a democracy in which all male citizens, some 10 percent of the city's population, could participate equally. In addition to being a military power, Athens was also a cultural center famous for its drama, art, and philosophy.

Greek Expansion in the Mediterranean, 2000–1200 B.C.E. When the Indo-European speakers arrived in Greece, they found that the rocky land of the Greek peninsula, the Aegean coast of Turkey, and the islands of the

Mediterranean offered little grass for their herds. No major rivers flowed in these areas. As the Indo-European migrants shifted from herding to farming, they used irrigation channels to distribute water over their fields. They usually planted barley, which was sturdier than wheat, in the lowlands, olive trees in the foothills, and grapes on the hillsides. It required so much labor to terrace the rocky soil and make fields suitable for cultivation that often the most efficient way to obtain new land was to set sail for the nearest land, frequently visible across a body of water.

The earliest trading centers of the Mediterranean have left ample archaeological evidence. Between 2000 and 1500 B.C.E., the Mediterranean island of Crete was home to a civilization with lavish palaces, well-built roads, bronze metallurgy, and a writing system called Linear A, which has not been deciphered. The archaeologist who discovered the site in the early twentieth century named the residents the Minoans (mih-NO-uhns) after the king Minos (mih-NOHS) who, Greek legends recounted, ruled a large empire with many ships. Archaeologists have found pottery made in the Minoan style all over the Mediterranean and western Asia, evidence of a wide-reaching Minoan trade network.

The remains of the Minoan civilization came to an abrupt end in 1500 B.C.E., probably because the Minoans were conquered by the Mycenaeans (1600–1200 B.C.E.), the earliest ancient civilization based on mainland Greece in the city of Mycenae. The Mycenaeans (my-see-NEE-uhns) used Linear B script, which remained undeciphered until 1952. In that year, an architect and amateur cryptographer, Michael Ventris, realized what no one else had: Linear B was a dialect of Greek. He used his high school ancient Greek to decipher four thousand surviving clay tablets, which unfortunately reveal much about the palace accounting system but little about Mycenaean society.

Archaeologists are not certain whether the Trojan Wars between the Greeks and the Trojans living across the Aegean in modern-day Turkey occurred as the poet Homer (ca. 800 B.C.E.) described them centuries later in his epic poems *The Odyssey* and *The Iliad*. If they did, it was during the time of the Mycenaean civilization. When the international system broke down in 1200 B.C.E. (see Chapter 2), Linear B fell into disuse, and the final archaeological evidence of Mycenaean culture dates to no later than 1200 B.C.E.

The Phoenicians and the World's First Alphabet

Around this time, another seafaring people, the **Phoenicians,** appeared in the western Mediterranean. The Greeks called this people "red men," *Phoinikes,* or Phoenicians in English, most likely because they produced an extremely rare reddish-purple dye made from the glands of snails. The Phoenicians began to expand outward from their homeland in modern-day Lebanon around 900 B.C.E. They used a new type of writing system: an alphabet of twenty-two letters, each representing a different consonant. Unlike cuneiform, this alphabet had no pictorial symbols and depicted only sounds. Like many other scripts, Phoenician did not record vowels, which most native speakers can readily supply. (Consider the following sentence from a subway advertisement for a secretarial school: f y cn rd ths, thn y cn lrn t wrt qckly.) The phonetic alphabet was surely one of the most influential innovations in the ancient world because it was much faster to learn an alphabet than to memorize a symbolic script like cuneiform.

By 814 B.C.E., the Phoenicians had established one outpost at Carthage (KARthudge) (modern-day Tunis in Tunisia) and subsequently built others at different ports along the North African coast as well as the southern coast of modern-day

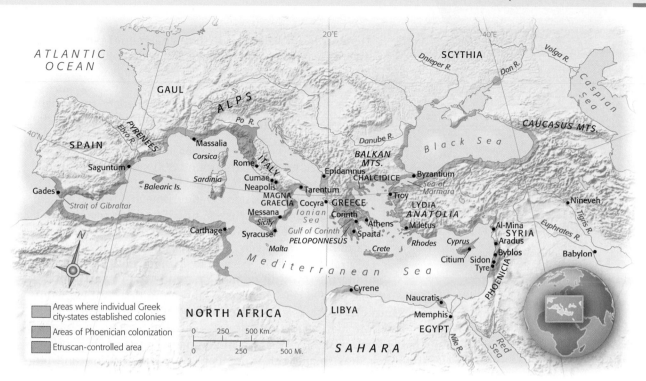

🌐 **MAP 6.1**

Greek and Phoenician Settlement in the Mediterranean   Starting in 900 B.C.E., the Phoenicians expanded westward into the Mediterranean from their base along the eastern shore; they settled on the island of Sardinia and the North African shore. In 800 B.C.E., settlers from different Greek-speaking city-states left their homelands and formed more than 250 city-states in the eastern Mediterranean and Black Seas.

Ⓒ Interactive Map

Spain (see Map 6.1). Herodotus credited the Phoenicians with the discovery that Africa was surrounded by water except where it joins Asia. He described a Phoenician voyage circumnavigating Africa sometime around 600 B.C.E.: "Every autumn they [the voyagers] put in where they were on the African coast, sowed a patch of ground, and waited for next year's harvest. Then, having got in their grain, they put to sea again, and after two full years rounded Gibraltar in the course of the third, and returned to Egypt." These early voyagers realized that prevailing winds and currents made sailing clockwise around Africa from the Red Sea much easier than sailing counterclockwise from Gibraltar.

The Phoenicians founded new colonies by sending groups of men and women to coastal towns around the Mediterranean and even beyond.[6] We learn this from a Greek account about the Phoenician explorer Hanno, who set off from Carthage in 500 B.C.E. with sixty vessels and thirty thousand men and women. Hanno passed a river and two large gulfs and then captured three "gorillas," probably chimpanzees or baboons. Then he turned back. The vagueness of the description makes it difficult to know how far the Phoenicians traveled, but they may have reached Sierra Leone.

The veracity of both of these accounts—the Phoenician circumnavigation of Africa and the Phoenician colonization of West Africa—is much debated because of the lack of independent confirmation, but it is certain that the oceangoing Phoenicians transmitted their knowledge of geography along with their alphabet to the Greeks. The Phoenicians retained control of the western and southern

Mediterranean throughout the Achaemenid period until their defeat by ancient Rome in 202 B.C.E. (see Chapter 7).

The Rise of the Greek City-State, 800–500 B.C.E.

Since no materials in ancient Greek survive from between 1200 and 900 B.C.E., there is a gap in our knowledge. A new era in Greek history starts around 800 B.C.E., when various regions—including mainland Greece, the islands of the Aegean and the eastern Mediterranean, and the Aegean coast of Turkey—coalesced into city-states (*polis;* plural, *poleis*). The residents of these different places began to farm more intensively, and the resulting increase in agricultural production permitted a diversification of labor among the growing population: while the vast majority of people farmed the agricultural land around the cities, a tiny minority were able to settle inside walled cities. These cities had both markets for agricultural goods and temples to different gods. Each of these city-states, including the surrounding agricultural area, was small, with a population of between five and ten thousand people, but it was self-sufficient, having its own courts, law code, and army (see Map 6.1).

■ Woman Temple Priest in Ancient Athens
Women temple priests played a major, if not always documented, role in ancient Greek religion. This amphora, dated to the 500s B.C.E., places a woman priest at the center of the painting because of her crucial role in the ritual being performed. She raises branches and sprinkles water on an altar in preparation for the sacrifice of the bull to the goddess Athena (*right*). This scene may portray an actual sacrifice performed on the Acropolis, where the Parthenon featured a similar giant statue of the goddess carrying a shield. (Staatliche Museen Antikensamlung 1686. Bildarchiv Preussischer Kulturbsitz/Art Resource, NY)

These city-states each had a guardian deity whose temple was located within the city walls. The Greeks believed in a pantheon of many gods headed by Zeus and his wife Hera. Each god possessed specific traits: Athena, the guardian god of Athens, was a goddess of war and of weaving. The Greeks told many myths about the gods and goddesses, often focusing on their attempts to intervene in the human world.

The citizens of the city-state gathered during festivals to offer animal sacrifices to the gods, with whom they communicated through prayers and oracles. The most famous oracle was at Delphi, on the Gulf of Corinth, where individuals and city-states consulted Apollo's priests to learn what would happen in the future before making any important decisions. People traveled all over the Aegean to pray for medical cures and to participate in temple festivals such as the Olympic games, which were held every four years since 776 B.C.E. at the temple to Zeus at Olympia in the Peloponnese (see the feature "World History in Today's World: The Olympics").

An important breakthrough in shipbuilding occurred around 800 B.C.E. that facilitated such travel. Greek shipbuilders added a partial deck to boats that covered the center but left an open aisle along the sides. (Earlier boats, whether powered by oars or sails, had no decks.) Easily capable of traversing the Mediterranean, these improved boats made it possible for the citizens of the different city-states of Greece to establish more than 250 different city-states along the coasts of the Mediterranean and Black Seas (see Map 6.1).

Like Mesopotamian city-states, the Greek city-states remained linked to the mother city through trade. Ships carried olive oil, wine, and pottery produced by

The Olympics

The Olympic games formally began in 776 B.C.E. (the earliest date that can be verified in ancient Greek history) at the temple to Zeus in Olympia, in the western Peloponnesus. In 720 B.C.E., one competitor started the race wearing some kind of garment but shed it by the end of the race; after his victory, no competitor ever wore clothes again.

At first competitors participated in only a 656-foot-long (200-m) footrace, but the number of events increased quickly. By the year 600 B.C.E., they included the 1,312-foot-long (400-m) footrace, the pentathlon of five different events in one, wrestling, boxing, and chariot races. At their height the games ran for five full days and included the first day, set aside for prayers and oath-taking, and a final day of competition and of feasting and crowning of the winners. Tens of thousands of people who did not participate traveled from all over the Mediterranean to see the races and to enjoy the feasting and drinking.

Only the victor of each event received a prize, always a simple wreath of leaves. Although the award of a wreath makes the Olympics seem an amateur event, most winners also received tangible rewards from their home city-states. Athletes sometimes competed for city-states where they had not been born simply to attain the higher rewards they offered. Winners from Athens were particularly fortunate: the city-state awarded them the equivalent of two years' income, a permanent tax break, and free meals for life.

Cheating did occur, even though it was considered an insult to the gods and was punished severely by fines or beatings. Athletes lied about their age so they could compete in the boys' events, which were less competitive. Wrestlers rubbed oil on their bodies so that their opponents could not get a grip on them.

The Olympic games occurred every four years until 393 C.E., when the Roman emperor forbade the worship of pagan gods (see Chapter 7). Inspired by the success of hundreds of festivals bearing the name *Olympics,* in 1896 a French aristocrat revived the games in Athens with the explicit intention of giving amateur athletes from all over the world a chance to compete. This inclusiveness, though, is new: the ancient games were for Greeks only.

the Greeks to other regions, where they obtained lumber to make more ships. The leaders of the mother city-state appointed a founder to lead the expedition; citizens of the mother city-state were always welcome, as were settlers from other city-states.

During this period of vibrant growth and expansion, the Greeks adopted the twenty-two original consonants of the Phoenicians, created vowels by using leftover Phoenician letters for sounds not present in Greek, and added three new letters. The first inscriptions in the new Greek alphabet date to 730 B.C.E. This new alphabet underlies many modern alphabets, including that of English, because the vowels and consonants of ancient Greek could be used to represent the sounds of other languages.

During the eighth and seventh centuries B.C.E., most Greek city-states were governed by powerful landowning families, but around 600 B.C.E. several city-states enacted reforms. Sparta became one of the first to grant extensive rights to its citizens. Only the descendents of original Spartans could be citizen-soldiers, who fought full-time and were not permitted to farm the land or engage in business. A second group, called "dwellers around," were descended from the first peoples to be conquered by the Spartans; entitled to own land, they also worked as craftsmen and traders but could not vote. The lowest-ranking group, full-time state slaves (Helots), cultivated the land of the citizens. Because their husbands were often away at war, Spartan women ran their estates and had more freedom than women in other city-states, yet they did not vote.

Future Spartan citizens joined the army as young children and received an austere military upbringing; only when successfully completed could they become citizens. Citizens (but not the state slaves) exercised a limited veto over the policies enacted by a council of elders who ruled in conjunction with two kings. This was the government system Herodotus chose as an example of oligarchy (see chapter opener).

It took more than one hundred years for Athens to establish democracy. The most famous reformer, Solon (SOH-luhn), became the civilian head of state of Athens in 594 B.C.E. and launched a reform that abolished the obligation to pay one-sixth of one's crop as tax to the state. He also cancelled debts, which made it possible for former debtors to acquire and farm their own land. Athenian citizens formed four groups, defined by how much property they owned; all citizens could participate in the assembly, the lawmaking body.

In 508 B.C.E., a group of aristocrats extended Solon's reforms further and established direct democracy. All citizens above the age of 20—roughly thirty thousand men, or 10 percent of the population—could join the assembly. Many, however, were too busy to attend the frequent meetings, which occurred as much as forty times a year.

Women, who could not serve as soldiers or become citizens, never participated in the assembly. The women who enjoyed the greatest security were married; only children born to such couples were legitimate. Athenian men had many other sexual partners, both male and female: prostitutes whom they visited occasionally, concubines whom they supported financially, and slaves who could not say no to their owners.

Roughly two-fifths of Athens's population, some 120,000 people, were slaves, who also did not participate in the assembly. Many different types of slaves existed: those who had skills and lived with their masters had less arduous lives than those who worked in the fields or in the silver mines, where working conditions were dangerous.

The Greco-Persian Wars, 490–479 B.C.E.

The Athenian army was particularly effective because it consisted of citizen-soldiers with a powerful commitment to defend their home city-state. Greek soldiers, called hoplites (HAHP-lites), could defeat the Persians in hand-to-hand combat because they had better shields, stronger armor, and more effective formations. The soldiers were divided into units, called phalanxes, eight men deep. If the first row of soldiers was broken, the row behind them pressed forward to meet the attack.

The first important Athenian victory came at the battle of Marathon in 490 B.C.E. The Persian ruler Darius sent a force to punish the Athenians for supporting an uprising against the Persians by the Greeks living on the east coast of the Aegean. The Athenian forces of 11,000 men attacked the Persian army of 25,000 when they were foraging for food and, in a stunning reversal of what every informed person expected, won a decisive victory on the plain of Marathon. (The English word *marathon* comes from a later legend about a messenger running over 20 miles [32 km] from Marathon to Athens to announce the victory.) Herodotus's tally of the casualties underlines the immensity of the Athenian victory: the Athenians lost 192 men; the Persians, 6,400.

After Darius died in 486 B.C.E. (see above), his son Xerxes (r. 486–465 B.C.E.) decided to avenge his father's defeat and gathered a huge army that he hoped would frighten the Greeks into surrendering. But Sparta and Athens for the first time organized a coalition of the Greek city-states that fought the Persians for control of a mountain pass north of Athens at Thermopylae (thuhr-MOP-uh-lie). The Greeks held the Persians off until an informer told the Persians about a secret path around the pass. Realizing that they had been betrayed, many of the Greeks fled, but three hundred Spartans fought to their deaths. The victorious Persians then sacked the deserted city of Athens.

The Greeks regrouped, and the Athenian naval commanders took advantage of their superior knowledge of the local terrain to secure a surprising Greek victory at Salamis. Xerxes fell for a Greek trap: he believed an infiltrator who reported that the Greeks planned to retreat from the narrow bay of Salamis (SAH-lah-miss). Xerxes ordered his men to stay up all night to watch for the Greek withdrawal, with the result that the Persians were exhausted when the naval battle began.

In recounting the battle, an important turning point in the war, Herodotus highlighted the role of **Artemisia** (fl. 480 B.C.E.), the woman ruler of Halicarnassus, Herodotus's hometown, who had become queen on the death of her husband and who, like all conquered peoples in the Persian Empire, fought alongside the Persians. The Persians had a fleet of 1,207 triremes (TRY-reems), three-story boats powered by rowers on each level, of which Artemisia (ar-TEM-ee-zee-uh) commanded 5. "She sailed with the fleet," Herodotus explains, "in spite of the fact that she had a grown-up son and that there was consequently no necessity for her to do so," implying that he would not have found her participation worthy of comment if her son had still been a child. Artemisia fascinated Herodotus because she differed so much from well-off Athenian women, who stayed indoors and devoted themselves to managing their households.

Herodotus employed contrasts to heighten his comparisons between Greeks and non-Greeks. The Athenians enjoyed the benefits of democracy while the Persians suffered under the tyranny of Xerxes. Greek men were strong while Persian men were weak, which is why Xerxes had to depend on Artemisia. In the inverted world of the war, the only Persian commander worthy of mention in Herodotus's eyes is the Greek woman Artemisia.

Contrary to all expectations, the Greeks defeated the Persians. Defeat, however, had little impact on the Persian Empire except to define its western edge. Xerxes returned home to an empire just as large as his father's, and no Achaemenid ruler after Xerxes ever succeeded in adding Greece to his empire.

●Artemisia (fl. 480 B.C.E.) The woman ruler of Halicarnassus, on the Aegean coast of modern-day Turkey, who fought with the Persians against the Greeks at the battle of Salamis.

Politics and Culture in Athens, 480–404 B.C.E.

During the century after the defeat of the Persians, Athens experienced unprecedented cultural growth. The new literary genre of Greek tragedy took shape, and the Athenians constructed the great temple to Athena on the Acropolis (uh-KRAW-poe-lis), the great bluff overlooking the city, as a lasting monument to Greek victory against the Persians.

In 472 B.C.E., the playwright Aeschylus (525–456 B.C.E.) wrote *The Persians*, the earliest Greek tragedy surviving today. Set in the Persian capital at Susa, the play opens with a chorus of elderly men speculating about Xerxes' attempted invasion of Greece because they have had no news for so long. One-quarter of the way through the play, a lone messenger arrives and mournfully announces:

> A single stroke has brought about the ruin of great
> Prosperity, the flower of Persia fallen and gone.
> Oh oh! To be the first to bring bad news is bad;
> But necessity demands the roll of suffering
> Be opened, Persians.[7]

Writing only eight years after the war, Aeschylus (ESS-kih-luhs), himself a veteran, exaggerates the losses to make the audience sympathize with the Persians and emphasize the shared humanity of the Persians and the Greeks. Xerxes' mother, the Queen, struggles to understand why the Persians have lost: they have violated natural law, she eventually realizes, by trying to conquer what did not belong to them. *The Persians* is the first of over one hundred tragedies written during the fifth century B.C.E. by three great playwrights—Aeschylus, Sophocles (sof-uh-KLEEZ) (496–406 B.C.E.), and Euripides (you-RIP-uh-deez) (ca. 485–406 B.C.E.)—that show individuals, both male and female, struggling to understand their fates.

In 478 B.C.E., the Athenians formed the Delian (DEE-lih-yuhn) League, a group of city-states whose stated purpose was to drive the Persians from the Greek world. After several victories in the 470s against the Persians, the Persian threat was eliminated, prompting some of the league's members to withdraw. Athens invaded these cities and forced them to become its subjects. In the 460s a general named Pericles (PER-eh-kleez) (ca. 495–429 B.C.E.) emerged as the most popular leader in the city, and in 454 B.C.E. the Athenians moved the league's treasury to Athens, ending all pretence of an alliance among equals. This was the closest that Athens came to having an empire, but its possessions were all Greek-speaking, and its control was short-lived.

■ **The Acropolis: A Massive Construction Project Completed in Only Fifteen Years**   Built between 447 and 432 B.C.E., the Parthenon was a two-roomed building surrounded by columns over 34 feet (10 m) tall; one of the interior rooms held a magnificent statue of Athena, now lost. Beautiful friezes inside the roofs and above the columns portrayed the legendary battles of the Trojan War, in which the Greek forces (symbolizing the Athenians and their allies) defeated the Trojans (the ancient counterpart of the Persian enemy), whom the Athenians had only recently defeated.   (Georg Gerster/Photo Researchers, Inc.)

In the early years after the victory at Salamis, the Athenians had vowed never to build anything on the Acropolis so that they would not forget the Persian destruction of their city. But the city's mood changed as the memory of the war receded. In 449 B.C.E., Pericles signed a peace treaty with Persia on behalf of the Delian League and used the league's funds to finance a building campaign to make Athens as physically impressive as it was politically powerful.

The centerpiece of the city's reconstruction, the Parthenon, was both a temple to Athena, the city's guardian deity, and a memorial to those who had died in the wars with Persia. As the many artists and artisans worked together over the course of fifteen years, they developed a collective style that many regard as the pinnacle of Greek artistic achievement. Once completed, the Parthenon expressed the Athenians' desire to be the most advanced people of the ancient world.

The Spartans, however, felt that they, not Athens, should be the leader of the Greeks. Since the 460s, tensions had been growing between the two city-states, and from 431 to 404 B.C.E. Athens and Sparta, and their allied city-states, engaged in the Peloponnesian

War. Since Athens was a naval power and Sparta a land power, the struggle was protracted, and Sparta, with the help of the Persians, finally defeated Athens in 404 B.C.E. Much as the long wars between the city-states of Tikal and Kalak'mul resulted in the decline of the Maya (see Chapter 5), the long and drawn-out Peloponnesian War wore both Sparta and Athens down, creating an opportunity for the rulers of the northern region of Macedon to conquer Greece (see below).

Athens as a Center for the Study of Philosophy

Even during these years of conflict, Athens was home to several of the most famous philosophers in history: Socrates (469–399 B.C.E.) taught Plato (429–347 B.C.E.), and Plato in turn taught **Aristotle** (384–322 B.C.E.). Their predecessors, the earliest Greek philosophers, were active around 600 B.C.E. in the city-state of Miletus, just north of Halicarnassus on the eastern coast of the Aegean Sea. Members of this school argued that everything in the universe originated in a single element: some proposed water; others, air. Their findings may seem naive, but they were the first to believe in rational explanations rather than crediting everything to divine intervention, and the Athenian philosophers developed this insight further.

One of the most famous Athenian philosophers, Socrates (sock-ruh-TEEZ), wrote nothing down, so we must depend on the accounts of his student Plato (PLAY-toe). He perfected a style of teaching, now known as the Socratic (suh-KRAT-ick) method, in which the instructor asks the student questions without revealing his own views. Many of the dialogues reported by Plato stress the Greek concept of *aretê* (virtue or excellence), which people can attain by doing right. Virtue was the highest good for Socrates, who believed that wisdom allows one to determine the right course of action.

Immediately after Sparta defeated Athens in the Peloponnesian War, a small group of men formed an oligarchy in Athens in 404–403 B.C.E., but they were overthrown by a democratic government. Some of those in the new government suspected Socrates of opposing democracy because he had associated with those in the oligarchy. In 399 B.C.E. they brought him to trial on vague charges of impiety (not believing in the gods) and corrupting the city's youth. Found guilty by a jury numbering in the hundreds, Socrates did not apologize but insisted that he had been right all along. His death in 399 B.C.E. from drinking poisonous hemlock, the traditional means of execution, became one of the most famous infamous executions in history. After his death the Athenians tried to modify their democratic government in various ways, but democratic rule ended in 322 B.C.E.

Plato continued Socrates' method of teaching by asking questions. He founded the Academy, a gymnasium where he could teach students a broad curriculum emphasizing ethics. Gymnasiums had begun simply as an open ground for soldiers to train, but they had evolved into schools for young boys where they engaged in exercise and studied texts. Plato taught that people could choose the just course of action by using reason to reconcile the conflicting demands of spirit and desire. Reason alone determined the individual's best interests. Plato admitted boys to the Academy as well as some girls. Scholars debate the extent of literacy among Greek women; some contend that all well-off women could read and write, while others think that only a small minority could.

Plato's student, Aristotle (AH-riss-tot-uhl), was not a native of Athens but was born in Macedon, a northern peripheral region. He entered Plato's Academy at the age of 17 in 367 B.C.E. and studied with him for twenty years. He left Athens after the death of Plato in 347 B.C.E. and returned to Macedon, where he later served as

● **Aristotle** (384–322 B.C.E.) Greek philosopher who encouraged his students to observe the natural world and explain logically how they proceeded from their starting assumptions. This system of reasoning shapes how we present written arguments today.

CL **Primary Source: Apologia** *Learn why Socrates was condemned to death, and why he refused to stop questioning the wisdom of his countrymen.*

CL **Primary Source:**
Aristotle Describes a
Well-Administered Polis
*Aristotle discusses how a
state and its citizens must
become virtuous in order to
achieve the best form of
government.*

a tutor to Alexander, the son of the Macedonian ruler Philip (382–336 B.C.E.). Aristotle did not share Socrates' and Plato's optimism that knowledge alone would result in ethical behavior because he did not accept their view that human nature was good. He emphasized, instead, that people had to study hard so that they could gain control over their desires.

Aristotle had a broad view of what constituted a proper education. Observing the round shadow the earth cast on the moon during eclipses, he concluded that the earth was a sphere and lay at the center of the universe. He urged his students to observe live animals in nature and was one of the first to realize that whales and dolphins were mammals, a discovery ignored for nearly two thousand years. Aristotle required that his students identify their starting assumptions and explain logically how they proceeded from one point to the next. This system of reasoning remained influential in the Islamic world and Europe long after his death and continues to shape how we present written arguments today.

⬤ Alexander the Great and His Successors, 334 B.C.E.–30 B.C.E.

• **Alexander of
Macedon** (r. 336–323
B.C.E.) Also known as
Alexander the Great.
Son of Philip of Mace-
don. Defeated the last
Achaemenid ruler in 331
B.C.E. and ruled the
former Achaemenid
Empire until his death.

In the course of his lifetime Aristotle witnessed the decline of Athens, which never recovered from the costs of the Peloponnesian War, and the rise of his native region of Macedon. Philip and his son **Alexander of Macedon** (also called Alexander the Great) were autocrats untouched by the Athenian tradition of democracy: as generals they ordered their professional armies to obey them and governed conquered territory as if the inhabitants were part of their army. Many scholars use the term *Helenization* to describe the process by which societies, peoples, and places during Alexander's rule became more Greek (the Greek word for Greece is *Hellas*). As Alexander's army conquered territory, his Greek-speaking soldiers encountered many different peoples living in West, Central, and South Asia. Some settled in these regions and built communities that resembled those they had left behind in Greece.

Recent historians have questioned this depiction of Alexander as a champion of Greek culture, noting how much he emulated the Persians. After the death of the last Achaemenid ruler, Darius III, Alexander portrayed himself as a defender of the Achaemenid tradition and adopted many Achaemenid practices, sometimes to the dismay of his Greek followers. Newly discovered leather scrolls show that four years after defeating the Achaemenids, Alexander's government issued orders under his name in the same format and language as the Achaemenids.[8] The borders of his empire overlapped almost entirely with those of the Achaemenid Empire, and his army, administration, and tax system were all modeled on those of the Achaemenids. After his death, Alexander's empire broke into three major sections, each ruled by a successor dynasty which followed Achaemenid practice.

Philip and Alexander: From Macedon to Empire, 359–323 B.C.E.

Lying to the north of Greece, Macedon was a peripheral region with no cities and little farming where Greek was spoken. Originally a barren region, it became a powerful kingdom under Philip II (r. 359–336 B.C.E.), who reorganized the army into a professional fighting force of paid soldiers. Philip and Alexander built empires by amassing wealth from the peoples they conquered.

Philip created, and Alexander inherited, an army more powerful than any of its rivals. Philip reorganized his army by training them to use close-packed infantry formations and by arming some of the infantry with pikes 17 feet (5 m) long. Alexander's infantry, who carried the same long pikes, formed two formidable groups on the battlefield. The infantry phalanx had 15,000 men who fought in rows and were almost invincible; 1,800 cavalry aided them by attacking the enemy on either side.

Following his father's assassination, Alexander defeated the Persian forces in 331 B.C.E., and in 330 B.C.E. one of the Persian satraps killed the reigning Achaemenid emperor Darius III (r. 336–330 B.C.E.). This turn of events allowed Alexander to take over the Persian Empire intact; he did not alter the administrative structure of satrapies. A brilliant military strategist, Alexander led his troops over eleven thousand miles in eight years, going as far as Egypt and north India, but did not significantly expand the territory of the Persian Empire (see Map 6.2).

Alexander constantly wrestled with the issue of how to govern. Should he rule as a Macedonian or adopt the Achaemenid model? To the horror of his Macedonian troops, he donned Persian clothing and expected them to prostrate themselves before him as the Achaemenid subjects honored the Persian king. When his senior advisers protested, Alexander made one of many compromises during his thirteen-year reign: he required the Persians, but not the Macedonians, to prostrate themselves. Like the Achaemenids, Alexander married women to cement his political alliances; his wife Roxane was a native of Samarkand, one of the cities that most vigorously resisted his rule.

The farther they traveled from Greece, the more unhappy Alexander's men grew. In 326 B.C.E., when they reached the banks of the Hyphasis River in India, they refused to go on, forcing Alexander to turn back. After a long and difficult march along the northern edge of the Indian Ocean, Alexander and the remnants of his army returned to Babylon, where Alexander died in 323 B.C.E.

The Legacy of Alexander the Great

The aftereffects of Alexander's conquests lasted far longer than his brief thirteen-year reign. Initially the greatest impact came from his soldiers. Thousands traveled with him, but thousands more chose to stay behind in different parts of Asia. Some could not continue at his breakneck pace because of battle wounds or age, and some preferred to live with their local wives. These men were responsible for the spread of Greek culture over a large geographic region.

Archaeologists have unearthed an entire Greek city in the Afghan town of Ai Khanum (aye-EE KAH-nuhm), which had all the usual buildings of a Greek town: a theater, a citadel where the army was stationed, a gymnasium, and temples. The temples built by Alexander's men contained statues of gods made by local artists following Greek prototypes. The population of Ai Khanum and other similar settlements included both the local Iranian peoples and descendants of Alexander's soldiers.

After Alexander's death, his empire broke into three sections, each ruled by one of his generals: Egypt went to Ptolemy (TOHL-uh-mee), Greece and Macedon to Antigonas (an-TIG-uh-nass), and all other territories—including Mesopotamia, the Mediterranean coast, and satrapies all the way to the Indus River Valley—to Seleucus (seh-LOO-kuhs), who sent Megasthenes as his ambassador to the Maury-ans in 302 B.C.E. (see Chapter 3). Each general founded a regional dynasty named

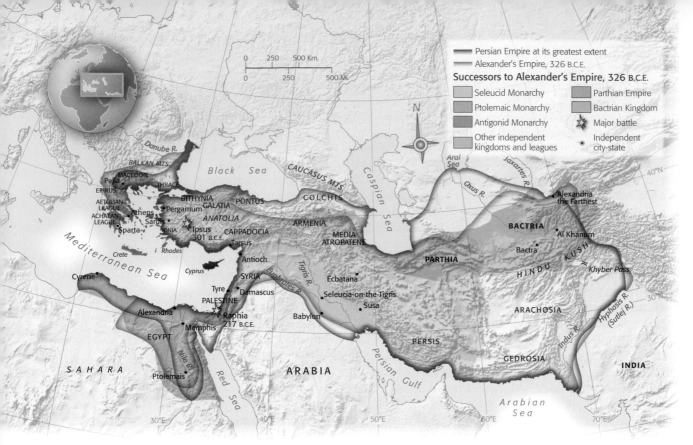

🌐 **MAP 6.2**

The Empires of Persia and Alexander the Great   The Achaemenids (550–330 B.C.E.), the Parthians (247 B.C.E.–224 C.E.), and the Sasanians (224–651) all formed powerful dynasties in Iran. The largest (shown with a green border) was that of the Achaemenids. After conquering it in 330 B.C.E., Alexander of Macedon enlarged its territory only slightly. Under the Achaemenids, this large region remained united for over two hundred years; under Alexander, for only thirteen. After Alexander's death, the empire split into three.

for himself: the Ptolemies (TOHL-uh-meze), the Antigonids (an-TIG-uh-nidz), and the Seleucids (seh-LOO-sidz). These successor regimes continued to administer their territories using the Achaemenid system of administration.

The city of Alexandria in Egypt, founded by Alexander in 332 B.C.E., became a major center of learning within the territory of the Ptolemies. At Alexandria, the Ptolemies built the Museum, a temple to the Muses (the goddesses of the arts), and they welcomed scholars in many different fields, including mathematics, medicine, astronomy, history, and geography. Archaeologists have found thirteen lecture halls of the same size, each with benches for a lecturer and his audience, an indication of the size of the city's schools. The city's library was particularly impressive because customs officials confiscated all papyrus rolls that travelers brought to Alexandria; the library retained the originals and returned copies to the owners.

In 240 B.C.E. the Greek astronomer Eratosthenes (eh-ruh-TOSS-thih-nees) was appointed librarian. Since Aristotle, the Greeks had believed that the earth was spherical, but they had no idea how big it was. Eratosthenes devised an ingenious experiment. He had heard that, on the day of the solstice, when the sun shone straight above a city named Syene (SIGH-ee-nee) to the south of

Alexandria, it cast no shadow. At high noon on June 21, the day of the solstice, Eratosthenes measured the angle of the sun's shadow in Alexandria at nearly one-fiftieth of a 360-degree circle. He then drew an imaginary triangle connecting Alexandria, Syene, and the center of the earth (see Figure 6.1). He concluded that since Syene was 5,000 stadia (488 miles, 785 km) away from Alexandria, the earth's circumference must be fifty times larger, or 250,000 stadia (24,427 miles, 39,311 km). The actual circumference of the earth is 24,857 miles (40,000 km), meaning that his error was less than 2 percent. Eratosthenes' brilliant experiment taught the Greeks that the known world occupied only a small section of the earth's northern hemisphere.

The Romans defeated the last of the Antigonids in 168 B.C.E. when they conquered Macedonia (see Chapter 7) and won Egypt from the Ptolemies in 30 B.C.E., but they never conquered the Iranian Plateau. A people based in northern Iran, the Parthians, broke off from the Seleucids in 247 B.C.E. and took Iran from the Seleucids by 140 B.C.E.

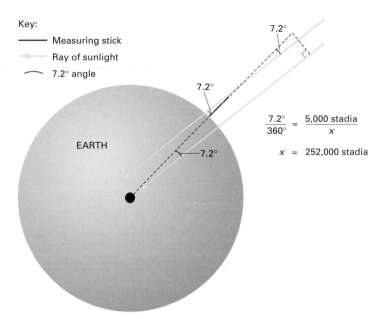

Key:
—— Measuring stick
← Ray of sunlight
⌒ 7.2° angle

EARTH

$$\frac{7.2°}{360°} = \frac{5{,}000 \text{ stadia}}{x}$$

$$x = 252{,}000 \text{ stadia}$$

FIGURE 6.1

Eratosthenes' Measurement of the Earth   Eratosthenes knew that, on June 21, a ray of light entering a well at the city of Syene cast no shadow because the sun was directly above. At Alexandria, 5,000 stadia away, also at noon, a parallel sun ray cast a shadow of 7.2 degrees on the ground next to a measuring stick. Using the law of congruent angles, Eratosthenes reasoned that 1/50th of the earth's circumference was 5,000 stadia, and therefore the circumference of the earth was 250,000 stadia. His result (24,427 miles, or 39,311 km) was less than 2 percent from the correct figure of 24,857 miles (40,000 km).   (Illustration by Lydia Stepanek)

The Parthians and the Sasanians, Heirs to the Achaemenids, 247 B.C.E.–651 C.E.

After the defeat of the Seleucids, two dynasties—the **Parthians** (247 B.C.E.–224 C.E.) and the **Sasanians** (224–651 C.E.)—governed Iran for nearly nine hundred years. The two dynasties frequently emulated the Achaemenids; they built monuments like theirs, retained their military and tax structures, and governed the different peoples under them flexibly. The Parthians followed the Achaemenid precedent closely, while the Sasanians experimented more.

The homeland of a seminomadic people who lived near the modern city of Gorgan in northern Iran, Parthia had been a satrapy within both the Achaemenid and Seleucid Empires. In 247 B.C.E., according to a legend, Arsaces I formed a conspiracy to found his own dynasty with six other men. It was no coincidence that he had exactly the number of conspirators that his role model Darius had. Like the Achaemenids, the Parthians were Zoroastrians who worshiped fire, but they allowed their subjects to practice their own religions.

● **Parthians** (247 B.C.E.–224 C.E.)   The ruling dynasty of Iran, who defeated the Seleucids and took over their territory in 140 B.C.E. Famous for their heavily armored cavalry, they posed a continuous problem for the Roman Empire.

●**Sasanians** The ruling dynasty (224–651 C.E.) of Iran who defeated the Parthians and ruled for more than four centuries until the Islamic conquest of Iran. Introduced innovations such as non-satrap royal lands and government support of Zoroastrianism.

The dynastic founder and his successors eventually conquered the Tigris and Euphrates River Valleys and the Iranian Plateau extending up to the Indus River Valley in Pakistan (see Map 6.2). The Parthians were famous for their fine and fast horses, which were heavily coated with armor. Parthian archers tricked the enemy by pretending to retreat and then turning backwards on their mounts to shoot, in a display of archery prowess still known as the Parthian shot. Starting in the first century B.C.E. and continuing through the first and second centuries C.E., the Romans (see Chapter 7) attacked the Parthians at periodic intervals, but the powerful Parthian military always kept them at bay.

Parthian soldiers were retainers to the nobles, for whom they performed military service. The king, who called himself "king of kings" in the Persian tradition, stood at the top of Parthian society, and the upper nobility ranked just below him but above the lower nobility. Though not slaves, the retainers had to perform a certain amount of labor and to pay a fixed amount of goods to the nobles they served. Doctors, artists, singing storytellers, and traders formed a middle level between the nobles and the retainers.

Trade was important because the Parthians occupied the territory between the Greco-Roman world and their Asian trading partners. In times of peace with Rome the Parthians traded spices and textiles for Roman metals and manufactured goods, but during the frequent periods of war, trading routes were blocked and smugglers became active.

The Parthians ruled for nearly five hundred years, far longer than the two-hundred-year reign of the Achaemenids, and their rule came to an end in 224 C.E. when Ardashir, one of their satraps based in the Iranian heartland of Persis, overthrew them and founded the Sasanian empire (named for his ancestor, Sasan). After defeating the Parthians, the Sasanians incorporated the Parthian forces into their army, of which the armored cavalry continued to be the strongest section. The Sasanian rulers led their powerful army to conquer all the territory of the former Parthian empire in addition to Sogdiana, Georgia, and the northeastern Arabian peninsula (see Map 6.2).

Sasanian society remained as hierarchical as in earlier Achaemenid and Parthian times, and the greater number of surviving documents means that we know more about it. The upper nobility was divided into four ranks, with the king's direct relatives ranking highest and those unrelated to the king lowest. Royal women continued to exercise considerable power, as in Achaemenid times; some of the most powerful rulers' mothers were called "queen of queens." Under the upper nobility were a lower group of nobles, some of whom received their lands and positions directly from the king. The middle ranks included craftsmen, traders, doctors, and singers. At the bottom of society were the cultivators, who had to give a share of their crop to the nobles in addition to the taxes they paid.

Once the Sasanians conquered a region, they divided the territory into two types of land: some was reserved for the king, while that portion entrusted to a satrap was divided into smaller districts. Only on the royal lands could the king establish cities, which he populated with deported peoples, most often skilled craftsmen, drawn from prisoners of war. The practice of forcible resettlement had a long history in western Asia going back to the Assyrians and the Babylonians (see Chapter 2). The resettled peoples could not leave their assigned cities, but they were free to marry local women, practice their own religions, and speak their native languages. These skilled craftsmen received high pay for their work as weavers and as builders and engineers who constructed roads and bridges.

The Sasanians realized that many different peoples lived within their empire, and to propagate knowledge they encouraged the translation of certain books from Sanskrit, Greek, and Syriac (the language spoken in Mesopotamia). They appointed officials to supervise Zoroastrian observances in each province at the local level, and the state constructed fire altars all over the empire. These government policies made Sasanian Iran actively Zoroastrian, and the Sasanians had difficulty managing the great religious diversity of their subjects.

By the third century C.E. two new religions, each with sizable followings, appeared in Iran: Christianity (see Chapter 7) and Manichaeism (mah-nih-KEE-iz-uhm). Mani (mah-KNEE) (216–ca. 274) was an Iranian preacher born in Mesopotamia who believed that his Manichaean teachings incorporated all the teachings of earlier prophets, including Zarathustra, the Buddha, and Jesus Christ. He deliberately recorded his teachings in written form so that his followers could translate them into other languages to encourage conversion. Like Zoroastrianism, his was a dualistic system in which the forces of light and dark were engaged in a perpetual struggle. Ordinary people could strengthen the forces of light by supporting the Manichaean clergy, who ate only vegetarian food provided by the laity, lived celibate lives, and conducted Manichaean rituals.

The Sasanians saw both the Christians and the Manichaeans as threats because they had their own religious hierarchy and refused to perform Zoroastrian rituals. Some kings tried to strengthen Zoroastrianism by commissioning a written version of *The Avesta* to rival Manichaean scriptures and the Bible. Other rulers directly persecuted members of the two churches: Manichaeism was banned even before Mani's death, and some Christians, suspected of being allies of the enemy Roman forces, were killed.

The third major religious community, the Jews, fared better under the Sasanians than did the Christians and the Manichaeans. The Sasanians allowed the Jews to govern their own communities as long as the Jews paid their taxes. Yet, whenever the Jews united behind a leader who challenged the legitimacy of Sasanian rule, the Sasanians put down the rebellion.

Adherence to the Achaemenid model of flexible empire allowed the Sasanians to rule for over four centuries. Surviving several military defeats and forfeiting large chunks of their empire, the Sasanians ruled until 651, when their capital at Ctesiphon fell to the Islamic armies of the caliphate (see Chapter 9).

For over a thousand years, the model of a flexible empire based on satrapies was so successful that the Achaemenids, Alexander, the successor states, the Parthians, and the Sasanians all used it to govern their empires. During this time, a very different empire and a powerful military rival to both the Parthians and the Sasanians arose in Rome in modern-day Italy, as the next chapter will explain.

■ **The Sasanian Palace, Ctesiphon, Iran**   The ruins of the Sasanian palace at Ctesiphon demonstrate the ingenuity and great skill of the brickmasons, who came from all over the empire and were resettled there by the emperors. The vaulted arch stands 118 feet (36 m) high, making it one of the world's largest brick arches. Its open doorways and fine brickwork inspired Islamic architects who incorporated these same features into early mosques.   (Gerard Degeorge/AKG Images)

Chapter Review

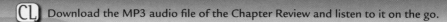 Download the MP3 audio file of the Chapter Review and listen to it on the go.

Born in the decade of the most intense fighting between Athens and the Achaemenid Empire, Herodotus devoted his life to understanding the conflict between the two. Indeed, he defined the goal of *The Histories* as "to show why the two peoples fought with each other." Although, as a Greek, Herodotus sympathized with the Athenians, he attributed much of the Persians' success to their monarchical form of government.

What administrative and military innovations enabled the Achaemenid dynasty to conquer and rule such a vast empire?

The Achaemenids succeeded in conquering the 30 to 35 million people who populated the entire world known to them; they did not conquer Greece or the area south of the Black Sea. The decentralized structure of the Persian Empire, divided into satrapies, allowed for diversity; as long as each region fulfilled its tax obligations to the center, its residents could practice their own religion and speak their own languages. Conquered peoples were recruited into the powerful infantry, cavalry, archers, and engineers of the Achaemenids. Hundreds of thousands of soldiers marched by foot over Eurasia on a fine system of roads whose major artery was the Royal Road.

What were the important accomplishments of the Greek city-states? Consider innovations in politics, intellectual life, fine arts, and science.

For all their military success, the Persians proved unable to defeat the Athenians and their allied city-states, who were able to outwit and outfight the Persian army and its navy twice in the late fifth century B.C.E. The city's democracy survived for more than two centuries until 322 B.C.E. The city-state's wealth supported an extraordinary group of dramatists who wrote plays, artists and craftsmen who built the Acropolis, and philosophers who debated the importance of reason. The Athenians knew that the world was round, and a later Greek scholar in Alexandria even calculated the world's circumference to within 2 percent of its actual length.

Who was Alexander, and what was his legacy?

Alexander conquered the entire extent of the Persian Empire and completely adopted its administrative structure. He died young after ruling only thirteen years, but thousands of his men stayed behind, building Greek-style cities like Ai Khanum throughout Central Asia. On his death, his empire broke into three smaller Achaemenid-style empires: the Antigonids in Greece, the Ptolemies in Egypt, and the Seleucids in western Asia.

How did the Parthians and the Sasanians modify the Achaemenid model of empire?

Parthia, originally a satrap in northern Iran, overthrew the Seleucids and largely adopted the Achaemenid model of empire. The Parthians and their successors, the Sasanians, broke from the Achaemenid model by creating royal lands on which the king resettled captured skilled craftsmen who built impressive cities. Zoroastrians like the Achaemenids, the Sasanians departed from earlier policies of religious tolerance by occasionally persecuting the Manichaean, Christian, and Jewish communities in their realm.

 **WEB RESOURCES**

Pronunciation Guide

Interactive Maps

MAP 6.1 Greek and Phoenician Settlement in the Mediterranean

MAP 6.2 The Empires of Persia and Alexander the Great

Primary Sources

Chapter Objectives

ACE Multiple-Choice Quiz

Flashcards

For Further Reference

Casson, Lionel. *Travel in the Ancient World*. Baltimore: Johns Hopkins University Press, 1974.

Harley, J. B., and David Woodward. *The History of Cartography*. Vol. 1, *Cartography in Prehistoric, Ancient, and Medieval Europe*. Chicago: University of Chicago Press, 1987.

Herodotus. *The Histories*. Translated by Aubrey De Sélincourt. Further rev. ed. New York: Penguin Books, 1954, 2003.

Hornblower, Simon, and Antony Spawforth. *The Oxford Companion to Classical Civilization*. New York: Oxford University Press, 1998.

Insler, Stanley. *The Gāthās of Zarathustra*. Leiden: E. J. Brill, 1975.

Markoe, Glenn E. *Peoples of the Past: Phoenicians*. Berkeley: University of California Press, 2000.

Martin, Thomas R. *Ancient Greece from Prehistoric to Hellenistic Times*. New Haven: Yale University Press, 1996.

Nylan, Michael. "Golden Spindles and Axes: Elite Women in the Achaemenid and Han Empires." In *Early China/Ancient Greece: Thinking Through Comparisons*, ed. Steven Shank-man and Stephen W. Durrant. Albany: State University of New York Press, 2002.

Pollitt, J. J. *Art and Experience in Classical Greece*. Cambridge: Cambridge University Press, 1972.

Wiesehöfer, Josef. *Ancient Persia from 550 BC to 650 AD*. Translated by Azizeh Azodi. New York: I. B. Tauris, 2001.

Websites

Evolution of Alphabets (http://www.wam.umd.edu/~rfradkin/alphapage .html).   Introduction to the history of many alphabets.

The Parthian Empire (www.parthia.com).   Introduction to Parthia Empire with excellent maps.

The Perseus Digital Library (www.perseus.tufts.edu).   A wealth of searchable texts from the classical world in both the original language and English translation.

The Roman Empire and the Rise of Christianity, 509 B.C.E.–476 C.E.

The events of 168 B.C.E. cut short the promising career of a young Greek statesman named **Polybius** (ca. 200–ca. 118 B.C.E.). In that year, after defeating the ruler of Macedon, the Romans demanded that the Greeks send over one thousand hostages to Italy for indefinite detention. Polybius (poh-LIH-bee-us) was deported to Rome, which remained his home even after his sixteen years of detention ended. His one surviving book, *The Rise of the Roman Empire*, explains why he felt that Rome, and not his native Greece, had become the major power of the Mediterranean:

(Alinari/Art Resource, NY)

There can surely be nobody so petty or so apathetic in his outlook that he has no desire to discover by what means and under what system of government the Romans succeeded . . . in bringing under their rule almost the whole of the inhabited world, an achievement which is without parallel in human history. . . .

The arresting character of my subject and the grand spectacle which it presents can best be illustrated if we consider the most celebrated empires of the past which have provided historians with their principal themes, and set them beside the domination of Rome. Those which qualify for such a comparison are the following. The Persians for a certain period exercised their rule and supremacy over a vast territory, but every time that they ventured to pass beyond the limits of Asia they endangered the security not only of their empire but of their existence. . . . The rule of the Macedonians in Europe extended only from the lands bordering the Adriatic to the Danube, which

POLYBIUS

 This icon will direct you to interactive activities and study materials on the *Voyages* website: www.cengage.com/history/hansen/voyages1e

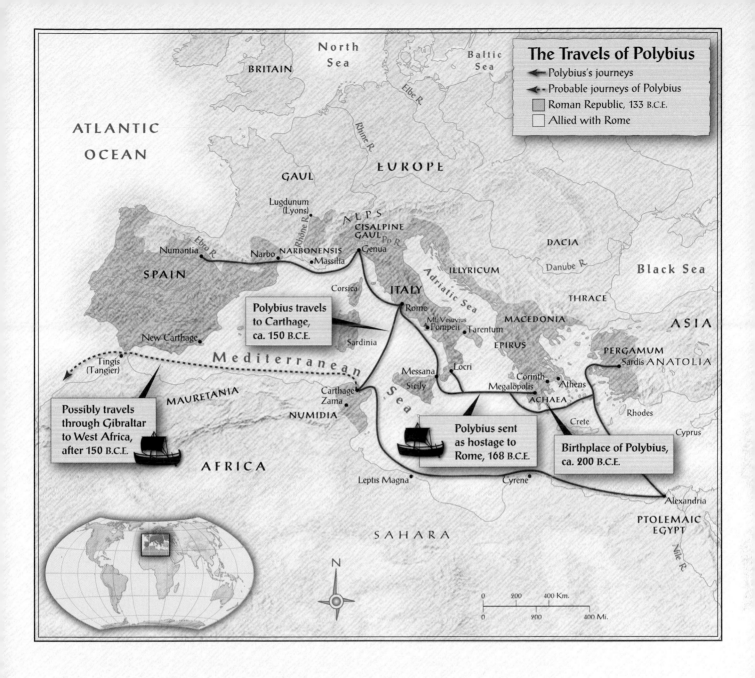

The Travels of Polybius

← Polybius's journeys
◄--- Probable journeys of Polybius
▨ Roman Republic, 133 B.C.E.
☐ Allied with Rome

ATLANTIC OCEAN

North Sea
BRITAIN
Baltic Sea
GAUL
EUROPE
Elbe R.
Rhine R.
Lugdunum (Lyons)
ALPS
CISALPINE GAUL
Po R.
DACIA
Danube R.
Ebro R.
Numantia
Narbo
NARBONENSIS
Genua
Massilia
SPAIN
Corsica
ITALY
Rome
ILLYRICUM
Adriatic Sea
Black Sea
THRACE
ASIA
New Carthage
Mt. Vesuvius
Pompeii
Tarentum
MACEDONIA
PERGAMUM
Sardis ANATOLIA
Polybius travels to Carthage, ca. 150 B.C.E.
Sardinia
EPIRUS
Mediterranean Sea
Tingis (Tangier)
MAURETANIA
Messana
Sicily
Locri
Corinth
Megalopolis
Athens
ACHAEA
Rhodes
Possibly travels through Gibraltar to West Africa, after 150 B.C.E.
Carthage
Zama
Crete
Cyprus
NUMIDIA
Polybius sent as hostage to Rome, 168 B.C.E.
Birthplace of Polybius, ca. 200 B.C.E.
AFRICA
Leptis Magna
Cyrene
Alexandria
SAHARA
PTOLEMAIC EGYPT
Nile R.

N

0   200   400 Km.
0   200   400 Mi.

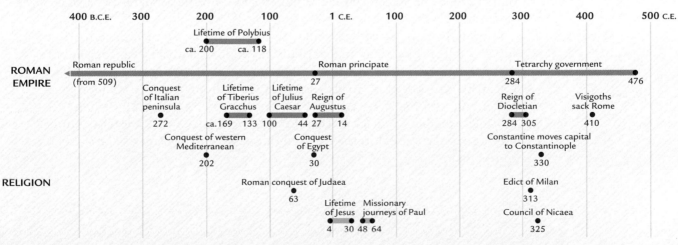

	400 B.C.E.	300	200	100	1 C.E.	100	200	300	400	500 C.E.

Lifetime of Polybius
ca. 200   ca. 118

ROMAN EMPIRE
Roman republic
(from 509)
Roman principate
27
Tetrarchy government
284   476

Conquest of Italian peninsula
272

Lifetime of Tiberius Gracchus
ca.169   133

Lifetime of Julius Caesar
100   44

Reign of Augustus
27   14

Reign of Diocletian
284   305

Visigoths sack Rome
410

Conquest of western Mediterranean
202

Conquest of Egypt
30

Constantine moves capital to Constantinople
330

RELIGION
Roman conquest of Judaea
63

Lifetime of Jesus
4   30

Missionary journeys of Paul
48   64

Edict of Milan
313

Council of Nicaea
325

would appear to be no more than a small fraction of the continent. Later, by overthrowing the Persian Empire, they also became the rulers of Asia; but although they were then regarded as having become the masters of a larger number of states and territories than any other people before them, they still left the greater part of the inhabited world in the hands of others. . . . The Romans, on the other hand, have brought not just mere portions but almost the whole of the world under their rule, and have left an empire which far surpasses any that exists today or is likely to succeed it.[1]

• **Polybius** (ca. 200–ca. 118 B.C.E.) A Greek historian who was deported to Rome. Author of *The Rise of the Roman Empire,* a book that explained how Rome acquired its empire. Believed the task of the historian was to distinguish underlying causes of events.

Most historians today would challenge Polybius's decision to rank Alexander of Macedon above the Achaemenids, whose empire he inherited (see Chapter 6). Polybius was also unaware of the Han dynasty in China (see Chapter 4), which probably had as many subjects as the Romans (some fifty-five million). Yet Rome did bring under its rule "almost the whole of the world" if we grant that Polybius meant the entire Mediterranean region, including western Asia, North Africa, and much of Europe. Even after the empire broke apart, the Mediterranean remained a coherent geographical region with shared cultural and linguistic ties forged during the nearly one thousand years of Roman rule.

During his detention, Polybius stayed in the city of Rome, where he lived with the descendants of a prominent general. After 152 B.C.E., when he was freed, Polybius accompanied his host's grandson to modern-day Spain and Carthage in North Africa and sailed down the Atlantic coast of West Africa. (The chapter opening map shows Polybius's travels and the extent of the Roman Empire after the conquests of Greece, Macedonia, and Carthage.) Travel around and across the Mediterranean was much more common in Polybius's lifetime than before, and it became even easier in the centuries after his death. Officials, soldiers, and couriers of the Roman Empire proceeded along a network of straight paved roads that ringed the Mediterranean Sea, the heart of the Roman Empire. Large boats crisscrossed the sea, while smaller vessels hugged its shore. Roman armies protected travelers from attacks, and the Roman navy lessened the threat of piracy.

During Polybius's lifetime Rome was a republic, but after his death, a century of political chaos culminated in the adoption of monarchy as the empire's new political system. In the beginning of the Common Era, the new religion of Christianity spread on roads and waterways throughout the Mediterranean region and eventually became the empire's official religion. The empire, increasingly unable to defend itself from powerful tribes in western Europe, moved to a new capital in the east and ultimately lost control of Rome and its western half.

Focus Questions

 How did Rome, a small settlement in central Italy, expand to conquer and control the entire Mediterranean world of Europe, western Asia, and North Africa?

 How did the political structure of the Roman Empire change as it grew?

 What were the basic teachings of Jesus, and how did Christianity become the major religion of the empire?

 What allowed Rome to retain such a large empire for so long, and what caused the loss of the western half of the empire?

●The Roman Republic, 509–27 B.C.E.

In its early years Rome was but one of many city-states on the Italian peninsula, but one with an unusual policy toward defeated enemies: once a neighboring city-state surrendered to Rome, Rome's leaders offered its citizens a chance to join forces with them. As a result, more and more men joined Rome's army. This policy increased the size of the Roman army and made it almost unstoppable, and by 272 B.C.E. Rome had conquered the Italian peninsula. In 202 B.C.E., after defeating Carthage, it gained dominance in the western Mediterranean, and in 146 B.C.E., after defeating a Greek coalition, it controlled the eastern Mediterranean as well. Those conquests were the crucial first step in the formation of the Mediterranean as a geographical region. After 146 B.C.E., Rome's armies continued to win territory, but the violence and civil wars of the first century B.C.E. brought an end to the republic in 27 B.C.E.

Early Rome to 509 B.C.E. The city of Rome lies in the middle of the boot-shaped peninsula of Italy, which extends into the Mediterranean. One chain of mountains, the Apennines (AP-puh-nines), runs down the spine of Italy, while the Alps form a natural barrier to the north. Italy's volcanic soil is more fertile than Greece's (see Chapter 6), and many different crops flourished in the temperate climate of the Mediterranean. Several large islands, including Sardinia and Corsica, lay to the west of Italy; immediately to the south, the island of Sicily formed a natural steppingstone across the Mediterranean to modern-day Tunisia, Africa, only 100 miles (160 km) away.

Written sources reveal little about Rome's origins. The earliest surviving history of Rome, by Livy, dates to the first century B.C.E., nearly one thousand years after the site of Rome was first settled in 1000 B.C.E. (Polybius's history starts in 264–260 B.C.E., long after the city's founding.) The city's original site lay 16 miles (26 km) from the Tyrrhenian Sea at a point where the shallow Tiber River could be crossed easily. The seven hills surrounding the settlement formed a natural defense, and from the beginning people gathered there to trade.

Romans grew up hearing a myth, also recorded by Livy, about the founding of their city by two twin brothers, Romulus and Remus, grandsons of the rightful king. An evil king who had seized power ordered a servant to kill them, but the servant abandoned them instead. Raised by a wolf, the twins survived, and Romulus went on to found Rome in 753 B.C.E. This legend is not unique to Rome; it is a Romanized version of a western Asian myth. Archaeologists have found that small communities surrounded by walls existed in Rome by the eighth century B.C.E.

During the sixth and fifth centuries B.C.E., when the Persian and the Greek Empires were vying for power, Rome was an obscure backwater (see Chapter 6). Greek colonists had settled in the south of Italy, and their cities were larger and far better planned than Rome. To the north lived the Etruscans (ee-TRUS-kunz), who built impressive fortresses dug into the sides of the hills. The Romans learned city planning, sewage management, and wall construction from their Etruscan neighbors. The Etruscans modified the Greek alphabet to write their own language, which the Romans in turn adopted around 600 B.C.E. to record their first inscriptions in their native Latin, a language in the Indo-European family.

The Early Republic and the Conquest of Italy, 509–272 B.C.E.

The earliest form of government in the Roman city-state was a monarchy. The first kings governed in consultation with an assembly composed of men from Rome's most prominent and wealthiest families, the patricians (puh-TRISH-uhns) who owned large landholdings. The origins of the patricians are unclear, but they formed a propertied, privileged social group distinct from the plebians (pluh-BEE-uhns), or commoners. Each time the king died, the patrician assembly chose his successor, not necessarily his son; the early kings included both Etruscans and Latins.

After overthrowing an Etruscan king, the Romans founded the **Roman Republic** in 509 B.C.E. In a republic, unlike direct democracy, the people choose the officials who govern. The power to rule was entrusted to two elected executives, called consuls, who served a one-year term. The consuls consulted regularly with an advisory body, the **Roman senate,** which was composed entirely of patricians, and less often with the plebian assembly, in which all free men, or citizens, could vote. The Romans never allowed a simple majority to prevail; instead they divided each assembly into smaller groups and reached a decision by counting the votes of the rich more heavily than the poor.

After 400 B.C.E., the republic continuously fought off different mountain peoples from the north who hoped to conquer Rome's fertile agricultural plain. The Celts or Gauls were residents of the Alps region who spoke Celtic, also an Indo-European language. In 387 B.C.E., Rome suffered a crushing military defeat at the hands of the Gauls, who took the city but left after plundering it for seven months.

Rome recovered and began to conquer other city-states. To speakers of Latin among their defeated enemies, the Romans offered all the privileges of citizenship

---

• **Roman Republic**
Type of Roman government between 509 B.C.E. and 27 B.C.E. Ruled by two elected executives, called consuls, who served one-year terms. The consuls consulted regularly with the senate, composed entirely of patricians, and less often with the plebian assembly, where all free men could vote.

• **Roman senate**
Roman governing body, composed largely of appointed patricians. During the years of the republic (509–27 B.C.E.), membership was around three hundred men and grew slightly in later periods, when the senate became an advisory body.

and the accompanying obligations; those who did not speak Latin had to pay taxes and serve as soldiers but could not participate in the political system.

The Romans learned much from the different peoples they conquered; they worshiped Greek gods to whom they gave Roman names (see below), and they adopted elements of Greek law. They also constructed roads linking Rome with their new possessions. This combination of policies provided a winning formula for Roman military success, and by 321 B.C.E. Roman troops had gained control of the entire Italian peninsula except for the south (the toe and heel of the Italian boot), a region where the Greek settlers' presence was so pronounced that the Romans referred to it as Magna Graecia ("Greater Greece"). It took almost fifty years before Rome conquered the final Greek city-state in Italy.

The Conquest of the Mediterranean World, 272–146 B.C.E.

In 272 B.C.E., the year that Rome gained control of the Italian peninsula, six different powers held territory around the coastline of the Mediterranean, and the residents of these different regions had no shared cultural identity. To the east, the three successors to Alexander (see Chapter 6) still occupied territory: the Antigonids in Macedon, the Seleucids in Syria, and the Ptolemies in Egypt. In addition, two separate leagues of city-states controlled the Greek peninsula. **Carthage,** a city originally founded by the Phoenicians (see Chapter 6), prospered by taxing trade. With an oligarchic government, Carthage controlled the north coast of Africa between today's Tunis and Morocco, the

● **Carthage** A city in modern-day Tunisia originally founded by the Phoenicians. Rome's main rival for control of the Mediterranean. Between 264 and 146 B.C.E., Rome and Carthage fought three Punic Wars, and Rome won all three.

🔳 **A Modern Reconstruction of the Port of Carthage**   The city's most prominent feature was its protected port. During peace, ships used the port behind the sea-wall, but during war, all the ships could retreat behind the city walls into the interior circular harbor, where they were well-protected.   (Museum of Carthage/Gianni Dagli Orti/The Art Archive)

southern half of modern-day Spain, Corsica, Sardinia, and half of Sicily. The only two actively expansionist states among these different powers, Rome and Carthage, collided in 264 B.C.E.

In that year Rome sent troops to support one city-state in Sicily against a different city-state allied with Carthage, triggering the first of the **Punic Wars.** (The Latin word for Phoenicians was *Poeni,* the origin of the English word *Punic* [PYOO-nik].) Whereas Rome had an army of citizens who fought when they were not farming, Carthage's army consisted almost entirely of mercenary troops paid to fight. Previously a land power, Rome built its first navy of sailing ships powered by multiple levels of oarsmen. After more than twenty years of fighting—some on land, some on sea—Rome won control of Sicily in 241 B.C.E., but Carthage continued to dominate the Mediterranean west of Sicily.

Rome and Carthage faced each other again in the Second Punic War (sometimes called the Hannibalic War) from 218 to 202 B.C.E. This war matched two brilliant generals: Carthage's **Hannibal** (ca. 247–ca. 182 B.C.E.) with Rome's Scipio Africanus (236–183 B.C.E.), the grandfather of Polybius's host Scipio Aemilianus (ca. 185–ca. 129 B.C.E.). Writing about events that occurred before he was born, Polybius believed that while an army might use a pretext to attack an enemy and a battle could begin a war, the historian should distinguish the underlying causes of war from both their pretexts and their beginnings. The underlying cause of the Second Punic War, Polybius argued, dated back to Hannibal's childhood and his father's anger at losing the First Punic War. Hannibal probably hoped, too, to cut Rome off from its territories so that Carthage could regain control over Roman territory in Spain. Launching his attack from New Carthage (modern-day Cartagena) in Spain, Hannibal led a force of 50,000 infantry, 9,000 cavalry, and 37 elephants on a five-month march across southern France and then through the Alps.

Polybius believed that the historian had to do on-site research; as he said, "I . . . have personally explored the country, and have crossed the Alps myself to obtain first-hand information and evidence." Hannibal's decision to cross the Alps was audacious: "These conditions were so unusual as to be almost freakish," Polybius learned from interviews with the locals. "The new snow lying on top of the old, which had remained there from the previous winter, gave way easily, both because it was soft, having just fallen, and because it was not yet deep." Many of Hannibal's men froze or starved to death, and Polybius estimated that less than half the original army, and a single elephant, survived the fifteen-day march through the Alps.

Carthage's army included Africans, Spaniards, Celts, Phoenicians, Italians, and Greeks. Although all of Hannibal's soldiers came from the Mediterranean region, Polybius noted that they "had nothing naturally in common, neither in their laws, their customs, their language, nor in any other respect," because the region had not yet become a coherent unit. The varied composition of Hannibal's army intimidated the Romans: "The troops were drawn up in alternate companies, the Celts naked, the Spaniards with their short linen tunics bordered with purple—their national dress—so that the line presented a strange and terrifying appearance."

Polybius attributed much of the Romans' success to the rules governing their army. Like the Qin army in China (see Chapter 4), the Roman commanders enforced a complex policy of rewards and punishments. Men who fought bravely in battle could win a spear, cup, or lance. The punishments for failure to fight were severe. If a group of men deserted, their commander randomly selected one-tenth

● **Punic Wars** The three wars between Rome and Carthage. The First Punic War, fought from 264 to 241 B.C.E., was for control of Sicily. In the second, between 218 and 202 B.C.E., Hannibal was defeated. In the third, in 146 B.C.E., Rome defeated Carthage and ordered all the city's buildings leveled and its residents enslaved.

● **Hannibal** (ca. 247–ca. 182 B.C.E.) The leader of Carthage's armies during the Second Punic War. A brilliant military strategist who led his troops over the Alps into Rome but who was defeated by Rome's superior army in 202 B.C.E.

of the deserters to be beaten to death. "This is carried out as follows," explains Polybius. "The tribune takes a cudgel and lightly touches the condemned man with it, whereupon all the soldiers fall upon him with clubs and stones, and usually kill him in the camp itself." Fear of this punishment kept Roman soldiers at their posts even when defeat was certain.

Diminished as their numbers were by the trip across the Alps, Hannibal's army entered Italy and won several major battles in succession, yet Hannibal never attacked Rome directly. When the two armies finally met in 202 B.C.E. at Zama, on the North African coast, Rome defeated Carthage. In 201 B.C.E., Rome and Carthage signed a peace treaty that imposed heavy fines on Carthage, granted Carthage's holdings in Spain to Rome, and limited the size of its navy to only ten vessels. With the elimination of Carthage as a rival power, the Roman Empire gained control of the entire western Mediterranean.

After the Second Punic War, Roman forces fought a series of battles with the three successor states to Alexander. Fighting in Greece and Anatolia, the Romans defeated the Seleucids in 188 B.C.E. yet allowed them to continue to rule in Syria. After several wars, Rome defeated the Antigonids in 168 B.C.E., the year Polybius came to Rome as a hostage, and brought the Antigonid dynasty to an end. In the same year, Ptolemaic Egypt became a client state of Rome, nominally ruled by a Ptolemy king. Rome secured control of the eastern Mediterranean only in 133 B.C.E. Before that time, Rome's power in the eastern Mediterranean was due to a series of treaties that created dependent and allied states through the region.

In 146 B.C.E. Rome defeated Carthage a third time. After he had taken the city, Scipio Aemilianus (SIP-ee-o ay-mill-YAN-us), the commander in charge of Roman forces, ordered all the buildings in the city leveled and the survivors sent to Rome to be sold as slaves. The Roman senate passed a bill forbidding anyone to rebuild Carthage and in place of Carthage's empire established the province of Africa (the origin of the continent's name), an area of about 5,000 square miles (13,000 sq km) along the North African coast. As we have seen in previous chapters, conquering rulers frequently exacted a high price from the people of a newly subjugated territory, but the order to destroy a city and enslave all its inhabitants marked a new level of brutality.

Each conquest brought new territory to be administered by the Roman Empire. Before the First Punic War, the newly conquered lands usually acquired the same governing structure as the city-state of Rome; in later periods the conquered territories, including Sicily, Sardinia, and Spain, were ruled as military districts by a governor, usually a former consul, appointed by the senate. The residents of these military districts did not receive citizenship.

Like the Achaemenid satraps (see Chapter 6), each Roman governor was in charge of an extremely large area; the district of North Africa stretched across the Mediterranean coastline of the three modern nations of Libya, Tunisia, and Algeria. The governor had a tiny staff: one official to watch over the province's finances, an advisory panel of his friends and high-ranking clients, and a small entourage composed of lower-ranking freedmen or slaves. The low number of officials meant that the governor almost always left the previous governmental structures in place.

The greatest challenge for the provincial governors was the collection of taxes, which their small staffs were supposed to forward to Rome. Unlike the Achaemenid satraps, who retained control over tax collection, the Roman governors delegated tax collection to others. The governors divided their provinces into regions

●**tax farmers**   Under the Roman empire, businessmen who paid in advance for the right to collect taxes in a given territory and who agreed to provide the governor with a fixed amount of revenue. Anything else they collected was theirs to keep.

and auctioned off the right to collect taxes in each region to the highest bidder. The **tax farmers,** the businessmen who paid in advance for the right to collect taxes in their territory, agreed to provide the governor with a certain amount of revenue; anything above that was theirs to keep. The residents of provinces suffered because the tax farmers took much more than they were entitled to. Most of the men who applied for the position of tax farmer belonged to a new commercial class of entrepreneurs and businessmen, called equites (EH-kwee-tays) because they were descended from soldiers who rode on horseback.

Roman Society Under the Republic

In 168 B.C.E., the family of the general Scipio Africanus (SIP-ee-o ah-frih-KAHN-us) persuaded the authorities to allow Polybius to stay with them. In *The Rise of the Roman Empire,* Polybius explains how he became acquainted with the grandson of Scipio Africanus, named Scipio Aemilianus. One day Scipio Aemilianus asked Polybius, "Why is it, Polybius, that although my brother and I eat at the same table, you always speak to him, address all your questions and remarks in his direction and leave me out of them?" Polybius responded that it was only natural for him to address the older brother, but he offered to help the 18-year-old Scipio Aemilianus launch his public career: "I do not think you could find anybody more suitable than myself to help you and encourage your efforts."

This conversation illustrates how influential Romans gained clients, or dependents not in their families. The people most likely to become clients were newcomers to a city, traders, or people who wanted to break from their own families. Patrons had the same obligation to help their clients as the head of the family had to help his own family members. They gave their clients food and money or assistance with legal matters, and clients in turn demonstrated loyalty by accompanying their patrons to the Forum, the marketplace where the residents of every Roman town gathered daily to transact business.

Scipio, like most important patrons in Rome, belonged to an eminent patrician family. Both his father and mother were the children of consuls. When he met Polybius, he was living with his adopted father, who was the head of his family, or the **paterfamilias** (pah-tehr-fah-MIL-lee-us). In Roman society only the paterfamilias could own property. He made all decisions affecting his wife, children, and son's wives, including, for example, the decision of whether the family could afford to raise a newborn baby or should deny it food and expose it to the elements. When the head of the family died, the sons might decide to split up the immediate family or to stay together under a new paterfamilias.

●**paterfamilias**   The legal head of the extended family in Rome and the only person who could own property. Made all decisions affecting his wife, children, and son's wives.

The Romans had a marriage ceremony, but most people did not bother with it; a man and a woman simply moved in together. Women were allowed to inherit, own, and pass on property in their own right, but under the stewardship of a male guardian, usually the paterfamilias. Marriage among more prominent families, like the Scipios, required a formal contract stipulating that the father would recognize as heirs any children resulting from the match. Roman men took only one wife, but the shorter life spans of the ancient world meant that remarriage among the widowed was common. Either the husband or wife could initiate divorce, which was accomplished by simple notification; the main legal issue was the settlement of property. Scipio Aemilianus's parents divorced two or three years after his birth, but he remained close to both.

Roman women devoted considerable energy to educating their children, whose marriages they often helped to arrange. The biographer of Cornelia, the widowed aunt of Scipio Aemilianus, praised her for being "proper in her behavior" and "a good and principled mother." She refused to marry the ruler of Ptolemaic Egypt so that she could devote herself to her twelve children, of whom only three survived to adulthood. Late in her life, "she had a wide circle of friends and her hospitality meant that she was never short of dinner guests. She surrounded herself with Greek and Roman scholars, and used to exchange gifts with kings from all over the world. Her guests and visitors used particularly to enjoy the stories she told of the life and habits of her father, Africanus."[2] Cornelia's example shows how Roman women were able to exert considerable influence even though they were formally barred from holding public office.

Well-off Roman households like the Scipios also owned slaves, who were usually captured in military campaigns abroad, brought to Rome, and sold to the highest bidder. Those who worked the fields or inside the homes of their masters were more fortunate than those who toiled in gold and silver mines, where mortality rates were high because the underground tunnels often collapsed. Some estimate that a ratio of three free citizens to one slave prevailed in the republic, one of the highest rates in world history.[3] On the rare occasions when Roman slaves obtained their freedom, they gained the full rights of citizens. However, many more slaves remained slaves for their entire lives, as did their children, because a child born to a slave mother, regardless of the father's status, remained a slave unless freed by the owner.

The Late Republic, 146–27 B.C.E.

Polybius and his contemporaries were well aware of the strains on Roman society that came with the rapid acquisition of so much new territory. During the years of Rome's conquests, the political system of the republic had functioned well. But soon after the victories of 146 B.C.E., the republic proved unable to resolve the tensions that came with the expanded empire.

In the early years of the republic, most Roman soldiers lived on farms, which they left periodically to fight in battles. As the Roman army fought in more distant places, like Carthage, soldiers went abroad for long stretches at a time and often sold off their fields to rich landowners, who invested in large-scale agricultural enterprises that grew fruit or vegetables, pressed olive oil, or produced wine. With few freedmen for hire, the rich landowners turned increasingly to slaves, and privately held estates, called latifundia (lat-uh-FUN-dee-uh), grew larger and larger. The gulf widened between the well-off owners of latifundia estates and the ordinary people who had lost their land. Many of the landless moved to Rome, where they joined the ranks of the city's poor because they had no steady employment.

Cornelia's son Tiberius Gracchus (ty-BEER-ee-us GRAK-us) (ca. 169–133 B.C.E.) was one of the first to propose economic reforms to help the poor. Each time Rome conquered a new region, the government set aside large amounts of public land, much of it controlled by the wealthy landed families of the city. Tiberius wanted to enforce an existing limit on the amount of land any individual family could own and give the remainder to the poor. Such land grants, he hoped, would ease unemployment among the city's poor while increasing the number of landed peasants eligible for military service.

Elected tribune in 133 B.C.E., Tiberius Gracchus brought his proposals before the plebian assembly, not the senate. The bill passed because Tiberius removed the other tribune, who was opposed to the measure. Furious that he did not follow the usual procedures, a gang of senators and their supporters killed him. This was the first time since the founding of the republic that participants in a political dispute used murder as a weapon. Even after his death, calls for agrarian reform persisted. In 123 B.C.E. Tiberius's younger brother Gaius Gracchus (GUY-us GRAK-us) launched an even broader program of reform that urged purchase of grain by the state and guaranteed sale to the poor living in Rome at low cost. He, too, was killed during the violence that broke out between his supporters and their political opponents.

Polybius and his contemporaries were shocked by the sudden violent turn in Roman politics, but the trend grew only more pronounced in the first century B.C.E., when many institutions of the republic ceased to function. In order to raise an army, one general, Marius (157–86 B.C.E.), did the previously unthinkable: he enlisted volunteers from among the working poor in Rome, waiving the traditional requirement that soldiers had to own land. Unlike the traditional farmer-soldiers, these troops had to be paid, and the leader who recruited them was obliged to support them for their entire lives. The troops eagerly looked forward to military campaigns because they received a share of the plunder each time they won a battle. Their loyalties were to the commander who paid them, not the republic.

After Marius died, Sulla, another general with his own private army, came to power. In 81 B.C.E. Sulla was not content to serve only a single year as consul and so arranged for the senate to declare him **dictator,** or temporary commander with full authority for a fixed amount of time. In earlier periods, the senate had the power to name a dictator for a six-month term during a crisis, but Sulla used the position to secure his hold on the government. In the different years after Sulla's death in 78 B.C.E., different generals vied to lead Rome. The senate continued to meet and to elect two consuls, but the generals with their private armies controlled the government, often with the senate's tacit consent.

Large privatized armies staffed by the clients and slaves of generals conquered much new territory for Rome in the first century B.C.E. They defeated the much-weakened Seleucids in 64 B.C.E. in Syria, bringing the dynasty to an end, but they never defeated the powerful Parthian cavalry (see Chapter 6). The most successful Roman commander was **Julius Caesar** (100–44 B.C.E.), who conquered Gaul, a region that included northern Italy and present-day France. Although the Romans looked down on the peoples of Gaul as barbarians, or less civilized people who could not read and write, the Gauls participated actively in trade and had a strong economy. After his term as governor ended in Gaul, Caesar led his armies to Rome, and in 49 B.C.E. the senate appointed Caesar dictator. Between 48 and 44 B.C.E. Caesar continued as dictator and served as consul every other year.

Caesar named himself dictator for life in 44 B.C.E. This move antagonized even his allies, and a group of senators killed him in March that year. Caesar's death, however, did not end Rome's long civil war. In his will, Caesar had adopted as his heir his great-nephew Octavian (63 B.C.E.–14 C.E.), the future Augustus. In 30 B.C.E. Octavian conquered Egypt, bringing the rule of the Ptolemies, the last successor state to Alexander, to an end. Egypt joined the Roman Empire as a province.

With this move Octavian eliminated all his rivals and brought nearly a century of political chaos and civil war to a close. The battles fought in Greece, Macedonia, Egypt, North Africa, and Spain demonstrate that commanders could move their armies easily around and across the Mediterranean in pursuit of their rivals.

● **dictator** A position given by the Roman senate before the first century B.C.E. to a temporary commander that granted him full authority for a limited amount of time, usually six months.

● **Julius Caesar** (100–44 B.C.E.) Rome's most successful military commander in the first century B.C.E. Conquered and governed much of Gaul, the region of modern-day France. Named dictator by the senate in 49 B.C.E.

CL Primary Source:
A Man of Unlimited Ambition: Julius Caesar
Find out how Roman attitudes toward kingship led to the assassination of Julius Caesar.

When the republic came to an end, Octavian had to devise a new political system capable of governing the entire Mediterranean region.

⬤ The Roman Principate, 27 B.C.E.–284 C.E.

In 27 B.C.E. Octavian became the sole ruler of Rome and made all of the important decisions governing the empire. He never named himself emperor. Instead he called himself *"princeps"* (PRIN-keps), or first citizen, even though he made all the important decisions governing the empire. The new political structure he devised, in which he held almost all power, is called the **Roman principate** (PRIN-sih-pate) (government of the princeps). The principate remained in place until 284 C.E. Historians call the period between 27 B.C.E., when Octavian took power, and 180 C.E. the "Pax Romana" (PAHKS ro-MAHN-uh), or Roman Peace, because the entire Mediterranean region benefited from these centuries of stability. People moved easily across the empire, which became even more integrated as a result.

● **Roman principate** The system of government in Rome from 27 B.C.E. to 284 C.E., in which the *princeps*, a term meaning "first citizen," ruled the empire as a monarch in all but name.

The Political Structure of the Principate

Octavian wanted to establish a regime that would last beyond his own life. He hoped, too, to prevent a future general from seizing the government, yet he did not want to name himself perpetual dictator or king for fear that he would antagonize the Roman political elite. In 27 B.C.E. the senate awarded him a new title, **Augustus,** meaning "revered," the name by which he is usually known.

Augustus transferred the power to tax and control the army from the senate to the princeps. Fully aware that the armies were dangerously big, Augustus ordered many soldiers demobilized and used his own private funds to buy land for them— some in Italy, some in the provinces. Augustus made sure that the senate approved the measures he enacted. The most important of his changes concerned the provinces; he asserted the right to appoint all military leaders and the governors of the important provinces, thus ensuring that no one could form an army in the provinces and challenge him in Rome.

● **Augustus** The name, meaning "revered," that Octavian (63 B.C.E.–14 C.E.) received from the senate when he became princeps, or first citizen, of Rome in 27 B.C.E. and established the monarchy that ruled the empire.

The one issue that Augustus did not resolve was who would succeed him: with no son of his own, he named his wife's son from a previous marriage as his heir, establishing a precedent that a princeps without a son of his own could name his successor. The best solution was the product of chance; since the three princeps who ruled from 98 to 161 C.E. did not have sons, they were able to choose their successors while still in office. The last century of the principate was not as smooth; between 211 and 284 C.E., the empire had thirty-six emperors, of whom nineteen were murdered, were executed, or died in battle with their successors.

The Social Changes of the Principate

Ever since the second century B.C.E., when the government classified Sicily and other new conquests as provinces, the men who had staffed the provincial governments had not received the privileges of citizens. They did not have access to Roman courts, and they could not participate in the political system of Rome. In the first century C.E. Augustus had deliberately increased the number of citizens by awarding Roman citizenship to discharged soldiers. On Augustus's death in

14 C.E. about four million people had become citizens,[4] and the number continued to increase. In 212 C.E. the emperor granted citizenship status to all free men anywhere in the empire, possibly in the hope of increasing tax revenues.

Roman law also changed during the course of the principate. Originally the magistrates and provincial governors who decided judicial cases applied Roman law to citizens and local law to noncitizens. They considered both unwritten laws, or customary practices, and written laws, which included laws passed by the senate or the plebian assembly, edicts from the emperor, and sometimes the writings of learned jurists. Many of the principles they developed still inform the modern practice of law. A person charged with a crime had the right to appear before a judge, who was to consider all the evidence fairly before deciding on the person's guilt. Everyone was innocent until proven guilty.

The Roman justice system did not, however, treat everyone equally. The sharp differences of the republic among patricians, equites, and plebians gradually faded, and, over the course of the principate, as more people gained the rights of citizens, two new social groups subsumed the earlier divisions: the elite *honestiores* (hoh-NEST-ee-or-eez) and the *humiliores* (HUGH-meal-ee-or-eez), or the humble. Membership in these groups did not overlap with citizenship: noncitizen honestiores existed, as did citizen humiliores. Courts tended to treat the two groups very differently, allowing the wealthy to appeal their cases to Rome while sentencing the humble to heavier punishments for the same crime.

The years of the principate also saw some gradual changes in the legal position of women. Most people lived in small families consisting of a couple, their children, and whichever slaves or servants they had. On marriage, women moved in with their husbands but technically remained in their father's families and so retained the right to reclaim their dowries when their husbands died. Dowries were small, often about a year of the father's income, because daughters were entitled to a share of their father's property on his death, which granted them financial independence during the marriage.

Although they had greater control over their property than women in most other societies, Roman women continued to assume a subordinate role in marriage, possibly because many were much younger than their husbands. Men tended to marry in their late twenties and early thirties, women in their teens or early twenties. Most families arranged their children's marriages to form alliances with families of equal or better social standing.

Some marriages turned out to be quite affectionate. One well-known writer in the first century who was also a lawyer, Pliny (PLIH-nee) the Younger (ca. 61–113 C.E.), wrote to his wife's aunt about his wife:

> She is highly intelligent and a careful housewife, and her devotion to me is a sure indication of her virtue. In addition, this love has given her interest in literature: she keeps copies of my works to read again and again and even learn by heart. She is so anxious when she knows that I am going to plead in court, and so happy when all is over! . . .
>
> Please accept our thanks for having given her to me and me to her as if chosen for each other.

Pliny married in his 40s, at the peak of his legal career, while his third wife Calpurnia was still a teenager. Despite their closeness, she must have often deferred to Pliny, who was much older.

House of the Faun, Pompeii, Italy One of the loveliest surviving villas at Pompeii is the House of the Faun, named for the figure in the fountain. The well-off residents of Pompeii, a provincial Roman town, lived in lovely villas like this one with hot and cold running water, lush gardens, and exquisite tiled fountains. (Casa del Faune, Pompeii, Italy/Scala/Art Resource, NY)

Pliny also wrote about the famous eruption from Mount Vesuvius, which he witnessed from his home in the Bay of Naples in the early afternoon on August 24, 79 C.E. He described the cloud of smoke as "white, sometimes blotched and dirty, according to the amount of soil and ashes carried with it."[5] Many of the residents of nearby Pompeii (POMP-ay) did not realize how dangerous the situation was and stayed in town, and Pliny's uncle, Pliny the Elder, actually traveled to the site of the erupting volcano to see if he could rescue anyone.

When Pliny the Elder arrived, "ashes were already falling, hotter and thicker as the ships drew near, followed by bits of pumice [PUH-miss] and blackened stones, charred and cracked by the flames." That evening Pliny the Elder went to bed inside his house; he awoke to find his door blocked. His servants dug him out, and the entire household went outside; even though the sun had come up, the ash-filled sky was "blacker and denser than any ordinary night." The uncle tried to escape by boat, but the waves were too high, and he collapsed. Two days later, when the cloud lifted, Pliny the Elder had died, killed by the poisonous fumes from the volcano. The sites of Pompeii and Herculaneum have afforded historians new understanding of Roman society in a provincial town during the first century C.E. (See the feature "Visual Evidence: Pompeii.")

Travel and Knowledge of the Outside World

While Romans had been traveling for business and pleasure ever since the conquests of the second century B.C.E., travel continued to increase throughout the principate and contributed to the further integration of the Mediterranean

POMPEII

The eruption of Mount Vesuvius in 79 C.E. preserved the entire provincial city of Pompeii—not just an individual building or a tomb—under a layer of ash, where it remained undiscovered until 1748. Pompeii possessed all the important features of a typical Roman city: a theater, temples to Roman and non-Roman gods, baths, a gymnasium, an amphitheater, shops, paved streets, and a forum where the residents met each day and carried out their business transactions.

The city's twenty thousand residents participated in a highly commercialized economy. No one baked bread because it was available fresh from bakeries every day. The bakeries at Pompeii are easily identified by their millstones of volcanic tufa stone, which slaves or draft animals rotated to grind the grain. Other shops also sold pastries and cakes. Farmers sold local products, like onions and herbs, at the markets, where people also purchased wine or *garum*, a sauce made from fermented fish.

One of the most developed industries in the city processed raw wool from sheep into luxurious woolen textiles. After the sheep were sheared, women slaves in many households washed the dirt and oils from the wool and carded it to make thread for spinning. After they wove the spun thread into cloth on looms, householders brought the homespun cloth to workshops to be finished. Workshop employees moistened, heated, and pressed the wool so that it would shrink and thicken. Only then could the cloth be dyed, often bright yellow or deep purple, or bleached

with sulphur. The painting on the facing page shows male and female workers processing wool.

This particular wall painting was probably commissioned by the owner of a textile workshop. The residents of Pompeii lived in lavish houses whose walls were filled with frescoes showing scenes of daily life and legendary exploits of the gods. Painted on wet plaster, these frescoes retain their original brilliant pigments, particularly the dark red so characteristic of Pompeii's art.

The large houses of the rich had extensive gardens and stables outside and lavish interior rooms. One tile floor portrayed Alexander the Great defeating Darius III, the last emperor of the Achaemenids (see Chapter 6). Large houses often had a dining room, called the triclinium, with three couches on which diners reclined as they ate. A sophisticated system of pipes supplied these houses with hot and cold running water.

The remains at Pompeii provide a valuable reminder of the high living standards of the Romans, even those living in a provincial town. Few people elsewhere in the world in the first century C.E. had hot running water, large gardens, or exquisite art. True, not everyone in Pompeii occupied such houses; poor people lived crowded together in small apartments without gardens or plumbing. The extraordinary archaeological remains at Pompeii afford a glimpse of exactly how rich and poor lived in 79 C.E., a view unmatched by any other site in the ancient world.

QUESTION FOR ANALYSIS

 What does this fresco reveal about the attire and working conditions of men and women of different social levels in Pompeii?

Craftsmen made this pigment by mixing red-colored minerals with powdered lime, soap, and wax and applying them to the wet plaster, which they polished after it dried.

An owl, the symbol of the Roman goddess Minerva (the Latin name of the Greek Athena), an expert weaver, rides on top of the wicker frame.

(Museo Archeologico Nazionale, Naples, Italy/Scala/Art Resource, NY)

A seated woman—a customer? a supervisor?—examines a piece of cloth shown to her by a young girl worker.

A male textile worker brushes a piece of wool hanging on a wooden frame with a thorned implement to smooth out the tangled threads.

This lightly clad man carries a metal bowl filled with burning sulphur, a bleaching agent, and carries a frame for hanging bleached textiles on his back.

189

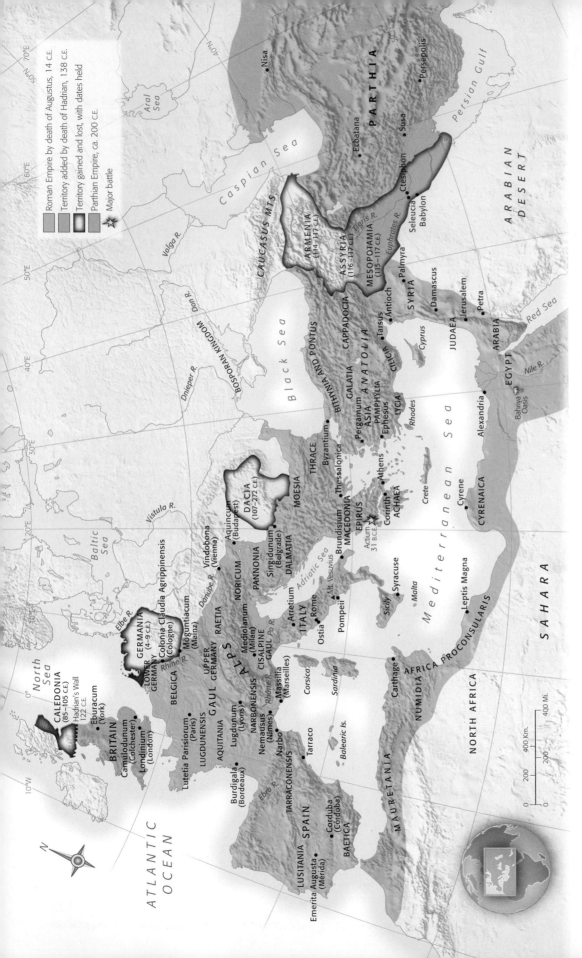

MAP 7.1

The Roman Empire at Its Greatest Extent Some fifty-five million people lived in the 2 million square miles (5 million sq km) of the Roman Empire in the second century C.E. A network of roads and shipping lanes bound the different regions together, as did a unified currency. Two common languages—Latin in the western Mediterranean and Greek in the eastern Mediterranean—helped to integrate the Mediterranean world even more closely.

CL Interactive Map

Roman Empire by death of Augustus, 14 C.E.

Territory added by death of Hadrian, 138 C.E.

Territory gained and lost, with dates held

Parthian Empire, ca. 200 C.E.

Major battle

ATLANTIC OCEAN

North Sea

Baltic Sea

CALEDONIA (85–105 C.E.)

Hadrian's Wall 122 C.E.

BRITAIN

Eburacum (York)

Camulodunum (Colchester)

Londinium (London)

Lutetia Parisiorum (Paris)

LUGDUNENSIS

AQUITANIA

Burdigala (Bordeaux)

Emerita Augusta (Mérida)

LUSITANIA

SPAIN

Corduba (Córdoba)

BAETICA

TARRACONENSIS

Tarraco

Ebro R.

Balearic Is.

NARBONENSIS

Narbo

Nemausus (Nîmes)

Rhône R.

Massilia (Marseilles)

Corsica

Sardinia

BELGICA

GAUL

Colonia Claudia Agrippinensis (Cologne)

LOWER GERMANY

UPPER GERMANY

GERMANIA (4–9 C.E.)

Moguntiacum (Mainz)

Rhine R.

Elbe R.

Vistula R.

RAETIA

ALPS

CISALPINE GAUL

Mediolanum (Milan)

Po R.

Vindobona (Vienna)

NORICUM

PANNONIA

Aquincum (Budapest)

DACIA (107–272 C.E.)

Singidunum (Belgrade)

DALMATIA

Adriatic Sea

Arretium

ITALY

Rome

Ostia

Mt. Vesuvius

Pompeii

Sicily

Syracuse

Malta

Leptis Magna

SAHARA

NORTH AFRICA

NUMIDIA

MAURETANIA

Carthage

AFRICA PROCONSULARIS

Mediterranean Sea

Crete

Cyrene

CYRENAICA

MOESIA

THRACE

Byzantium

Thessalonica

MACEDONIA

EPIRUS

Actium 31 B.C.E.

Brundisium

ACHAEA

Corinth

Athens

BITHYNIA AND PONTUS

Black Sea

Don R.

Dnieper R.

Volga R.

BOSPORAN KINGDOM

Aral Sea

Caspian Sea

CAUCASUS MTS.

ARMENIA (114–117 C.E.)

ASSYRIA (116–117 C.E.)

MESOPOTAMIA (115–117 C.E.)

Tigris R.

Euphrates R.

PARTHIA

Nisa

Ecbatana

Ctesiphon

Seleucia

Babylon

Susa

Persepolis

Persian Gulf

CAPPADOCIA

GALATIA

ASIA ANATOLIA

Pergamum

Ephesus

PAMPHYLIA

LYCIA

CILICIA

Rhodes

Cyprus

Tarsus

Antioch

SYRIA

Damascus

Palmyra

Jerusalem

JUDAEA

Petra

ARABIA

ARABIAN DESERT

Red Sea

EGYPT

Alexandria

Nile R.

Bahriya Oasis

N

0 200 400 Mi.

0 200 400 Km.

10°W 0° 10°E 20°E 30°E 40°E 50°E 60°E 70°E

40°N

50°N

world. The empire reached its largest extent in the second century C.E. (see Map 7.1), with an estimated population of fifty-five million people living in an area of 2 million square miles (5 million sq km).[6] Rome controlled not only the entire Mediterranean coast of North Africa, western Asia, and Europe but also large amounts of territory inland from the Mediterranean: modern-day Spain, France, England, Germany west of the Rhine River, the Balkans, and Turkey. Roman roads connected the different parts of the empire, and sea transport, even with its dangers, remained even cheaper. Travelers needed to carry only one type of currency, Roman coins. Just two languages could take them anywhere within the empire: Latin was used throughout the western Mediterranean and in Rome itself, while Greek prevailed in the eastern Mediterranean.

The appearance of new maps and guides testifies to the frequency of travel. Some simply listed each place on a given road and the distance to the next city; others portrayed the information visually. When papyrus was not available, the Romans used parchment, or treated animal skin, for writing material. One of the longest surviving texts on parchment, the Peutinger Map, occupies a piece of

◼ The Peutinger Map: The Roman Equivalent of the Mobil Guide?   This detail from the Peutinger Map shows Jerusalem, where many Christians traveled in the late 300s and 400s. (This is a twelfth- or thirteenth-century copy of a map dating to the 300s). The cartographer devised symbols for the different type of lodging at each stopping place: a square building with a courtyard, for example, indicated the best kind of hotel. Modern guidebooks use exactly the same type of system.   (akg-images)

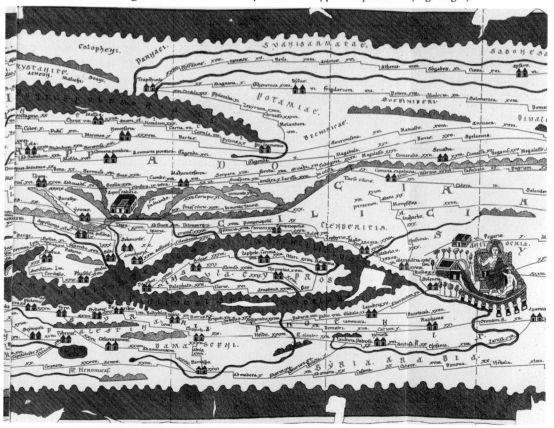

parchment 13 inches (34 cm) wide and over 22 feet (6.75 m) long. It depicts the full 64,600 English miles (104,000 km) of the empire's road system.

The study of geography flourished throughout the empire and particularly in the city of Alexandria, Egypt, which continued to be a center of learning even after the Roman conquest of Egypt in 30 B.C.E. The geographer Ptolemy (ca. 100–170 C.E.) (not related to the Ptolemy royal family), devoted his life to making a map of all the world's known countries. Ptolemy's data survive in a list of longitudinal and latitudinal coordinates for eight thousand places. We do not know whether he made an actual map, but his work marks the high point of geographic knowledge in the Roman Empire. China and Southeast Asia marked the eastern edge of the world known to the Romans; the Canary Islands in the Atlantic Ocean marked the western end. To the north lay the British Isles and the Scythian region (north of the Black Sea in Russia); to the south, below Ethiopia, lay Africa. Although he made some errors, Ptolemy knew where more places were located on the globe than did any geographer elsewhere in the world. His comprehensive knowledge of geography remained influential in the Islamic world (see Chapter 9) and Europe until 1500 (see Chapters 10 and 13).

The Rise of Christianity, ca. 30–284 C.E.

During these years, as Rome was consolidating its empire, people and religious teachings moved easily and widely throughout the Mediterranean world as never before. The Romans had their own gods, to whom officials offered regular sacrifices, and they worshiped many deities originating in other parts of the empire. Christianity began as a faith professed by a small group of Jews in the province of Judaea (joo-DAY-uh) and began to spread throughout the Mediterranean in the first and second centuries C.E. The emperor Constantine's decision to support Christianity in 313 proved to be the crucial step in its extension throughout the Mediterranean world.

Roman Religion and Judaism

Throughout the republic and the principate, the state encouraged the worship of many different gods in the Roman polytheistic religion. Most Romans worshiped major deities, like Jupiter, the most powerful of all the gods, or Mars, the god of war, both of which have given their names to the planets. Many of these gods were originally Greek; for example, the Roman Jupiter was the same as the Greek Zeus. Officials frequently spent tax monies in support of public cults, sometimes to a deity and sometimes to the current or former deified princeps.

In addition to their public obligations to state-supported gods, many people privately worshiped mystery cults that drew on the symbolism of fertility deities. A female deity, sometimes with a male partner, disappeared in the fall and had to be coaxed to return in the spring. Mystery cults promised adherents immortality and a closer personal relationship with the divine. Throughout the Mediterranean, believers worshiped deities not originally from Rome, including Isis (EYE-sis), the Egyptian goddess of the dead, thought to have power to cure the sick, and Mithra (MIH-thruh), the Iranian sun-god sent by Ahura Mazda (see Chapter 6) to struggle against evil. Gathering in small groups to sacrifice bulls, the worshipers of Mithra believed that the souls of the dead descended into earth before ascending into heaven.

Unlike almost everyone else in the Roman Empire, Jews were monotheistic (see Chapter 2). Worshiping a single god, whom they never depicted in images or paintings, Jews refused to worship any of the Roman gods or former princeps, a stance that was tolerated by the Roman government. Their center of worship was the Jerusalem Temple, a building that housed their scriptures. After the Babylonians destroyed the First Temple (see Chapter 2), the Jews built the Second Temple under King Cyrus of the Achaemenids (see Chapter 6). The Second Temple survived the Roman conquest of Judaea in 63 B.C.E., when Judaea came under indirect Roman rule.

The Romans initially delegated the task of governing the region to the leadership of the Temple, yet many Jews challenged the authority of the Temple's leaders. One group of reformers, the Pharisees (FAIR-uh-seez), believed that Jews should also obey a body of oral law in addition to the written laws of the Hebrew Bible. Unlike the traditional leaders, the Pharisees did not believe that Jews should exclusively worship in the Temple and encouraged them to worship in separate buildings called synagogues.

The discovery of the Dead Sea Scrolls, a group of texts on leather, papyrus, and copper, has revealed the diversity of beliefs among Jewish groups. The scrolls mention a Teacher of Righteousness, a figure who the authors believed would bring salvation, called a Messiah (muh-SIGH-uh) in Hebrew. Many Jewish groups at the time believed that a Messiah would come, yet they disagreed about how to identify him.

The Life and Teachings of Jesus, ca. 4 B.C.E.–30 C.E.

Almost every surviving record about early Christianity written before 100 C.E., whether about the life of **Jesus** or the early ministry, is written by a Christian believer.[7] The earliest sources, and so the most reliable, are the four gospels of Mark, Matthew, Luke, and John, written between 70 and 110 C.E. Accordingly, historians use the gospels to piece together the chronology of Jesus' life, all the while remembering that, like sources about Zarathustra or the Buddha, they were written by devotees, not outsiders.

The gospels relate that Jesus was born around 4 B.C.E. to a well-off Jewish family near the Sea of Galilee, where residents made a good living fishing. They say little about his life before about 26 C.E., when his cousin John the Baptist baptized him. Jewish tradition held that baptism, or ritual washing with water, could cleanse someone from impurities; converts to Judaism sometimes were baptized, and women bathed to mark the end of their menstrual periods. Invoking this tradition, John claimed to be a prophet and urged Jews to undergo baptism in preparation for the kingdom of God. However, John's message was new because he urged everyone to be baptized.

In 28 and 29 C.E. Jesus began preaching publicly in Galilee and, like John, urged Jews to repent and undergo baptism. Illness was a sign of Satan's presence, Jesus taught, and many of the miracles recorded in the gospels are anecdotes about his curing the sick. Historians, particularly those who do not subscribe to the teachings of a given belief system, are often skeptical about whether the events described in miracle tales actually occurred. But they realize that many religious figures were able to win converts because of them.

● **Jesus** (ca. 4 B.C.E.– 30 C.E.) Jewish preacher believed by Christians to be the Messiah, the figure who would bring salvation. The Christian doctrine of atonement holds that God sent Jesus to the world to bring eternal life to all those who believed in him.

As he explained in the Sermon on the Mount, Jesus welcomed the poor and downtrodden: "Blessed are the poor in spirit, for theirs is the kingdom of heaven" (Matthew 5:3). According to the gospels, Jesus' preaching in Galilee culminated in the feeding of five thousand supporters, possibly in the summer of 29 C.E. Jesus summed up his teachings succinctly in response to a Pharisee who asked him what the most important commandment was:

> "'You shall love the Lord your God with all your heart, and with all your soul, and with all your mind.' This is the great and first commandment. And a second is like it: 'You shall love your neighbor as yourself.'" (Matthew 22:36–39)

Jesus also taught his followers that a time of great difficulty was coming and that God would send a Messiah to usher in a new age. *Christos* was the Greek word for Messiah, and Jesus came to be known as Jesus Christ because his followers believed that he was the Messiah. Jesus' teachings attracted converts because the egalitarian religion promised salvation to all, including the poor, and welcomed all to join the new church, regardless of their background.

Jesus also wanted to reform and challenge the abuses he saw. His criticisms provoked the Jewish community leaders, who may also have feared that he would lead the residents of Palestine, where there was already a great deal of unrest, in an uprising against Roman rule. They asked the Roman governor, Pontius Pilate, to convict Jesus on the grounds that he claimed to be king of the Jews and thus posed a political threat to Rome. The gospels portray Pontius Pilate as being hesitant to punish Jesus, who refused to directly answer Pilate's question "Are you the King of the Jews?" Fearful of possible disorder, in 30 C.E. Pilate agreed to crucify Jesus. At the time of his death Jesus had been actively preaching for only three years.

On the third day after he died, Christians believe, several of Jesus' female disciples visited his tomb and found it empty, and some of the disciples then had visions of Jesus. The gospels concur that Jesus was resurrected, or raised from the dead. The gospel of John explains: "For God so loved the world that he gave his only Son, so that everyone who believes in him may not perish but may have eternal life" (John 3:16). This teaching, that Jesus died so that all believers will be able to overcome death, is called atonement, and it became one of the most important teachings of the Christian church.

Paul and the Early Church, 30–284 C.E.

Jesus preached that a new age of salvation would come soon after his death, yet his disciples realized that they had to devise a governing structure for the church no matter how temporary they expected the wait to be. The early church followed the model of Jewish synagogues and established churches in each community where a sufficient number of Christians lived. Bishops headed these districts; below them were deacons and deaconesses, a position of genuine authority for the many women who joined the church.

The teachings of another early Christian leader, Paul, were highly influential. **Paul** (ca. 5–ca. 64 C.E.) was born to a wealthy family of Roman citizens living in Tarsus in modern-day Turkey. Like many Jews living outside Judaea, Paul had grown up in a bilingual household in which both Greek and Hebrew were spoken,

●**Paul** (ca. 5–ca. 64 C.E.) An influential early Christian leader. Born in Tarsus (in modern-day Turkey) and grew up in a Greek-speaking Jewish household. Traveled widely in modern-day Turkey, Cyprus, and Greece to teach about early Christianity.

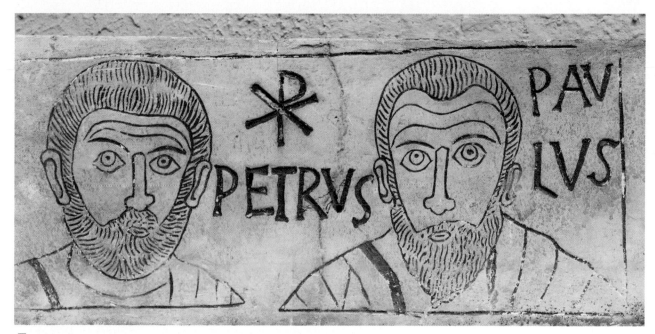

■ **Picturing the Apostles Peter and Paul**   After the government in 313 permitted Christians to worship openly (see page 200), many Romans began to decorate their stone coffins with Christian images. This is a very early depiction of Peter and Paul, who are identified by name. The symbol between them combines two Greek letters, *chi* and *ro*, the first two letters in the word Greek word for Christ, *Christus*, a symbol used throughout the Christian world.   (Vatican Museums, Vatican State/ Erich Lessing/Art Resource, NY)

but he received a traditional education in Jerusalem, where he studied with the Pharisees.

As described in the book of Acts, the turning point in Paul's life came when Jesus appeared to him in a vision, probably in the year 38 C.E., as he traveled to Damascus. After deciding to become a Christian, Paul was baptized in Damascus. The Christian leadership in Jerusalem, however, never granted that Paul's vision was equal to their own experience of knowing Jesus personally and hearing him teach. Understandably suspicious of him, they sent Paul to preach in his native Tarsus in 48 B.C.E.

Paul initially focused on converting the Jewish communities scattered throughout the eastern half of the Mediterranean, preaching and writing letters in Greek. Written with the sophistication of an educated Roman, his letters carried the teachings of Christianity to many fledgling Christian communities. When he arrived in a new place, he went first to the local synagogue and preached. (See the feature "Movement of Ideas: Early Christianity in the Eastern Provinces.") Whereas Jesus had preached to the poor and to slaves, Paul's potential audience consisted of more prosperous people. He did not call for the abolition of slavery or propose any genuine social reform. Accepting the right of the Roman Empire to exist, he, like Jesus before him, urged his audiences to pay their taxes.

Early Christianity in the Eastern Provinces

What did early Christians believe? The book of Acts in the New Testament contains this very interesting summary of a sermon given by Paul in Pisidian Antioch (in modern-day Turkey), one of the first cities he visited in 46. Local Jews constituted the bulk of his audience, and Paul expected them to be familiar with the predictions about the coming of prophets in the Old Testament, which they read in a Greek translation of the original Hebrew Bible. His sermon concludes with a statement of the important doctrine of atonement: Jesus died so that the sins of everyone who believed in his teachings could be forgiven. He closes with a pointed contrast between the law of Moses, or traditional Jewish teachings, and the teachings of Jesus, which he says offer more benefits.

The second selection is from Pliny the Younger, who was not a Christian. He served as a provincial governor in a region of present-day Turkey, south of the Black Sea, between 111 and 113. In one letter, he wrote to ask the emperor Trajan exactly how he should determine who was a Christian and who deserved punishment. The details in his letter offer a vivid description of the impact of Christianity on local religious practice during a period when it was officially banned. Unlike Pliny, many Roman officials did not persecute the Christians in their districts.

Sources: Acts 13:16–39 (New Revised Standard Version); Betty Radice, *The Letters of the Younger Pliny* (New York: Penguin Books, 1963), pp. 293–295.

Paul's Sermon at Antioch

You Israelites, and others who fear God, listen. The God of this people Israel chose our ancestors and made the people great during their stay in the land of Egypt, and with uplifted arm he led them out of it.... Then they asked for a king...; he [God] made David their king. In his testimony about him he said, "I have found David, son of Jesse, to be a man after my heart, who will carry out all my wishes." Of this man's posterity God has brought to Israel a Savior, Jesus, as he promised; before his coming John had already proclaimed a baptism of repentance to all the people of Israel. And as John was finishing his work, he said, "What do you suppose that I am? I am not he. No, but one is coming after me; I am not worthy to untie the thong of the sandals on his feet."

My brothers, you descendants of Abraham's family, and others who fear God, to us the message of this salvation has been sent. Because the residents of Jerusalem and their leaders did not recognize him nor understand the words of the prophets that are read every sabbath, they fulfilled those words by condemning him. Even though they found no cause for a sentence of death, they asked Pilate to have him killed. When they had carried out everything that was written about him, they took him down from the tree, and laid him in a tomb. But God raised him from the dead; and for many days he appeared to those who came up with him from Galilee to Jerusalem, and they are now his witnesses to the people. And we bring you the good news that what God promised to our ancestors, he has fulfilled for us, their children, by raising Jesus; as also it is written in the second psalm,

"You are my son; today I have begotten you."

... Let it be known to you therefore, my brothers, that through this man [Jesus] forgiveness of sins is proclaimed to you; by this Jesus everyone who believes is set free from all those sins from which you could not be freed by the law of Moses.

Pliny to Emperor Trajan

I have never been present at an examination of Christians. . . .

For the moment this is the line I have taken with all persons brought before me on the charge of being Christians. I have asked them in person if they are Christians, and if they admit it, I repeat the question a second and third time, with a warning of the punishment awaiting them. If they persist, I order them to be led away for punishment;[*] for, whatever the nature of their admission, I am convinced that their stubbornness and unshakeable obstinacy ought not to go unpunished. There have been others similarly fanatical who are Roman citizens. I have entered them on the list of persons to be sent to Rome for trial. . . .

Others, whose names were given to me by an informer, first admitted the charge and then denied it; they said that they had ceased to be Christians two or more years previously, and some of them even twenty years ago. They all did reverence to your statue and the images of the gods in the same way as the others, and reviled the name of Christ. They also declared that the sum total of their guilt or error amounted to no more than this: they had met regularly before dawn on a fixed day to chant verses alternately among themselves in honor of Christ as if to a god, and also to bind themselves by oath, not for any criminal purpose, but to abstain from theft, robbery, and adultery, to commit no breach of trust and not to deny a deposit when called upon to restore it. After this ceremony it had been their custom to disperse and reassemble later to take food of an ordinary, harmless kind; but they had in fact given up this practice since my edict, issued on your instructions, which banned all political societies. This made me decide it was all the more necessary to extract the truth by torture from two slave-women, whom they call deaconesses. I found nothing but a degenerate sort of cult carried to extravagant lengths.

I have therefore postponed any further examination and hastened to consult you. The question seems to me to be worthy of your consideration, especially in view of the number of persons endangered; for a great many individuals of every age and class, both men and women, are being brought to trial, and this is likely to continue. It is not only the towns, but villages and rural districts too which are infected with contact with this wretched cult. I think though that it is still possible for it to be checked and directed to better ends, for there is no doubt that people have begun to throng the temples which had been almost entirely deserted for a long time; the sacred rites which had been allowed to lapse are being performed again, and flesh of sacrificial victims is on sale everywhere, though up till recently scarcely anyone could be found to buy it. It is easy to infer from this that a great many people could be reformed if they were given an opportunity to repent.

* The Latin text has *puniri,* which Radice translates as "execute," but "punishment" is more accurate.

QUESTIONS FOR ANALYSIS

▶ How do these descriptions of Christianity by a believer and a nonbeliever differ? Which Jewish teachings and which Christian teachings does Paul present?

▶ Which of Pliny's points support his contention that Christianity can be controlled? Which do not?

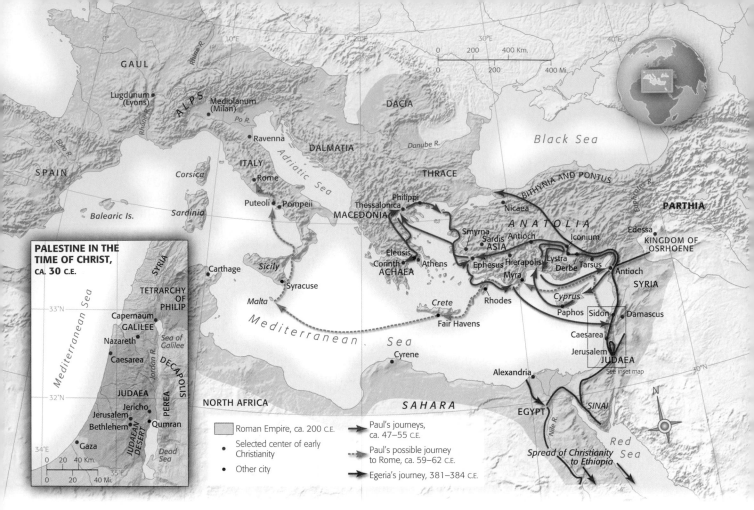

PALESTINE IN THE
TIME OF CHRIST,
CA. 30 C.E.

Roman Empire, ca. 200 C.E.

• Selected center of early
  Christianity

• Other city

→ Paul's journeys,
  ca. 47–55 C.E.

- - → Paul's possible journey
  to Rome, ca. 59–62 C.E.

→ Egeria's journey, 381–384 C.E.

Spread of Christianity
to Ethiopia

CL Interactive Map

⊕ **MAP 7.2**

The Spread of Christianity   During his lifetime, Jesus preached in the Roman
province of Judaea. After his death, Paul and other missionaries introduced Christian
teachings to the eastern Mediterranean. By the late 300s, Christianity had spread
throughout the Mediterranean, making it possible for pilgrims like Egeria to travel all
the way from Rome to Jerusalem and Egypt, where she visited the earliest Christian
monasteries.

Paul took advantage of the ease of travel within the Roman Empire to propagate his views. A list of the cities he visited vividly conveys how much he traveled:
Antioch, Iconium, Lystra, Derbe, and Ephesus in modern-day Turkey; Paphos on
the island of Cyprus; and Thessalonica, Philippi, and Corinth in Greece. By the
time Paul died, circa 64, a Christian community had arisen in each of these cities.
In Rome, according to Christian tradition, Jesus' apostle Peter, who died about the
same time as Paul, headed the Christian community (see Map 7.2). A Jewish uprising in 66 prompted the Roman authorities to intervene with great brutality: they
destroyed the Second Temple in 70, and many Jews fled Jerusalem. After 70, Rome
replaced Jerusalem as the center of the Christian church.

In subsequent centuries the Christian church must have expanded, more than
the spotty historical record indicates. We see early Christian centers proliferate
around the Mediterranean like the tips of icebergs, but surviving sources do not
indicate how deep or wide the icebergs were at the base. The church grew steadily
during the first, second, and third centuries.

The Decline of the Empire and the Loss of the Western Provinces, 284–476

Although the principate was still nominally the structure of the government, the Pax Romana ended in the third century. In 226 C.E. Rome faced new enemies on its northern borders, as a Germanic tribal people called the Goths launched a series of successful attacks in the region of the Danube River. (In later centuries, the word *Goth* came to mean any social movement, whether Gothic architecture or today's Goth styles, that challenged existing practices.) The attacks by Germanic peoples continued in the following centuries. As a result, different Roman rulers repeatedly restructured the Roman Empire and shifted the capital east. During these same centuries, they lifted the ban on Christianity and increasingly offered government support to the religion, which led to its further spread. Although the Romans lost chunks of their empire and even the city of Rome to barbarian invaders, the region of the Mediterranean remained a cultural unit bound by a common religion—Christianity—and the same two languages—Latin and Greek—that had been in use since the time of the republic.

Political Changes of the Late Empire

The principate came to a formal end early in the reign of Diocletian (r. 284–305). Diocletian (dy-oh-KLEE-shun) increased the size of Rome's armies by a third so that they could fight off their various enemies, including the Goths and the Sasanians, the dynasty established in Iran in 224 (see Chapter 6). In 260, the Sasanians had captured the Roman emperor Valerian and forced him to crouch down so that the Sasanian emperor could step on his back as he mounted his horse. Realizing that the new threats made the empire too large to govern effectively, Diocletian divided the empire into an eastern and western half and named a senior emperor and a junior emperor to govern each half. Diocletian ruled with the assistance of appointed advisers, no longer pretending to consult the senate. He reorganized the empire into twelve units called dioceses. This new structure of government, which replaced the principate, is generally referred to as the tetrarchy (teh-TRAR-kee) because two senior and two junior emperors ruled the empire.

The structure of the tetrarchy did not make it easier to defend the empire. **Constantine** (272–337, r. 312–337), the son of one of the junior emperors named by Diocletian, defeated each of the other emperors in battle until he was the sole ruler of the reunited empire. In 330, to place himself near threatened frontiers, Constantine established a new capital 800 miles (1,300 km) to the east at Byzantium (bizz-AN-tee-um) on the Bosphorus, which he named for himself, Constantinople (modern-day Istanbul, Turkey). At the time the population of Byzantium was around fifty thousand, while that of Rome was over one million. The move was strategic: it was difficult to maintain control of the empire from a base in Rome, and the emperors of the tetrarchy had already established individual capitals outside of Rome. Constantinople, located near the Danube and the Euphrates frontiers, could be defended more easily than Rome.

●**Constantine** (272–337, r. 312–337) May have converted to Christianity late in life. In 313 C.E. issued the Edict of Milan, the first imperial ruling to allow the practice of Christianity. Shifted the capital from Rome to the new city of Constantinople (modern-day Istanbul, Turkey) in 330 C.E.

When Constantine died in 337, he left the empire to his three sons, who immediately began fighting for control. After the last of Constantine's sons died in 364, no ruler succeeded in reuniting the empire for more than a few years at a time. In 395 the emperor formally divided the empire into western and eastern halves.

The fourth century was a time, particularly in the west, of economic decline. Repeated epidemics struck Rome and killed many of those living in the overcrowded city. In addition, armies had difficulty recruiting soldiers to staff their units. The central government, chronically short of revenues, minted devalued coins that contained far less metal than indicated by their face value. People living in regions where the use of coins had been common were forced to barter simply because fewer coins were in use. As the economy contracted, many urban dwellers moved to the countryside to grow their own crops.

During the fourth century, the armies of Germanic-speaking peoples repeatedly defeated the overstretched Roman army. These peoples, including the Vandals (see below), the Visigoths and Ostrogoths (both branches of the Goths), and other tribes (see Map 7.3), lived north and west of the empire and spoke a variety of languages in the Germanic language family (see Chapter 10). Although the residents of the Roman Empire looked down on these preliterate peoples, who lived in simple villages, the Goths and Vandals proved to be highly mobile and ferocious fighters. They had little to defend and so could devote their energies to attacking the long Roman frontier. In 410 the Visigoths sacked Rome for three days and then retreated; this was the first time since the fourth-century B.C.E. attack of the Gauls (see page 178) that foreign armies had entered the city.

Religious Changes of the Late Empire

Diocletian launched the last persecution of Christianity in 303. In addition to ordering that Christian scriptures be destroyed and churches torn down, he called for the punishment of all practicing Christians. Since officials implemented these measures unevenly, the eastern section of the empire, which Diocletian ruled, was more severely affected than the west. The suppression was brief because his successor issued an edict of toleration in 311.

In that year Constantine defeated one of the other claimants to the throne. Initially he claimed to have had a vision of the Roman sun-god Apollo and the Roman numeral for 30, which is written XXX; he interpreted the vision to mean that Apollo chose him to rule for the next thirty years. However, Constantine later began to worship the Christian God alongside other Roman deities, and according to his biographer, a Christian bishop, Constantine had actually seen a Christian cross.

Whatever the precise nature of Constantine's own beliefs, we know for certain that he ended Diocletian's persecution of Christianity in 313. With his co-emperor, Constantine issued the Edict of Milan, which compensated Christians for any property confiscated during Diocletian's persecution and officially allowed the practice of Christianity. This decision proved crucial to Christianity, in the same way as had Ashoka's support for Buddhism and the Achaemenid emperors' support for Zoroastrianism. (See the feature "World History in Today's World: Snapshot of Christianity.") In 380 Christianity was declared the only permissible religion in the empire, the final step to its becoming the official religion of the Roman Empire.

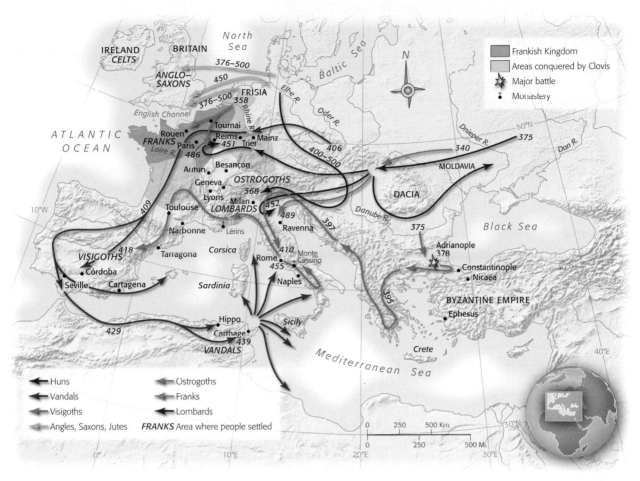

MAP 7.3

The Germanic Migrations   Although the Romans looked down on the pre-literate Germanic peoples living on their borders, the Germanic armies proved surprisingly powerful and launched wave after wave of attack on the empire and Rome itself. In 410, the Visigoths came from the east and sacked Rome. In 430 Augustine (354–430) witnessed 80,000 Vandals attack his home city of Hippo on the north African coast. After his death, the Vandals crossed the Mediterranean and looted Rome for two weeks in 455.

(CL) **Interactive Map**

In 325 Constantine summoned different church leaders to Nicaea (ny-SEE-uh) (modern-day Iznik, Turkey) and encouraged them to reach an agreement about the nature of the Trinity, which consisted of God, Jesus Christ, and the Holy Spirit, often mentioned in the book of Acts in conjunction with healing and exorcism. By the fourth century, many Christians had come to believe that God, Jesus, and the Holy Spirit were equal. Arius (AIR-ee-us), a teacher from Alexandria, Egypt, disagreed. He maintained that God the Father was superior to Jesus and the Holy Ghost because he had created them. The council drew up a basic statement of faith, the Nicene (ny-SEEN) Creed, which was worded specifically to counter the teachings of Arius and to assert that God and Jesus were

Snapshot of Christianity

Of the 6.1 billion people in the world today, 2.1 billion people identify themselves as Christian, making Christianity the world's largest religion. The largest groupings belong to Catholic, Protestant, or Eastern Orthodox churches, while the smaller Christian churches include Jehovah's Witnesses, Quakers, and the Copts of Egypt, among many others. The degree of observance varies enormously: some attend services at least once a week and possibly more often, while others have not been inside a church since being baptized.

The heartland of Christianity has shifted since the early centuries of the religion, when most early Christians lived in the Mediterranean region governed by the Roman Empire. After the seventh century, many people in North Africa and western Asia converted to Islam (see Chapter 9), while the number of Christians in Europe continued to grow. In 1900, 95 percent of Europeans identified themselves as Christian, yet in 2000, only 77 percent did.

The area of greatest growth is unquestionably in Africa, where 45 percent of the population identifies itself as Christian (versus 9 percent in 1900). One of the fastest-growing branches of African Christianity is Pentecostalism, whose ministers perform healings in the name of Jesus. Many Africans are drawn to Christianity because of Christian churches' promise to provide good health, money, and a better standard of living.

In 2000, the world area with the greatest concentration of Christians (93 percent) was Latin America. Yet the percentage of Latin Americans who identify themselves as Christian is shrinking slightly, while the number of Christians in Africa and Asia is growing. In short, fully 60 percent of the world's Christians in 2000 lived in Africa, Latin America, and Asia.

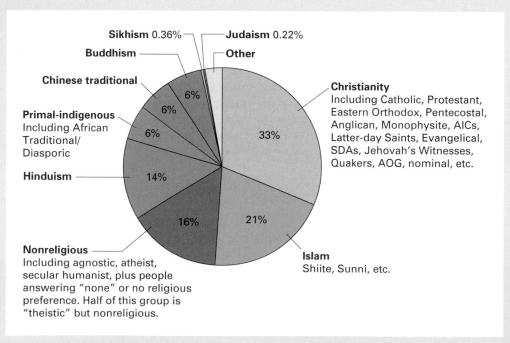

Chart from www.adherents.com. Used by permission.

made of the same substance.[8] When Arius refused to sign the Nicene Creed, which became the basic statement of Christian belief, the Council of Nicaea excommunicated, or expelled, him from the church. In subsequent centuries the church convened many similar meetings to ensure doctrinal agreement among the different Christian branches.

During the third and fourth centuries, church leaders met to decide which books of the Bible, both in the Hebrew Bible (which Christians call the Old Testament) and the New Testament, should be included in the canon and which should be viewed as less reliable, or apocryphal. One of Arius's main opponents, Saint Athanasius (293–373), lived in Alexandria, Egypt, an important Christian center. He was the first person to list the twenty-seven books of the New Testament as canonical, the final step in the formation of the Bible.

As part of his support for the Christian church, Constantine also ordered churches built at sites in Jerusalem that Jesus had visited. Although more difficult than in earlier, more peaceful centuries, travel was still possible in the fourth and fifth centuries, and Christian pilgrimages, often to Jerusalem, became increasingly popular. Travel was safe enough that ordinary women could also make the trip, as we learn from a travel account written by a woman named Egeria, who, sometime between 380 and 400 C.E., traveled all the way from her homeland in Spain to the Holy Land, the Christian name for Judaea. She went to Egypt, the Sinai, Jordan, and modern-day Turkey to visit the important sites of Judaism and early Christianity. After a three-year stay in Jerusalem, Egeria decided to continue her journey before returning home: "by the will of God, I wished to go to Mesopotamia of Syria [modern-day Edessa, Turkey], to visit the holy monks who were said to be numerous there and to be of such exemplary life that it can scarcely be described."[9] The devout Egeria wanted to see monasteries because they were a new institution.

Christianity in North Africa

As we can see from Egeria's itinerary, North Africa had already become an important center of Christianity by the fourth century. An Egyptian Christian, Pachomius (ca. 290–346), had founded the first monastic communities early in the fourth century. Before Pachomius, Christians who wanted to devote themselves full-time to a religious life had lived alone as hermits. Pachomius designed a monastic community whose members worked in the fields and prayed each day. In the centuries after his death, monasteries became so popular that they spread from Egypt to all over the Mediterranean.

One important Christian center lay to the east of Egypt in Aksum, in modern-day Ethiopia, whose rulers converted soon after Constantine issued the Edict of Milan. Their kingdom profited by taxing the trade from Egypt that went via the Red Sea to India. Merchants, who exported ivory from Africa and imported frankincense and myrrh from Arabia, encountered Christians while on trading voyages to the Mediterranean and introduced the religion to their countrymen.

The pre-Christian inscriptions commissioned by the rulers of Aksum mention local deities, including the southern Arabian goddess of the evening star, while the later ones mention the Lord of Heaven. One inscription, in Greek, names the Father, the Son, and the Holy Ghost, a definite indication of the ruler's support for Christianity. The Aksum Christians looked to the Egyptian church for leadership; the first bishop of Aksum and all his successors received their appointments from Egyptian bishops.

■ Stone Stele at Axum, Ethiopia

Supported by a counterweight placed underground, this stone tower stands 67 feet (21 m) tall. It represents a building ten stories high, with closed windows and a door bolted shut. Notice the lock on the ground floor level. Some two hundred stone towers like this were built in the 300s and 400s, when the rulers of Aksum converted to Christianity, but, unlike coins from the same period that show the cross, these towering monuments give no hint that the rulers who built them had converted to Christianity. (Werner Forman/Art Resource, NY)

To the west of Egypt was another Christian center at Hippo, now Annaba, Algeria, home to one of the most important thinkers in early Christianity, Augustine (354–430). Educated in North Africa, Augustine wrote over five million words in his lifetime. His book *The Confessions* detailed his varied experiences, which included fathering a child and belonging to the Manichaean order (see page 171), before he joined the Christian church and became the bishop of Hippo. According to Augustine, God's grace was so great that all, no matter how much they had violated the church's teachings, would be forgiven if they joined the church. Augustine encouraged the practice of confessing one's sins to a member of the clergy, and confession became an important rite in early Christianity.

• **Vandals** A Germanic tribe that attacked North Africa in 430 C.E. and sacked Rome for two weeks in 455 C.E. Their fighting techniques and looting were so brutal that the word *vandal* came to mean any deliberate act of destruction.

The Barbarian Invasions: The Fall of Rome

In 430, the last year of Augustine's life, the **Vandals** led a force of eighty thousand men from different Germanic tribes across the Mediterranean and laid siege to Hippo. Augustine witnessed

whole cities sacked, country villas razed, their owners killed or scattered as refugees, the churches deprived of their bishops and clergy, and the holy virgins and ascetics dispersed; some tortured to death, some killed outright, others, as prisoners, reduced to losing their integrity, in soul and body, to serve an evil and brutal enemy.[10]

For him, the invasions indicated the breakdown of the Roman Empire and the end of the civilized world.

After taking Hippo, the Vandals went on to conquer all of North Africa and the Mediterranean islands of Sardinia, Corsica, and Sicily. Their fighting techniques and looting were so brutal that the word *vandal* came to mean any deliberate act of destruction. In 455, the Vandals moved north to Italy and sacked Rome for two weeks, exposing again the city's vulnerability.

For the next twenty years different Germanic tribes gained control of the city and placed puppet emperors on the throne. In 476, the final emperor of the west-

(CL) **Primary Source:**
Augustine Denounces Paganism and Urges Romans to Enter the City of God
In The City of God, *Augustine uses sarcasm to condemn the rituals of Rome's pre-Christian religion.*

ern empire was deposed and not replaced. This date marks the end of the western empire, and many earlier historians declared that the Roman Empire fell in 476.

Most recent historians, however, prefer not to speak in these terms. They note that the Eastern Roman Empire, the Byzantine Empire, continued to be governed from Constantinople for another thousand years (see Chapter 10). The cultural center of the Mediterranean world, thoroughly Christianized by this time, had shifted once again—away from the Latin-speaking world centered on Rome to the Greek-speaking world, where it had been before Polybius was deported to Rome in 168 B.C.E.

Three different governments—a republic, a principate, and a tetrarchy—had ruled Rome for nearly one thousand years. During that time the Mediterranean world had taken shape, and, with the support of Rome's rulers, a single religion, Christianity, had spread throughout the Roman Empire. The next chapter will analyze how decisions made by many different rulers led to the spread of two different religions, Buddhism and Hinduism, throughout Asia.

Chapter Review

 Download the MP3 audio file of the Chapter Review and listen to it on the go.

In the second century B.C.E., travel around the Mediterranean was so convenient that Polybius, the client of a Roman general, was able to visit many places in Italy, Spain, Carthage, and North Africa and even to sail down the Atlantic coast of Africa. With each passing century, transportation, both overland and by sea, improved, and even in the last years of the western empire Egeria was able to travel throughout the Holy Land and western Asia. The roads around the Mediterranean and the waterways across it provided wonderfully effective channels for the spread of Christian teachings. With the emperor's support, Christianity became the sole religion of the empire at the end of the fourth century, and the Mediterranean region governed by the Roman Empire became the core area of Christianity.

 How did Rome, a small settlement in central Italy, expand to conquer and control the entire Mediterranean world of Europe, western Asia, and North Africa?

The Roman Republic was gradually able to gain control of the Italian peninsula through a series of conquests; it then granted the victorious citizen-soldiers land, allowed the Latin speakers among the defeated to join the republic on an equal footing with its citizens, and welcomed the defeated soldiers to serve in its army. By 272 B.C.E. Rome had conquered the Italian peninsula. The treaty ending the Second Punic War with Carthage granted Rome control of the western Mediterranean in 201 B.C.E., and Rome's defeat of both the Macedonians and the Greeks brought control of the eastern Mediterranean in 133 B.C.E.

KEY TERMS
Polybius (174)
Roman Republic (178)
Roman senate (178)
Carthage (179)
Punic Wars (180)
Hannibal (180)
tax farmers (182)
paterfamilias (182)
dictator (184)
Julius Caesar (184)
Roman principate (185)
Augustus (185)
Jesus (193)
Paul (194)
Constantine (199)
Vandals (204)

How did the political structure of the Roman Empire change as it grew?

The structure of the republic proved incapable of handling the huge empire. During the first century B.C.E., privatized armies of slaves and clients led by generals plunged the empire into civil war, and peace came only with Augustus's creation of the principate, a monarchy in all but name, in 27 B.C.E. Rome expanded to its widest borders under the principate, and until 180 C.E. it enjoyed nearly two centuries of peace, called the Pax Romana. In 284 C.E. the Romans adopted yet another governmental system, the tetrarchy, which had two senior emperors and two junior emperors.

 What were the basic teachings of Jesus, and how did Christianity become the major religion of the empire?

According to the gospels, Jesus distilled his teachings to two major points: everyone should love God, and everyone should love his or her neighbor. His disciple Paul taught that God had sent his son Jesus as the Messiah to atone for the sins of all Christians. Although banned during the principate, Christianity spread throughout the empire, and Emperor Constantine's support for the new religion proved crucial. By the end of the fourth century, when the emperor forbade worship of the different Roman gods, Christianity had become the only permitted religion of the empire.

 What allowed Rome to retain such a large empire for so long, and what caused the loss of the western half of the empire?

The empire was able to retain so much territory for so long because of its rulers' willingness to adopt new structures. At the end of the third century, the emperor Diocletian created the tetrarchy, a government headed by two senior and two junior emperors, in the hope of bringing greater order. He also reorganized the provincial structure. Diocletian's successor Constantine established a new capital at Constantinople, a measure that strengthened the empire but left the city of Rome vulnerable. Sustained attacks by different barbarian tribes, including the Visigoths and the Vandals, weakened the western half of the empire so much that in 476 its governing tribes did not even bother to name a puppet emperor. But even after the empire shifted east to the new capital, the Mediterranean remained a coherent region bound by the Christian religion and the common languages of Greek and Latin.

For Further Reference

Boardman, John, Jasper Griffin, and Oswyn Murray. *The Oxford History of the Roman World*. New York: Oxford University Press, 1986.

Casson, Lionel. *Travel in the Ancient World*. Baltimore: Johns Hopkins University Press, 1974.

Etienne, Robert. *Pompeii: The Day a City Died*. New York: Harry N. Abrams, 1992.

Frend, W. H. C. *The Rise of Christianity*. Philadelphia: Fortress Press, 1984.

Garnsey, Peter, and Richard Saller. *The Roman Empire: Economy, Society and Culture*. Berkeley: University of California Press, 1987.

Hornblower, Simon, and Antony Spawforth, eds. *The Oxford Companion to Classical Civilization*. New York: Oxford University Press, 1998.

Kebric, Robert B. *Roman People*. 4th ed. New York: McGraw-Hill, 2005.

Polybius. *The Rise of the Roman Empire*. Translated by Ian Scott-Kilvert. New York: Penguin Books, 1979.

Scarre, Chris. *The Penguin Historical Atlas of Ancient Rome*. New York: Penguin Books, 1995.

Tingay, G. I. F., and J. Badcock. *These Were the Romans*. Chester Springs, Pa.: Dufour Editions, 1989.

Wilken, Robert L. *The Christians as the Romans Saw Them*. New Haven: Yale University Press, 2003.

Websites

In Old Pompeii
(http://edsitement.neh.gov/view-lesson-plan.asp?ID=271). A field trip to ancient Pompeii.

 WEB RESOURCES

Pronunciation Guide

Interactive Maps

MAP 7.1 The Roman Empire at Its Greatest Extent

MAP 7.2 The Spread of Christianity

MAP 7.3 The Germanic Migrations

Primary Sources

Chapter Objectives

ACE Multiple-Choice Quiz

Flashcards

Internet Medieval Sourcebook: End of Rome
(http://www.fordham.edu/halsall/sbook.html). Extremely valuable collection of primary sources about the fifth century C.E. and the "fall" of the Roman Empire.

The Perseus Digital Library
(www.perseus.tufts.edu). A wealth of searchable texts from the classical world in both the original language and English translation.

World Religions
(www.adherents.com). Takes an informed Religious Studies approach to the world's many religions.

Films

A Funny Thing Happened on the Way to the Forum

Gladiator

Spartacus

Hindu and Buddhist States and Societies in Asia, 100–1000

The year was 629, only eleven years after the founding of the Tang dynasty (618–907). Emperor Taizong (TIE-zohng) (r. 626–649) had banned all foreign travel because he had not yet secured control of the Chinese empire. Undeterred, the Chinese monk **Xuanzang** (ca. 596–664) departed on foot from the capital of Chang'an (CHAHNG-ahn) and headed overland for India so that he could obtain the original Sanskrit versions of Buddhist texts. One of his first stops after leaving China was the Central Asian oasis kingdom of Gaochang (GOW-chahng) on the western edge of the Taklamakan Desert, whose rulers—like many others throughout Asia at the time—adopted from Indian and Chinese models to strengthen their governments. At Gaochang, we learn from a biography written decades later by a disciple, the Buddhist king politely requested that Xuanzang (SHUEN-zahng) give up his trip and preach to his subjects. Xuanzang courteously explained that he preferred to go to India. The conversation suddenly turned ugly:

CHINESE BUDDHIST
MONK, TANG DYNASTY

(Musée des Arts Asiatiques-Guimet, Paris, France/
Réunion des Musées Nationaux/Art Resource, NY)

The king's face flushed. He pushed up his sleeves, bared his arms, and shouted, "Your disciple has other ways to deal with you. How can you go on your own! Either you stay or I send you back to your country. Please consider my offer carefully. I think it is better for you to do what I say."

The Master replied, "I have come on my way to seek the Great Dharma and now have encountered an obstacle. Your majesty may detain my body but never my spirit."

CL This icon will direct you to interactive activities and study materials on the *Voyages* website: www.cengage.com/history/hansen/voyages1e

208

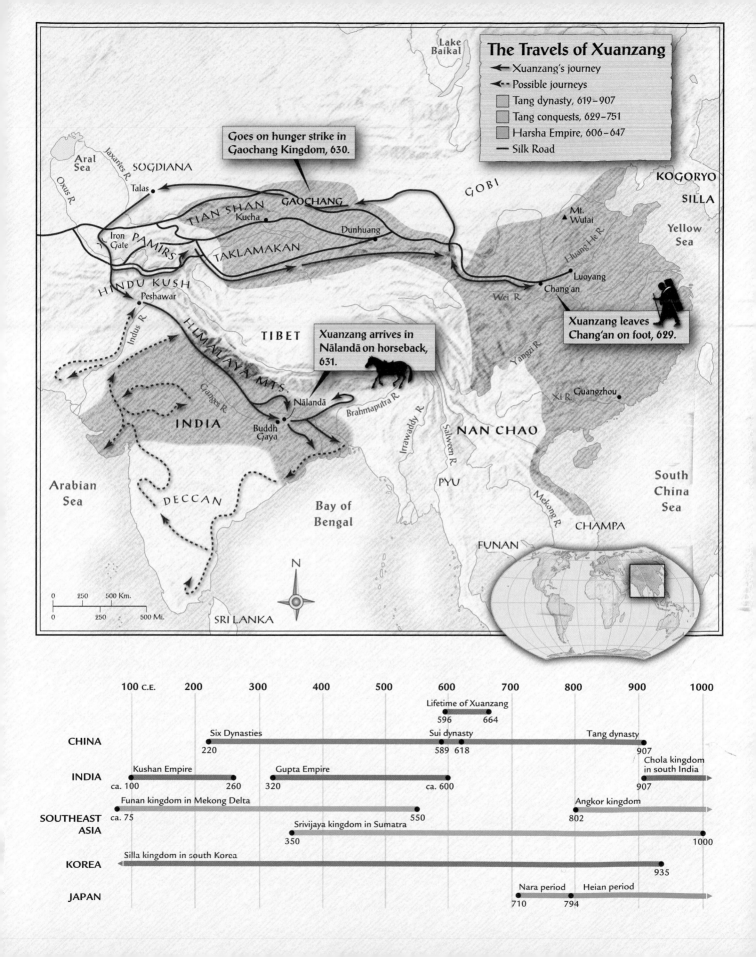

The Travels of Xuanzang

← Xuanzang's journey
◄-- Possible journeys
☐ Tang dynasty, 619–907
☐ Tang conquests, 629–751
☐ Harsha Empire, 606–647
— Silk Road

Goes on hunger strike in Gaochang Kingdom, 630.

Xuanzang arrives in Nālandā on horseback, 631.

Xuanzang leaves Chang'an on foot, 629.

Lake Baikal

Aral Sea
Oxus R.
Jaxartes R.
SOGDIANA
Talas
TIAN SHAN
Iron Gate
Kucha
PAMIRS
TAKLAMAKAN
GAOCHANG
Dunhuang
GOBI
KOGORYO
SILLA
Mt. Wutai
Huang He R.
Yellow Sea
HINDU KUSH
Peshawar
Indus R.
HIMALAYA MTS.
TIBET
Ganges R.
Nālandā
Buddh Gaya
INDIA
Brahmaputra R.
Wei R.
Luoyang
Chang'an
Yangzi R.
Xi R.
Guangzhou
Irrawaddy R.
Salween R.
NAN CHAO
Arabian Sea
DECCAN
Bay of Bengal
PYU
Mekong R.
South China Sea
CHAMPA
FUNAN

0 250 500 Km.
0 250 500 Mi.

N

SRI LANKA

	100 C.E.	200	300	400	500	600	700	800	900	1000

Lifetime of Xuanzang
596   664

CHINA
Six Dynasties
220
Sui dynasty
589 618
Tang dynasty
907
Chola kingdom in south India
907

INDIA
Kushan Empire
ca. 100   260
Gupta Empire
320   ca. 600

SOUTHEAST ASIA
Funan kingdom in Mekong Delta
ca. 75   550
Srivijaya kingdom in Sumatra
350
Angkor kingdom
802
1000

KOREA
Silla kingdom in south Korea
935

JAPAN
Nara period
710
Heian period
794

His sobs made it impossible for him to say more. Even so, the king did not give in but increased the gifts he gave. Every day at mealtimes, the king presented a tray of food to Xuanzang. Since Xuanzang was detained against his will and his plans thwarted, he vowed not to eat so that the king would change his mind. Accordingly, for three days he sat erect and refused all water.

On the fourth day, the king discovered that the Master's breathing had become very faint. Feeling deeply ashamed of himself and afraid, the king bowed with his head touching the ground and apologized: "I will allow you to go to the West. Please eat immediately."[1]

Xuanzang (ca. 596–664) A monk who traveled to Central Asia and India between 629 and 644 to obtain original Buddhist texts.

chakravartin Literally "turner of the wheel," a Buddhist term for the ideal ruler who patronized Buddhism but never became a monk.

Silk Routes Overland routes through Central Asia connecting China and India, as well as the sea routes around Southeast Asia, along which were transmitted teachings, technologies, and languages.

Xuanzang's three-day hunger strike succeeded. The contrite king offered to provide his travel expenses, and Xuanzang in turn agreed to teach the king's subjects before continuing his journey.

We might wonder why the Gaochang king so desperately wanted a lone monk to remain in his kingdom. As this chapter explains, Xuanzang represented an important element of the revised Chinese blueprint for empire. After reuniting China, the Sui (SWAY) (589–617) and Tang (TAHNG) emperors introduced important additions to the Qin/Han synthesis of Legalist and Confucian policies (see Chapter 4), including civil service examinations, a new system of taxation, and a complex law code. They also aspired to fulfill Ashoka's model of the ideal **chakravartin** king who patronized Buddhism. The Gaochang king applied the new Chinese model to his kingdom in the hope of strengthening his rule. After the hunger strike, he realized that if he could not persuade Xuanzang to stay, at least he could provide him with travel expenses and become known as a generous donor, a key component of being a chakravartin. (Conversely, if Xuanzang had died while staying with him, it would have permanently damaged his reputation as a pious ruler.)

When Xuanzang returned to China in 644, he had covered over 10,000 miles (16,000 km). The Gaochang kingdom had fallen to the armies of the Tang dynasty, and Emperor Taizong welcomed Xuanzang enthusiastically. He sought both Xuanzang's skills as a translator and the valuable information he brought about distant lands. Historians of India and Central Asia are particularly grateful for Xuanzang's detailed accounts of his trip, which supplement sparse indigenous sources. After he returned, Xuanzang translated over seventy Buddhist texts, many still read today because of their accuracy.

The overland routes through Central Asia that Xuanzang took to India—and the sea routes around Southeast Asia taken by others—are known today as the **Silk Routes.** These routes were conduits not just for pilgrims like Xuanzang but also for merchants plying their goods, soldiers dispatched to fight in distant lands, and refugees fleeing dangerous areas for safety. These travelers told of powerful rulers in India and China, whose accomplishments inspired chieftains in border areas to imitate them. These Asian leaders introduced new writing systems, law codes, ways of recruiting government officials, and taxation systems, often modifying them to suit their own societies. Some, like the Gaochang king and the rulers of Korea, Japan, and Tibet, patronized Buddhism and adopted Tang policies. Others, particularly in South and Southeast Asia, emulated South Asian monarchs and built temples to deities such as Shiva (SHIH-vah) and Vishnu (VISH-new), the most important deities in the emerging belief system of **Hinduism.**

> ● **Hinduism** Temple-based religious system that arose between 300 and 700 in India. Hinduism has two dimensions: public worship in temples and daily private worship in the home.

The individual decisions of these rulers resulted in the religious reorientation of the region. In 100 C.E., a disunited India was predominantly Buddhist, while the unified China of the Han dynasty embraced Legalist, Confucian, and Daoist beliefs. By 1000 C.E., the various kingdoms of India and Southeast Asia had become largely Hindu, while China, Japan, Korea, and Tibet had become Buddhist. This religious shift did not occur because a ruler of an intact empire, such as Constantine in the West (see Chapter 7), recognized a single religion. It was the result of many decisions taken by multiple rulers in different places over the course of centuries.

Focus Questions

 How did Buddhism change after the year 100? How did Hinduism displace it within India?

 How did geography, trade, and religion shape the development of states and societies in Southeast Asia?

 How did the Sui and Tang dynasties modify the Qin/Han blueprint for empire?

 Which elements of the revised Chinese blueprint for empire did Korea and Japan borrow intact? Which did they modify?

● Religion and the State in India, 100–1000

By the year 100, India had broken up into different regional kingdoms, all much smaller than the Mauryan Empire ruled by Ashoka (see Chapter 3) but bound by common cultural ties of Buddhism, social hierarchy, and respect for classical Sanskrit learning. Although the Ashokan inscriptions claim that Buddhist missionaries went to other countries to spread the dharma, the first evidence of the spread of Buddhism beyond South Asia dates to the Kushan empire (ca. 50–260 C.E.). The most important Kushan ruler, Kanishka (r. ca. 120–140 C.E.), launched a missionary movement that propelled the new Greater Vehicle teachings of Buddhism (see next page) into Central Asia and China.

Between 100 and 1000 C.E., Buddhism gained many adherents outside India but increasingly lost ground to new deities inside India. When Xuanzang traveled to north India in the early 600s, he noticed Buddhism in decline everywhere, and he recorded, often regretfully, the rise of a new religion taught by Brahmins. We know this religion as Hinduism, a name not used until the nineteenth century, when British scholars of Indian religion coined the term to denote Indians who were not Zoroastrian, Christian, or Muslim.[2] By the year 1000, in many regions in India, particularly south India, the largest religious institutions were temples to Hindu deities such as Vishnu and Shiva, and kings recorded magnificent gifts to Hindu temples in long inscriptions.

The Rise of Greater Vehicle Teachings in Buddhism

Buddhism changed a great deal between Ashoka's time in the third century B.C.E. and Kanishka's reign in the second century C.E. Most importantly, Buddhist teachings no longer required an individual to join the Buddhist order to gain enlightenment. New interpreters of Buddhism referred to their own teachings as the Greater Vehicle (Mahayana) and denigrated those of earlier schools as the Lesser Vehicle (Hinayana). For this reason, scholars sometimes call the earlier schools Theravada, meaning "the Tradition of the Elders."

The Buddha had also taught that he was not a deity and that his followers should not make statues of him. Yet Indians began to worship statues of the Buddha in the first and second centuries C.E. (see Chapter 3). They also began to pray to **bodhisattvas** (BODE-ee-saht-vahz) for easier childbirth or the curing of illness. A bodhisattva—literally, a being headed for Buddhahood—refers to someone on the verge of enlightenment who chooses, because of his or her compassion for others, to stay in this world for this and future lives and help other sentient beings (the Buddhist term for all living creatures, including humans) to attain nirvana.

The proponents of the Greater Vehicle schools emphasized that Buddhists could transfer merit from one person to another: if someone paid for a Buddhist text to be recited, he or she acquired a certain amount of merit that could be transferred to someone else, perhaps an ill relative. Buddhist inscriptions frequently state that someone gave a gift to the Buddhist order, such as paying for part of a monastery, in someone else's name.

During the early centuries of the Common Era, Buddhist monasteries appeared throughout India. This, too, was a departure from earlier times. The Buddha had wandered from place to place with his followers and had stayed in one place only during the rainy season. Over the centuries, though, most Buddhist monks ceased the daily walk in which they asked for offerings from townspeople and instead moved into permanent monasteries. Since monastic rules forbade the monks from working in the fields, most monasteries hired laborers to do their farming for them. One monastery erected a giant stone begging bowl by its front gate. Rather than feed monks as they had in the past, the monastery's supporters placed large gifts in the stone bowl for the monks and nuns.

King Kanishka certainly supported the Buddhist order, and rich merchants probably did as well. Many Buddhist texts encouraged donors to make gifts of gold, silver, lapis lazuli, crystal, coral, pearls, and agate. These valuable items, often referred to as the Seven Treasures, were traded overland between India and China. The blue mineral lapis lazuli could be mined only in present-day Afghanistan, and one of the world's best sources of pearls was the island of Sri Lanka, just south of India.

• bodhisattva
Buddhist term denoting a being headed for Buddhahood.

The Buddhists, like the Christians at the Council of Nicaea (see Chapter 7), met periodically to discuss their teachings, and Buddhist sources credit Kanishka with organizing the Fourth Buddhist Council, whose primary task was to determine which versions of orally transmitted texts were authoritative. Because the few writing materials available in ancient India, such as leaves and wooden tablets, decayed in India's tropical climate, Buddhist texts were not recorded. Monks specialized in a specific text, or a group of texts, and they transmitted them to their disciples by teaching them to memorize them.

The Kushan dynasty was only one of many regional dynasties in India during the first to third centuries C.E. After 140 C.E., Kanishka's successors fought in various military campaigns, and Chinese sources report the arrival of refugees fleeing the political upheavals of their homeland in north India. The earliest Buddhists to arrive in China in the first and second centuries C.E. were missionaries from the Kushan empire, and their propagation of Buddhist teachings was particularly influential (see below). In 260 C.E. the Sasanians (see Chapter 6) defeated the final Kushan ruler, bringing the dynasty to an end.

The Rise of Hinduism, 300–900

In the centuries after the fall of the Kushan dynasty, various dynasties arose in the different regions of South Asia, which continued to be culturally united even as it was politically divided. One of the most important was the **Gupta dynasty,** which controlled much of north India between 320 and 600. An admirer of the Mauryan dynasty (ca. 320–185 B.C.E.), Chandragupta (r. 319/320–ca. 330), the founder of the Gupta (GOO-ptah) dynasty took the same name as the Mauryan founder and governed from the former capital at Pataliputra (modern-day Patna).

In an important innovation, the Gupta rulers issued land grants to powerful families, Brahmins, monasteries, and even villages. These grants gave the holder the right to collect a share of the harvest from the cultivators who worked his land. Inscriptions on stone and copper record the details of these gifts: the dimensions of the land, the share of the harvest given to the grantee and to village officials, and the names of the accountants responsible for implementing these arrangements. Scribes developed a decimal system that allowed them to record the dimensions of each plot of land. Certainly by 876, and quite possibly during the Gupta reign, they also started to use a small circle to hold empty places; that symbol is the ancestor of the modern zero.[3] On the other side of the globe, the Maya started to use zero at roughly the same time (see page 125).

The Gupta rulers, inscriptions reveal, made many grants of land to Brahmins, members of the highest-ranking varna (see Chapter 3) who conducted rituals honoring Hindu deities like Vishnu and Shiva. The two deities, who appear only briefly in the *Rig Veda* of ancient India, became increasingly important in later times. Both deities took many forms with various names. Worshipers of Vishnu claimed that the Buddha was actually Vishnu in an earlier incarnation.

In 631, when Xuanzang reached Gandhara, which had been a center of Buddhism under Kanishka, he noticed many abandoned monasteries: "On both banks of the Shubhavastu River there were formerly fourteen hundred monasteries with eighteen thousand monks, but now the monasteries were in desolation and the number of monks had decreased."[4] Buddhist monasteries were not as large as they had been in earlier centuries, and the number of Buddhist monks had also declined. (See the feature "World History in Today's World: Snapshot of Hinduism and Buddhism.")

Gupta dynasty (ca. 320–600) Indian dynasty based in north India; emulated the earlier Mauryan dynasty. The Gupta kings pioneered a new type of religious gift: land grants to Brahmin priests and Hindu temples.

Snapshot of Hinduism and Buddhism

Hinduism, with 900 million adherents worldwide, is the world's third-largest religion (after Christianity and Islam); Buddhism, with 350 million believers, is the fourth. Almost all Hindus live in South Asia or are of South Asian descent. The largest group of Hindus, 780 million, resides in India.

Modern India is home to a Buddhist community as well. Indian Buddhists are not the descendants of long-established Buddhist families but members of untouchable groups, as they were called in the British colonial period, who converted to Buddhism at the urging of Dr. Bhimrao Ramji Ambedkar (1891–1956). A member of a jati who traditionally had been sweepers and messengers, Ambedkar became a leader of untouchables after receiving his Ph.D. from Columbia University. In 1935, he announced his decision to stop being a Hindu because he felt that Hinduism reinforced discrimination against members of lower castes.

On October 14, 1956, nine years after India gained independence, Ambedkar took the traditional vows to become a lay Buddhist and composed twenty-two new vows that he administered to nearly 400,000 followers. The nineteenth vow explained: "I renounce Hinduism, which is harmful for humanity and impedes the advancement and development of humanity because it is based on inequality, and adopt Buddhism as my religion."

Ambedker objected to Hindu teachings because they ranked Brahmins as the most pure of all jati.

Only two months later, Ambedkar died. Since then others have organized similar mass conversions. One occurred on October 14, 2006, fifty years after Ambedkar took his vows. The Buddhism movement has been most successful in Ambedkar's home state of Maharashtra and in neighboring Uttar Pradesh. Of the 7.95 million Indians who said that they were Buddhist in the 2001 census, 5.83 million, or 73 percent, lived in Maharashtra.

Many of the world's Buddhists are not as explicit about their religious adherence as are Ambedkar's followers. Several Southeast Asian nations subscribe to Theravada Buddhist teachings, including Thailand, Cambodia, and Sri Lanka. Almost all young Thai men undergo temporary ordination and spend a year or so studying Buddhism at Buddhist monasteries. The largest numbers of Buddhist adherents, however, live in China, with an estimated 100 million Buddhists, or in Japan, with 90 million. While many modern Chinese or Japanese may identify themselves as Buddhists if asked, they visit Buddhist temples only rarely and are much less actively Buddhist than Thais.

Sources: www.adherents.com and www.columbia.edu/itc/mealac/pritchett/00ambedkar/ambedkar_buddha/.

Xuanzang's time in India from 630 to 643 coincided with the long reign of King Harsha (606–647) in Kanauj (KAHN-awj) (modern-day Kanpur), one of the successor dynasties to the Guptas. Remarking on the caste system, which was so different from that in China, he ranked the four varna in the traditional order according to purity: Brahmins, royal caste, merchant class, and agricultural class.[5] Brahmin priests played an important role in Hindu worship, but unlike the Brahmins of Vedic times, who had conducted large public ceremonies with animal sacrifices, the Brahmins of the Gupta era performed offerings to Vishnu and Shiva at temples.

Hindu worship of Shiva and Vishnu had two dimensions: public ceremonies conducted by Brahmins in temples, which allowed local rulers to proclaim their power for all visiting the temple to see, and private worship in the home. In private worship, devotees daily sang songs of love or praise to their deities. This strong personal tie between the devotee and the deity is known as **bhakti.** The main evidence for the rise of bhakti devotionalism is a large corpus of poems

● **bhakti** Literally "personal devotion or love," a term for Hindu poetry or cults that emphasizes a strong personal tie between the deity and a devotee, who did not use priests as intermediaries.

written in regional languages such as Tamil, a language of great antiquity spoken in the southernmost tip of India.

The Beginnings of the Chola Kingdom, ca. 900

The Tamil-speaking Chola (CHOH-la) kings, who established their dynasty in south India in 907, were among the most powerful leaders who patronized Hindu temples. In their capital at Tanjore, they bestowed huge land grants on the Shiva temple in the hope that their subjects would associate the generosity of the royal donors with the power of the deity.

The Tanjore temple to Shiva, like many other Hindu temples, had an innermost chamber, called the womb room, that housed a stone lingam, to which

■ **Brihadeshwara Temple at Tanjore, with Womb Room**   Rajaraja I (r. 985–1014) built this imposing temple (*below*) to Shiva at Tanjore. The temple's ornate exterior contrasts sharply with the austere interior. The innermost sanctuary of the Hindu temple, the womb room (*right*), held the lingam, on which devotees placed offerings, like the flowers shown here. A Hindu goddess sits on the peacock on the wall. Many temples allowed only Hindus, sometimes only Hindu priests, to enter the womb room.   (below: Dinodia Photo Library; right: Robert Harding/Jupiter Images)

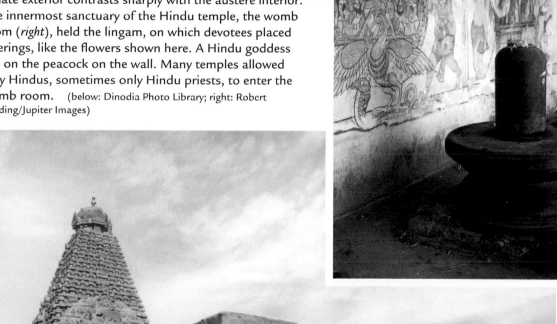

Hindu priests made ritual offerings. *Lingam* means "sign" or "phallus" in Sanskrit. The lingam was always placed in a womb room because male and female generative power had to be combined. On a concrete level, the lingam symbolized the creative force of human reproduction; on a more abstract level, it stood for all the creative forces in the cosmos.

The Shiva temple lands lay in the agricultural heartland of south India and, when irrigated properly, produced a rich rice harvest whose income supported the thousands of Brahmins who lived in the temple. These Brahmins performed rituals, memorized and transmitted different texts, and taught local boys in temple schools. The Chola kings controlled the immediate vicinity of the capital and possibly the other large cities in their district, but not the many villages surrounding the cities. Many of these villages were self-governing. But since their temples were subordinate to the larger temple in the Chola capital, they also acknowledged the Chola kings as their spiritual overlords.

One of the most successful Chola rulers was Rajaraja (RAH-jah-rah-jah) I (r. 985–1014), who conquered much of south India and sent armies as far as Srivijaya (sree-VEE-jeye-ah) (modern Indonesia, on the southern Malay Peninsula and Sumatra). Although he did not conquer any territory there, the people of Southeast Asia learned of the Chola king's accomplishments from these contacts. As a direct result, local rulers encouraged priests literate in Sanskrit to move to Southeast Asia to build Hindu temples and teach them about Chola governance (see page 218).

State, Society, and Religion in Southeast Asia, 300–1000

The term *Southeast Asia* encompasses a broad swath of land in subtropical Asia and over twenty thousand islands in the Pacific. In most periods, travel among islands and along the shore was easier than overland travel, which was possible only on some of the region's major rivers like the Irrawaddy and the Salween in modern Myanmar (Burma), the Red River in Vietnam, and the Mekong in Laos, Thailand, Cambodia, and Vietnam. Most of the region's sparse population (an estimated fifteen people per square mile [six people per sq km] in the seventeenth century,[6] and even lower in earlier centuries) lived in isolated groups separated by forests and mountains, but the coastal peoples went on sea voyages as early as 1000 B.C.E.

Like India, Southeast Asia received heavy monsoon rains in the summer; successful agriculture often depended on storing rainwater in tanks for use throughout the year. While people in the lowlands raised rice in paddies, the different highland societies largely practiced slash-and-burn agriculture. Once farmers had exhausted the soil of a given place, they moved on, with the result that few states with fixed borders existed in Southeast Asia.

With no equivalent of caste, the shifting social structure of the region was basically egalitarian. People lived in different groups in the forested mountains without settling permanently in any given spot. From time to time, a leader unified some of the groups, dedicated a temple to either the Buddha or a Hindu deity, and adopted other policies in hopes of strengthening his new state.

Buddhist Kingdoms Along the Trade Routes

Merchants and religious travelers going from India to China (and back) by boat traveled along well-established routes (see Map 8.1). Before 350 C.E., ships usually landed at a port on the Isthmus of Kra, and travelers crossed the 35-mile (56-km) stretch of land dividing the Andaman Sea from the Gulf of Thailand by foot before resuming their sea voyages. This overland route could reduce an often treacherous sea route by 1,600 miles (2,500 km). The Buddhist kingdom of Funan, centered on the Mekong River Delta, arose in this area and thrived between the first and sixth centuries C.E. Surprisingly little is known about Funan; scholars debate its exact location and refer to it by its Chinese name, *Funan,* because they do not know its indigenous name.

Prevailing winds and the types of boat available determined which routes merchants and pilgrims took. During the spring and summer, while the Eurasian landmass heated up, travelers could follow the monsoon winds that blew toward India; during the fall and winter, as the landmass cooled, they could leave India and follow the winds that blew away from the landmass. Most boats had to wait in Southeast Asian ports for the winds to change. The long periods of waiting meant that entire ships—sometimes with several hundred crew and passengers—needed food and shelter for three to five months, and port towns grew up to accommodate their needs. Local rulers discovered that they could tax the travelers, and merchants realized that there was a market for Southeast Asian aromatic woods and spices in both China and India.

Funan declined as a Buddhist center sometime after 350 C.E., when the mariners of Southeast Asia discovered a new route between China and India. Merchants and monks boarded ships at Sri Lanka and traveled all the way to either the Strait of Malacca or the Sunda Strait. They disembarked in the kingdom of Srivijaya in modern-day Indonesia, waited for the winds to shift, and then continued through the South China Sea to China. The main port for the kingdom was located at the modern-day city of Palembang, which has a deep natural harbor. The kingdom traded with many regional kingdoms in central Java, where the world's largest Buddhist monument, at Borobudur (boh-roh-BUH-duhr), provides a powerful example of religious architecture connected with early state formation. (See the feature "Visual Evidence: Borobudur: A Buddhist Monument in Java, Indonesia.")

Srivijaya's ruler welcomed Buddhist travelers and made extensive contributions to local Buddhist monasteries as well as non-Buddhist deities. The Srivijayan kings called themselves "Lord of the Mountains" and "Spirit of the Waters of the Sea," titles from the local religious traditions. The kingdom of Srivijaya flourished between 700 and 1000 C.E.

Buddhist and Hindu Kingdoms of Inland Southeast Asia, 300–1000

Buddhist images made in stone appeared throughout interior Southeast Asia between 300 and 600. In the pre-Buddhist period, all the different societies of the region recognized certain individuals as "men of prowess" who used military skill and intelligence to rise to the leadership of their tribes. They succeeded against other claimants to power because they had more active networks of loyal supporters whom they could lead in times of war. Sometimes a leader was so successful that various tribal leaders acknowledged him as a regional overlord.

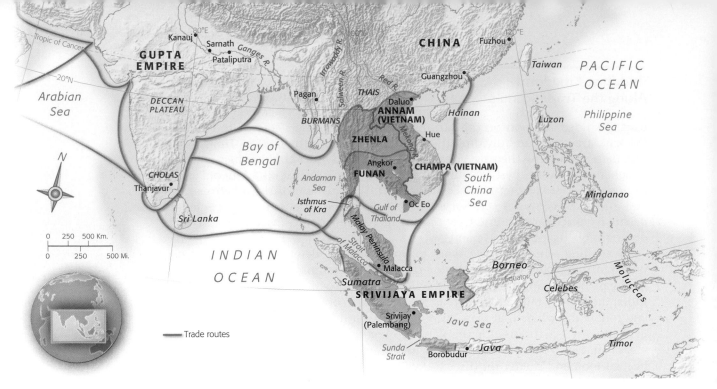

🌐 **MAP 8.1**

The Spread of Buddhism and Hinduism to Southeast Asia Sea routes connected Southeast Asia with both India and China, facilitating travel by missionaries to the region and by devotees from the region. The regions closest to China, particularly Vietnam, became predominantly Buddhist, like China, while the rulers of other regions, including Cambodia, patronized both Buddhism and Hinduism, as did most rulers in India.

Most societies in Southeast Asia recognized descent through both the mother and the father. In practice this meant that the son of a man of prowess was not necessarily the leading candidate to succeed him as leader; a nephew, particularly the child of his sister, had the same claim as the son. As a result, no group hung together for very long. People were loyal to a given individual, not to a dynasty, and when he died, they tended to seek a new man of prowess to support. After these men of prowess died, they became honored ancestors.

Burial practices varied widely throughout Southeast Asia. In modern Cambodia alone, archaeologists have found evidence of cremation, burial in the ground, burial by disposal in the ocean, and exposure of the dead above ground. Many people conceived of a natural world populated by different spirits usually thought to inhabit trees, rocks, and other physical features. Specialists conducted rituals that allowed them to communicate with these spirits.

This was the world into which literate outsiders came in the fourth, fifth, and sixth centuries C.E. Most of the visitors, some identified as Brahmins, came from India and knew how to read and write Sanskrit. Southeast Asians also traveled to India, where they studied Sanskrit and returned after they memorized both sacred texts and laws. Inscriptions often refer to men literate in Sanskrit as *purohita*, a Sanskrit word meaning a chief priest, who conducted rituals for leaders and served in their governments as an adviser or administrator. The teachings of devotional Hinduism, or bhakti (see above), encouraged devotees to study with a teacher, or purohita, so that they could get closer to the divinity they worshiped.

Literate teachers, whether native or not, brought different teachings—some we now identify as Buddhist, some as Hindu—to the rulers of Southeast Asia. We can see how they came together in one ruler's mind in the case of Jayavarman II (JAI-ah-var-mahn) (ca. 770–850), who ruled the lower Mekong basin in Cambodia between 802 and 850. (Jayavarman II was named for a seventh-century ruler of the same name.) Before the Mekong River empties into the South China Sea, much of its waters flow into Tonle Sap (the Great Lake). The lake served as a holding tank for the monsoon rains, which were channeled into nearby rice fields.

Historians view Jayavarman II's reign as the beginning of the Angkor period (802–1431), named for the **Angkor dynasty,** whose rulers spoke the Khmer (KMEHR) language. Because Jayavarman II is closely identified with the Hindu deity Shiva, this dynasty is often called a Hindu dynasty. Jayavarman II was a devotee of Shiva, who was believed to preside over the entire universe, with other less powerful deities having smaller realms. Similarly, Jayavarman II presided over the human universe, while the surrounding chieftains had their own smaller, inferior,

> **• Angkor dynasty**
> Khmer-speaking dynasty in modern-day Cambodia founded by Jayavarman II. His combination of Hindu and Buddhist imagery proved so potent that it was used by all later Angkor kings.

▪ **Bayon Gate, Angkor Thom, Cambodia**   In the 1180s and 1190s, the ruler Jayavarman VII built a series of monuments and temples, including this one at Angkor Thom, a fortified city just north of Angkor Wat. The figures on the road leading up to the Bayon Gate are Buddhist guardians: on the left stands a line of warrior deities; on the right, a row of gods. The faces on the four sides of the tower are those of a bodhisattva, but the multiple faces also seem Hindu, in an artful blending of Hindu and Buddhist imagery.   (Gavin Hellier/Robert Harding Picture Library Ltd./Alamy)

BOROBUDUR: A BUDDHIST MONUMENT IN JAVA, INDONESIA

The largest Buddhist monument in the world lies not in the homeland of the Buddha in India but over 1,000 miles (1,600 km) to the southeast at Borobudur on the island of Java in Indonesia. The Shailendra (SHAI-len-drah) kings (ca. 775–860) built the monument out of volcanic rock sometime in the eighth or ninth century, just as they were consolidating their rule. When they moved their capital to a different location in east Java, they abandoned the magnificent complex, and it lay unknown until the early nineteenth century, when Sir Thomas Raffles, founder of Singapore, saw it covered with mold and lichen plants in the middle of a dense forest.

Since no surviving documents explain the meaning of the elements of the monument, analysts must study the different sections of the enormous monument to reconstruct its possible meaning. Rising over 100 feet (31.5 m) above the ground, the monument rests on a large squarish base measuring 400 feet (122 m) on each side. The overall effect resembles the ziggurat temples of Mesopotamia. Staircases at the center of each level lead up to the next, and visitors walk around each level for a total of 3 miles (5 km) until they reach the top.

The lowest level of the monument, originally below ground, depicts an underground hell for those who do not obey Buddhist teachings. The four square terraces above contain over 2,500 panels, most showing scenes from the earlier lives of the Buddha. Monks and guides probably explained the meaning of these scenes to pilgrims. Near the top, the visitor reaches the three terraces holding seventy-two bodhisattvas, each sitting under a bell-shaped stone with holes to look through. At the top of the monument stands an empty stupa, which may have originally held a relic.

Borobudur was a pilgrimage site for people all over Southeast Asia. Pilgrims brought simple clay objects in the shape of stupas and buried them underground at the site. Archaeologists have unearthed 2,397 clay stupas and 252 clay tablets with writing on them. Pilgrims also buried clay pots and sheets of silver covered with written Buddhist charms, either to keep away evil spirits or to bring good health. The many languages on the tablets indicate that people came from great distances to see Borobudur and to make offerings to the Buddha who came to be worshiped so far from his original home.

Most analysts concur that the monument was designed to lead pilgrims from the underworld, shown in the base, up through the five platforms showing human existence, through the world of the seventy-two bodhisattvas to the single Buddha on top who had attained enlightenment. While the content of the different panels is clearly inspired by Buddhism, the design of the monument, with its multiple ascending levels, is distinctly local. No other Buddhist monument is like it.

Borobudur is made of two million separate blocks of yellow-brown andesite, volcanic rock found throughout Java. Each year over 70 inches (2 m) of rain falls on the rocks, creating the perfect environment for moss and lichen to thrive. Between 1973 and 1983, with UNESCO support, workers dismantled the monument, removed and cleaned each of the blocks, and restored the monument for the third time since its rediscovery in the early 1800s.

QUESTION FOR ANALYSIS

 How had Buddhist worship at stupas changed from the first century B.C.E. at Sanchi (see Visual Evidence, Chapter 3) to the eighth and ninth centuries at Borobudur?

These three circular terraces hold seventy-two smaller stupas, each housing an image of a bodhisattva.

This large stupa, 36 feet (11 m) in diameter and 460 feet (43 m) above the ground, is empty. It probably originally held an image of the Buddha.

(Robert Harding Picture Library Ltd.)

All of the stones today are grayish-black, but they were originally covered with a layer of white plaster and then painted different eye-catching colors.

The galleries on the four square levels hold 1,460 six-foot-wide stone panels, each showing a different scene from Buddhist songs, poems, sacred texts, and the earlier lives of the Buddha.

The heavy stone monument rests on an unstable core of earth. After construction first started, the monument sagged, prompting a reconfiguration of the subterranean level, which now is surrounded by a terrace to prevent it from slipping even further. Some observers have compared the resulting uneven profile to a cake that did not rise properly.

realms. Jayavarman II did not have to conquer them militarily because they acknowledged him as a bhakti teacher who could provide them with closer access to Shiva.

Devotees of Shiva built temples that incorporated pre-existing local shrines, usually on sites where local spirits were thought to live. If the spirit inhabited a rock, that rock could be worshiped as the lingam of the new Shiva temple. When devotees conducted a Hindu ceremony to request children, they poured a sacred liquid over the lingam, a practice that echoed earlier fertility cults. The largest temple in the kingdom came to be known as Angkor Wat (en-CORE waht). Built in the early twelfth century, it used motifs borrowed from Hinduism to teach its viewers that they were living during a golden age, when peace reigned and the Angkor dynasty controlled much of modern-day Cambodia. Jayavarman II also invoked Buddhist terminology by calling himself a chakravartin ruler. This combination of Hindu and Buddhist imagery proved so potent that all subsequent Angkor kings, and many other Southeast Asian rulers, used it.

With the exception of Vietnam, which remained within the Chinese cultural sphere even when not under direct Chinese rule, Southeast Asia faced toward India, where Buddhism and Hinduism often coexisted. Buddhism and Hinduism came to Southeast Asia not because of conquest but because local rulers aspired to create new states as powerful as those they heard existed in India.

Buddhism and the Revival of Empire in China, 100–1000

With the fall of the Han dynasty in 220 C.E., China broke up into different regions, each governed by local military leaders. When the first Buddhist missionaries from the Kushan empire arrived in China during the first and second centuries C.E., they faced great difficulties in spreading their religion. Buddhist teachings urged potential converts to abandon family obligations and adopt a celibate lifestyle, yet Confucian China was one of the most family-oriented societies in the world. The chakravartin ideal of the universal Buddhist ruler, though, appealed to leaders of regions no longer united under the Han dynasty. During the Sui dynasty, which reunited China, and its long-lived successor, the Tang dynasty, Chinese emperors introduced important additions to the Qin/Han blueprint for empire, additions that remained integral to Chinese governance until the end of dynastic rule in the early 1900s.

Buddhism in China, 100–589

The first Buddhists in China came to the Han dynasty capitals at Chang'an and Luoyang early in the Common Era, most likely by sea and overland through Central Asia. The first Chinese who worshiped the Buddha did so because they thought him capable of miracles; some sources report that his image shone brightly and could fly through the air. The earliest Chinese document to mention Buddhism, from 65 C.E., tells of a prince worshiping the Buddha alongside the Daoist deity

Laozi, the purported author of *The Way and Integrity Classic* (see Chapter 4), indicating that the Chinese initially thought the Buddha was a Daoist deity.

The Han dynasty ended in 220 C.E. when a general decided to end the fiction of ruling through a puppet emperor and founded a new dynasty. He was never able to unite the entire empire, and no other regional dynasty succeeded in doing so until 589. Historians call this long period of disunity the Six Dynasties (220–589 C.E.).

During the Six Dynasties, Buddhist miracle workers began to win the first converts. Historians of Buddhism treat these miracle accounts in the same way as historians of Christianity do biblical accounts (see Chapter 7). Nonbelievers may be skeptical that the events occurred as described, but people at the time found (and modern devotees continue to find) these tales compelling, and they are crucial to our understanding of how these religions gained their first adherents.

One of the most effective early missionaries was a Central Asian man named **Fotudeng** (d. 349), who claimed that the Buddha had given him the ability to bring rain, cure the sick, and foresee the future. In 310, Fotudeng managed to convert a local ruler named Shi Le (274–333) just as he was about to lead an army into Luoyang, the former Han dynasty capital. Shi Le asked Fotudeng to perform a miracle to demonstrate the power of Buddhism. A later biography explains what happened: "Thereupon he took his begging bowl, filled it with water, burned incense, and said a spell over it. In a moment there sprang up blue lotus flowers whose brightness and color dazzled the eyes."[7] A Buddhist symbol, the lotus is a beautiful flower that grows from a root coming out of a dirty lake bottom; similarly, Fotudeng explained, human beings could free their minds from the impediments of worldly living and attain enlightenment. As usual with miracle tales, we have no way of knowing what actually happened, but Fotudeng's miracle so impressed Shi Le that he granted the Buddhists tax-free land so they could build monasteries in north China.

The son of a Xiongnu (SHEE-awng-new) chieftain (see Chapter 4), Shi Le could never become a good Confucian-style ruler because he spoke but could not read or write Chinese. Buddhism appealed to him precisely because it offered an alternative to Confucianism. He could aspire to be a chakravartin ruler.

Fotudeng tried to persuade ordinary Chinese to join the new monasteries and nunneries, but most people were extremely reluctant to take vows of celibacy. If they did not have children, future generations would not be able to perform ancestor worship for their parents and grandparents. A Buddhist book written in the early sixth century, *The Lives of the Nuns*, portrays the dilemma of would-be converts. When one young woman told her father that she did not want to marry, he replied, "You ought to marry. How can you be like this?" She explained, "I want to free all living beings from suffering. How much more, then, do I want to free my two parents!"[8] But her father was not persuaded by her promise that she could free him from the endless cycle of birth, death, and rebirth. When Fotudeng met the woman's father, he promised: "If you consent to her plan [to become a nun], she indeed shall raise her family to glory and bring you blessings and honor." Deeply impressed, the father agreed to let her enter a nunnery.

Similar encounters between parents and children took place all over China during the Six Dynasties. Many families made a compromise between the demands of Buddhism and Confucianism; they allowed one child to join the Buddhist order and transfer merit to the other children, who married and had children.

● **Fotudeng** (d. 349) Central Asian Buddhist missionary who persuaded the ruler Shi Le to convert to Buddhism; Shi Le's decision to grant tax-free land to Buddhist monasteries was a crucial first step in the establishment of Buddhism in China.

Buddhist missionaries found that they could use miracles to convert uneducated people like Shi Le, but they needed accurate Chinese translations of Buddhist texts to impress China's scholars. Still, the structure and vocabulary of Sanskrit, an Indo-European language, differed greatly from Chinese, and no dictionaries or other translation aids existed. The first understandable translations in Chinese appeared only in the year 400, long after Buddhists had been active in China, when a monk who knew both Chinese and Sanskrit founded a translation bureau with teams of bilingual translators.

Buddhists continued to win converts during the fifth and sixth centuries. They gained support because Buddhist teachings offered more hope about the afterlife than did Confucian and Daoist teachings. Confucius had refused to discuss the afterlife, except to urge his students to mourn their parents, yet many Chinese envisioned an underground prison where the dead languished forever while remaining recognizably themselves.

The original Indian belief in the transmigration of souls as expressed in the *Upanishads* (oo-PAHN-ih-shahdz; see Chapter 3) presumed that someone's soul in this life stayed intact and could be reborn in a different body. But the Buddhists propounded the no-self doctrine, which taught that there is no such thing as a fixed self. Each person is a constantly shifting group of five aggregates—form, feelings, perceptions, karmic constituents, and consciousness—that change from one second to the next. Accordingly, there is no self that can be reborn in the next life. This idea proved extremely difficult for people to grasp and was much debated as a result.

Gradually, Chinese Buddhists abandoned the strict no-self doctrine and began to describe a series of hells, much like the indigenous Chinese concept of the underground prison, where people went when they died. A few people could attain nirvana and ascend to a Buddhist paradise, they taught, but most people went to these hells and awaited their rebirth as one of six different types of being, depending on whether they had accrued good or bad karma in their previous existences. The willingness of Buddhist teachers to modify their original no-self teachings won them many converts. (See the feature "Movement of Ideas: Teaching Buddhism in a Confucian Society.")

By the year 600, Buddhism was firmly implanted in the Chinese countryside. A history of Buddhism written in that year explained that three types of monasteries existed. The largest 47 monasteries were completely financed by the central government; educated monks who lived in them conducted regular Buddhist rituals on behalf of the emperor and his immediate family. In the second tier were 839 monasteries that depended on royal princes and other powerful families for support. The final category included over 30,000 smaller shrines that dotted the Chinese countryside. Dependent on local people for contributions, the monks who worked in these shrines were often uneducated and could recite only a handful of Buddhist texts from memory. Some could not even read and write. The number of monks, educated and not, varied over the centuries, but it never exceeded more than 1 percent of China's total population, which was about fifty million in 600.[9]

China Reunified, 589–907

After more than three hundred years of disunity, the founder of the Sui dynasty reunified China in 589. Then, in less than thirty years, the **Tang dynasty** succeeded it. The Sui and Tang emperors embraced the chakravartin ideal, for they hoped Buddhism would help to bind their many subjects together. Tang dynasty China represented a high point in Chinese history; the Tang emperors ruled more territory than any

● **Tang dynasty**
Dynasty (618–907) that represented a political and cultural high point in Chinese history. The Tang emperors combined elements of the Qin/Han blueprint for empire with new measures to create a model of governance that spread to Tibet, Korea, and Japan.

dynasty until the mid-eighteenth century, and Chinese openness to the influences of Central Asia made Tang art and music particularly beautiful.

The Sui founder consciously modeled himself on the great chakravartin ruler Ashoka, whose support for the Buddhist order was well known in China. He gave money for the construction of monasteries all over China and ordered prayers to be chanted in them on the Buddha's birthday. He also built a new capital at Chang'an, the former capital of the Han dynasty, with a gridded street plan (see Figure 8.1). The city housed 120 new Buddhist monasteries. When the emperor turned 60, in 601, he explicitly followed Ashoka's lead and ordered stupas for Buddhist relics to be built throughout the empire.

In 604, when the Sui founder died, his son succeeded him and led his armies on a disastrous campaign in Korea. He was soon overthrown by one of his generals, who went on to found the Tang dynasty. After only eight years of rule, in 626, the Tang founder's son, Emperor Taizong, overthrew his father in a bloody coup in which he killed one brother and ordered an officer to kill another.

In 645, when Xuanzang wrote asking permission to return, the emperor had defeated his domestic opponents, and his brilliant military leadership had succeeded in extending Tang China's borders deep into Central Asia. Taizong was able to fulfill the chakravartin ideal by making generous donations of money and land to Buddhist monasteries and by supporting famous monks like Xuanzang. He built a special brick pagoda where Xuanzang could translate the hundreds of texts he brought from India.

One of Taizong's greatest accomplishments was a comprehensive law code, the *Tang Code,* that was designed to help local magistrates govern and adjudicate disputes, a major part of their job. It taught them, for example, how to distinguish between manslaughter and murder and specified the punishments for each. Tang

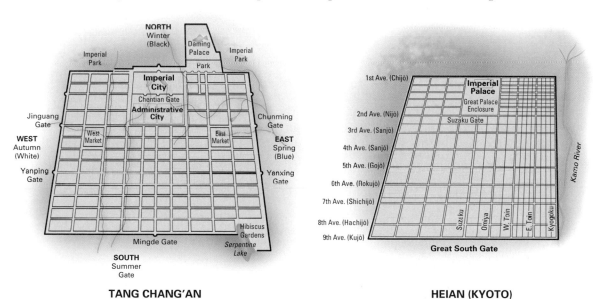

TANG CHANG'AN   **HEIAN (KYOTO)**

FIGURE 8.1

Layout of Chang'an and Heian (Kyoto)   Many rulers in East Asia followed Tang models very closely. Compare the city plans of Chang'an, the Tang capital, and Kyoto, the Heian capital. Both cities had square walls enclosing a gridded street plan, and the imperial palace was located in the north. Unlike Chang'an, Kyoto did not have a city wall or two central markets.

Teaching Buddhism in a Confucian Society

Monks frequently told stories to teach ordinary people the tenets of Buddhism. The story of the Indian monk Maudgalyayana (mowd-GAH-lee-yah-yah-nah) survives in a Sanskrit version, composed between 300 B.C.E. and 300 C.E., and a much longer Chinese version from a manuscript dated 921. This story has enormous appeal in China (it is frequently performed as Chinese opera or on television) because it portrays the dilemma of those who wanted to be good Confucian sons as well as good Buddhists. Maudgalyayana may have been filial, but he was unable to fulfill his Confucian obligations as a son because he did not bear a male heir. The Buddhist narrator takes great pains to argue that he can still be a good son because Confucian offerings have no power in a Buddhist underworld.

In the Sanskrit version, Maudgalyayana, one of the Buddha's disciples, realizes that his mother has been reborn in the real world and asks the Buddha to help her to attain nirvana. Maudgalyayana and the Buddha travel to find the mother, who attains nirvana after hearing the Buddha preach.

In the Chinese version, the protagonist retains his Indian name but acts like a typical Chinese son in every respect. The tale contrasts the behavior of the virtuous, if slightly dim, Maudgalyayana with his mother, who never gave any support to her local monastery and even kept for herself money that her son had asked her to give the monks. As a filial son, he cannot believe her capable of any crime, and he searches through all the different compartments of the Chinese hell to find her. Unrepentant to the very end of the tale, she explains that traditional Confucian offerings to the ancestors have no power in the underworld. Only offerings to the Buddhist order, such as paying monks to copy Buddhist texts, can help to ease her suffering. At the end of the story, the Buddha himself frees her from the underworld, a grim series of hells that do not exist in the Sanskrit original.

Sources: John Strong, "Filial Piety and Buddhism: The Indian Antecedents to a 'Chinese' Problem," in *Traditions in Contact and Change: Selected Proceedings of the XIVth Congress of the International Association for the History of Religions,* ed. Peter Slater and Donald Wiebe (Winnipeg, Man: Wilfrid Laurier University Press, 1980), p. 180; Victor H. Mair, trans., *Tun-huang Popular Narratives* (New York: Cambridge University Press, 1983), pp. 109–110.

Sanskrit Version

From afar, [Maudgalyayana's mother] Bhadrakanya [bud-DRAH-kahn-ee-ya] saw her son, and, as soon as she saw him, she rushed up to him exclaiming, "Ah! At long last I see my little boy!" Thereupon the crowd of people who had assembled said: "He is an aged wandering monk, and she is a young girl—how can she be his mother?" But the Venerable Maha Maudgalyayana replied, "Sirs, these skandhas• of mine were fostered by her; therefore she is my mother."

Then the Blessed One, knowing the disposition, propensity, nature and circumstances of Bhadrakanya, preached a sermon fully penetrating the meaning of the Four Noble Truths. And when Bhadrakanya had heard it, she was brought to the realization of the fruit of entering the stream.

- **skandhas** The five aggregates—form, feelings, perceptions, karmic constituents, and consciousness—which in Buddhism are the basis of the personality.

QUESTIONS FOR ANALYSIS

▶ What are the main differences between the Indian and Chinese versions?

▶ How do they portray the fate of the mother after her death?

▶ What is the Chinese underworld like?

Chinese Version

This is the place where mother and son see each
    other: . . .
Trickles of blood flowed from the seven openings
    of her head.
Fierce flames issued from the inside of his
    mother's mouth,
At every step, metal thorns out of space entered
    her body;
She clanked and clattered like the sound of five
    hundred broken-down chariots,
How could her waist and backbone bear up
    under the strain?
Jailers carrying pitchforks guarded her to the left
    and the right,
Ox-headed guards holding chains stood on the
    east and the west;
Stumbling at every other step, she came forward,
Wailing and weeping, Maudgalyayana embraced
    his mother.
Crying, he said: "It was because I am unfilial,
You, dear mother, were innocently caused to
    drop into the triple mire of hell;
Families which accumulate goodness have a sur-
    plus of blessings,
High Heaven does not destroy in this manner
    those who are blameless.
In the old days, mother, you were handsomer
    than Pan An•,
But now you have suddenly become haggard and
    worn;
I have heard that in hell there is much suffering,
Now, today, I finally realize, 'Ain't it hard, ain't
    it hard.'
Ever since I met with the misfortune of father's
    and your deaths,
I have not been remiss in sacrificing daily at your
    graves;
Mother, I wonder whether or not you have been
    getting any food to eat,
In such a short time, your appearance has be-
    come completely haggard."
Now that Maudgalyayana's mother had heard
    his words,
"Alas!" She cried, her tears intertwining as she
    struck and grabbed at herself:

"Only yesterday, my son, I was separated from
    you by death.
Who could have known that today we would be
    reunited?
While your mother was alive, she did not
    cultivate blessings,
But she did commit plenty of all the ten evil
    crimes•;
Because I didn't take your advice at that time,
    my son,
My reward is the vastness of this Avici Hell•.
In the old days, I used to live quite
    extravagantly,
Surrounded by fine silk draperies and
    embroidered screens;
How shall I be able to endure these hellish
    torments,
And then to become a hungry ghost for a
    thousand years?
A thousand times, they pluck the tongue from
    out of my mouth,
Hundreds of passes are made over my chest with
    a steel plough;
My bones, joints, tendons, and skin are
    everywhere broken,
They need not trouble with knives and swords
    since I fall to pieces by myself.
In the twinkling of an eye, I die a thousand
    deaths,
But, each time, they shout at me and I come
    back to life;
Those who enter this hell all suffer the same
    hardships.
It doesn't matter whether you are rich or poor,
    lord or servant.
Though you diligently sacrificed to me while you
    were at home,
It only got you a reputation in the village for
    being filial;
Granted that you did sprinkle libations of wine
    upon my grave,
But it would have been better for you to copy a
    single line of sutra."

• **Pan An** A well-known attractive man.

• **ten evil crimes** The ten worst offenses according
  to Buddhist teachings.
• **Avici Hell** The lowest Buddhist hell, for those who
  had committed the worst offences.

● **equal-field system**
The basis of the Tang dynasty tax system as prescribed in the *Tang Code*. Dividing households into nine ranks on the basis of wealth, officials allocated each householder a certain amount of land.

dynasty governance continued many Han dynasty innovations, particularly respect for Confucian ideals coupled with Legalist punishments and regulations.

The *Tang Code* also laid out the **equal-field system,** which was the basis of the Tang dynasty tax system. The Tang state adopted the system, named for an ideal agricultural society in the Chinese classics, from a regional dynasty that had ruled in the north during the Six Dynasties period. Under the provisions of the equal-field system, the government conducted a census of all inhabitants and drew up registers listing each household and its members every three years. Dividing households into nine ranks on the basis of wealth, it allocated to each householder a certain amount of land—some for temporary use and some for permanent use. It also fixed the tax obligations of each individual. Historians disagree about whether the equal-field system took effect throughout all of the empire, but they concur that Tang dynasty officials had an unprecedented degree of control over their sixty million subjects.

Emperor Taizong made Confucianism the basis of the educational system. As in the Han dynasty, most officials continued to be appointed on the basis of another official's recommendation, but the Tang recruited some 5 percent of officials by testing their knowledge of the Confucian classics in a written examination. This policy set an important precedent: it reserved the highest posts in the government for those who had passed the exams. Taizong combined the chakravartin ideal with Confucian policies to create a new model of rulership for East Asia.

● **Emperor Wu** (r. 685–705)   The sole woman to rule China as emperor in her own right; she called herself emperor and founded a new dynasty, the Zhou (690–705), that replaced the Tang dynasty.

One Tang emperor extended the chakravartin ideal to specific government measures: **Emperor Wu** (r. 685–705), the only woman to rule China as emperor in her own right. Many English-language books incorrectly refer to her as Empress Wu, even though she called herself emperor and founded a new dynasty, the Zhou, that supplanted the Tang from 690 to 705. Originally the wife of the emperor, she engineered the imperial succession so that she could serve first as regent to a boy emperor and then as emperor herself.

The chakravartin ideal appealed to Emperor Wu because an obscure Buddhist text, *The Great Cloud Sutra,* prophesied that a kingdom ruled by a woman would be transformed into a Buddhist paradise. (The word *sutra* means the words of the Buddha recorded in written form.) Emperor Wu ordered the construction of Buddhist monasteries in each part of China so that *The Great Cloud Sutra* could be read aloud. She issued edicts forbidding the slaughter of animals or the eating of fish, both violations of Greater Vehicle teachings, and in 693 she officially proclaimed herself a chakravartin ruler. In 705 she was overthrown in a palace coup, and the Tang dynasty was restored. Although today we often focus on Emperor Wu's gender, contemporary documents and portrayals do not indicate that she was particularly aware of being female. Like the female pharaoh Hatshepsut (see Chapter 2), Emperor Wu portrayed herself as a legitimate dynastic ruler.

The Long Decline of the Tang Dynasty, 755–907

Historians today divide the Tang dynasty into two halves: 618–755 and 755–907. In the first half, the Tang emperors ruled with great success. They enjoyed extensive military victories in Central Asia, unprecedented control over their subjects through the equal-field system, and great internal stability. The first signs of decline came in the early 700s, when tax officials reported insufficient revenues from the equal-field system. In 751, the Tang sent an army deep into Central Asia to Talas (modern-day Dzhambul, Kazakhstan) to fight an army sent by the Abbasid caliph, ruler of much of the Islamic world (see Chapter 9). The Tang army lost the battle, marking the end of Tang expansion into Central Asia.

The defeat drew little notice in the capital, where all officials were transfixed by the conflict between the emperor and his leading general, who was rumored to be having an affair with the emperor's favorite consort, a court beauty named Precious Consort Yang. In 755 General An Lushan led a mutiny of the army against the emperor. The Tang dynasty suppressed the rebellion in 763, but it never regained full control of the provinces. The equal-field system collapsed, and the dynasty was forced to institute new taxes that produced much less revenue.

In 841, a new emperor, Emperor Huichang, came to the throne. Thinking that he would increase revenues if he could collect taxes from the 300,000 tax-exempt monks and nuns, in 845 he ordered the closure of almost all Buddhist monasteries except for a few large monasteries in major cities. Although severe, Huichang's decrees had few lasting effects. Since the central government controlled little territory outside the capital, the ban was not carried out in the provinces. When a new emperor took the throne two years later, in 847, he rescinded the ban and rebuilt the damaged monasteries.

The eighth and ninth centuries saw the discovery by faithful Buddhists of a new technology that altered the course of world history. Ever since the founding of the religion, Buddhists had encouraged their followers to propagate Buddhist teachings, usually by memorizing a text or paying someone else to recite it. In China, devout Buddhists paid monks to copy texts to generate merit for themselves and their families. Sometime in the eighth century, believers realized that they could make multiple copies of a prayer or picture of a deity if they used **woodblock printing.** The carver made an image in reverse on a block of wood and then pressed the block onto sheets of paper.

At first Buddhists printed multiple copies of single sheets; later they used glue to connect the pages into a long book. The world's earliest surviving printed book, from 868, is a Buddhist text, *The Diamond Sutra.* During the Tang dynasty, almost all printing was religious, but later the Chinese realized that they could use the same technique for nonreligious books as well.

After 755, no Tang emperor managed to solve the problem of dwindling revenues. In 907, when a rebel deposed the last Tang emperor, who had been held prisoner since 885, China broke apart into different regional dynasties and was not reunited until 960 (see Chapter 12).

▣ Woodblock Printing   This single sheet of paper is slightly larger than a standard sheet of computer paper. With a drawing of a bodhisattva above and the words of prayers below, it demonstrates how believers used woodblock printing to spread Buddhist teachings. The new medium reproduced line drawings and Chinese characters equally well, and printers could make as many copies as they liked simply by inking the woodblock and pressing individual sheets of paper on it. The more copies they made, they believed, the more merit they earned.

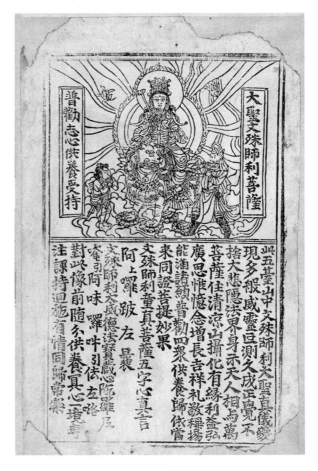

● **woodblock printing** Printing technique developed by the Chinese in which printers made an image in reverse on a block of wood and then pressed the block onto sheets of paper. An efficient way to print texts in Chinese characters.

The Tang dynasty governed by combining support for Buddhist clergy and monasteries with strong armies, clear laws, and civil service examinations. In so doing, it established a high standard of rulership for all subsequent Chinese dynasties and all rulers of neighboring kingdoms.

The Tibetan Empire, ca. 617–ca. 842

The rulers of the Tibetan plateau were among the first to adopt the Tang model of governance. Most of the Tibetan plateau lies within today's People's Republic of China, but historically it was a borderland not always under Chinese control. Located between the Kunlun Mountains to the north and the Himalayan Mountains to the south, the Tibetan plateau is high, ranging between 13,000 and 15,000 feet (4,000 and 5,000 m), and contains extensive grasslands suitable for raising horses and some river valleys where barley can be grown. The inhabitants used knotted cords and tallies to keep records, Chinese sources report, because they had no writing system.

Sometime between 620 and 650, during the early years of the Tang, a ruler named Songtsen Gampo (ca. 617–649/650) unified Tibet for the first time and founded the Yarlung dynasty (ca. 617–ca. 842), named for the valley to the southeast of Lhasa. Hoping to build a strong state, he looked to both India and China for models of governance. In 632, an official he had sent to India to study Buddhism returned and introduced a new alphabet, based on Sanskrit, for writing Tibetan.

Songtsen Gampo learned that the Tang emperor had provided Chinese brides for the leaders of several peoples living in western China and demanded that he be given a Chinese bride as well. At first Emperor Taizong refused, but when a Tibetan army nearly defeated the Tang forces in Sichuan, he sent a bride in 641. Later sources credit this woman, the princess of Wencheng (ONE-chuhng) (d. 684), with introducing Buddhism and call her a bodhisattva because of her compassion for Tibetans.

Songtsen Gampo saw China as more than a source of Buddhist teachings. He requested that the Tang court send men to his court who could read and write, and he dispatched members of his family to Chang'an to study Chinese. He also asked the Chinese to send craftsmen to teach Tibetans how to make silk and paper and how to brew wine. He was the first to record traditional laws on Chinese paper with ink.

The Tibetans took advantage of Tang weakness during the An Lushan rebellion and briefly invaded the capital of Chang'an in 763 before retreating. They conquered territory in western China, in modern-day Xinjiang (SHIN-jyahng) and Gansu provinces, which they ruled for nearly a century until 842, when the confederation of peoples who had supported the Yarlung dynasty suddenly broke apart. The Tibetan experience demonstrates the utility of the Sui/Tang model of governance for a people in the early stages of state formation, and subsequent Tibetan dynasties periodically returned to it.

State, Society, and Religion in Korea and Japan, to 1000

Because of the Han dynasty military garrisons stationed in Korea, Koreans had some contact with China as early as the Qin and Han dynasties (see Chapter 4), while their neighbors to the east in Japan, who were surrounded by water, did not (see Map 8.2).

In Korea and Japan, as in Tibet, rulers introduced Buddhism to their subjects because they hoped to match the accomplishments, particularly the military success, of the Tang dynasty. By the year 1000, both Korea and Japan had joined a larger East Asian cultural sphere in which people read and wrote Chinese characters, studied Confucian teachings in school, emulated the political institutions of the Tang, and even ate with chopsticks.

Buddhism and Regional Kingdoms in Korea, to 1000

The northern part of the Korean peninsula, around modern-day Pyongyang, North Korea, was easily accessible to Chinese armies and had come under Han dynasty rule in 108 B.C.E. It remained under Chinese dominance until 313 C.E., when the king of the northern Koguryo (KOH-guh-ree-oh) region overthrew the last Chinese ruler. Because the Chinese presence had been limited to military garrisons, there was little lasting influence.

During this time, Korea was divided into different small chiefdoms on the verge of becoming states. The three most important ones were Koguryo (traditionally 37 B.C.E.–668 C.E.), Paekche (traditionally 18 B.C.E.–660 C.E.), and Silla (traditionally 57 B.C.E.–935 C.E.). Historians call these dates "traditional" because they are based on much later legends, not contemporary evidence. Constantly vying with each other for territory and influence, the three kingdoms adopted Buddhism at different times but for the same reason: their rulers hoped to strengthen their dynasties.

Before the adoption of Buddhism, the residents of the Korean peninsula prayed to local deities or nature spirits for good health and good harvests. The vast majority lived in small agricultural villages and grew rice. Most Koreans, particularly the people in the north, had contact with Chinese, from whom they learned about Buddhism. In the 370s and 380s, the ruling families of the Koguryo and Paekche (PECK-jeh) kingdoms adopted Buddhism to strengthen their kingdoms. Believing that Buddhist rituals could bring this-worldly benefits, particularly if performed by trained religious specialists, they welcomed Buddhist missionaries from China, who brought statues of the Buddha and Chinese-language sutras to their kingdoms.

Like Chinese rulers, the Koguryo and Paekche kings combined patronage for Buddhism with support for Confucian education. Koreans used Chinese

🌐 MAP 8.2
Korea and Japan, ca. 550   The Japanese island of Kyushu lies some 150 miles (240 km) from the Korean peninsula, and the island of Tsushima provided a convenient stepping stone to the Japanese archipelago for those fleeing the warfare on the Korean peninsula. The Korean migrants introduced their social structure, with its bone-rank system, and Buddhism to Japan.

Ⓒ Interactive Map

characters as their writing system but not always easily, since Chinese word order differed from that of Korean. Accordingly, the Koguryo and Paekche kings established Confucian academies where students could study Chinese characters, Confucian classics, the histories, and different philosophical works in Chinese.

The circumstances accompanying the adoption of Buddhism by the **Silla** (SHE-luh) royal house illustrate how divided many Koreans were about the new religion. King Pophung (r. 514–540), whose name means "King who promoted the Dharma," wanted to patronize Buddhism but feared the opposition of powerful families who had passed laws against it. Sometime between 527 and 529, he persuaded one of his courtiers to build a shrine to the Buddha. However, since such activity was banned, the king had no choice but to order the courtier's beheading. The king and his subject prayed for a miracle. An early history of Korea describes the moment of execution: "Down came the sword on the monk's neck, and up flew his head spouting blood as white as milk." The miracle, we are told, silenced the opposition, and Silla became Buddhist.

By the middle of the sixth century, all three Korean kingdoms had adopted pro-Buddhist policies, and all sent government officials and monks to different regional kingdoms within China. When the delegations returned, they taught their countrymen what they had learned. With the support of the royal family, Buddhist monasteries were built in major cities and in the countryside, but ordinary people continued to worship the same local deities they had in pre-Buddhist times.

The Sui dynasty reunification of China in 589 had repercussions on the Korean peninsula. In 598, the Koguryo king attacked the Sui, and the Sui retaliated by trying to invade but failed because of bad weather and the strength of the Koguryo armies. In 612, in a second attempted invasion, 300,000 Sui dynasty soldiers attacked the Koguryo capital, but only 2,700 Chinese are reported to have survived the defeat. The Sui attacked three more times, each time unsuccessfully, until the Sui dynasty was fatally weakened and fell to the Tang dynasty in 618. Chinese armies did not return to the Korean peninsula again until the 640s, when Emperor Taizong led several attacks against Koguryo. All were defeated. As a result,

• Silla Korean kingdom that adopted Buddhism and united with the Tang dynasty in 660 to defeat the Koguryo and Paekche kingdoms, unifying Korea for the first time in 668.

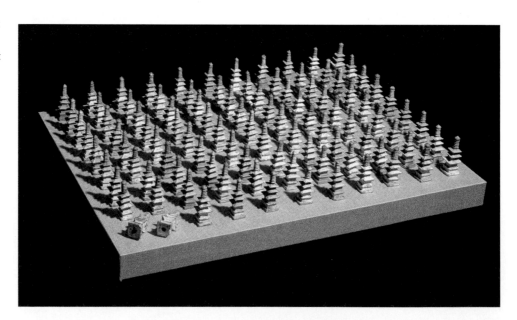

Miniature Buddhist Pagodas, Korea During the ninth century, Buddhist believers in the Silla kingdom placed this set of ninety-nine tiny clay pagodas inside a stone pagoda. Each pagoda stands 3 inches (7.5 cm) tall and contains a small hole at the base for a small woodblock-printed prayer. Rulers throughout East Asia sponsored similar projects in the hope of generating merit. (Japan Society Catalog, May 2003, *Transmitting the Forms of Divinity*, Gyeongu National Museum)

in the middle of the seventh century, the same three kingdoms—Paekche, Koguryo, and Silla—still ruled a divided Korea.

The Silla kingdom cultivated ties with the Tang dynasty in hopes of defeating the Paekche and Koguryo kingdoms. One of the most influential monks in Silla was Chajang (active 635–650), who studied Buddhism for seven years at the Chinese pilgrimage center of Mount Wutai in Shanxi province from 636 to 643. When he returned to Silla, the king named him to the highest religious post in the government, in charge of overseeing all the monks in the kingdom.

In 660, the Silla kingdom allied with the Tang. The combined Silla-Tang forces defeated first the Paekche and then, in 668, the Koguryo dynasty. The Silla ruler paid lip service to Tang sovereignty by accepting the inferior status of a tributary that sent annual gifts to the Tang emperor, but by 675 the Silla forces had pushed Tang armies back to the northern edges of the Korean peninsula, and the Silla king ruled a united Korea largely on his own.

Silla's rule ushered in a period of stability that lasted for two and a half centuries. Silla kings offered different types of support to Buddhism. Several Silla rulers followed the example of Ashoka and the Sui founder in building pagodas throughout their kingdom. One Chinese Buddhist text that entered Korea offered Buddhist devotees merit if they commissioned sets of identical pagodas that contained small woodblock-printed texts, usually Buddhist charms. A gift of ninety-nine miniature pagodas with texts inside, the text promised, was the spiritual equivalent of building ninety-nine thousand life-size pagodas (see the photo on the facing page). The Koreans adopted the brand-new Chinese innovation of woodblock printing as part of their efforts to learn from China.

The Silla rulers adopted some measures of Tang rule, such as Confucian academies and extensive support for Buddhism, but not the equal-field system or the Confucian examination system, which were not suited to the stratified Korean society of the seventh and eighth centuries. Aristocratic families were quite separate from ordinary peasant families. The **bone-rank system** classed all Korean families into seven different categories. The true-bone classification was reserved for the highest-born aristocratic families, those eligible to be king. Below them were six other ranks in descending order. No one in the true-bone classification could marry anyone outside that group, and the only way to lose true-bone status was to be found guilty of a crime.

The Silla rulers found that they could govern better if they granted entire villages to members of the true-bone families. In turn, these families appointed government officials and paid their salaries. The rigid stratification of the bone-rank system prevented the Silla rulers from attempting to implement civil service examinations.

The Silla kingdom entered a period of decline after 780 with the death of the first Silla king to be assassinated while in office. From that time on, different branches of the royal family fought each other for control of the throne, yet no one managed to rule for long.

bone-rank system Korean social ranking system used by the Silla dynasty that divided Korean families into seven different categories, with the "true-bone" rank reserved for the highest-born families.

The Emergence of Japan

Japan is an island chain of four large islands and many smaller ones. Originally connected by a land bridge to the Asian mainland, it was cut off about 15,000 years ago. Like Korea, Japan had no indigenous writing system, so archaeologists must piece together the island's early history from archaeological materials and later sources like the

Chronicle of Japan (*Nihon shoki*) (knee-HOHN SHOW-kee), a year-by-year account written in 720. The royal Yamato (YAH-mah-toe) house, this book claims, was directly descended from the sun-goddess Amaterasu (AH-mah-TAY-rah-soo). The indigenous religion of Japan, called Shinto (SHIN-toe), included the worship of different spirits of trees, streams, and mountains, as well as rulers. Because people believed that the spirit of a deceased chieftain might threaten the living, they buried their chieftains with goods used in daily life and distinctive clay figurines, called haniwa (HAH-knee-wah), a modern term meaning "clay rings."

In the fifth and sixth centuries, many Koreans fled the political instability of the disunited peninsula to settle in the relative peace of Japan only 150 miles (240 km) away. These Korean refugees significantly influenced the inhabitants of the islands. The Yamato kings gave titles modeled on the Korean bone-rank system to powerful Japanese clans. They had the most sustained contact with the Paekche kingdom because the two states had been allied against the Silla kingdom, which was geographically closest and the most threatening to Japan.

Once the Paekche royal house adopted Buddhism, it began to pressure its clients, the Yamato clan, to follow suit. In 538, the Paekche ambassador brought a gift of Buddhist texts and images for the ruler of Japan, but the most powerful Japanese families hesitated to support the new religion. The conflict among supporters and opponents of Buddhism lasted for nearly fifty years, during which the Paekche rulers continued to send the Japanese gifts of Buddhist writings, monks, and nuns.

• **Soga family**
Powerful Japanese family that ruled in conjunction with the Yamato clan from 587 to 645; introduced Buddhism to Japan.

Two miracles played a key role in persuading the Japanese to adopt Buddhism. The first occurred in 584, when Soga no Umako, the leader of the powerful **Soga family,** which had provided the Yamato clan with many wives, saw a small fragment of bone believed to be from the original Buddha's body. Skeptical of the relic's authenticity, he tried to pulverize it, but his hammer broke, and when he threw the relic into water, it floated up or down on command. As a result, Soga no Umako became an enthusiastic supporter of Buddhism. This miracle tale illustrates the early stages of state formation as the Soga family tried to unify the region through Buddhism. Three years later, in 587, the 13-year-old Soga prince Shotoku (574–622) went into battle against the powerful families opposed to Buddhism. Prince Shotoku vowed that, if the Soga clan won the battle, their government would support Buddhism, an indication of how the new religion helped the Soga family to consolidate its hold on power. The pro-Buddhist forces won.

Because Prince Shotoku was too young to be king, his mother, Queen Suiko (r. 592–628), was named regent, and Soga no Umako became the chief minister. Throughout Queen Suiko's regency, the Japanese court depended on Korean monks to learn about Buddhism. Only in the 630s were there enough knowledgeable Japanese monks at court to conduct Buddhist rituals correctly without Korean guidance.

(CL) **Primary Source:**
Chronicles of Japan
These guidelines for imperial officials show how the Soga clan welcomed Chinese influence in an attempt to increase the authority of the Japanese imperial family.

Queen Suiko's reign coincided with the Sui dynasty and the founding of the Tang, but Chinese forces never threatened Japan as they had Korea. Japan embarked on an ambitious program to learn from China. Between 600 and 614, it sent four missions to China, and then a further fifteen during the Tang dynasty. A large mission could have as many as five hundred participants, including officials, Buddhist monks, students, and translators. Some Japanese stayed in China for as many as thirty years.

In 645, the Fujiwara clan overthrew the Soga family, and the Yamato clan remained the titular rulers of Japan. The Fujiwara continued to introduce Chinese institutions, particularly those laid out in the *Tang Code* like the equal-field system. However, they modified the original Chinese rules so that members of powerful families received more land than they would have in China. It is not clear whether the Japanese state was actually able to implement the redistribution of land every three years.

The Fujiwara rulers sponsored Buddhist ceremonies on behalf of the state and the royal family at state-financed monasteries. Like the Chinese, they established a head monastery at their capital with branch temples elsewhere. The Fujiwara clan built their first Chinese-style capital at Fujiwara and the second at Nara in 710, which marked the beginning of the Nara period (710–794). Both were modeled on the gridded street plan of Chang'an. In 794, the start of the Heian (HEY-on) period (794–1185), the Fujiwara shifted their capital to Kyoto, where it remained for nearly one thousand years (see Figure 8.1 on page 225).

Gradually the Fujiwara lessened their efforts to learn from the Chinese. The final official delegation went to China in 838. Some Chinese-style reforms lasted longer than others: for example, educated Japanese continued to study Buddhist and Confucian texts written in Chinese characters. Because Japanese, like Korean, was in a different language family from Chinese, characters did not capture the full meaning of Japanese. In the ninth century, the Japanese developed an alphabet, called kana (KAH-nah), that allowed them to write Japanese words as they were pronounced.

A Japanese woman named Murasaki Shikibu (MOO-rah-sock-ee SHE-key-boo) used only kana to write one of the world's most important works of literature, *The Tale of Genji,* in 1000. Some have called it the world's first novel. The book relates the experiences of a young prince

■ **Horyuji Pagoda, Nara, Japan**   Built before 794, this five-story pagoda is possibly one of the oldest wooden buildings in the world. Like the stupa at the Indian site of Sanchi, it was built to hold relics of the Buddha. Not certain how the building survived multiple earthquakes without sustaining any damage, architects speculate that the central pillar is not directly connected to the ground below, allowing it to float slightly above the ground.   (Christopher Rennie/Robert Harding Picture Library Ltd./Alamy)

as he grows up in the court. Lady Murasaki spent her entire life at court, and her novel reflects the complex system of etiquette that had developed among the Japanese aristocracy. For example, lovers choose sheets of paper from multiple shades, each with its own significance, before writing notes to each other. While the highest members of Japan's aristocracy could read and write—men using both Chinese characters and kana and women more often only kana—the vast majority of their countrymen remained illiterate.

By 1000, Japan had become part of the East Asian cultural realm. Although its rulers were predominantly Buddhist, they supported Confucian education and used the *Tang Code* as a model of governance. The Fujiwara family modified some Chinese institutions, like the equal-field system, to better suit Japanese society.

Chapter Review

KEY TERMS

Xuanzang (208)

chakravartin (210)

Silk Routes (210)

Hinduism (211)

bodhisattva (212)

Gupta dynasty (213)

bhakti (214)

Angkor dynasty (219)

Fotudeng (223)

Tang dynasty (224)

equal-field system (228)

Emperor Wu (228)

woodblock printing (229)

Silla (232)

bone-rank system (233)

Soga family (234)

 Download the MP3 audio file of the Chapter Review and listen to it on the go.

India gave two models of royal governance to the world. Ashoka pioneered the Buddhist chakravartin ideal in the third century B.C.E., and the Kushan and Gupta dynasties developed it further. When Xuanzang visited India, he witnessed the decline of this model and the appearance of a new model in which kings patronized Brahmin priests and Hindu temples. Although it died out in India, the chakravartin model traveled to China, where the Sui and Tang rulers added new elements: the equal-field system, civil service examinations, and a legal code. Tibetan, Korean, and Japanese rulers all adopted variations of the Tang model, with the result that, by 1000, East Asia had become a culturally unified region in which rulers patronized Buddhism, which coexisted with local religious beliefs, and subjects studied both Confucian and Buddhist teachings. In South Asia and Southeast Asia, on the other hand, rulers worshiped Hindu deities and supported Sanskrit learning.

How did Buddhism change after the year 100? How did Hinduism displace it within India?

Greater Vehicle teachings, which gradually replaced earlier Theravada teachings, emphasized that everyone—not just monks and nuns—could attain nirvana. They could do so with the help of bodhisattvas who chose not to attain enlightenment themselves but to help all other beings. Indian rulers like Kanishka of the Kushan dynasty supported Buddhism with gifts to monasteries, but between 320 and 500 Gupta rulers pioneered a new type of gift: land grants to Brahmin priests and to Hindu temples. Over time, as more rulers chose to endow temples to Vishnu and Shiva, support for Hinduism increased, and Buddhism declined.

How did geography, trade, and religion shape the development of states and societies in Southeast Asia?

The timing of the monsoon winds meant that all boats traveling between India and China had to stop in Southeast Asia for several months before they could resume their journeys. The rulers of coastal ports such as Funan and Srivijaya taxed the trade brought by these boats and used the revenues to construct Buddhist centers of worship. At the same time, different local rulers—some along the sea route between India and China, some in the forested interior—patronized purohita and built monuments to Buddhist and Hindu deities, all in the hope of strengthening their states as they were taking shape.

How did the Sui and Tang dynasties modify the Qin/Han blueprint for empire?

The emperors of both the Sui and Tang dynasties took over the Qin/Han blueprint for empire with its Legalist and Confucian elements and governed as chakravartin rulers who patronized Buddhism. The Sui founder designed the gridded street plan of his capital at Chang'an, which the Tang retained. Emperor Taizong of the Tang, who welcomed Xuanzang back from India, promulgated the *Tang Code,* which established the equal-field system throughout the empire. In addition, the Tang emperors used the civil service examinations to recruit the highest-ranking 5 percent of officials in the bureaucracy.

 ## Which elements of the revised Chinese blueprint for empire did Korea and Japan borrow intact? Which did they modify?

Korean and Japanese rulers patronized Buddhism and supported the introduction of Chinese characters and education in the Confucian classics. The Silla rulers tried to introduce civil service examinations and the equal-field system but had no success in the hierarchical bone-rank society of Korea. Similarly, the Fujiwara clan had to modify the equal-field system to suit Japan's aristocratic society. The Fujiwara clan modeled all three of their capitals—at Fujiwara, Nara, and Kyoto—on the gridded street plan of Chang'an.

WEB RESOURCES

Pronunciation Guide

Interactive Maps

MAP 8.1 The Spread of Buddhism and Hinduism to Southeast Asia

MAP 8.2 Korea and Japan, ca. 550

Primary Sources

Chapter Objectives

ACE Multiple-Choice Quiz

Flashcards

FOR FURTHER REFERENCE

Ebrey, Patricia Buckley, Anne Walthall, and James B. Palais. *East Asia: A Cultural, Social, and Political History.* 2d ed. Boston: Wadsworth/Cengage Learning, 2009.

Hansen, Valerie. *The Open Empire: A History of China to 1600.* New York: Norton, 2000.

Holcombe, Charles. *The Genesis of East Asia, 221 B.C.–A.D. 907.* Honolulu: Association of Asian Studies and the University of Hawai'i Press, 2001.

Kapstein, Matthew. *The Tibetan Assimilation of Buddhism: Conversion, Contestation, and Memory.* New York: Oxford University Press, 2000.

Keown, Damien. *Buddhism: A Very Short Introduction.* New York: Oxford University Press, 1996.

Mair, Victor H. *Tun-huang Popular Narratives.* New York: Cambridge University Press, 1983.

Ray, Himanshu Prabha. "The Axial Age in Asia: The Archaeology of Buddhism (500 BC to AD 500)." In *Archaeology of Asia,* ed. Miriam T. Stark. Malden, Mass.: Blackwell, 2006, pp. 303–323.

Tarling, Nicholas, ed. *The Cambridge History of Southeast Asia.* Vol. I, *From Early Times to c. 1500.* New York: Cambridge University Press, 1992.

Thapar, Romila. *Early India from the Origins to AD 1300.* Berkeley: University of California Press, 2003.

Washizuka, Hiromitsu, et al. *Transmitting the Forms of Divinity: Early Buddhist Art from Korea and Japan.* New York: Japan Society, 2003.

Wolters, O. W. *History, Culture, and Region in Southeast Asian Perspectives.* Singapore: Institute of Southeast Asian Studies, 1982.

Wriggins, Sally Hovey. *Xuanzang: A Buddhist Pilgrim on the Silk Road.* Boulder: Westview Press, 1996.

Websites

Borobudur (http://rubens.anu.edu.au/htdocs/bycountry/indonesia/borobudur/).   Information on the Borobudur monument in Java, Indonesia.

The Buddha and His Dhamma (http://www.columbia.edu/itc/mealac/pritchett/00ambedkar/ambedkar_buddha/).   B. R. Ambedkar's explanation of the Buddha's teachings.

Silk Road Narratives: A Collection of Historical Texts (http://depts.washington.edu/silkroad/texts/texts.html).   A valuable collection of primary sources in translation about the Silk Road, including Xuanzang's *Record of the Western Regions,* which describes the different countries he visited.

Islamic Empires of Western Asia and Africa, 600–1258

Khaizuran (ca. 739–789) grew up as a slave girl but became the favored wife of the supreme religious and political leader of the Islamic world, the caliph Mahdi (MAH-dee), who reigned from 775 to 785 as the third ruler of the Abbasid (ah-BAHS-sid) caliphate (750–1258). As the wife of Mahdi and the mother of the caliph who succeeded him, Khaizuran (HAY-zuhr-ahn) played an active role in court politics. A slave dealer brought her, while still a teenager, to Mecca, where she met Mahdi's father. He had come to perform the hajj pilgrimage that is the religious obligation of all Muslims. In reply to his asking where she was from, she said:

ABBASID SINGING GIRL

(Los Angeles County Museum of Art, The Nasil M. Heeramaneck Collection, gift of Joan Palefsky. Photograph © 2007 Museum Associates/LACMA)

Born at Mecca and brought up at Jurash (in the Yaman)."[1]

Of course we would like to know more, but she has left no writings of her own. The written record almost always says more about men than about women, and more about the prominent and the literate than about the ordinary and the illiterate. To understand the experience of everyone in a society, historians must exercise great ingenuity in using the evidence at hand. Khaizuran provides a rare opportunity to study the life of an ordinary Muslim woman who rose to become a leader in her own right.

In its support for Islam, the Abbasid dynasty (see page 250) played a role in world history similar to that of the Roman Empire, which patronized Christianity (see Chapter 7), and the Tang dynasty in China, which supported Buddhism (see Chapter 8). Under the Abbasids, Islam was a world religion with millions of

CL This icon will direct you to interactive activities and study materials on the *Voyages* website:
www.cengage.com/history/hansen/voyages1e

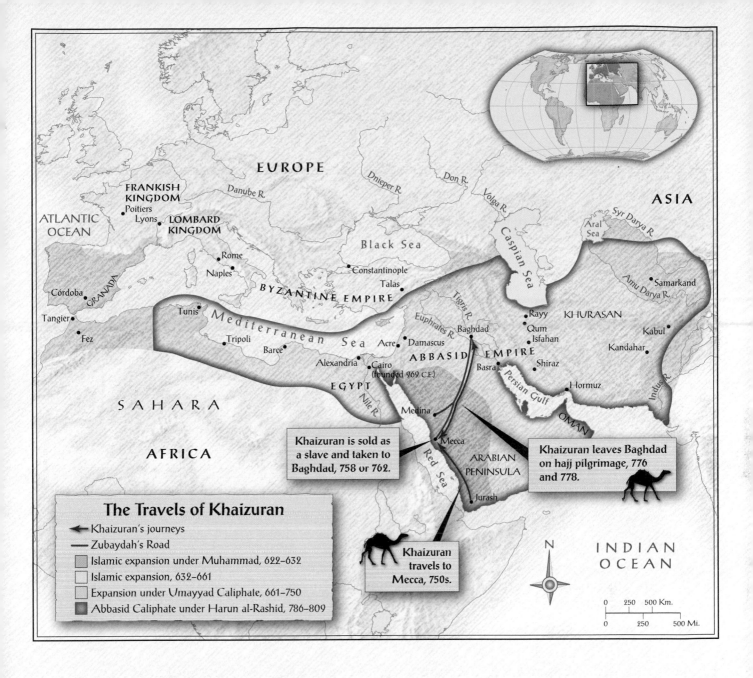

The Travels of Khaizuran

Khaizuran is sold as a slave and taken to Baghdad, 758 or 762.

Khaizuran leaves Baghdad on hajj pilgrimage, 776 and 778.

Khaizuran travels to Mecca, 750s.

Legend:
- ← Khaizuran's journeys
- — Zubaydah's Road
- Islamic expansion under Muhammad, 622–632
- Islamic expansion, 632–661
- Expansion under Umayyad Caliphate, 661–750
- Abbasid Caliphate under Harun al-Rashid, 786–809

Map labels:
EUROPE • ASIA • ATLANTIC OCEAN • FRANKISH KINGDOM • Poitiers • Lyons • LOMBARD KINGDOM • Rome • Naples • Córdoba • GRANADA • Tangier • Fez • Tunis • Tripoli • Barce • Danube R. • Dnieper R. • Don R. • Volga R. • Black Sea • Constantinople • Talas • BYZANTINE EMPIRE • Caspian Sea • Aral Sea • Syr Darya R. • Amu Darya R. • Samarkand • Mediterranean Sea • Acre • Damascus • Euphrates R. • Tigris R. • Baghdad • Rayy • KHURASAN • Qum • Isfahan • Kabul • Kandahar • Alexandria • Cairo (founded 969 C.E.) • ABBASID EMPIRE • Basra • Shiraz • Persian Gulf • Hormuz • Indus R. • EGYPT • Nile R. • SAHARA • AFRICA • Medina • Red Sea • Mecca • ARABIAN PENINSULA • OMAN • Jurash • INDIAN OCEAN • Samarkand

Scale: 0 250 500 Km. / 0 250 500 Mi.

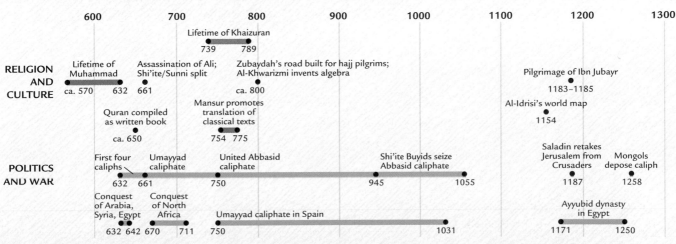

Timeline (600–1300)

Lifetime of Khaizuran 739 789

RELIGION AND CULTURE

Lifetime of Muhammad ca. 570 – 632

Assassination of Ali; Shi'ite/Sunni split 661

Zubaydah's road built for hajj pilgrims; Al-Khwarizmi invents algebra ca. 800

Pilgrimage of Ibn Jubayr 1183–1185

Quran compiled as written book ca. 650

Mansur promotes translation of classical texts 754 775

Al-Idrisi's world map 1154

POLITICS AND WAR

First four caliphs 632

Umayyad caliphate 661

United Abbasid caliphate 750

Shi'ite Buyids seize Abbasid caliphate 945 1055

Saladin retakes Jerusalem from Crusaders 1187

Mongols depose caliph 1258

Conquest of Arabia, Syria, Egypt 632 642

Conquest of North Africa 670 711

Umayyad caliphate in Spain 750 1031

Ayyubid dynasty in Egypt 1171 1250

● **Khaizuran** Slave girl (ca. 739–789) who became the wife of the caliph Mahdi (r. 775–785), the third ruler of the Abbasid caliphate. Khaizuran played an active role in court politics.

● **Muhammad** (ca. 570–632) Believed by Muslims to be the last prophet who received God's revelations directly from the angel Gabriel. The first leader of the Muslim community.

adherents in Africa, Europe, and Asia. At the peak of their power, around the year 800, the Abbasids governed over thirty-five or forty million people living in North Africa and Southwest Asia.[2]

But the Abbasid Empire differed in a crucial way from either the Roman or the Tang Empire. When the Roman emperor Constantine issued the Edict of Milan in 313 (see Chapter 7), he recognized a religion already popular among his subjects. And when the early Tang emperors supported Buddhism, they did so because many Chinese had come to embrace Buddhism since its entry into China in the first century C.E. Yet the Roman and Tang emperors could withdraw their support for these religions, and they sometimes did.

In contrast, the Abbasid rulers were religious leaders who claimed a familial relationship with the prophet **Muhammad** (ca. 570–632) through his uncle Abbas (ah-BAHS). They could not withdraw their support from the Islamic religious community because they led that very religious community. At the same time, they were also political leaders; the founder of the Abassid dynasty seized power from the Umayyad (oo-MY-uhd) dynasty in 750. Even when it became no longer possible for the Abbasid caliphs to serve as political leaders, the caliphs retained their religious role. Others could be king, but the Abbasids had a unique claim to being caliph.

This chapter will examine the history of Islam, from the first revelations received by Muhammad to the final collapse of the Abbasid Empire in 1258.

Focus Questions

Who was the prophet Muhammad, and what were his main teachings?

Between Muhammad's death in 632 and the founding of the Abbasid caliphate in 750, what were the different ways that the Islamic community chose the new caliph?

Which economic, political, and social forces held the many peoples and territories of the Abbasid caliphate together?

After the fragmentation of the Abbasid Empire in 945, which cultural practices, technologies, and customs held Islamic believers in different regions together?

The Origins of Islam and the First Caliphs, 610–750

Muhammad began to preach sometime around 613 and won a large following among the residents of the Arabian peninsula before his death in 632. The man who succeeded to the leadership of the Islamic religious community was called the caliph, literally "successor." The caliph exercised political authority because the Muslim religious community was also a state, complete with its own government and a powerful army that conquered many neighboring regions. The first four caliphs were chosen from different clans on the basis of their ties to Muhammad, but after 661 all the caliphs came from a single clan, or dynasty, the Umayyads, who governed until 750.

The Life and Teachings of Muhammad, ca. 570–632

Muhammad was born into a family of merchants sometime around 570 in Mecca, a trading community in the Arabian peninsula far from any major urban center. At the time of his birth, the two major powers of the Mediterranean world were the Byzantine Empire (see Chapter 10) and the Sasanian Empire of the Persians (see Chapter 6).

On the southern edge of the two empires lay the Arabian peninsula, which consisted largely of desert punctuated by small oases. Traders traveling from Syria to Yemen frequently stopped at the few urban settlements, including Mecca and Medina, near the coast of the Red Sea. The local peoples spoke Arabic, a Semitic language related to Hebrew that was written with an alphabet.

The population was divided between urban residents and the nomadic residents of the desert, called Bedouins (BED-dwins). The Bedouins moved from place to place, tending their flocks of sheep, horses, and camels, and were divided into different clans. Even though they no longer followed a nomadic way of life, many city people maintained a strong clan identity.

All Arabs, whether nomadic or urban, belonged to clans who worshiped protective deities that resided in an individual tree, a group of trees, or sometimes a rock with an unusual shape. One of the most revered objects was a large black rock in a cube-shaped shrine, called the Kaaba (KAH-buh) at Mecca. Above these tribal deities stood a creator deity named Allah (AH-luh). (The Arabic word *allah* means "the god" and, by extension, "God.") When, at certain times of the year, members of different clans gathered to worship individual tribal deities, they pledged to stop all feuding. During these pilgrimages to Mecca, merchants like Muhammad bought and sold their wares. Extensive trade networks connected the Arabian peninsula with Palestine and Syria, and both Jews and Christians lived in its urban centers.

While in his forties and already a wealthy merchant, Muhammad had a series of visions in which he saw a figure. Muslims believe that God spoke to Muhammad through the angel Gabriel, after which Muhammad called on everyone to submit to God. The religion founded on belief in this event is called Islam, meaning "submission" or "surrender." Muslims do not call Muhammad the founder of Islam because God's teachings, they believe, are timeless. Muhammad taught that his predecessors included all the Hebrew prophets from the Hebrew Bible as well as Jesus and his disciples. Muslims consider Muhammad the last messenger of

God, however, and historians place the beginning date for Islam in the 610s because no one thought of himself or herself as Muslim before Muhammad received his revelations. Muhammad's earliest followers came from his immediate family: his wife Khadijah (kah-DEE-juh) and his cousin Ali, whom he had raised since early childhood.

Unlike the existing religion of Arabia, but like Christianity and Judaism, Islam was monotheistic; Muhammad preached that his followers should worship only one God. He also stressed the role of individual choice: each person had the power to decide to worship God or to turn away from God. Those who submitted to God became the first Muslims. Men who converted to Islam had to undergo circumcision, a practice already widespread throughout the Arabian peninsula.

Islam developed within the context of Bedouin society, in which men were charged with protecting the honor of their wives and daughters. Accordingly, women often assumed a subordinate role in Islam. In Bedouin society, a man could repudiate his wife by saying "I divorce you" three times. Although women could not repudiate their husbands in the same way, they could divorce an impotent man.

(CL) **Primary Source:**
The Quran: Muslim Devotion to God
This excerpt articulates the Muslim faith in a heavenly reward for believers and a hellish punishment for unbelievers.

■ **Certificate of Pilgrimage to Mecca** Islamic artists often ornamented manuscripts, tiles, and paintings with passages from the Quran. This document, written on paper, testifies that the bearer completed the pilgrimage to Mecca in 1207 and thus fulfilled the Fifth Pillar of Islam. Arabic reads from right to left; the red lines and dots guide the reader's pronunciation. (Turkish and Islamic Art Museum, Istanbul/Alfredo Dagli Orti/The Art Archive)

Although Muhammad recognized the traditional right of men to repudiate their wives, he introduced several measures aimed at improving the status of women. For example, he limited the number of wives a man could take to four. His supporters explained that Islamic marriage offered the secondary wives far more legal protection than if they had simply been the unrecognized mistresses of a married man, as they were before Muhammad's teachings. He also banned the Bedouin practice of female infanticide. Finally, he instructed his female relatives to veil themselves when receiving visitors. Although many in the modern world think the veiling of women an exclusively Islamic practice, women in various societies in the ancient world, including Greeks, Mesopotamians, and Arabs, wore veils as a sign of high station.

Feuding among different clans was a constant problem in Bedouin society. In 620, a group of nonkinsmen from Medina, a city 215 miles (346 km) to the north, pledged to follow Muhammad's teachings in hopes of ending the feuding. Because certain clan leaders of Mecca had become increasingly hostile to Islam, even threatening to kill Muhammad, in 622 Muhammad and his followers moved to Medina. Everyone who submitted to God and accepted Muhammad as his messenger became a member of the umma (UM-muh), the community of Islamic believers.

The Kaaba, Mecca   This photograph, taken in 2006, shows hajj pilgrims circumambulating the cube-shaped shrine of the Kaaba, which means "cube" in Arabic. Muhammad instructed all Muslims who could afford the trip to make the pilgrimage to Mecca. Today some two million pilgrims perform the hajj each year. (Interfoto Pressebildagentur/Alamy)

This migration, called the *hijrah* (HIJ-ruh), marked a major turning point in Islam. All dates in the Islamic calendar are calculated in the year of the hijrah (Anno Hegirae, a Latin term usually abbreviated A.H.). (Because of the differences in the calendars, Islamic years often straddle two Common Era years. For example, 165 A.H. = 781–782 C.E.) The Islamic calendar calculated each year as twelve lunar months of 29.5 days each, with no adjustment for the remaining days (each solar year has 365.25 days). As a result, each day falls at a slightly different time each year. For example, the first day of the month of Ramadan, when Muslims fast during daytime, falls ten or eleven days earlier than it did the previous year.

Muhammad began life as a merchant, became a religious prophet in middle age, and assumed the duties of a general at the end of his life. In 624, Muhammad and his followers fought their first battle against the residents of Mecca. Muhammad said that he had received revelations that holy war, whose object was the expansion of Islam—or its defense—was justified. He used the word **jihad** (GEE-hahd), whose root in Arabic means "striving or effort," to mean struggle or fight in military campaigns against non-Muslims. (In addition to its basic meaning of holy war, modern Muslims use the term in a more spiritual or moral sense to indicate an individual's striving to fulfill all the teachings of Islam.)

In 630, Muhammad's troops conquered Mecca and removed all tribal images from the pilgrimage center at the Kaaba. Muhammad became ruler of the region and exercised his authority by adjudicating among feuding clans. The clans, Muhammad explained, had forgotten that the Kaaba had originally been a shrine to God dedicated by the prophet Abraham (Ibrahim in Arabic) and his son Ishmael. Muslims do not accept the version of Abraham's sacrifice given in the Old Testament, in which the elderly couple, Abraham and Sarah, have a son, Isaac, whom Abraham spares at God's command. In contrast, Muslims believe that Abraham offered God another of his sons: Ishmael, whose mother was the slave woman Hajar (Hagar in Hebrew). The pilgrimage to Mecca, or **hajj** (HAHJ), commemorates that moment when Abraham freed Ishmael and sacrificed a sheep in his place. Later, Muslims believe, Ishmael fathered his own children, the ancestors of the clans of Arabia.

The First Caliphs and the Sunni-Shi'ite Split, 632–661

Muhammad preached his last sermon from Mount Arafat outside Mecca and then died in 632. He left no male heirs, only four daughters, and did not designate a successor, or **caliph** (KAY-lif). Clan leaders consulted with each other and chose Abu Bakr (ah-boo BAHK-uhr) (ca. 573–634), an early convert and the father of Muhammad's second wife, to lead their community. Because Abu Bakr could not receive divine revelations, he had to govern on the basis of what he and his advisers remembered of Muhammad's teachings. Although not a prophet, he held political and religious authority and also led the Islamic armies. Under Abu Bakr's skilled leadership, Islamic troops conquered all of the Arabian peninsula and pushed into present-day Syria and Iraq.

When Abu Bakr died only two years after becoming caliph, the Islamic community again had to determine a successor. This time the umma chose Umar ibn al-Khattab (oo-MAHR ibn al-HAT-tuhb) (586?–644), the father of Muhammad's third wife. Muslims brought their disputes to Umar, as they had to Muhammad. As the number of cases increased, the caliph appointed jurists (*qadi* in Arabic), who listened to the aggrieved parties often after the close of Friday prayers in the Islamic house of worship, or mosque.

CL Primary Source:
The Quran: Call for Jihad
Discover what the Quran says about the duty of Muslims to defend themselves from their enemies.

• **jihad**   (Arabic root for "striving" or "effort"). A struggle or fight against non-Muslims. In addition to its basic meaning of holy war, modern Muslims use the term in a spiritual or moral sense to indicate an individual's striving to fulfill all the teachings of Islam.

• **hajj**   The pilgrimage to Mecca, required of all Muslims who can afford the trip. The pilgrimage commemorates that moment when, just as he was about to sacrifice him, Abraham freed Ishmael and sacrificed a sheep in his place.

• **caliph**   Literally "successor." Before 945, the caliph was the successor to Muhammad and the supreme political and religious leader of the Islamic world. After 945, the caliph had no political power but served as the religious leader of all Muslims.

During Muhammad's lifetime, a group of Muslims had committed all of his teachings to memory, and soon after his death they began to compile them as the **Quran** (also spelled Koran), which Muslims believe is the direct word of God as revealed to Muhammad. In addition, early Muslims recorded testimony from Muhammad's friends and associates about his speech and actions. These reports, called **hadith** (HAH-deet) in Arabic, formed an integral part of the Islamic textual tradition, second in importance only to the Quran (kuh-RAHN).

Umar reported witnessing an encounter between Muhammad and the angel Gabriel in which Muhammad listed the primary obligations of each Muslim, which have since come to be known as the **Five Pillars of Islam:** (1) to bear witness to Allah as the sole god and to accept Muhammad as his messenger, (2) to pray five times a day in the direction of Mecca, (3) to pay a fixed share of one's income to the state in support of the poor and needy, (4) to refrain from eating, drinking, and sexual activity during the daytime hours of the month of Ramadan, and, (5) provided one has the necessary resources, to do the hajj pilgrimage to Mecca. (See the feature "Movement of Ideas: The Five Pillars of Islam.")

When Umar died in 644, the umma chose Uthman to succeed him. Unlike earlier caliphs, Uthman was not perceived as impartial. He gave all the top positions to members of his own Umayyad clan, which angered many. In 656, a group of soldiers mutinied and killed Uthman. With their support, Muhammad's cousin Ali, who was also the husband of his daughter Fatima, became the fourth caliph. Ali was unable to reconcile the different feuding groups, and in 661 he was assassinated. Ali's martyrdom became a powerful symbol for all who objected to the reigning caliph's government.

The political division that occurred with Ali's death led to a permanent religious split in the Muslim community. The **Sunnis,** the "people of custom and the community," held that the leader of the Islamic community could be chosen by consensus and that the only legitimate claim to descent was through the male line. In Muhammad's case, his uncles could succeed him, since he left no sons. Although Sunnis accept Ali as one of the four rightly guided caliphs that succeeded Muhammad, they do not believe that Ali and Fatima's children, or their descendants, can become caliph because their claim to descent was through the female line of Fatima.

Opposed to the Sunnis were the "shia" or "party of Ali," usually referred to as **Shi'ites** in English. Shi'ites not only support Ali's claim to succeed Muhammad but also believe that the grandchildren born to Ali and Fatima should lead the community. They denied the legitimacy of the three caliphs before Ali, who were related to Muhammad only by marriage, not by blood.

The breach between Sunnis and Shi'ites became the major fault line within Islam down to the present. (Today, Iran, Iraq, and Bahrain are predominantly Shi'ite, and the rest of the Islamic world is mainly Sunni.) The two groups have frequently come into conflict, not only over the issue of succession but also over other issues, like property rights. For example, Shi'ite Muslims grant direct female kin, such as daughters, preference in inheritance law over more distant male relatives, such as uncles, a direct consequence of their view that descent from Muhammad could be traced through his daughter Fatima.

Early Conquests, 632–661

The early Muslims forged a powerful army that attacked non-Muslim lands, including the now-weak Byzantine and Sasanian Empires, with great success. When the army attacked a

---

● **Quran** The bo[ok] that Muslims believe i[s] the direct word of God as revealed to Muhammad. Written sometime around 650.

CL Primary Source:
The Quran
These selections contain a number of the tenets of Islam and shed light on the connections among Islam, Judaism, and Christianity.

● **hadith** Testimony recorded from Muhammad's friends and associates about his speech and actions. Formed an integral part of the Islamic textual tradition, second in importance only to the Quran.

● **Five Pillars of Islam** (1) To bear witness to Allah as the sole god and accept Muhammad as his messenger; (2) to pray five times a day in the direction of Mecca; (3) to pay a fixed share of one's income to the state in support of the poor and needy; (4) to refrain from eating, drinking, and sexual activity during day-time hours in the month of Ramadan; and (5) if feasible, to do the hajj pilgrimage to Mecca.

● **Sunnis** The larger of the two main Islamic groups that formed after Ali's death. Sunnis, meaning the "people of custom and the community," hold that the leader of Islam should be chosen by consensus and that legitimate claims to descent are only through the male line. Sunnis do not believe Ali and Fatima's descendants can become caliph.

...ars of Islam

...important Islamic texts, the
...riel, is associated with the sec-
...who described an encounter he
...ween the prophet Muhammad and
th... ...I. The Hadith of Gabriel summarizes
the cor... ...s of Islam as they were understood in
Muhammad s lifetime. The Five Pillars proved crucial to the expansion of Islam because these concise
teachings encapsulated its most important practices.
One did not have to learn Arabic or memorize the
entire Quran to be a Muslim; nor did one require access to a mosque or to educated teachers. The second passage, from the Islamic geographer al-Bakri
writing in 1068, describes how a Muslim teacher persuaded a king in Mali, in West Africa, to convert to
Islam. Al-Bakri lived in Spain his entire life and did
not himself witness the Mali king's conversion or the
rain that followed it. Thus his account may not be
entirely factual, but it shows how an educated Muslim scholar believed one ruler's conversion occurred
at the edge of the Islamic world. Observe how, according to al-Bakri, the teacher condensed the Five
Pillars even further.

Sources: Hadith of Gabriel as translated in Vincent J. Cornell,
"Fruit of the Tree of Knowledge: The Relationship Between Faith
and Practice in Islam," in *The Oxford History of Islam,* ed. John L.
Esposito (New York: Oxford University Press, 1999), pp. 75–76
(brackets removed to enhance readability); al-Bakri's *The Book of
Routes and Realms,* as translated in *Corpus of Early Arabic Sources for
West African History,* ed. N. Levtzion and J. F. P. Hopkins (New York:
Cambridge University Press, 1981), pp. 82–83.

From the Hadith of Gabriel

Umar ibn al-Khattab reported: One day, while we
were sitting with the Messenger of God (may God
bless and preserve him), there came upon us a
man whose clothes were exceedingly white and
whose hair was exceedingly black. No dust of
travel could be seen upon him, and none of us
knew him. He sat down in front of the Prophet
(may God bless and preserve him), rested his
knees against the Prophet's knees and placed his
palms on the Prophet's thighs. "Oh Muhammad,
tell me about Islam," he said. The Messenger of
God (may God bless and preserve him) replied:
"Islam means to bear witness that there is no god
but Allah, that Muhammad is the Messenger of
Allah, to maintain the required prayers, to pay
the poor-tax, to fast in the month of Ramadan,
and to perform the pilgrimage to the House of
God at Mecca if you are able to do so."

"You are correct," the man said. We were
amazed at his questioning of the Prophet and
then saying that the Prophet had answered correctly. Then he said, "Tell me about faith." The
Prophet said: "It is to believe in Allah, His angels,
His books, His messengers, and the Last Day, and
to believe in Allah's determination of affairs,
whether good comes of it or bad."

"You are correct," he said. "Now tell me
about virtue [*ihsan*]." The Prophet said: "It is to
worship Allah as if you see Him; for if you do not
see Him, surely He sees you." . . . Then the man
left. I remained for a while, and the Prophet said
to me: "Oh, Umar, do you know who the ques-
tioner was?" "Allah and His Messenger know
best," I replied. He said: "It was the angel
Gabriel, who came to you to teach you your
religion."

From al-Bakri's *The Book of Routes and Realms,* about the Malal region (modern-day Mali)

Beyond this country lies another called Malal, the king of which is known as al-musulmani [the Muslim]. He is thus called because his country became afflicted with drought one year following another; the inhabitants prayed for rain, sacrificing cattle till they had exterminated almost all of them, but the drought and the misery only increased. The king had as his guest a Muslim who used to read the Quran and was acquainted with the Sunna [the model of behavior that all Muslims were expected to follow]. To this man the king complained of the calamities that assailed him and his people.

The man said: "O King, if you believed in God (who is exalted) and testified that He is One, and testified as to the prophetic mission of Muhammad (God bless him and give him peace), and if you accepted all the religious laws of Islam, I would pray for your deliverance from your plight and that God's mercy would envelop all the people of your country, and that your enemies and adversaries might envy you on that account."

Thus he continued to press the king until the latter accepted Islam and became a sincere Muslim. The man made him recite from the Quran some easy passages and taught him religious obligations and practices which no man be excused from knowing. Then the Muslim made him wait till the eve of the following Friday, when he ordered him to purify himself by a complete ablution, and clothed him in a cotton garment which he had. The two of them came out towards a mound of earth, and there the Muslim stood praying while the king, standing at this right side, imitated him. Thus they prayed for a part of the night, the Muslim reciting invocations and the king saying "Amen." The dawn had just started to break when God caused abundant rain to descend upon them. So the king ordered the idols to be broken and expelled the sorcerers from his country. He and his descendants after him as well as his nobles were sincerely attached to Islam, while the common people of his kingdom remained polytheists. Since then their rulers have been given the title of al-musulmani [the Muslim].

QUESTIONS FOR ANALYSIS

▶ Which of the Five Pillars marked one's conversion to Islam?

▶ Which, according to the Hadith of Gabriel, was optional?

▶ Which Pillar do you think would have been the most difficult for the king of Mali to observe?

new region, the front ranks of infantry advanced using bows and arrows and crossbows. Their task was to break into the enemy's frontlines so that the mounted cavalry, the backbone of the army, could attack.

In the first stage of conquest, the troops seized all the movable property of the conquered people and reserved a fixed share, called *zakat* (literally "purification," officially set at one-fifth), for the commander. The remaining four-fifths were distributed among the troops and provided a powerful incentive to keep on fighting. The caliph headed the army, which was divided into units of one hundred men and subunits of ten.

Once the Islamic armies pacified a new region, a process that sometimes took generations, the regional governor had to implement a more regular system of taxation. The Muslims levied the same tax rates on conquering and conquered peoples alike, provided that the conquered peoples converted to Islam.

Islam stressed the equality of all believers before God, and all Muslims, whether born to Muslim parents or converts, paid two types of taxes: one on the land, usually fixed at one-tenth of the annual harvest, and the zakat tax, originally set by Muhammad at one-fifth of all plunder. The zakat tax evolved into a property tax with different rates for different possessions. Because the revenue was to be used to help the needy or to serve God, it is often called an "alms-tax" or "poor tax." Exempt from the zakat tax, non-Muslims paid the *jizya* tax, usually set at a higher rate than the taxes paid by Muslims.

Islamic forces conquered city after city and ruled the entire Arabian peninsula by 634. Then they crossed overland to Egypt from the Sinai Peninsula. Although Egypt had a majority Christian population, Egyptians chose to ally with the invading Islamic armies to throw off Byzantine rule. By 642 the Islamic armies controlled Egypt, and by 650 they controlled an enormous swath of territory from Libya to Central Asia. In 650, they vanquished the once-powerful Sasanian empire.

The new Islamic state in Iran aspired to build an empire as large and long-lasting as the Sasanian empire, which had governed modern-day Iran and Iraq for more than four centuries. The caliphate's armies divided conquered peoples into three groups. Those who converted became Muslims. Those who continued to adhere to Judaism or Christianity were given the status of "protected subjects" (*dhimmi* in Arabic), because they too were "peoples of the book" who honored the same prophets from the Hebrew Bible and the New Testament that Muhammad had. Non-Muslims and nonprotected subjects formed the lowest group. Dhimmi status was later extended to Zoroastrians as well.

The Umayyad Caliphate, 661–750

Although the Islamic community had not resolved the issue of succession, by 661 Muslims had created their own expanding empire whose religious and political leader was the caliph. After Ali was assassinated in 661, Muawiya, a member of the Umayyad clan like the caliph Uthman, unified the Muslim community. In 680, when he died, Ali's son Husain tried to become caliph, but Muawiya's son defeated him and became caliph instead. Since only members of this family became caliphs until 750, this period is called the Umayyad dynasty.

The Umayyads built their capital at Damascus, the home of their many Syrian supporters, not in the Arabian peninsula, the original homeland of Islam. Initially they used local languages for administration, but after 685 they chose Arabic as the language of the empire.

■ **Portraying Paradise on Earth: The Umayyad Mosque of Damascus**   The most beautiful building in the Umayyad capital of Damascus was the mosque, where some 12,000 Byzantine craftsmen incorporated mosaics, made from thousands of glass tiles, into the building's structure. Notice how the trees grow naturally from the columns at the bottom of the photograph and how the twin windows allow viewers to glimpse the beautiful flowers on the ceiling above. These compositions portray the paradise that Muhammad promised his followers would enter after their deaths. (© Bernard O'Kane/Alamy)

In Damascus, the Umayyads erected the Great Mosque on the site of a church housing the relics of John the Baptist (see Chapter 7). Architects modified the building's Christian layout to create a large space where devotees could pray toward Mecca. This was the first Islamic building to have a place to wash one's hands and feet, a large courtyard, and a tall tower, or minaret, from which Muslims issued the call for prayer. Since Muslims honored the Ten Commandments, including the Second Commandment, "You shall not make for yourself a graven image," the Byzantine workmen depicted no human figures or living animals. Instead their mosaics showed landscapes in an imaginary paradise.

The Conquest of North Africa, 661–750

Under the leadership of the Umayyads, Islamic armies conquered the part of North Africa known as the Maghrib—modern-day Morocco, Algeria, and Tunisia. Strong economic and cultural ties dating back to the Roman Empire bound the Maghrib to western Asia. Its fertile fields provided the entire Mediterranean with grain, olive oil, and fruits like figs and bananas. In addition, the region exported handicrafts such as textiles, ceramics, and glass. Slaves and gold moved from the interior of Africa to the coastal ports, where they, too, were loaded into ships crossing the Mediterranean.

While Egypt had fallen in only a few years, the conquest of the rest of the Maghrib took many years. Islamic armies took Tunis (formerly Carthage, Tunisia) in 670 and Fez (Morocco) in 711, and then crossed the Strait of Gibraltar to enter Spain.

Arab culture and the religion of Islam eventually took root in North Africa, expanding from urban centers into the countryside. By the tenth century, Christians had become a minority in Egypt, outnumbered by Muslims, and by the twelfth century, Arabic had replaced both Egyptian and the Berber languages of the Maghrib as the dominant language. Annual performance of the hajj pilgrimage strengthened the ties between the people of North Africa and the Arabian peninsula. Starting from different places along the Mediterranean coast and along the Nile, pilgrim caravans converged in Cairo, from where large groups then proceeded to Mecca.

Islamic rule reoriented North Africa. Before it, the Mediterranean coast of Africa formed the southern edge of the Roman Empire, where Christianity was the dominant religion and Latin the language of learning (see Chapter 7). Under Muslim rule, North Africa lay at the western edge of the Islamic realm, and Arabic was spoken everywhere.

●The Abbasid Caliphate United, 750–945

In 744, a group of Syrian soldiers assassinated the Umayyad caliph, prompting an all-out civil war among all those hoping to control the caliphate. In 750, a section of the army based in western Iran, in the Khurasan region, triumphed and then shifted the capital some 500 miles (800 km) east from Damascus to Baghdad, closer to their base of support. Because the new caliph claimed descent from Muhammad's uncle Abbas, the new dynasty was called the Abbasid dynasty and their empire the **Abbasid caliphate.** Under Abbasid rule, the Islamic empire continued to expand east into Central Asia. At its greatest extent, it included present-day Morocco, Tunisia, Egypt, Saudi Arabia, Iraq, Iran, southern Pakistan, and Uzbekistan. In Spain, however, the leaders of the vanquished Umayyad clan established a separate Islamic state.

● **Abbasid caliphate**
Dynasty of rulers (750–1258) who ruled a united empire from their capital at Baghdad until the empire fragmented in 945. They continued as religious leaders until 1258, when the last Abbasid caliph was killed by the Mongols.

Baghdad, City of Learning

The new Abbasid capital was built by the second Abbasid caliph Mansur (r. 754–775). Baghdad was on the Tigris River in the heart of Mesopotamia, near the point where the Tigris and Euphrates Rivers come closest together (see Chapter 2). Several canals linked the two rivers. Mansur explained his choice:

> Indeed, this island between the Tigris in the East and the Euphrates in the West is the harbor of the world. All the ships that sail up the Tigris . . . and the adjacent areas will anchor here. . . . It will indeed be the most flourishing city in the world.[3]

Baghdad more than fulfilled his hopes. Located at the crossroads of Africa, Europe, and Asia, it was home to a half a million residents who included the majority Muslim community and smaller communities of Christians, Jews, and Zoroastrians. The city's residents lived side by side, celebrated each other's festivals, and spoke Arabic, Persian, Greek, and Hebrew.

Mansur, we learn from the historian Masudi,

> was the first caliph to have foreign works of literature translated into Arabic . . . various of Aristotle's treatises on logic and other subjects; Ptolemy's *Almagest;* the *Book of Euclid;* the treatise on arithmetic and all the other ancient works. . . . Once in possession of these books, the public read and studied them avidly.[4]

Local scholars benefited from the support of both the caliph and the city's residents, who paid for the manuscripts to be copied and studied them in their schools. The city's cosmopolitan environment encouraged scholars to study the scientific and mathematical discoveries of Greece, India, and Mesopotamia. Historians call their collective efforts, which lasted several centuries, the **translation movement.** In translating astronomy, medical, mathematical, and geography books from ancient Greek, Sanskrit, and Persian into Arabic, they created a body of scientific knowledge unsurpassed in the world. Certain works by ancient Greek scholars, such as the medical scholar Galen, survive only in their Arabic translations. When, beginning in the eleventh and twelfth centuries, Europeans once again became interested in the learning of the Greeks, they gladly used the Arabic translations, which preserved the legacy of the past while adding many distinguished advances (see the "Movement of Ideas" feature in Chapter 13).

• **translation movement** The collective effort of Islamic scholars, many living in Baghdad, between 750 and 1000 to translate astronomy, medical, mathematical, and geography books from ancient Greek, Sanskrit, and Persian into Arabic.

Islamic scholars also made many scientific and mathematical discoveries of their own. The great mathematician al-Khwarizmi (al-HWAR-ez-mee) (d. 830) combined the Indian and Babylonian number systems to create the world's first workable decimal system. Al-Khwarizmi invented algebra (from the Arabic word *al-jabr,* meaning "transposition") to solve math problems more easily through the use of equations. He also developed a system of computation that divided complex problems into shorter steps, or algorithms (the word *algorithm* is derived from al-Khwarizmi's name).

One of the Five Pillars of Islam (see page 245) is to pray five times a day facing toward Mecca. Islamic scholars developed increasingly sophisticated instruments to determine this position for prayer. The **astrolabe** allowed observers to calculate their location on earth once they had set the appropriate dials for the date, the time of day, and the angle of the sun's course through the sky; they could then determine the direction of Mecca for their prayers. The astrolabe also functioned as a slide rule, one of the world's first hand-held mathematical calculators. It became the most significant computational tool of its time.

• **astrolabe** Computational instrument that allowed observers to calculate their location on earth to determine the direction of Mecca for their prayers. Also functioned as a slide rule, one of the world's first hand-held mathematical calculators.

In a significant technological advance, a paper-making factory was opened in Baghdad in 794–795 that used Chinese techniques (see Chapter 4) to produce the first paper in the Islamic world. Muslim scholars had previously written on either papyrus, a dried plant grown in Egypt, or dried, scraped leather, called parchment. Both were much more costly than paper, and the new writing material spread quickly throughout the empire. By 850, Baghdad housed one hundred paper-making workshops.

The low cost of paper greatly increased the availability of books. Manuals on agriculture, botany, and pharmacology contributed to the spread of agricultural

■ **Determining the Direction of Mecca: The Astrolabe**   This astrolabe, made in 1216, is a sophisticated mathematical device. After holding the astrolabe up to the sun to determine the angle of the sun's rays and thus fix the viewer's latitude on earth, one inserted the appropriate metal plate (this example has three) into the mechanism, which allowed one to chart the movement of the stars.   (Musée Paul Dupuy, Toulous, France/Eric Lessing, Art Resource, NY)

techniques and crops from one end of the empire to the other. Cookbooks show the extent to which the empire's residents embraced Asian foodstuffs like rice, eggplant, and processed sugar. Cotton for clothing, grown by Persians at the time of the founding of the Abbasid dynasty, gradually spread to Egypt, and, by the twelfth century, West Africans began to cultivate the crop as well.

Abbasid Governance

Baghdad, the city of learning, was the capital of an enormous empire headed by the caliph, who presided over the military, the bureaucracy, and the judiciary. His chief minister, or vizier, stood at the head of a bureaucracy based in the capital. In the provinces, the caliph delegated power to regional governors, who were charged with maintaining local armies and transmitting revenues to the center; however, they often tried to keep revenues for themselves.

In the early centuries of Islamic rule, local populations often continued their pre-Islamic religious practices. For example, in 750 fewer than 8 percent of the people living in the Abbasid heartland of Iran were Muslims. By the ninth century, the Muslim proportion of the population had increased to 40 percent, but only in the tenth century did converts become a majority—70 or 80 percent—of the population.[5]

The caliphate offered all of its subjects access to a developed judicial system that implemented Islamic law. He appointed a chief judge, or qadi, for the city of Baghdad and a qadi for each of the empire's provinces. These judges were drawn from the learned men of Islam, or **ulama** (also spelled *ulema*), who gained their positions after years of study. The ulama took no special vows and could marry and have families. Some specialized in the Quran, others scrutinized records of Muhammad's sayings in the hadith to establish their veracity, and still others concentrated on legal texts. Scholars taught at schools, sometimes in mosques and sometimes in separate buildings. On Fridays, at the weekly services, the ulama preached to the congregation (women and men sat separately, with the men in front), and afterward they heard legal disputes in the mosques.

The judiciary enjoyed an unusually high position, for even members of the caliph's immediate family were subject to their decisions. In one example, an employee who brought goods for Zubaydah, the wife of the caliph Harun al-Rashid, refused to pay a merchant. When the merchant consulted a judge, the judge advised the merchant to file suit and then ordered the queen's agent to pay the debt. The angry queen ordered the judge transferred and Harun complied with his wife's request, but only after he himself paid the money owed to the merchant.

At first glance, it might seem that the queen had prevailed; after all, she managed to have the judge transferred. But she had not ordered him killed, and the judge continued to hear cases in his new post. A comparison with other contemporary empires demonstrates the power of the judiciary in the Abbasid empire: no Chinese subject of the Tang dynasty would have dared to sue the emperor, and no one in Europe had access to a comparable judicial system.

● **ulama** Learned Islamic scholars who studied the Quran, the hadith, and legal texts. They taught classes, preached, and heard legal disputes; they took no special vows and could marry and have families.

Abbasid Society

When compared with its Asian and European contemporaries, Islamic society appears surprisingly egalitarian. It had divisions, of course: rural/urban, Muslim/non-Muslim, free person/slave. Apart from gender differences, however, none of these divisions were insurmountable. Rural people could move to the city, non-Muslims could convert to Islam, and slaves could be, and often were, freed.

In the royal ranks, however, much had changed since the time of Muhammad, whose supporters treated him as an equal. The Abbasid rulers rejected the egalitarianism of early Islam to embrace the lavish court ceremonies of the Sasanians. To the horror of the ulama, the caliph received visitors from behind a curtained throne, and visitors had to kiss the ground in front of his throne even though only God, the learned felt, should receive such a form of submission. Equally reprehensible in the eyes of the ulama, his subjects addressed the caliph as "the shadow of God on earth," a title modeled on the Sasanian "king of kings." At the right of the caliph stood an executioner, ready to kill any visitor who might offend the caliph.

The one group in Islamic society to inherit privileges on the basis of birth were those who could claim descent from Muhammad's family. All the Abbasid caliphs belonged to this group, and their many relatives occupied a privileged position at the top of Baghdad society. Descent from Muhammad did not bring any financial advantage; it simply commanded more respect.

Under the royal family, two large groups enjoyed considerable prestige and respect: the ulama, on the one hand, and the cultured elite, who included courtiers surrounding the caliph, bureaucrats staffing his government, and educated land-owners throughout the empire. These groups often patronized poets, painters, and musicians, themselves also members of the cultured elite. Generally speaking the cultured elite were not as observant as the ulama.

Like the caliph's more educated subjects, ordinary people varied in the extent of their compliance with the religious teachings of Islam. In the cities they worked carrying goods, and in the countryside they farmed. Most farmers prayed five times a day and attended Friday prayers at their local mosques, but they could not always afford to go on the hajj.

Farmers aspired to send their sons, but not their daughters, to study at the local mosque for a few years. Here they acquired the rudiments of Arabic so that they could recite the Quran before starting work full-time as cultivators. Families that educated their daughters did so at home. Boys who demonstrated scholarly ability hoped to become members of the ulama, while those gifted in mathematics might become merchants.

Muhammad and two of his immediate successors had been merchants, and trade continued to enjoy a privileged position in the Abbasid caliphate. Merchants were supposed to adhere to a high standard of conduct: to be true to their word and to sell merchandise free from defects. Many merchants contributed money for the upkeep of mosques or to help the less fortunate. Because Islamic law forbade usury (charging interest on loans), Muslim merchants used credit mechanisms like checks, letters of credit, and bills of exchange.

While the most successful merchants became bankers and traders who specialized in large-scale transactions that spanned the empire, other merchants ran single shops or peddled their goods, some of which they made themselves, from town to town. The state regulated the quality of goods such as textiles, which had to be stamped by the government before being placed on sale.

The shift of the capital to Baghdad in the eighth century brought a dramatic increase in trade within the empire and beyond. Long-distance merchants sent ships to India and China that were loaded with locally produced goods—such as Arabian horses, textiles, and carpets—and nonlocal goods, such as African ivory and Southeast Asian pearls. The ships returned with spices, medicines, and textiles. Islamic merchants were at home in a world stretching from China to Africa; Aladdin, the famous fictional hero of a tale from *The Thousand and One Nights,* was born in China and adopted by an African merchant. As early as the ninth century, ships traveled routinely between the Arabian Sea and south Chinese ports, and the China-Mecca route was the longest regularly traveled sea route in the world before 1500.

Slavery   Much long-distance trade involved the import of slaves from three major areas: Central Africa, Central Asia, and central and eastern Europe, by far the largest source (see Map 9.1). The Arabs referred to the region of modern Poland and Bohemia as the "slave country." (The English word *slave* is derived from the Latin word for *slav,* because so many slaves were originally Slavic.)

An extraordinary sailor's tale from the mid-tenth century tells of the abduction of an East African slave.[6] Although the tale is clearly a literary creation, the narrator, a Muslim slave trader, describes real-world trading routes. In 922, an Arab ship set out from the port of Oman in the Persian Gulf, was caught in a storm, and landed on the coast of East Africa, in modern Somalia or Kenya, regions that had become Islamicized under the Abbasids. "The canoes of the negroes

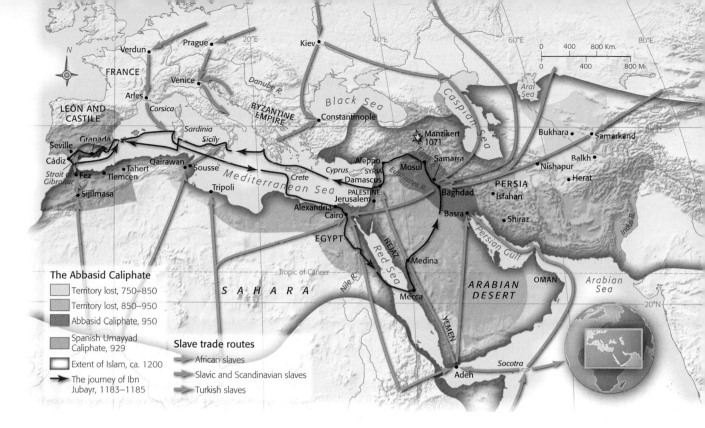

MAP 9.1

The Abbasid Caliphate Between 750 and 950, the Abbasid caliphate lost huge chunks of territory in North Africa, the Arabian peninsula, Iran, and Central Asia, yet a shared Islamic identity held the former empire together, as Ibn Jubayr learned in his 1183–1185 journey (see page 262). The people living in the empire's core around Baghdad imported slaves, many of whom converted to Islam, from Africa, northern Europe, and Central Asia.

surrounded us and brought us into the harbour," the narrator explains, and the local king gave him permission to trade.

At the conclusion of their trip, the African king and seven companions boarded the ship to bid the Arab merchants good-bye. The narrator explains the ship's captain's thoughts:

> When I saw them there, I said to myself: In the Oman market this young king would certainly fetch thirty dinars [a *dinar* coin contained 4.25 grams of gold], and his seven companions sixty dinars. Their clothes are not worth less than twenty dinars. One way and another this would give us a profit of at least 3,000 dirhams [a silver coin] and without any trouble. Reflecting thus, I gave the crew their orders. They raised the sails and weighed anchor.

The captain's split-second calculation of the king's value chills the blood. Unable to escape, the captive king joined two hundred other slaves in the ship's hold and was sold when the ship reached Oman.

Several years later, the same captain and the same ship were caught in a storm, and, to their horror, they landed in the same harbor. They were brought to the king, and to their amazement, it was the same king they had sold at the Oman slave market. The king explained that he had been purchased by a Muslim in the Persian Gulf port of Basra, who had first taught him the Quran and then had sold him to a man living in Baghdad. After converting to Islam, the king joined a group of hajj pilgrims on their way to Mecca, and in Mecca he joined a group going to Cairo. On the way home from Cairo, slave traders captured him twice, he escaped both times, and finally he reached his former kingdom where his countrymen welcomed him back.

The king then explained why he had forgiven the narrator and his fellow slave traders: "And here I am, happy and satisfied with the grace God has given me and mine, of knowing the precepts of Islam, the true faith, prayers, fasting, the pilgrimage, and what is permitted and what is forbidden." In short, the chain of events that began with his capture led to his conversion and finally his freedom.

Although fictional, this tale sheds light on a poorly documented process: under the Abbasids, the coastal cities of East Africa, particularly those north of Madagascar, became Muslim, not because they were conquered by invading armies but because traveling merchants introduced Islam to them. The merchants came to the coast to buy slaves and other products, including gold and ivory. In many cases, the rulers converted first, and the population later followed.

Like this fictional enslaved king, most Islamic slaves worked as servants or concubines, not as field hands like the slaves of the American South before the Civil War. The caliph's household purchased thousands of slaves each year. The women entered the secluded women's quarters in the palace, or harem, where they were guarded by eunuchs, or castrated men. Many slave buyers particularly valued eunuchs because they could trust them with their female kin.

Since Islamic law held that no Muslim could be sold as a slave, any slave who converted to Islam had to be freed. Former slaves often continued to work for their original owners for wages. All levels of society, from the caliph with his hundreds of female slaves down to the petty trader who could afford only one, respected the teaching that children born to a slave woman and a Muslim father should be raised as free Muslims. As a result, these children were granted identical rights as their siblings born to Muslim mothers.

Harun al-Rashid was himself the child of a slave mother, Khaizuran. Like many young slave children, she learned to read and write because educated slaves could command a higher price on the slave market. When the caliph Mansur gave her to his son Mahdi sometime in the late 750s, Mahdi took an immediate liking to the young girl, who was "slender and graceful as a reed," the root meaning of her name *khaizuran*.

Politics of the Harem   Like most ordinary people living within the Abbasid Empire, Khaizuran had grown up in a nuclear family headed by her father and his one wife, her mother. Islamic law permitted Muslim men to marry as many as four wives, but most men could afford to support only one. The caliphs took the four wives Islamic law entitled them to, and their enormous revenues also permitted them to support unlimited numbers of concubines.

When Khaizuran joined the royal household, she left behind her life in the streets of Mecca, where women had some freedom of movement, and entered a world whose customs were completely unfamiliar. The higher a woman's class, the greater the degree of seclusion, and the caliph's wives were the most secluded of all. An army of eunuchs guarded the secluded women's quarters and prevented illicit contact with any men. Khaizuran was free to leave the palace only on rare occasions, and then only under escort.

When Khaizuran entered the harem, she told everyone she had no living kin. Only after giving birth to two sons, and only after she was certain of her status as one of the future caliph's favorites, did she reveal that her mother, two sisters, and a brother were still alive in Yemen. The caliph Mansur immediately summoned them to live in the palace and arranged for Khaizuran's sister to marry another of his sons. The sister subsequently gave birth to a daughter, whose nickname was "little butter ball," or Zubaydah.

Khaizuran's relations with her son Hadi soured soon after he, and not Harun, became caliph in 785. Hadi was particularly upset to discover that his mother was meeting with his generals and courtiers on her own. He chastised her, saying: "Do not overstep the essential limits of womanly modesty.... It is not dignified for women to enter upon affairs of state. Take to your prayer and worship and devote yourself to the service of Allah. Hereafter, submit to the womanly role that is required of your sex."[7]

But Khaizuran did not back down. Hadi then asked his generals how they would feel if their mothers interfered in politics, and they all agreed, "Not any one of us would like that."[8] This description by the historian al-Tabari (at-TAH-bah-ree) (d. 923) seems to suggest that all the commanders felt the same: that no woman, and certainly not Khaizuran, should intervene in matters of state. Contrary to the expectation of these men, Khaizuran did, however, intervene in court politics. Hadi died suddenly, in mysterious circumstances, and Khaizuran made sure that Harun succeeded him as caliph. (No one knows exactly how.)

Unlike her mother and her famous aunt Khaizuran, who had come to the harem as adults, Zubaydah grew up entirely within the women's quarter of the palace. After her marriage she devoted herself to public works. While in Mecca, she contributed an additional 1,700,000 dinars, or nearly eight tons of gold, from her own funds to construct a giant reservoir. She also ordered wells dug to provide hajj pilgrims with fresh water. The resulting stone water tunnels, running above and below ground for 12 miles (20 km), constituted a genuine feat of engineering. Finally, she made extensive repairs to the road linking Kufa, a city outside Baghdad, with Mecca and Medina. (See the feature "Visual Evidence: Zubaydah's Road.")

The Breakup of the Abbasid Empire, 809–936

Like her mother-in-law Khaizuran, Zubaydah tried to manipulate the succession after Harun's death in 809, but she sided with the losing son, who was defeated by his brother Mamun in 813. The empire Mamun won, however, was not as prosperous as it appeared. The costs of governing the Abbasid Empire often exceeded its revenues. Even during Harun's reign the caliphs were often forced to seek emergency loans. The central government frequently ran short of money because regional governors did not forward the taxes they collected to the caliph. The frequent civil wars between rivals for the caliphate destroyed the irrigation works that underpinned the agrarian economy, and, because no one rebuilt them, tax revenues continuously declined.

As a temporary expedient, the caliph occasionally appointed someone, usually called a tax farmer, to collect a fixed amount in a region where the caliph's bureaucrats had trouble raising revenue. In these cases the caliph still retained direct political control. If tax farmers failed to raise the necessary revenues, the caliph

ZUBAYDAH'S ROAD

Zubaydah devoted considerable resources to the project that brought her lasting fame: the road linking Kufa, a city outside Baghdad, with Mecca and Medina. Although the road existed before her reign, she made so many improvements to it that it came to be called Darb Zubaydah, or Zubaydah's Road.

When Saudi archaeologists surveyed the desert in the 1970s, they found identifiable traces of a roadway 18 yards (17 m) yards wide. The road's builders had faced the challenge of designing a road for pedestrians even though it ran through long stretches of sand, some muddy ground, and rough lava fields. They cleared the road of stones, paved the sections of the road that went through the mud, and smoothed rough lava fields before covering them with soft sand on which pilgrims could easily walk. One archaeologist has called the project "the finest and most remarkable and extensive road system in the earlier period of Islamic history."*

_____
*Saad A. al-Rashid, _Darb Zubaydah: The Pilgrim Road from Kufa to Mecca_ (Riyad: Riyad University, 1980), p. 330.

• The stones of the lava field were so sharp that they hurt the feet of the pilgrims and their camels.

• After clearing the road, engineers covered it with a smooth layer of sand for the convenience of the pilgrims and their camels, who traveled over 700 miles (1,100 km).

(John Herbert)

QUESTION FOR ANALYSIS

 What preparations did hajj travelers going overland have to make, and how would these differ for those traveling by boat?

Because Zubaydah was particularly concerned about poorer pilgrims who traveled the difficult route on foot, she added nine new rest stations at convenient intervals between existing stations, for a total of fifty-four rest stops. All the new stations had a pool, and they often included some kind of shelter and sometimes even a small mosque. This painting, from an illustrated thirteenth-century manuscript of collected anecdotes, shows what a resting place on the Darb Zubaydah might have looked like.

The nimbus, or cloud, behind the head was originally an Iranian artistic convention used to show royalty. In this picture, however, the nimbus seems purely decorative, since all the human figures have one.

This figure uses bellows to light a fire below a cooking pot.

This is a shrine, most likely to a prominent Islamic teacher whose grave lies inside it, where Muslims came to pray.

Two camels bray with their mouths open. Although often ill-tempered, camels were the one draft animal that could withstand the hot, dry climate of the desert.

Inside a tent made from beautiful textiles, these two men lean on portable wooden furniture as they converse with each other.

(Institute of Oriental Studies, St. Petersburg, Russia/The Bridgeman Library)

Three camels feed from saddlebags placed on the ground. Able to survive for up to nine days without water, camels can carry loads over 300 pounds (140 kg).

259

• **iqta grant** A grant given by the caliph to someone who promised to collect taxes from a certain region and pay the caliph a certain amount of money. Grant holders became military governors and rulers of their regions, over which the caliph had only nominal control.

might go a step further and make an **iqta grant,** ceding all political control to the man who promised to pay a certain amount. The iqta (ICK-tah) grant-holder became the military governor and ruler of the area, and the caliph retained only nominal control. In 789 and 800, Harun granted independence to two Islamic states in North Africa in exchange for annual tax payments; his successors made similar arrangements with other regions.

Until the middle of the tenth century, none of the iqta holders directly challenged the authority of the caliph. Then, in 936, the caliph took the final step and ceded all his power to an Iraqi grant holder, giving him the title *commander of commanders.* The grant holder disbanded the entire Abbasid army and replaced it with an army loyal to himself. He eliminated the Abbasid bureaucracy as well, sentencing the last vizier to life imprisonment in a dungeon.

This new arrangement did not last long. In 945, the Buyids, a group of Shi'ite Iranian mercenaries based in the mountains south of the Caspian Sea, conquered Baghdad and took over the government. Rather than depose the caliphs and risk alienating their Muslim subjects, the Buyids retained them as figureheads who led the Islamic caliphate but had no political power. The caliph received a small allowance so that he could reside in his crumbling palace in Baghdad, and Islamic preachers continued to cite his name in their Friday prayers. The extensive territory of the Abbasid Empire proved ungovernable as a single political unit, and it broke up into different regions, all still part of the Islamic cultural and religious world.

The Rise of Regional Centers After the Abbasids, 945–1258

Although no one knew how the caliph's loss of political authority would affect the caliphate, Muslims found it surprisingly easy to accept the new division of political and religious authority. The caliphs continued as the titular heads of the Islamic religious community, but they were entirely dependent on temporal rulers for financial support. No longer politically united, the Islamic world was still bound by religious ties and the obligation to perform the hajj. Under the leadership of committed Muslim rulers, Islam continued to spread throughout South Asia and the interior of Africa. Rulers all over the Islamic world continued to patronize Islamic scholars, and Islamic learning, particularly in the field of geography, continued to thrive.

Regional Islamic States, 945–1258

Many different states formed in the centuries after the caliph's loss of political authority. In 1055, Baghdad fell to yet a different group of soldiers, the Turkish-speaking Seljuqs (also spelled Seljuk) from Central Asia. With the accession of the Seljuqs (sell-JOOKs), other sections of the empire broke off and, like Baghdad, experienced rule by different dynasties. In most periods, the former Abbasid Empire was divided into four regions: the former heartland of the Euphrates and Tigris River basins, Egypt and Syria, North Africa and Spain, and the Amu Darya and Syr Daria River Valleys in Central Asia.

Two centuries of Abbasid rule had transformed these four regions into Islamic realms whose residents, whether Sunni or Shi'ite, observed the tenets of Islam. Their societies retained the basic patterns of Abbasid society. When Muslims traveled anywhere in the former Abbasid territories, they could be confident of finding mosques, being received as honored guests, and having access to the same basic legal system (even if some legal schools differed in their interpretations). As in the Roman Empire, where Greek and Latin prevailed, just two languages could take a traveler through the entire realm: Arabic, the language of the Quran and high Islamic learning, and Persian, the Iranian language of much poetry, literature, and history.

■ Map of Eurasia, 1182 This map, like all Islamic maps, is oriented with the south on top and the north below. It is a copy of a silver map made by the geographer al-Idrisi, which no longer survives. With greater precision than any other contemporary map, it shows the blue Mediterranean Sea in the middle with Africa above (notice the three sources of the Nile on the right) and Eurasia below. (National Library [Dar-al-Katub], Cairo, Egypt/Erich Lessing/Art Resource, NY)

Sometime around 1000, the city of Córdoba in Islamic Spain replaced Baghdad as the leading center of Islamic learning. The Umayyad capital from around 750 to 1031, Córdoba served as the capital for the Almoravid (1031–1147) and Almohad (1130–1269) dynasties who succeeded the Umayyads and ruled North Africa and Spain in the eleventh through thirteenth centuries. All visitors to Córdoba admired its gardens, fountains, paved streets, and most of all, its running water (the first in Europe since the fall of Rome).

Córdoba played a crucial role in the transmission of learning from the Islamic world to Christian Europe. Craftsmen learned how to make paper in the eleventh century and transmitted the technique to the rest of Europe. Córdoba's residents, both male and female, specialized in copying manuscripts and translated treatises from Arabic into Latin for European audiences.

The study of geography also flourished in the eleventh and twelfth centuries as Muslims learned about the most distant places within the Islamic community. Al-Bakri, a geographer based in Córdoba, provided a rare, detailed description of Central Africa. He reported that the two kingdoms of Ghana and Gao had capital cities with separate districts for Muslims and for local religious practitioners who prayed to images. He explained that although rulers often converted to Islam after contact with Muslim traders, their subjects, as in the case of Mali, did not always follow suit.

This religious division between rulers who converted to Islam and subjects who did not held true in the other major area that was brought into the Islamic world in the eleventh and twelfth centuries: Afghanistan, Pakistan, and north India. Muslim conquerors moved into north India from their base in Afghanistan. During the actual conquest they tore down Hindu temples, but once they gained power they allowed Hindu temples to remain, even as they endowed mosques. Ordinary Indians continued to worship Hindu deities (see Chapter 8), while the ruling family, who were based in Delhi and who are thus known as the Delhi sultanate, observed the tenets of Islam.

During this long period of division, Muslim cartographers made some of the most advanced maps of their day. Working in Sicily, the geographer al-Idrisi (1100–1166) drew a map of the world engraved on a silver tablet 3 yards by 1.5 yards (3 m by 1.5 m). Although the map was destroyed during his lifetime, the book al-Idrisi wrote to accompany his map is so detailed that scholars have been able to reconstruct the seven climatic zones, each with ten sections, that appeared on his original map. Like all Islamic maps, his looks upside down to modern viewers because he oriented the map to the south. His map showed the outlines of the Mediterranean, Africa, and Central Asia with far greater accuracy than contemporary maps made elsewhere in the world.

Ibn Jubayr's Hajj in 1183

By the twelfth century, different Islamic governments ruled the different sections of the former Abbasid Empire. Since the realm of Islam was no longer unified, devout Muslims had to cross from one Islamic polity to the next as they performed the hajj. Local Islamic rulers might take advantage of the pilgrims by charging them extra taxes or exacting customs duties, but sometimes they also facilitated the pilgrims' journey. Pilgrims were often unsure of the correct rituals to perform in Mecca, and as the number of pilgrims increased over the centuries, a new genre of book, called "travels" (*rihla* in Arabic), appeared that described the trip to Mecca and the most

The Hajj Today

The world's fastest-growing religion, Islam is second only to Christianity in the number of adherents, with a total of 1.2 billion Muslims in the world today. The four countries with the greatest number of Muslims lie far from the heartland of Islam in Saudi Arabia: Indonesia (170 million), Pakistan (136 million), Bangladesh (106 million), and India (103 million). The world region with the greatest number of recent converts is Africa.

Each Muslim hopes to go on the hajj at least once in his or her lifetime, and more than two million people travel to Saudi Arabia each year on this pilgrimage. The number would be even greater except that the government of Saudi Arabia limits the number of visas issued annually to one thousand pilgrims for each one million citizens in each country.

Because the visitors all want to visit the different sites in the prescribed order on the same days, crowding poses a major problem. As in Ibn Jubayr's day, the stoning of the Devil at Mina is one of the most dangerous rites. After staying up most of the night, pilgrims throw rocks, yell insults, or hurl their shoes at one of three stone pillars. The highest number of casualties occurred in 1990, when 1,426 pilgrims died in a stampede in a tunnel. Stampedes have also occurred in 1998, 2001, 2004, and 2006. Still, because it is such an important part of the hajj experience, authorities are reluctant to limit the number of people visiting Mina.

Sources: adherents.com; various newspaper reports accessed via Lexis Nexus.

important rituals performed there. Although Muslims came from different regional states and spoke different languages, their participation in the same rituals of the hajj bound them together. (See "World History in Today's World: The Hajj Today.")

The most famous travel book is *The Travels* of **Ibn Jubayr** (1145–1217), a courtier from Granada, Spain, who went on the hajj in 1183–1185. Ibn Jubayr (IH-buhn joo-BAH-eer) decided to go to Mecca to repent for drinking seven cups of wine, a drink forbidden to Muslims. He financed his trip with a gift of seven cups of gold coins received from the governor of Granada, his superior, who felt contrite about having forced Ibn Jubayr to drink so much. Ibn Jubayr's book serves as a guide to the sequence of hajj observances that had been fixed by Muhammad; Muslims today continue to perform the same rituals (see Table 9.1, "The Nine Steps of the Hajj").

• **Ibn Jubayr** (1145–1217) Spanish courtier from Granada, Spain, who went on the hajj pilgrimage in 1183–1185. Wrote *The Travels,* the most famous example of a travel book, called a *rihla* in Arabic, that described the author's trip to Mecca.

After thirty days' sail across the Mediterranean, Ibn Jubayr arrived in the port of Alexandria, Egypt, then under the rule of Saladin (1137/38–1193), the founder of the Ayyubid dynasty (1171–1250) in Egypt. When Saladin, whose father had served in the Seljuq army, defeated the Fatimid dynasty, the caliph in Baghdad granted him an iqta for all of Egypt and Syria.

Because their boat was from another country, all the travelers with Ibn Jubayr had to go through customs. Ibn Jubayr praised Saladin's generosity as a host but criticized the port officials for requiring the pilgrims to pay the zakat tax on the goods they carried. From Egypt, Ibn Jubayr traveled south and crossed the Red Sea; on his arrival, he once again had to pay a tax. Before 945, all territory was under Abbasid rule, and there were no border crossings; after 945, Muslim travelers, even those going in the hajj, had to pay the costs of leaving one country and entering another.

Table 9.1   The Nine Steps of the Hajj

1. To put on pilgrim's robes
2. To walk around the Kaaba seven times counterclockwise
3. To stand at Arafat on the ninth day of the twelfth month
4. To stay overnight near Arafat
5. To throw stones at three different locations where, Muslims believe, Satan tempted the prophet Ishmael
6. To sacrifice an animal at Mina
7. To repeat the circumambulation of the Kaaba (see step 2)
8. To drink water from the Zamzam well
9. To recite two sets of prayers at the Station of Abraham, where Abraham and Ishmael, Muslims believe, prayed together after the Kaaba was built

Source: Vincent J. Cornell, "Fruit of the Tree of Knowledge: The Relationship Between Faith and Practice in Islam," in *The Oxford History of Islam,* ed. John Esposito (New York: Oxford University Press, 1999), pp. 84–87.

When Ibn Jubayr arrived at the outskirts of Mecca, he put on the two pieces of unsewn cloth permitted to the male pilgrim. (Because women pilgrims were obliged to cover all but their face, hands, and feet, they required more cloth.) While Sunni and Shi'ite rules differed slightly, all concurred that pilgrims should refrain from having sex, eating meat, and cutting their hair or nails during the hajj. Muslims could fulfill their obligation to go on the hajj only once a year: on the eighth, ninth, and tenth days of the twelfth month in the Islamic lunar calendar. After Ibn Jubayr had been in Mecca for some eight months, the month of the hajj arrived.

The number of Muslims going on the hajj had increased dramatically over time. By 1184, Ibn Jubayr writes that the total number of pilgrims from Iraq alone "formed a multitude whose number only God Most High could count."[9] The more unruly pilgrims (especially from Yemen, in Ibn Jubayr's opinion) forced the Meccan authorities to replace the Kaaba's wooden covering with a strong iron dome.

Once pilgrims arrived in Mecca, they walked around the Kaaba seven times in a counterclockwise direction. On the eighth day of the month Ibn Jubayr and all the other pilgrims departed for Mina, which lay halfway to Mount Arafat. The hajj celebrated Abraham's release of his son Ishmael. The most important rite, the Standing, commemorated the last sermon given by the prophet Muhammad.

Fear of bandits prevented the pilgrims from spending the night at Arafat as was customary. When they arrived at Mount Arafat early in the morning of the ninth day, they first climbed the mountain and then descended to the plain, where they remained on their feet throughout the Standing:

> When, on Friday, the midday and afternoon prayers were said together, the people stood contrite and in tears, humbly beseeching the mercy of Great and Glorious God. The cries of "God is Great" rose high, and loud were the voices of men in prayer. Never has there been seen a day of such weeping, such penitence of heart, and such bending of the neck in reverential submission and humility before God.

As soon as the sun had set, the pilgrims proceeded quickly in the dark toward a mosque some three hours away for final prayers. They spent the rest of the night there.

When the pilgrims arrived at Mina the next day, their religious observance shifted suddenly from solemn piety to raucous celebration. They first threw stones at the wall where Muslims believe Satan tempted Ishmael, and they then slaughtered sheep to celebrate Abraham's substitution of a sacrificial ram for his son Ishmael. The change of pace was abrupt, and disturbances often broke out at Mina. Ibn Jubayr saw "dissension and riot between the negro inhabitants of Mecca and the Turks of Iraq in which there were some hurts. Swords were drawn, arrow notches were put to the bow-string, and spears were thrown, while some of the goods of the merchants were plundered."

After the religious observances were completed, giant bazaars sprang up in which Ibn Jubayr saw "wares ranging from precious jewels to the cheapest strings of beads, together with other articles and various merchandises of the world." The hajj may have been a religious duty, but it also had a distinctly commercial side: merchants from all over the Islamic world found a ready market among the pilgrims.

Finally, Ibn Jubayr, like almost all pilgrims, went to see Muhammad's tomb and mosque at Medina, even though this was not an obligatory part of the hajj. From Medina to Baghdad, Ibn Jubayr traveled along Zubaydah's Road, which he covered at a rapid 30 miles (50 km) per day:

> These tanks, pools, wells, and stations on the road from Baghdad to Mecca are monuments to Zubaydah. . . . But for her generous acts in this direction this road could not have been traversed.

In Baghdad, he visited the palace where the family members of the figurehead caliph "live in sumptuous confinement in those palaces, neither going forth nor being seen."

For the return trip, Ibn Jubayr chose a different route: after going to Damascus, he traveled to the kingdom of Jerusalem, which was under the rule of the Crusader states (see Chapter 13). In 1185, Saladin had already begun his campaign to win Jerusalem back (he did so in 1187), and on his way to Jerusalem, Ibn Jubayr saw hundreds of Christian prisoners taken captive by Saladin. The incongruity of the situation struck him: "One of the strangest things in the world is that Muslim caravans go forth to Frankish [meaning the Christians from modern-day France and Germany] lands, while Frankish captives enter Muslim lands." Ibn Jubayr's caravan entered the Crusader-ruled territory without paying any taxes, and he caught a ship to Europe from Acre [Akka], in modern Israel. Because of several months' delay caused by a shipwreck, he arrived back in Spain more than two years after his departure in 1185.

Ibn Jubayr's rihla offers a precious eyewitness account of the Islamic world in the late twelfth century, when the Abbasid caliphs continued as figureheads in Baghdad but all real power lay with different regional rulers. This arrangement came to an abrupt end in 1258, when the Mongols (see Chapter 14) invaded Baghdad and ended even that minimal symbolic role for the caliph.

Chapter Review

KEY TERMS

Khaizuran (238)

Muhammad (240)

jihad (244)

hajj (244)

caliph (244)

Quran (245)

hadith (245)

Five Pillars of Islam (245)

Sunnis (245)

Shi'ites (245)

Abbasid caliphate (250)

translation movement (251)

astrolabe (251)

ulama (253)

iqta grant (260)

Ibn Jubayr (263)

 Download the MP3 audio file of the Chapter Review and listen to it on the go.

When Muhammad instructed his followers to perform the annual hajj pilgrimage, the Islamic world was limited to the west coast of the Arabian peninsula. In the eighth century, Khaizuran was able to fulfill her obligation with a journey only a few weeks long, and Ibn Jubayr traveled all the way from Spain to Mecca in a few months. However, Muslims who lived at the edges of the Islamic world in Central Africa, Central Asia, or Afghanistan measured their journeys in years. Although living in widely dispersed areas, they were bound together by many ties, including loyalty to the caliph.

 Who was the prophet Muhammad, and what were his main teachings?

Muhammad was a merchant who, in the early 600s, had a series of visions in which, according to Muslim belief, he received revelations from God as transmitted by the angel Gabriel. The Five Pillars of Islam specified the obligations of each Muslim: (1) to bear witness to Allah as the sole god and to accept Muhammad as his messenger, (2) to pray five times daily in the direction of Mecca, (3) to pay a fixed share of one's income to the state in support of the poor and needy, (4) to refrain from eating, drinking, and sexual activity during the daytime hours of the month of Ramadan, and (5) provided one has the necessary resources, to do the hajj pilgrimage to Mecca.

 Between Muhammad's death in 632 and the founding of the Abbasid caliphate in 750, what were the different ways that the Islamic community chose the new caliph?

At first, the Islamic community chose the caliph by consensus, but the murder of the third caliph threw the umma into turmoil. Sunnis believed that only those chosen by consensus, even if not related to Muhammad, could serve as caliphs. Shi'ites believed that only those like Muhammad's cousin and son-in-law Ali were qualified. During the first century after Muhammad's death, Muslims struggled with the question of choosing his successor, until they eventually accepted the idea of dynastic succession in 680, when the son of the first Umayyad caliph succeeded him.

 Which economic, political, and social forces held the many peoples and territories of the Abbasid caliphate together?

Between its founding in 750 and its disintegration in 945, the Abbasid rulers used a common political structure—of provinces paying taxes to the center at Baghdad—to tie the empire together. Muslims throughout the empire honored the caliph as their political and religious leader and revered the learned religious teachers of the ulama; they also went on the hajj. Those who knew Arabic (the language of the Quran) and Persian (the language of learning) could make themselves understood anywhere in the Abbasid Empire.

 ### After the fragmentation of the Abbasid Empire in 945, which cultural practices, technologies, and customs held Islamic believers in different regions together?

After the breakup of the Abbasid Empire in 945, Muslims in different regions accepted the deposed caliph as their religious leader even as they served the different regional rulers based in Spain and North Africa, sub-Saharan Africa, Egypt and Syria, Iraq, and Central and South Asia.

Although originally a religious obligation, by 1200 the hajj had a profound effect on trade, navigation, and technology. The hajj, and the resulting trade, pushed Muslims to adopt or to discover the fastest and most efficient means of transport from different places to Mecca and to equip those vessels with the best astronomical instruments, maps, and navigational devices. Despite the hardships, all Muslims viewed a trip to Mecca, no matter how distant, as an obligation to be fulfilled if at all possible. The result was clear: ordinary Muslims were far better traveled and more knowledgeable than their contemporaries in other parts of the world.

In the years after 945, multiple political and cultural centers arose that challenged Baghdad's position in the previously united Islamic world. As the next chapter will show, something similar happened in Europe as political and cultural centers first appeared and then overtook the Byzantine capital at Constantinople.

WEB RESOURCES

Pronunciation Guide

Interactive Maps
MAP 9.1 Abbasid Caliphate

Primary Sources

Chapter Objectives

ACE Multiple-Choice Quiz

Flashcards

For Further Reference

Abbott, Nadia. *Two Queens of Baghdad: Mother and Wife of Harun al-Rashid.* London: Al Saqi Books, 1986, reprint of 1946 original.

Allen, Roger. *An Introduction to Arabic Literature.* New York: Cambridge University Press, 2000.

Broadhurst, R. J. C., trans. *The Travels of Ibn Jubayr.* London: Jonathan Cape, 1952.

Esposito, John L., ed. *The Oxford History of Islam.* New York: Oxford University Press, 1999.

Freeman-Grenville, G. S. P. *The East African Coast: Select Documents from the First to the Earlier Nineteenth Century.* Oxford: Clarendon Press, 1962.

Gutas, Dmitri. *Greek Thought, Arabic Culture: The Graeco-Arabic Translation Movement in Baghdad and Early 'Abbāsid Society (2nd–4th/8th–10th centuries).* New York: Routledge, 1998.

Hodgson, Marshall. *Venture of Islam.* Vols. 1–3. Chicago: University of Chicago Press, 1974.

Hourani, George F. *Arab Seafaring.* Exp. ed. Princeton: Princeton University Press, 1995.

Kennedy, Hugh. *The Prophet and the Age of the Caliphates.* 2d ed. London: Pearson Education Limited, 2004.

Levtzion, N., and J. F. P. Hopkins, eds. *Corpus of Early Arabic Sources for West African History.* New York: Cambridge University Press, 1981.

Lunde, Paul, and Caroline Stone, trans. *The Meadows of Gold: The Abbasids by Mas'udi.* New York: Kegan Paul International, 1989.

Turner, Howard R. *Science in Medieval Islam: An Illustrated Introduction.* Austin: University of Texas Press, 1995.

Websites

Adherents.com
(www.adherents.com). Takes an informed Religious Studies approach to the world's many religions, including Islam.

Discover Islam
(http://www.Islamicity.com). An introduction to Islam on an educational website that also sells products related to Islam.

Internet Medieval Sourcebook
(http://www.fordham.edu/halsall/sbook.html). Many primary sources listed under the link "Islam."

The Multiple Centers of Europe, 500–1000

Sometime around the year 1000, Leif Eriksson (LEAF ERIC-son) sailed with some forty companions from Greenland across the North Atlantic to Newfoundland in today's Canada. His former sister-in-law **Gudrid** and her second husband **Thorfinn Karlsefni** followed in a subsequent voyage. The travelers were originally from Norway in the Scandinavian region of Europe, which also includes Sweden, Finland, and Denmark. The Europe of 1000 differed dramatically from the Europe of 500. In 500, it contained only one major empire, Byzantium, with its capital at Constantinople (modern Istanbul, Turkey). Over the next five hundred years, migrating peoples completely reshaped Europe. By 1000, it was home to multiple centers—modern-day France and Germany, Scandinavia, and Russia—that today are still the most important European powers.

Competition among these multiple centers provided a powerful stimulus to develop, as the Scandinavian voyages to the Americas amply demonstrate. An account recorded several hundred years later, but based on oral history, reports that, after the Scandinavians arrived in the Americas, Karlsefni set off to explore with a man named Snorri:

Karlsefni sailed south along the coast. . . . Karlsefni and his men sailed into the estuary and named the place Hope (Tidal Lake). Here they found wild wheat growing in fields on all the low ground and grape vines on all the higher ground. Every stream was teaming with fish. They dug trenches at the high-tide mark, and when the tide went out there were halibut trapped in all the trenches. In the woods there was a great number of animals of all kinds.

They stayed there for a fortnight [two weeks], enjoying themselves and noticing nothing untoward. They had their livestock with them. But early one morning as they looked

GUDRID AND THORFINN KARLSEFNI

(Arni Magnusson Institute, Reykjavik, Iceland/ The Bridgeman Art Library)

CL This icon will direct you to interactive activities and study materials on the *Voyages* website: www.cengage.com/history/hansen/voyages1e

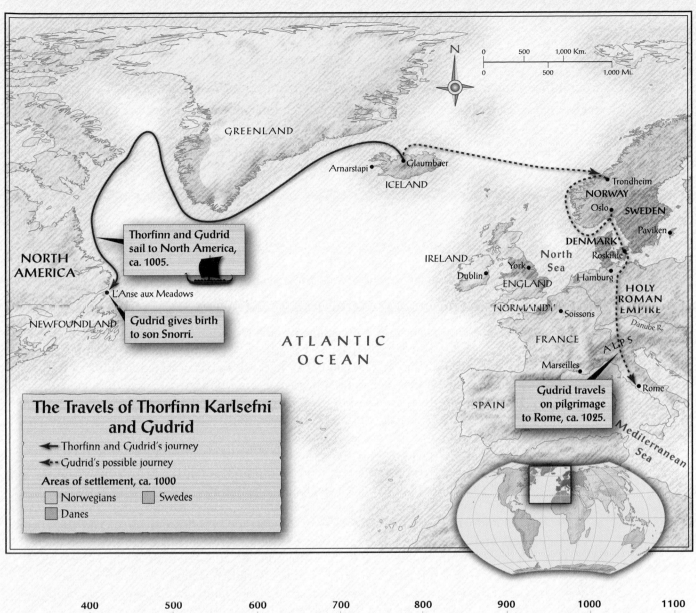

N

| | 0 | 500 | 1,000 Km. |
| | 0 | 500 | 1,000 Mi. |

GREENLAND

Arnarstapi • Glaumbaer •
ICELAND

Trondheim •
NORWAY
Oslo •
SWEDEN
Paviken •
DENMARK
Roskilde •
IRELAND
North Sea
Dublin • York • Hamburg •
ENGLAND
NORMANDY
Soissons •
HOLY ROMAN EMPIRE
Danube R.
FRANCE
ALPS
Marseilles •
Rome •

NORTH AMERICA

L'Anse aux Meadows •

NEWFOUNDLAND

ATLANTIC OCEAN

SPAIN

Mediterranean Sea

Thorfinn and Gudrid sail to North America, ca. 1005.

Gudrid gives birth to son Snorri.

Gudrid travels on pilgrimage to Rome, ca. 1025.

The Travels of Thorfinn Karlsefni and Gudrid

← Thorfinn and Gudrid's journey
◄-- Gudrid's possible journey

Areas of settlement, ca. 1000
☐ Norwegians   ☐ Swedes
☐ Danes

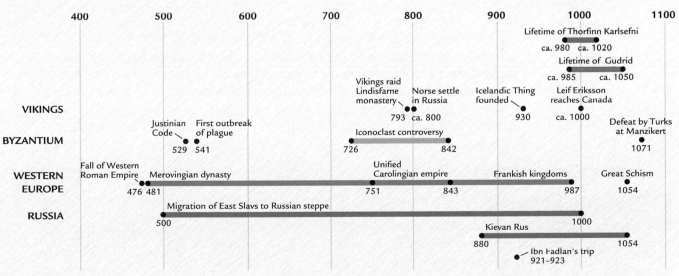

| | 400 | 500 | 600 | 700 | 800 | 900 | 1000 | 1100 |

Lifetime of Thorfinn Karlsefni
ca. 980   ca. 1020

Lifetime of Gudrid
ca. 985   ca. 1050

VIKINGS
Vikings raid Lindisfarne monastery — 793
Norse settle in Russia — ca. 800
Icelandic Thing founded — 930
Leif Eriksson reaches Canada — ca. 1000

BYZANTIUM
Justinian Code — 529
First outbreak of plague — 541
Iconoclast controversy — 726 842
Defeat by Turks at Manzikert — 1071

WESTERN EUROPE
Fall of Western Roman Empire — 476
Merovingian dynasty — 481
Unified Carolingian empire — 751
843
Frankish kingdoms — 987
Great Schism — 1054

RUSSIA
Migration of East Slavs to Russian steppe — 500 1000
Kievan Rus — 880 1054
Ibn Fadlan's trip — 921–923

around they caught sight of nine skin-boats; the men in them were waving sticks which made a noise like flails [tools used to thresh grain], and the motion was sunwise [clockwise].

Karlsefni said, "What can this signify?"

"It could well be a token of peace," said Snorri. "Let us take a white shield and go to meet them with it."[1]

● **Gudrid and Thorfinn Karlsefni** A couple originally from Iceland who settled in about 1000 in Greenland and then Canada, which the Scandinavians called Vinland. Eventually left the Americas and returned to Iceland.

Karlsefni and Snorri went out to meet the men in boats, who stared at them and then left without incident. Although this incident is recorded in a later source, archaeological evidence shows that these Scandinavians built at least one settlement; evidence of their presence has been found in the Canadian town of L'Anse aux Meadows in today's Newfoundland.

Possessing faster and more maneuverable wooden boats than any of their contemporaries, the Scandinavians went as far as Russia, Greenland, Iceland, and Canada (see the map on page 269). Although we are accustomed to think of the distance between Europe and the Americas as enormous, the voyage from Greenland to the northeastern coast of Canada was only 1,350 miles (2,200 km). If the Scandinavians had hugged the coast of Greenland and Canada, they could have traveled farther but still within constant sight of land.

The Scandinavians were one of several different groups speaking Germanic languages that lived in western and northern Europe after the loss of the western half of the Roman Empire (see Chapter 7). Around 500, the residents of the late Roman Empire looked down on these Germanic peoples because they could not read and write, worshiped a variety of different deities rather than the Christian God, and lived in simple villages much smaller than Rome or the eastern capital of Constantinople. But by 1000, the situation had changed dramatically. The rise of Germanic states paralleled the rise of the Buddhist states of East Asia that borrowed the Tang dynasty blueprint for empire (see Chapter 8). These new European states, like Byzantium, were Christian, but their political structures differed from those of Rome because they were based on the war-band.

This chapter begins in Constantinople, the successor to the Roman Empire. As the Byzantine Empire contracted, new centers arose: first in Germany and France, then in Scandinavia, and finally in modern-day Russia. The residents of Constantinople viewed these regions as uncivilized backwaters, good only as sources of raw materials and slaves. They did not recognize the vitality of these new centers.

Focus Questions

 What events caused the urban society of the Byzantines to decline and resulted in the loss of so much territory to the Sasanian and Abbasid Empires?

- What was the war-band of traditional Germanic society? How did the political structures of the Merovingians and the Carolingians reflect their origins in the war-band?

- When, where, how, and why did the Scandinavians go on their voyages, and what was the significance of those voyages?

- What were the earliest states to form in the area that is now Russia, and what role did religion play in their establishment and development?

- What did all the new states have in common?

● Byzantium, the Eastern Roman Empire, 476–1071

To distinguish it from the western empire based in Rome, historians call the Eastern Roman Empire, with its capital at Constantinople, the **Byzantine Empire,** or simply Byzantium (see Map 10.1). The Byzantine Empire lasted for over a thousand years after the western empire ended, in spite of continuous attacks by surrounding peoples. Far worse than any attack by a foreign power, the bubonic plague struck the empire in 541 and then at regular intervals for two more centuries. The massive decline in population, coupled with the cutting off of shipping lines across the Mediterranean, resulted in a sharp economic downturn. Through all these events the empire's scholars continued to preserve Greek learning, systematize Roman law, and write new Christian texts. Over the centuries, however, the amount of territory under Byzantine rule shrank, providing an opportunity for other European centers to develop.

- **Byzantine Empire** (476–1453) Eastern half of the Roman Empire after the loss of the western half in 476. Sometimes simply called Byzantium. Headed by an emperor in its capital of Constantinople (modern-day Istanbul).

Justinian and the Legacy of Rome, 476–565

Constantinople, the city named for the emperor Constantine, had been a capital of the Eastern Roman Empire since 330. Between 395 and 476 different rulers governed the eastern and western sections of the empire, but after 476 the eastern emperor often had no counterpart in Rome. The Christian church at this time had five major centers: in Constantinople, Alexandria, Jerusalem, Antioch, and Rome. The top church bishops in the first four cities were called **patriarchs,** but by 1000 the highest-ranking bishop in Rome had the title of **pope.**

Culturally the residents of the eastern and western halves of the empire had much in common: educated people often spoke both Greek and Latin, almost everyone was Christian, and citizens accepted Roman law. Sometimes people in the west referred to those living in the eastern half as "Greeks" since nearly everyone there, including Armenians, Syrians, and Egyptians, spoke Greek, not Latin, although not always as their mother tongue. In the year 500, few observers realized that the urbanized life of the Roman Empire was soon to decline, but decline did begin with the first outbreak of plague in 541, which occurred during the long reign of the emperor Justinian I and had lasting repercussions.

- **patriarch** In the 400s and 500s, the highest-ranking bishop of the four major Christian church centers at Constantinople, Alexandria, Jerusalem, and Antioch. By 1000, the patriarch of Constantinople had become head of the Orthodox church of Byzantium.

- **pope** In the 400s and 500s the pope was the highest-ranking bishop in Rome, equal in rank to the patriarchs of Constantinople, Alexandria, Jerusalem, and Antioch. By 1000, the pope was recognized as leader of the Catholic Church in Rome.

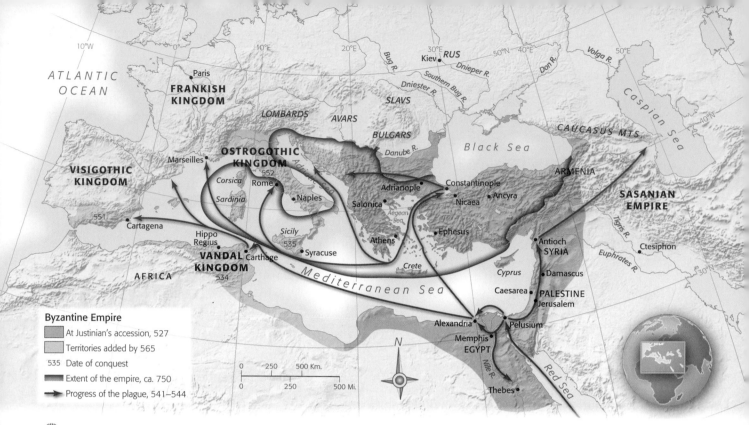

Byzantine Empire
- ▮ At Justinian's accession, 527
- ▯ Territories added by 565
- 535 Date of conquest
- ▬ Extent of the empire, ca. 750
- → Progress of the plague, 541–544

🌐 **MAP 10.1**

The Byzantine Empire

The Byzantine empire grew dramatically during the reign of Justinian (r. 527–565), expanding its territory in North Africa, the Balkans, and Italy. Yet the plague struck for the first of at least fifteen times in 541–544, killing seven million of his twenty-six million subjects.

CL Interactive Map

Justinian I was a native of Thrace, the region north of Greece, and grew up speaking the local language and Latin. Like many Byzantine emperors, he was chosen by his predecessor, an illiterate soldier also from Thrace, who adopted him and raised him in Byzantium. In 520, Justinian met his future wife: an actress and circus performer named Theodora (497–548), who had given birth to at least one child before she met Justinian. She did not fulfill Byzantine ideals of modesty, yet Justinian succeeded in changing the law so that he could marry her, and the two ruled together for more than twenty years.

In 532, early in their reign, a commission of legal scholars completed one of the most important legal works ever written: the Justinian Corpus of Civil Law. The corpus consists of three works: the Code (completed in 529), the Digest (533), and the Institutes (also 533). Working for three years, the commission gathered together all the valid laws of the Roman Empire and reduced some three million laws, many no longer in effect, to a manageable body 1,500 pages long in its modern edition. The texts of the laws and the extensive legal commentary were written in Latin, still the official language of the central government, but the laws issued by Justinian himself were in Greek, which was rapidly becoming the administrative language of the empire. The Justinian Corpus preserved the core of Roman law not just for sixth-century jurists but also for all time.

Justinian and Theodora managed the empire's relations with its neighbors with considerable success. Unlike his predecessors, Justinian challenged the Vandals, one of the Germanic peoples who had conquered North Africa in the fifth century (see Chapter 7). His successful military campaigns in Northwest Africa, coastal Spain, and Italy added territory to the empire. Yet, on the eastern front, the armies of the Sasanian empire in Iran (see Chapter 6) captured Antioch, the third-largest city in the Byzantine Empire. This Persian display of military might revealed how vulnerable the eastern empire was.

The Impact of the Plague and the Arab Conquests, 541–767

The fighting on both the eastern and western frontiers subsided immediately after the first recorded outbreak of the bubonic plague in Europe in 541. Many people, including Justinian himself, became terribly ill. In modern usage, the term **plague** refers to two distinct illnesses, bubonic plague and pneumonic plague, which form two phases of an outbreak. First, fleas that have drunk the blood of infected rodents transmit the bubonic plague to people. Lymph glands on the neck, under the arm, and on the groin swell up and turn black. Once part of the human population is infected with bubonic plague, the pneumonic plague spreads as one victim sneezes or coughs onto another. Pneumonic plague is almost always fatal.

One contemporary observer, the historian Procopius (pro-COE-pee-uhs), observed that the disease first appeared in towns along the coast and then moved inland, but he did not know why. Only in the late nineteenth century did scientists realize that black rats living on ships were the main agents responsible for spreading the disease.

The first outbreak hit the Egyptian port of Pelusium (pell-OOZE-ee-uhm) on the mouth of the Nile in 541 and spread across the Mediterranean to Constantinople in the following year. Ports such as Carthage, Rome, and Marseilles were affected in 543. Further outbreaks followed; historians have counted at least fifteen different outbreaks between 541 and 767, when the plague finally came to an end.

In the absence of accurate population statistics, historians have to estimate the deaths resulting from the plague. The deaths in the large cities were massive: some 230,000 out of 375,000 died in Constantinople alone.[2] High estimates put the death toll from the plague at one-quarter of the empire's population during Justinian's reign: of 26 million subjects, only 19 million survived.

Before the plague the Roman Empire had been an urban society where powerful people met at the marketplace each day to discuss their affairs, enjoying theater and circus performances alongside their poorer neighbors. By 600 such an urban type of life had become a memory. Constantinople may have begun as the emperor's glorious second capital, but the deaths resulting from the Justinian plague severely damaged the empire's economy.

Starting in 541 and continuing to sometime in the ninth century, the population declined, cities shrank, the economy contracted, and tax revenues plummeted. In these centuries of declining tax revenues, the government minted far fewer coins than earlier, and a barter economy replaced the partially monetized economy. Craftsmen and merchants gave up their occupations to become farmers.

Another consequence of these catastrophes was that the government could no longer afford to pay its soldiers. Instead, militias were formed by part-time soldiers who farmed the land during peacetime. When Islamic forces began to expand around 640 (see Chapter 9), the Sasani and Byzantine Empires had just finished an exhausting war, and the Byzantine Empire ceded to the victorious Islamic forces large chunks of territory in Armenia and Africa.

In contrast to the multiple officials of Roman times, the basic administrative unit of the Byzantine Empire during the seventh and eighth centuries was the *theme* (Greek plural form: *themata*) headed by a single governor rather than the multiple officials of Roman times. This governor heard legal disputes, collected taxes, and commanded the local militia. Society had also changed from Roman times. The high and low in rank led almost identical lives, and people no longer used a clan name and a personal name; a simple Christian name (first name) sufficed. Fewer

● **plague** Refers to two distinct illnesses, bubonic plague and the almost always fatal pneumonic plague, forming two phases of an outbreak. The plague struck Byzantium more than fifteen times between 541 and 767.

people knew Latin. Some people possessed more land than others, but they now worked the land alongside their poorer dependents. Slavery declined as well because no one could afford to feed slaves. Most of the people in the countryside were legally independent peasants who farmed the land intensively, often with two oxen and a plow, and grew only enough food to feed their own families.

The final outbreak of plague hit Constantinople in 747 and ended in 767. In the following years a slow revival began. The government minted more small coins, and trade and commerce increased slightly. The writing of manuscripts resumed, especially in monasteries, where scribes devised a new, smaller minuscule script that allowed them to write more words on a piece of parchment, the most common writing material. (Parchment was made by scraping the hair from the skin of sheep, goats, or calves and then stretching and cleaning it.) Literacy was mainly concentrated among monks and nuns. Although monasteries had little land and not much wealth, like the monasteries of Egypt (see Chapter 7), they offered an appealing alternative to family life.

■ **The Striking Dome of Hagia Sophia**   Built in a mere five years, the dome of the Hagia Sophia cathedral in Constantinople (modern Istanbul, Turkey) is more than 100 feet (30 m) in diameter and over 180 feet (55 m) tall. Forty windows at the bottom of the dome give the impression that it floated in the air, and later observers believed that such a beautiful dome could only have been made with divine help.   (Color lithograph from the original drawing by Chevalier Caspar Fussati/© Historical Picture Archive/Corbis)

Religion and State, 767–1071

The Byzantine emperor ruled the empire, while the patriarch of Constantinople presided over the church, which held property throughout the empire. While the Christian emperors sometimes tried to impose their own views on the church, they also served as patrons. For example, the emperor Justinian financed the rebuilding of the most beautiful cathedral in Constantinople, the Hagia Sophia (hah-GHEE-ah so-FEE-ah), whose literal meaning "Divine Wisdom" refers to an attribute of Jesus.

Byzantine opinion during the eighth century was sharply divided over the use of images in Christian worship. The iconoclasts, literally "image-breakers," advocated the removal of all images of Jesus, Mary, and any saints yet permitted prayers directed to crosses. Like the Umayyads, who also banned images (see Chapter 9), the iconoclasts justified their position by citing the Second Commandment of the Hebrew Bible forbidding the worship of graven images. The iconoclast movement appalled many Christians in western Europe, however, who frequently prayed to the statues of saints. When one emperor ordered the removal of a statue of Jesus from the main entrance to his palace, an angry crowd of women killed the man who took the image down.

In 780, the widow of the emperor Leo IV came to power when in her mid-20s and served as regent for her 9-year-old son. Few expected Irene to rule for long, but she surprised her opponents by tackling some of the major issues facing the empire. Whenever Byzantine rulers wanted to resolve a controversy within the church, they summoned a church council that included the patriarch (the top-ranking cleric in Constantinople) and bishops from all over the Christian world. Irene summoned such a council in the hope of working out a compromise to end the iconoclast controversy. In 787, the Second Council of Nicaea met and condemned iconoclasm. Those at the meeting cited passages from the Bible approving the veneration of images, and they permitted all previous iconoclasts to repudiate their earlier positions against icons. Images that had been removed from different churches were returned.

During her reign, Irene tried, not always successfully, to negotiate foreign relations with the Abbasid caliphate and the Franks, the powerful Germanic group that controlled most of modern France (see next page). By agreeing to make various large payments of both books and money, she managed to keep the Abbasid armies under the leadership of Harun al-Rashid from taking the city of Constantinople (see Chapter 9), but she could not prevent the powerful Islamic army from making incursions into the empire's shrunken territory.

Irene and her son did not share power easily. First he tried to seize power from her, then they ruled together, and then, in 797, she tried to overthrow him. Her allies blinded her son, possibly without her knowledge, and he died soon after. Irene then became the first woman to rule the Byzantine Empire in her own right and called herself emperor (not empress).

■ **The Sin of Iconoclasm**   The ninth-century Byzantine artist who painted this miniature equated the application of whitewash to a round icon of Jesus (*lower center*) with the Roman centurions giving vinegar to the dying Jesus on the cross at Jerusalem (*upper right*). The text in the upper left hand is written in minuscule script, first developed in the eighth century, that allowed scribes to squeeze more words onto each page of costly parchment.   (State Historical Museum, Moscow. Photo courtesy the Weitzmann Collection, Department of Art and Archaeology, Princeton University)

A great blow to the Byzantines came from Rome in 800 when the pope crowned the ruler of the Franks, Charlemagne, emperor of Rome (see page 281). The pope used the pretext that Irene could not be emperor because she was female. The Byzantines were horrified. They thought of Charlemagne as the unlettered leader of primitive peoples, not as a monarch comparable to their own. The pope's crowning of Charlemagne was significant because it marked the rise of a new state outside the Byzantine Empire that claimed to be the legitimate heir to the Roman Empire.

In 802, the empress's courtiers deposed the elderly Irene and installed a general as her successor. The empire that Irene relinquished was less than a third the size it had been in the mid-sixth century. Justinian had ruled over an empire that controlled the eastern half of the Mediterranean, but Islamic forces had conquered large blocks of territory throughout the seventh century. By 800, the Byzantine Empire, consisting largely of the region of Anatolia, could easily fit inside the modern borders of Turkey, and its population was only seven million.

In the centuries after 800 Byzantium, though small, continued to be an important intellectual center where scholars studied, copied, and preserved Greek texts from the past, analyzed Roman law, and studied Christian doctrine. Between 800 and 1000, Byzantine rulers sometimes won military victories to the east in modern-day Bulgaria or farther west in Anatolia, but in 1071 they suffered a massive defeat at the battle of Manzikert (modern-day Malazgirt, Turkey) at the hands of the Seljuq Turks, who captured the emperor himself. A new emperor took power in Constantinople. After 1071, the Byzantine emperors continued to rule from their capital at Constantinople, but with a much-weakened army over much less territory.

The Germanic Peoples of Western Europe, 481–1000

After the fall of the Western Roman Empire, the Byzantines often referred to the peoples living in the north of Europe as *barbarians,* a Greek word meaning "uncivilized." The largest group were the Franks in modern-day France and Germany. Although uncivilized in Byzantine eyes, they commanded powerful armies who defeated the Byzantine armies in battle. The Franks were ruled first by the kings of the Merovingian dynasty (481–751) and then by the Carolingians (751–ca. 1000). And in 800, as we have seen above, the pope crowned the king of the Franks, Charlemagne, the emperor of Rome. Unlike the Byzantine emperors, who governed an empire divided into regular administrative districts called *themata,* the Merovingian and Carolingian monarchs ruled as the leaders of war-bands, the most important unit of Germanic society.

Germanic Society Before 500

Many different peoples lived in the regions of northern and central Europe and crowded the borders of the Western Roman Empire before it fell in 476. They spoke a group of related languages now classed as Germanic, about which little is known because none was written down. Even so, analysts have been able to sketch some broad similarities among Germanic peoples, usually on the basis of archaeological evidence.

The basic unit of Germanic society was the extended family, which was headed by the father, who might have more than one wife, as well as children and slaves. Since cattle herding was the basis of the economy, the more cattle an individual had, the higher his rank. Freemen looked down on slaves, who were usually war captives.

Beyond the immediate family were larger kinship groups consisting of several households bound by family ties on both the male and female sides. These groups feuded often and developed a complex set of rules for determining the correct handling of disputes. The best source for understanding the practices of the Germanic peoples is the Salic Law, a list of punishments for different crimes recorded early in the sixth century. Although written in Latin, the Salic Law shows little Roman influence.

One of the most important Germanic legal concepts was that of **wergeld** (literally "man-payment"), which set the monetary value of a human life. Wergeld (WEAR-geld) payments served to prevent an endless cycle of killing and counter-killing among feuding families. Different wergeld penalties were specified for men and women, both free and unfree. For example, the section of the Salic Law "On Killing Pregnant Women" says the following:

> • **wergeld** Literally "man-payment," an important Germanic legal concept that set the monetary value of a human life. The function of wergeld payments was to prevent an endless cycle of killing and counterkilling among feuding families.

1. He who kills a pregnant woman shall be liable to pay twenty-four thousand denarii [six hundred solidi, or 6 pounds, or 2.73 kg, of gold]. And if it is proved that the fetus was a boy, he shall also be liable to pay six hundred solidi for the child.

2. He who kills a girl less than twelve years old or up to the end of her twelfth year shall be liable to pay two hundred solidi [2 pounds, or .9 kg, of gold].

3. He who kills a woman of mature age up to her sixtieth year, as long as she is able to bear children, shall be liable to pay twenty-four thousand denarii [six hundred solidi, or 6 pounds, or 2.73 kg, of gold].

4. But if she is killed afterwards when she is no longer able to bear children he shall be liable to pay two hundred solidi [2 pounds, or .9 kg, of gold].[3]

Penalties were levied in either silver denarius coins or gold solidus coins and varied depending on whether a woman had reached or passed child-bearing age, and if pregnant, whether she was carrying a male or female child. These payments were the sole form of punishment: no one was imprisoned or banished.

In times of war, groups of warriors called **war-bands** gathered behind a leader, whose main claim to their allegiance was the distribution of plunder. A successful leader took his men into battle and rewarded them liberally with the spoils of victory. He not only fed and clothed them but also provided them with horses, armor, and a place to live. His supporters, in turn, fought next to him in battles and banqueted with him when at peace.

> • **war-band** The most important social unit of Germanic society. In times of war, warriors formed bands behind a leader, who provided them with horses, armor, and a place to live. Successful leaders rewarded their men with the spoils of victory to claim their allegiance.

Germanic society was extremely fluid, because war-bands could form rapidly and collapse equally quickly. Members of a war-band distinguished themselves from others by wearing a certain kind of clothing, having similar hairstyles, or carrying similar weapons. They often believed that they and the other members of the war-band had a common ancestor, sometimes a god, from whom they all claimed descent. According to Germanic custom, freemen were obliged to fight in wars while slaves were not. The freemen in these bands often gathered in assemblies, called Thing (TING), to settle internal disputes or to plan military campaigns.

The Merovingians, 481–751

The most important leader to emerge from the constantly evolving alliances of Frankish society was Clovis (r. 481–511), who established the **Merovingian dynasty** that ruled modern-day France and Germany from 481 to 751. He combined great military successes, such as defeating the Visigoths of Spain, with skillful marriage alliances to build a dynasty that lasted two centuries, far longer than any earlier Germanic dynasty. The Merovingian army consisted of different war-bands linked by their loyalty to Clovis.

One incident, recounted by the chronicler Gregory of Tours (538/39–594?), vividly illustrates the ties between Clovis and his followers. In 486, Clovis and his men removed many items from the treasuries of several churches, including a "vase of marvelous size and beauty" from Soissons. The bishop of the robbed church requested the vase's return. After Clovis and his followers had divided the goods they had stolen, Clovis addressed his men: "I ask you, O most valiant warriors, not to refuse to me the vase in addition to my rightful part." Most of his men agreed to do so, but one man crushed the vase with his battle-ax because he felt that Clovis, although their leader, was not entitled to more than his fair share. The humiliated Clovis returned the pieces of the broken vase to the bishop.

One year later, Clovis summoned his troops for a review so that he could inspect their spears, swords, and axes, the iron weapons that helped to make his armies invincible. When he reached the man who had destroyed the vase, he threw the soldier's ax to the ground. As the soldier bent down to pick it up, Clovis grabbed his head and smashed it down on the weapon. "Thus," he said, "didst thou to the vase at Soissons."[4]

This incident shows that, though called a king, Clovis was a war-band leader who ruled his men only as long as he commanded their respect, and he had to use brute strength coupled with rewards to do so. One sign of the Merovingian king's power was his hair, which only he was allowed to grow long. If someone challenged the ruler's hold on power and defeated the leader, he was forced to shave off his hair — a visible reminder that he was no longer fit to rule — and the challenger took over.

The Franks, a tiny minority of perhaps 200,000 people, lived among 7 million Gallo-Romans in modern-day France and Germany.[5] Like many of his subjects, Clovis worshiped both Roman and Germanic deities. However, as Gregory of Tours reports, Clovis converted to Christianity a few years before his death in 511, thus eliminating the largest cultural barrier between the Germanic peoples and the Gallo-Romans they governed. Like the Roman emperor Constantine (see Chapter 7), Clovis promised to convert if Jesus Christ brought him victory in battle; when his enemy surrendered, he was baptized, along with three thousand of his men. This battle may have occurred in 496, 498, or 506. So few records about the early Merovingians survive that even the basic chronology of Clovis's reign is unknown. When Clovis died in 511, he divided his realm among his four sons, according to Germanic custom, and they and their descendents continued to rule until the mid-eighth century.

Under the Romans, large landowners had lived with their slaves in widely dispersed estates. Under the Merovingians, the basic farming unit changed to the Germanic village. The many wars with Rome during the fourth and fifth centuries forced Roman villa owners to leave their homes and move near streams or forests, where they lived with others in small settlements and reclaimed small plots from Roman agricultural land that had been allowed to go wild. They engaged in slash-and-burn agriculture and changed plots whenever a field's productivity gave out.

Ordinary people consumed a diet composed largely of hunted animals, fish caught in rivers, or plants foraged from the forest.

At the beginning of the Merovingian dynasty, many urban residents had embraced Christianity, while most of those living in the countryside continued to pray to shrines housing Germanic or Roman gods. In the fourth and fifth centuries, early Christians had experimented with extreme forms of asceticism and different types of religious communities. Monasteries—small communities under the supervision of the local bishop—gradually spread to western Europe from the eastern Mediterranean. Many were modeled on a monastery founded in 529 near Rome by Benedict of Nursia (ca. 480–545), who composed a concise set of practical rules for running a monastery. Benedictine monks devoted themselves full-time to manual labor and the worship of God, usually through public prayer conducted eight times each day. Unlike monks in more extreme monasteries, they ate an adequate diet and received enough sleep. The adult members of the community selected their leader, or abbot, who was to obey the local bishop.

Around 590 an Irish monk named Saint Columbanus (543–615) arrived in the Merovingian kingdom and founded many monasteries that encouraged monks to be even more devout and disciplined. Columbanus (COH-luhm-bahn-us) taught that laypeople could contribute land and money to monasteries, read religious texts (or have them read aloud), and recite Psalms from the Hebrew Bible. Irish monks copied, and so preserved, many manuscripts that would have otherwise been lost.

Bishops were among the few educated men in Merovingian society. Bishops tended to have varied backgrounds. While some had served as priests, others had worked for the king; still others had been monks or abbots in monasteries, and some had no ties to the church except that they belonged to an important lay family, often one that controlled a fair amount of land. Many learned to read and write by studying with other bishops or in monasteries.

Most Merovingian bishops had married before assuming office. After they became bishops, their wives continued to assist them with their duties, but the popes in Rome frequently urged them to treat their wives as their sisters and stop sleeping with them. In some cases bishops slept surrounded by their male assistants so that everyone could see that they maintained their vows of celibacy.[6]

The head cleric of the Western church, the pope, was elected by the clergy in Rome. Before the rise of Islam, Rome and the Christian church had been securely under the control of the Byzantines, who controlled Italy. As Byzantine power declined, and after 568, when the Byzantines lost control of northern and central Italy to a Germanic people

CL **Primary Source:**
The Rule of Saint Benedict: Work and Pray
In this selection from his rules for monastic life, Benedict urged monks to avoid idleness by devoting themselves to physical labor, prayer— and reading!

■ **Lindisfarne Gospel**   In 793, the Vikings raided the island of Lindisfarne, an important center of Christian learning famed for its illuminated manuscripts. Here, the artist monk portrays Matthew using a stylus to write the first page of the gospel named for books. The artist first made a sketch on the reverse side of an individual sheet of parchment, turned it over, and shone a candle through the animal skin so that they could see the outline, which they then filled in with paint.   (British Library, London/HIP/Art Resource, NY)

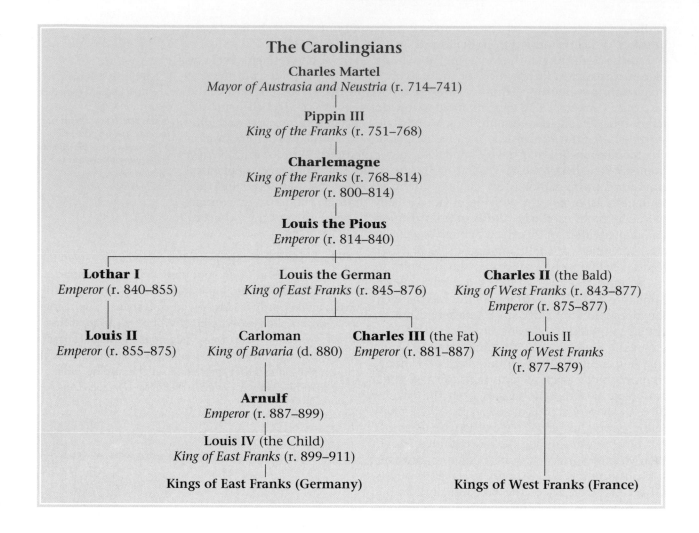

The Carolingians

Charles Martel
Mayor of Austrasia and Neustria (r. 714–741)
|
Pippin III
King of the Franks (r. 751–768)
|
Charlemagne
King of the Franks (r. 768–814)
Emperor (r. 800–814)
|
Louis the Pious
Emperor (r. 814–840)

Lothar I
Emperor (r. 840–855)

Louis the German
King of East Franks (r. 845–876)

Charles II (the Bald)
King of West Franks (r. 843–877)
Emperor (r. 875–877)

Louis II
Emperor (r. 855–875)

Carloman
King of Bavaria (d. 880)

Charles III (the Fat)
Emperor (r. 881–887)

Louis II
King of West Franks
(r. 877–879)

Arnulf
Emperor (r. 887–899)
|
Louis IV (the Child)
King of East Franks (r. 899–911)
|
Kings of East Franks (Germany)

Kings of West Franks (France)

called the Lombards, the popes needed military protection because they had no armies of their own. Moreover, the Lombards were Arians, and the popes did not accept Arius's teachings that God the Father was superior to Jesus and the Holy Ghost (see Chapter 7). The pope eventually turned to the Carolingians, an important family living in the Merovingian realm, for help.

•Carolingian dynasty (751–ca. 1000) An important aristocratic family who overthrew the Merovingian rulers in 751. Their most powerful ruler was Charlemagne. After his death, the empire split into three sections, each under a different Carolingian ruler.

Charlemagne and the Carolingians, 751–ca. 1000

In 751, the **Carolingian dynasty,** an important aristocratic family living in the eastern part of the Merovingian realm, overthrew the Merovingian rulers. (See the chart "The Carolingians.") The most powerful Carolingian ruler was Charles "the Great" ("le Magne" in old French), or Charlemagne (SHAHR-leh-maine). The events of his reign (768–814) demonstrated that the Carolingian realm (the region of modern-day France and Germany) exceeded Byzantium in importance. By 800, Europe had two powerful centers: Byzantium, which had inherited the legacy of Rome, and the new kingdom of the Franks.

Since the pope needed protection against the Lombards, he looked north to the Franks, and in 753 he formed an alliance with the Carolingians against the

MAP 10.2
The Carolingian Realms

After coming to power in 768, Charlemagne continuously expanded the area under Carolingian rule. The unified empire did not last long. In 843, his grandsons divided his realm into three separate regions. The West Frankish kingdom eventually became modern-day France, while the East Frankish kingdom developed into modern Germany. The two states regularly vied for control of the territory between them.

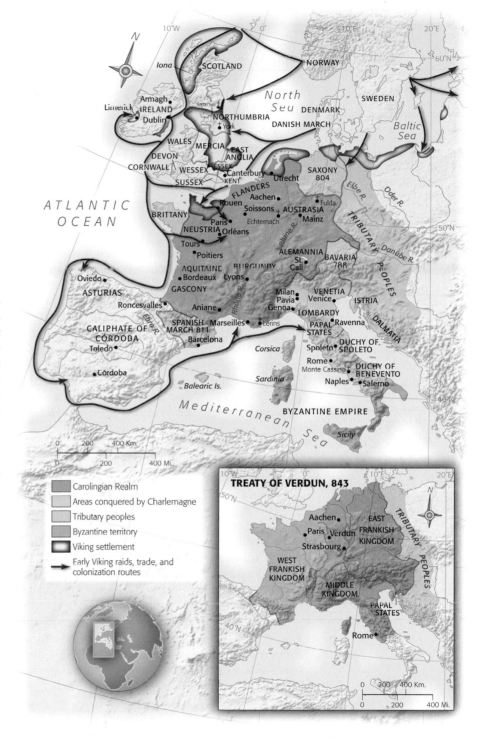

Carolingian Realm
Areas conquered by Charlemagne
Tributary peoples
Byzantine territory
Viking settlement
Early Viking raids, trade, and colonization routes

TREATY OF VERDUN, 843

Lombards. The geographical origins of the popes changed almost immediately. Of the seventeen popes in office between 654 and 752, five came from Byzantium and five from Rome. After 753, there was never again another Greek-speaking pope. Most were Roman, and a few came from Frankish lands.[7]

Charlemagne became king of the Franks in 768 and then launched a series of wars against the neighboring Germanic peoples. The pope in Rome supported him against the Lombards, who controlled much of Italy, and Charlemagne rapidly conquered northern and central Italy, some parts of Spain, and much of Germany (see Map 10.2). In 800, during Irene's reign as Byzantine emperor (see page 275), the pope crowned Charlemagne emperor. By accepting this title, Charlemagne claimed that he, and not Irene, was the rightful successor of the emperors of Rome.

CL Interactive Map

Diverging from its roots in the war-band, Carolingian society was divided into two groups: the powerful (potentes) and the powerless (paupers), literally the poor. The powerful owned their own land and could command others to obey them. Although some paupers owned land, they had no one to command. Among the powerless were slaves, a minority of the laborers in the countryside.

During Charlemagne's many conquests, his armies took vast numbers of prisoners from enemy forces; they sold these slaves to buyers, sometimes in distant lands. Writers in the eighth and ninth centuries used the word *captive*, not *slave*, for these prisoners of war. Charlemagne's Christian advisers urged him to stop the sale of Christian slaves to non-Christians, but he continued to do so. One of Europe's main exports to the Abbasids under Charlemagne and his successors was slaves (see Chapter 9).

Despite his title of emperor, Charlemagne was still very much a Germanic warband leader. Although he had conquered more territory than any Germanic leader, he was much less educated than the Byzantine or Abbasid rulers of his day. His biographer, Einhard, reports that "he also attempted to learn how to write, and, for this reason, used to place wax-tablets and notebooks under the pillows on his bed, so that, if he had any free time, he might accustom his hand to forming letters. But his effort came too late in life and achieved little success."[8] Unable to write his name, Charlemagne liked having books read aloud to him.

Nevertheless, Charlemagne founded an academy where the sons of the powerful could be educated. He and his successors also established schools, one at the imperial court, others in monasteries. As in the Byzantine Empire, a new minuscule script came into use that permitted more words to be written on a single page of parchment. (Carolingian minuscule is the basis of today's lowercase Roman fonts.) During this revival of learning, monastic authors wrote Latin grammars, medical texts, and liturgies with detailed instruction for church ceremonies.

When Charlemagne died in 814, he left his empire intact to his son Louis the Pious (r. 814–840), but when Louis died in 840, his feuding sons divided the kingdom into thirds. The West Frankish kingdom would eventually become modern France, and the East Frankish kingdom, modern Germany. The East and West kingdoms continuously fought over the territory of the former Middle kingdom, which today contains portions of France, Germany, Italy, the Netherlands, and Switzerland. The Carolingians ruled until 911 in Germany and until 987 in the region of modern France, when they were succeeded by new dynasties.

Historians often describe the Carolingians as more centralized than the Merovingians, but in fact the two Frankish dynasties were more alike than different. Both dynasties were led by rulers who rewarded their followers with gifts and whose main source of revenue was plunder. Throughout this period, literacy remained extremely restricted, with only a tiny number of officials able to read and write. The rulers of both dynasties were Christian, but many of their subjects did not observe basic Christian teachings.

By the tenth century, when Carolingian rule came to an end, the region of the Franks, sometimes called the Latin West, was no longer united. Its major sections—modern-day France and Germany—were beginning to become powerful centers in their own right. By 1000, Byzantium was no longer the only empire in Europe.

The Age of the Vikings, 793–1050

In 793, a group of **Viking** raiders came by boat and seized the valuables held in an island monastery off the English coast. The term *Viking* refers to those Scandinavians who left home to loot coastal towns. For the next three centuries the

Vikings were the most successful plunderers in Europe, and no one could withstand their attacks. The peoples living in Scandinavia had many of the same Germanic customs as the Franks: their leaders commanded the loyalty of war-bands, plunder was their main source of income, and they gradually adopted Christianity and gave up their traditional Germanic gods. Some Scandinavian boatmen lived by stealing from coastal peoples, while others eventually settled in Iceland, Greenland, England, Scotland, Ireland, and Russia; ultimately, however, they decided not to stay on the Atlantic coast of Canada. Between 800 and 1000, several new states formed in Greenland, Iceland, Denmark, Norway, and Sweden, creating even more centers in Europe (see Map 10.3).

> • **Viking** Term used for those Scandinavians who left home to loot coastal towns and who were most active between 793 and 1066.

🌐 **MAP 10.3   The Viking Raids, 793–1066**   From their homeland in Scandinavia, the Vikings launched their first raid on Lindisfarne on the North Sea in 793 and moved on to attack Iceland, Greenland, France, Spain, and Russia for more than two hundred years. They often settled in the lands they raided. In around 1000, they even reached North America.

CL Interactive Map

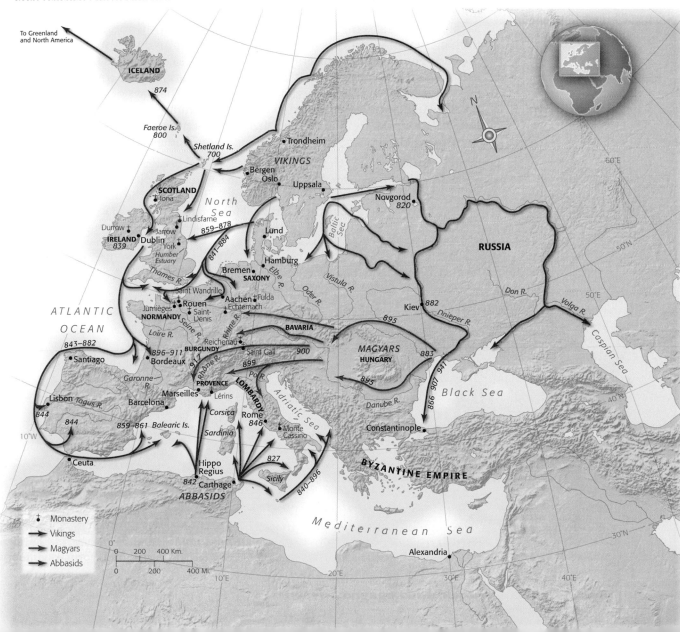

Viking Raids on Great Britain, 793–1066

The Viking homeland was north of Charlemagne's realm in Scandinavia, a region consisting of modern-day Norway, Sweden, and Denmark (see the map on page 269), where the languages spoken were Germanic. The region had a cold climate with a short growing season, and many of its residents hunted walrus and whale for their meat or maintained herds on farms.

Since the Scandinavians conducted their raids by sea, the greatest difference between the Viking and the Frankish war-bands was the **longboat,** a large wooden boat held together by iron rivets and washers. The combination of oars and sails made these boats the fastest mode of transport in the world before 1000. Like the ancient Polynesians (see Chapter 5), the Scandinavian navigators recognized the shapes of different landmasses, sometimes sighting them from mountaintops. No evidence of Scandinavian navigational instruments survives. Their first targets were the monasteries of the British Isles in England, Ireland, and Scotland, which lay closest to the southwestern coast of Norway.

Before 500, Britain was home to a group of indigenous peoples whom the Romans had encountered, but after 500 these groups were absorbed by the Anglo-Saxons, a general term for the many Germanic groups who migrated to Britain from present-day Denmark and northern Germany. Anglo-Saxon society retained the basic characteristics of Germanic society on the continent: a sharp distinction between free and unfree, with a legal system emphasizing the concept of wergeld. (See the feature "World History in Today's World: The Days of the Week.")

The Anglo-Saxons converted to Christianity during the sixth and seventh centuries. Bede (ca. 672–735) became their most famous Christian thinker. He also

● **longboat** Boat used by the Vikings to make raids, made of wood held together by iron rivets and washers. Equipped with both oars and sails, they were the fastest mode of transport before 1000.

🔳 **The Longboats of the Scandinavians** Sewn between 1066 and 1082, the Bayeux tapestry (held in northern France) is an embroidered piece of linen that stretches 231 feet (70 m). This detail shows the longboats in full sail. The boats are moving so quickly that the men seated in the first and third boats do not need to row. Notice that the middle and last boats are large enough to transport horses. (© Michael Holford)

The Days of the Week

Where do Tuesday, Wednesday, Thursday, and Friday come from? Each of these names combines the name of a Scandinavian god with the suffix -*day*. Thursday, or Thor's day, is named for the vigorous god who ruled the sky and controlled thunder, wind, rain, and the harvest. Germanic peoples prayed to him to prevent famine and disease. Friday is named for Frey, the powerful god of fertility, who was honored at weddings. Odin, the powerful god of war, was thought to have created the first man and the first woman. His name is also spelled Wodin, the root of the modern Wednesday. Odin's son Tiu gave his name to Tuesday.

What about Sunday, Monday, and Saturday? They date back to 321 C.E., when the Romans adopted the seven-day week; Emperor Constantine named the days for different astronomical bodies: the sun, the moon, and the planet Saturn. The English names for the days of the week, which combine both the Scandinavian and Roman names, date to the fifth and sixth centuries C.E., when the Anglo-Saxons migrated to England from Germany.

Source: www.indepthinfo.com/weekdays/index.shtml.

wrote a history of the Anglo-Saxons that dated events before and after Christ's birth, the same system used in most of the world today.

Monasteries made an appealing target for Viking raiders because they contained much detailed metalwork, whether reliquaries that held fragments of saints' bones or bejeweled gold and silver covers for illustrated manuscripts. The raiders also captured many slaves, keeping some for use in Scandinavia and selling others to the Byzantine and Abbasid Empires. In 866, a large Viking army arrived in England, just north of London, and established a long-term base camp. This was the first Scandinavian settlement in England.

Between 866 and 954, the Scandinavians retained tenuous control of much of northern and eastern England, a region called the **Danelaw.** The residents paid an annual indemnity to their conquerors, and the Scandinavians settled throughout the Danelaw, Ireland, and Scotland. Alfred I (r. 871–899), who called himself "king of the Anglo-Saxons," managed to survive in the face of Viking attacks. After his death, various English, Anglo-Saxon, and Scandinavian leaders vied with each other for control of England, but no one succeeded for very long. In the tenth century, some Scandinavians settled in Normandy ("Northman's land") in northern France. From this base William the Conqueror launched an invasion of England in 1066, and his descendants ruled England for more than a hundred years.

● **Danelaw** Region including much of northern and eastern England, over which the Scandinavians maintained tenuous control between 866 and 954. The conquered residents paid an annual indemnity to the Scandinavians.

Scandinavian Society

Since the Scandinavians left only brief written texts on runestones, historians must draw on archaeological evidence and orally transmitted epics. Composed in Old Norse, a Germanic language, these epics were written down between 1200 and 1400. Two fascinating works, entitled *Erik the Red's Saga* and *The Greenlanders' Saga*, recount events around the year 1000. Together they are called **The Vinland Sagas,** since the Scandinavians called the Americas Vinland, meaning either grape land or fertile land. Like all oral sources, they must be used cautiously; both epics glorify certain ancestors while denigrating others, and both exaggerate the extent of Christian belief while minimizing the extent of non-Christian practices.

● *The Vinland Sagas* Term for *Erik the Red's Saga* and *The Greenlanders' Saga,* two sagas composed in Old Norse that recount events around the year 1000. Both were written between 1200 and 1400.

285

The peoples of Scandinavia lived in communities of small farms in large, extended families of parents, children, grandchildren, unmarried siblings, and their servants. Women had considerable authority in Scandinavian society. They had property rights equal to those of their husbands and could institute divorce proceedings.

Leif Eriksson's sister-in-law Gudrid plays such a major role in *Erik the Red's Saga* that some have suggested that it should have been named for her, and not for Leif's father Erik. She married three times, once to Leif Eriksson's brother, was widowed twice, and possibly went to Rome on a pilgrimage at the end of her life. In the saga, whereas Gudrid is virtuous, Leif's illegitimate sister Freydis (FRY-duhs) is a murderer who will stop at nothing to get her way. Both women, however one-dimensional, are intelligent, strong leaders.

Like the Germanic peoples living on the European continent, the Scandinavians formed war-bands around leaders. Leaders recruited their retinues with gifts, and their followers accompanied them into battle and fought vigorously for shares of the plunder they took from the defeated. In the years before 1000, new trade routes appeared linking Scandinavia with the Abbasid Empire. Muslims bought slaves and furs from Scandinavians with silver dirham coins, over 130,000 of which have been found around the Baltic Sea.

At this time Scandinavian society produced a leader who played a comparable role to King Clovis of the Merovingians: Harald Bluetooth, who ruled the region of modern Denmark between approximately 940 and 985. After unifying Denmark, he conquered southern Norway. In 965 he became the first Scandinavian ruler to convert to Christianity, and the rulers of Norway and Sweden did so around 1030.

Scandinavian Religion

Women played an especially active role in pre-Christian religion because some served as seers who could predict the future. Once when famine hit a Greenland community, *Erik the Red's Saga* relates, a wealthy landowner hosted a feast to which he invited a prophetess. The next day she asked the women of the community who among them knew "the spells needed for performing the witchcraft, known as Warlock songs." Gudrid reluctantly volunteered and "sang the songs so well and beautifully that those present were sure they had never heard lovelier singing." When she finished, the seer explained that the famine would end soon, since "many spirits are now present which were charmed to hear the singing."[9]

The Scandinavians worshiped many gods. One traveler described a pre-Christian temple in Sweden that held three images. In the center was Thor, the most powerful deity who controlled the harvest. On either side of him stood the war-god Odin and the fertility goddess, Frey. Scandinavian burials often contain small metal items associated with Thor, such as hammers.

Burial customs varied. In some areas burials contained many grave goods, including full-size boats filled with clothing and tools, while in other areas the living cremated the dead and burned all their grave goods. (See the feature "Movement of Ideas: Ibn Fadlan's Description of a Rus Burial" on page 294.) When people converted to Christianity, they were not supposed to bury grave goods because Christians believed that the dead could not bring these goods to the afterlife, but many who still believed in the gods were reluctant to follow this prohibition for fear that the dead might starve or freeze as a result. In one gruesome anecdote from *The Vinland Sagas,* the ghost of a dead man comes to Gudrid and instructs her to give the dead a Christian burial in consecrated ground near a church but to burn the body of a bad man, presumably to stop him from haunting the living. The tale captures the dilemma of those deciding between Christian and pre-Christian burial.

The Scandinavian Migrations to Iceland and Greenland, 870–980

As in Merovingian and Carolingian society, slaves and former slaves ranked at the bottom of society. When a former slave proposes to Gudrid, her father is furious: "I never expected to hear such a suggestion from you—that I should marry my daughter to the son of a slave! My lack of money must be very obvious to you!" The proposal prompts him to give up his farm and leave for Greenland, where he hopes to find more fertile land. This was the impetus for migration: everyone hoped to get more fertile land than was available in Scandinavia, which was becoming increasingly crowded.

In the first wave, between 870 and 930, Scandinavians went to Iceland. In 930 they established an assembly, called the Thing, that resembled the assemblies of other Germanic peoples to their south. The Thing had the power to pass laws and to hear disputes. Some have called Iceland's Thing the world's first legislature, but wealthy landowners had a greater say than the poor.

The Vinland Sagas describe events occurring in Iceland sometime around 980, when Erik the Red and his father had already left Norway "because of some killings." They were forced to give up their home, where Leif was born, after Erik killed two neighbors. When they became involved in a second dispute, the Thing assembly exiled Erik for being a thief.

Erik then told a group of followers that he was going to look for an island that he had heard about. He sailed west 200 miles (320 km) to Greenland, which he so named because he hoped to entice more people to settle there. After his term of exile ended, he returned to Iceland, which was becoming increasingly crowded with a population of thirty thousand, and recruited Scandinavians to go with him. In 985 or 986, Erik led a fleet of twenty-five boats on a migration to Greenland; fourteen reached Greenland, and the others either turned back to Iceland or perished.

These stories roughly describe how migrations occurred. Scandinavian explorations generally began with a ship being blown off course. Those navigators who successfully steered their way home described what they had seen. Then someone, such as Erik the Red, sailed in search of the new place. Finally, a small expedition of ships led a group of settlers to the new lands.

The Scandinavians established two settlements on Greenland, the Eastern and Western Settlements. At that time Greenland was slightly warmer than it is now. The settlers lived much as they had on Iceland, grazing animals on the narrow coast between the ocean and the interior ice, fishing for walrus, whales, and seals, and hunting polar bears and reindeer. They had to trade furs and walrus tusks to obtain the grain, wood, and iron they needed to survive. The Greenlanders established their own Thing assembly, which voted to adopt Christianity soon after the Icelandic Thing voted to do so in 1000.

The Scandinavians in Vinland, ca. 1000

Around 1000, Leif Eriksson, the son of Erik the Red, decided to lead an exploratory voyage because he had heard from a man named Bjarni Herjolfsson (bee-YARN-ee hair-YOLF-son) of lands lying to the west of Greenland. It is possible that others had preceded Bjarni to the Americas, but *The Vinland Sagas* do not give their

THE SCANDINAVIAN SETTLEMENT AT L'ANSE AUX MEADOWS

In 1960, a Norwegian diplomat-turned-explorer, Helge Ingstad, and his archaeologist wife, Anne Stine Ingstad, explored the Canadian coastline hoping to find a place where, as *The Vinland Sagas* said, "the country was flat and wooded, with white sandy beaches wherever they went; and the land sloped gently down to the sea."* This description fit an inlet near the town of L'Anse aux Meadows on the northern tip of Newfoundland, and here Helge and Anne Ingstad found a small settlement.

Pollen analysis revealed that the climate in about 1000 was similar to today's and could have easily supported a settlement. Lumber, whether live trees or driftwood, was abundant. It was so cold that in most years the ice did not melt until June or July, an impossible climate for wild grapes. Still, the growing season was long enough for cloudberries, raspberries, blueberries, and red and black currants to thrive. Caribou, wolves, and foxes lived on the land, while walruses, whales, and seals flourished in the bay.

Originally, the Ingstads were not certain whether local Amerindians or Scandinavians had lived at the site. The small settlement contained eight houses that dated to between 980 and 1020, precisely at the time of the Scandinavian exploration of Vinland. Many finds indicated that it was a Scandinavian settlement.

---

*Magnus Magnusson, ed., *The Vinland Sagas* (New York: Penguin Books, 1965), p. 55.

Identical in structure to Icelandic buildings of the same period, the houses had walls and roofs made of sod that rested on wooden supports. Three were quite large halls for perhaps fifty people measuring 65 feet (20 m) long, with five smaller structures nearby. They formed three clusters of houses, each with a main dwelling for the group's leader and smaller, outlying houses for his dependents and slaves. Archaeologists found no large objects, an indication that the residents of the site systematically packed their possessions and left for home. The most revealing artifact was a small ringed pin, identical in design to thirteen others found on Iceland.

Many small artifacts indicate the kinds of tasks done on site. Needles and spindle whorls point to textile manufacture and mending, which, according to the sagas, were traditional women's work. The residents also collected iron ore, which forms naturally in bogs containing iron and manganese, and melted it in a furnace to obtain metal, which they hammered into nails for their boats. The place where the Scandinavians worked iron (the smith) contained an anvil and a big stone for hammering iron, iron fragments, and lumps of iron found in local bogs. The presence of a single locally produced iron nail makes this the earliest site of ironworking in the Americas (since none of the indigenous peoples living in the Americas could work iron).

Butternuts, a kind of a walnut, were found at the site but do not grow that far north. Archaeologists reason that the Scandinavians probably traveled

QUESTIONS FOR ANALYSIS

➤ What finds from the site of L'Anse aux Meadows indicated that it was a Scandinavian settlement and not an Amerindian site?

➤ What activities did men and women do separately in the different rooms of Hall F, and which together?

➤ How did archaeologists use information from *The Vinland Sagas* to analyze the site?

south to collect them and possibly the grapes mentioned so often in the sagas. The site may have been a base camp for launching different expeditions to southern regions.

Some analysts believe that l'Anse aux Meadows was the main settlement of the Scandinavians where Leif Eriksson landed. The site was not occupied for long because little garbage was found, and no one was buried there. Even if it was not actually Leif's settlement, it is undeniable that the Scandinavians lived at l'Anse aux Meadows, however briefly, before deciding to return home.

• Archaeologists injected a chemical preservative to harden the original walls, which were 5 feet (1.5 m) thick.

• The bay, which opens onto the Atlantic Ocean, remains icy until June and freezes again in November or December.

• This picture shows Hall F, the great hall, 65 feet (20 m) long and 16 feet (5 m) wide, that occupied the center of the structure.

(Parks Canada National Photo Collection)

• Here, archaeologists found a sandstone whetstone for sharpening needles and scissors as well as the flywheel of a handheld spindle, both signs of a women's sewing area.

• Archaeologists found iron rivets in this iron-smelting workshop.

• This hearth produced a small soapstone lamp of Icelandic design.

• **Bjarni Herjolfsson**
The first European,
according to *The Vinland
Sagas,* to sail to the
Americas, most likely
sometime in the 990s.

• **Skraelings**   Term in
The Vinland Sagas for
the Amerindians living
on the coast of Canada
and possibly northern
Maine, where the Scan-
dinavians established
temporary settlements.

names, so we should probably credit **Bjarni Herjolfsson**—and not Christopher Columbus—with being the first European to sail to the Americas. First Leif and then Thorfinn Karlsefni made several voyages to the Americas, landing in modern-day L'Anse aux Meadows, Newfoundland, Canada, and possibly farther south in Maine. The Scandinavians landed in North America after the end of the Maya classic era and before the great Mississippian cities of the Midwest were built (see Chapter 5). (See the feature "Visual Evidence: The Scandinavian Settlement at L'Anse aux Meadows.")

Leif's brother-in-law, Thorfinn Karlsefni (see the beginning of the chapter), decided to lead a group of sixty men and five women to settle in Vinland, the Scandinavian name for their settlements in North America. Their first year went well because they found much wild game. Then "they had their first encounter with **Skraelings**" (literally "wretches"), the term that the Scandinavians used for indigenous peoples. At first the Skraelings traded furs for cow's milk or scraps of red cloth, because Karlscfni would not allow his men to trade their iron weapons. But relations soon deteriorated, and the Scandinavians and the Skraelings fought each other in several battles involving hand-to-hand combat. *Erik the Red's Saga* reports that the Skraelings "were using catapults. Karlsefni and Snorri saw them hoist a large sphere on a pole; it was dark blue in color. It came flying in over the heads of Karlsefni's men and made an ugly din when it struck the ground."

The settlers in this story probably belonged to Karlsefni's war-band. Many had kin ties to him, whether direct or through marriage, and they probably gave him a share of the lumber they shipped to Greenland, much as they would have given him a share of any loot they collected in battle. Whenever the Scandinavians went to a new place, they captured slaves, and North America was no exception. Karlsefni enslaved two Skraeling boys, who lived with the Scandinavians and later learned their language. The boys told them about their homeland: "there were no houses there and that people lived in caves or holes in the ground. They said that there was a country across from their own land where the people went about in white clothing and uttered loud cries and carried poles with pieces of cloth attached." This intriguing report is one of the earliest we have about Amerindians.

The Scandinavians had a technological advantage over the Amerindians because they could fight using metal knives and daggers, which the indigenous peoples lacked because they did not know how to work iron. But while iron weapons gave the Scandinavians a slight advantage over a band of Amerindians equal in size to their own small population, they could never have prevailed against a much larger force. The sagas succinctly explain why the Scandinavians decided to leave the Americas: "Karlsefni and his men had realized by now that although the land was excellent they could never live there in safety or freedom from fear, because of the native inhabitants."

After a few years on the Canadian coast, the Scandinavians returned to Greenland, and in later centuries they sometimes returned to Canada to gather wood but never to settle. Sometime in the fifteenth century they also abandoned their settlements on Greenland because a drop in global temperature made life there much more difficult. The Scandinavian voyages are significant because they were the first Europeans to settle in the Americas. Their decision to leave resulted in no long-term consequences, a result utterly different from that of Columbus's voyages in the 1490s (see Chapter 15).

Russia, Land of the Rus, to 1054

Long before they set foot in Iceland, Greenland, or the Americas, around 800, early Scandinavians, mostly from Sweden, found that they could sail their longboats along the several major river courses, including the Volga and Dnieper Rivers, through the huge expanse of land lying to their east (see Map 10.4). The peoples living in this region called themselves and their polity **Rus,** the root of the word *Russia*. This region offered many riches, primarily furs and slaves, to the raiders. Local rulers sometimes allied with a neighboring empire, such as Byzantium or the Abbasids, to enhance their power. When forming such an alliance the rulers

• **Rus** Name given to themselves by people who lived in the region stretching from the Arctic to the north shore of the Black Sea and from the Baltic Sea to the Caspian Sea.

🌐 **MAP 10.4 Kievan Rus** Before 970, the leaders of different war-bands controlled the region between the Baltic, Black, and Caspian Seas. In the 970s Prince Vladimir gained control of the trading post at Kiev and gradually expanded the territory under his rule to form the state of Kievan Rus.

CL Interactive Map

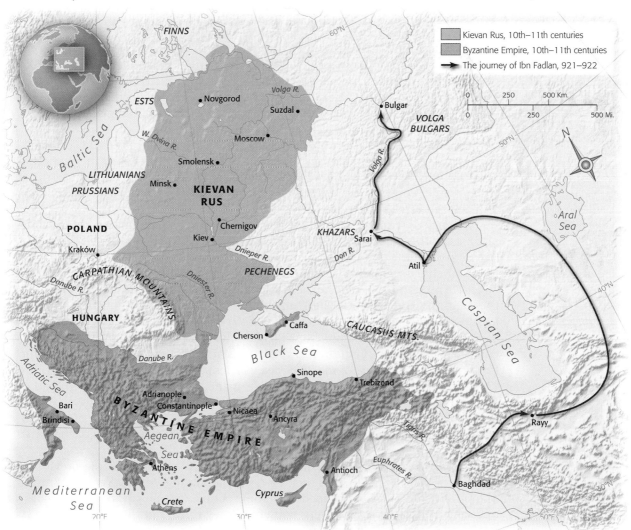

Kievan Rus, 10th–11th centuries
Byzantine Empire, 10th–11th centuries
The journey of Ibn Fadlan, 921–922

had to choose among Judaism, Islam, or the Christianity of Rome or Constantinople, and the decisions they made had a lasting effect. The region of modern-day Russia also saw the rise of important centers before 1000, contributing to even more centers in Europe.

The Peoples Living in Modern-Day Russia

Stretching from the Arctic to the north shore of the Black Sea and from the Baltic Sea to the Caspian, the region of Russia (which was much larger than today's modern nation) housed different ecosystems and different peoples deriving their living from the land. To the north, peoples exploited the treeless tundra and the taiga (sub-Arctic coniferous forest) to fish and to hunt reindeer, bear, and walrus. On the steppe grasslands extending far to the west, nomadic peoples migrated with their herds in search of fertile pasture. In the forests, where most people lived, they raised herds and grew crops on small family farms. Too poor to dedicate much land to raising hay, they had no draft animals and could clear the land only with fire and hand-tools. The lack of natural fertilizer from draft animals forced them to clear new lands every few years, with the result that their agriculture resembled slash-and-burn cultivation. These cultivators and foragers never could have survived had they depended entirely on agriculture.

The various peoples living in Russia spoke many different languages, none of which were written down. In 500, the **Slavs** occupied much of the territory in the lower Danube River Valley near the Black Sea. As they moved north and east for the next five hundred years, they enlarged the area in which their language, an ancestor of Russian, Ukrainian, Polish, and Czech, was spoken.

All these peoples, whatever their ecological niche, lived on the edge of subsistence and were vulnerable to Scandinavian slave raiders. After 700, the Scandinavians established trade outposts on the southeast coast of the Baltic and on the Dnieper and Volga Rivers. By 800, they had learned how to navigate these rivers to reach the Black and Caspian Seas.

The lack of written sources, whether by outsiders or Slavs, makes it difficult to reconstruct the early history of the Rus. Scholars have intensely debated their identity, some arguing that they were entirely Scandinavian, and others, entirely Slav. Modern scholars tentatively agree that the Rus were a multiethnic group including Balts, Finns, and Slavs, with Scandinavians the most prominent among them. Of these groups, the Balts and the Finns stayed in the region of the Baltic and Finland, while the Slavs and the Scandinavians traveled throughout the region.

Much of what we know about Russia before 900 comes from Byzantine accounts. The Byzantine Empire had the most sustained contact with the peoples who lived on the north shore of the Black Sea, particularly the Crimean peninsula. The Khazars, a formerly nomadic Turkic people, gained control of the southern part of Kievan Russia. In 900 their rulers converted to Judaism, a religion of the book that was neither the Christianity of their Byzantine enemies nor the Islam of their Abbasid rivals. The Khazar state continued to rule the Crimea for much of the tenth century.

During the tenth century, the Bulgars, a Turkic nomadic people previously subject to the Khazars, formed their own state along the Volga River. The Bulgars of modern Bulgaria are descended from these people. The Bulgars paid the Khazars one sable pelt each year for every household they ruled, but they converted to Islam partially in the hope of breaking away from the Khazars and avoiding this

● **Slavs** The people who, around 500, occupied much of the lower Danube River Valley near the Black Sea. They moved north and east for the next five hundred years and enlarged the area where their language, an ancestor of Russian, Ukrainian, Polish, and Czech, was spoken.

payment. After they received a visit by an envoy from the Abbasid caliph in 921–923, the ruler of the Bulgars assumed the title *emir,* and this state is therefore known as the Volga Bulgar Emirate.

Ibn Fadlan, an envoy from the Abbasid court, says that one merchant prayed, saying, "Lord, I have come from a distant land, bringing so and so many slave-girls priced at such and such per head and so many sables priced at such and such per pelt."[10] He then asked the deity to find him a merchant who would accept his asking price without haggling. (See "Movement of Ideas: Ibn Fadlan's Description of a Rus Burial.")

Rus traders used the currency of the Abbasid Empire: gold dinars and silver dirhams. The Rus gave their wives a gold or silver neckband for each ten thousand dirhams they accumulated. Archaeologists have found many such neckbands, frequently decorated with small Thor's hammers like those found in Scandinavian graves.

In addition to amber, swords, and wax, the main goods the Rus sold to the Islamic world were furs and slaves. Scandinavian merchants sold so many Slavs into slavery that, in the tenth century, the Europeans coined a new word for slaves: the Latin *sclavus* (SCLAV-uhs), derived from the Latin word for the Slavic peoples. This is the source of the English word *slave.*

Kievan Rus, 880–1054

Before 930, the Rus consisted of war-bands who paid tribute to rulers like the Khazars and the Volga Bulgar Emirate so that they could sell slaves and furs in their territories. After 930, the Rus war-bands evolved into early states called principalities, political units led by princes who exercised control over their own trading posts. The history of Kiev, a trading outpost on the Dnieper River, illustrates this development. Before 900, Kiev had a population of only one or two hundred residents who lived in villages. After 900, as trade grew, its population increased to several thousand, including specialized craftsmen who made goods for the wealthy. In 911, and again in 945, the Rus **Principality of Kiev** signed a treaty with Byzantium that specified the terms under which the Rus were to do business in Constantinople. Throughout the tenth century, the princes of Kiev eliminated their political rivals, including the Khazars and the Bulgars.

Since the middle of the ninth century, Byzantine missionaries had been active among the Rus and had modified the Greek alphabet to make the Cyrillic alphabet, named for a Byzantine missionary, Saint Cyril (827–869), who had been active a century earlier in modern-day Moravia. Using this alphabet, they devised a written language, called Old Church Slavonic, into which they translated Christian scriptures.

In the 970s Prince Vladimir emerged as leader of the Kievan Rus. Like the Khazar and Bulgar rulers, he had to decide which religion would best unify his realm, so he summoned the leaders of his kingdom and asked their advice. Our main source for this period, *The Primary Chronicle,* written down around 1100, gives a year-by-year chronology after 850 for the Rus (leaving many years blank). Its detailed entry for 987 explains that Vladimir decided to send ten "good and wise men" to compare the religions of the Volga Emirate, the Germans (the successors of the Carolingians), and the Byzantines. When the men returned, they criticized both the Islamic practices of the Volga Emirate and the Christianity of the Germans.

■ **Tangible Evidence of the European Slave Trade** European slave traders used this set of shackles, found in modern Bulgaria, to restrain a slave. They wrapped the long chain of iron links around his arms and legs and then connected it to the large ring, which they fastened around the captive's neck. Iron was expensive, though, so wooden and rope restraints would have been more common. (Krivina Museum, Ruse, Bulgaria)

● **Principality of Kiev** A new state that began as a trading post on the Dnieper River and evolved into a principality, led by a prince, around 900.

Ibn Fadlan's Description of a Rus Burial

Although Ibn Fadlan, an envoy from the Abbasid court, looked down on the Rus as coarse and uncivilized, his account of a king's funeral is the most detailed description of pre-Christian Rus religious beliefs and practices surviving today. It is particularly moving because he was able to observe a young girl who died so that she could be buried with her lord. The Angel of Death who kills the girl may have been a priestess of either Frey or Odin, whose devotees some-times engaged in sex as part of their fertility rites. While Ibn Fadlan clearly finds the Rus funerary practices strange, the Scandinavian he quotes at the end of this selection finds the Islamic practice of burial equally alien.

Source: James E. Montgomery, "Ibn Fadlan and the Rusiyyah," *Journal of Arabic and Islamic Studies* 3 (2000): 12–20. Online at www.uib.no/jais/content3.htm.

I was told that when their chieftains die, the least they do is cremate them. I was very keen to verify this, when I learned of the death of one of their great men. They placed him in his grave and erected a canopy over it for ten days, until they had finished making and sewing his funeral garments.

In the case of a poor man they build a small boat, place him inside and burn it. In the case of a rich man, they gather together his possessions and divide them into three, one third for his family, one third to use for his funeral garments, and one third with which they purchase alcohol which they drink on the day when his slave-girl kills herself and is cremated together with her master. (They are addicted to alcohol, which they drink night and day. Sometimes one of them dies with the cup still in his hand.)

When their chieftain dies, his family ask his slave-girls and slave-boys, "Who among you will die with him?" and some of them reply, "I shall." Having said this, it becomes incumbent on the person and it is impossible ever to turn back. Should that person try to, he is not permitted to do so. It is usually slave-girls who make this offer.

When that man whom I mentioned earlier died, they said to his slave-girls, "Who will die with him?" and one of them said, "I shall." So they placed two slave-girls in charge of her to take care of her and accompany her wherever she went, even to the point of occasionally washing her feet with their own hands. They set about attending to the dead man, preparing his clothes for him and setting right all that he needed. Every day the slave-girl would drink alcohol and would sing merrily and cheerfully.

On the day when he and the slave-girl were to be burned I arrived at the river where his ship was. To my surprise I discovered that it had been beached and that four planks of birch and other types of wood had been placed in such a way as to resemble scaffolding. Then the ship was hauled and placed on top of this wood. They advanced, going to and fro around the boat uttering words which I did not understand, while he was still in his grave and had not been exhumed.

Then they produced a couch and placed it on the ship, covering it with quilts made of Byzantine silk brocade and cushions made of Byzantine silk brocade. Then a crone arrived whom they called the "Angel of Death" and she spread on the couch the coverings we have mentioned. She is responsible for having his garments sewn up and putting him in order and it is she who kills the slave-girls. I myself saw her: a gloomy, corpulent woman, neither young nor old.

When they came to his grave, they removed the soil from the wood and then removed the wood, exhuming him still dressed in the *izar* [clothing] in which he had died. . . . They carried him inside the pavilion on the ship and laid him to rest on the quilt, propping him with cushions. . . . Next they brought bread, meat, and onions, which they cast in front of him, a dog, which they cut in two and which they threw onto the ship, and all of his weaponry, which they placed beside him. . . .

At the time of the evening prayer on Friday, they brought the slave-girl to a thing they had constructed, like a door-frame. She placed her feet on the hands of the men and was raised above the door-frame. She said something and they brought her down. [This happened two more times.] They next handed her a hen. She cut off its head and threw it away. They took the hen and threw it on board the ship.

I quizzed the interpreter about her actions and he said, "The first time they lifted her, she said, 'Behold, I see my father and my mother.' The second time she said, 'Behold, I see all of my dead kindred, seated.' The third time she said, 'Behold I see my master, seated in Paradise. Paradise is beautiful and verdant. He is accompanied by his men and his male-slaves. He summons me, so bring me to him.'" . . .

The men came with their shields and sticks and handed her a cup of alcohol over which she chanted and then drank.

Six men entered the pavilion and all had intercourse with the slave girl. They laid her down beside her master and two of them took hold of her feet, two her hands. The crone called the "Angel of Death" placed a rope around her neck in such a way that the ends crossed one another and handed it to two of the men to pull on it. She advanced with a broad-bladed dagger and began to thrust it in and out between her ribs, now here, now there, while the two men throttled her with the rope until she died.

Then the deceased's next of kin approached and took hold of a piece of wood and set fire to it. . . . A dreadful wind arose and the flames leapt higher and blazed fiercely.

One of the Rus stood beside me and I heard him speaking to my interpreter. I quizzed him about what he had said, and he replied, "He said, 'You Arabs are a foolish lot!'" So I said, "Why is that?" and he replied, "Because you purposely take those who are dearest to you and whom you hold in highest esteem and throw them under the earth, where they are eaten by the earth, by vermin and by worms, whereas we burn them in the fire there and then, so that they enter Paradise immediately." Then he laughed loud and long.

QUESTIONS FOR ANALYSIS

As you read the above passage carefully, note the events that Ibn Fadlan did not witness himself.

▶ Which of these events do you think could have occurred?

▶ Which events seem less likely?

▶ How did Muslim and Scandinavian burial customs differ?

▶ What is Ibn Fadlan's attitude toward peoples whose practices differ from those in the Islamic world?

But when they went to the Hagia Sophia church in Byzantium (see photo on page 274), they reported the following:

> We knew not whether we were in heaven or on earth. For on earth there is no such splendor or such beauty, and we are at a loss how to describe it. We know only that God dwells there among men, and their service is fairer than the ceremonies of other nations. For we cannot forget that beauty.[11]

Vladimir did not immediately accept their recommendation, but instead asked the reigning Byzantine emperor Basil II (r. 963–1025) to send his sister Anna to him as his bride. Although the Byzantine emperors rarely allowed imperial princesses to marry foreign rulers, Basil agreed because he desperately needed the assistance of Vladimir's troops to suppress a rebellion. He agreed, the *Primary Chronicle* reports, to the engagement on the condition that Vladimir be baptized before the marriage. Vladimir made a counteroffer: he would receive baptism only from the priests accompanying Anna to the wedding. Basil acceded. Once baptized, Vladimir then ordered, on penalty of death, all the inhabitants of Kiev to come to the riverbank and surprised them all by performing a mass baptism. Kiev and all its inhabitants converted to Christianity.

The Growing Divide Between the Eastern and Western Churches

Prince Vladimir and his ten advisers conceived of the Christianity of the Germans and of the Byzantines as two separate religions, which we now call Roman Catholicism and Eastern Orthodoxy. The two churches used different languages, Latin in Rome and Greek in Constantinople, and after 500 they became increasingly separate. Since 751, the pope had been allied with the rulers of the Franks, not the Byzantine emperors.

By 1000, the practices of the Eastern and Western clergy diverged in important ways. Members of the Western church accepted the pope as head, while members of the Eastern church recognized the patriarch of Constantinople as leader. Western priests were supposed to be celibate, even if not all were; their Eastern counterparts could marry. Eastern priests were required to have beards, while Western priests did not. Orthodox Christians put yeast in the communion bread, while Roman Catholics ate unleavened bread.

Although the cultural differences were greater, the teachings of the two churches also diverged on certain doctrinal points. Sometime in the sixth century, probably in Spain, Western Christians had added a new phrase to the basic statement of Christian belief, the Nicene Creed, saying that the Holy Spirit proceeded from both the Father (God) and the Son (Jesus). Charlemagne adopted this phrasing. In contrast, Eastern theologians held that the Holy Spirit proceeded from God alone and did not approve of the phrasing introduced by the Western church. The dispute was not just about a doctrinal point: the Eastern church objected to the Roman church making such a fundamental change on its own.

In 1054, a bishop in Bulgaria wrote to an Italian bishop criticizing certain practices of the Western church, such as the use of unleavened bread in communion and the failure to fast on Saturdays. The pope responded by sending an envoy who carried two letters (one was 17,000 words long) to the patriarch in Constantinople defending these practices and asserting his right as the pope to lead the Western church. As the level of rhetoric escalated, the pope's envoy excommunicated the patriarch of Constantinople, and the patriarch did the same to the pope's envoy. Historians call this the Great Schism of 1054.

Although similar disputes had been resolved in the past, 1054 marked the final break between the two churches. (The dispute was resolved only in 1965, but the two churches stayed separate.) After 1054, the pope in Rome, whose wealth and influence made him the equal of European monarchs, led the Roman Catholic Church. In Constantinople, the patriarch led the Eastern Orthodox Church, the church of both the Byzantine Empire and its close ally, the Kievan princes.

The new Christian states of Europe that formed between 500 and 1000 provided slaves and different raw materials, like fur, to the Abbasids, their powerful neighbors to the southeast. So many of the enslaved captives came from the homeland of the Slavs that Europeans coined the Latin word *sclavus* (meaning "slave") from Slav. As we have seen in Chapter 9, slaves entered the Islamic world from three major sources: Scandinavia, Russia, and Africa, but the expanding trade with Europe and the Islamic world had different results in Africa, as we will see in the next chapter.

Chapter Review

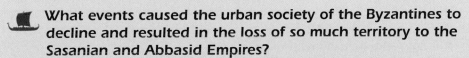 Download the MP3 audio file of the Chapter Review and listen to it on the go.

Between 500 and 1000, Europe became multicentered. In 500 the Byzantine Empire was the sole power throughout Europe, but by 1000 many other centers had formed: in Germany, Scandinavia, and Russia. Gudrid, *Erik the Red's Saga* reports, personally visited Greenland and the Scandinavian settlement in Canada before returning to live in Iceland; at the end of her life, she may have traveled to the center of the Christian church in Rome. Thorfinn, who came originally from Iceland, also visited Greenland, Canada, and Norway.

What events caused the urban society of the Byzantines to decline and resulted in the loss of so much territory to the Sasanian and Abbasid Empires?

After the fall of Rome in 476, only one empire existed in Europe: the Eastern Roman Empire of Byzantium. In 500, the urban life of Constantinople varied little from ancient Rome's: urban residents continued to gather at marketplaces, watch the circus, and attend the theater. But when plague struck in 541 and continued for more than two centuries, the cities of the empire contracted, trade fell off, and people took up subsistence farming. Their urban way of life all but disappeared. The weakened army lost extensive lands in Anatolia to the Sasanians and in Armenia and Africa to the powerful Abbasid Empire. After its disastrous defeat by the Seljuq armies at Manzikert in 1071, Byzantium retained control only of Constantinople and parts of Anatolia, a fraction of its original empire.

KEY TERMS

Gudrid and Thorfinn Karlsefni (268)

Byzantine Empire (271)

patriarch (271)

pope (271)

plague (273)

wergeld (277)

war-band (277)

Merovingian dynasty (278)

Carolingian dynasty (280)

Viking (282)

longboat (284)

Danelaw (285)

The Vinland Sagas (285)

Bjarni Herjolfsson (290)

Skraelings (290)

Rus (291)

Slavs (292)

Principality of Kiev (293)

What was the war-band of traditional Germanic society? How did the political structures of the Merovingians and the Carolingians reflect their origins in the war-band?

To the west in Germany and France lived various Germanic peoples whose primary social unit was the war-band. Each war-band had a leader who provided his followers with food, clothing, housing, and plunder from the places they raided; the followers in turn remained loyal to him in peace and fought with him in war. The Merovingians and the Carolingians called their leaders king, but their greatest leaders, including Clovis and Charlemagne, commanded the respect of their war-bands only as long as they could provide them with the spoils of battle.

 When, where, how, and why did the Scandinavians go on their voyages, and what was the significance of those voyages?

To the north, in Scandinavia, lived a different group of Germanic peoples, the Scandinavians. Unlike the Franks, who moved overland, they traveled by longboat, first to England and Ireland in the 790s, then to Iceland in 870, to Greenland in 980, and finally to the Atlantic coast of Canada around the year 1000, some fifteen years after Bjarni Herjolfsson first spotted land there. All the Scandinavian settlers shared the same goal: they wanted more farmland than was available to them in Scandinavia.

Their voyages were significant because they were the first Europeans to settle in the Americas. Their short-lived settlement in Canada preceded Columbus's by nearly five hundred years; unlike his, theirs had no long-term consequences.

 What were the earliest states to form in the area that is now Russia, and what role did religion play in their establishment and development?

In the centuries that some Scandinavians traveled west, others went east. The Rus took their longboats down the rivers of Russia, where they captured slaves, collected furs from subject peoples, and traded with the Islamic world. Before 970, these Rus traders paid taxes to the Khazars, who had adopted Judaism, and to the Volga Bulgars, who had converted to Islam. After 970, the Rus formed their own state, the Kievan Rus principality, whose ruler Prince Vladimir converted to Eastern Orthodoxy, the state church of Byzantium.

What did all the new states have in common?

The new states that formed in France and Germany, Scandinavia, and Russia had much in common. The Germanic peoples who settled these regions all grouped into war-bands, and the first kings convened assemblies with their subjects as war-band leaders. The early kings gave up their multiple deities for Christianity, although they often continued to worship their gods for a few generations. Unlike the complex legal system of the Romans, the legal systems of these societies were wergeld-based systems with clearly defined offenses and fines.

For Further Reference

Biraben, J. N., and Jacques Le Goff. "The Plague in the Early Middle Ages." In *Biology of Man in History: Selections from Annales Economies, Sociétés, Civilisations,* ed. Robert Forster et al. Baltimore: Johns Hopkins University Press, 1975, pp. 48–80.

Fitzhugh, William W., and Elisabeth I. Ward. *Vikings: The North Atlantic Saga.* Washington, D.C.: Smithsonian Institution Press, 2000.

Fletcher, Richard. *The Barbarian Conversion: From Paganism to Christianity.* Berkeley: University of California Press, 1999.

Geary, Patrick. *Before France and Germany: The Creation and Transformation of the Merovingian World.* New York: Oxford University Press, 1988.

Kazhdan, A. P., and Ann Wharton Epstein. *Change in Byzantine Culture in the Eleventh and Twelfth Centuries.* Berkeley: University of California Press, 1985.

Lynch, Joseph H. *The Medieval Church: A Brief History.* New York: Longman, 1992.

Magnusson, Magnus, and Hermann Palsson, trans. *The Vinland Sagas: The Norse Discovery of America.* New York: Penguin Books, 1965.

Martin, Janet. *Medieval Russia 980–1584.* New York: Cambridge University Press, 1995.

McCormick, Michael. *Origins of the European Economy: Communications and Commerce AD 300–900.* New York: Cambridge University Press, 2001.

McKitterick, Rosamond, ed. *The New Cambridge Medieval History,* vol. 2, c. 700–c. 900. New York: Cambridge University Press, 1995. Particularly the essays by Michael McCormick.

Reuter, Timothy. "Plunder and Tribute in the Carolingian Empire." *Transactions of the Royal Historical Society,* 5th ser., 35 (1985): 75–94.

Reuter, Timothy, ed. *The New Cambridge Medieval History,* vol. 3, c. 900–1024. New York: Cambridge University Press, 1999. Particularly the essay by Thomas S. Noonan.

Rosenwein, Barbara H. *A Short History of the Middle Ages.* Orchard Park, N.Y.: Broadview Press, 2002.

Southern, R. W. *Western Society and the Church in the Middle Ages.* New York: Penguin Books, 1970.

Treadgold, Warren. *A History of the Byzantine State and Society.* Stanford: Stanford University Press, 1997.

Wallace, Birgitta L. *Westward Vikings: The Saga of L'Anse aux Meadows.* St. John's, Newfoundland, Canada: Historic Sites Association of Newfoundland and Labrador, 2006.

(CL) WEB RESOURCES

Pronunciation Guide

Interactive Maps

MAP 10.1 The Byzantine Empire

MAP 10.2 The Carolingian Realms

MAP 10.3 The Viking Raids, 793–1066

MAP 10.4 Kievan Rus

Primary Sources

Chapter Objectives

ACE Multiple-Choice Quiz

Flashcards

Websites

L'Anse aux Meadows
(http://www.pc.gc.ca/progs/spm-whs/itm2-/site1-E.asp). Canada Parks Service website about the Viking colony at L'Anse aux Meadows.

Internet Medieval Sourcebook
(http://www.fordham.edu/halsall/sbook.html). Excellent collection of primary sources under the following headings: Carolingians, The Early Germans, France, and England.

Vikings
(http://www.mnh.si.edu/vikings/). Information about the Vikings from the Smithsonian National Museum of Natural History.

11

Expanding Trade Networks in Africa and India, 1000–1500

In 1325, a 20-year-old legal scholar named **Ibn Battuta** (1304–1368/69[1]) set off on a hajj pilgrimage from his home in Tangier (tan-jeer), a Mediterranean port on the westernmost edge of the Islamic world (see Chapter 9). In Mecca Ibn Battuta (ibin bah-TOO-tuh) made a decision that changed his life: instead of returning home, he decided to keep going. A world traveler with no fixed destination and no set time of return, he followed trade routes that knitted the entire Islamic world together. These routes connected places like Mecca, which had been at the center of the Islamic world since Muhammad's first revelations (see Chapter 9), to others that had more recently joined that world, such as the sub-Saharan kingdom of Mali and the Delhi sultanate of north India. After his travels were over, Ibn Battuta dictated his adventures to a ghost writer. His account began:

MUSLIM TRAVELER, CA. 1300

(Bibliothèque nationale de France/Superstock, Inc.)

My departure from Tangier, my birthplace, took place . . . in the year seven hundred and twenty-five [1325] with the object of making the Pilgrimage to the Holy House at Mecca and of visiting the tomb of the Prophet . . . at Medina. I set out alone, having neither fellow-traveller in whose companionship I might find cheer, nor caravan whose party I might join, but swayed by an over-mastering impulse within me, and a desire long-cherished in my bosom to visit these illustrious sanctuaries.[2]

This icon will direct you to interactive activities and study materials on the *Voyages* website: www.cengage.com/history/hansen/voyages1e

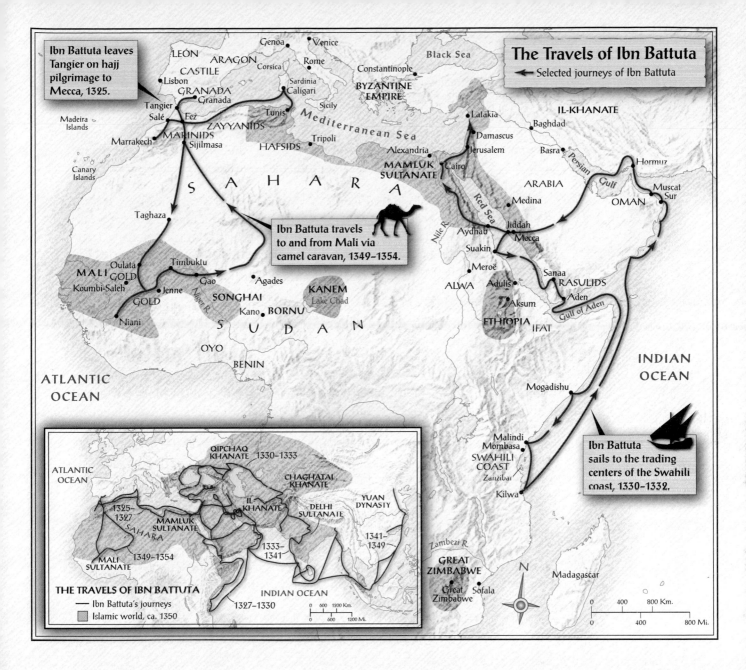

The Travels of Ibn Battuta

← Selected journeys of Ibn Battuta

Ibn Battuta leaves Tangier on hajj pilgrimage to Mecca, 1325.

Ibn Battuta travels to and from Mali via camel caravan, 1349–1354.

Ibn Battuta sails to the trading centers of the Swahili coast, 1330–1332.

León · ARAGON · Genoa · Venice · Rome · Black Sea
CASTILE · Corsica · Constantinople
Lisbon · Sardinia · BYZANTINE
GRANADA · Caligari · Sicily · EMPIRE · IL-KHANATE
Granada · Tunis · Lalakia · Baghdad
Tangier · Fez · Mediterranean Sea · Damascus
Salé · ZAYYANIDS · Tripoli · Jerusalem · Basra · Hormuz
Madeira Islands · MARINIDS · Alexandria · ARABIA · Muscat
Marrakech · HAFSIDS · MAMLUK · Cairo · OMAN · Sur
Sijilmasa · SULTANATE
Canary Islands · S A H A R A · Medina
Taghaza · Red Sea · Jiddah
Mecca
MALI · Timbuktu · Aydhab
Oulata · GOLD · Suakin · Sanaa · RASULIDS
Koumbi-Saleh · Jenne · Gao · Agades · Meroë · ALWA · Adulis · Aden
GOLD · SONGHAI · KANEM · Aksum · Gulf of Aden
Niani · Kano · BORNU · Lake Chad · ETHIOPIA
S U D A N · IFAT
OYO
BENIN · INDIAN OCEAN
ATLANTIC OCEAN
Mogadishu

Malindi · Mombasa
SWAHILI COAST
Zanzibar
Kilwa

Zambezi R.
GREAT ZIMBABWE · Madagascar
Great Zimbabwe · Sofala

THE TRAVELS OF IBN BATTUTA

QIPCHAQ KHANATE 1330–1333
CHAGHATAI KHANATE
ATLANTIC OCEAN
1325–1327 · IL-KHANATE
MAMLUK SULTANATE · DELHI SULTANATE · YUAN DYNASTY
SAHARA · 1341–1349
MALI SULTANATE · 1349–1354 · 1333–1341
1327–1330
INDIAN OCEAN

— Ibn Battuta's journeys
▨ Islamic world, ca. 1350

0   600   1200 Km.
0   600   1200 Mi.

0   400   800 Km.
0   400   800 Mi.

N

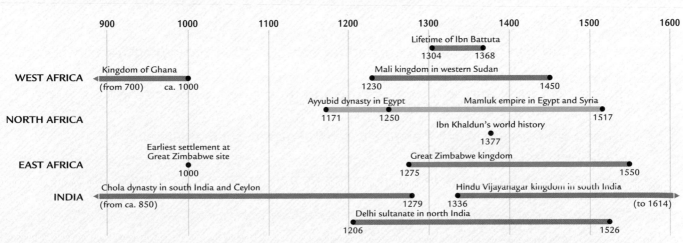

	900	1000	1100	1200	1300	1400	1500	1600

Lifetime of Ibn Battuta
1304 — 1368

WEST AFRICA
Kingdom of Ghana (from 700) ca. 1000
Mali kingdom in western Sudan
1230 — 1450

NORTH AFRICA
Ayyubid dynasty in Egypt
1171 — 1250
Mamluk empire in Egypt and Syria
1517
Ibn Khaldun's world history
1377

EAST AFRICA
Earliest settlement at Great Zimbabwe site
1000
Great Zimbabwe kingdom
1275 — 1550

INDIA
Chola dynasty in south India and Ceylon (from ca. 850)
1279
Hindu Vijayanagar kingdom in south India
1336 — (to 1614)
Delhi sultanate in north India
1206 — 1526

● **Ibn Battuta** (1304–1368/69) Legal scholar from Tangier, Morocco, who traveled throughout the Islamic world between 1325 and 1354 and wrote *The Travels* recounting his experiences in Africa, India, Central Asia, Spain, and China.

So begins the account of the longest known journey taken by any single individual before 1500. Proceeding on foot, riding camels and donkeys, and sailing by boat, Ibn Battuta covered an estimated 75,000 miles (120,000 km)—an extraordinary distance in the preindustrial world. Because the Five Pillars of Islam (see Chapter 9) obligated all Muslims to give alms, not just to the poor and the sick but also to travelers, Ibn Battuta was able to continue his travels even when his own funds were exhausted.

After setting out alone, Ibn Battuta soon fell in with a caravan of traders on their way to Cairo. Because he always traveled with Islamic merchants on established caravan routes, his itinerary provides ample evidence of the extensive trade networks connecting northern Africa, much of East and West Africa, and northern India. Many of the people he met accepted the teachings of the Quran, and he was able to communicate in Arabic everywhere he went. In each place he visited, he named the rulers, identified the highest-ranking judges, and then listed the important holy men of the town and their most important miracles. This narrow focus means that he rarely reported on some important topics, such as the local economy or the lives of women and non-Muslims.

Ibn Battuta was the first traveler to leave an eyewitness description of Africa south of the Sahara Desert, where he stayed in the kingdom of Mali. He visited Cairo, the capital city of the Mamluks (MAM-lukes) of Egypt, a powerful dynasty founded by military slaves, as well as several East African ports south of the equator. He remained for seven years in north India, then under Muslim rule, and visited many Indian Ocean ports. He did not, however, go to the interior of southern Africa or see the majestic site of Great Zimbabwe.

Many legs of Ibn Battuta's journey would not have been possible three hundred years earlier. In 1000 many parts of Africa were not connected to the broader Islamic world, including the rainforest of the West African coastlands and Central Africa, the densely populated Great Lakes region around Lake Victoria, and the southern African savannah. By 1450, however, expanding networks of trade had brought West and East Africa into increasing contact with the Islamic world of northern Africa and western Asia.

Focus Questions

⛵ How was sub-Saharan Africa settled before 1000 C.E.? What techniques have historians used to reconstruct the past?

⛵ What role did trade play in the emergence and subsequent history of the kingdoms of Ghana and Mali?

⛵ How and why did the Mamluk empire based in Egypt become the leading center of the Islamic world after 1258?

⛵ What was the nature of the Indian Ocean trade network that linked India, Arabia, and East Africa?

Reconstructing the History of Sub-Saharan Africa Before 1000 C.E.

The Sahara Desert divides the enormous continent of Africa into two halves: sub-Saharan Africa in contrast to North and East Africa. As we have seen in Chapter 9, Islamic armies conquered North Africa in the seventh century, and East Africans had much contact with Muslim traders throughout the Abbasid period (750–1258). We know much less about sub-Saharan Africa before 1000 because few Muslims, the source of so much of our information, traveled there. Apart from Arabic accounts, historians of Africa must draw on archaeological excavation, oral traditions, and analysis of vocabulary from different languages to piece together sub-Saharan Africa's history before 1000.

The Geography and Languages of Sub-Saharan Africa

Africa is a large continent, with an area greater than that of the United States (including Alaska), Europe, and China combined. As we saw in Chapter 1, the first anatomically modern humans crossed the Sinai Peninsula from Africa into western Asia at least 150,000 years ago, possibly earlier. The Nile River Valley was the site of Africa's earliest complex societies, first in Egypt and then in Nubia (see Chapter 2). Rome's greatest rival, Carthage, operated from a base in North Africa, and after its defeat in 202 B.C.E., Romans bought much of their grain from Egypt. In the 300s, Christianity spread throughout the Mediterranean to Egypt, northern Africa, and Ethiopia (see Chapter 7). After 650, Islam replaced Christianity in much of northern Africa, but not Ethiopia.

A glance at Map 11.1 shows why only North and East Africa had such close contacts with the larger world: 3,000 miles (4,800 km) across and around 1,000 miles (1,600 km) from north to south, the Sahara Desert posed a formidable barrier between the coast and the sub-Saharan regions. The first traders to cross the Sahara did so riding camels. The single-humped camel they used originated in Arabia and reached North Africa sometime in the first century B.C.E. Domesticated in the third or fourth centuries C.E., camels were much cheaper than human porters because they were hardier—capable of going for long periods without water and carrying much heavier loads. Camels did not need roads and crossed the desert on sandy tracks.

Immediately to the south of the Sahara is a semidesert region called the Sahel (meaning "shore" in Arabic). South of the Sahel (SAH-hel), enough rainfall fell to support the tall grasses of the dry savanna, and then farther south, a band of wooded savanna where many trees grew. Rainfall was heaviest in Central Africa, and rainforest stretched from the Atlantic coast all the way to the Great Lakes region. The pattern repeated itself south of the rainforest: first a band of woodland savanna, then dry savanna, and then the Kalahari Desert near the tip of southern Africa.

Africans today speak nearly two thousand different languages, one-third of the total number of languages spoken in the world (see Map 11.1). Several languages spoken in North Africa, including Egyptian, Nubian, Ethiopian, and Arabic, have had written forms for a thousand years or longer (see Chapters 2, 7, and 9). But none of those spoken south of the Sahara were written down before 1800. Today about five hundred of Africa's two thousand languages have written forms.

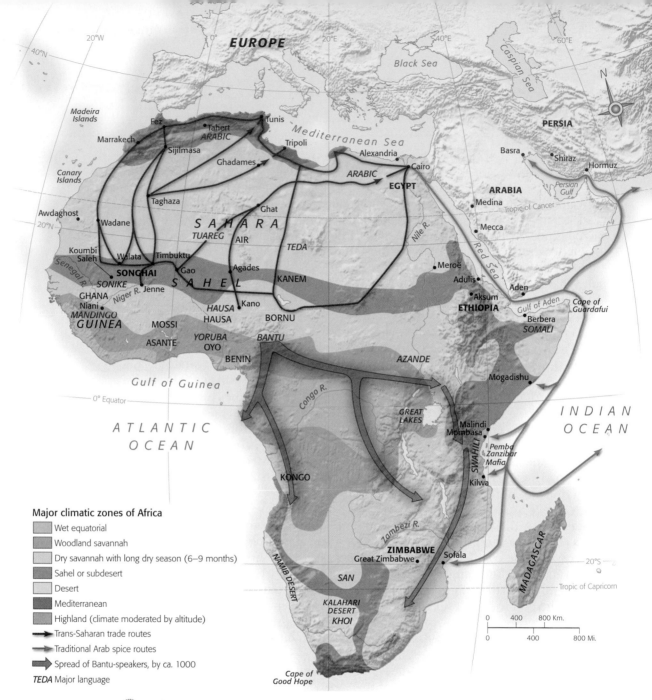

Major climatic zones of Africa

- Wet equatorial
- Woodland savannah
- Dry savannah with long dry season (6–9 months)
- Sahel or subdesert
- Desert
- Mediterranean
- Highland (climate moderated by altitude)
- → Trans-Saharan trade routes
- → Traditional Arab spice routes
- → Spread of Bantu-speakers, by ca. 1000
- *TEDA* Major language

CL Interactive Map

🌐 **MAP 11.1**

African Trade Routes, 1200–1500   The Sahara Desert forms a natural boundary between Saharan Africa and sub-Saharan Africa. Overland camel routes across the Sahara Desert linked Mali with the Mediterranean coast, while Indian Ocean sea routes connected the important center of Great Zimbabwe in East Africa to the Islamic world and Asia.

The Spread of Bantu Languages	Africa's languages cluster in several major groups. Arabic is spoken throughout the Islamic regions, while the **Bantu** languages of the Niger-Congo language family are widely

distributed throughout sub-Saharan Africa. Since many of these languages show surprising uniformity over a wide area, earlier analysts posited that the migration of a single people, all speaking an earlier form of the Bantu language, accounted for this modern language distribution.

Accordingly, many analysts assumed that the Bantu speakers set out from their homeland in Nigeria and Cameroon, in the western bend of Africa, and migrated all over central, eastern, and southern Africa. When they came to a new place, they conquered the indigenous peoples with their iron weapons and then used iron tools to till the land. This view, like earlier understandings of the Indo-European migrations discussed in Chapter 3, presumes that a single people were responsible for the spread of a single language family. It also credits them with technological superiority over the original residents of the regions who hunted, fished, and gathered wild plants.

But this model of a single wave of Bantu migration presents many problems, the most basic of which is timing. Agriculture and ironworking did spread throughout sub-Saharan Africa sometime before 1000 C.E., but not necessarily at the same time as the Bantu languages did.

African historians have pioneered the use of a linguistic method called *glottochronology* to analyze the history of languages. By comparing vocabulary lists, linguists can count how many words in two languages are the same and how many have changed. The greater the number of shared words, the closer two languages are; the fewer the number, the more distant. Those who practice glottochronology believe that linguistic change holds constant over time: some, for example, estimate that sixteen words out of one hundred will change over a five-hundred-year period.[3] Most analysts find glottochronology useful for determining which languages broke off from others and in what order; not everyone, however, is convinced of claims about the timing of those changes. The linguistic variation among modern Bantu languages suggests multiple waves of change. Accordingly, scholars today have discarded the theory of a single wave of Bantu migration.

A more persuasive model for the spread of Bantu languages sees three different, and often overlapping, processes taking place over an extended period of time: the planting of the first crops, the development of metallurgy, and the spread of the Bantu languages. First, archaeological evidence shows that, sometime between 1000 and 500 B.C.E., different peoples began to cultivate crops. Those in the drier regions grew sorghum, millet, and rice, while those in the rainforest raised tubers such as yams. Like the Maya (see Chapter 5), many of these peoples engaged in slash-and-burn agriculture, meaning they farmed the same place for only one or two seasons. Once the fertility of a plot gave out, cultivators moved to a new site, where they cleared fields by setting fire to the brush. As in other parts of the world, it took hundreds, possibly thousands, of years before people shifted to full-time agriculture.

During this transition to agriculture, different peoples learned how to work iron. Iron tools were much more effective than stone and wood tools in turning the earth and preparing it for seed, and Africans developed sophisticated technologies for making them. Archaeologists have traced the spread of ironworking techniques throughout sub-Saharan Africa. The first evidence of ironworking in Africa dates to about 600 B.C.E. Interestingly, people living north of the Sahara, along the Nile River in modern Sudan, and south of the Sahara in central Nigeria learned how to work iron at about the same time. The metallurgical techniques used north of the Sahara differ markedly from those used in the south, an indication that the peoples of the two regions discovered how to work iron independently of each other.

The African experience differs from that of other societies because most sub-Saharan African peoples started to work iron without any previous experience in

● **Bantu** Name for the languages of the Niger-Congo language family, which are widely distributed throughout sub-Saharan Africa. By extension, the word also refers to the speakers of those languages.

working copper. In Eurasia the usual pattern was first to combine copper and tin into bronze and then, as the Hittites did in 2000 B.C.E., build on that expertise to smelt iron (see Chapter 2); the peoples of the Americas, in contrast, never worked iron (see Chapter 5).

Africans built a greater variety of furnaces for smelting iron than people anywhere else in the world. Some furnaces had tall shafts; others used preheated air. These smelting techniques allowed Africans to make iron from much leaner ores than those used elsewhere. The technology for smelting iron spread throughout southern Africa by 300 C.E.

Although iron is an extremely useful metal that can be made into agricultural implements and military weapons, it is relatively soft and rusts. Steel is much stronger and more resistant to rusting. The difference between iron and steel is the amount of carbon in the metal: iron that has been worked by a blacksmith, or wrought iron, usually contains less than .2 percent carbon, while steel may contain up to 1.5 percent. African smelting furnaces often made iron with enough dissolved carbon to have the properties of steel.

In the same centuries that the sub-Saharan Africans were developing agriculture and refining their production of iron, the Bantu languages spread in a southward direction to the regions where rainfall was heavier. It is possible that different groups moved out from the heartland of the Bantu languages in modern-day Nigeria and Cameroon and that their ability to farm and to make iron tools enabled them to displace the indigenous populations, who hunted and gathered. Yet it is equally likely that indigenous peoples adopted the new farming and iron-smelting technologies and the Bantu languages in different phases in different regions.

By 1000, agricultural peoples who used iron tools had settled throughout sub-Saharan Africa, many of them speaking Bantu languages. Their iron tools allowed them to move into and settle heavily forested areas such as the Great Lakes regions.

Society and Family Life

The final centuries of these changes overlap with the first written records. As early as the eighth century, Arab geographers began to record some preliminary notes, often on the basis of hearsay, about sub-Saharan Africa (see the "Movement of Ideas" feature in Chapter 9), and Arabic sources dominate the historical record through the sixteenth century, particularly for North and East Africa. The lack of indigenous historical records means that, like their colleagues elsewhere, historians of sub-Saharan Africa must rely on **oral histories,** recited accounts passed from one generation to the next. Exciting breakthroughs in African history have come when historians have determined the exact date and location of a given event by linking events from oral histories with Arabic-language sources. Ibn Battuta's account occupies pride of place among these Arabic sources because he went to so many places and wrote at such great length. (The English translation of his account fills nearly a thousand pages in four volumes.)

Historians have been able to reconstruct the past through careful examination of historic accounts and judicious consideration of which aspects of social and economic life remained unchanged over the centuries. Jan Vansina, a prominent historian of Africa, coined the term *up-streaming* for their task because it resembles standing on a riverbank, observing what is in front of them, and making an intelligent guess about what happened upstream.[4]

● **oral histories**
Historical accounts passed from one generation to the next. In Africa, griots often recited the events of the past to the monarchs they advised. Particularly important in societies where no written accounts survive.

Up-streaming has led historians to concur that certain generalizations probably hold true for most of sub-Saharan Africa before 1000. While no estimates for Africa's overall population at this time exist, it is clear that people lived in villages of several hundred to several thousand residents and that fertile areas were more heavily populated than barren regions like the Sahara Desert. Often the people of one village claimed descent from the same ancestor, whether legendary or historical, and historians use the term **lineage** or *clan* for such family units. (Historians today avoid the word *tribe* because of its negative associations and condescending use in the past.)

Lineages and clans organized into villages were the bedrock of Africa's diverse societies. Men often dominated the tasks with the greatest prestige, like hunting or metallurgy, as well as anything requiring long-distance travel, such as military conquest, long-distance trade, and diplomatic negotiations. Women usually tilled the soil, gathered wild fruits and vegetables, made pottery, and prepared meals. Marriage patterns varied from village to village: a man might take a single wife or multiple wives, sometimes from within his own lineage, sometimes from other groups.

Men formed tight bonds with other men of the same age while undergoing initiations into adulthood. Men in the junior age grades respected the men of the more senior age grades, and when they grew old, they in turn expected younger men to obey them. A man who fathered many children and attained great wealth was called a "great man." Great men earned their position at the top of village society, often by military prowess.

Great men led villages, and, if continuously successful in battle, they might form larger political units such as a chieftaincy; if more successful, a kingdom. Historians usually describe villages as evolving into chieftaincies, and then chieftaincies into kingdoms or states, but the different stages were not sharply defined. The same political unit might seem to be a kingdom to an observer in the capital but more like a chieftaincy to someone in an outlying area. During the lifetimes of the great men who led them, the villages they had conquered would submit gifts to them; after their deaths, however, the fragile political units they formed could easily break apart. In the course of his travels, Ibn Battuta met several great men who headed their own kingdoms, one of whom was the ruler of Mali.

• **lineage** Group of people claiming descent from the same ancestor, whether legendary or historical, who are not necessarily biologically related but see themselves as a family unit.

The Kingdom of Mali in Sub-Saharan Africa

The kingdom of **Mali,** centered on the Niger River basin, occupied much of West Africa south of the Sahara Desert. It straddled the Sahel (see above) and the vast savannah grasslands to the south. Because this territory included some of the world's biggest gold mines, merchants crossed the Sahara to this region perhaps as early as 500 C.E. Urbanization began in the West African Sahel with the development of the trans-Saharan trade. Ghana (ca. 700–1000) was the first kingdom to take advantage of its location at an important node of trade, and the kingdom of Mali built on these earlier achievements in using trans-Saharan trade as a pathway to power. Ibn Battuta offers a verbal snapshot of Mali's trade with the north in the 1350s: caravans brought slaves and gold from the south and exchanged them for cloth, pottery, and glass trinkets from the north.

• **Mali** Kingdom founded ca. 1230 by Sundiata in West Africa south of the Sahara Desert and in the Niger River basin. Generated revenue by taxing the caravans of the trans-Saharan trade. Declined around 1450 after losing trading cities to the Songhai Empire.

The Kingdom of Ghana, ca. 700–1000

The Muslim geographer al-Bakri (d. 1094) provided the earliest and most detailed description of the kingdom of Ghana in his *Book of Routes and Realms* (see "Movement of Ideas," Chapter 9). Since al-Bakri never left his native Spain, he drew all of his information from earlier geographic accounts and from named informants who had been to the Sahara and the sub-Saharan trading kingdoms.

These kingdoms originated as small settlements located at points where different routes crossed each other. Sijilmasa (sih-jil-MAHS-suh), located on the northern edge of the Sahara in modern Morocco, began, al-Bakri reports, as a periodic market on a "bare plain" where local people came to buy and sell goods, like iron tools, only at certain times of year. He says, "That [the periodic market] was the beginning of its being populated, then it became a town." Sijilmasa grew into an important trade depot ruled by a royal lineage whose founder claimed descent from a family who sold iron tools at the earliest periodic market. Towns like Sijilmasa became city-states whose main source of revenue was the taxes their rulers collected from traders.[5]

The kingdom of Ghana arose through a similar process. In the mid-1000s, al-Bakri reported that the kingdom contained two cities: preachers and scholars lived in the Islamic one, which had twelve mosques where Friday prayers were said; and "six miles" away, the king and his "sorcerers" lived in the other. Al-Bakri's informants drew a sharp line between Muslims and "polytheists," whose "religion is paganism and the worship of idols." The king did not convert to Islam, but he welcomed Muslim visitors.

Archaeologists have not found any sites that match al-Bakri's description and have concluded that the kingdom did not have a fixed capital. Instead, the king and his retinue regularly moved among different cities. Excavations at Jenne (JENN-eh) and Koumbi Saleh (KOOM-bi sah-LEH) (200 miles north of Bamako, Mali) have found evidence of large cities: the population of Jenne in the 700s was around 20,000, with smaller surrounding towns of 500 to 1,500 people.[6]

The king taxed the goods going in and out of the cities he ruled. Merchants paid a tax in gold on each donkey load of goods they brought into the city. The tax was higher for more valuable goods, like copper, and lower for cheaper commodities, like salt. These revenues financed the king's military campaigns. The king, al-Bakri reported, could raise an army of 200,000 men, of whom 40,000 were archers.

Some states in pre-1500 Africa, like Ghana, controlled large amounts of territory, but usually they exercised direct political control over only a small core area. Even where such states existed, however, kings normally had little independent political power, usually serving as mediators and consensus-builders of councils of elders. The lineage and clan elders made the most important decisions at the local level.

Unlike Mesopotamia, Egypt, India, China, or the Americas, where the first complex societies tapped agricultural surplus, most African states arose through control of strategic natural resources like water or gold. The loss of several key trading depots to the Almoravid dynasty of Spain (see Chapter 9) drastically reduced the tax revenues paid to the kings of Ghana, and they lost their kingdom to a local lineage named the Sosso (SUE-sue) around 1150.

Sundiata and the Founding of the Mali Kingdom, ca. 1230

The best source about the rise of Mali is an oral epic, written down only in the twentieth century, that recounts the life and exploits of the founder of the Mali kingdom, Sundiata (soon-JAH-tuh) (r. ca. 1230).[7] The peoples of

West Africa spoke a group of related languages called Mande (MAHN-day), which included the Malinke (muh-LING-kay) language spoken in Mali. The Malinke version of the tale *Sundiata* tells how the son of a local ruler overthrew the Sosso king Soumaoro (sue-MAO-row) and united the different peoples of the region.

Each king of Mali had his own storyteller, or **griot** (GREE-oh; a French word), who had been taught the story of his dynastic predecessors and whose task was to compose new sections about the reigning king. The griots' extensive knowledge of the ancestral teachings granted them a prominent position in Mali society, and they often advised rulers on matters of state and accompanied them on diplomatic missions. Since Ibn Battuta did not speak Malinke, an interpreter must have told him about the griots; his description is one of the earliest we have of the griots and their close relationship to the **sultan.** Ibn Battuta used the word *sultan,* meaning "ruler" in Arabic, for the Mali king because his predecessors had converted to Islam sometime around 1000.

Ibn Battuta saw the sultan's griots when he visited Mali: "Each of them is inside a costume made of feathers resembling the green woodpecker on which is a wooden head with a red beak. . . . They stand before the Sultan in this laughable get-up and recite their poems. I have been told that their poetry is a sort of admonition. They say to the Sultan: 'This platform, formerly such and such a king sat on it and performed noble actions, and so and so did such and such; do you do noble acts which will be recounted after you.'" Once they were done reciting, the griots climbed up the platform on which the sultan was sitting and placed their head on his right shoulder, his left, and then his lap to show their respect. (See the feature "World History in Today's World: Griottes in Mali.")

The story of Sundiata remains our most detailed source about the early years of Mali. Mali's founder, Sundiata, was born to a king and his hump-backed wife,

- **griot/griotte** Royal storytellers who served as advisers to the rulers of Mali and other West African states. (A griotte is a female storyteller.)

- **sultan** "Ruler" in Arabic. Any head of an Islamic state. The states they governed were often called *sultanates.*

🔲 **A Modern Headdress from Mali** When Ibn Battuta visited the sultan of Mali, he described griots who wore a feathered costume topped by a bird's head with a beak. Perhaps he saw something like this bird mask, made in the twentieth century out of feathers, porcupine quills, antelope horns, and mud, from the same region of Mali that he visited. (Gift of Mr. William W. Brill. Photograph courtesy of the Herbert F. Johnson Museum of Art, Cornell University)

Griottes in Mali

When the historian D. T. Niane studied the epic of *Sundiata* in 1960, he transcribed the tale from a male griot named Mamadou Kouyaté (mah-mah-DEW koh-yah-TAY), who had learned the tale from his father and grandfather. Although the narrative presents a few vivid female characters, the story is focused on one man's exploits. One can easily imagine a largely male audience listening to a male griot tell the story of Sundiata.

Before 1960, it was difficult for women to leave home for extended periods so that they could learn new epics from experienced griots. Women storytellers therefore specialized in singing shorter narratives with little historical content, which did not attract large audiences. Now that epics are often performed on radio or television, women can learn to recite them from cassette recordings. As a result, the number of women griottes (GREE-ohts) has increased so much that they now dominate the storytelling profession in Mali, and the genre of the oral epic seems much less male-centered. Scholars are uncovering new tales, some with female heroines, told by griottes. Often women tell the stories while men accompany them on musical instruments.

Sources: Thomas A. Hale, *Griots and Griottes: Masters of Words and Music* (Bloomington: Indiana University Press, 1998). Video resource: *Griottes of the Sahel: Female Keepers of the Songhay Oral Tradition in Niger* (made by Thomas A. Hale; 11-minute video distributed by Audio-Visual Services, the Pennsylvania State University).

and he walked only at the age of 7. These traits indicated to the audience that both mother and son possessed unusual spiritual powers. In the hope that Sundiata would someday succeed to the throne, his father assigned him his own griot. One day, when his exasperated mother yelled at Sundiata because he was still entirely dependent on others for food, his griot sent word to the village blacksmith to send an iron bar so heavy that six men were needed to carry it. Sundiata easily picked up the bar with one hand and then stood up and walked. He grew into a strong and powerful warrior, eventually forced into exile by one of his father's envious wives. After nearly ten years away, Sundiata returned to his kingdom to find it under the oppressive rule of Soumaoro, the leader of the Sosso lineage that Sundiata resolved to overthrow.

The *Sundiata* narrative sketches the process of state formation as a series of conquests, some within Mali, others beyond; some of human enemies, others of supernatural forces. By the end of the epic, Sundiata rules the kingdom of Mali. (See the feature "Movement of Ideas: Mali Religion in the Epic of *Sundiata*.")

How many of the events described in *Sundiata* can be confirmed by other sources? Arab chronicles confirm that the kingdom of Mali existed in the thirteenth century, and the great Arab historian Ibn Khaldun (1332–1406), a native of Tunis in North Africa, recorded the names of the Mali kings and the major events of their reigns. Ibn Khaldun (IH-buhn hal-DOON), perhaps the most important Muslim historian of all times, formulated an entirely original definition of history as the study of human society and its transformations. His work makes it possible to date Sundiata's reign to around 1230.

The process of state formation that the *Sundiata* narrative describes is plausible: armies several thousand strong did fight with iron-tipped bows and other metal weapons. At its largest, reached some one hundred years after Sundiata's reign, the kingdom of Mali extended more than 1,000 miles (1,600 km) east to west and included the basins of both the Senegal and Niger Rivers.

As the *Sundiata* narrative shows, the Mali army consisted of different independent armies, each led by a local leader, who decided in each instance which leader he would support. When Soumaoro lost, a number of kings changed sides and supported Sundiata.

Although these kings may have exchanged gifts with Sundiata, the government's primary source of revenue was taxes on trade. One of Sundiata's most wealthy successors was Mansa Musa (r. 1307–1332), who visited Cairo on his way to Mecca in 1324. (*Mansa* is a word in the Malinke language meaning "supreme ruler," and *Musa* is Arabic for Moses; *Mansa Musa* means King Moses.) Five hundred servants, each carrying a staff of gold weighing 6 pounds (2.7 kg), walked in front of him. One hundred camels were required to carry his travel money, which was some 700 pounds (315 kg) of gold, making Mansa Musa one of the most talked-about and most welcome travelers of his day. A map of Afro-Eurasia made one hundred years after his death pictured Mansa Musa as a symbol of great wealth.[8]

Trans-Saharan Trade Networks

In 1352, twenty years after Mansa Musa's death, Ibn Battuta went to Mali, then ruled by his grandson. The only eyewitness description we have of the fabulously wealthy kingdom, his

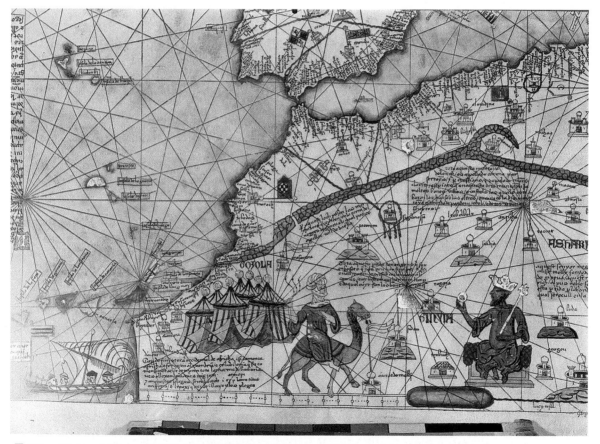

■ **The Richest King in the Land? Mansa Musa of Mali** In 1375, a European cartographer mapped Afro-Eurasia with unprecedented accuracy. This detail of the Catalan Atlas shows the green Mediterranean Ocean, southern Spain, and North Africa. The mapmaker has also included written labels that identify the seated figure on the lower right as Mansa Musa, the richest king in the land because of the abundant gold in his country. (Bibliothèque nationale de France/Bridgeman Art Library)

Mali Religion in the Epic of *Sundiata*

The *Sundiata* epic reveals much about African religions. Sundiata's enemy Soumaoro is a sorcerer who knows how to make small figurines, or fetishes, and recite spells to wound his enemies. Still, Soumaoro is not invincible. He tells his wife that he must observe a taboo against touching a cock's spur, the sharp talon a rooster uses to attack his enemies. If he does not, he will lose the power granted to him by his ancestors. Both Sundiata and his half-sister use the same word for the sorcerer's power: *jinn*, the Arabic word for a spirit or ghost (also the root of the English word *genie*), which they are able to overcome by attaching a cock's spur to the arrow that kills Soumaoro. The epic illustrates how local African religion absorbed religious conceptions from Islam. Notice that Sundiata never mentions God or the power of Islam, even though Mali's ruler converted to Islam around 1000, two centuries before the events described in the epic occurred. The selections below are taken from different parts of the epic.

Source: D. T. Niane, *Sundiata: An Epic of Old Mali*, trans. G. D. Pickett (London: Longman, 1965), pp. 52–53, 57–58, 65.

Sundiata's Description of Soumaoro's Powers

Soumaoro was now within spear range and Sundiata reared up his horse and hurled his weapon. It whistled away and bounced off Soumaoro's chest as off a rock and fell to the ground. Sogolon's son [Sundiata] bent his bow but with a motion of the hand Soumaoro caught the arrow in flight and showed it to Sundiata as if to say "Look, I am invulnerable."

Furious, Sundiata snatched up his spear and with his head bent charged at Soumaoro, but as he raised his arm to strike his enemy he noticed that Soumaoro had disappeared. Manding Bory [man-DING BORE-ee] riding at his side pointed to the hill and said, "Look, brother."

Sundiata saw Soumaoro on the hill, sitting on his black-coated horse. How could he have done it, he who was only two paces from Sundiata? By what power had he spirited himself away on to the hill? . . . The sun was already very low and Soumaoro's smiths gave way but Sundiata did not give the order to pursue the enemy. Suddenly Soumaoro disappeared!

How can I vanquish a man capable of disappearing and re-appearing where and when he likes? How can I affect a man invulnerable to iron? Such were the questions which Sogolon's son asked himself. He had been told many things about Sosso-Soumaoro but he had given little credence to so much gossip. Didn't people say that Soumaoro could assume sixty-nine different shapes to escape his enemies? According to some, he could transform himself into a fly in the middle of the battle and come and torment his opponent; he could melt into the wind when his enemies encircled him too closely—and many other things.

The battle of Neguéboria [neh-GAY-BOH-ria] showed Djata [Sundiata], if he needed to be shown, that to beat the king of Sosso [Soumaoro] other weapons were necessary.

The evening of Neguéboria, Sundiata was master of the field, but he was in a gloomy mood. He went away from the field of battle with its agonized cries of the wounded, and Manding Bory and Tabon Wana [TAY-ban WAH-nah] watched him go. He headed for the hill where he had seen Soumaoro after his miraculous disappearance from the midst of his troops. From the top of the hill he watched the compact mass of Soumaoro's smiths withdrawing in a cloud of dust.

"How was he able to escape me? Why did neither my spear nor my arrow wound him?" he wondered. "What is the jinn that protects Soumaoro? What is the mystery of his power?"

He dismounted from his horse and picked up a piece of the earth which Soumaoro's horse had trampled on. Complete darkness had already fallen, the village of Neguéboria was not far away and the Djallonkés came out in a crowd to greet Sundiata and his men. The fires were already lit in the camp and the soldiers were beginning to prepare a meal, but what was their joy when they saw a long procession of girls from Neguéboria carrying on their heads enormous gourds of rice. All the sofas [warriors] took up the girls' song in chorus. The chief of the village and its notables followed behind. Djata came down from the hill and received the Djallonké chief of Neguéboria, who was a vassal of Tabon Wana. For the sofas the day had been a victory because Soumaoro had fled, so the drums of war became drums of joy and Djata let his men celebrate what they called a victory. He stayed in his tent. In the life of every man there comes a moment when doubt settles in and the man questions himself on his own destiny, but on this evening it was not yet doubt which assailed Djata, for he was thinking rather of what powers he could employ to injure Sosso-Soumaoro.

Sundiata's Half-Sister Questions Her Husband Soumaoro Directly About the Source of His Powers

"Tell me, oh you whom kings mention with trembling, tell me Soumaoro, are you a man like others or are you the same as the jinn who protects humans? No one can bear the glare of your eyes, your arm has the strength of ten arms. Tell me, king of kings, tell me what jinn protects you so that I can worship him also." These words filled him with pride and he himself boasted to me of the might of his Tana•. That very night he took me into his magic chamber and told me all.

• **Tana**   the taboo he observed to keep his powers

The Loss of Soumaoro's Powers

Sogolon's son looked for Soumaoro and caught sight of him in the middle of the fray. Sundiata struck out right and left and the Sossos scrambled out of his way. The king of Sosso, who did not want Sundiata to get near him, retreated far behind his men, but Sundiata followed him with his eyes. He stopped and bent his bow. The arrow flew and grazed Soumaoro on the shoulder. The cock's spur no more than scratched him, but the effect was immediate and Soumaoro felt his powers leave him. His eyes met Sundiata's. Now trembling like a man in the grip of a fever, the vanquished Soumaoro looked up towards the sun. A great black bird flew over above the fray and he understood. It was a bird of misfortune.

QUESTIONS FOR ANALYSIS

▶ Where does Sundiata's power come from?

▶ What about Soumaoro's?

▶ Does this epic provide evidence about the religious beliefs of the storyteller? Of the audience?

▶ What evidence does the epic contain of Islamic beliefs?

• trans-Saharan caravan trade network A network of overland trade linking sub-Saharan Africa with the Mediterranean. Starting around 500 C.E., camel caravans brought slaves and gold from the south and traded them for cloth, pottery, and glass trinkets from the north.

account provides our best source about the **trans-Saharan caravan trade network** connecting Mali with northern Africa. Traveling in caravans on well-established trade routes, Ibn Battuta witnessed the highly developed commercial network that traversed the sharply different geographic zones of the Sahara Desert, the Sahel, the grasslands, and the more heavily populated forests of Central Africa.

Those like Ibn Battuta who crossed the desert usually bought camels and provisions at towns like Sijilmasa, whose rise al-Bakri described (see above). After twenty-five days in the desert, Ibn Battuta's exhausted caravan arrived in Taghaza, one of the major salt-producing centers on the southern edge of the Sahara. "It is a village with no attractions," remarks Ibn Battuta, who describes only dwellings and a mosque with walls of salt blocks and roofs of camel skins. Salt structures were long-lasting because there was less than 8 inches (200 mm) of rain each year. The slaves who mined the salt lived on a monotonous diet of camel meat, dates from North Africa, and millet from Mali, so even they were enmeshed in a trading economy.

Salt is an essential nutrient for all human beings, and it is even more important in hot areas because it allows the body to replenish nutrients lost by sweating. Pure salt was so valuable that it was used as a currency. "The Blacks," Ibn Battuta remarks, "trade with salt as others trade with gold and silver; they cut it in pieces and buy and sell with these." As Ibn Battuta made his way south of the Sahara, he learned that travelers did not have to carry either food or silver coins because they could trade small amounts of salt, small glass trinkets, or spices for whatever food and lodging they required.

At the end of his stay, Ibn Battuta visited Timbuktu (tim-buk-TOO), a great trading city on the Niger River, whose ruler gave him a young male slave, a typical gift for an honored guest. The slave traders of Mali did not enslave their own countrymen; they captured slaves in the forest belt to the south. When Ibn Battuta returned to Morocco, he traveled with a caravan carrying six hundred female slaves. This figure is one of the few reliable statistics available to historians trying to measure the volume of the slave trade across the Sahara. Ibn Battuta's observation, combined with a handful of other sources, has led one historian to estimate that 5,500 slaves crossed the desert each year between 1100 and 1400.[9]

Ibn Battuta's caravan was indeed typical: more women than men crossed the Sahara because more buyers wanted female slaves than male slaves. Once sold in the markets of Morocco, women slaves would work as servants and concubines for urban dwellers, or perhaps for the royal court. Since slave owners feared that male slaves might impregnate the female members of the household, they preferred castrated males.

At the time of Ibn Battuta's visit, Mali had two major exports: slaves and gold. One historian has estimated that, in the thirteenth and fourteenth centuries, two-thirds of all the gold entering Europe passed through the North African cities of Tunis, Fez, and Cairo.[10] The gold originated in the mines of Bambuk (bam-BOOK) and Bure (boo-RAY) in Mali. Working conditions in the gold mines were grim: shafts could be over 60 feet (20 m) deep and frequently collapsed. Men dug out the ore while women extracted the gold. Since individual veins were not that rich, both tasks were laborious, but the mining allowed subsistence farmers to augment their incomes.

Society in Mali

Ibn Battuta visited Mali because it was on an established caravan route and he was confident that he would be received there as he was throughout the Islamic world. The first ruler of Mali to convert to Islam did so around 1000, but his subjects, according to the geographer al-Bakri, did not (see the "Movement of Ideas" feature in Chapter 9). By the time of Ibn Battuta's visit, Mali had become a Muslim kingdom, but people in Mali did not behave as Ibn Battuta felt observant Muslims should. Although he wrote as though there was a single standard of behavior that prevailed throughout the Islamic world, there was not. Within the structure of Islam, no supreme authority existed that could establish such a standard, which explains why Islamic religious and cultural practices were (and are) so diverse.

On his arrival in Mali, Ibn Battuta commented how unusual the kingdom was:

> No one takes his name from his father, but from his maternal uncle. Sons do not inherit, only sister's sons! This is something I have seen nowhere in the world except among the infidel Indians of al-Mulaibar [Malabar, on the east coast of India].

In short, Mali society was matrilineal, with descent determined by the mother, not the father. Royal women had much more power than their North African counterparts, but the rulers were male.

Ibn Battuta did not mince words when what he saw in Mali fell short of his expectations. He disdainfully described the social practices of the provincial town of Walata, where women were not secluded. On one occasion he visited his caravan leader and his wife, who were hosting a male friend of the wife. Indignantly, Ibn Battuta inquired: "Are you happy about this, you who have lived in our country and know the content of the religious law?" His host defended himself, explaining that the local women "are not like the women of your country," but Ibn Battuta refused to return to his host's house.

Ibn Battuta concluded his discussion of Mali with an "account of what I found good," namely, its secure roads, its high attendance at Friday services, and, most of all, the "great attention to memorizing the Holy Quran." He was deeply impressed by the example of several different children who had been placed in shackles because they had failed to memorize assigned passages from the Quran.

The kings of Mali continued to govern after Ibn Battuta's departure in 1353, but they faced rival armies as cavalry warfare became more common around 1400. To fight these battles, they had to import large horses from the north because horses bred locally often died from sleeping sickness and other parasitic diseases. They also bought saddles, iron stirrups, and bits to control their mounts. By 1400, they had added helmets and chain mail armor to their equipment. The kings lost control of several major cities, such as Timbuktu in 1433, and around 1450 Songhai (SONG-high), a neighboring kingdom that similarly profited by controlling the trans-Saharan trade, conquered Mali and brought Sundiata's dynasty to an end.

■ **Mali Horseman**   This terracotta figurine of a mounted warrior dates to around 1200 C.E., the time of Sundiata's reign. Local rulers began to import horses from North Africa around 1000 C.E., but initially only the most important leaders, like the imposing man shown here, rode on horses. By 1400, the kings of the Mali regularly led armies of mounted warriors into battle.   (Photo © Heini Schneebeli/Bridgeman Art Library)

Islamic North Africa and the Mamluk Empire

By the time of Ibn Battuta's travels, North Africa had split into three separate sultanates, each ruled by a sultan. Each year these kingdoms sent thousands of pilgrims, like Ibn Battuta, to Cairo, where they joined pilgrims coming from North and West Africa to form even larger caravans for the final trip to Mecca. Cairo had become the cultural capital of the Islamic world in 1261, when the rulers of the **Mamluk empire** announced the re-establishment of the caliphate after the fall of Baghdad in 1258 to the Mongols (see Chapter 9). Ibn Battuta traveled through Mamluk territory in Egypt, Syria, and Arabia and personally experienced the ravages of the plague, which struck Eurasia for the first time since the eighth-century outbreaks in Constantinople (see Chapter 10).

• **Mamluk empire** (1250–1517). Dynasty founded by mamluk military slaves in Cairo that ruled Egypt, Syria, and the Arabian peninsula. In 1261, following the Mongol destruction of the caliphate of Baghdad, the Mamluk empire re-established the caliphate in Cairo.

The Sultanates of North Africa

Three months after his departure from Tangier in 1325, Ibn Battuta arrived at the trading port of Tunis, the capital of one of the three sultanates in North Africa, with a population near 100,000. Located on a point sticking out into the Mediterranean, it was ideally situated as a port for trade across the Strait of Gibraltar to southern Europe. European merchants traded fine textiles, weapons, and wine for animal hides and cloth from North Africa as well as gold and slaves transshipped from the interior.

In almost all the North African states, a sultan headed the government. In exchange for taxes paid by the inhabitants (Muslims paid a lower rate than non-Muslims), the government provided military and police protection. In addition, the sultan appointed a *qadi,* or chief jurist, who was assisted by subordinate jurists in settling disputes in court. Anyone who had studied law at Islamic schools was eligible to be appointed a qadi. These courts implemented Islamic law, called **sharia** (sha-REE-ah), which consisted of all the rules that Muslims were supposed to follow; legal authorities compiled these rules on the basis of the Quran, the hadith, and earlier legal decisions. Interpretation of certain points varied among the jurists belonging to different legal schools. Ibn Battuta had studied the legal interpretations of the Maliki school, one of the four major Sunni schools that interpreted the sharia.

• **sharia** Islamic law: all the rules that Muslims were supposed to follow, compiled on the basis of the Quran, the hadith, and earlier legal decisions.

The chief jurist in Tunis, Ibn Battuta informs us, heard disputes every Friday after prayers in the mosque: "people came to ask him to give a decision on various questions. When he had stated his opinion on forty questions he ended that session." The qadi's decision, called a *fatwa,* had the force of law and was enforced by the sultan's government.

Although Ibn Battuta had come to Tunis as an individual pilgrim, he left the city as the qadi for a caravan of Berber pilgrims going on the hajj. The caravan functioned like a small, mobile sultanate, with the caravan leader making all the important decisions about the route and Ibn Battuta serving as the traveling qadi. His new salary made it possible for him to marry the daughter of a fellow pilgrim, but the marriage did not last. "I became involved in a dispute with my father-in-law which made it necessary for me to separate from his daughter," Ibn Battuta comments without explaining further.

According to Islamic law, when a man and a woman married, they drew up a contract specifying the terms of the marriage and the property arrangements should they divorce. While a man could divorce his wife simply by saying "I divorce thee" three times, a woman had to demonstrate genuine maltreatment. Both husband and wife could remarry after divorce.

The Mamluk Empire, 1250–1517

Sometime in the spring of 1326, not quite a year after his departure from Tangier, Ibn Battuta arrived in the port city of Alexandria and went immediately to see the city's most famous tourist attraction: the lighthouse overlooking the Mediterranean. Alexandria marked the westernmost point of the Mamluk empire, which ruled all the way to Damascus.

The word **mamluk** originally referred to a type of non-Muslim slave used by Islamic states as warriors. In the ninth and tenth centuries, Islamic rulers in Afghanistan, North Africa, Spain, and Egypt, unable to recruit and train an efficient army from among their own populace, purchased large numbers of Turks from Central Asia to staff their armies. The number of slaves swelled in succeeding centuries.

Bought as children, the young mamluks studied Islam in preparation for their mandatory conversion. Living in isolation from the rest of the population, they continued to speak their own Turkic dialects and often could not read Arabic. They did no manual labor and could rise to high military rank. Once a mamluk soldier converted to Islam, he was freed, and his children would be born Muslim. This made his children ineligible for service as mamluks, a powerful check on the ability of any commander to develop his own power base.

Many of these mamluk slaves rose to high positions in the Ayyubid dynasty (1171–1250) founded by Saladin (which Ibn Jubayr visited in 1183–1185; see Chapter 9). Taking advantage of their growing power, the mamluk slave soldiers staged a coup in 1250 and founded the Mamluk dynasty. Only ten years later, Mamluk generals masterminded one of the greatest military victories in premodern times; in 1260, 120,000 Mamluk troops defeated 10,000 Mongol archers in 1260 at the battle of Ayn Jalut, north of Jerusalem in modern Israel (see Chapter 14). Hailing from the Central Asian grasslands and intimately familiar with horses, many Mamluk soldiers were skilled in the same fighting techniques used by the Mongols. The Mamluk forces were one of the few armies in the world to defeat the Mongols in direct combat.

Cairo, Baghad's Successor as the Cultural Capital of the Islamic World

Although the Mamluks were neither originally Muslim nor native speakers of Arabic, they positioned themselves as the protectors of the Islamic world. In 1261, they announced the re-establishment of the caliphate in Cairo, three years after its destruction by the Mongols in 1258 (see Chapter 9). Thousands of refugees, particularly Islamic teachers, poured into Cairo, where they taught in the city's many colleges, called *madrasas* in Arabic. The high number of Islamic schools, many located in mosques, impressed Ibn Battuta.

The thirteenth and fourteenth centuries saw the rise throughout the Islamic world of a new type of Islamic mystic, or **Sufi,** who taught that the individual could experience God directly without the intercession of others. Followers of individual Sufis also believed that their teachers had *baraka,* or divine grace, and could help others gain direct access to God. When alive, these Sufi teachers usually formed their own lodges where they taught groups of disciples and hosted visitors. When they died, their tombs became pilgrimage sites because their devotees believed that they retained their occupant's *baraka.*

• **mamluk** Non-Muslim slaves purchased by Islamic states in Afghanistan, North Africa, Spain, and Egypt as warriors to staff their armies. Mamluks were forced to convert to Islam.

• **Sufi** Islamic mystic who taught that the individual could experience God directly without the intercession of others. Followers of individual Sufis believed their teachers had *baraka,* or divine grace, and could help others gain direct access to God.

Ibn Battuta stayed three days with a Sufi teacher named Burhan al-Din the Lame, whom he described as "learned, self-denying, pious and humble." Burhan al-Din urged Ibn Battuta to visit three teachers in India, Pakistan, and China. His advice is certain evidence of a Sufi network stretching all the way from Egypt to China, and Ibn Battuta eventually met all three men.

With a population between 500,000 and 600,000, Cairo was larger than most contemporary cities; only a few Chinese cities outranked it.[11] The city's population fell into distinct social groups. At the top were the Mamluk rulers, military commanders, and officials who kept records and supervised the tax system. Independent of the military were the Islamic notables, or *ulema,* who included religious teachers, scholars, preachers, and judges in the Islamic court system. Merchants, traders, and brokers formed a third influential group, who were often as wealthy and as respected as members of the Mamluk ruling class.

Below the military, religious, and mercantile elites were those who worked at respectable occupations: tradesmen, shopkeepers, and craftsmen. Farmers worked agricultural plots located in the center of Cairo and the outlying suburbs. At the bottom of society were the people whose occupations violated Islamic teachings, such as usurers (who lent money for interest) and slave dealers. Cairo residents looked down on their neighbors who sold wine or performed sex for a fee, and they shunned those whose occupations brought them into contact with human corpses or dead animals.

Eyewitness to the 1348 Outbreak of Plague in Damascus

The sultan of the Mamluk empire provided camels, food, and water for the poorer hajj travelers and guaranteed the safety of the pilgrims who gathered in Cairo before they journeyed together to Mecca. The number of pilgrims to Mecca in any given year varied enormously, depending on weather conditions and political uncertainty, but Ibn Battuta was probably traveling in the company of some ten thousand pilgrims. On his first pilgrimage (he arrived in Cairo in 1326), he hoped to journey to Mecca by boat, which was the most direct route from Cairo, but the closing of the sea route forced him to retrace his steps to Cairo, where he joined a group of pilgrims going overland to Damascus, a detour hundreds of miles out of his way. Damascus was the second-largest city in the Mamluk empire and a great cultural center in its own right, having been the capital of the Umayyads in the seventh century.

In Damascus, Ibn Battuta's route converged with Ibn Jubayr's, and his account borrowed, often without acknowledgment, as much as one-seventh of Ibn Jubayr's twelfth-century narrative.[12] From Damascus, Ibn Battuta proceeded to Mecca. After some time there (scholars are not certain how long), he decided to continue east on his journey.

Some twenty years later, Ibn Battuta again passed through Damascus on his journey home. This time he was unwittingly traveling with the rats that transmitted one of the most destructive diseases to strike humankind: the plague. Historians reserve the term *Black Death* for the outbreak in the mid-1300s. Because Europe, the Middle East, and North Africa had experienced no major outbreaks of plague since the eighth century (see Chapter 10), the effects of the Black Death were immediate and devastating.

The first new outbreak in western Europe occurred in 1346 in the Black Sea port of Kaffa. From there the dread disease traveled to Italy and Egypt (see Map 13.2). In May or June 1348, Ibn Battuta first heard of the plague in Ghazza, Syria, where "the number of dead there exceeded a thousand a day." He returned to Damascus, where the city's residents stayed up all night praying at the Great Mosque, and then joined a barefoot march in hopes of lowering the death toll: "The entire population of the city joined in the exodus, male and female, small and large; the Jews went out with their book of the Law and the Christians with their Gospel, their women and children with them; the whole concourse of them in tears and humble supplications, imploring the favour of God through His Books and His Prophets." Damascus lost two thousand people "in a single day," yet Ibn Battuta managed to stay well.

Modern historians estimate that the plague wiped out 33 to 40 percent of the population in Egypt and Syria alone.[13] By the beginning of 1349, daily losses began to diminish, but it would take two to three hundred years for the populations of Egypt and Syria to return to their pre-plague levels.

East Africa, India, and the Trade Networks of the Indian Ocean

The Indian Ocean touched three different regions, each with its own languages and political units: the East African coast, the southern edge of the Arabian peninsula, and the west coast of India. Much as the rulers of the trading posts on the Sahara survived by taxing overland trade, the sultans of the **Indian Ocean trade network**—the city-states and larger political units encircling the Indian Ocean—taxed the maritime trade. Some sultanates consisted of only a single port city like Kilwa in modern Tanzania, while others, like the Delhi sultanate, controlled as much Indian territory as the Mauryan and Gupta dynasties of the past (see Chapters 3 and 8). Although politically decentralized, the Indian Ocean was bound together by frequent boat crossings to its different ports. Merchants who had grown up along the African coast had operations in Arabia or India, and much intermarriage among the residents of different coasts took place, contributing to a genuine mixing of cultures along the coastlines of the Indian Ocean. Interior regions supplied goods to the coastal cities, but because so few outsiders visited them, we know much less about them.

> **Indian Ocean trade network** Network that connected the ports around the Indian Ocean in East Africa, Arabia, and western India. Dhows traveled from port to port along the coast carrying goods.

The East African Coast

In January 1329, after leaving Mecca, Ibn Battuta traveled south to the port of Aden, on the Arabian peninsula, and sailed to East Africa, most likely in a **dhow** (DOW). Among the earliest and most seaworthy vessels ever made, dhows served as the camels of the Indian Ocean trade. Boatmakers made dhows by sewing teak or coconut planks together with a cord and constructing a single triangular sail. Because dhows had no deck, passengers sat and slept next to the ship's cargo. Traders frequently piloted their dhows along the coastline of East Africa, the Arabian peninsula, and India's west coast. Their expenses were low: dhows required no fuel and traders and their family members could staff their own boats.

> **dhow** Among the earliest and most seaworthy vessels and the main vessel used by Indian Ocean traders. Was made from teak or coconut planks sewn together with a cord; had a single triangular sail and no deck.

Everywhere Ibn Battuta traveled, he saw Indian, Persian, and Arabian ships and merchants. After leaving Aden, he sailed for fifteen days before he reached the port city of Mogadishu, Somalia, which exported woven cotton textiles to Egypt and other destinations. Mogadishu's political structure resembled that of other East African ports: headed by a sultan, the government maintained an army and administered justice through a network of qadi justices.

The sultan spoke his native Somali in addition to a little Arabic. The farther Ibn Battuta traveled from the Islamic heartland, the fewer people he would find who knew Arabic. Still, he could always be confident of finding an Arabic speaker, and the Mogadishu sultan's chief legal adviser turned out to be an Egyptian.

Because Ibn Battuta's stay in Mogadishu was brief, he did not go inland, where he would have seen villages growing the strange, colorful foodstuffs he ate, fewer people of Arabian descent, and more non-Islamic religious practices. After a short stop in Mombasa, Ibn Battuta proceeded to Kilwa, a small island off the coast of modern Tanzania (modern Kilwa Kivinye, 140 miles south of Dar es Salaam); there he saw "a large city on the seacoast, most of whose inhabitants are Zinj, jet-black in colour. They have tattoo marks on their faces." Ibn Battuta used the word *zinj*, meaning black, to refer to the indigenous peoples of East Africa. The people he encountered may have already begun to speak the creole mixture that later came to be called Swahili (swah-HEE-lee), a Bantu language that incorporated many vocabulary words from Arabic. (*Swahili* means "of the coast" in Arabic.)

Ibn Battuta arrived at Kilwa during a period of prosperity: a newly established dynasty had taken control of Sofala, a small port near the Zambezi River, which was a major entrepôt (trading center) for gold coming from the interior. Archaeological excavations have revealed that the city had a mosque and a palace built of stone, and its inhabitants lived in stone houses with indoor toilets, ate in kitchens equipped with Chinese porcelains, and wore imported silks and gold and silver ornaments.

We know more about the history of Kilwa than about many other East African ports because of the survival of *The Chronicle of the Kings of Kilwa* in both Portuguese and Arabic versions. This work gives the name of individual rulers but not their dates. By matching the names of rulers in *The Chronicle* with Ibn Battuta's detailed account, historians have concluded that the Kilwa dynasty began in the

■ **The Dhows of the Indian Ocean**
Unlike most other boats, the dhows of the Indian Ocean were sewn and not nailed together. Boatmakers sewed planks of teak or coconut trees together with a cord and added a single sail. This boat design was so practical that it is still in use today. (Hauke Dressler/LOOK Die Bildagentur der Fotografen GmbH/Alamy Images)

1200s. The kings of Kilwa were descended from Arabic-speaking settlers who came to the region from Yemen, further evidence of the ties linking the different societies on the Indian Ocean.

The sultan of Kilwa was a generous man, Ibn Battuta reports, who regularly gave gifts of slaves and ivory from elephant tusks, which he obtained in the interior: "He used to engage frequently in expeditions to the land of the Zinj people, raiding them and taking booty." Slaves and ivory, and less often gold, were Kilwa's main exports. Like the other East African ports, Kilwa imported high-fired ceramics from China, glass from Persia, and textiles from China and India.

Great Zimbabwe and Its Satellites, ca. 1275–1550

Although the interior of southern Africa supplied the Kilwa sultan with slaves and ivory, we know much less about it because Ibn Battuta and other travelers never described the region. There, on the high plateau between the Zambezi and Limpopo Rivers, stood a state that reached its greatest extent in the early 1300s. Its center was the imposing archaeological site of **Great Zimbabwe** (see Map 11.1).

Like other speakers of Bantu languages in sub-Saharan Africa, the people living on the Zimbabwe plateau cultivated sorghum with iron tools. Before 1000 C.E., most lived in small villages in houses made from wood beams held together by plaster. Even at this early date they traded ivory, animal skins, and gold.

Sometime around 1000 C.E., some villagers became wealthy enough to build stone enclosures for themselves. By the thirteenth and fourteenth centuries, the population had reached 10,000[14] and they built three hundred smaller stone enclosures over a large area on the plateau. The word for these enclosures in the local Shona language is *zimbabwe,* which means "venerated houses." Archaeologists use this name for the people who built the enclosures, and it is also the name of the modern nation of Zimbabwe where they are located.

The Elliptical Building is the largest single stone structure in sub-Saharan Africa built before 1500. One estimate holds that four hundred laborers could have built the wall of this building during the slack period of the agricultural season over the course of four years.[15] Because the walls of Great Zimbabwe do not resemble any Islamic buildings along the coast, including those at nearby Kilwa, all analysts concur that Great Zimbabwe was built by the local people, not by the Arabic-speaking peoples of the coast.

Since the people who lived there did not keep written records, archaeological finds provide our only information about local religion. Nothing indicates Islamic beliefs. On the northern edge of the site, the Eastern Enclosure held six stylized birds carved from soapstone, which may depict ancestors or deities. The Zimbabwe people also made and probably worshiped phalluses and female torsos with breasts in the hope of increasing the number of children. (See the feature "Visual Evidence: The Ruins of Great Zimbabwe.")

When excavated, the site contained a single hoard that one archaeologist has called "a cache of the most extraordinary variegated and abundant indigenous and imported objects ever discovered at Great Zimbabwe or, indeed, anywhere else in the interior of south-central Africa." Pieces of broken, imported, Chinese green high-fired celadon ceramic pots and colorful Persian earthenware plates with script on them make it possible to date the site's occupation to the thirteenth and fourteenth centuries. The presence of a single coin at the site, embossed with the name of the king Ibn Battuta met at Kilwa, reveals that the site's residents traded with the coastal towns and were part of existing trade networks.

● **Great Zimbabwe** Large city in Zimbabwe surrounded by smaller outlying settlements, all distinguished by stone enclosures called "zimbabwe" in the local Shona language. The location of the largest stone structure built in sub-Saharan Africa before 1500.

THE RUINS OF GREAT ZIMBABWE

Located near Masvingo, Zimbabwe, the Great Zimbabwe site contains several large ruins and many smaller stone structures whose original purpose is undocumented and therefore still not well understood. The ruins, covering almost 1,800 acres (7.2 sq km), fall into three groups: the Hill Complex, the Valley Complex, and the Great Enclosure. The site was first settled before 1000, when the first stone structures were built, and continued to grow through the 1300s. Little evidence of cereal agriculture survives, indicating that the city's population depended largely on cattle for their food supply.

Like other Bantu peoples, the Zimbabwe people living at the site knew how to work iron. Archaeolo-

The Hill Complex, a group of stone buildings forming a ritual space, stood above a granite cliff 330 feet (100 m) long and 100 feet (30 m) high on the northern edge of the site.

Area of detail

(© Georg Gerster/Photo Researchers, Inc.)

QUESTIONS FOR ANALYSIS

What methods have archaeologists used to analyze the function of the stone buildings at Great Zimbabwe? Whose analysis do you find more convincing?

gists have found nodules of iron ore from mines and alluvial gold collected from riverbeds. The site also contained a workshop where metal-smiths heated copper ingots in crucibles to make wire.

The Great Enclosure holds two large structures: the Elliptical Building and the solid Conical Tower inside it. The outer wall of the Elliptical Building is made of evenly cut granite blocks, fitted together without mortar, that are elegantly trimmed with an intricate (V-shaped) design on the top. What was the purpose of these two buildings? Two analysts, Peter S. Garlake and Thomas N. Huffman, have taken radically different approaches to the problem.

Garlake bases his analysis on close examination of the construction techniques used to make the different types of walls and the location of different artifacts. The sheer size of the Elliptical Building suggests to him that it was the palace of the ruler. Its walls, he contends, stood too high to be mere guard walls:

they made a statement about the ruler's power to all his subjects.

Huffman, in contrast, examines the settlements of the Shona-speaking peoples who live near the site today. Since many of their houses are divided into areas for men to work and women to work, he wonders whether this might not be true of Great Zimbabwe as well. The one hundred smaller soapstone carvings of phalluses and female torsos with breasts found in the Elliptical Building resemble some figurines used in modern schools to teach adolescent girls about family life. The high walls of the Elliptical Building, Huffman believes, kept outsiders from observing the activities at a girls' initiation school.

Sources: P. S. Garlake, *Great Zimbabwe* (New York: Stein and Day, 1973); Thomas N. Huffman, "Where You Are the Girls Gather to Play: The Great Enclosure at Great Zimbabwe," in *Frontiers: Southern African Archaeology Today*, ed. M. Hall et al., *Cambridge Monographs in African Archaeology* 10 (Oxford: B. A. R., 1984), pp. 252–265.

The Eastern Enclosure contained six stone bird statues, suggesting that it was a ritual center.

Detail

In the Valley Complex, Enclosure 12 contained the largest hoard found on the site: over 220 pounds (100 kg) of iron hoes, 44 pounds (20 kg) of iron for wire, warthog and elephant tusks, thousands of Indian beads, and broken ceramic vessels from China and Iran.

With three entrances, the Great Enclosure contains the Elliptical Building, the Conical Tower, and mud and thatch huts where individual families lived.

The Conical Tower—possibly a symbolic granary—is a completely solid stone structure with an outer wall over 30 feet (9 m) high.

The Elliptical Building has an outer wall that runs 800 feet (250 m) long and contains 182,000 cubic feet (5,150 cubic m) of stone.

Kilwa was most prosperous at exactly the same time that Great Zimbabwe was—in the thirteenth and fourteenth centuries when Ibn Battuta visited the city. When the Portuguese arrived on the East African coast after 1500, both Kilwa and the Great Zimbabwe site had already declined dramatically from their earlier, glorious days, but we do not know why.

The Delhi Sultanate and the Hindu Kingdoms of Southern India

When Ibn Battuta sailed away from Kilwa, he embarked on a fifteen-year-long journey along the trade routes linking Africa with India and China. He traveled first to Constantinople and to Central Asia, where he learned that the Muslim ruler of India, Muhammad Tughluq (r. 1324–1351), had defeated his rivals to become the ruler of the **Delhi sultanate** (1206–1526), a powerful sultanate that ruled from their capital at Delhi.

The Delhi sultanate, like the Mamluk empire of Egypt and Syria, was founded by former mamluk slaves. It was not the first Islamic dynasty in South Asia. In the eighth century, conquering caliphate armies had established Islamic states in the Sind region of modern Pakistan. In the 1200s, when a group of mamluks based in today's Afghanistan conquered large sections of northern India, they considerably expanded the extent of territory under Muslim control. These Afghans established their capital in Delhi, which remained the capital of many later northern Indian dynasties and is India's capital today.

Ibn Battuta's patron Muhammad Tughluq, the son of a Turkish slave and an Indian woman, was a powerful leader. His armies, fueled by a desire for plunder, succeeding in conquering almost all of India, including south India. To be closer to the lands he had conquered, in 1326, he ordered his officials to move the capital 400 miles (650 km) south. This measure had disastrous consequences, including the loss of much territory by his enraged subordinates.

● **Delhi sultanate** (1206–1526). Islamic state led by former mamluk slaves originally from Afghanistan, who governed north India from their capital at Delhi. At their height, in the early 1300s, they controlled nearly all of the Indian subcontinent.

🔳 **The Earliest Islamic Building in Delhi, India**   In 1311, the ruler of the Delhi sultanate planned to build an enormous mosque with four gates, but construction stopped after only the southern gate, the Alai Darwaza shown here, was completed. The Indian architects who built the gate had little familiarity with the classic Islamic elements of arches and domed roofs, so they used extremely thick walls (10.5 feet, or 3.2 m, deep) to support a very shallow dome. (Alai Darwaza/DK Images)

In yet another departure from the practices of earlier rulers, Muhammad Tughluq decided to hire only foreigners to administer his empire. He named Ibn Battuta to be the highest qadi jurist in Delhi, a very high-ranking position, even though Ibn Battuta did not speak Persian, the language of the government, and had studied the writings of a different legal school from that of the Delhi sultanate. In fact, Ibn Battuta kept so busy attending court ceremonials and hunting expeditions that he heard no legal cases.

Throughout this reign, south India remained largely Hindu. After Muhammad Tughluq's government withdrew from the failed new capital, Hindu rulers gained control of urban centers in the south and established temple-centered kingdoms like that of the earlier Cholas (see Chapter 8). The most important Hindu empire was based at **Vijayanagar** (vihj-eye-NUH-gah), which means "city of victory" in Sanskrit, in the modern Indian state of Karnataka. The Vijayanagar rulers (ca. 1336–1614) patronized Sanskrit learning and Hindu temples while creating a powerful army that enabled them to rule for more than two centuries.

● **Vijayanagar** (ca. 1336–1614) "City of victory" in Sanskrit. Important Hindu empire based in the modern Indian state of Karnataka. Vijayanagar rulers created a powerful army that enabled them to rule in central India for more than two centuries.

Ibn Battuta remained in Delhi for seven years before the sultan named him his emissary to China. When he departed in August 1341, he was traveling with fifteen Chinese envoys, over two hundred slaves, one hundred horses, and various lavish gifts of textiles, dishes, and weapons—all intended for the Mongol rulers of China. His party traveled overland until they reached the Indian Ocean port of Cambay, where they boarded ships.

As Ibn Battuta made his way down the west coast of India, he visited towns that resembled the ports on the African side of the Indian Ocean. A sultan governed each port, where qadis administered justice, and each town had a bazaar and a mosque. Ibn Battuta arrived in Calicut at the head of a large embassy carrying Muhammad Tughluq's gifts for the ruler of China and accompanied by several concubines, one pregnant with his child. At the time of his visit, thirteen Chinese-built vessels were in the port waiting for the winds to shift so they could return to China. "On the sea of China," Ibn Battuta comments, "traveling is done in Chinese ships only."

The Chinese ships docked at Calicut differed markedly from dhows. Unlike dhows, the Chinese-built ships had wooden decks and multiple levels with compartments with doors. Some had up to twelve sails, made of "bamboo rods plaited like mats." These enormous ships, over 100 feet (30 m) long, carried six hundred sailors and four hundred armed men; Ibn Battuta took their massive size as an indication of China's prosperity: "There is no people in the world wealthier than the Chinese."

Ibn Battuta much preferred the Chinese-built ships with their private cabins to dhows, which had no deck and no cabins. On the day he sailed, he discovered that the best staterooms, those with lavatories, were taken by Chinese merchants. He indignantly changed to a smaller vessel, where he could have a room big enough for him to stay with his female companions, "for it is my habit," he said, "never to travel without them." Since it was a Friday, Ibn Battuta went to the mosque for prayers and arranged for his luggage to be transferred to the smaller boat, leaving his traveling companions on the larger vessel.

A violent storm broke that night, and the captains of the two ships removed their vessels from the shallow harbor to the safety of the sea. The smaller boat survived, but the big ship was totally destroyed. Ibn Battuta stood horror-struck on the beach, watching corpses whose faces he recognized float to the top of the water. Having utterly failed to protect the envoys he accompanied, Ibn Battuta fled. Eight years more in India, the Maldive Islands, and China passed before he returned home to Morocco.

Chapter Review

KEY TERMS

Ibn Battuta (300)

Bantu (304)

oral histories (306)

lineage (307)

Mali (307)

griot/griotte (309)

sultan (309)

trans-Saharan
    caravan trade
    network (314)

Mamluk empire (316)

sharia (316)

mamluk (317)

Sufi (317)

Indian Ocean trade
    network (319)

dhow (319)

Great Zimbabwe (321)

Delhi sultanate (324)

Vijayanagar (325)

Download the MP3 audio file of the Chapter Review and listen to it on the go.

As Ibn Battuta discovered, many roads led to Mecca. His travels along existing trade routes brought him to much of the Islamic world of the 1300s: overland across the Sahara to Mali, to the ports of northern and eastern Africa, around the Indian Ocean, and to China. He encountered Islamic practices everywhere he went: rulers and the well-off received him generously; students learned to recite the Quran in Arabic; Friday prayers were conducted in mosques; and he could always find companions, often hajj pilgrims or merchants, to accompany him on another leg of his journey. Yet some places, like southern Africa, remained beyond his reach even though they, too, were embedded in the expanding trade networks of Africa and India. The arrival of the Europeans after 1500 did not mark a break with the past but simply extended further the well-developed trade routes already linking the interior of Africa with its coastal ports on the Mediterranean and the Indian Ocean.

How was sub-Saharan Africa settled before 1000 C.E.? What techniques have historians used to reconstruct the past?

Historians have combined oral histories, glottochronology, and archaeological analysis to reconstruct the different phases of the Bantu migrations before 1000 C.E. Most people in sub-Saharan Africa lived in villages, which varied in size and were usually ruled by great men who had demonstrated military prowess and had large families. Sometime around 500 B.C.E., some sub-Saharan peoples planted their first crops. Over the centuries, as they refined their techniques of cultivation, they learned how to make tools and weapons from smelted iron. Iron technology spread throughout sub-Saharan Africa by 300 C.E. The Bantu languages spread in multiple waves until 1000 C.E., when they blanketed much, but not all, of sub-Saharan Africa.

What role did trade play in the emergence and subsequent history of the kingdoms of Ghana and Mali?

The kingdoms of Ghana and Mali both arose at important nodes on trade networks linking the Mediterranean with the Sahel. The Islamic historian al-Bakri described how Sijilmasa began as a periodic market and then became a year-round trading center, then a town, and finally a city. Ghana and Mali followed this same pattern. Their rulers taxed trade, charging merchants for each donkey cart loaded with goods that they brought in and led out of major cities. They used these tax revenues to finance their armies; when they lost important trading cities to rival armies, tax revenues dwindled, and their kingdoms contracted.

How and why did the Mamluk empire based in Egypt become the leading center of the Islamic world after 1258?

The rulers of Cairo, the Mamluks, started as military slaves brought to Egypt from Central Asia and the Caucasus Mountains. After a coup in 1250 in which they seized power from their predecessors, they became great patrons of Islam. In 1261 they announced the establishment in Cairo of the caliphate, which had been destroyed in 1258 when the Mongols took Baghdad. The Mamluks gave large donations to many mosques, hostels, and Islamic schools.

WEB RESOURCES

Pronunciation Guide

Interactive Maps
MAP 11.1 African Trade Routes, 1200–1500

Primary Sources

Chapter Objectives

ACE Multiple-Choice Quiz

Flashcards

 What was the nature of the Indian Ocean trade network that linked India, Arabia, and East Africa?

Dhows crisscrossed the Indian Ocean, carrying African slaves, gold, textiles, and ivory; Iranian glass; Chinese porcelains; and Indian textiles and beads from one port to the other. All along the coast, different sultanates, some big, some small, survived by taxing the trade. The ports on the Indian Ocean were Islamic city-states governed by sultans and administered by qadi jurists. The merchants who spoke the different languages in this area—Swahili, Arabic, various Indian languages—intermarried with local people and created a new composite Indian Ocean culture.

For Further Reference

Childs, S. Terry, and David Killick. "Indigenous African Metallurgy: Nature and Culture." *Annual Reviews Anthropology* 1993 (22): 317–337.

Dunn, Ross. *The Adventures of Ibn Battuta: A Muslim Traveler of the 14th Century.* Berkeley: University of California Press, 2005.

Garlake, P. S. *Great Zimbabwe.* New York: Stein and Day, 1973.

Hale, Thomas A. *Griots and Griottes: Masters of Words and Music.* Bloomington: Indiana University Press, 1998.

Hall, Martin. *Farmers, Kings, and Traders: The People of Southern Africa 200–1860.* Chicago: University of Chicago Press, 1990.

Hopkins, J. F. P. *Corpus of Early Arabic Sources for West African History.* New York: Cambridge University Press, 1981.

Huffman, Thomas N. "Where You Are the Girls Gather to Play: The Great Enclosure at Great Zimbabwe." In *Frontiers: Southern African Archaeology Today,* ed. M. Hall et al. *Cambridge Monographs in African Archaeology* 10. Oxford: B. A. R., 1984, pp. 252–265.

Irwin, Robert. *The Middle East in the Middle Ages: The Early Mamluk Sultanate 1250–1382.* London: Croom Helm, 1986.

Isichei, Elizabeth. *A History of African Societies to 1870.* Cambridge: Cambridge University Press, 1997.

Lapidus, Ira M. *Muslim Cities in the Later Middle Ages.* Cambridge: Harvard University Press, 1967.

Letzvion, Nehemia, and Randall L. Pouwels, eds. *The History of Islam in Africa.* Athens: Ohio University Press, 2000.

Schoenbrun, David Lee. *A Green Place, a Good Place: Agrarian Change, Gender, and Social Identity in the Great Lakes Region to the 15th Century.* Portsmouth, N.H.: Heineman, 1998.

Vansina, J. "New Linguistic Evidence and 'The Bantu Expansion.'" *Journal of African History* 36 (1995): 173–195.

Vansina, J. *Paths in the Rainforest: Towards a History of Political Tradition in Equatorial Africa.* Madison: University of Wisconsin Press, 1990.

Websites

National Geographic: Xpeditions (http://www.nationalgeographic.com/xpeditions/lessons/10/g35/tgbattuta.html).   This website is a lesson plan on Ibn Battuta and his travels.

PBS: Africa (http://www.pbs.org/wnet/africa/.   Various resources about Africa. Teacher Tools are particularly helpful.

African Studies Center Outreach Program at Boston University (www.bu.edu/africa/outreach).   Offers some online materials, as well as a list of materials for borrowing.

CHAPTER 12

China's Commercial Revolution, ca. 900–1276

- The Five Dynasties Period and the Song Dynasty, 907–1276 (p. 331)
- The Commercial Revolution in China, 900–1300 (p. 335)
- Book Publishing and the Education Boom (p. 341)
- Religious Life During the Song (p. 345)
- Vietnam, Korea, Japan, and the World Beyond (p. 347)

In 1127, **Li Qingzhao** (LEE CHING-jow) (ca. 1084–ca. 1151) and her husband Zhao Mingcheng (JOW MING-chung) (1081–1129), a low-ranking Chinese official, abandoned their home in Shandong (SHAN-dong) province and joined half a million refugees fleeing to the south. After Zhao's death only two years later, Li recorded her memoir, which depicts the long-term economic changes of the Song (soong) dynasty (960–1276), when China's prosperity made it the world's most advanced economy, and the short-term consequences of military defeat, when the Song emperors were forced to surrender all of north China to a non-Chinese dynasty named the Jin (GIN) (1115–1234).

As she explains, Li and Zhao fled from their home in north China and traveled 500 miles (800 km) to the Yangzi River:

LI QINGZHAO

(The Collected Works of Li Qingzhao [Beijing: Zhonghua shuju, 1962], plate 3)

In 1126, the first year of the Jingkang [JEENG-kong] Reign, my husband was governing Zichuan [DZE-chwan; in Shandong province] when we heard that the Jin Tartars were moving against the capital. He was in a daze, realizing that all those full trunks and overflowing chests, which he regarded so lovingly and mournfully, would surely soon be his possessions no longer.... Since we could not take the overabundance of our possessions with us, we first gave up the bulky printed volumes, the albums of paintings, and the most cumbersome of the vessels. Thus we reduced the size of the collection several times, and still we had fifteen cartloads of books. When we reached Donghai [DONG-high; Jiangsu], it took a string of boats to ferry them all across the Huai, and again across the Yangzi River to Jiankang [JI-AHN-kong; modern Nanjing, Jiangsu].[1]

 This icon will direct you to interactive activities and study materials on the *Voyages* website: www.cengage.com/history/hansen/voyages1e

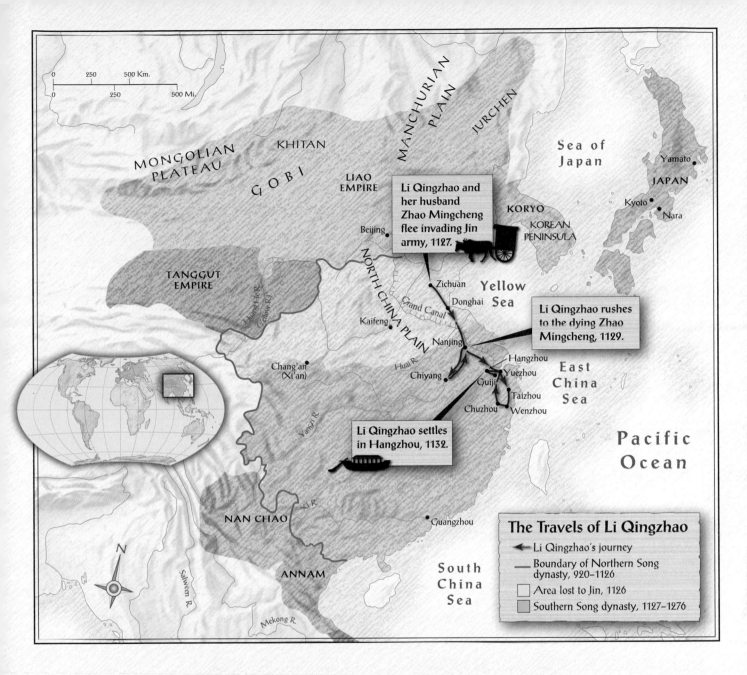

Li Qingzhao and her husband Zhao Mingcheng flee invading Jin army, 1127.

Li Qingzhao rushes to the dying Zhao Mingcheng, 1129.

Li Qingzhao settles in Hangzhou, 1132.

The Travels of Li Qingzhao

← Li Qingzhao's journey

— Boundary of Northern Song dynasty, 920–1126

□ Area lost to Jin, 1126

■ Southern Song dynasty, 1127–1276

MONGOLIAN PLATEAU

KHITAN

GOBI

MANCHURIAN PLAIN

JURCHEN

Sea of Japan

LIAO EMPIRE

KORYO

KOREAN PENINSULA

JAPAN

Yamato

Kyoto

Nara

Beijing

TANGGUT EMPIRE

Huang He R.

(Yellow R.)

NORTH CHINA PLAIN

Grand Canal

Zichuan

Donghai

Yellow Sea

Kaifeng

Nanjing

Hangzhou

Yuezhou

Guiji

Taizhou

Chuzhou

Wenzhou

East China Sea

Chang'an (Xi'an)

Huai R.

Chiyang

Yangzi R.

Pacific Ocean

NAN CHAO

+ R.

Guangzhou

ANNAM

Salween R.

Mekong R.

South China Sea

N

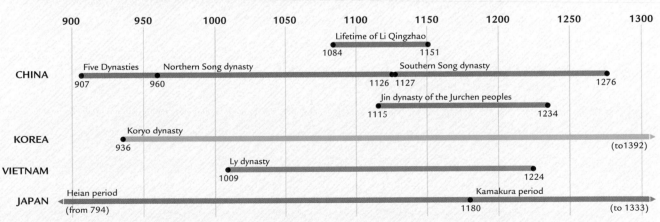

	900	950	1000	1050	1100	1150	1200	1250	1300

Lifetime of Li Qingzhao
1084 — 1151

CHINA
Five Dynasties
907
Northern Song dynasty
960
Southern Song dynasty
1126 1127
1276

Jin dynasty of the Jurchen peoples
1115 — 1234

KOREA
Koryo dynasty
936
(to 1392)

VIETNAM
Ly dynasty
1009 — 1224

JAPAN
Heian period
(from 794)
Kamakura period
1180
(to 1333)

After they reached Nanjing (NAHN-jeeng), Li explains, they were forced to abandon their last fifteen carts of books. Li was in her early 40s at the time of her flight. She and her husband Zhao had been born into the top level of Song society, and their fathers had both served as high officials. The couple went by boat to south China, where they hoped they would be safe from the invading armies.

Li Qingzhao's memoir permits a glimpse of Chinese life at a time of wrenching political chaos. Seldom has the world seen such a mass panic as when the Jin armies defeated the Northern Song dynasty. While half a million other people made the same trip south as Li Qingzhao, her account stands out. For one, a woman wrote it. Highly educated in an age when the vast majority of women could not read, Li Qingzhao was the only woman of her time to achieve lasting fame as a poet. Even though only fifty of her poems survive today, many people consider her China's greatest woman poet, and she remains some people's favorite poet, male or female.

The fall of the Northern Song intensified a long-term migration from north to south China that had started centuries before Li Qingzhao's lifetime and continued centuries after it. Starting around 750, farmers realized they could grow more food in south China than in north China. In addition, during the years following the An Lushan rebellion of 755–763 (see Chapter 8), north China suffered continuous political instability that pushed people to migrate to the south.

These long-term migrations resulted in economic growth so dramatic that this period is called China's "commercial revolution." Before the revolution, most of China's farmers grew the food they ate. Largely self-sufficient, they bought little at markets. After the revolution, farmers and craftsmen produced full-time for the market, and China's economic growth affected her neighbors in Korea, Japan, and Vietnam as well.

Focus Questions

- What political events pushed people to migrate south?
- What were the causes of the commercial revolution?
- How did the changes of the commercial revolution affect education—for men and for women—and religious life?
- How did China's economic growth influence its immediate neighbors of Japan, Korea, and Vietnam?

The Five Dynasties Period and the Song Dynasty, 907–1276

The Tang dynasty (618–907), permanently weakened by the An Lushan rebellion of 755, came to an end in 907 (see Chapter 8). China then broke apart until 960, when the founder of the Song dynasty (960–1276) reunited the empire. The dramatic rise and fall of Chinese dynasties sometimes left the political structure basically unchanged, and this happened during the transition from the Tang dynasty to the Song. The new Song emperor presided over the central government. Almost all government officials were recruited by means of the civil service examinations, making the Song the world's first genuine bureaucracy. Despite the loss of north China to the Jin, Song officials successfully managed the transfer of the central government to a new capital in the south, where they presided over two centuries of unprecedented economic growth.

The Rise of the Northern Song Dynasty, 960–1126

The fifty-three years between the Tang and Song dynasties is known as the Five Dynasties period (907–960) because during this time China was ruled by different regional governments, of which five were most important. The Five Dynasties, in turn, came to an end when a powerful general overthrew a boy ruler of one of the regions and founded the **Song dynasty** in 960. By 976, he had united both north and south China and made his capital in Kaifeng (kie-fuhng). Since the reign of the First Emperor (see Chapter 4), China's capital had always been in the heartland of China, in the valley of the Yellow River. When the founder of the Song dynasty established his capital in Kaifeng (in Henan province) in 976, he was also continuing this tradition.

The Song founder kept in place the old political structure, with the emperor at the top of a central bureaucracy that oversaw local government. But there was one major difference. After unifying the empire in 976, the emperor summoned his most important generals and explained that the Tang dynasty had fallen apart because the regional governors, many of them also generals, exercised too much power. His generals agreed to retire, setting an important precedent. The Song initiated a period of greater civilian rule, as opposed to military rule, with genuine power remaining in the hands of bureaucrats, not generals.

Those officials stationed in the capital held the highest positions in the Song bureaucracy. The Song government referred all matters of state to six ministries: Revenue, Civil Appointments, Rites, Works, Punishments, and War. The heads of these six ministries all reported to the grand councilor, the highest official in the government, who was named to office by the emperor. If the emperor chose, he could, like the Song founder, be active in government matters. However, some emperors preferred to delegate their authority to the grand councilor and devote themselves to leisurely pursuits like the study of calligraphy and art.

The largest administrative districts during the Tang had been the prefectures. There were 220 such prefectures during the Song dynasty. Officials grouped these into over twenty larger units called circuits. Each prefecture in a circuit was further divided into subprefectures headed by a magistrate, who was in charge of collecting

Song dynasty (960–1276) Dynasty that ruled a united China from the northern capital of Kaifeng from 960 to 1126 and only the southern half of the empire from 1127 to 1276.

taxes and implementing justice. Aided by two or three subordinate officials and a clerical staff, the magistrate depended on powerful local families to help him govern. When he encountered problems that he could not solve, he could petition his superiors in the prefecture and in the larger circuit. At every level of the bureaucracy, officials were required to carry out the directives of the central government.

The Collapse of the Northern Song, 1126–1127

Since its founding, the Song dynasty faced a problem common to earlier dynasties: keeping peace with the nomads to the north, in this case the Khitan (KEE-tan), a nomadic people living in modern-day Mongolia. To counter this threat, the Song formed an alliance with the Jurchen (JIR-chen), a forest-dwelling, fishing people based in Manchuria who proved to be skilled horsemen and who raised a powerful army of their own. They spoke Jurchen, an Altaic language similar in structure to Japanese. Originally a subject people of the Khitan, the Jurchen declared their independence by founding their own dynasty, the **Jin dynasty** ("gold" in Chinese), in 1115. The Song-Jurchen forces defeated the Khitan in 1125, yet their alliance proved to be short-lived. As soon as victory was certain, the Jurchen leader ordered his troops to attack the Song. The Jurchen army, with its superior horses, defeated the Song handily and conquered Kaifeng.

•**Jin dynasty** (1115–1234) Dynasty of the Jurchen people of Manchuria that ruled north China from 1127 to 1234, when the Mongols defeated their armies. They modeled their government on that of the Song dynasty.

The superiority of the Jurchen cavalry proved decisive in battles with the Song army, but a powerful cavalry alone could not conquer the huge walled cities of north China like Kaifeng. For that, the Jurchen had to use weapons fueled by gunpowder, a Chinese invention. Gunpowder is an explosive material made with different ratios of potassium nitrate (also called saltpeter), sulfur, and charcoal. Before 900, the Chinese used different combinations of these materials, primarily for fireworks. But sometime around 900 they realized that they could use gunpowder as a weapon.

Chinese soldiers employed gunpowder in both simple and complex ways. In the most basic use, archers tied small bags of gunpowder onto their arrows, which then detonated on impact. One of the most complex and powerful weapons used in the siege of Kaifeng was the flame-thrower, which emitted a continuous stream of fire. Military engineers used gunpowder to keep the fuse lit and designed a cart of high-quality brass that did not melt when the lit fuel touched it.

When the Jurchen armies first attacked Kaifeng in early 1126, forty-eight thousand Song defenders fended them off with stone-throwers and flame-throwers. The Jurchen troops retreated and then returned a second time in the winter of 1126 and built siege towers, taller than the city's walls, from which they could shoot incendiary bombs made of bamboo shells containing gunpowder and fragments of porcelain that shot in all directions. Unable to devise an effective defense to this horrific new weapon, the residents of Kaifeng surrendered in January 1127.

The loss of the capital marked the end of the Northern Song dynasty (960–1126) and the beginning of the Southern Song dynasty (1127–1276). When the Jurchen captured Kaifeng, they took two emperors prisoner. One, Huizong (HWAY-dzong), had reigned from 1101 to 1125 and then abdicated in favor of his eldest son. The most artistically talented of China's emperors, Huizong did many paintings of birds and flowers and also perfected his own distinctive calligraphic style. His Jurchen captors forced him and his son to wear the plain clothes of commoners. They gave Huizong the humiliating title *Marquis of Muddled Virtue,* and his son, *Doubly Muddled Marquis.*

The Emperor as Painter Emperor Huizong (r. 1101–1125) is famous for his bird-and-flower paintings and his distinctive calligraphy, but recently art historians have carefully analyzed the brushstrokes in several paintings labeled "imperially brushed" and have discovered that they were made by different artists, probably those in the imperial workshop. They argue that Huizong's idiosyncratic calligraphy, in fact, lent itself to replication by others. (Palace Museum, Beijing, China/Cultural Relics Press)

Despite their success, Jurchen armies could not conquer the region south of the Huai River. One of Huizong's ten living sons managed to escape from Kaifeng and was named emperor in May of 1127. He did not realize it at the time, but both his father and his brother would die in captivity, making him the first emperor of the Southern Song dynasty. He named Hangzhou (HAHNG-jo), in Zhejiang province, his temporary capital. This placed China's capital south of the Yangzi River for the first time in Chinese history and marked the new importance of southern China. He and his supporters hoped that they would eventually reconquer north China, but they never did, and Hangzhou became the capital of the Southern Song. Historians refer to the period when the capital was in Kaifeng as the Northern Song (960–1126) and the period when the capital was in Hangzhou as the Southern Song (1127–1276). The period of the Song dynasty covers its founding in 960 to its collapse in 1276.

The military defeat of the Northern Song triggered one of the greatest migrations in human history. Most of the people who left Kaifeng worked for the Song government; they included 20,000 officials, 100,000 clerks, and 400,000 army soldiers and their families. In sum, nearly 500,000 people, out of a population in north and south China of an estimated 100 million, crossed the Yangzi River in 1126 and 1127. Like Li Qingzhao, most never returned to north China.

China Divided: The Jin and the Southern Song, 1127–1234

Life in the south was extremely difficult for many northerners, who viewed the north and south as two distinct cultural regions. Northerners ate wheat and millet, often in the form of noodles or bread, while southerners ate rice. Worse, their spoken dialects were mutually incomprehensible. Many of the refugees moved to Hangzhou, which had been a small, regional city, and its population was hard-pressed to accept 500,000 new residents. Within a few years the migrants built housing, and the population of Hangzhou soon reached one million, making it a worthy successor to the Northern Song capital of Kaifeng.

Li Qingzhao's memoir provides a rare eyewitness account of the migration south. She and her husband Zhao Mingcheng fled their home in 1127 to avoid the invading troops. They left behind belongings and artwork that filled ten rooms in their home, which was burnt to the ground by the Jurchen invaders a few months later. In the south, crisscrossed by many rivers and lakes, the couple moved more rapidly by boat.

In the summer of 1129, when the Southern Song emperor summoned Zhao Mingcheng to Nanjing for a personal audience, the couple were forced to separate, with Li Qingzhao remaining behind. Six weeks later, Li Qingzhao received a letter from her husband saying that he had contracted malaria. She frantically traveled the 100 miles (160 km) to Nanjing in twenty-four hours by boat, reaching his side just in time to watch him succumb to dysentery and die at the age of 49.

Li Qingzhao closes her memoir with this sentence: "From the time I was eighteen until now at the age of fifty-two—a span of thirty years—how much calamity, how much gain and loss I have witnessed!" Alone and widowed, Li Qingzhao wrote some of her most moving poems:

> The wind subsides—the dust carries a fragrance of fallen petals;
> It's late in the day—I'm too tired to comb my hair.
> Things remain but he is gone, and with him everything.
> On the verge of words, tears flow.
>
> I hear at Twin Creek spring's still lovely;
> How I long to float there on a small boat—
> But I fear that at Twin Creek my frail grasshopper boat
> Could not carry this load of grief.[2]

Li Qingzhao gave voice to the losses suffered by the many people displaced by the Jurchen conquest. In the south, the Southern Song dynasty governed some sixty million people from the capital at Hangzhou, where Li Qingzhao settled. For more than a century and a half after 1127, China was divided. With a government structure modeled after the Song dynasty, one million Jurchen ruled a population of some forty million Chinese in the north until 1234.

After fourteen years of more fighting, the Southern Song and the Jurchen signed a peace treaty in 1142, but it came at a high price for the Southern Song. According to the humiliating terms of the treaty, the Southern Song, an "insignificant state," agreed to pay the Jurchen, a "superior state," tribute of 250,000 ounces of silver and 250,000 bolts of silk each year. This tribute was an enormous burden on the Song state and its people, who were well aware that earlier dynasties had received tribute from weaker neighbors, not paid it. The payments, however, stimulated trade and economic growth because the Jurchen used the money to buy Chinese goods. After the peace treaty of 1142 was signed, the people of south China turned to the task of rebuilding the economy, and theirs became one of the richest societies in the world.

The Commercial Revolution in China, 900–1300

The expansion of markets throughout China between 900 and 1300 brought such rapid economic growth that scholars refer to these changes as a commercial revolution. We do not usually think of a change that takes place over more than four hundred years as revolutionary, and the commercial revolution affected different regions at different times. But for the people who personally experienced the expansion of markets, the changes were indeed dramatic.

Before the commercial revolution, farmers grew their own food in a largely self-sufficient barter economy and bought salt, if that, at the market. Officials strictly monitored all trade, and markets opened only at noon and closed promptly at dusk. As markets sprang up in different towns and more people went to them, these restrictions became increasingly difficult to enforce, and, by Li Qingzhao's day, they had long been forgotten. At the height of the commercial revolution in the Song dynasty, China's farmers sold cash crops such as tangerines and handicrafts such as pottery, baskets, and textiles at markets. They used their earnings to buy a variety of products, including food. Dependent on the marketplace for their incomes, they led totally different lives from those who had lived before the commercial revolution.

Changes in Agriculture and the Rise of the South

The origins of the commercial revolution go back centuries before Li Qingzhao's lifetime. In north China, where rainfall was lower (see Chapter 4), farmers planted wheat and millet; in south China, where rainfall was greater, farmers grew rice, which produced a larger surplus. This surplus freed others to grow cash crops or to produce handicrafts.

Before the commercial revolution, south China was universally viewed as a remote backwater whose many swamps provided a breeding ground for malaria and other diseases. When northerners moved south in search of more land, they settled in the highlands and drained the swamps. They used pumps to regulate the flow of water into walled fields. After planting rice seeds in small gardens, they transplanted the rice plants into a field drained of water. Once the plants had taken root, they flooded the fields with water until the crop ripened.

Southern farmers experimented with different rice strains, and in the late tenth century they realized that a type of rice imported from Vietnam had a higher yield than indigenous rice. The Vietnamese rice had a shorter growing season, making it possible to harvest two crops a year rather than just one. Initially this double-cropped rice tasted and smelled bad, but farmers mixed different strains of rice and eventually developed high-yielding hybrids that tasted better.

The shift from wheat and millet to rice had a dramatic impact on China's population. In 742, 60 percent of the population of sixty million lived in north China, where wheat and millet were grown. By 980, 62 percent were living in south China, where they cultivated the higher-yielding rice. With more food available, the overall population increased to one hundred million in the year 1000. Thus one of the most important changes in China's history was this shift south. During the Song dynasty, for the first time, the majority of China's population lived in the south, a trend that continues today.

The Currency of the Song Dynasty

● **paper money**
Money issued around 1000 by the Song dynasty that could be used instead of bronze coins. The Song dynasty was the first government in world history to issue paper money.

● **New Policies**
Reforms introduced by Wang Anshi, a grand councilor of the Song dynasty, implemented between 1069 and 1086. These included paying all government salaries in money and extending interest-free loans to poor peasants.

As more and more people began to produce for markets, they needed a way to pay for their purchases. In response, Song authorities greatly increased the money supply, which consisted of round bronze coins with square holes; a string consisted of a thousand coins strung together. By the eleventh century, the Song government was minting twenty times more coins than had the Tang dynasty at its height.[3]

Li Qingzhao's description of her husband's many shopping trips offers a rare glimpse into the new market economy under the Northern Song: "On the first and fifteenth day of every month, my husband would get a short vacation from the Academy: he would 'pawn some clothes' for five hundred cash and go to the market at Xiangguo [SHE-AHNG-gwaw] Temple, where he would buy fruit and rubbings of inscriptions." Many people in the Song enjoyed tangerines and oranges, which were grown in south China but were available at reasonable cost at markets all over the empire. Zhao used bronze coins to purchase rubbings of inscriptions, art objects that only the richest people could afford. Sometime near the year 1000, the government introduced **paper money,** which was printed on paper and could be used instead of bronze coins. Paper money was much lighter than bronze coins; a string of one thousand coins could weigh as much as 2 pounds (1 kg). The new currency appeared at a time when China's paper-making technology was just reaching the Islamic world (see Chapter 9) and had not yet spread to Europe. While people continued to use coins, paper money expanded the money supply, further contributing to the economic growth of the commercial revolution.

Right from its start, the question of how much paper money to print was intensely controversial. Some wanted to print vast quantities of paper money; other officials urged caution. The debate came to a head in 1069, when the reigning emperor appointed a new grand councilor, named Wang Anshi (WAHNG AHN-shih), who held more radical views. He instituted the **New Policies,** which included paying all government salaries in money and extending interest-free loans to poor peasants. But peasants could not earn enough money to pay back their loans, and by 1086 the reforms had failed.

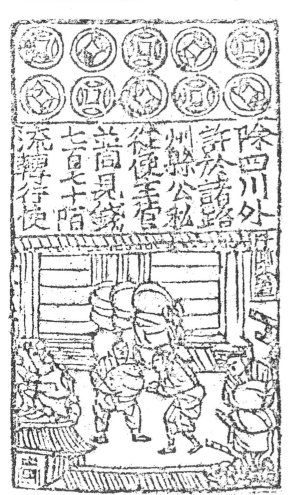

■ **The World's First Paper Money**   This early example of paper money, which the Song dynasty first issued around the year 1000, has three frames. The top section shows ten round bronze coins with square centers, the distinctive currency of the Chinese that paper money supplemented. The middle band of text explains that this sheet of money is worth 770 coins and valid everywhere in the empire except for Sichuan (which had its own iron currency), while the bottom shows men carrying grain into a storehouse.   (Neimenggu jinrong yanjiusuo [The Research Center for Finance in Inner Mongolia], *Zhongguo guchao tuji,* 1987, plate 1.1)

Iron and Steel   The commercial revolution led to the increased production of all goods, not just of rice and fruit. Iron production boomed as entrepreneurs built large-scale workshops to make iron products in factory-like spaces with hundreds of workers. Song metallurgists made two kinds of iron: cast and wrought. Cast iron was poured into a mold and was so hard that it could not be worked with a hammer; wrought iron was malleable enough that blacksmiths could work it. The capital's demand for both types of iron was considerable. For centuries Chinese metallurgists had used blast furnaces to make cast iron, and by the Song their technology was so advanced that they cast an entire pagoda 78 feet (24 m) high, section by section.

Soldiers needed iron armor and weapons, while government workshops produced iron tools and iron fittings, like nails and locks, for buildings and bridges. These goods were not mass-produced in the modern sense, with assembly lines and factories. But they were made in large quantities and at low prices and so were available to rural and urban residents.

The metal-smiths of the Song even learned to how to produce steel, one of the strongest metals known. They heated sheets of wrought and cast iron together in a superheated furnace and then worked them by hand to make steel swords. After the forests around Kaifeng had been depleted for fuel and housing, Chinese metal-smiths fired their smelters with coke, a fuel made from preheated coal that produced high temperatures.

The area around Kaifeng became the world's leading producer of iron. By 1078, China was producing 125,000 tons of iron or 3.1 pounds per person in the entire country, a ratio matched in Europe only in 1700, on the eve of the Industrial Revolution. China's iron and steel production has prompted historians to ask why, if the Song reached such an advanced stage of metal production, China did not experience a sustained industrial revolution. The answer most often given is that Britain's Industrial Revolution occurred under a unique set of circumstances. For example, the British invented machines to make up for a labor shortage, while the Song had no corresponding shortage of labor and therefore no need to develop labor-saving machinery.

Urban Life   As newlyweds, Li Qingzhao and her husband had lived in Kaifeng, one of the world's most prosperous cities and possibly the largest city in the world, rivaled only by Cairo, with a population of 500,000. (At that time London and Paris each had fewer than 100,000 residents.) After one of her husband's shopping expeditions, Li and her husband played a drinking game that shows how close they were:

> I happen to have an excellent memory, and every evening after we finished eating, we would sit in the hall called "Return Home" and make tea. Pointing to the heaps of books and histories, we would guess on which line of what page in which chapter of which book a certain passage could be found. Success in guessing determined who got to drink his or her tea first. Whenever I got it right, I would raise the teacup, laughing so hard that the tea would spill in my lap, and I would get up, not having been able to drink anything at all. I would have been glad to grow old in such a world.

Li Qingzhao and her husband clearly enjoyed each other's company, and he treated her as his intellectual equal. As wealthy urbanites living in Kaifeng before 1127, they were able to enjoy all the fruits of the commercial revolution.

THE COMMERCIAL VITALITY OF A CHINESE CITY

Li Qingzhao's memoir makes the reader wonder what the markets and cities of the Northern Song looked like. One of the masterpieces of Song painting, an extraordinary hand scroll sometimes called the *Mona Lisa* of China, depicts a city with many markets during the Northern Song. We are told in a brief biographical notice at the end of the painting that the scroll's painter, Zhang Zeduan (JAHNG zehdwon) (flourished 1150), specialized in technical drawing: "He showed talent for fine-lined architectural drawing, and especially liked boats and carts, markets and bridges, moats and paths." The artist

(National Palace Museum, Beijing/Cultural Relics Press)

• This vendor has laid out his tools on a cloth for customers to see.

• Three lightly clothed carriers put down their loaded baskets outside a stand serving drinks under two large umbrellas.

QUESTIONS FOR ANALYSIS

What are people buying and selling in the Qingming scroll? What do these transactions reveal about the commercial revolution of the Song dynasty?

intended that viewers look at the hand scroll slowly, rolling it out inch by inch, from right to left, and savoring the extraordinary detail that extends a full 17.25 feet (5.25 m) long. The painting, often referred to as the Qingming scroll, was completed sometime before 1186. Entitled *Peace Reigns over the River*, the scroll celebrates commercial life.

The dramatic high point of the painting comes right in the middle of the scroll. At first one views a boat with sailors hurriedly pulling the mast down. Then, as the scroll unfurls, the viewer understands why: the boat is going under the rainbow bridge, yet its towline has snapped. In his efforts to keep the boat from crashing, one sailor grabs a rope thrown by a passerby standing on the bridge, just as the men at the ship's bow gesture frantically to the oncoming boat to stay out of the way.

The bridge scene vividly illustrates the major change of the commercial revolution: commerce had exploded out of restricted market districts to blanket the cities of the twelfth century. Restaurants and food stands line the side of the river, and they have even crept up the bridge where passersby can eat a snack purchased from a seated baker or can buy ropes or scissors from vendors who have laid out their goods on the ground. As the scroll ends, when one goes through a large gate and finally enters the city proper, it dawns on the viewer that all the commercial activity seen so far has taken place outside the city walls—a location where all markets were banned during the Tang dynasty.

The detail of the scroll is so mesmerizing that one can easily forget that one is looking at a painting by an artist and not at a photograph. Zhang Zeduan has fit the city into an artfully constructed composition, complete with the rainbow bridge at the exact midpoint of the scroll, and has depicted a city without dirt, illness, or crowding. Curiously, Zhang has nearly omitted women from his cityscape. Of the over five hundred people in the scroll, only twenty or so are female. Surely a real city would have had more women outside, even if women from prestigious families, like Li Qingzhao, often remained indoors.

A collision is about to occur on top of the bridge: an official riding a horse confronts someone (a woman?) in a sedan chair. Several feisty servants gesture emphatically to the horseman to get out of the way.

A bystander on top of the bridge tosses a rope to the boat's frantic crew, who hope to avert a crash with a boat coming toward them from under the bridge.

The details of the bridge's construction—a round arch made from straight wooden beams wrapped together with iron—are clear from this angle. A wooden walkway at the water's edge allows pedestrians to pass underneath the bridge.

Kaifeng was a city with many sensual pleasures for those who could afford them, and the prosperity of the commercial revolution meant that many people could. Restaurants were the most prominent establishments catering to consumers. Kaifeng alone had seventy-two major restaurants, each standing three floors high and licensed by the government. Many smaller establishments had menus listing over one hundred kinds of different dishes. Even working people could afford to eat noodles or a snack at the many stands dotting the city.

Although Li Qingzhao does not write about crowding, Kaifeng's one million residents were packed into a small space just over 23 square miles (60 sq km), resulting in a density of 32,000 people per square mile (2,000 per sq km). With people so crowded, sanitation posed a genuine problem, and disease must have spread quickly. (See the feature "Visual Evidence: The Commercial Vitality of a Chinese City.")

Footbinding   The southward migration eventually brought greater wealth to most people and eroded the distinctions among social groups. Although merchants continued to be at the bottom of the ideal social hierarchy—below scholars, peasants, artisans, and merchants—others envied their wealth. The continued expansion of the market turned many peasants into part-time and full-time artisans. Many of those making money selling goods at the market aspired to the high social position of the officials they saw above them.

Both in cities and the countryside, wealthy men sought second and third wives, called concubines, whom they hoped would give them more children. Being able to support a large family with concubines and many children was a mark of prestige. Many observers complained about unscrupulous merchants who kidnapped women and sold them as concubines to newly wealthy men.

Brokers in women found that those with bound feet attracted a higher price than those with natural feet. Li Qingzhao's mother did not bind her daughter's feet, but by 1300 the wives and daughters of officials throughout south China did. The practice appeared first in the tenth century, when dancers at the imperial court, who were probably in their late teens, had begun to wrap their own feet to make them smaller. By the Southern Song, women from good families began to wrap their daughters' feet in the hopes of enhancing their chances of making a good match. The mothers started when the girls were young, around 10, so that their feet would never grow to their natural size.

In the Song period, feet were shortened only slightly, to around 7 or 8 inches (18 or 20 cm), but by the nineteenth century a foot only 3 inches

A Bound Foot Superimposed on a Normal Foot   When girls turned 10, their mothers started to bind their feet by wrapping long strips of cloth around them and gradually tightening them until the foot shrank. During the Song dynasty, bound feet were only slightly smaller than normal feet, but in the nineteenth century the ideal bound foot measured only 3 inches (8 cm) long. (Illustration from John K. Fairbank, Edwin O. Reischauer, and Albert M. Craig, *East Asia: Tradition and Transformation*, rev. ed. [Boston: Houghton Mifflin, 1989], p. 142.)

(8 cm) long was the ideal. To bind her daughter's feet, a mother took a long cloth, some 10 feet (3 m) long, and wrapped it around her daughter's foot so that the small toes were bent inward toward the sole while the big toe was left unbound. Over the years, the mother would tighten the bindings to make the foot smaller. The initial binding was very painful, but eventually girls could resume walking, though always with difficulty. Footbinding transformed a woman's foot into a sexual object that only her husband was supposed to see, wash, or fondle.

Book Publishing and the Education Boom

The commercial revolution brought an information revolution parallel to today's Internet boom, brought on by a deceptively simple innovation, woodblock printing. Before 700, creating a book was a slow, laborious process, since all manuscript copies were done by hand (see Chapter 8). The introduction of woodblock printing sped up book publishing dramatically and significantly lowered the cost of books.

The effect on everyday life was profound, as many more men and women could afford books and learned to read. Because people had more disposable income, they could finance the education of their children. The rise in wealth and educational opportunity also prompted more people to take the government's civil service examination, the door to a job in the bureaucracy (see Chapters 4 and 8).

Woodblock Printing and the Invention of Movable Type

For centuries Chinese scholars had made ink rubbings from stone carvings of Buddhist, Daoist, and Confucian texts. Woodblock printing applied this technique to woodblocks. First, a literate but low-level craftsman with good, clear handwriting wrote the desired text on a piece of paper, which was glued face down on the wood. When the paper was scraped off, the ink from the text remained on the surface of the wood. Then a carver removed the wood around the characters. When the block was completed, the text remained in relief. He then inked the woodblock, placed a sheet of paper over it, and rubbed with a brush. Printers could make hundreds of copies from the same block of wood. Folding each page in half, they sewed the pages into bound chapters of thirty or so pages. Often people calculated the size of libraries in sewn chapters, which were stored in boxes.

Shortly after 1040, a Chinese bookmaker invented **movable type,** in which each character is made separately and arranged on a frame to form a page. An eleventh-century description explains:

> Bi Sheng [bee shung], a man of unofficial position, made moveable type. His method was as follows: he took sticky clay and cut in it characters as thin as the edge of a coin. . . . When he wished to print, he took an iron frame. . . . In this he placed the types, set close together. . . . If one were to print only two or three copies, this method would be neither simple nor easy. But for printing hundreds or thousands of copies, it was marvelously quick.[4]

• movable type
First developed in China after 1040. Printers made individual characters from clay, fired them in a kiln, set them in an iron frame, and printed pages by pressing paper against the inked type.

◼ The World's First Movable Type

This model reconstructs the movable type Bi Sheng invented for printing in the 1040s. Because the printer had to cut out an individual type for each character out of clay, the cost of movable type was much higher than the traditional Chinese method of woodblock printing. For large print runs of over one hundred thousand, however, movable print made sense. The world's earliest surviving books printed with movable type were made in Korea around 1400, some fifty years before the German printer Gutenberg used movable type to print the Bible. (Ontario Science Centre, Toronto, Canada)

Since Chinese has thousands of different characters, making a different piece of type for each character was a slow and expensive process. For this reason, it was cheaper to carve woodblocks for smaller runs, such as a thousand books. Movable type made sense only for few large-scale printing projects.

The low cost of books combined with sustained economic growth produced an education boom that intensified the competition for government jobs. More and more families hired scholars who had failed the civil service examinations as tutors for their sons and daughters, buying books and study aids in large numbers. Though only a few passed the exams, many boys gained basic literacy.

The Education of Women

• **epitaph** A biography of someone who has died that was placed in their tomb. An important source for Chinese ideals about model women in the twelfth and thirteenth centuries.

Some women began to enjoy increased educational opportunities in the twelfth and thirteenth centuries, exactly the time when footbinding began to spread. Although they were not allowed to take the civil service exams, many women learned to read and write and take care of their families' finances. We know a good deal about wealthy women in the Song dynasty from biographies, called **epitaphs,** that were buried in their tombs.

The epitaphs reveal what kind of woman was most admired in the twelfth and thirteenth centuries. Whereas Tang dynasty epitaphs emphasized women's physical appearance and ancestry, Song epitaphs frequently praised women for successfully managing their household finances, a skill requiring knowledge of math. In 1250, one official wrote an epitaph for Lady Fang, the wife of his younger brother:

> My brother was untalented at making a living but loved antiques and would spend every cent to collect famous paintings and calligraphies. Lady Fang calmly made secret economies and never complained of lacking anything. . . .
>
> Lady Fang was a widow for over ten years. During this time she arranged for her husband's tomb, completed marriage arrangements for her children, repaired the old house, and brought new fields into cultivation in order to continue the thread of our family and preserve the orphans. . . .[5]

Note that the author commends her ability to manage her family's income after her husband's death. Widows frequently figure in epitaphs from the twelfth and thirteenth centuries, and they are often praised for tutoring their young children at home and for making economies that allow their offspring to attend school when older.

The Growth of Civil Service Examinations

The Song dynasty was the only government in the twelfth- and thirteenth-century world to recruit its bureaucrats via merit, as measured by a grueling series of examinations. At the time of the dynasty's founding in 960, civil service examinations had been in use for over a thousand years (see Chapters 4 and 8). But the system had expanded slowly. It was only in the Song era that the proportion of the bureaucracy who had passed the civil service examinations exceeded 90 percent. The tests were not always fair, but they were more equitable than the system of appointments by heredity or social position used elsewhere in the world.

During the Song dynasty, exam candidates took two rounds of exams: the first in their home prefecture and the second in the capital. Originally examiners often met the candidates and knew whose paper they were grading; after 1000, the candidates' names were covered up and the exam papers recopied so that examiners could not recognize their acquaintances' handwriting. The emperor himself conducted the final stage, the palace examinations, in which those placing highest in the written exams were examined orally, with one lucky man named number one in the empire. Those placing highest in the exams were given prestigious entry-level jobs, often drafting decrees for the emperor, because even they had to work their way up the bureaucracy.

The government examiners devised different types of exams over the centuries. Successful candidates had to demonstrate mastery of a classic text, often within the Confucian tradition, by explaining from which text an unidentified passage had been taken. They were asked to compose poetry or essays with a fixed number of lines and a set number of words per line (like a sonnet in English). The candidates also wrote essays about problems the central government had faced in the past or might face in the future, such as inflation or defeating border peoples. Many of these literary skills did not relate directly to what officials would do once in office. Still, those who wrote the questions were seeking to test a broad range of learning with the expectation that they could select the most educated, and so, they believed, the most virtuous, men to become officials.

By 1046, more than 89 percent of the estimated 10,000 to 20,000 officials[6] in China's bureaucracy had received examination degrees, compared to 5 percent under the Tang. As a result, the Song era saw a decisive shift from government by aristocracy to government by merit-based bureaucracy.

Exams in Today's China

In 2007, 10.1 million people competed for 5.67 million spots in China's colleges; only 2.6 million slots are in four-year universities. For the two days in early June when the exams are held, officials implore—not always successfully—construction workers to stop the pounding of jackhammers and partygoers to turn off their outdoor karaoke machines. Urban couples often accompany their only child (one-child families are the norm among China's urban middle class) to the examination site and wait outside for them with meals and snacks; in 2007, one 46-year-old father in the northeastern city of Harbin even attended high school so that he could take the examinations alongside his 18-year-old son.

Cheating is a problem. In 2005, the authorities caught 1,300 people cheating; in 2006, they apprehended 3,000. A new system allows officials to monitor each of the 346 test sites (each with an average of just under 3,000 people) throughout the country. Some officials require that exam-takers sign written pledges, while others equip examination halls with mobile phone detectors (so that exam-takers cannot call people outside for the answers).

In 2007, police captured three men in Anhui province who had hired current university students to sit the exams using the false names of current high school students. If the cheaters did well on the exams, they could make over $1,000. Students and their ambitious parents are not the only ones cheating. Some school principals have leaked the contents of the exams ahead of time so that students from their schools can do better than students from rival schools.

Nowadays, many college graduates have trouble finding jobs, especially in the cities where most want to live. Increasing numbers are turning to the civil service examinations, which were introduced in 1995. (Before that year, the universities placed their graduates in various positions.) In 2007, 530,000 college graduates took the first round of the civil service examinations, which consisted of a general multiple-choice test, an essay question, and a specialized test in law or various types of management. Those who do well on the examination are then interviewed in person. Twelve thousand people—one out of forty-two—will receive positions in different ministries, such as Commerce, Information, Construction, and Justice.

In recent years, as competition to enter universities has eased, many people see the civil service examinations as the true heir to the examinations of the Song dynasty.

The examinations were not open to everyone. Local officials permitted only young men from well-established families to register for the first round of exams. Unlike farmers' sons, who were lucky to attend village school for a year or two, the sons of privileged families had the time and money to study for the exams, often at home with a tutor. Preparation required long years of study. A few brilliant men passed the exams after fifteen years of study, but most continued to study part-time in their 20s and 30s, and some did not pass the examinations until later. (See the feature "World History in Today's World: Exams in Today's China.")

In the eleventh century, successful exam candidates tended to come from a small group of one hundred families living in the capital, Kaifeng. This was the elite into which Li Qingzhao and Zhao Mingcheng were born, and both her father and her father-in-law had received the highest possible degree of advanced scholar.

As the population grew and printed books became more widely available, examinations became more competitive. In 1100, some 80,000 men participated in the civil service exams; in 1270, the number had increased to 400,000, or about 1 out of every 250 people. By that time, in some prefectures in southeast China (particularly in modern Fujian), as many as 700 men competed for a single place in the first round of the examinations. The high number of candidates must have increased the literacy rate: some historians believe that one in ten men, but many fewer women, could read.[7]

The examinations maintained the anonymity of candidates and were outwardly fair. But in fact, the examinations favored the sons of powerful families. Sons and relatives of high officials were eligible to take a less competitive series of examinations, often with a pass-rate of 50 percent, an advantage called the **shadow privilege.** Since Zhao Mingcheng's father was grand councilor, the highest official in the bureaucracy, his shadow privilege extended to his sons, grandsons, sons-in-law, brothers, cousins, and nephews. In the twelfth and thirteenth centuries, as more men became eligible for the shadow privilege, fewer candidates took the open examinations.

● **shadow privilege**
Privilege extended to sons and relatives of Song dynasty officials who were allowed to take a less competitive series of examinations, often with a pass-rate of 50 percent.

As competition increased, so did the pressure to cheat. Some candidates paid others to take the exams in their place, or they copied others' answers. In one scandal in Sichuan province, officials grading the exams took bribes, changed the names on the exams, and secretly marked the booklets to which they were supposed to give passing grades. Crafty students also bought commercial aids, like miniature books with tiny characters the size of a fly, that they could smuggle into the examination halls.

Cheating and heightened competition prompted many men to turn away from the examinations and government service altogether. In 1101, when Li Qingzhao married, she assumed that her husband would become an official, and he did. One hundred years later, many families of equally prominent rank chose instead to educate their sons at private academies and to keep them at home to run their family estates once their education was completed. As a book critical of the examination system explained:

> If the sons of a gentleman have no hereditary stipend to maintain and no permanent holdings to depend on, and they wish to be filial to their parents and to support children, then nothing is as good as being a scholar. . . . For those who cannot be scholars, then medicine, Buddhism and Daoism, agriculture, trade, or crafts are all possible.[8]

This author uses the word *scholar* for everyone who earned a living by reading, writing, teaching, or editing. Many young men followed the book's advice. After studying at private academies, they returned to their family estates and pursued the alternate careers the author suggested.

● Religious Life During the Song

The prosperity created by the commercial revolution allowed the Chinese to give money to practitioners of many different religions. Most Chinese did not adhere to a specific religion: they worshiped the deities and consulted the religious specialists they thought most powerful. Lay Chinese made offerings to their ancestors, to Buddhist and Daoist deities, and to gods not associated with any organized religion. Many educated families, particularly those whose sons did not do well on the civil service examinations, were drawn to the teachings of Neo-Confucianism.

• **Zhu Xi** (1130–1200) The leading thinker of Neo-Confucianism.

Neo-Confucian Teachings

The most influential private academy, the White Deer Academy, was founded in 1181 by the thinker **Zhu Xi** (1130–1200). Zhu Xi's curriculum emphasized moral cultivation. He wanted his students to become true Confucian gentlemen, not civil service officials, and he thought the best guidelines were the Confucian classics. Four texts: *The Analects* (which contained the conversations of Confucius with his students), *Mencius* (written by a follower of Confucius), and two chapters from a ritual manual. These writings are known collectively as *The Four Books*.

Zhu Xi (JOO She) criticized Buddhism as a non-Chinese religion and urged his followers to give up all Buddhist practices, yet Buddhist teachings about meditating and reaching enlightenment clearly influenced Zhu Xi's understanding of the transmission of the Way. He also claimed that studying and thinking on his own had allowed him to understand the Way as it had passed from Confucius to Mencius, from Mencius to a Tang dynasty thinker named Han Yu (768–824), and then to himself. Moreover, he was not the first thinker to focus on the two chapters from the ritual manual included in *The Four Books:* Buddhist teachers in the early 1000s had noticed that these books contained ideas that overlapped with Buddhism, and the two chapters had already circulated as independent texts studied in Buddhist monasteries.

• **Neo-Confucianism** Teachings of a thinker named Zhu Xi (1130–1200) and his followers, based on Confucianism but introducing major revisions. Rather than focusing on ritual and inner humanity, Zhu Xi urged students to apprehend the principle in things.

Because Zhu Xi's teachings were based on Confucianism but introduced major revisions, they are called **Neo-Confucianism.** Rather than focusing on ritual and inner humanity as Confucius had (see Chapter 4), Zhu Xi urged students to apprehend the principle in things. If students examined the world around them and studied *The Four Books* carefully, Neo-Confucians believed that they could discern a coherent pattern underlying all human affairs. Armed with that knowledge, an individual could attain sagehood, the goal of all Neo-Confucian education. (See the feature "Movement of Ideas: The Teachings of Neo-Confucianism.")

Zhu Xi did not attract a great following during his lifetime, and the government banned his teachings during the last years of his life. But after the ban was rescinded in 1202, his teachings gained in popularity, and, in the fourteenth century, his edition of *The Four Books* became the basis of the civil service examinations—an outcome Zhu Xi could never have anticipated. Zhu Xi's teachings continued to be influential in China long after his death, and by the seventeenth century they had gained a wide following in Japan, Korea, and Vietnam.

Day-to-Day Religious Life

At the time that Zhu Xi and his followers were formulating their teachings, Neo-Confucian shrines spread throughout south China. At the beginning of the Song dynasty, a few community leaders and teachers had erected shrines to classical thinkers in their schools, but, by the end of the dynasty, shrines to worthies had proliferated throughout the empire. A "worthy" was someone who had lived a virtuous life and embodied the Neo-Confucian virtues of being educated, honest, and concerned about his community's welfare. All worthies were male.

These shrines provided a physical reminder of Neo-Confucian teachers and teachings to ordinary people who might not otherwise have encountered them. They often housed a portrait of the person to be worshiped. Members of the local community or the school that housed the shrine gathered on certain holidays to make offerings to the worthy: bolts of cloth, food, and drinks like wine or tea. A member of the community led a prayer asking the worthy to descend, listen to the prayer, and receive offerings. [9]

Many other types of religion coexisted with the shrines to worthies. Li Qing-zhao's account mentions ancestor worship in particular. When she and her husband parted, Zhao instructed her to "carry the sacrificial vessels for the ancestral temple yourself; live or die with them; don't give *them* up." Each household had an altar for ancestor worship. The wealthy put bronze vessels on their altars; ordinary people used pottery or wooden bowls and cups.

Much religious activity took place outside the home. Some religious practitioners going from market-town to market-town were associated with organized religions, like Daoism and Buddhism, while others, like the spirit mediums, tended to work on their own. Believing that evil spirits caused illness, many people consulted religious specialists, such as exorcists, in the hope of curing sick family members. Daoist practitioners claimed to intervene with the spirits of the underworld and dead ancestors on behalf of the ill, while spirit mediums professed the ability to communicate directly with the spirit world.

Buddhist monasteries offered many women a place where they could go unaccompanied by men and listen to Buddhist texts recited aloud (see Chapter 8). At home the educated few could read Buddhist texts themselves, while the wealthy could afford to hire monks to come to their homes to read to them. Thousands forswore marriage and became monks and nuns living in monasteries and nunneries. Male clerics outnumbered women six to one during the Song dynasty.

Vietnam, Korea, Japan, and the World Beyond

At the beginning of the Song dynasty, few knew much about the regions beyond China's frontiers, with the exception of places like Central Asia that could be reached overland. As the commercial revolution led to technological breakthroughs, particularly in ocean exploration, the vastness of the larger world became apparent to educated Chinese. Chinese navigators continued to modify their designs for ships, whose large wooden construction profoundly impressed Ibn Battuta (see Chapter 11), and techniques for surveying extensive stretches of territory—so crucial to mapmaking—also improved.

After the Song ruler signed the peace treaty of 1142 with the Jurchen, his dynasty entered a multistate world. The Southern Song was only one of several regional powers in East Asia at the time, of whom the Jurchen were the most powerful. Foreign trade with these powers played an important role in China's commercial revolution. Anyone traveling to Vietnam, Korea, or Japan in the thirteenth century would have seen signs of Chinese influence everywhere: people using chopsticks, Buddhist monasteries and Confucian schools, books printed in Chinese, and Chinese characters on all signposts and government documents. Chinese bronze coins, or local copies, circulated throughout the region, forming a Song dynasty currency sphere. But Vietnam, Korea, and Japan also had their own distinctive political structures and their own ways of modifying the collection of institutions, laws, education systems, and religions they had adopted from the Tang (see Chapter 8).

The Teachings of Neo-Confucianism

The first selection is from a Chinese primer. During the Song dynasty, children learned to read by using primers that taught a core vocabulary. One of the most popular, *The Three-Character Classic*, written circa 1200, consisted of rhyming lines of three Chinese characters each, which students had to learn by heart. Because almost everyone studied *The Three-Character Classic* while only more advanced students studied Zhu Xi's teachings, this version of Confucianism had great influence, not only in China but also all over East Asia, where many students learned to read Chinese characters (even if they pronounced them in Japanese or Korean) using this primer.

The second selection is a memorial to the emperor in which Zhu Xi provides a succinct description of Neo-Confucianism. Zhu Xi formulated his curriculum of the Four Books for advanced students who could read difficult texts. Again and again, he returns to the importance of education. One could apprehend the "principle in things" only through education, by which Zhu Xi meant careful study of the Confucian classics. Here he cites both Confucius (see "Movement of Ideas," Chapter 4) and his later follower Mencius in support of his views.

In the fourteenth century, when Zhu Xi's teachings were chosen as the basis of the civil service examinations, one of his followers included this essay in a widely read anthology. Zhu Xi's teachings spread to Korea around 1400 and to Japan around 1600. One Japanese proponent summarized them in this way: "Study widely. Question thoroughly. Deliberate carefully. Analyze clearly. Act conscientiously."* Although neither the Japanese nor Korean governments recruited bureaucrats via exams as the Song had, both valued Zhu Xi's emphasis on education.

Sources: (*The Three-Character Classic*) Pei-yi Wu, "Education of Children in the Sung," in *Neo-Confucian Education: The Formative Stage*, ed. Wm. Theodore de Bary and John W. Chaffee (Berkeley: University of California Press, 1989), pp. 322–323; (Zhu Xi's memorial) Patricia Buckley Ebrey, *Chinese Civilization and Society: A Sourcebook* (New York: The Free Press, 1981), pp. 116–117.

Selections from *The Three-Character Classic*

Men, one and all, in infancy are virtuous at heart.
Their moral tendencies the same, the practice wide apart.
Without Instruction's friendly aid, our instinct grew less pure;
But application only can proficiency ensure. . . .

To feed the body, not the mind—fathers, on you the blame!
Instruction without discipline, the idle teacher's shame.
Study alone directs the course of youthful minds aright;
How, with a youth of idleness, can age escape the blight?
Each shapeless mass of jade must by the artisan be wrought,
And man by constant study moral rectitude be taught.

Be wise in time, nor idly spend youth's fleeting days and nights;
Love tutor, friend, and practice oft Decorum's sacred rights. . . .

Father and son should live in love, in peace the married pair:
Kindness the elder brother's and respect the younger's care.
Let deference due to age be paid, comrades feel friendship's glow,
Princes treat well their minister—*they* loyalty should show.
These moral duties binding are on all men here below. . . .

Men's hearts rejoice to leave their children wealth and golden store!
I give my sons this little book and give them nothing more.

*Totman, *Japan Before Perry* (Berkeley: University of California Press, 1981), p. 152.

Zhu Xi on Learning

Of all the methods of learning, the first is to explore the basic principle of things. To get at the basic principle of things, one must study. The best way to study is to proceed slowly and in sequence, so as to learn everything well. In order to learn everything well, one must be serious-minded and able to concentrate. These are the unchanging principles of study.

There is a principle for everything under the sun: there is a principle behind the relationship between an Emperor and his subjects, between a father and his son, between brothers, between friends, and between a man and wife. Even in such trivial matters as entering and leaving a house, rising in the morning and going to bed at night, dealing with people and conducting daily affairs, there are set principles. Once we have explored the basic principles of things, we will understand all phenomena as well as the reasons behind them. There no longer will be doubts in our minds. We will naturally follow good and reject evil. Such are the reasons why learning should begin with the exploration of the true principles of things.

There are many theories about the principles of things in our world, some simple, others subtle, some clear, others obscure. Yet only the ancient sages were able to formulate a constant, eternal theory of the world, and their words and deeds have become the model for the ages. If we follow the teachings of these ancient sages, we can become superior men; if not, we will become ignorant fellows. We are inspired by the superior men who govern the realm within the four seas; we are frightened by the ignorant ones who lose their lives. All these deeds and results are recorded in the classics, historical writings, and memorials to the throne. A student who wishes to comprehend the basic truth of things yet fails to study these materials might as well place himself in front of a wall—he will not get anywhere. This is why I say that study is the only key to the comprehension of the principles of the world. . . .

The comprehension of essential knowledge depends on the mind. The mind is the most abstract, most mysterious, most delicate, and most unpredictable of all things. It is always the master of a person, for everything depends on it, and it cannot be absent for even a second. Once a person's mind wanders beyond his body, he will no longer have control over himself. Even in movements and perception he will not be the master of himself, let alone in the comprehension of the teachings of the ancient sages or in the investigation of the true nature of the myriad of things. Therefore Confucius said, "If a gentleman is not serious-minded, he will not inspire awe and his learning will not be solid." And Mencius said, "There is no principle in learning other than the freeing of the mind." . . . This is why concentration is the basis of learning. I, your humble subject, have tried these principles in the course of my own studies and found them most effective. I believe that even if the ancient sages should return to life, they would have no better methods for educating people. I believe these principles are fit even for the education of Kings and Emperors.

QUESTIONS FOR ANALYSIS

▶ Compare and contrast the two different texts: how do their authors view education?

▶ Which of Zhu Xi's ideas do not appear in *The Three-Character Classic* or in *The Analects* (see "Movement of Ideas," Chapter 4)?

▶ Which ideas do you think students in Japan and Korea would have found most understandable?

Technological Breakthroughs Although Chinese ships traveled to Southeast Asia and India as early as the fifth century, they stayed close to the coastline because their ships did not have compasses. Already in the fourth century B.C.E. the Chinese had known that naturally magnetic lodestones would point north when placed on a board. The lodestones, however, eventually lost their magnetism and so were not suited to long sea voyages.

Sometime between 850 and 1050, Chinese metallurgists realized that, if they heated steel needles to a high temperature that we now call the Curie point (which varies depending on the metal in question) and then cooled them rapidly, they could magnetize the needles. Placed in water on a float of some kind, the buoyant needles pointed north. The use of a steel-needle compass floating in water made deep-water navigation possible in the twelfth and thirteenth centuries and facilitated travel to distant places like Vietnam and Cambodia in Southeast Asia, farther than Chinese navigators had gone before.

Two maps (shown below), carved back to back on a stone tablet in 1136, illustrate the limits of Song dynasty knowledge of the outside world. Drawn sometime

■ **What Song Dynasty Cartographers Knew About the World Beyond China** These two maps were carved back to back on a single stone tablet in 1136. The map on the front of the tablet (*left*), "The Map of the Tracks of Yu," uses a grid to map the territory under Northern Song rule. This map shows nothing beyond China's borders. The cartographer of the map on the back of the stone tablet (*right*), "The Map of China and Foreign Countries," depicts China's major rivers and provinces spatially and provides short verbal descriptions of foreign peoples. (left: Zhengjiang Museum; right: Shaanxi Provincial Museum; both from Cao, Wan-Ru, with Zheng Xihuang, *An Atlas of Ancient Maps in China* [Beijing: Cultural Relics Publishing House, 1990], maps 56 and 62)

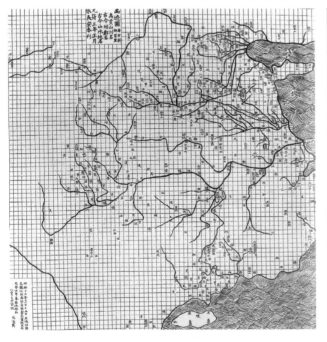
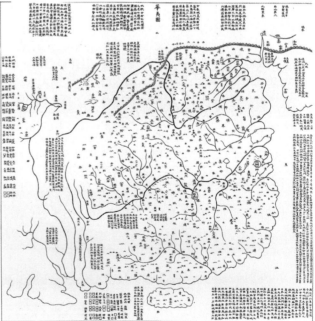

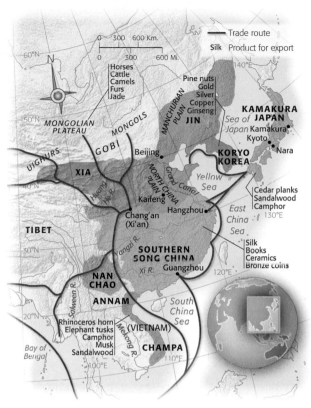

🌐 **MAP 12.1**

China's Trade Relations with the External World, 1225 In 1225, most of Song dynasty China's foreign trade was with Japan, Korea, and Vietnam. China exported silk and high-quality ceramics, while these different societies traded different minerals, raw materials, and foodstuffs in return. Chinese bronze coins circulated throughout the region, creating a currency sphere.

between 1081 and 1084, the map on the front, "The Map of the Tracks of Yu," maps the rivers and coastline of north and south China onto a grid. The map is named for Yu, a legendary ruler of ancient China who controlled floods. Each square covers the same amount of territory. Drawn to a scale of 1:3,500,000, the map is so accurate that it has been called "the most remarkable cartographic work of its age in any culture."[10] Depicting the territory under Northern Song rule, this map shows nothing beyond China's borders, so it omits Vietnam, Korea, and Japan.

As the title reveals, the second map, "The Map of China and Foreign Countries," includes non-Chinese areas. Composed in 1117, it covers much of the same territory as "The Map of the Tracks of Yu" but without a grid and so with much less precision. The map's anonymous cartographer had a good reason for leaving outlying areas blank: he simply did not know the locations of many foreign peoples. Accordingly, he devised a different way to show what he knew about them: he used words, not graphics. In tiny black characters surrounding the map, he provided capsule descriptions of certain foreign peoples. These written descriptions provide the names of Vietnam, Korea, and Japan yet give no further information, an indication that even mapmakers knew little about China's immediate neighbors in the early twelfth century.

The tradition of writing about foreign peoples continued with the publication in 1225 of *The Description of Foreign Peoples*[11] by **Zhao Rugua** (see Map 12.1). Zhao Rugua (JAO RUE-gwah) served as the director of the Department of Overseas Trade in Quanzhou, China's largest international trade port, in Fujian province on the southeast coast. Not a traveler himself, he combined information from encyclopedias with what he learned from speaking with foreign and Chinese traders, which enabled him to go beyond the 1117 map and describe the three states of East Asia most influenced by the Tang: Vietnam, Korea, and Japan.

Interactive Map

• Zhao Rugua (fl. 1225) Author of *The Description of Foreign Peoples* (published in 1225), a compendium of information about China's closest trading partners—Korea, Vietnam, and Japan—and distant places such as the east coast of Africa and Spain.

• Ly dynasty (1009–1224) The independent rulers of Vietnam who claimed to have the Mandate of Heaven to rule the southern empire. Adopted the *Tang Code* in 1042 and accepted tributary status, acknowledging the superiority of the Chinese emperor.

Vietnam Since Vietnam directly bordered China on the south, it received the most extensive Chinese influence. Zhao did not consider it a separate country. Under direct Chinese rule during the Han and Tang dynasties, Vietnam, under the **Ly dynasty** (1009–1224), remained nominally independent during the

Song. Because it was a tributary of China, its king acknowledged the superiority of the Chinese emperor and periodically sent delegations to the Chinese capital to present him with gifts. The Chinese emperor bestowed gifts on the emissaries in return.

The Chinese-educated scholars of the Ly (LEE) dynasty argued that their king, the southern emperor, ruled the southern kingdom of Vietnam because he, like the Chinese emperor, had the Mandate of Heaven (see Chapter 4). The Vietnamese kings credited local spirits with protecting the royal house and supported Buddhism. Since at least the fourth century, Buddhist monks had traveled back and forth between China and Vietnam, and Buddhist texts had circulated in both directions (see Chapter 8).

The Vietnamese king and his courtiers had received a Chinese-style education and could read and write Chinese. In 1042, the Ly emperor adopted a modified form of the *Tang Code* (see Chapter 8) so that his subjects would understand the laws of the kingdom. In fact, though, the dynasty's control beyond the major administrative centers was weak. In much of the kingdom's territory, largely independent chieftains ruled groups who lived in bands in the highlands and submitted valued items like rhinoceros horns and elephant tusks to the king. At the time of Zhao's writing, the Vietnamese exported to China the same unprocessed goods, including rhinoceros horns, elephant tusks, camphor, musk, and sandalwood, that they had for the previous thousand years.

Korea

Korea Like Vietnam, Korea did not strike Zhao Rugua as foreign: "Their houses, utensils and implements, their mode of dressing and their methods of administration are," Zhao remarked, "more or less copies of what we have in China." In 936, the founder of the **Koryo dynasty** (936–1392) defeated his last rival and founded the dynasty that gave its name to the modern country of Korea. He modeled the structure of the central government on the Tang dynasty and divided the region into administrative districts like those in China.

The king used a Chinese-style exam to recruit officials and thereby reduce the influence of his main rivals, powerful families who formed a hereditary local aristocracy who controlled their own troops. This policy succeeded for over two hundred years until 1170, when aristocrats and their military supporters overthrew the Chinese-style administration. Military officers took over all government positions, and men of letters retreated to the countryside, where they continued their studies. Kings continued to rule as figureheads, but the top generals could and did replace them at will.

Trade with China persisted even during these politically unstable times. Korea exported precious metals like gold, silver, and copper and edible goods like ginseng and pine nuts in exchange for Chinese silks, books, and high-quality ceramics. Korean potters built high-firing kilns in which they made pale green celadon pots even more beautiful than Chinese export ware.

Koreans also embraced woodblock printing. In 1251, Korean printers created a library of Buddhist texts several thousand sewn chapters long that is universally acknowledged to be the highest-quality set made anywhere in East Asia. Much more so than their Chinese counterparts, Korean printers adopted the technology of movable type. The world's first surviving book printed with movable type was made in Korea and dates to around 1400, some three centuries after the Chinese first

• Koryo dynasty (936–1392) Dynasty that gave its name to the modern country of Korea. Its founder modeled the structure of the central government on the Tang dnasty and divided the region into administrative districts like those in China.

invented movable type and half a century before Johannes Gutenberg printed the first Bible in Germany using movable type (see Chapter 15).

Japan

Zhao Rugua called Japan the "Land of the Rising Sun," because "this country is situated near the place where the sun rises." The Japanese, Zhao reported, exported cedar trees, some as tall as 15 yards (15 m). "The natives split them into planks, which they transport in large junks to our port of Quanzhou for sale."

Although the Japanese emperors had earlier looked to China as a model (see Chapter 8), after 900 certain warrior clans gradually gained power and forced the emperor to retire to Kyoto, abandon Chinese-style government, and remain as a figurehead. In 1185, the Minamoto (ME-nah-MOE-toe) clan defeated its rivals and established a new capital at Kamakura, a city just outside modern Tokyo.

During the **Kamakura period** (1185–1333), political power rested in the hands of the shogun, or general, who claimed to govern on behalf of the emperor. The shogun did not conduct Chinese-style civil service examinations but appointed members of powerful clans to office. Still, scholars continued to study both Buddhist and Confucian texts, many of them imported from China and written in Chinese characters; they also used the kana alphabet to represent the sounds of spoken Japanese.

The shogun patronized Buddhism, and the teachings of Zen Buddhism attracted many followers. Zen masters posed puzzling questions with no clear answer: for example, what is the sound of one hand clapping? As disciples meditated on these questions, their masters hoped that they would suddenly understand the teachings of the master and attain enlightenment.

> • **Kamakura period** (1185–1333) Era in Japanese history when political power rested in the hands of the shogun, or general, who governed on the emperor's behalf. The shogun appointed members of powerful clans to office without civil service examinations.

The World Beyond East Asia

Going beyond East Asia, Zhao Rugua's book covers the Islamic heartland of Arabia and Mecca and the Islamic periphery; the southern coast of Europe; and the northern and eastern coasts of Africa. Clearly dependent on Arab geographers for his knowledge of these places, Zhao's entries mix accurate information with sheer fantasy. For example, he begins his description of Madagascar in vague terms—"The country is in the sea to the south-west"—and then reports that a giant bird lives there who swallows camels whole.

But Zhao's information is not all myth. He is particularly knowledgeable about foreign products, such as dark-skinned African slaves, that he has seen with his own eyes in Quanzhou. "In the West there is an island in the sea on which there are many savages, with bodies as black as lacquer and with frizzed hair. They are enticed by offers of food and then caught and carried off for slaves to the Arabian countries, where they fetch a high price."

Zhao's knowledge of the non-Chinese was the product of the trading environment of Quanzhou. Almost every place on his list is located on a seacoast, and the goods he describes came to China on seagoing vessels. Knowing nothing of the nomadic peoples of the north, Zhao was completely unaware that as he was writing a powerful confederation of Mongols was taking shape on the grasslands of Eurasia (see Chapter 14).

> CL **Primary Source:**
> A Description of Foreign Peoples
> *Discover the rich commodities and unusual customs of Arabia and southern Spain, as seen by Zhao Rugua, a thirteenth-century Chinese trade official.*

Chapter Review

CL Download the MP3 audio file of the Chapter Review and listen to it on the go.

When later Chinese looked back on the Song dynasty, they had much reason to be proud. To be sure, the dynasty's military forces had suffered the massive loss in 1126 of all north China to the Jurchen, as Li Qingzhao so movingly recorded. Her memoir captures the civilized, cosmopolitan life of the Song dynasty. The expansion of markets during the commercial revolution had changed people's lives dramatically for the better. The sustained prosperity made it possible for couples like Li Qingzhao and Zhao Mingcheng to attain a high level of education. In the next chapter, we will meet a similarly talented couple who lived through a period of comparable economic growth in Europe.

What political events pushed people to migrate south?

The turmoil of the An Lushan rebellion of 755–763 prompted many living in north China to move south, and the migrations continued in the closing years of the Tang dynasty and the Five Dynasties period. The fall of north China in 1126–1127 to the invading armies of the Jin dynasty accelerated the migrations south. Some 20,000 officials, including Li Qingzhao's husband Zhao Mingcheng, 100,000 clerks, and 400,000 soldiers and their families moved to the new capital at Hangzhou.

What were the causes of the commercial revolution?

The more productive rice agriculture of south China produced a surplus that freed some family members to grow cash crops, like tangerines, or to make handicrafts, like baskets and textiles, to sell at market. The Song dynasty government increased the money supply, both by minting more bronze coins and, after 1100, by printing the world's first paper money.

How did the changes of the commercial revolution affect education—for men and for women—and religious life?

The era's prosperity, coupled with the development of woodblock printing, sustained an educational boom. While sons of official families might have bemoaned the increased competition in the open civil service examinations, hundreds of thousands of boys and even girls learned to read and write in schools or at home with tutors. The economic growth also meant that more people had money to give to religious practitioners who claimed to be able to cure the ill and to pray on behalf of the dead. Devotees gave money to Buddhist and Daoist monasteries, temples to deities, and Confucian shrines to worthies. The teachings of Zhu Xi attracted a wide following, particularly among elite families whose sons did not attain positions in the bureaucracy.

How did China's economic growth influence its immediate neighbors of Japan, Korea, and Vietnam?

Consumers in Vietnam, Korea, and Japan purchased Chinese ceramics, textiles, and books even as they exported metals, food, and lumber to the Song Empire. They did not accept Chinese culture passively but modified it to suit their own societies. Korean potters and printers surpassed Chinese accomplishments in high-fired porcelain and movable type printing.

For Further Reference

Bol, Peter K. "The Sung Examination System and the Shih." *Asia Major,* 3rd ser., 3.2 (1990): 149–171.

Chaffee, John. *The Thorny Gates of Learning in Sung China: A Social History of Examinations.* New York: Cambridge University Press, 1985.

Ebrey, Patricia. *The Inner Quarters: Marriage and the Lives of Chinese Women in the Sung Period.* Berkeley: University of California Press, 1993.

Ebrey, Patricia Buckley, Anne Walthall, and James B. Palais. *East Asia: A Cultural, Social, and Political History.* 2d ed. Boston: Wadsworth/Cengage Learning, 2009.

Franke, Herbert. "The Chin Dynasty." In Denis C. Twitchett and Herbert Franke, eds., *Alien Regimes and Border States, 907–1368,* vol. 6 of *The Cambridge History of China.* New York: Cambridge University Press, 1994.

Hansen, Valerie. *The Open Empire: A History of China to 1600.* New York: W. W. Norton, 2000.

Heng Chye Kiang. *Cities of Aristocrats and Bureaucrats: The Development of Medieval Chinese Cityscapes.* Singapore: University of Singapore Press, 1999.

Owen, Stephen. "The Snares of Memory." In *Remembrances: The Experience of the Past in Classical Chinese Literature.* Cambridge: Harvard University Press, 1986, pp. 80–98.

Tarling, Nicholas, ed. *The Cambridge History of Southeast Asia.* Cambridge: Cambridge University Press, 1999.

Temple, Robert. *The Genius of China; 3,000 Years of Science, Discovery, and Invention.* New York: Simon and Schuster, 1986.

Totman, Conrad. *A History of Japan.* Malden, Mass: Blackwell Publishers, 2000.

 **WEB RESOURCES**

Pronunciation Guide

Interactive Maps

MAP 12.1 China's Trade Relations with the External World, 1225

Primary Sources

Chapter Objectives

ACE Multiple-Choice Quiz

Flashcards

Websites

The Beijing Qingming Scroll and Its Significance for the Study of Chinese History, by Valerie Hansen (http://www.yale.edu/history/faculty/materials/hansen-qingming-scroll.html).   Introduction to the Qingming Scroll, with captions and detailed images of the painting.

Li Qingzhao (http://home.infionline.net/~ddisse/liquinzh.html).   A short biography and translations of poems by Li Qingzhao.

Nova Online: Secrets of Lost Empires: China Bridge (http://www.pbs.org/wgbh/nova/lostempires/china/). A website to accompany the show "China Bridge," including resources and teacher's guide.

Europe's Commercial Revolution, 1000–1400

Sometime around 1132, when he was in his early 40s, **Peter Abelard** (1079–1142/44) wrote an account of his own life entitled *The Story of His Misfortunes*. The title was apt. Abelard wrote about his love affair with **Heloise** (ca. 1090–1163/64), a woman at least ten years younger than he was; when her guardian discovered that Heloise was pregnant, he ordered several of his men to castrate Abelard. After the assault, Abelard and Heloise separated and lived in religious institutions for the rest of their lives, he as a learned teacher, she as the abbess of a nunnery. Over the course of their event-filled lives, Heloise and Abelard personally experienced the changes occurring in Europe between 1000 and 1400. Like China of the Song dynasty (see Chapter 12), Europe underwent a dramatic commercial revolution, especially in agriculture. Most of the land in Europe was brought under cultivation in a process called *cerealization*. The economic surplus financed the first universities of Europe, new religious institutions, the Crusades, and trade with East Asia, all of which made the Europeans in 1400 richer and more knowledgeable about distant places than they had been in 1000.

We can learn about the dramatic changes of this period from Abelard's memoir, which begins with the story of his childhood:

ABELARD
AND HELOISE

(Musée Condé, Chantilly, France/Giraudon/Art Resource, NY)

I was born on the borders of Brittany, about eight miles I think to the east of Nantes (NAHNT), in a town called Le Pallet (luh PAH-lay). I owe my volatile temperament to my native soil and ancestry and also my natural ability for learning. My father had acquired some knowledge of letters before he was a knight, and later on his passion for learning was such that he intended all his sons to have instruction in letters before they were trained to arms. His purpose was fulfilled. I was his first-born, and being specially dear to him had the greatest care taken over my education. For my part, the more rapid and easy my progress in my

CL This icon will direct you to interactive activities and study materials on the *Voyages* website: www.cengage.com/history/hansen/voyages1e

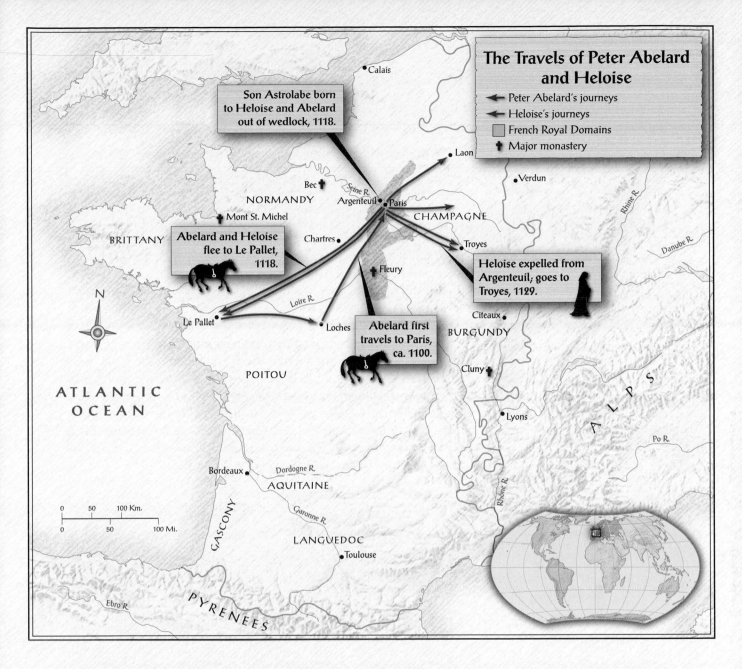

The Travels of Peter Abelard and Heloise

← Peter Abelard's journeys
← Heloise's journeys
▢ French Royal Domains
✝ Major monastery

Calais

Son Astrolabe born to Heloise and Abelard out of wedlock, 1118.

Laon

Verdun

Bec ✝

Seine R.

Rhine R.

NORMANDY

Argenteuil • Paris

CHAMPAGNE

Danube R.

Mont St. Michel ✝

Chartres •

BRITTANY

Abelard and Heloise flee to Le Pallet, 1118.

Troyes •

Fleury ✝

Heloise expelled from Argenteuil; goes to Troyes, 1129.

Loire R.

Le Pallet •

Loches •

Abelard first travels to Paris, ca. 1100.

Cîteaux •

BURGUNDY

N

POITOU

Cluny ✝

Lyons •

A L P S

ATLANTIC OCEAN

Po R.

Bordeaux •

Dordogne R.

AQUITAINE

Rhône R.

Garonne R.

0   50   100 Km.
0   50   100 Mi.

GASCONY

LANGUEDOC

Toulouse •

Ebro R.

P Y R E N E E S

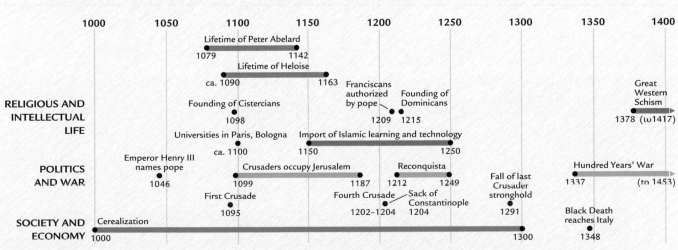

	1000	1050	1100	1150	1200	1250	1300	1350	1400

Lifetime of Peter Abelard
1079   1142

Lifetime of Heloise
ca. 1090   1163

RELIGIOUS AND INTELLECTUAL LIFE

Founding of Cistercians
1098

Franciscans authorized by pope
1209

Founding of Dominicans
1215

Great Western Schism
1378 (to 1417)

Universities in Paris, Bologna
ca. 1100

Import of Islamic learning and technology
1150   1250

POLITICS AND WAR

Emperor Henry III names pope
1046

Crusaders occupy Jerusalem
1099   1187

Reconquista
1212   1249

Fall of last Crusader stronghold
1291

Hundred Years' War
1337   (to 1453)

First Crusade
1095

Fourth Crusade
1202–1204

Sack of Constantinople
1204

SOCIETY AND ECONOMY

Cerealization
1000   1300

Black Death reaches Italy
1348

studies, the more eagerly I applied myself, until I was so carried away by my love of learning that I renounced the glory of a military life. . . . I began to travel about in several provinces disputing, like a true peripatetic philosopher, wherever I had heard there was a keen interest in the art of dialectic.[1]

• Peter Abelard (1079–1142/44) Prominent scholastic thinker who wrote about his affair with Heloise in his autobiography, *The Story of His Misfortunes.*

• Heloise (ca. 1090–1163/64) French nun who wrote many letters to Peter Abelard, her former lover and the father of her child Astrolabe, which survive in the *Letters of Abelard and Heloise.*

Abelard's speaking abilities and ferocious intelligence made him one of the best-known philosophers and most famous teachers in Europe. He traveled from one French town to another until he arrived in the great intellectual center of Paris, where one of the first universities in the world was taking shape. Students from all over Europe flocked to hear his lectures before returning home to serve their kings as officials or their churches as clergy.

During this time, new methods of farming produced much higher yields, and Europe's population increased as a result. Many landowning families initiated new inheritance practices that gave only the eldest sons the right to inherit their father's estates, forcing the other sons to go into education, as Abelard chose to do voluntarily, or the church, which, after undergoing many different reforms, became one of the most vibrant institutions in medieval European society. The century from 1300 to 1400 saw a temporary halt in growth caused by a massive outbreak of plague but also changes that strengthened European monarchies.

Focus Questions

What caused the cerealization of Europe, and what were its results?

What led to the foundation of Europe's universities? How did they gain the right to govern themselves?

How did economic prosperity affect the Christian church and different monastic orders?

What did the Crusaders hope to achieve outside Europe? Within Europe?

How did the major developments of the century from 1300 to 1400 strengthen European monarchies?

The Cerealization and Urbanization of Europe

Europe experienced sustained economic prosperity between 1000 and 1300. The growth resulted not from migration to rice-growing regions as in China (see Chapter 12) but from the intensification of agriculture. Quite simply, Europeans grew the same staple crops of wheat and barley, but they reclaimed more land and farmed it more intensively than they had before. The main innovations—crop rotation, horse-drawn plows, use of iron tools, and water mills and windmills—were known in earlier times but became widespread after 1000. Europe's population grew dramatically as a result. As in China, the creation of a large agricultural surplus freed some people from having to work the land and allowed them to pursue a variety of careers.

Agricultural Innovation

The agricultural innovations from 1000 to 1300 can be summed up in a single word: *cerealization*. Like the term *industrialization,* the word **cerealization** indicates a broad transformation that profoundly affected everyone who experienced it. Before cerealization, much of the land in Europe was not cultivated regularly; after it, much of it was. In Carolingian France at the time of Charlemagne in 800 (see Chapter 10), many farmers had engaged in slash-and-burn, or swidden, agriculture. Since they worked different plots at different times, as much as half of the land remained uncultivated at any moment. Farmers had to fish and hunt to supplement their diets. But the advanced agricultural techniques that came into use after 1000 allowed them to keep more land under cultivation.

Not all these changes occurred at the same time throughout Europe. Northern France and England were the most advanced regions. Farmers before 1000 realized that land became less fertile if they planted the same crop year after year, so each year they allowed a third to half of their land to lie fallow. After 1000, a few farmers began to rotate their crops so that they could keep their land under continuous cultivation. One popular rotation of turnips, clover, and grain took advantage of different nutrients in the soil each year. This practice, so crucial to increasing agricultural yield, spread only slowly.

European farmers also began to exploit more sheep, horses, and cows in their farming. They raised sheep for their wool, while they could use both horses and oxen for transport. In the centuries after 1100, horses, which worked harder and faster, gradually replaced oxen on European farms. By 1200, very few farmers in northern France used oxen any longer.

Before 1000, most of the plows used in Europe to prepare the earth for planting had wooden blades, which broke easily and could not penetrate far into the soil. Gradually farmers, particularly in northern France, added pieces of iron to their blades, which allowed them to dig deeper and increase productivity. In addition, iron horseshoes protected the hooves of the horses that pulled the plows. Farmers also experimented with better harnesses for draft horses that allowed them to pull plows more efficiently. By 1200, many villages had their own blacksmiths who repaired horseshoes and plow blades.

The final innovation left the deepest imprint on the landscape. As early as 500, but particularly after 1000, farmers began to harness the water in flowing rivers to

> **cerealization** Term comprising many agricultural practices that allowed Europeans between 1000 and 1300 to cultivate most of the land in Europe: crop rotation, use of draft animals, the addition of iron blades to plows, and the spread of water mills and windmills.

operate mills. Water mills were first used to grind grain and then were adapted to other uses, such as beating wool to make it thicker ("fulling" cloth), sawing wood, and sharpening or polishing iron. By 1100, records show that at least 5,600 water mills existed throughout England, or one mill for every thirty-five families.

Even more powerful than water mills were those powered by wind. The world's first windmills were built in Iran around 700; positioned on a vertical axis, the blades drove pumps that moved water from one irrigation channel to another. They came into use in Europe just before 1200. Since windmills required a steady wind, they could only be used in certain regions, often by the sea.

Each farming family performed a wide variety of tasks. Women tended to do the jobs closer to the home, like raising children, cooking food, tending the garden, milking cows, and caring for the other livestock. Men did the plowing and sowed seed, but both sexes helped to bring in the harvest. Many households hired temporary help, both male and female, at busy times of year to assist with shearing sheep, picking hops for beer, and mowing hay.

Population Growth and Urbanization

The clear result of Europe's cerealization was the marked population growth that occurred between 1000 and 1340. In 1000, Europe had a population of less than 40 million; by 1340 the population had nearly doubled to around 75 million. Even more significant was the geographic pattern of population growth. The number of people living in southern and eastern Europe—in Italy, Spain, and the Balkans—increased 50 percent, from 17 to 25 million. But the population of northern Europe shot up by a factor of three, with the result that half of Europe's people lived in northern Europe by 1340.[2]

■ **Cutting-Edge Farming Techniques in Europe, 1300–1340** At first glance, the two men working the land may seem to be using traditional farming techniques. In fact, though, this detail from a manuscript illustrates two of the most important innovations in the cerealization of Europe: horse-drawn plowing equipment and the use of iron tools. The horse is pulling a harrow, a large rakelike tool with many teeth that broke up lumps of earth after the soil had already been plowed. (British Library, London/HIP/ Art Resource, NY)

The process of cerealization freed large numbers of people from working the land full-time. Individual households began to produce food products such as butter, cheese, and eggs or handicrafts like textiles and soap to sell at local markets. At first, people went to periodic markets to trade for the goods they needed. This began to change around 1000, when rulers minted the first coins since the fall of the Western Roman Empire. With the new currency, many periodic markets gradually evolved into permanent markets that opened daily. Markets were usually located near castles or large monasteries; inside the walls of most European market towns were the marketplace, the lord's castle, and several churches.

These market towns arose first on the coasts of the Mediterranean, the English Channel, and the Baltic or along inland rivers like the Rhine. During the 1000s and 1100s, more and more people traveled from one market to another, sometimes going overland on new roads, to attend the fairs that occurred with increasing frequency.

Before 1000, only a handful of cities, all the sites of castles or church centers, existed north of the Alps. After 1000, the number of cities there increased sharply. European cities between 1000 and 1348 were not large. One of the largest, Paris, had a population of 80,000 in 1200, much less than the 450,000 people living in Islamic Córdoba and a mere fraction of Song dynasty Hangzhou's one million.

Yet the people who lived in Europe's cities had crossed an important divide: because they had stopped working the land, they were dependent on the city's markets for their food supply. Many urban artisans worked either in food preparation, like butchers and bakers, or in the field of apparel, like tailors and shoemakers. Because one-third to one-half of these artisans worked with no assistants, they depended on their wives and children to sell their goods. Some merchants specialized in transporting goods from one place to another; for example, a German woman in 1420 bought and sold "crossbows, saddle bags, bridles, harnesses, halters, spurs, and stirrups, as well as sulphur, copperas [a chemical used in tanning], verdigris [a green pigment], arrow quivers, soap, parchment, wax, paper, and spices."[3]

The people who lived in cities were intensely aware that they differed from those who worked the estates and those who owned them. Tradesmen in the same occupations formed **guilds** that regulated prices and working hours; they also covered their members' burial costs. Most important, they decided who could enter the guild and who could not; only those who belonged to the guild could engage in the business the guild regulated. One visible sign of the guilds' influence was the cathedrals they financed throughout Europe, sometimes with contributions from others. (See the feature "Visual Evidence: The Gothic Cathedral at Chartres.")

After 1000, urban residents frequently petitioned their rulers for the right to pass regulations concerning trade and to mint coins. Local rulers often granted these rights in the hope that the guilds would support them against their rivals.

● **guilds** Associations formed by members of the same trade that regulated prices and working hours and covered members' burial costs. Only those who belonged to the guild could engage in the business the guild regulated.

Land Use and Social Change, 1000–1350

The sharp increases in productivity brought dramatic changes throughout society. These changes did not occur everywhere at the same time, and in some areas they did not occur at all, but they definitely took place in northern France between 1000 and 1200.

One change was that slavery all but disappeared, while serfs did most of the work for those who owned land. Some of the most informative sources are the lists of customs that detail the obligations of serfs to their landlords. Although their

THE GOTHIC CATHEDRAL AT CHARTRES

Starting around 1150, people throughout Europe built cathedrals in the Gothic style, of which the Cathedral of Notre Dame at Chartres, France, is one of the best examples. The cathedral has an unusual front because the south tower (on the left) was built in 1160, while the much more opulent north tower was added in 1513 after a fire destroyed the original.

High arched ceilings inspired awe in those who entered cathedrals, but medieval builders faced a major engineering challenge. Arches built in the traditional manner required thick walls to support them; otherwise the walls would buckle from the outward pressure. Two innovations allowed stoneworkers to deflect the pressure away from the walls and build taller structures: vaults with ribs inside the church and flying buttresses outside the walls. With the help of these supports, the ceiling of Chartres rises a glorious 121 feet (37 m) above the ground.

Since the walls did not bear the weight of the ceiling, they could be cut away to hold glass windows. Unlike many other cathedrals, Chartres preserves much of its original stained glass. Of 186 original stained-glass windows, 152 have survived. Many

(Sandro Vannini/Corbis)

The north tower, completed in 1507, is so heavily decorated that architectural historians call its style "flamboyant style." It contrasts sharply with the original Gothic style of the south tower.

Half arches connect these flying buttresses outside to the cathedral wall, which they support, making it possible to build a high interior roof.

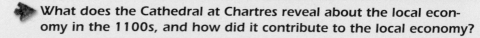

QUESTION FOR ANALYSIS

What does the Cathedral at Chartres reveal about the local economy in the 1100s, and how did it contribute to the local economy?

windows were dedicated by guild members and portray biblical scenes above and scenes of that guild's work below.

The window shown here was dedicated to Saint Lubin (Saint Leobinus), the bishop of Chartres in 558, whose devotees believed that he performed miracles, including curing people afflicted with edema, an illness that caused excess swelling. Wine merchants and local innkeepers paid for the window, which was completed in 1210.

Chartres was both a religious and an economic center. Pilgrims flocked to the cathedral to worship Mary, the Virgin Mother of Jesus, and her robe, which they believed survived, inside the cathedral. The pilgrims hoped that Mary would heal their illnesses and grant their prayers. Wealthy worshipers could afford to buy copies of her robe made for tourists, while others could purchase cheaper, lead figurines that they could pray to at home.

The young Lubin studies his alphabet while behind him his companion quaffs a glass of wine. All the round windows portray scenes from the life of Saint Lubin.

His hand holding a whip, a wine merchant transports a cask of wine tied onto a donkey cart.

In each of the side panels, people wearing different-colored robes hold cups of wine.

A wine seller gives a goblet of wine to a seated traveler, while the young boy behind him announces that a new barrel of wine has been opened. Above his head is a barrel hoop, the sign of a tavern.

(Erich Lessing/Art Resource, NY)

363

landlords did not own them, and they were not slaves, a series of obligations tied serfs to the land. Each year, their most important duty was to give their lord a fixed share of the crop and of their herds. Serfs were also obliged to build roads, give lodging to guests, and perform many other tasks for their lords. After 1000, a majority of those working the land became serfs.

Many serfs lived in settlements built around either the castles of lords or churches. The prevailing mental image of a medieval castle town is one in which a lord lives protected by his knights and surrounded by his serfs, who go outside the walls each day to work in the fields. Some use the term **feudal** for such a society. Yet historians today often avoid the word *feudal* because no one alive between 1000 and 1350 used such a word, and the term came into use only after 1600 as a legal concept.

> • **feudal** The legal and social system in Europe from 1000 to 1400 in which serfs worked the land and subordinates performed military service for their lords in return for protection. The term came into use after 1600 as a legal concept.

The prominent French historian Georges Duby has described the social revolution of the eleventh and twelfth centuries in the following way. In Carolingian society, around 800, the powerful used loot and plunder to support themselves, usually by engaging in military conquest. Society consisted of two major groups: the powerful and the powerless. In the new society after 1000, the powerful comprised several clearly defined social orders—lords, knights, clergy—who held specific rights over the serfs below them. Many lords also commanded the service of a group of warriors, or knights, who offered them military service in exchange for military protection from others.

Knights began their training as children, when they learned how to ride and to handle a dagger. At the age of 14, knights-in-training accompanied a mature knight into battle. They usually wore tunics made of metal loops, or chain mail, as well as headgear that could repel arrows. This type of clothing was heavy and hot. Their main weapons were iron-and-steel swords and crossbows that shot metal bolts.

One characteristic of the age was weak centralized rule. Although many countries, like England and France, continued to have monarchs, these kings' power was severely limited because their armies were no stronger than those of the nobles who ranked below them. They controlled the lands immediately under them but not much else. The king of France, for example, ruled the region in the immediate vicinity of Paris, but other nobles had authority over the rest of France. In other countries as well, kings vied with rival nobles to gain control of a given region, and they often lost.

In the eleventh and twelfth centuries, landowners frequently gave large tracts of land to various monasteries (see page 372). The monasteries did not pay any taxes on this land, and no one dared to encroach on church-owned land for fear of the consequences from God. By the end of the twelfth century, the church owned one-third of the land in northern France and one-sixth of all the land in France and Italy combined.

One of the most perplexing changes was the rise of primogeniture in northern France, England, Belgium, and the Netherlands. Before 1000, when the head of the family died, aristocratic families divided their property among their sons, and sometimes even granted their daughters a share of the estate. After 1000, they kept their estates intact by passing the property on to only one son. As we have seen, Peter Abelard explained that he, the first-born son, was entitled to his father's lands but chose to give up his inheritance to pursue his studies.

He was an exception. Much more often first-born sons kept their family estates, and their brothers pursued other careers, whether as bureaucrats, churchmen, or knights in someone else's service. In many cases these second sons attended schools and universities before embarking on their chosen careers.

The Rise of the European Universities, 1100–1400

Although schools had existed in Europe at least since the time of the Roman Empire, rates of literacy remained low throughout the continent. Starting around 1100, groups of teachers gathered in two major centers—Paris, France, and Bologna, Italy—and began to attract large numbers of male students, many of them from well-off families who used their surplus wealth, the product of cerealization, to finance their sons' education. In this early period, the universities were unregulated and free, as Peter Abelard experienced himself. Soon, however, the curriculum became more standardized. In a crucial development, cities, kings, and popes granted the universities a certain amount of self-rule and the right to grant degrees, rights that allowed universities to develop into independent centers of learning.

Education in Europe Before the Universities, ca. 1100

Latin remained the language of all educated people, the church, and administrative documents, and students had to learn to read and write Latin before they could advance to other subjects. The most basic schools also taught the simple mathematics needed by peddlers. Before 1100, most people who learned to read and write did so in local schools or at home with tutors or their parents. Some of these schools admitted girls, whether in separate classrooms or together with boys. Many schools were headed by a couple so that the father could teach the boys and the mother the girls. Often they were located close to the cathedrals that administered them. Heloise studied at a convent outside Paris.

Peter Abelard has little to say about his early education except that he loved learning and that his favorite subject was "dialectic," by which he meant the study of logic. Dialectic was one of three subjects, along with grammar and rhetoric, that formed the trivium. The roots of the trivium curriculum lay in ancient Greece and Rome: one studied the structure of language in grammar, expression in rhetoric, and meaning in dialectic, the most advanced subject of the three. Then one advanced to the quadrivium, which included arithmetic, astronomy, geometry, and music theory. The trivium and quadrivium formed the basic core of the curriculum and together were known as the **liberal arts.** The highest-level subjects, beyond the trivium and the quadrivium, were theology, church law, and medicine.

Abelard wrote a treatise called *Sic et Non* (Yes and No) whose prologue explained his method of instruction:

> It is my purpose, according to my original intention, to gather together the various sayings of the holy Fathers which have occurred to me as being surrounded by some degree of uncertainty because of their seeming incompatibility. These may encourage inexperienced readers to engage in that most

● liberal arts Basic core of the curriculum in Europe between 500 and 1500 that consisted of the trivium (logic, grammar, and rhetoric) and the quadrivium (arithmetic, astronomy, geometry, and music theory).

important exercise, enquiry into truth. . . . For by doubting we come to inquiry, and by inquiry we perceive the truth.[4]

Sic et Non poses a series of questions and then provides citations from classical sources and the Bible without directly providing any solutions. If one posed the question correctly and considered the proper authorities, one could draw on the powers of reasoning to arrive at the correct answer, Abelard and his contemporaries believed. This optimism about the ability of human reason to resolve the long-standing debates of the past characterizes **scholasticism,** the prevailing method of instruction in Europe between 1100 and 1500.

In 1114, Abelard was named to his first teaching position in Paris as master of the cathedral school at Notre-Dame. He became a canon, that is, a member of the small group of salaried clerics living close to the cathedral who served its religious needs. When Peter Abelard began teaching, he focused on explicating the single book Ezekiel of the Hebrew Bible. Teachers at universities explicated ideas and concepts slowly. The goal of most instructors was to cover an entire book in a year or two of instruction.

Books remained expensive. The main writing material was parchment, made by scraping the hair from the skin of a sheep or goat and drying it. One copy of the Bible made in Winchester, England, was made from the skins of 250 calves selected from 2,500 imperfect ones.[5] Booksellers formed copying workshops in which literate craftsmen copied texts at maximum speed. They no longer used the minuscule handwriting popular in Charlemagne's day: instead they adopted the even faster Gothic script, with short, upright strokes.

When the news of Abelard's affair with Heloise broke in 1118, he left Paris and returned only in the 1130s, when he again took up a teaching post. In 1136, when John of Salisbury arrived from England to study with Abelard, he reported that Paris had become the most important center of learning in Europe because more people taught there than anywhere else.

During the early 1100s, the university at Bologna in Italy became a center for the study of law. Legal study flourished as people realized that law could be used to resolve the disputes that occurred constantly between kings and subjects, churches and nobles, and merchants and customers. All kinds of groups, whether in monasteries, guilds, or universities, began to write down previously unwritten laws. The Magna Carta, which formalized the relationships between the English king and his barons in 1215, is a good example.

The Import of Learning and Technology from the Islamic World, 1150–1250

From about 1150 to 1250, scholars recovered hundreds of Greek texts that had disappeared from Europe after the loss of the Western Roman Empire in 476 (see Chapter 10). Arabic versions of these texts had been preserved in the Islamic world, and their recovery fueled a period of great intellectual growth. Between 1160 and 1200, all of Aristotle's works were first translated from Arabic into Latin and then checked against the original Greek. Like many of his contemporaries, Abelard did not know more than a few words of Greek (Heloise seems to have known more), so the translation of Greek texts into Latin had a direct impact on Europe's intellectual life. (See the feature "Movement of Ideas: Adelard of Bath.")

Sidebar

• **scholasticism**
Prevailing method of instruction in Europe between 1100 and 1500. Held that students could arrive at a correct answer if they used their powers of reasoning to derive the answer from multiple citations of classical sources and the Bible.

CL Primary Source:
Magna Carta: The Great Charter of Liberties
Learn what rights and liberties the English nobility, on behalf of all free Englishmen, forced King John to grant them in 1215.

As Islamic learning entered Europe, Europeans encountered paper, which the Chinese had first invented and which was transmitted to the Islamic world in the eighth century. Paper appeared first in Spain in the tenth century and then in Sicily in the eleventh, but it won wide use only between 1250 and 1350 as Italian-made paper spread throughout Europe. Following the same route as paper, the ship's compass and the adjustable rudder originated in China and came to Europe via the Islamic world.

Other technologies from the Islamic world, such as magnifying glasses, entered Europe around 1200. Eyeglasses were first made from transparent, naturally occurring quartz, and only later from glass. Europeans also profited from Islamic knowledge of medicine, which was much more advanced than European; students at European universities studied the works of the Greek doctor Galen (129–ca. 216) that had been updated by Islamic commentators. Muslim observers were shocked to see European surgeons cut off the legs of wounded soldiers with axes instead of with the precise metal instruments used throughout the Islamic world.

Some European scholars clearly admired Islamic learning. Among them were Peter Abelard and Heloise, who named their son Astrolabe (born in 1118, year of death unknown) for the Islamic navigation instrument. Others, however, remained suspicious of the Islamic world because it was not Christian, and the interest in Arab learning waned after 1250 once the important Greek thinkers had been translated into Latin.

The Universities Come of Age, 1150–1250

As contact with the Islamic world began to invigorate learning, the universities at Paris and Bologna gained significant independence in the century after Abelard's death in the 1140s. Although the two universities had arisen at the same time, they were quite different. In Paris, most of the masters had independent incomes provided by the church, so they were not dependent on the tuition paid by students. Their counterparts in Italy were more often laypeople without independent incomes who earned their living with the money the students paid. Accordingly, Bologna's students had far more power than those in Paris, and they hired the masters for the following year.

In 1200, Paris had a population of some eighty thousand, while Bologna, with forty thousand residents, was half its size. In both cities, the student population fluctuated around 10 percent. As trade guilds regulated their own membership, so too did students and instructors decide who could join the university.

Modern degrees have their origins in the different steps to full membership in the guild of university teachers. Starting students, like apprentices, paid fees, while more advanced bachelors, like journeymen, helped to instruct the starting students. Those who attained the level of masters were the equivalent of full members of the guild. In the 1170s, the masters of Paris gained the right to determine the composition of the assigned reading, the content of examinations, and the recipients for each degree. This structure was much more formalized than anything during Peter Abelard's lifetime.

Most students came from well-off families and had ample spending money; therefore, they formed a large body of consumers whose business was crucial to local shopkeepers. Whenever students had a dispute with local authorities, whether with the city government or the church, they could boycott all local merchants.

Adelard of Bath

Adelard of Bath (ca. 1080–ca. 1152) is best known for his translation of Euclid's geometry into Latin from an Arabic translation of the original Greek text, which was written around 300 B.C.E. He also translated other works, including al-Khwarizmi's astronomical tables (see Chapter 9), and he is credited with introducing the use of the abacus to the treasury officials of the English king Henry I. Born most likely in Bath, he studied first in France in Laôn and then went to Salerno, Italy, and Syracuse, Sicily, both centers of Islamic learning.

Although Adelard consistently praises Islamic learning, scholars have not found any quotations from Arabic books in his writing. Although he studied in Italy, his transcriptions of Arabic words reflect Spanish pronunciation, not Italian as one would expect. It seems likely, therefore, that he spoke Arabic to an informant, probably from Spain, who explained Islamic books to him, and he then wrote down what he had been told. This kind of translation using native informants is exactly how the early Buddhist translators in China handled difficult Sanskrit texts (see Chapter 8).

The selections below are drawn from Adelard's Questions on Natural Science, a series of dialogues with his "nephew," who may have been a fictitious conversational partner. Their conversation illustrates how the great teachers of the twelfth century, including Adelard, taught by using the Socratic method (see Chapter 6), in which they guided their students with pointed questions. The nephew's suspicion of Islamic learning was the typical European view. Few learned Arabic as Adelard had, and most saw Islam as the source of teachings that were contrary to Christianity. The uncle and nephew agree to accept reason as their guide, a conclusion that both the ancient Greeks and Adelard would have applauded.

Source: Charles Burnett et al., eds., Adelard of Bath: Conversations with His Nephew: On the Same and the Different, Questions About Natural Science, and on Birds (New York: Cambridge University Press, 1998), pp. 91, 103–105.

ADELARD: You remember, dear nephew, that, seven years ago, when I dismissed you (still almost a boy) with my other students in French studies at Laôn, we agreed amongst ourselves that I would investigate the studies of Arabs according to my ability, but you would become no less proficient in the insecurity of French opinions.

NEPHEW: I remember, and all the more so because when you left me you bound me with a promise on my word that I would apply myself to philosophy. I was always anxious to know why I should be more attentive to this subject. This is an excellent opportunity to test whether I have been successful by putting my study into practice, because since, as a listener only, I took note of you when often you explained the opinions of the Saracens [Muslims], and quite a few of them appeared to me to be quite useless. I shall for a brief while refuse to be patient and shall take you up as you expound these opinions, wherever it seems right to do so. For you both extol the Arabs shamelessly and invidiously accuse our people of ignorance in a disparaging way. It will therefore be worthwhile for you to reap the fruit of your labor, if you acquit yourself well, and likewise for me not to have been cheated in my promise, if I oppose you with probable arguments.

ADELARD: Perhaps you are being more bold in your presumption than you are capable. But because this disputation will be useful both to you and to many others, I shall put up with your impudence, as long as this inconvenience is avoided: that no one should think that when I am putting forward unknown ideas, I am doing this out of my own head, but that I am giving the views of the studies of the Arabs. For I do not want it to happen that, even though what I say may displease those who are less advanced, I myself should also displease them. For I know what those who profess the truth suffer at the hands of the vulgar crowd. Therefore, I shall defend the cause of the Arabs, not my own.

NEPHEW: Agreed, so that you may have no occasion for silence.

ADELARD: Well then, I think we should begin from the easier subjects. For if I speak sensibly about these, you may have the same hope concerning greater things. So let us start from the lowest objects and end with the highest.

(The two then discuss the sources of nourishment for plants, and then the nephew asks about animals.)

ADELARD: About animals my conversation with you is difficult. For I have learnt one thing from my Arab masters, with reason as guide, but you another: you follow a halter, being enthralled by the picture of authority. For what else can authority be called other than a halter? As brute animals are led wherever one pleases by a halter, but do not know where or why they are led, and only follow the rope by which they are held, so the authority of written words leads not a few of you into danger, since you are enthralled and bound by brutish credulity. Hence too, certain people, usurping the name of "an authority" for themselves, have used too great a license to write, to such an extent that they have not hesitated to trick brutish men with false words instead of true. For why should you not fill pages, why not write on the back too, when these days you generally have the kind of listeners that demand no argument based on judgment, but trust only in the name of an ancient authority? For they do not understand that reason has been given to each single individual in order to discern between true and false with reason as the prime judge. For unless it were the duty of reason to be everybody's judge, she would have been given to each person in vain. . . .

Rather I assert that first, reason should be sought, and when it is found, an authority, if one is at hand, should be added later. But authority alone cannot win credibility for a philosopher, nor should it be adduced for this purpose. Hence the logicians have agreed than an argument from authority is probable, not necessary. Therefore, if you wish to hear anything more from me, give and receive reason. . . .

NEPHEW: By all means let us do as you demand, since it is easy for me to oppose with reasonable arguments, nor is it safe to follow the authorities of your Arabs. Therefore, let us keep to this rule: between you and me reason alone should be the judge.

QUESTIONS FOR ANALYSIS

▶ What does Islamic learning represent to Adelard? To his nephew?

▶ How do the two view European learning?

▶ On what basis will they decide if a given explanation is true or false?

The most dramatic conflicts occurred in Paris. In 1229, during the Mardi Gras season, a disturbance broke out, and the authorities killed several students in the confusion. The masters of the university demanded that the city officials be punished, but the monarch sided with the officials. The masters left the city and returned only two years later when the ruler gave in. The pope then issued an order recognizing the masters as a guild with the right to boycott. Thereafter, the papacy always supported university masters in disputes with French rulers.

By 1200, Paris and Bologna were firmly established as Europe's first universities, and other universities formed in England, France, and Italy and later in Germany and eastern Europe. Universities offered their home cities many advantages, all linked to the buying power of a large group of wealthy consumer-students.

As in both the Islamic world and Song China, young men came to large cities to study with teachers to prepare for careers in government, law, religious institutions, or education. The largest schools provided facilities for a wide variety of instructors to teach many different topics. Unlike either Islamic schools or Song dynasty schools, however, only European universities had the power to grant degrees independently of the state or the church.

Most students did not study long enough to get their first degree, which was the equivalent of a modern master's degree. Instead, many concentrated on improving their command of Latin, which remained the language of educated people and the church throughout Europe before 1500. Learning to take notes in Latin during a lecture greatly enhanced a young man's ability to draft a Latin document quickly. Some knowledge of mathematics was also useful. University studies prepared young men for careers in government administration or the church. Many received employment as literate bureaucrats working for a noble or for members of the clergy, often near their hometown. Over time, as more and more families sent their sons to university, it became the norm for officials and clergy to be literate, and the proportion of students finishing their degrees consistently increased over time.

The Movement for Church Reform, 1000–1300

Although historians often speak of the church when talking about medieval Europe, Peter Abelard and Heloise's experiences make it clear that no single, unified entity called the church existed. The pope in Rome presided over many different local churches and monasteries, but he was not consistently able to enforce decisions. Below him, but not necessarily obedient to him, were many churches and monasteries throughout Europe that possessed their own lands and directly benefited from the greater yields of cerealization; in addition, their devotees often gave a share of their increasing personal wealth to religious institutions. As a result, monastic leaders had sufficient income to act independently, whether or not they had higher approval.

Starting in 1000, different reformers tried to streamline the church and reform the clergy. Yet reform from within did not always succeed. The new orders founded in the thirteenth century, like the Franciscans and the Dominicans, explicitly rejected what they saw as lavish spending in favor of new begging orders in which monks and nuns demonstrated their faith by renouncing wealth.

The Structure of the Church

By 1000, the European countryside was completely blanketed with churches, each one the center of a parish in which the clergy lived together with laypeople. Some churches were small shrines that had little land of their own, while others were magnificent cathedrals with extensive monasteries, and sometimes nunneries, attached to them. The laity were expected to pay a tithe of 10 percent of their income to their local parish priest, and he, in turn, performed the sacraments for each individual as he or she passed through the major stages of life: baptism at birth, confirmation and marriage at young adulthood, and funeral at death. The parish priest also gave communion to his congregation.

By the year 1000, this system had become so well established in western Europe that no one questioned it. Much as we agree to the obligation of all citizens to pay taxes, medieval Europeans accepted, for example, that all those born in a parish had to undergo baptism. Baptism guaranteed passage to heaven; failure to be baptized ensured permanent suffering in hell. The other sacraments and the tithe were similarly accepted.

The clergy fell into two categories: the secular clergy and the regular clergy. The secular clergy worked with the laity as local priests or schoolmasters. Those who lived in monasteries and had no contact with laypeople were called regular clergy because they lived by the rule, or *regula* in Latin, of the church or by monastic rules, such as those of Saint Benedict (see Chapter 10).

Reform from Above

In 1046, a crisis occurred in the papacy when three different Italian candidates vied for the position of pope; one had bought his position from an earlier pope who decided that he wanted to marry. A church office was considered sacred, and its sale, or **simony,** was universally considered a sin.

The ruler of Germany, Henry III (1039–1056), then intervened in the dispute and named Leo IX (in office between 1048 and 1056) pope. For the first time in over two hundred years, the pope traveled north of the Alps to modern-day Germany and France, where he conducted public ceremonies in which priests vowed, sometimes in the presence of saints' relics, that they had not bought their offices. This was the first reform campaign led by a pope. Leo's main goals were to end simony and to enforce celibacy.

Although many people recognized the dangers of simony in corrupting church officials, fewer agreed that marriage of the clergy should be forbidden. Many priests' wives came from locally prominent families who felt strongly that their female kin had done nothing wrong in marrying a member of the clergy. In 1072, when one French archbishop tried to punish priests who had married, the laity threw stones at him, and he barely escaped serious injury. Those who supported celibacy believed that childless clergy would have no incentive to divert church property toward their own family, and their view eventually prevailed.

Pope Gregory VII (1073–1085) also sought to reform the papacy by drafting twenty-seven papal declarations asserting the supremacy of the pope. Only the pope could decide issues facing the church, Gregory VII averred, and only the pope had

simony The sale of church office in Europe. Since church office was considered sacred, its sale was a sin.

Pope Innocent III Approves the Franciscan Rule One of the most famous painters of the fourteenth century, Giotto (1266–1336), painted the most important events in the life of Saint Francis (ca. 1181–1226) directly on fresh plaster, which preserved the intense reds and blues for all time. Here Pope Innocent III (*right*) grants Francis and his followers (*left*) the right to preach among the poor. Note the sharp contrast between the elegant robes of the pope and the cardinals and the coarse brown robes of the Franciscan friars. (Upper Church, S. Francesco, Assisi, Italy/Alinari/Art Resource, NY)

the right to appoint bishops. In his efforts to strengthen the papacy, he even claimed "that the Roman Church has never erred, nor will it ever err, as the scripture testifies."[6] Many of the twenty-seven points had been realized by 1200 as more Europeans came to accept the pope's claim to be head of the Christian church.

In 1215, Pope Innocent III (1198–1216) presided over the fourth Lateran Council. Over twelve hundred bishops, abbots, and representatives of different European monarchs met in the Lateran Palace in the Vatican to pass decrees regulating Christian practice, some of which are in effect today. For example, they agreed that all Christians should receive Communion at least once a year and should also confess their sins annually. The fourth Lateran Council marked the high point of the pope's political power; subsequent popes never commanded such power over secular leaders.

Reform Within the Established Monastic Orders

• **heresy** The offense of believing in teachings that the Roman Catholic Church condemned as incorrect.

Abelard was condemned twice, once after his affair with Heloise, and again near the end of his life for heresy. **Heresy,** the offense of believing in teachings that the church condemned as incorrect, was a grave charge. The details of the charges against Abelard are complex, and historians may never understand them fully because many of the original documents are lost. Though found guilty, Abelard was able to continue teaching and writing because powerful patrons protected him. In 1140, Peter the Venerable (abbot from 1122 to 1156) invited him to Cluny (CLUE-nee), the largest monastery in Europe, and refused to give him up to those who had condemned him. Peter's invitation quite possibly saved Abelard's life.

Cluny's holdings in land and money were greater than those of the church in Rome, and the abbot of Cluny, Peter the Venerable, was more powerful than anyone in the church, except for the pope. Founded in 910, the monastery at Cluny followed the rules of Saint Benedict. Three hundred monks, many from the most prominent families in France, lived at Cluny itself, and one thousand monasteries, home to twenty thousand monks, were associated with Cluny.

Since the abbot did not visit most of these monasteries, monastic discipline at Cluny suffered. In 1098, several monks broke away from Cluny because they wanted reform. This was the beginning of the Cistercian Order, which called for a return to the original rules of Saint Benedict. Unlike the Cluniac monasteries, each Cistercian monastery had its own abbot, and no one was admitted until he was over 15 and had served a full year as a novice. The Cistercian monasteries established a fixed procedure for the creation of new monasteries: a new abbot went with twelve monks to each new site. The resulting daughter monasteries retained close ties with their mother monasteries, whose abbots visited each year. All Cistercian abbots convened at regular intervals to ensure that everyone followed the same regulations. The Cistercians lived more austerely than the monks at Cluny, wearing simple clothes of undyed wool, eating only vegetarian food, and building undecorated churches. The Cistercian monasteries proved enormously popular, as did other movements for monastic reform. From 5 monasteries in 1119, the order mushroomed to 350 in 1150 and to 647 by 1250.

About half of the Cistercian monasteries were nunneries for women. After 1000, as Europe's population surged, many more women joined nunneries. But because their contemporaries did not think it appropriate for them to do the work monks did, a nunnery needed male staff to run its estates, farm the land, and perform religious services. The chronic lack of revenue created by this problem made the nunneries vulnerable to outside intervention.

The day after Abelard's castration, he ordered Heloise to become a nun at the convent in Argenteuil, France, where she had been educated as a child. She reluctantly agreed and left her son Astrolabe to be raised by Abelard's sister. Heloise rose to the rank of prioress, the second in command at the convent. When the king abruptly ordered the nuns to move elsewhere because he wanted their land, Heloise received a letter from Abelard for the first time since they had parted. He offered his own church, which had its own lands given by supporters, to Heloise. She accepted Abelard's invitation and served as abbess until her death in the 1160s.

Reform Outside the Established Orders

Although the Cistercians certainly thought of themselves as reformers, they still accepted the need for groups of men or women to live on landed monasteries or nunneries. But as the drive to reform continued, some asked members of religious orders to live exactly as Jesus and his followers had, not in monasteries with their own incomes but as beggars dependent on ordinary people for contributions. Between 1100 and 1200, reformers established at least nine different begging orders, the most important of which was the Franciscans founded by Saint Francis of Assisi (ca. 1181–1226). Members of these orders were called **friars.**

Francis was born to the well-off Italian family of a textile merchant, but while in his 20s he abandoned his family and began to live as a beggar. After attracting a small group of followers, he requested formal permission from Pope Innocent III

friars Members of the begging orders established in Europe between 1100 and 1200, of which the Franciscans were the best known.

CL Primary Source:
Summa Theologica:
On Free Will

This selection from Thomas Aquinas, on the question of free will, shows a synthesis of Aristotelian logic and Christian theology.

• **Thomas Aquinas**
(1224/25–1274)   One of the most famous scholastic thinkers and a member of the Dominican order. He wrote a book, *Summa Theologica* (Summary of Theology), juxtaposing the teachings of various church authorities on various difficult questions.

to be allowed to preach. In 1209, the pope granted the Franciscans the right to speak on simple topics like the correct conduct of a Christian but not on complex theological issues.

The Franciscan movement grew rapidly even though Francis allowed none of his followers to keep any money, to own books or extra clothes, or to live in a permanent dwelling. In 1217, Francis had 5,000 followers; by 1326, some 28,000 Franciscans were active. Francis also created the order of Saint Clare for women, who lived in austere nunneries where they were not allowed to accumulate any property of their own.

In 1215, Saint Dominic (1170?–1221) founded the order of Friars Preachers in Spain. Unlike Francis, he stressed education and sent some of his brightest followers to the new universities. Since he hoped to eliminate heresy everywhere, he created a structure in which all his followers, and not just bishops, could convert non-Christian peoples. **Thomas Aquinas** (1224/25–1274), one of the most famous scholastic thinkers, belonged to the Dominican order. Aquinas wrote *Summa Theologica* (Summary of Theology), a book juxtaposing the teachings of various church authorities on various difficult questions, just as Abelard had; but where Abelard had trusted each reader to determine the correct interpretation, Aquinas wrote detailed explanations that remained definitive for centuries.

The Crusades, 1095–1291

The founding of the Franciscans and the Dominicans was only one aspect of a broader movement to spread Christianity through Crusades. Some Crusades within Europe targeted Jews, Muslims, and members of other non-Christian groups. In addition, the economic surplus resulting from cerealization and urban growth financed a series of expeditions to the Holy Land. During the twelfth and thirteenth centuries, thousands of Crusaders left Europe in the hope that they could conquer Jerusalem, the symbolic center of the Christian world because Jesus had preached and died there, and make it Christian again (see Map 13.1). They succeeded in conquering Jerusalem but held it for only eighty-eight years.

The Crusades to the Holy Land

• **Crusader**   Term, meaning "one who is signed by the cross," that indicated anyone who attached a cross to his or her clothes as a sign of belonging to a large, volunteer force against Muslims. Between 1095 and 1291, eight different groups of Crusaders traveled to the Holy Land in the hope of capturing Jerusalem.

Historians use the term *Crusades* to refer to the period between 1095, when the pope first called for Europeans to take back Jerusalem, and 1291, when the last European possession in Syria was lost. The word **Crusader,** literally "one who is signed by the cross," indicates anyone who attached a cross to his or her clothes as a sign of belonging to a large, volunteer force against Muslims. In 1095, Pope Urban II (1088–1099) told a large meeting of church leaders that the Byzantine emperor requested help against the Seljuq Turks (see Chapters 9 and 10). He urged those assembled to recover the territory lost to "the wicked race" (meaning Muslims) so that they could govern it: his audience cried, "It is the will of God" in response.[7] If they died en route, the pope promised, they could be certain that God would forgive their sins because God forgave all pilgrims' sins. This marked the beginning of the First Crusade.

From the outset, the Crusader forces consisted of self-financed individuals who, unlike soldiers in an army, did not receive pay and had no line of command. The

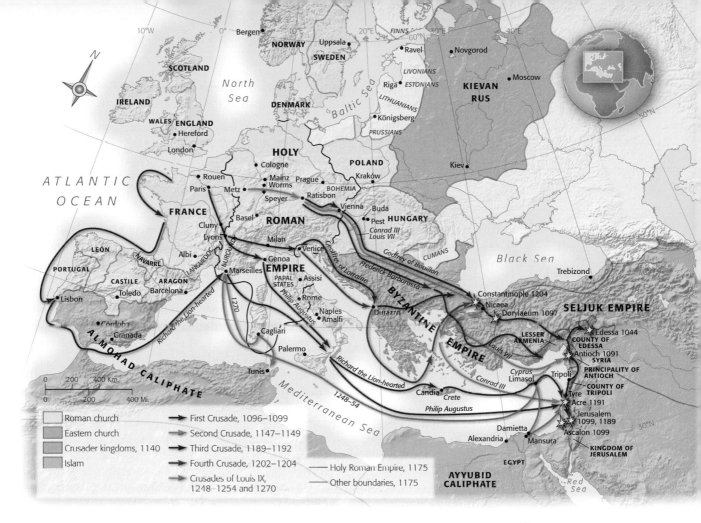

Map legend

- Roman church
- Eastern church
- Crusader kingdoms, 1140
- Islam

→ First Crusade, 1096–1099
→ Second Crusade, 1147–1149
→ Third Crusade, 1189–1192
→ Fourth Crusade, 1202–1204
→ Crusades of Louis IX, 1248–1254 and 1270

— Holy Roman Empire, 1175
— Other boundaries, 1175

problems of disorganization extended to the top ranks, which included some of France and England's most prominent nobles. Rarely agreeing with each other about military strategy, they often could not even decide on their main commander.

An estimated 50,000 combatants responded to the pope's plea in 1095; of these, only 10,000 reached Jerusalem. Of those 10,000, some 1,500 were knights, the only fighters properly equipped for siege warfare. Nevertheless, the Crusaders succeeded in taking Jerusalem in 1099 from the rulers of Egypt, who controlled it at the time. After the city fell, the out-of-control troops massacred everyone still in the city.

The Crusaders ruled Jerusalem for eighty-eight years, long enough that the first generation of Europeans died and were succeeded by generations who saw themselves first as residents of Outremer (OU-truh-mare), the term the Crusaders used for the eastern edge of the Mediterranean. The Crusaders' fervent belief that they had the right to remove the non-Christian government of Jerusalem led to the creation of the Crusader kingdom in the city. Despite the fact that Jerusalem was also a holy site for both Jews and Muslims, the Crusaders were convinced that the city belonged to them.

In 1169, Saladin overthrew the reigning Egyptian dynasty and in 1171 founded the Ayyubid dynasty (see Chapter 9). He then married the widow of the Seljuq ruler of Central Asia, effectively allying the two great powers of the Islamic world.

🌐 MAP 13.1
The Crusades In response to the pope's request, thousands of Europeans walked over 2,000 miles (3,200 km) overland through the Byzantine Empire to reach Jerusalem, which the Europeans governed from 1099 to 1187. Others traveled to the Holy Land by sea. The Europeans who lived in Jerusalem for nearly a century developed their own hybrid culture that combined French, German, and Italian elements with the indigenous practices of the eastern Mediterranean.

375

With this combined power, he was poised to fight the Crusaders. His biographer explained the extent of Saladin's commitment to jihad, or holy war:

> The Holy War and the suffering involved in it weighed heavily on his heart and his whole being in every limb: he spoke of nothing else, thought only about equipment for the fight, was interested only in those who had taken up arms.[8]

Saladin devoted himself to raising an army strong enough to repulse the Crusaders. By 1187 he had gathered an army of thirty thousand men on horseback carrying lances and swords like knights but without chain-mail armor. Half of his army consisted of light cavalry who could maneuver much more quickly than the twenty thousand Crusaders they faced. Saladin laid a trap for the Crusaders in an extinct Syrian volcano called the Horns of Hattin. While the Crusader forces had no way to replenish their water supply, the Muslim armies made sure that each camp had water storage tanks supplied by camels carrying goat skins filled with water. On the day of the battle, Saladin's well-rested forces baited the parched and exhausted Crusaders by pouring fresh water out on the ground instead of giving it to them to drink. They easily defeated the Crusaders.

When Saladin's victorious troops took Jerusalem back, they restored the mosques as houses of worship and removed the crosses from all Christian churches, although they did allow Christians to visit the city. The English king Richard the Lion-Hearted (1189–1199) led armies provided by different European rulers in an effort to recapture Jerusalem from Saladin. Traveling by sea, Richard conquered the Mediterranean island of Cyprus from its ruler in 1191. After several years of fighting, however, he realized that the Crusaders could not recapture Jerusalem unless they conquered Egypt first, and they returned to Europe without having taken Jerusalem.

In 1201, the Europeans decided to make one further attempt, in the Fourth Crusade, to retake Jerusalem. Because they did not have enough ships, they promised to pay the Venetian navy to transport them to the Holy Land. In June 1203, the Crusaders reached Constantinople and were astounded by its size: the ten biggest cities in Europe could easily fit within its imposing walls, and its population surpassed one million. One awe-struck soldier wrote home:

> If anyone should recount to you the hundredth part of the richness and the beauty and the nobility that was found in the abbeys and in the churches and the palaces and in the city, it would seem like a lie and you would not believe it.[9]

When one of the claimants to the Byzantine throne refused to pay the crusaders, the commanders gave the fateful command to their troops to attack the city in the hope that they could plunder what they needed to pay the Venetians to transport them to Jerusalem.

One of the worst atrocities in world history resulted: the Crusaders rampaged throughout the beautiful city, killing all who opposed them and raping thousands of women. They treated the Eastern Orthodox Christians of Constantinople precisely as if they were the Muslim enemy. (See the feature "World History in Today's World: The Memory of the Crusades in Istanbul.") The Crusaders' conduct in Constantinople turned the diplomatic dispute between the two churches, which had begun in 1054, into a genuine and lasting schism between Roman Catholics and Eastern Orthodox adherents (see page 296).

CL Primary Source: Annals
Read a harrowing, firsthand account of the pillage of Constantinople by Western Crusaders on April 13, 1204.

The Memory of the Crusades in Istanbul

After eight centuries, how can we not share the disgust and pain?" Pope John Paul asked Bartholomew I, the patriarch of Constantinople (modern Istanbul), who visited the Vatican on June 29, 2004. "In particular, in these circumstances we cannot forget what happened in the month of April in the year 1204. An army, which left to recover the Holy Land for Christianity, headed toward Constantinople to take and sack it, spilling the blood of brothers in faith."

Since 1964, the pope and the patriarch have exchanged annual visits in an attempt to maintain dialogue between the two churches. In April 2004, Bartholomew granted a formal pardon to the Catholics who had sacked Constantinople.

John Paul II's successor, Pope Benedict XVI, visited Istanbul in November 2006 and met with Bartholomew. The two church leaders issued a joint declaration that stated their shared desire to move toward "full unity" at some point in the future.

Pope Benedict's visit triggered protests by Turkish Muslims, who greatly outnumber Orthodox Christians. As one protestor explained: "The popes—were they not the ones who tried to destroy Turks and Islam? Who organized the crusades? They should not give lessons of peace here."

Sources: Religion News Service, June 29, 2004 (Tuesday 3:16 PM Eastern Time); *The Australian,* July 1, 2004; BBC Monitoring Europe—Political, November 30, 2006; *Los Angeles Times,* December 1, 2006, all accessed via Lexis/Nexis.

After 1204, individual European monarchs sent armies to attack Egypt or Jerusalem, but they never again sent a multinational force. Europeans did not regain control of Jerusalem, and by 1291 they had lost control of the little territory around it, like the port city of Acre in modern-day Israel, that they retained after the Battle of Hattin. Cyprus, however, remained in European hands until 1570 and provided an important precedent that gave subsequent generations of Europeans the belief that the conquest of foreign territory for Christianity was acceptable. When Europeans went to new lands in Africa and the Americas, they founded colonies similar to those of the Crusaders in the Mediterranean (see Chapter 15).

The Crusades Within Europe

Muslims in West Asia were not the Crusaders' only target. European Christians, convinced that they were right about the superiority of Christianity, also attacked enemies within Europe, sometimes on their own, sometimes in direct response to the pope's command.

Many European Christians looked down on Jews, who were banned from many occupations, could not marry Christians, and often lived in separate parts of cities, called *ghettos.* But before 1095, Christians had largely respected the right of Jews to practice their own religion; they neither forced them to convert nor attacked their temples. This fragile coexistence fell apart in 1096, as the out-of-control crowds traveling through on the First Crusade attacked the Jews living in the three German towns of Mainz, Worms, and Speyer and killed all who did not convert to Christianity. Thousands died in the violence. Anti-Jewish prejudice worsened over the next two centuries; England expelled the Jews in 1290 and France in 1306.

These spontaneous attacks on Jews differed from two campaigns launched by the pope against enemies of the church. The first was against the Cathars, a group of Christian heretics who lived in the Languedoc region of southern France. Like the Zoroastrians of Iran (see Chapter 6), the Cathars believed that the forces of good in the spiritual world and of evil in the material world were engaged in a perpetual fight for dominance. Jesus, they thought, never assumed material form but remained a spirit the entire time he was visible on earth.

In 1208, Pope Innocent III launched a crusade to Languedoc in which he promised that God would forgive the sins of those who fought the Cathars for forty days in France just as he would forgive those who went on the Crusades for a much longer time. The campaign attracted numerous supporters, and gradually the pope's forces killed many of the lords and bishops who supported Catharism.

Because mass campaigns against heretics often spun out of control, in the early thirteenth century the pope established a special court, called the **inquisition,** to hear charges against accused heretics. Unlike other church courts, which operated according to established legal norms, the inquisition used anonymous informants, forced interrogations, and torture to identify heretics. Those found guilty were usually burned at the stake. One inquisitor in south France, active between 1308 and 1323, sentenced 633 offenders, many to life imprisonment.[10] The inquisition remained active in the region of the Cathars until 1330, and later popes established inquisition courts whenever they felt it necessary.

The leader of the crusade against the Cathars begged to be allowed to continue his fight against non-Christians in Spain, and the pope granted his request in 1212. Historians use the Spanish word *Reconquista* ("Reconquest") to refer to these military campaigns by Christians against the Muslims of Spain and Portugal. Before 1200, various Christian rulers had recovered isolated cities, such as Toledo, Spain, and Lisbon, Portugal, and the Crusader army won a decisive victory in 1212 and captured Córdoba and Seville in the following decades. After 1249, only the kingdom of Granada, on the southern tip of Spain, remained Muslim.

• **inquisition** Special court established by the pope to hear charges against those accused of heresy. The inquisition used anonymous informants, forced interrogations, and torture to identify heretics. Those found guilty were usually burned at the stake.

Disaster and Recovery, 1300–1400

The three centuries of prosperity and growth caused by cerealization and urbanization came to a sudden halt in the early 1300s, when first a series of food shortages rocked the north European countryside and then the Black Death, which Ibn Battuta had seen in Damascus (see Chapter 11), traveled along established trade routes to reach Europe's major cities first in 1348 and several times thereafter. The fighting of the Hundred Years' War (1337–1453) between England and France caused more deaths. In the long run, however, the economy recovered, and by 1500 the population had returned to pre–Black Death levels. The structure of European society also changed, and European kings, especially in France and England, emerged from this difficult century with more extensive powers than their predecessors.

Continuing Expansion of Trade Outside Europe

The Crusaders who returned from the Holy Land were one source of information for those seeking to learn about the world beyond Europe. Europeans gained access to other sources of information as trade networks linking Europe with Asia expanded. During the 1300s, merchants, usually from the Italian city-states of Venice or Genoa, traveled to West Asia, and sometimes to East Asia, to pursue trading opportunities (see Map 13.2).

In the twelfth and thirteenth centuries, Europeans consumed huge quantities of the new spices—such as pepper, cinnamon, ginger, cloves, and nutmeg—that entered Europe from Southeast Asia. Europeans used spices to enhance dishes' flavor and as medicines, not to preserve rotten meat, as is often said. (Rotten meat could not be salvaged once it spoiled; the wealthy ate freshly killed meat.) Surprisingly large quantities of spices went into a single meal: in 1319, the pope presided at a dinner for six guests in which he served lamb, pork, chicken, and partridges seasoned with one pound each of ginger and cloves.[11] To obtain spices, European merchants often traveled to Constantinople, the Black Sea, or Iran, where they

⊕ **MAP 13.2**

Movement of the Plague and Trade Routes   The complex network of trade routes linking Europe with Asia and Africa facilitated the movement of goods, like Asian spices, but also disease, like the Black Death. Europeans learned about Asia from travelers like Marco Polo, who went to Mongolia and China, and John of Mandeville, who did not. Small communities of Europeans lived in the nodes of the network: in Constantinople, Kaffa, Khara Khorum, and the Chinese capital of Beijing.

CL Interactive Map

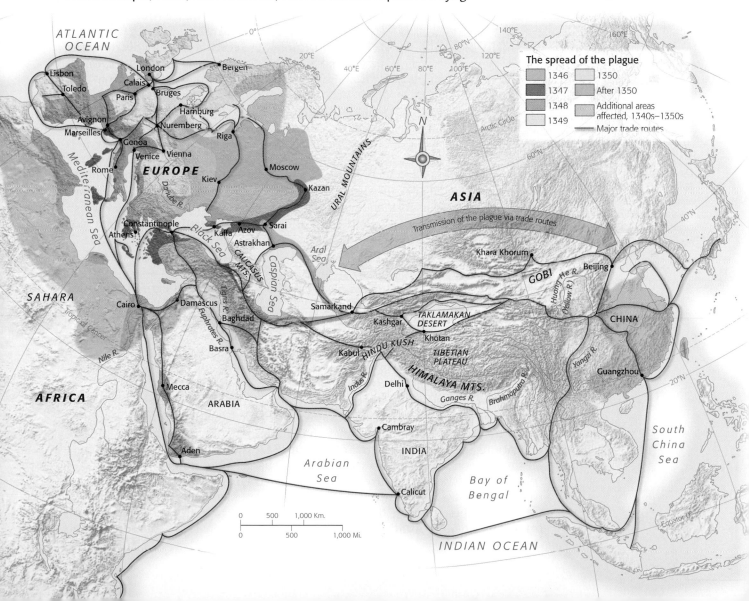

Primary Source:
Description of the World
Follow Marco Polo, and hear him relate the natural—and sometimes supernatural—wonders he encountered on his journey to Khubilai Khan.

■ **Tombstone for an Italian Girl Who Died in China** In 1342, the daughter of a Venetian merchant died in Yangzhou, near the mouth of the Yangzi River, and her family commissioned a tombstone for her. The tombstone shows scenes from the life of a haloed figure, most likely Saint Catherine of Alexandria, for whom the deceased was named. To the left of the Latin text, four Chinese characters appear in a small rectangle; the artist's signature in stone is the equivalent of the red-colored seals Chinese painters stamped on their paintings. (Harvard Yenching Library)

established small commercial colonies with warehouses and homes. During the 1330s and 1340s, a small group of merchants even lived in the Mongols' capital at Beijing, China, where a bishop served the Christian congregation.

During these years, readers avidly devoured books about distant foreign places, especially those that purported to describe the actual travels of their authors. Marco Polo (1254–1324), a Venetian merchant who traveled to Asia, portrayed the wonders of the known world and painted China as especially wealthy. Even more popular was *The Travels of Sir John Mandeville,* published in the 1350s, which described a legendary Christian king named Prester John who ruled over a realm distant from Europe. Polo combined some firsthand knowledge with hearsay; Mandeville's writing was based on pure hearsay. Even so, both books created an optimistic impression of Asian wealth that inspired later explorers like Columbus to found overseas colonies (covered in Chapter 15).

The Losses from Rural Famines and the Black Death

Europeans living in the 1300s could see signs of expansion but also troubling indications that the prosperity might end. The first signs that three centuries of growth had come to an end were internal. The Great Famine of 1315–1322 affected all of northern Europe, and it was the first of repeated food shortages. Many starved to death, and thousands fled the barren countryside to beg in the cities.

These difficult times caused financial strains that, in turn, led to changes in rural society as rulers and feudal lords struggled to increase their tax revenues. Rulers found that they needed more money than they could obtain from the traditional obligations tying peasants to their lords. In 1315, therefore, the French king freed all the serfs on royal land so that he could charge them new and higher taxes. Landlords in other places, like England and Germany, adopted short-term leases that replaced the lists of customary obligations and fixed rents at higher rates.

During these difficult decades, the Black Death came first to Europe's ports from somewhere in Asia, possibly North China (see Map 13.2). In 1346, the rats

■ **Portraying the Black Death**
This painting, made more than a century after the Black Death struck Europe between 1346 and 1348, shows Saint Sebastian praying for those who had fallen ill with the plague. The artist shows the plague victim wrapped in a white shroud, presumably because the black swellings on the bodies were too grisly to include in a painting displayed in a church. (Walters Art Museum, Baltimore/Bridgeman Art Library)

infected with the Black Death traveled by ship to the Genoese colony of Kaffa on the Black Sea. In 1348, the year in which Ibn Battuta observed the plague's toll in Damascus, the plague struck Italy, and then France and Germany one year later. Like the plague in sixth-century Byzantium (see Chapter 10), it had two phases: bubonic plague and pneumonic plague, which was almost always fatal. Historians reserve the term *Black Death* for the outbreak in the 1300s.

Since nearly six hundred years had passed since the most recent outbreak of 767, Europeans had lost whatever immunity they had developed, and the plague's initial toll was devastating. The Black Death reduced Europe's population from about seventy-five to about fifty-five million, and it only returned to pre-plague levels after 1500.

The losses of the first outbreak were greatest. One doctor in Avignon, France, reported that, in 1349, two-thirds of the city's population fell ill, and almost all died. In the second occurrence, in 1361, half the city's population was affected, and, again, almost all died. But in a third outbreak in 1371, only one-tenth of the people caught the illness, and some of them survived. By the fourth outbreak, in 1382, only one-twentieth of the population was afflicted, and almost everyone survived.[12]

The Hundred Years' War Between England and France, 1337–1453

During this difficult century, the rulers of England and France engaged in a long series of battles now known as the **Hundred Years' War** (1337–1453). In 1328, the French king died without leaving an heir. Edward III of England (1327–1377), who owned extensive lands, was next in line to the throne, but in 1337 the French nobles selected his cousin as king instead.

● **Hundred Years' War** War between the English and French fought entirely on French soil. At the end of the war (1337–1453), the kings of England and France had gained the power to tax and to maintain a standing army.

Edward III sent an army to France and launched a conflict that took more than a century to resolve.

France, with a population of some fifteen million, was far richer than England, which had only around four million. The war was conducted entirely on French soil, and the opportunity to obtain plunder provided a strong incentive for the English troops.

The long conflict saw the end of battles fought by mounted knights. Early in the war, the English won significant victories because they used a new type of long-bow 6 feet (1.8 m) tall that shot metal-tipped arrows farther and more accurately than the crossbows then in use. Knights donned even heavier armor to protect themselves, but they could not protect their horses. Moreover, the armor was so heavy that a knight who had fallen off his horse could not get up to fight an as-sailant armed with a staff. By the final years of the war, both sides were using gunpowder to shoot stones or cannonballs. Although difficult to aim accurately, these new weapons could destroy the walls surrounding a castle or town under siege and make it possible to take the city.

Not restricting their contest to the battlefield, the English and French kings both tried to enlist the support of the pope. In 1309, a pope moved to the French town of Avignon to avoid the factional disputes in Rome, and his seven successors, all French, acknowledged the supremacy of the French monarch. In 1378, a crisis oc-curred when two popes, one based in Rome, the other in Avignon, simultaneously claimed to be the rightful pope; each excommunicated the other. The French mon-arch backed the Avignon pope, while the English king supported the pope in Rome. Between 1409 and 1417, a third man claimed to be the legitimate pope as well. This **Great Western Schism** only ended in 1417, when a church council deposed all three claimants and appointed a new pope, who accepted the council's authority.

The Hundred Years' War continued through the time of the Great Western Schism, and in 1429 a young illiterate peasant woman named Joan of Arc (1412–1431), who claimed divine guidance, succeeded in rallying the French forces and won a surprise victory. After capturing her in 1430, the English burned her as a heretic in 1431. In the years after her death, the French forces won more victories, recovering all the territory that had been under English rule—with the sole excep-tion of the port of Calais—until they defeated the English in 1453, when the French and the English signed a treaty marking the end of the war.

• **Great Western Schism**   Dispute that divided the Roman Catholic Church (1378–1417), in which two, sometimes three, men claimed to be the legiti-mate pope. The French kings backed the popes living in Avignon; the English king supported the pope in Rome.

The Consolidation of Monarchy in France and England

When they assess the significance of the Hundred Years' War, historians note how the political structure of France and England changed: at the beginning of the war, the two kingdoms consisted of patchworks of territory ruled by a king who shared power with his nobles. By the end of the war, the two coun-tries had become centralized monarchies governed by kings with considerably more power.

This result had much to do with the changing nature of warfare. In conflicts during the early 1300s, the French and English kings summoned their nobles, who provided knights and soldiers. But the men best able to use first the longbow and then cannon were specialists who had to be paid. At first, when the kings needed money, they asked for it on an emergency basis, often allowing their subordinates to substitute financial payment for military aid. Over time, kings demanded money each year and so gained the right to tax the lords of their country.

In England, the king had summoned groups of advisers since the 1200s; contemporaries called these meetings "Parliament," which literally means "to talk." **Parliament** consisted of different groups, some nobles and some well-off city dwellers. It met whenever the English king convened his most powerful subordinates to inform them of new taxes. Though they always paid what he asked for, they were entitled to an explanation for why he needed the money. Most European rulers convened bodies similar to Parliament; the French equivalent, weaker than Parliament, was called the Estates General and included the nobles, clergy, and townsfolk.

The monarchy as it evolved in France and England differed from earlier political structures. France and England were smaller than the earlier Roman and Byzantine Empires, and their rulers consulted with their subordinates more often. The new monarchies, though, proved to be extremely effective, partially because they could command the allegiance of their subjects.

• **Parliament** (literally "to talk"). Name for the different councils that advised the English kings and approved their requests for taxation.

Chapter Review

Download the MP3 audio file of the Chapter Review and listen to it on the go.

Peter Abelard and Heloise experienced the changes of Europe's commercial revolution, particularly the changes in education, organization of the church, and city life. The losses of the 1300s caused by food shortages, the Black Death, and prolonged warfare brought a halt to Europe's developing economy, but only a temporary one.

What caused the cerealization of Europe, and what were its results?

Between 1000 and 1300, Europe experienced enormous growth, much of it fueled by cerealization, the reclamation and planting of land with grain. The European countryside in 1300 looked very different than it had in 1000: livestock, iron tools, and wind mills or watermills were in use everywhere, and crop rotation was systematically practiced. The increasing crop yields caused Europe's population to grow from some forty million in 1000 to around seventy-five million in 1340. In addition, society became more complex as lords, knights, and clergy acquired specific rights over serfs.

What led to the foundation of Europe's universities? How did they gain the right to govern themselves?

The universities had their roots in privately run schools or church-run schools like those at which Peter Abelard taught. Structured like commercial guilds, the universities gradually implemented rules about the curriculum, examinations, and the

KEY TERMS

Peter Abelard (356)
Heloise (356)
cerealization (359)
guilds (361)
feudal (364)
liberal arts (365)
scholasticism (366)
simony (371)
heresy (372)
friars (373)
Thomas Aquinas (374)
Crusader (374)
inquisition (378)
Hundred Years' War (381)
Great Western Schism (382)
Parliament (383)

granting of degrees. Because students and masters threatened to, and sometimes did, leave the towns that hosted them, the townspeople supported them in their quest for autonomy, which universities achieved by the mid-thirteenth century.

How did economic prosperity affect the Christian church and different monastic orders?

Since individual churches had their own lands and benefited from cerealization, their leaders often had their own incomes and considerable independence. Many people outside the church called for an end to the sale of church office, or simony, and for members of the clergy to be celibate. Reformers founded different monastic orders, each demanding greater sacrifices from its members. During the twelfth century, the pope granted permission for the founding of at least nine different begging orders, including the Franciscans and the Dominicans. The church, after undergoing many different reforms, became one of the most vibrant institutions in medieval European society.

What did the Crusaders hope to achieve outside Europe? Within Europe?

The Crusaders' main purpose was to recapture Jerusalem, the symbolic center of the Christian world where Jesus had lived and died. They held Jerusalem for eighty-eight years, and after it fell in 1187, they tried to recover it. In the same years that they fought Muslims for control of the Holy Land, they also tried to make Europe more Christian: out-of-control crowds attacked Jews, the pope authorized a Crusade against the Cathars of France, and Christian armies fought to reconquer the Muslim cities of Spain and Portugal. In later centuries, the Crusades provided an important precedent for those who believed that Europeans were entitled to colonize non-Christian lands outside Europe.

How did the major developments of the century from 1300 to 1400 strengthen European monarchies?

The tremendous growth of the twelfth and thirteenth centuries began to slow around the year 1300, when the first food shortages occurred, and then stopped almost entirely when the Black Death of 1348 struck. The fourteenth century was also a time of military conflict between France and England, which fought the Hundred Years' War between 1337 and 1453, and of conflict in the church, which had two, sometimes even three, candidates for pope during the Great Schism (1378–1417). The long years of fighting gave the monarchs new powers, most notably the power to tax their subordinates (who no longer provided them with armies of knights) and to keep standing armies. Once the difficult fourteenth century ended, a renewed Europe emerged.

For Further Reference

Baldwin, John W. *The Scholastic Culture of the Middle Ages, 1000–1300.* Prospect Heights, Ill.: Waveland Press, 1971, 1997.

Cipolla, Carlo M. *Before the Industrial Revolution: European Society and Economy, 1000–1700.* New York: W. W. Norton, 1994.

Clanchy, M. T. *Abelard: A Medieval Life.* Malden, Mass.: Blackwell, 1997.

Lynch, Joseph H. *The Medieval Church: A Brief History.* New York: Longman, 1992.

Madden, Thomas F. *The New Concise History of the Crusades.* Updated ed. New York: Rowman and Littlefield, 2005.

Moore, R. I. *The First European Revolution, c. 970–1215.* Malden, Mass.: Blackwell, 2000.

Opitz, Claudia. "Life in the Late Middle Ages." In *Silence of the Middle Ages,* ed. Chistiane Klapisch-Zuber, vol. 2 of *A History of Women in the West.* Cambridge, Mass.: Belknap Press of Harvard University Press, 1992, pp. 259–317.

Radice, Betty, trans. *The Letters of Abelard and Heloise.* Revised by M. T. Clanchy. New York: Penguin Books, 2003.

Rosenwein, Barbara. *A Short History of the Middle Ages.* Orchard Park, N.Y.: Broadview Press, 2002.

Spufford, Peter. *Power and Profit: The Merchant in Medieval Europe.* New York: Thames and Hudson, 2002.

 **WEB RESOURCES**

Pronunciation Guide

Interactive Maps

MAP 13.1 The Crusades

MAP 13.2 Movement of the Plague and Trade Routes

Primary Sources

Chapter Objectives

ACE Multiple-Choice Quiz

Flashcards

Websites

Chartres Cathedral (http://gallery.sjsu.edu/chartres/tour.html).   Photographs and information on Chartres.

The Cloisters (http://www.metmuseum.org/cloisters).   Introduction to America's most prominent museum of medieval art.

Internet Medieval Sourcebook (http://www.fordham.edu/halsall/sbook.html).   Many valuable primary sources under the entries for Crusades, Iberia, Empire and Papacy, France, and England.

The Mongols and Their Successors, 1200–1500

In 1255, after his return from Mongolia, **William of Rubruck** (ca. 1215–ca. 1295) wrote a confidential report about his attempt to convert the Mongols to Christianity. He addressed it to his sponsor, the pious French king Louis IX (1214–1270). William's letter runs nearly three hundred pages long in translation and contains the most detailed, accurate, and penetrating description of the Mongols and their empire that exists today. In 1206, the Mongols exploded out of their homeland just north of China and conquered most of Eurasia by 1242. For the first time in world history, it became possible for individual travelers, like William, to move easily across a united Eurasia. Such movement prompted an unprecedented exchange of ideas, goods, and technologies. William's report is just one example of the different cultural exchanges that resulted and whose effects persisted long after different successor states replaced the Mongol Empire. His description of his trip to the Mongol empire begins as follows:

WILLIAM OF RUBRUCK

(The Masters and Fellows of Corpus Christi College, Cambridge)

We began our journey, then, around June 1, with our four covered wagons and two others which the Mongols had provided for us, in which was carried the bedding for sleeping on at night. They gave us five horses to ride, since we numbered five persons: I and my colleague, Friar Bartholomew of Cremona; Gosset, the bearer of this letter; the interpreter Homo Dei, and a boy, Nichols, whom I had bought at Constantinople with the alms you gave me. They supplied us in addition with two men who drove the wagons and tended the oxen and horses. . . .

Now on the third day after we left Soldaia, we encountered the Tartars [the Mongols]; and when I came among them, I really felt as if I were entering some other world. Their life and character I shall describe for you as best I can.[1]

This icon will direct you to interactive activities and study materials on the *Voyages* website: **www.cengage.com/history/hansen/voyages1e**

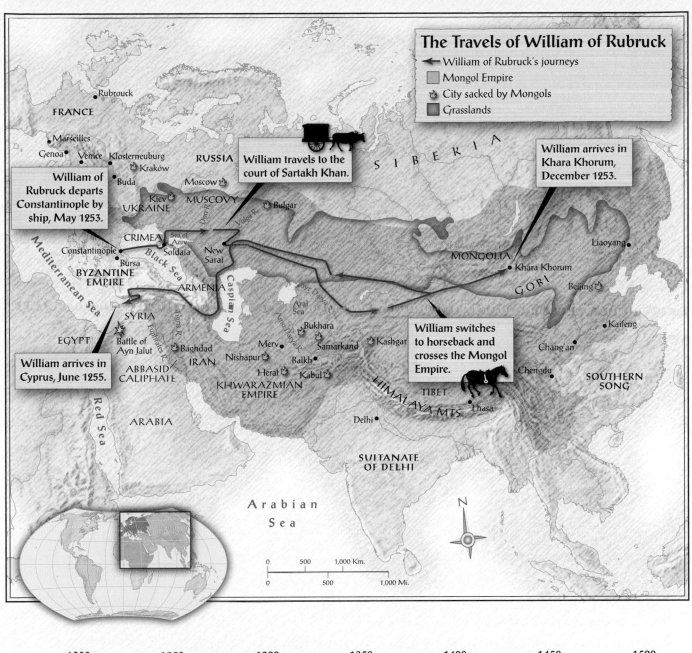

The Travels of William of Rubruck

- ← William of Rubruck's journeys
- ■ Mongol Empire
- ↻ City sacked by Mongols
- ■ Grasslands

William of Rubruck departs Constantinople by ship, May 1253.

William travels to the court of Sartakh Khan.

William arrives in Khara Khorum, December 1253.

William switches to horseback and crosses the Mongol Empire.

William arrives in Cyprus, June 1255.

FRANCE — Rubrouck · Marseilles · Genoa · Venice · Klosterneuburg · Kraków · Buda

RUSSIA · Moscow · MUSCOVY · Bulgar

UKRAINE · Kiev · Don R. · Volga R.

SIBERIA

CRIMEA · Sea of Azov · New Sarai

Constantinople · Bursa · Soldaia · Black Sea

BYZANTINE EMPIRE · ARMENIA · Caspian Sea

Mediterranean Sea · SYRIA · Tigris R. · Euphrates R. · Aral Sea · Syr Darya R. · Amu Darya R.

EGYPT · Battle of Ayn Jalut · Baghdad · ABBASID CALIPHATE · IRAN · Nishapur · Merv · Balkh · Herat · Bukhara · Samarkand · Kashgar

KHWARAZMIAN EMPIRE · Kabul

MONGOLIA · Khara Khorum · GOBI · Liaoyang · Beijing · Kaifeng · Chang'an · Chengdu · SOUTHERN SONG

HIMALAYA MTS. · TIBET · Lhasa

Red Sea · ARABIA · Delhi · SULTANATE OF DELHI

Arabian Sea

N

0 500 1,000 Km.
0 500 1,000 Mi.

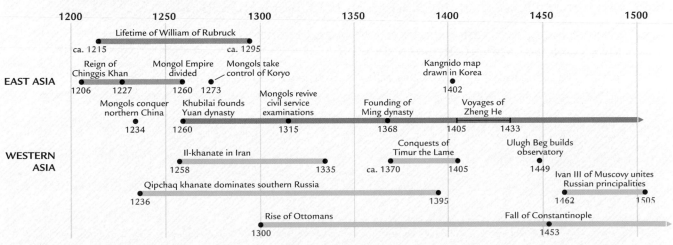

| 1200 | 1250 | 1300 | 1350 | 1400 | 1450 | 1500 |

Lifetime of William of Rubruck
ca. 1215 — ca. 1295

EAST ASIA

Reign of Chinggis Khan
1206 – 1227

Mongols conquer northern China
1234

Mongol Empire divided
1260

Mongols take control of Koryo
1273

Khubilai founds Yuan dynasty
1260

Mongols revive civil service examinations
1315

Founding of Ming dynasty
1368

Kangnido map drawn in Korea
1402

Voyages of Zheng He
1405 – 1433

WESTERN ASIA

Il-khanate in Iran
1258 – 1335

Qipchaq khanate dominates southern Russia
1236 – 1395

Conquests of Timur the Lame
ca. 1370 – 1405

Ulugh Beg builds observatory
1449

Ivan III of Muscovy unites Russian principalities
1462 – 1505

Rise of Ottomans
1300

Fall of Constantinople
1453

• **William of Rubruck** (ca. 1215–ca. 1295) Franciscan monk from France who visited the court of the Mongol khan Möngke in 1253–1254. His long letter to King Louis IX of France is one of the most detailed surviving sources about the Mongols.

In December 1253, after nine months of traveling—first by cart, then on horseback—through modern-day Turkey, Russia, the Ukraine, Siberia, and Mongolia, William arrived at the court of the Mongol leader Möngke (MUNG-keh) (d. 1259), the grandson of Chinggis Khan (the Mongolian spelling; Genghis Khan in Persian).

Called William of Rubruck because he was born sometime around 1215 in the village of Rubrouck, France, William was educated at Paris. A follower of Saint Francis, he went to Syria, then under the control of the Crusaders (see Chapter 13) in 1248, from where he departed for Mongolia.

As an outsider, William writes about the appearance of Mongol men and women, the process for making fermented horse's milk, and their worship of household spirits. No comparably detailed account by a Mongol survives. William visited the Mongols at the height of their power, during the years after Chinggis Khan had united the empire and before it broke apart.

William's gripping description of the Mongols allows us to understand how the Mongols created the largest contiguous land empire in world history, stretching from Hungary to the Pacific. Once they conquered a region or the local rulers surrendered, the Mongols placed a governor in charge and granted him considerable autonomy. Their loosely structured empire allowed many people, including William, to cross Eurasia and resulted in the interaction of societies and cultures that had been previously isolated. This chapter will also examine the states that succeeded the Mongols: the principality of Muscovy (Moscow) in Russia, the Ottomans in Turkey, the Yuan and Ming dynasties in China, and the successor states of Korea, Japan, and Vietnam.

Focus Questions

How did the Mongols' nomadic way of life contribute to their success as conquerors?

What bound the different sectors of the Mongol Empire together? What caused its breakup in the 1260s?

What states succeeded the Qipchaq and Chaghatai khanates?

What military innovations marked Ottoman expansion, and what cultural developments typified Ottoman rule?

What was the legacy of Mongol rule in East and Southeast Asia?

From Nomads to World Conquerors, 1200–1227

Founded by **Chinggis Khan** (ca. 1167–1227), the Mongol Empire formed between 1200 and 1250. At the time of Chinggis's birth around 1167, the Mongols lived in modern-day Mongolia with their herds of sheep, cattle, and horses and pursued a nomadic existence, trading with their sedentary neighbors primarily for grain, tea, textiles, and metal goods. After conquering the different peoples in Mongolia, Chinggis forged them into a fearsome fighting force that conquered gigantic sections of Europe, Central Asia, and China. The Mongols' skill with horses and systematic use of terror brought them unprecedented military success.

> **Chinggis Khan** (ca. 1167–1227) Founder of the Mongol Empire who united the different peoples living in modern-day Mongolia in 1206, when he took the title Chinggis Khan.

The Mongols' Nomadic Way of Life Before 1200

Nomadic peoples lived in the Mongolian grasslands even before the Mongols moved into Central Asia around 1000. The Mongols spoke Mongolian and different Turkic languages that are the basis of modern Turkish. The only source in Mongolian about the Mongols' early history is *The Origin of Chinggis Khan,* an anonymous oral epic that took shape in 1228 and was committed to writing a century or more later. (Many English translations are entitled *The Secret History of the Mongols.*) In 1206, Chinggis Khan ordered a Central Asian prisoner of war to record something he said in Mongolian. The prisoner wrote in his native Uighur, a Central Asian language spoken in Central Asia and in modern-day Xinjiang in west China. After this incident, the Mongols used the Uighur script to write the Mongolian language.

The Origin of Chinggis Khan gives a vivid sense of how the Mongols lived before they were unified. The Mongols' traditional homeland occupies much of the modern-day Mongolian People's Republic as well as the Inner Mongolian autonomous region just northwest of Beijing. This steppe region consists largely of grasslands, watered by a few rivers. Few trees grow there. While the soil and limited rainfall could not support a sedentary, farming population, the extensive grasslands perfectly suited pastoral nomads grazing their herds. (See the feature "World History in Today's World: Modern Nomads.")

After exhausting the available grass in a location, the Mongols moved to new pastures. Ranging from ten to several hundred people, an individual band might travel 100 miles (160 km) in its annual migration, usually on a fixed route. When the Mongols began their conquests, the fighters covered much larger distances and left their parents, wives, and children behind to tend their herds.

Religious Practices of the Mongols

The Mongols worshiped a variety of nature spirits. Each of the Mongols' tents, William noticed, contained several figurines made of felt, a textile made by pressing layers of wool together. All these figurines represented protective spirits who watched over the tent's residents as they performed their daily tasks.

The supreme deities of the Mongols were the sky-god Tengri and his counterpart, the earth-goddess Itügen. Certain people, called **shamans,** specialized in interceding with these gods. Sometimes they traveled to high mountains thought

> **shamans** Mongol religious specialists who interceded with the gods. Traveled to high mountains, thought to be the residence of high gods, to prostrate themselves. Also contacted deities by burning bones and interpreting the cracks to interpret the gods' will.

Modern Nomads

The population of Mongolia today is 2.65 million; about one-third are nomadic and keep herds totaling twenty-five million sheep, goats, horses, cattle, camels, and yaks. (The other two-thirds live in cities.) Many are struggling to maintain their traditional nomadic way of life. From the 1920s to 1990, Mongolia, sometimes called Outer Mongolia, was a satellite state dependent on the Soviet Union. During those years many nomads stopped herding and lived instead on large state farms with collectively owned herds. In 1990, after the fall of the Berlin Wall, Mongolia became independent. The withdrawal of massive Soviet subsidies caused its economy to collapse, forcing many to return to private herding. The state farms were disbanded, and each person received thirty animals.

Many of these nomads live in the traditional felt tents with a wooden frame, called *ger* (GAIR), but have added some modern conveniences. Some use solar-energy generators to fuel small refrigerators, while others receive television signals from sat-ellite dishes. The most prosperous have bought dirt bikes, motorcycles, or pickup trucks, which they use if they move their ger to a new location. A few have tried tending their herds with motor vehicles, but the high cost of gasoline means that most rely on horses for herding.

Few modern nomads have retained traditional herding skills. In 2000 and 2001, two harsh winters in a row covered much of Mongolia's extensive grasslands with ice and snow, preventing millions of animals from grazing. A few knowledgeable families prepared by taking their animals on a traditional monthlong trek covering some 100 miles (160 km) in the fall, and their fattened animals survived the difficult winter. Others fared less well: 3.5 million livestock died in 2000, and 4.8 million in 2001. Many of those who lost their flocks have given up herding and moved to the capital, Ulan Bator, to seek their livelihood, where fully one-third of the population consists of migrants from the countryside.

to be the residence of the sky-god and the other high gods, where they prostrated themselves. On other occasions, shamans burned bones and interpreted the cracks as indicators of the gods' will, much like Shang dynasty diviners in ancient China (see Chapter 4).

The Mongols in central and western Mongolia had some contact with Christian missionaries from the Church of the East, which was based in Syria and used Syriac as its primary liturgical language. These missionaries, the Christians most active in Central Asia, spoke the Turkic language Uighur when they preached among the Mongols. Williams called them Nestorians after Nestorius, a Syrian patriarch in Constantinople in 428, but in fact the Church of the East did not accept the teachings of Nestorius, whom successive church councils had declared a heretic.

Throughout his travels William encountered Eastern Christians and acknowledged them as fellow Christians while profoundly disagreeing with them about their beliefs. Like other Roman Catholics, William believed that Jesus had a single nature, not two distinct ones, and that Mary was Jesus' mother. William gradually realized that the Mongols saw no contradiction between worshiping their traditional deities and praying to the Christian God. They also saw no significant differences between Western and Eastern teachings about Jesus.

Mongol Society

Mongol society had two basic levels: ordinary Mongols and the families of the chiefs. The chief's sons and grandsons formed a privileged group from which all future rulers were chosen. Differences in wealth certainly existed, with some men having larger herds or better clothes than others, but no rigid social divisions or inherited ranks separated ordinary Mongols. Below them in rank, however, were slaves who had often been captured in battle.

The chiefs periodically collected a 1 percent tax simply by taking one of every hundred animals. They could use this tax as they liked or to meet the group's needs. Unlike sedentary peoples, who collected taxes once a year, usually in the fall after the harvest was in, Mongol chiefs imposed the tax whenever they chose.

The Mongols lived in felt tents that could be put up and dismantled rapidly. While the men led their herds to new grazing areas, the women packed up their households and organized the pitching of tents at the new campsite. William described the Mongols' traditional division of labor:

> It is the women's task to drive the wagons, to load the dwellings on them and to unload again, to milk the cows, to make butter and curd cheese, and to dress the skins and stitch them together, which they do with a thread made from sinew. . . . They never wash clothes, for they claim that this makes God angry and that if they were hung out to dry it would thunder. . . .
>
> The men make bows and arrows, manufacture stirrups and bits, fashion saddles, construct the dwellings and the wagons, tend the horses and milk the mares, churn the khumis (that is, the fermented mare's milk), produce the skins in which it is stored and tend and load the camels. Both sexes tend the sheep and goats, and they are milked on some occasions by the men, on others by the women.

Because Mongol women ran their households when their menfolk were away and often sat at their husbands' side during meetings, they had much more decision-making power than women in sedentary societies, William realized. Living in close proximity to their animals, the Mongols used the products of their own herds whenever possible: they made their tents from felt, wore clothes of skins and wool, ate meat and cheese, and drank fermented horse's milk, or khumis. William describes his first reaction to this drink with unusual frankness: "on swallowing it I broke out in a sweat all over from alarm and surprise, since I had never drunk it before. But for all that I found it very palatable, as indeed it is."

The Mongols, however, could not obtain everything they needed from their herds and depended on their agricultural neighbors to provide grain, which they valued as a supplement to their monotonous diet. The Mongols also relied on settled peoples to obtain the silks and cottons that were so much softer and lighter than the Mongols' rough wool and felt. Although they could make do, if necessary, without grain, tea, or textiles, they required metal objects like the knives, daggers, and spears used in hunting and war.

Before 1200, an uneasy peace prevailed among the Mongols and their neighbors. Individual Mongol groups might occasionally plunder a farming community, but they never expanded outside their traditional homelands. Under the powerful leadership of Chinggis Khan, all that changed.

The Rise of Chinggis Khan

Sometime around 1167, *The Origin of Chinggis Khan* reports, a chieftain of a small Mongol band and his wife gave birth to a son they named Temüjin, the future Chinggis Khan. He enjoyed a normal family life for a mere nine years before a rival poisoned his father. His widowed mother and her children were able to eke out a living only by grazing a small herd of nine horses and eating wild plants.

Difficult as it was for his mother, his father's untimely death brought Temüjin some advantages. Though only a teenager, he could forge alliances with other leaders who declared their loyalty to him. He allied himself with one band to fight a third band, and when that band had been defeated and joined his forces, he would then attack another. In this way, Temüjin eventually formed a confederation of all the peoples in the grasslands of modern Mongolia. In 1206, in recognition of his leadership, the Mongols awarded the 39-year-old Temüjin the title of universal ruler: Chinggis (literally "oceanic") Khan ("ruler").

The Mongols used a political process called **tanistry** to choose a new leader. Its basic rule was that the most qualified member of the chief's family led the band.[2] In practice, this meant that each time a chief died or was killed by a challenger, all contenders for power had to prove their ability to lead by defeating their rivals in battle. Then the warriors gathered at an assembly, or **khuriltai,** to acclaim the new leader. When this leader died, the destabilizing and bloody selection process began again. Each time a Mongol leader died, his followers disbanded; only a powerful successor could reunite them.

• **tanistry** Process the Mongols used to choose a new leader. Under tanistry, the most qualified member of the chief's family led the band. All contenders for power had to prove their ability to lead by defeating their rivals in battle.

• **khuriltai** Name of the Mongols' assembly that gathered to acclaim the new leader after he had defeated his rivals. Not an electoral body.

Chinggis's Army

Once he had united the Mongols, Chinggis weakened their group loyalties by dividing all his soldiers into units that crossed group lines. Each soldier belonged to four units: a unit of ten was part of a unit of one hundred, within a larger unit of one thousand, which finally belonged to one of ten thousand men. All able-bodied men between the ages of 15 and 70 fought in the army, and women did so if necessary. Scholars estimate the total population of the Mongols at one million, far less than the populations of the lands they conquered and governed. With such a small population, the Mongols did not have enough warriors to staff an enormous army. Numbering only one hundred thousand in 1206, the Mongol forces reached several hundred thousand at the height of Chinggis's power in the 1220s.

🔲 **A Mongol Archer in Italian Eyes**
This Mongol warrior's skull-like face stares menacingly at the viewer. He clasps a compound bow in his left hand, an arrow in his right. Ordinary bows were too big for a mounted warrior to shoot, but the compound bow was short enough for use on horseback. When the Mongols laid siege to cities, row after row of mounted archers shot showers of arrows with devastating effect. (Louvre, Paris, France/Réunion des Musées Nationaux/ Art Resource, NY)

A Mongol Hunting Party as Seen by a Chinese Artist In painting the hunting party of Khubilai Khan (see page 410), the Chinese artist Liu Guandao rendered the horses' different stances and the varied facial features of the retainers in exquisite detail. Note the different animals the Mongols, but not the Chinese, used for hunting: a greyhound dog to the right of the khan and a cheetah, prized for its speed, on the saddle of the lowermost horse. The archer (*far left*) leans backward to shoot a bird flying high above in the sky; the skills the Mongols developed while hunting were directly transferable to warfare. (National Palace Museum, Taipei, Taiwan/The Bridgeman Art Library)

The Mongols started with only one significant advantage over the European and Asian powers they conquered: horses. Their grassy homeland provided them with an unending supply of horses, and, because Mongol children were raised on horseback, they matured into highly skilled riders who could shoot from horseback with their compound bows of wood, horn, and sinew. The Mongols had so many horses that they could change their mounts three times a day, and they frequently put dummies on riderless horses to make their army look larger.

The overriding goal of the Mongol armies was to conquer as much territory as quickly as possible. It was much cheaper and faster, the Mongols realized, to take a city whose occupants surrendered without a fight than to lay siege to a walled, medieval settlement that could take months to fall. The Mongols placed captives on their front lines to be killed by their own countrymen, in the hope that the rulers of the cities on their path could surrender. In exchange, the Mongols promised not to destroy their homes.

Mongol traditions held that Chinggis Khan could command the total obedience of his warriors in wartime but not in peacetime. Accordingly, he had good reason to keep conquering new territory. In war, the Mongols viewed all plunder as their due, but they limited their requisition to one-tenth of all the enemy's movable property if the enemy submitted voluntarily. Because the ruler shared the spoils with his men whenever he conquered a city, his followers had a strong incentive to follow him, and the ruler had no reason to stop fighting. Under Chinggis's leadership, the Mongols built one of the most effective fighting forces the world had ever seen.

At first Chinggis led his troops into north China, which was under the rule of the Jin dynasty (see Chapter 12), and conquered the important city of Beijing in 1215, forcing the Jin dynasty to occupy a small sliver of land between the Southern Song and the Mongol realms. In 1219, Chinggis turned his attention to Transoxiana, the region between the Amu Darya and Syr Darya Rivers, then under the rule of the Islamic Khoresmian empire. In rapid succession the Mongols conquered the glorious cities of Bukhara (in modern Uzbekistan), Balkh (Afghanistan), Nishapur (Iran), Merv (Turkmenistan), and Herat (Afghanistan). The Persian historian Juvaini (1226–1283) quotes an eyewitness: "They came, they sapped, they burnt, they slew, they plundered, and they departed."[3]

Mongol Governance

● **darughachi**
Regional governor appointed by the leaders of the Mongols after they had conquered a new territory. The darughachi's main tasks were to administer the region and to collect taxes.

Before departing from Bukhara, Chinggis summoned all the local notables to explain how the new regime would work. He appointed one man, usually a Mongol, to be governor, or **darughachi** (dah-roo-GAH-chee), of the conquered region. The darughachi's main responsibility was to collect the required taxes.

The darughachi were free to try different types of taxes in the various parts of the empire as long as they produced sufficient revenue. The Mongols continued to levy irregular taxes, like their traditional 1 percent tax on herds, in addition to taxes on agriculture, and in many locations they also instituted a 5 percent tax on commercial transactions. Since the Mongols allowed the local governments to rule as they had before the conquest, the darughachi resembled the satraps of the Achaemenid Empire of Persia (see Chapter 6).

The Mongols reserved the highest positions in the occupying government, such as the darughachi, for Mongols. Above the darughachi were the Mongol khan and his kin, who did not hold official titles but made all the major decisions affecting the empire. Below the darughachi were the conquered peoples, who staffed the lower branches of government and were permitted to continue their own religious practices. Religious institutions did not have to pay taxes. The Mongols' willingness to leave much of the local government and customs intact meant that they could conquer enormous swaths of territory quickly without having to leave behind a large occupying force to rule the conquered lands.

The United Mongol Empire After Chinggis, 1229–1260

When Chinggis Khan died in 1227, no one knew whether his empire would survive him. From 1229 to 1260, the Mongols remained united but were led by different rulers (see the chart "Mongol Rulers, 1206–1260"). They continued their conquests and took eastern Europe and northern China. During this time, they also introduced important innovations, such as the postal relay system, and began

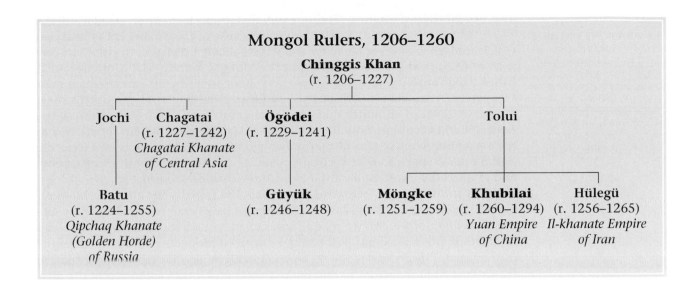

Mongol Rulers, 1206–1260

Chinggis Khan
(r. 1206–1227)

Jochi   **Chagatai**
(r. 1227–1242)
*Chagatai Khanate
of Central Asia*

Ögödei
(r. 1229–1241)

Tolui

Batu
(r. 1224–1255)
*Qipchaq Khanate
(Golden Horde)
of Russia*

Güyük
(r. 1246–1248)

Möngke
(r. 1251–1259)

Khubilai
(r. 1260–1294)
*Yuan Empire
of China*

Hülegü
(r. 1256–1265)
*Il-khanate Empire
of Iran*

work on the Mongol capital at Khara Khorum. The postal relay system, the requirements for receiving envoys, and the court-financed merchant networks were the only institutions holding the different parts of the far-flung Mongol Empire together, as William of Rubruck discovered when he traveled to Khara Khorum in the 1250s. His trip exemplifies the ease of movement across Eurasia and the resulting cultural exchanges that came with the Mongol conquest.

The Reign of Ögödei, 1229–1241

Chinggis Khan died in Mongolia in 1227 at the age of 60. Before he died, Chinggis had divided his entire realm into four sections, each for one of his sons. If the Mongols had followed the traditional election process, the succession dispute could have been protracted. Instead, at a khuriltai held two years after Chinggis's death, they acquiesced to Chinggis's request that his third son, Ögödei (r. 1229–1241), govern all four sections of the Mongols' realm.

In the 1230s, the Mongols attacked Russia repeatedly and subdued the Russian principalities. With nothing now standing between the Mongols and Europe, western European rulers, including the king of France and the pope, belatedly realized how vulnerable they were to Mongol attack. Until then, they had been preoccupied with taking back Jerusalem (see Chapter 13). Ignorantly assuming that any enemy of Islam had to be Christian and so a natural ally of theirs, the Europeans hoped to enlist the Mongols in the Crusades. Each European envoy returned with the same report: the Mongols demanded that the Europeans submit to them and give up one-tenth of all their wealth. The Europeans refused. In 1241–1242, the Mongols attacked Poland, crossed the Danube, and reached Klosterneuburg, only a few miles from Vienna, Austria.

There, on the brink of overrunning western Europe, the Mongols suddenly halted. News of Ögödei's death reached the troops, and, according to custom, all the warriors returned home to attend the khuriltai. They were unable to choose a new leader quickly from among the brothers, sons, and nephews of Chinggis Khan, and the troops never returned to eastern Europe. The western European powers were spared invasion by the Mongols.

• postal relay system
Mongol institution of
fixed routes with regular
stops where messengers
could eat and get fresh
mounts, which took
shape during Ögödei's
reign. Functioned as the
central nervous system
of the sprawling empire.

The Postal Relay System

The warriors in Europe learned of Ögödei's death fairly quickly because of the **postal relay system,** which took shape during his reign and which allowed the ruler to communicate with officials in the furthest regions of the Mongol Empire. The Mongols established fixed routes, with regular stops every 30 or so miles (50 km) at which messengers could eat and get fresh mounts. As official messengers, they carried a silver or bronze tablet of authority that entitled them to food and horses. Because the riders could cover some 60 miles (100 km) a day, the relay system functioned as the central nervous system of the sprawling empire. The Mongols also used the postal relay stations to host visiting envoys, to provide them with escorts, food, and shelter, and, most important, to guarantee their safe return.

William of Rubruck began his journey in 1253, two years after the Mongols had finally settled on Möngke, one of Chinggis Khan's grandsons, as Ögödei's successor. William wore a brown robe and went barefoot because he was a Franciscan missionary, not a diplomat. Just before he entered Mongol territory, however, he learned that if he denied he was an envoy, he might lose his safe-conduct guarantee and the right to provisions and travel assistance. He decided to accept the privileges granted to envoys.

The system for receiving envoys functioned well but not flawlessly, as William discovered. When he crossed the Don River, local people refused to help. To his dismay William found that the money he brought from Europe was useless: in one village, no one would sell him food or animals. After three difficult days, William's party once again received the mounts to which they were entitled. For two months, William reported, he and his compatriots "never slept in a house or a tent, but always in the open air or underneath our wagons."

On July 31, 1253, they arrived at the court of Sartakh, a great-grandson of Chinggis. Earlier envoys had reported that Sartakh was an observant Christian, and William hoped that Sartakh would permit him to stay. In his quest to obtain permission to preach, William personally experienced the decision-making structure of the Mongol government. Although the Mongols respected envoys, they feared spies. Sartakh said that, to preach, William needed the approval of Sartakh's father, Batu, a grandson of Chinggis Khan who ruled the western section of the empire. Batu in turn decided that William needed the approval of the highest ruler of all, Möngke, before he could preach among the Mongols. Each ruler chose to send William in person to see his superior.

William and his companion Bartholomew departed for Khara Khorum with a Mongol escort who told them: "I am to take you to Möngke Khan. It is a four month journey, and the cold there is so intense that rocks and trees split apart with the frost: see whether you can bear it." He provided them each with a sheepskin coat, trousers, felt boots, and fur hoods. At last, taking advantage of the postal relay system, William began to travel at the pace of a Mongol warrior, covering some 60 miles (100 km) each day:

> On occasions we changed horses two or three times in one day; on others we would travel for two or three days without coming across habitation, in which case we were obliged to move at a gentler pace. Out of the twenty or thirty horses we, as foreigners, were invariably given the most inferior, for everyone would take their pick of the horses before us; though I was always provided a strong mount in view of my very great weight.

William's reference to his bulk provides a rare personal detail. The Mongols ate solid food only in the evening and breakfasted on either broth or millet soup. They had no lunch. Although William and Bartholomew found the conditions extremely trying, the speed at which they traveled illustrates the postal relay system's crucial role in sending messages to officials and orders to the armies throughout the Mongol Empire.

At Möngke's Court   On December 27, 1253, William arrived at the winter court of Möngke on the River Ongin in modern Mongolia, where he and his retinue pitched their tents and where their herds stayed with them. On January 4, 1254, the two Franciscans entered the ruler's tent, whose interior was covered with gold cloth. Möngke "was sitting on a couch, dressed in a fur which was spotted and very glossy like a sealskin. He is snub-nosed, a man of medium build, and aged about forty-five." William asked Möngke for permission to preach in his territory. When his interpreter began to explain the khan's reply, William "was unable to grasp a single complete sentence." To his dismay, he realized that Möngke and the interpreter were both drunk.

His interpreter later informed him that he had been granted permission to stay two months, and William ended up staying three months at Möngke's court and another three at the capital of Khara Khorum, where he arrived in the spring of 1254. Khara Khorum was home to a small but genuinely international group of foreigners, who introduced important innovations from their home societies to the Mongols. Although they had originally come as captives and were not free to go home, these Europeans possessed valuable skills and enjoyed a much higher standard of living than the typical Mongol warrior. Whenever the Mongols conquered a new city, they first identified all the skilled craftsmen and divided them into two groups: siege-warfare engineers and skilled craftsmen. These engineers made catapults to propel large stones that cracked holes in city walls, and Chinese and Jurchen experts taught the Mongols how to use gunpowder (see Chapter 12). Mongol commanders sent all the other skilled craftsmen to help build Khara Khorum. The Mongols' willingness to learn from their captives prompted extensive cultural exchange.

The Mongol rulers designated a group of Central Asian merchants as their commercial agents who would convert the Mongols' plunder into money and then buy goods the rulers desired. As a nomadic people, the Mongols particularly liked textiles because they could be transported easily. Instead of a fixed salary, rulers gave their followers suits of clothes at regular intervals. The Mongols had two types of tents: their traditional felt tents held up with poles on the interior and new-style tents with guy ropes on the outside. Both could be very large, holding as many as a thousand people, and could be lined with thousands of yards of lavishly patterned silks. Most of the merchants traveling along caravan routes and supplying the Mongol rulers were Central Asian Muslims, whom William does not mention in his account.

Understandably, William writes much about the Europeans resident in Khara Khorum, including a French goldsmith named William. Captured in Hungary and technically a slave, the goldsmith worked for Möngke, who paid him a large amount for each project he completed. The goldsmith made an elaborate drinking fountain that dispensed khumis, honey wine, grape wine, and rice ale. This fountain illustrates the many cultural exchanges of the time: the technology was French, while the drinks were both European and Mongol. The goldsmith generously offered his bilingual son as a replacement for William's incompetent interpreter, and the son interpreted for William when Möngke invited him to debate with Nestorian, Muslim, and Buddhist representatives at court. (See the feature "Movement of Ideas: A Debate Among Christians, Buddhists, and Muslims at the Mongol Court.")

A Debate Among Christians, Buddhists, and Muslims at the Mongol Court

In May 1254, Möngke sent word to William that, before departing, the Christians, Muslims, and Buddhists should meet and debate religious teachings, since Möngke hoped to "learn the truth." William agreed to participate, and he and the Nestorians had a practice session in which he even took the part of an imaginary Buddhist opponent. On the appointed day, Möngke sent three of his secretaries—a Christian, a Muslim, and a Buddhist—to be the judges.

Since William's report is the only record that survives, historians cannot compare it with other descriptions of what happened. It is possible, for example, that he exaggerated his own role in the debate or misunderstood the arguments of his opponents.

The debate began with William arguing points with a Chinese Buddhist, whom William identifies by the Mongolian word *tuin* (TWUN). Like the Crusaders, William refers to the Muslims as Saracens and reports that they said little.

Source: Peter Jackson, trans., *The Mission of Friar William of Rubruck: His Journey to the Court of the Great Khan Möngke 1253–1255* (London: The Hakluyt Society, 1990), pp. 231–235.

The Christians then placed me in the middle and told the tuins to address me; and the latter, who were there in considerable numbers, began to murmur against Möngke Khan, since no Khan had ever attempted to probe their secrets. They confronted me with someone who had come from Cataia [China]: he had his own interpreter, while I had Master William's son.

He began by saying to me, "Friend, if you are brought to a halt, you may look for a wiser man than yourself."

I did not reply.

Next he enquired what I wanted to debate first: either how the world had been made, or what becomes of souls after death.

"Friend," I answered, "that ought not to be the starting-point of our discussion. All things are from God, and He is the fountain-head of all. Therefore we should begin by speaking about God, for you hold a different view of Him from us and Möngke wishes to learn whose belief is superior." The umpires ruled that this was fair.

They wanted to begin with the issues I have mentioned because they regard them as more important. All of them belong to the Manichaean heresy, to the effect that one half of things is evil and the other half good, or at least that there are two principles; and as regards souls, they all believe that they pass from one body to another.

Even one of the wiser of the Nestorian priests asked me whether it was possible for the souls of animals to escape after death to any place where they would not be compelled to suffer. In support of this fallacy, moreover, so Master William told me, a boy was brought from Cataia [China], who to judge by his physical size was not three years old, yet was fully capable of rational thought: he said of himself that he was in his third incarnation, and he knew how to read and write.

I said, then, to the *tuin*: "We firmly believe in our hearts and acknowledge with our lips that God exists, that there is only one God, and that He is one in perfect unity. What do you believe?"

"It is fools," he said, "who claim there is only one God. Wise men say that there are several. Are there not great rulers in your country, and is not Möngke Khan the chief lord here? It is the same with gods, inasmuch as there are different gods in different regions."

"You choose a bad example," I told him, "in drawing a parallel between men and God: that way any powerful figure could be called a god in his own dominions."

But as I was seeking to demolish the analogy, he distracted me by asking, "What is your God like, of Whom you claim that there is no other?"

"Our God," I replied, "beside Whom there is no other, is all-powerful and therefore needs assistance from no one; in fact we all stand in need of His. With men it is not so: no man is capable of all things, and for this reason there have to be a number of rulers on earth, since no one has the power to undertake the whole. Again, He is all-knowing and therefore needs no one as counsellor: in fact all wisdom is from Him. And again He is the supreme Good and has no need of our goods: rather, 'in Him we live and move and are.' This is the nature of our God, and it is unnecessary, therefore, to postulate any other."

"That is not so," he declared. "On the contrary, there is one supreme god in Heaven, of whose origin we are still ignorant, with ten others under him and one of the lowest rank beneath them; while on earth they are without number."

As he was about to spin yet more yarns, I asked about this supreme god: did he believe he was all-powerful, or was some other god?

He was afraid to answer, and asked: "If your God is as you say, why has He made half of things evil?"

"That is an error," I said. "It is not God who created evil. Everything that exists is good." All the *tuins* were amazed at this statement and recorded it in writing as something erroneous and impossible. . . .

He sat for a long while reluctant to answer, with the result that the secretaries who were listening on the Khan's behalf had to order him to reply. Finally he gave the answer that no god was all-powerful, at which all the Saracens burst into

loud laughter. When silence was restored I said: "So, then, not one of your gods is capable of rescuing you in every danger, inasmuch as a predicament may be met with where he does not have the power. Further, 'no man can serve two masters': so how is it that you can serve so many gods in Heaven and on earth?" The audience told him to reply; yet he remained speechless. But when I was seeking to put forward arguments for the unity of the Divine essence and for the Trinity while everyone was listening, the local Nestorians told me it was enough, as they wanted to speak themselves.

At this point I made way for them [the Nestorians]. But when they sought to argue with the Saracens, the latter replied: "We concede that your religion is true and that everything in the Gospel is true; and therefore we have no wish to debate any issue with you." And they admitted that in all their prayers they beg God that they may die a Christian death. . . .

Everybody listened without challenging a single word. But for all that no one said, "I believe, and wish to become a Christian." When it was all over, the Nestorians and Saracens alike sang in loud voices, while the *tuins* remained silent; and after that everyone drank heavily.

QUESTIONS FOR ANALYSIS

▶ What is William's main point?

▶ How does William present the main teachings of Buddhism? Of Islam?

▶ In William's account of the debate, does anyone say anything that you think they probably did not? Support your position with specific examples.

Möngke's invitation to debate illustrates the Mongols' tolerance for and interest in other religious beliefs. Yet, on the one occasion he had a competent interpreter, even William realized that he had made no converts. William returned to Acre, the city in the Holy Land from which he departed, and then proceeded to France, where, in 1257, he met Roger Bacon (ca. 1214–1294), who preserved William's letter. After 1257, William disappears from the historical record, leaving the date of his death uncertain.

William's lack of success as a missionary is confirmed by one contemporary: in 1259, the king of Armenia, Hetum I (1226–1269), reported what the Mongols had told him about William. When William "appeared before the great king of the Tartars [Batu], he began to press on him the Christian faith, saying that the Tartar—and every infidel—would perish eternally and be condemned to everlasting fire." William might have been more successful as a missionary, the Mongol ruler Batu wryly commented, if he had tried to persuade the Mongols of the benefits of being a Christian, rather than threatening them with "everlasting punishment." The Armenian king's report seems all too believable: we can easily imagine William haranguing the unconvinced Mongol ruler.

The Empire Comes Apart, 1259–1263

William's letter to his monarch reveals that only the postal relay stations bound the different parts of the Mongol Empire together. The Mongols granted the darughachi governors wide latitude in governing, and they never developed an empire-wide bureaucracy. Officials from one part of the empire were not transferred to other regions, and they did not implement uniform standards and policies.

Because the Mongols allowed the darughachi governors to use the local language for administration and the recruitment of local officials, Chinese, Persian, and Turkish continued to be spoken throughout the empire. The Mongols did not impose Mongolian as the language of administration. During William's trip, the different sections of the empire continued to forward some taxes to the center, but the empire broke apart after Möngke's death in 1259.

A year earlier, Möngke's brother Hülegü had led the Mongols on one of the bloodiest campaigns in their history, the conquest of Baghdad, in which some 800,000 people died. Hülegü also ordered the execution of the caliph and so, in 1258, put a final end to the Abbasid caliphate, founded in 750 (see Chapter 9). In 1260, the Mamluk dynasty of Egypt (see Chapter 11) defeated the remnants of Hülegü's army in Syria at the battle of Ayn Jalut.

This defeat was the first time the Mongols had lost a battle and also marked the end of a united Mongol Empire. One of Möngke's surviving brothers, Khubilai (KOO-bih-leye) (d. 1294), engineered a khuriltai that named him the rightful successor, while a rival khuriltai named his brother Arigh Boke (d. 1264) the new khan. After 1260 it was impossible to maintain any pretense of imperial unity.

Another setback occurred in 1263, when the ruler of the Qipchaq (KIP-chack) khanate in Russia actively sought an alliance with the Mamluks against his cousin Hülegü in Iran. Never before had a Mongol allied with a non-Mongol force against another Mongol leader, and the alliance provides a clear date for the end of the unified Mongol Empire.

Successor States in Western Asia, 1263–15

After this breakup the Mongol Empire divided into four sections, each ruled by a different Mongol prince, generally the son or grandson of a former ruler (see Map 14.1). The eastern sector consisted of the Mongolian heartland and China (discussed later in this chapter). In the western sectors, each time a ruler died his living sons divided his territory, and succession disputes were common, fragmenting authority even further. Three important realms dominated the western sector. The Il-khanate in Iran governed the Tigris and Euphrates River basins, the Iranian Plateau, and Anatolia in Turkey. Their northern neighbor, the Qipchaq khanate or the Golden Horde, ruled the region north of the Black, Caspian, and Aral Seas (modern Ukraine, Russia, and Kazakhstan). Both the Il-khanate and the Qipchaq khanate shared a border with the third region, the Chaghatai khanate, which controlled the Syr Darya and Amu Darya Rivers of Central Asia around Samarkand. Each of these khanates inherited the legacy of the larger Mongol Empire but could not build territories as large. Border disputes often prompted war among these three realms. The Mongol tradition of learning from other peoples continued as each of the three ruling families converted to Islam, the religion of their most educated subjects (see Chapter 9).

The Il-khanate in Iran, 1256–1335

Since the Mongols had conquered Iran in 1258, only two years before the empire broke apart in 1260, they were not well established there. Hülegü took the title *il-khan* ("subordinate khan" in Persian) to indicate that he was lower in rank than his brother Möngke; he ruled the **Il-khanate.** As elsewhere, the Mongols faced the immediate problem of establishing order and ensuring the continued flow of taxes from the Muslim peoples of Iran.

Hülegü, like his brother Möngke, was primarily a believer in shamanism. Five of Hülegü's sons and grandsons ruled Iran between 1265 and 1295. They, like other Mongol rulers, allowed Muslims, Buddhists, and Nestorian Christians to continue to worship their own belief systems. When Hülegü's great-grandson Ghazan (r. 1295–1304) took the throne in 1295, he announced his conversion to Islam, the religion of most of his subjects, and his fellow Mongols followed suit.

The Il-khanate never succeeded in establishing an efficient way to tax Iran. Infamous for collecting taxes twenty or more times a year, officials frequently resorted to force before they could get Iran's cultivators to pay. The end result was severe impoverishment of the countryside, which had already been devastated in the 1250s during the Mongol invasions. The Il-khanate had regular contact with the Yuan dynasty in China (covered later in this chapter), and in the 1290s the government introduced paper money (using the Chinese word for it) in the hopes that people would turn in all their gold and silver to the government. The paper money failed completely, bringing commerce to a standstill, but the experiment testifies to the Il-khanate's willingness to borrow from neighboring peoples.

After 1295, several Il-khanate rulers, in an attempt to bring reform, stipulated how much taxation should occur and when, encouraged farmers to reclaim abandoned land, and closely supervised Islamic judges, or qadi. Revenues seem to have

• Il-khanate Mongol government of the region of Iran (1256–1335), founded by Hülegü, who took the title *il-khan* ("subordinate khan" in Persian) to indicate that he was lower in rank than his brother Möngke.

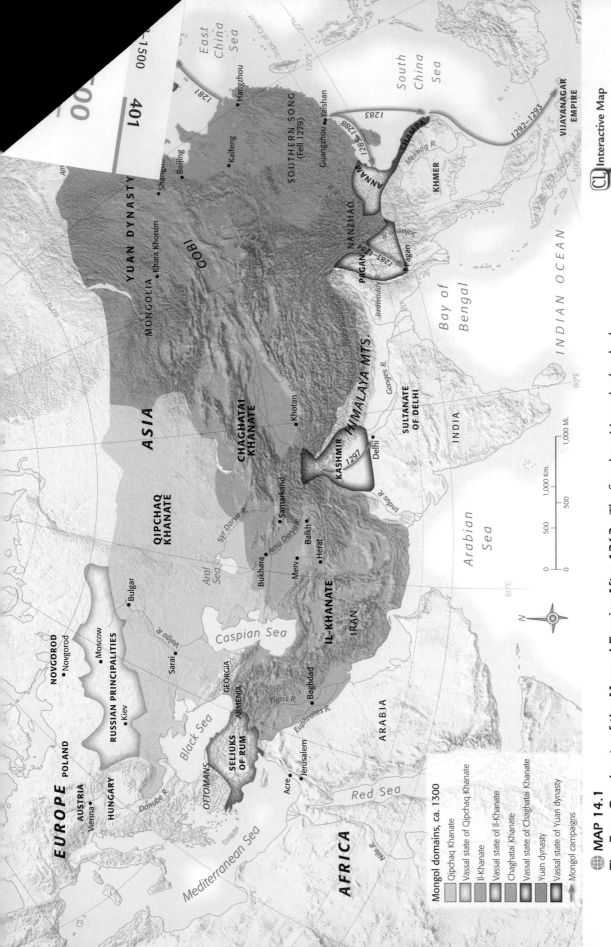

MAP 14.1

The Four Quadrants of the Mongol Empire After 1263   The first three Mongol rulers had governed the largest contiguous land empire in world history. But the Mongols were unable to choose a single successor to Möngke, the grandson of Chinggis Khan who died in 1259. The empire broke into four quadrants, each governed by a different member of the founder's family.

CL Interactive Map

Mongol domains, ca. 1300
- Qipchaq Khanate
- Vassal state of Qipchaq Khanate
- Il-Khanate
- Vassal state of Il-Khanate
- Chaghatai Khanate
- Vassal state of Chaghatai Khanate
- Yuan dynasty
- Vassal state of Yuan dynasty
- Mongol campaigns

increased, but the Il-khanate ended in 1335 when the last of Hülegü's descendants died, and Iran broke up into many small regions.

The Qipchaq Khanate and the Rise of Moscow

Although individual rulers of the Qipchaq khanate converted to Islam as early as the 1250s, Islam became the official religion only during the reign of Muhammad Özbeg (r. 1313–1341). The Qipchaq ruled the lower and middle Volga River valley, the home of the Bulgars, who had converted to Islam in the tenth century (see Chapter 10). Many Qipchaq subjects in Russian cities to the north and west continued to belong to the Eastern Orthodox Church.

Before the Mongols conquered the region in the 1230s, the descendants of Prince Vladimir of Kiev had governed the various Rus principalities (see Chapter 10). Unable to mount a successful defense against the Mongols, the different Russian princes surrendered. At the beginning of the Mongol era, Kiev had been the most important city in Russia, but the conquests devastated the city, prompting many to move to other places. Like all conquered peoples, the Russian princes of various cities paid the Mongols tribute, and the Qipchaq khanate, in turn, gave certain princes written permission to govern a given territory.

The **principality of Muscovy** (Moscow) eventually emerged as Kiev's successor, partially because the rulers of Moscow were frequently better able to pay their share of tribute and so were favored by the Qipchaq khanate. Ivan III (r. 1462–1505) defeated other Russian families to become the undisputed leader of the region; in 1480 he stopped submitting tribute to the Qipchaq khanate, and in 1502 he brought the khanate to an end. Ivan III controlled large chunks of modern-day Russia: from the Black Sea in the south to Novgorod in the north and much of modern-day Poland.

Primary Source: Russia's Conquest by the Mongols: A Song to Lost Lands
This song mournfully describes Russia before its conquest by the Mongols.

• **principality of Muscovy** Successor to the Qipchaq khanate in modern-day Russia. Its most important leader, Ivan III, defeated other Russian families to become the region's undisputed leader; overthrew the Qipchaq khanate in 1502.

The Chaghatai Khanate and Timur the Lame

Straddling the Amu Darya and Syr Darya River valleys, the Chaghatai khanate included the eastern grasslands in what is now modern Mongolia and a western half that included the great Silk Road cities of Bukhara and Samarkand. In the grasslands to the east, the Mongols could follow their traditional nomadic way of life, and different chieftains continued to rule this region after the breakup of the empire.

Starting around 1350, a Turkish-speaking leader of Mongol descent took power first in the city of Samarkand and then in the surrounding western section of the Chaghatai khanate. This leader, known to his Persian enemies as **Timur the Lame** (1336?–1405), contracted to *Tamerlane* in English, succeeded in forming a powerful confederation.

Timur the Lame united the different peoples of the steppe much as Chinggis Khan had done around 1200: fighting one band until he defeated them, and then allying with them against another. In this way, he conquered much of modern Iran, Uzbekistan, Afghanistan, and the Anatolian region of Turkey. He married a descendant of Chinggis so that he could claim to be his successor, and he, too, used terror to reduce resistance. Timur was famous for setting his enemies on fire or throwing them off cliffs.

Like the Mongols, Timur the Lame forcibly resettled artisans and architects from among the conquered townspeople of India, Iran, and Syria. In his capital of

• **Timur the Lame** Also known in English as Tamerlane. Successor to the Chaghatai khanate, he conquered much of modern Iran, Uzbekistan, Afghanistan, and the Anatolian region of Turkey.

■ **The Tomb of Timur the Lame in Samarkand** Completed in 1401, this building was originally intended as a madrasa, or school, but, when Timur died suddenly in 1405, his son buried his father there. The dome has a diameter of 49 feet (15 m) and is 41 feet (12.5 m) tall, but its design, with sixty-four distinctive ribs, gives an impression of lightness. The brilliant mosaic of light and dark blue tiles, the culmination of several centuries of experimenting, makes this one of the most striking buildings in modern Samarkand. (© Tom Ang/drr.net)

Samarkand, these craftspeople built foreign-influenced buildings with elaborate mosaic tilework that is still visible today. As a result of this work, Samarkand became one of the most beautiful of all Central Asian cities.

Timur died in 1405 as he was preparing to lead his troops into China. Continuing the Mongol legacy of patronizing learning, his grandson Ulugh Beg (1394–1449, r. 1447–1449) built an enormous astronomical observatory and compiled a star chart based on ancient Greek and Islamic learning. Ulugh Beg ruled for only two years before his son ordered him killed and took over as ruler, in keeping with the Mongol tradition of tanistry. Timur's empire soon fragmented because the different members of the royal house, unable to decide on a successor, simply divided it among themselves.

By 1500, almost all the Mongol successor states had ceased to exist in western Asia. The region of Iran had broken into smaller states, as had the territory of the former Chaghatai khanate. Muscovy emerged as the major power in the Volga region, leaving only a small Mongol successor state in the Crimea.

⬤ The Ottomans, 1300–1500

In the centuries that saw the fragmentation of the khanates in the west, a new power arose that initially replicated many elements of Mongol rule but then made crucial innovations that allowed it to build an empire that outlasted all the Mongol successor states. The **Ottomans,** a group of Turkic Muslim nomads, first gained control of Anatolia, in modern Turkey, which lay between the eastern edge of the Byzantine Empire and the western edge of the Il-khanate. Like the Mongols, the Ottomans were a nomadic people who conquered their sedentary neighbors and paid their soldiers with plunder. They put local rulers in place and granted them considerable autonomy in exchange for the regular payment of tribute and provision of troops when needed. Over time, however, they shifted from a Mongol-type army to an army who received a fixed salary—and not a share of plunder. Their conquest of Constantinople in 1453 marked the end of the Byzantine Empire and the establishment of a major Islamic power in western Asia.

● **Ottomans** Group of Turkic Muslim nomads who gained control of the Anatolia region in modern Turkey around 1300. Their conquest of Constantinople in 1453 marked the end of the Byzantine Empire and the establishment of a major Islamic power in western Asia.

The Rise of the Ottomans, 1300–1400

Even at the height of their power during the thirteenth century, the Mongols sent few troops to Anatolia, which lay on the western edge of their empire. After sacking Constantinople in 1204 (see Chapter 13), the Crusader forces occupied the city, while different Byzantine contenders tried to organize the opposition; as a result they, too, neglected the region of Anatolia. Around 1300 a man named Osman (the origin of the name *Ottoman*) emerged as the leader of a group of nomads who successfully conquered different sections of the Anatolian peninsula.

In 1326, the Ottomans conquered the port city of Bursa, which lay across the Sea of Marmora from Constantinople, and made it their first fixed capital. Because their armies were powerful, different claimants to the throne of the Byzantine Empire formed alliances with them. In 1354, Ottoman forces bypassed Constantinople and crossed the narrow straits of Dardanelles into modern-day Bulgaria. From this base, they conquered much of Greece and the Balkans by 1400, when they became the most powerful group professing loyalty to the Byzantine ruler, who controlled only the city of Constantinople and its immediate environs.

As the Ottomans swallowed up large chunks of the Byzantine territory, they became less hostile to the Christian residents of Anatolia and the Balkans, who were, after all, peoples of the book. The Ottomans could not stand up to the armies of Timur the Lame, but they resumed their conquests after his death in 1405.

As the Ottoman realm expanded, Ottoman rulers began to see themselves as protectors of local society, with Islamic law as their main tool. They paid mosque officials salaries and included them as part of their government bureaucracy. Agriculture thrived under their rule, and they were able to collect high revenues from their agricultural taxes, which they used to build roads for foot soldiers.

The Ottoman Military

The Ottomans enjoyed unusual military success because of their innovative policies. Unlike their enemies, they paid market prices for food and did not simply steal supplies from the local people. As a result, farmers willingly brought their produce to market to sell to the Ottomans.

As the Ottomans moved through the countryside, they frequently captured soldiers from among the conquered Christians. These enslaved prisoners of war were forced to join the army. Many eventually converted to Islam. They were called **Janissaries,** a Turkish word that means "new soldier." To prevent the Janissaries from building up large private estates, the Ottomans required them to be celibate so that they would not have descendants. Even so, many local people volunteered their sons for Janissary units because the boys could rise to a much higher position than if they remained on family farms.

The Ottomans also took advantage of new weapons using gunpowder. Although the Mongols had used some gunpowder, their most effective troops were mounted cavalry with bows and arrows. Nomadic peoples had the advantage over sedentary peoples because people living in cities could not defend themselves against the mobile, mounted nomad warriors armed with crossbows.

Around 1400, however, gunpowder weapons improved noticeably. Siege engineers realized that they could use wrought-iron launches powered by gunpowder to propel stone cannonballs weighing 440 pounds (200 kg) against city walls. While settled peoples could store gunpowder in safe stone storehouses, called *magazines,* nomadic peoples could not transport large quantities of gunpowder because they exploded too easily. Sedentary peoples then gained the advantage over nomadic peoples.

The Ottoman Conquest of Constantinople, 1453

The Ottomans demonstrated their command of the new gunpowder technology in 1453. When the Byzantine emperor requested the doubling of an annual subsidy from the Turks, the young Ottoman emperor Mehmet II (r. 1451–1481) decided to end the fiction of Byzantine rule. Mehmet, who is known as **Mehmet the Conqueror,** began construction of a large fort on the western shore of the Bosphorus, just across from Constantinople, and positioned three cannon on the fort's walls where they could hit all ships that entered the harbor to provision the Byzantine troops. (See the feature "Visual Evidence: The Siege of Constantinople, 1453.")

Eight thousand men on the Byzantine side faced an Ottoman force of some eighty thousand, assisted by a navy of over one hundred ships and armed with powerful cannon that could shoot a ball weighing 1,340 pounds (607 kg). Even so, the walls of Constantinople were so strong that it took two long months before the Ottomans defeated the Byzantine Empire.

When the city fell, Mehmet promised his troops the customary three days of looting a fallen non-Islamic city, but he called an end to the sacking after a single day. At the end of that day he led a small group of guards and advisers to the Hagia Sophia, the largest and most striking church in the city, which he planned to convert into a mosque. The Ottomans transformed Constantinople from a Christian into a Muslim city by turning many churches into mosques, often by adding four minarets around the original church building and clearing a prayer hall inside. The official name of the city was Qustantiniyya, "city of Constantine," but its residents referred to it as Istanbul, meaning simply "the city" in Greek.

Once the city came under Ottoman rule, the Greek, Slavic, and Turkic peoples living in the region moved to the city, bringing great prosperity. Priding himself

■ **Converting a Church into a Mosque**   In 1453, on the day Mehmet's troops took Constantinople, he summoned his advisers to the most beautiful church in the city, the Hagia Sophia, to discuss their postconquest plans. The Ottomans transformed the Hagia Sophia into a mosque by adding four minarets outside the original church building and by clearing a giant hall for prayer inside. They also constructed a traditional Islamic garden, complete with fountain, behind the mosque.   (Steve McCurry/ Magnum Photos)

on his patronage of scholars and artists, Mehmet commissioned scholars to copy the ancient Greek classics, to write epic poetry in Italian, and to produce scholarly works in other languages, like Arabic and Persian. Realizing that the state needed educated officials, he established Islamic schools (madrasas) in the different cities of the realm.

Fresh from their 1453 victory, the Ottomans consolidated their control of the former Byzantine lands. Although they had started in 1300 as nomadic warriors who, like the Mongols, attacked sedentary peoples to take their agricultural surplus, by 1500 they had become the undisputed rulers of western Asia, and the salaried Janissary army was much more stable than the Mongol army, which had been propelled by the desire for plunder. Like the Mongols, the Ottomans adopted new technologies from the peoples they conquered.

THE SIEGE OF CONSTANTINOPLE, 1453

Although the fall of Constantinople was one of the major turning points in world history, surprisingly few portrayals of the event survive. One of the most detailed illustrations is from a manuscript describing the travels of Bertrandon de la Broquière (BEAR-trahn-dohn duh lah BROKE-ee-air) (d. 1459) from Dijon, France, to the Ottoman Empire in 1432–1433. Traveling on a mission for a French nobleman, Bertrandon hoped to find out whether it was feasible to launch a new crusade to free the Holy Land from Muslim rule. Although he visited Constantinople twenty years before 1453, his book included a picture of the fall, which he must have learned about after his return to France and before his death in 1459.

Bertrandon's *Voyage d'Outremer,* or *Voyage to Outremer,* offered European readers an eyewitness description of the Ottomans' power during the reign of Murad II (r. 1421–1451). The sultan's army impressed Bertrandon because his men ate only small amounts when traveling and rode strong horses. The soldiers' armor, made of chain mail, was lighter than the plated armor of the French, and their level of discipline seemed high to Bertrandon.

Bertrandon visited Adrianople (modern-day Edirne, Turkey), where the ambassador of Milan hosted him and took him to court. Here he saw the Ottoman sultan, who, he reported, had four major advisers who had to approve anyone's request to speak in person to the ruler. The painting (see inset 3 on the facing page) shows two of these advisers standing in an ornate tent in the foreground.

(Bibliothèque nationale de France/The Bridgeman Art Library)

This label, in medieval French, reads, "The headquarters of the Grand Turk with two of his principal advisers; The headquarters of the captain-general of the Turks."

QUESTION FOR ANALYSIS

Which different weapons and fighting techniques does the painting portray?

The artist painted a view of Constantinople, the peninsula of the Golden Horn, from the western shore of the Bosphorus. To protect the city, the Byzantines connected a giant chain (not shown in the painting) across the entrance to the Golden Horn to block the Ottoman warships, but the Ottomans simply transported their ships overland in wooden cradles along metal tracks to just outside the city, where they could fire on the walls. They carried a total of seventy ships, of which the artist shows only a handful, over the 200-foot-tall (60-m-tall) hill on the left of the painting. Outside the city the Ottomans arrayed a force of eighty thousand to lay siege; inside the city, a combined force of eight thousand Byzantines and their non-Byzantine allies succeeded in defending the city for two months before it fell.

This painting, though based on secondhand information, is surprisingly accurate. The artist captures the city's vulnerability: on all sides the Ottoman forces gather, while the Byzantines are concentrated in the central walled triangle extending into the Bosphorus. The painting does not convey the noise and confusion of cannon warfare; the scene is sunny and the setting idyllic. But it is not hard to imagine that all the forces arrayed outside the walls will soon be able to conquer the city.

These men are pulling the Ottoman boats on wooden carriages along a metal track to get around the chain blocking water access.

The Byzantines had triremes, or boats with three tiers of rowers, which could row faster than the one- or two-tiered Ottoman boats, but the Ottomans commanded many more ships than the Byzantines.

Ottoman engineers constructed this pontoon bridge so that their armies could get closer to the city walls, where their artillery was more effective.

A fishmonger offers fish for sale, a reminder that daily life continued in the city during the two-month-long siege.

The headquarters of the Ottomans. An elderly prisoner kneels before an officer.

East Asia During and After Mongol Rule, 1263–1500

At the time the empire broke apart in 1260, Chinggis's grandson Khubilai Khan (r. 1260–1294) controlled the traditional homeland of Mongolia as well as north China. Conquering south China, where the wet terrain proved extremely difficult for the Mongol horsemen to traverse, posed a genuine challenge. Only after building a Chinese-style navy did the Mongols succeed in taking south China, but they never conquered Japan or Southeast Asia. The Mongols ruled China for nearly one hundred years, until, in 1368, a peasant uprising overthrew them. The cultural exchanges of the Mongols continued to influence Ming dynasty (1368–1644) China, most clearly in the sea voyages of the 1400s.

● **Khubilai Khan**
(1215–1294) Grandson of Chinggis Khan who became ruler of Mongolia and north China in 1260 and who succeeded in 1276 in conquering south China, but not Japan or Vietnam.

The Conquests of Khubilai Khan and Their Limits

Of the Mongol rulers who took over after 1260, **Khubilai Khan** (1215–1294) lived the longest and is the most famous. Suspicious of classical Chinese learning, Khubilai learned to speak some Chinese but not to read Chinese characters. During his administration in China, the Mongols suspended the civil service examinations (see Chapter 12); preferring to appoint officials, they tried to pair a non-Chinese official, either a Mongol or a Central Asian, with each Chinese appointee, though the small number of Mongol officials available made it difficult to do so. Even so, the Mongol administration in China absorbed many local customs. For example, in 1271, Khubilai adopted a Chinese name for his dynasty, the Yuan, meaning "origin."

Khubilai Khan's most significant accomplishment was the conquest of south China, resulting in the unification of north and south China for the first time since the tenth century. Demonstrating a genuine willingness to learn from other peoples, Khubilai Khan commissioned a giant navy that conquered all of south China by 1276. The Mongols became the first non-Chinese people in history to conquer and unify north and south China. As elsewhere in the Mongol Empire, they left much of the machinery of local government intact.

Like all Mongol armies, Khubilai's generals and soldiers wanted to keep conquering to obtain even more plunder. The Mongols made forays into Korea, Japan, and Vietnam even before 1260, and they continued their attacks under Khubilai's rule.

Of these three places, Korea, under the rule of the Koryo dynasty (936–1392), was the only one to come under direct Mongol rule. In 1231, a Mongol force active in north China invaded, prompting the Korean ruler to surrender. He agreed to disband his army, made heavy payments to the Mongols, and sent five hundred young men and five hundred young women as hostages to the Mongol court. Sporadic fighting continued, and the Mongols gained firm control only in 1273. Acknowledging the Mongols as their overlords, the Koryo rulers continued on the throne, but the Mongols forced them to intermarry with Mongol princesses, and the Koreans adopted many Mongol customs.

Once they had subdued Korea and gained control of north and south China, the Mongols tried to invade Japan, then under the rule of the Kamakura (see Chapter 12), in 1274 and 1281. To this end the Mongols forced the Koreans to provide nine hundred ships as well as many soldiers and supplies. Later sources report that a powerful wind destroyed the Mongol ships, an event described to this day by Japanese as *kamikaze* or "divine wind." (In World War II, Japanese fliers who went on suicide missions were called kamikaze pilots.) Contemporary sources do not mention the weather but describe a Mongol force of no more than ten thousand on either occasion being turned back by the fortifications the Japanese had built on their coastline. The costs of repelling the invasion weakened the Kamakura government, which fell in 1333, and Japan began three centuries of divided political rule that would end only in 1600 when the country was reunified.

The Mongols also proved unable to invade Vietnam, then under the rule of the Tran dynasty (1225–1400). Mongol armies sacked the capital city at Hanoi three times (in 1257, 1284, and 1287), but on each occasion an army staffed by local peoples regained the city and promised to pay tribute to the Mongols, who then retreated.

When Khubilai Khan died in 1294, a new generation of leaders took over who had grown up in China, spoke and wrote Chinese, and knew little of life on the steppes. The fourth emperor in the Yuan dynasty, Renzong (r. 1312–1321), received the classical Chinese education of a Chinese scholar and reinstated the civil service exams in 1315. Under his direction, the Mongols introduced a new Neo-Confucian examination curriculum testing the candidates' knowledge of Zhu Xi's commentary on *The Four Books* (see Chapter 12). Adopted by subsequent dynasties, this curriculum remained in use until 1905.

After Emperor Renzong's death, the Yuan government entered several decades of decline. The 1330s and 1340s saw outbreaks of disease that caused mass deaths; a single epidemic in 1331 killed one-tenth of the people living in one province. Scholars suspect that these deaths may have been linked to the Black Death that hit Europe in 1348, but they cannot be certain because the Chinese sources do not describe the symptoms of those who died.

Faced with a sharp drop in population and a corresponding decline in revenue, the Yuan dynasty raised taxes, causing a series of peasant rebellions. In 1368, a peasant who had been briefly educated in a monastery led a peasant revolt that succeeded in overthrowing the Yuan dynasty and driving the Mongols back to their homeland, from which they continued to launch attacks on the Chinese. He named his dynasty the Ming, meaning "light" or "bright" (1368–1644).

The Reign of the First Ming Emperor, 1368–1398

The founder of the **Ming dynasty,** Ming Taizu, prided himself on founding a native Chinese dynasty but in fact continued many Mongol practices. In addition to the core areas ruled earlier by the Northern Song dynasty, the Ming realm included Manchuria, Inner Mongolia, Xinjiang in the northwest, and Tibet, which had all been conquered by the Mongols. The Ming also took over the provincial administrative districts established by the Mongols, which still define modern China.

When the Ming founder assumed office, he appointed all new officials and suspended the civil service examinations because he was suspicious of Confucian learning. Later, though, he came to believe that bureaucrats were best able to govern China and in 1381 reinstated the civil service examinations with a Confucian curriculum identical to that of the Mongols. Competition for the exams intensified in succeeding centuries, and the ruling elite remained Confucian because of this decision.

● **Ming dynasty** (1368–1644) Ruling dynasty in China founded by the leader of a peasant rebellion against the Yuan. Its founder prided himself on founding a native Chinese dynasty but in fact continued many of the practices of his Mongol predecessors.

Oddly, the Ming founder, the one emperor in Chinese history who was born a peasant, had a conservative vision of China's society and believed that no one could change his or her social position. Ming officials assigned each household a category of labor such as agriculture, military service, or salt mining and required that each household contribute a fixed number of days of that type of labor annually. In fact, many people paid others to fulfill their labor obligations.

When the Ming founder died in 1398, he hoped that his grandson would succeed him, but one of the emperor's brothers led an army to the capital and set the imperial palace on fire. The unfortunate new emperor, only 21 at the time, probably died in the fire, making it possible for his uncle to name himself the third emperor of the Ming dynasty, or the Yongle emperor (r. 1403–1424).

The Chinese Voyages to South and Southeast Asia and Africa, 1405–1433

Viewed as a usurper his entire life, the Yongle emperor pursued several policies to show that he was the equal of the Ming founder. He ordered all written materials to be copied into a single, enormous set of books called *The Yongle Encyclopedia*. He moved the capital from Nanjing, where many remained sympathetic to the deposed emperor, to Beijing, the former capital of the Mongols. He sent five military expeditions to Mongolia in the hope of vanquishing the Mongols, but none succeeded. The Yongle emperor also launched a series of imperially sponsored voyages to demonstrate the strength of his dynasty to all of China's trading partners.

Chinese geographical knowledge of the world had grown considerably since the maps of the mid-twelfth century (see the maps on page 350). No maps made under the Mongols survive today, but a Korean map copied around 1470, the Kangnido map, was based on earlier maps and includes both the Islamic world and Europe, a vivid illustration of how the Mongol unification of Eurasia led to a dramatic increase in geographic knowledge.

This increase in geographical knowledge prompted the most ambitious voyages in Chinese history, which were led by the admiral named Zheng He (JUHNG huh) (1371–1433). Zheng He's ancestors had moved from Bukhara (Uzbekistan) to southwest China to serve as officials under the Yuan dynasty. Both his father and grandfather went on the hajj pilgrimage to Mecca, and the family was well informed about the geography of the larger Islamic world.

Zheng He was captured at the age of 10, castrated, and forced into the Chinese military, where he rose quickly and eventually put in charge of maritime expeditions to display the power of the Yongle emperor. The Chinese junks of the **Zheng He expeditions** visited Sumatra (SOO-mah-trah), Sri Lanka, and the western Indian ports of Calicut, Cochin, and Quilon (KEE-lahn), and they also crossed the Persian Gulf. The farthest they went was the coast of East Africa, which they visited in 1418, 1421–1422, and 1431–1433. In leading China's navy to India and Africa, Admiral Zheng He was following well-established hajj routes taken by both pilgrims and Muslim merchants. His route to East Africa from China was simply the mirror image of Ibn Battuta's from East Africa to China (see Chapter 11). Although they covered enormous distances, Zheng He's ships never ventured into unknown waters. They were not exploring: their goal was to display the might of the Yongle emperor.

Admiral Zheng He's fleet must have impressed everyone who saw it. Twenty-eight thousand men staffed the full fleet of over three hundred massive wooden

•**Zheng He expeditions** From 1405 to 1433, a fleet of Chinese junks under the leadership of the eunuch admiral Zheng He (1371–1433) traveled on well-established hajj routes from China to Southeast Asia, India, the Islamic world, and East Africa to display the might of the Yongle emperor.

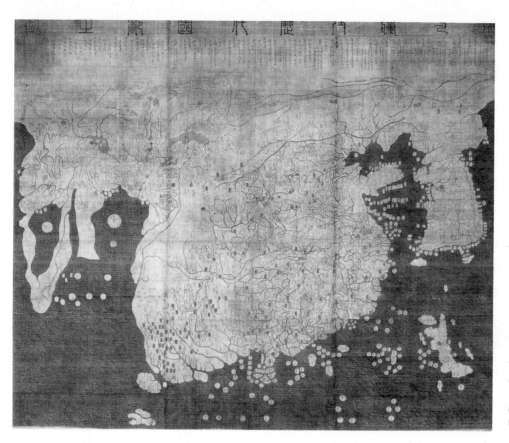

State-of-the-Art Cartography in 1470: The Kangnido Map   In 1470, Korean cartographers made this map of Afro-Eurasia. Although the proportions are wrong (Korea is disproportion-ately large) and India is missing, the map testifies to the wide circulation of informa-tion under the Mongols. The three sources of the Nile are exactly the same as those on the map shown in Chapter 9 (see page 261), the Islamic map of al-Idrisi com-pleted in 1182, because the Korean mapmakers copied Africa from an Islamic original. (Ryukoku University Library, Kyoto, Japan)

ships. The biggest Chinese ships—200-foot-long (61-m-long) "treasure ships"—were the largest ships in the world at that time.[4] In 1341, at Calicut, Ibn Battuta had praised Chinese ships for their wooden compartments that offered individual travelers privacy; Zheng He's sailors filled similar compartments with fresh water and stocked them with fish for their dining pleasure.

Although none of the sailors has left an eyewitness account of the East African coast, one of Zheng He's men, Fei Xin (1385–1436?), did record what he had been able "to collect as true facts from the explanations" of others about Africa. Much more detailed than Zhao Rugua's 1225 descriptions of Africa (see Chapter 12) are Fei Xin's descriptions of Mogadishu in modern-day Somalia: "This place lies on the sea-shore. Piles of stones constitute the city-wall. . . . The houses are of layers of stone and four or five storeys high, the places for dwelling, cooking, easing oneself [going to the bathroom], and entertaining guests all being on the upper floors."[5] Fei Xin's informant describes what he saw from onboard ship; the Chinese did not venture inland.

Because Zheng He's ships also engaged in trade, usually giving suits of cloth-ing in exchange for horses, animal skins, gold, and silver, his men were well in-formed about local trading conditions. The commodities traded at Mogadishu included such things as "gold and silver, colored satins, sandalwood, rice and cere-als, porcelain articles, and colored thin silk." Fei Xin's description of the known world ends with a description of Mecca, an indication that his account, although written in Chinese, was modeled on the Islamic genre of rihla travel accounts used by Ibn Jubayr, Ibn Fadlan, and Ibn Battuta to record their journeys (see Chapters 9, 10, and 11), further evidence that the Chinese of the Ming dynasty inherited the shared intellectual traditions of the Mongols.

The Chinese voyagers who participated in the trade did so as members of the imperial navy, not as independent entrepreneurs. When the Ming government suspended the voyages in 1433, the year Admiral Zheng He died, the trips to Africa came to an abrupt halt. Placed in storage, the treasure ships subsequently rotted away. The Ming dynasty shifted its resources from the sea to the north and rebuilt the Great Wall (see Chapter 4) in the hope of keeping the Mongols from invading. (The Great Wall visitors see today is the Ming wall.) The Ming stayed in power until 1644, with its attention fixed firmly on its main foreign enemy, the Mongols to the north.

Chapter Review

KEY TERMS

William of Rubruck (386)

Chinggis Khan (389)

shamans (389)

tanistry (392)

khuriltai (392)

darughachi (394)

postal relay system (396)

Il-khanate (401)

principality of Muscovy (403)

Timur the Lame (403)

Ottomans (405)

Janissaries (406)

Mehmet the Conqueror (406)

Khubilai Khan (410)

Ming dynasty (411)

Zheng He expeditions (412)

Download the MP3 audio file of the Chapter Review and listen to it on the go.

In 1253–1254, William of Rubruck traveled through a unified Mongol territory; in 1263, the empire split apart. The rulers of the different successor dynasties, like Chinggis and his descendants, led powerful armies fueled by the desire for plunder; once they conquered a given region, they proved unusually willing to learn from conquered peoples and adopt their technologies. Although their empire was short-lived, the Mongols unified much of Eurasia for the first time. They were able to conquer so much territory because their cavalry was more powerful than that of the various sedentary peoples they defeated. After 1400, the development of new weapons powered by gunpowder, particularly cannon and small firearms, shifted the military advantage away from nomadic peoples decisively in favor of sedentary societies. As we will see in the next chapter, the Europeans who landed in the Americas in the 1490s used the same gunpowder weapons with far-reaching consequences.

How did the Mongols' nomadic way of life contribute to their success as conquerors?

Before 1200, the Mongols moved within the region of modern Mongolia with their flocks in search of fresh grass. After Chinggis unified them in 1206, their mobility allowed them to conquer much of Eurasia. The Mongols' skillful use of terror prompted many people to surrender rather than fight, enabling the Mongols to conquer vast amounts of territory rapidly.

What bound the different sectors of the Mongol Empire together? What caused its breakup in the 1260s?

Even when the Mongol Empire was at its strongest, during the first fifty years of its existence, only the postal relay system and the system of hosting envoys held it together. After the third Mongol ruler Möngke died in 1259, the traditional method for selecting a new ruler, tanistry, did not work because two rival candidates each held their own khuriltai and the empire broke into western and eastern halves. In 1263, the alliance between the Qipchaq khanate in Russia and the Mamluks of Egypt against the Il-khanate of Iran provides a clear date for the end of the unified Mongol Empire.

 What states succeeded the Qipchaq and Chaghatai khanates?

In the western half, all the Mongol rulers eventually converted to Islam. Ivan III's principality of Moscow emerged as the strongest power in Russia after the breakup of the Qipchaq khanate, and Timur the Lame succeeded the Chaghatai khanate.

 What military innovations marked Ottoman expansion, and what cultural developments typified Ottoman rule?

Although the Ottomans were a nomadic people whose army initially resembled that of the Mongols, they shifted to a more stable army of Janissaries. The Ottomans took advantage of the new gunpowder weapons, particularly cannon, when they attacked and conquered Constantinople in 1453. After taking the city, the Ottoman rulers commissioned scholars to copy the ancient Greek classics, to write epic poetry in Italian, and to produce scholarly works in other languages.

 What was the legacy of Mongol rule in East and Southeast Asia?

The legacy of the Mongols was most visible in Ming dynasty China, whose borders overlapped with those of the Yuan dynasty. The Ming founder implemented the Neo-Confucian examination curriculum of the Mongols. Although the Mongols ruled Korea only briefly and never conquered either Japan or Vietnam, all peoples in East Asia knew more about Eurasia than they had before the Mongol conquests. The Kangnido map of the world and the Zheng He voyages vividly illustrate this increase in knowledge.

For Further Reference

Allsen, Thomas T. *Mongol Imperialism: The Politics of the Grand Qan Möngke in China, Russia, and the Islamic Lands, 1251–1259.* Berkeley: University of California Press, 1987.

Dawson, Christopher, ed. *The Mongol Mission: Narratives and Letters of the Franciscan Missionaries in Mongolia and China in the Thirteenth and Fourteenth Centuries.* New York: Sheed and Ward, 1955.

De Rachewiltz, Igor. *Papal Envoys to the Great Khans.* London: Faber and Faber, 1971.

Finlay, Robert. "How Not to (Re)Write World History: Gavin Menzies and the Chinese Discovery of America." *Journal of World History* 15, no. 2 (2004): 225–241.

Fletcher, Joseph. "The Mongols: Ecological and Social Perspectives." *Harvard Journal of Asiatic Studies* 46, no. 1 (1986): 1–56.

Hodgson, Marshall G. S. *The Venture of Islam: Conscience and History in a World Civilization,* vol. 2, *The Expansion of Islam in the Middle Periods.* Chicago: University of Chicago Press, 1974.

Inalcik, Halil. *The Ottoman Empire: The Classical Age, 1300–1600.* Translated by Norman Itzkowitz and Colin Imber. London: Weidenfeld and Nicolson, 1973.

Jackson, Peter, trans. *The Mission of Friar William of Rubruck: His Journey to the Court of the Great Khan Möngke 1253–1255.* London: The Hakluyt Society, 1990.

Kennedy, Hugh. *Mongols, Huns and Vikings.* London: Cassell, 2002.

Latham, Ronald, trans. *The Travels of Marco Polo.* New York: Penguin Books, 1958.

Morgan, David. *The Mongols.* 2d ed. New York: Blackwell, 2007.

Wood, Frances. *Did Marco Polo Go to China?* London: Secker and Warburg, 1995.

 **WEB RESOURCES**

Pronunciation Guide

Interactive Maps

MAP 14.1 The Four Quadrants of the Mongol Empire After 1263

Primary Sources

Chapter Objectives

ACE Multiple-Choice Quiz

Flashcards

Websites

The Mongols in World History (http://afe.easia.columbia.edu/mongols/).   This website provides general information on the Mongols.

Popular History and Bunkum (http://maritimeasia.ws/topic/1421bunkum.html). A detailed critique of the evidence that allegedly shows that Zheng He visited the Americas.

Silk Road Narratives: A Collection of Historical Texts (http://depts.washington.edu/silkroad/texts/texts.html).   A valuable collection of primary sources, including Rubruck's, with helpful introductions.

Film

Mongol, a commercial movie epic released in 2008 about Chinggis Khan's rise to power, departs from *The Origin of Chinggis Khan* in many places but still gives a vivid sense of Mongol society in the early 1200s.

CHAPTER 15

Maritime Expansion in the Atlantic World, 1400–1600

With two of his ships separated from the third in a storm and uncertain that he would make it back to Spain, **Christopher Columbus** (1451–1506) summarized his journey and then wrapped the parchment document in cloth, sealed it with wax, and dropped it overboard in a wine casket. He survived the storm and returned to Spain, where he presented a long letter describing his first voyage to his backers Queen Isabella (1451–1504) and King Ferdinand (1452–1516) of Spain. Columbus's voyage connected Europe with the Americas in a way that no previous contact had; the resulting exchange of plants, animals, people, and disease shaped the modern world. In his letter describing the people he encountered in the Caribbean, he voices the twin motivations of the Spanish and the Portuguese: in search of gold, they also hoped to convert the indigenous peoples to Christianity.

CHRISTOPHER COLUMBUS

(The Metropolitan Museum of Art, New York. Image copyright © The Metropolitan Museum of Art/Art Resource, NY)

Hispaniola is a wonder. The mountains and hills, the plains and the meadow lands are both fertile and beautiful. They are most suitable for planting crops and for raising cattle of all kinds, and there are good sites for building towns and villages. The harbors are incredibly fine and there are many great rivers with broad channels and the majority contain gold. . . .

The inhabitants of this island, and all the rest that I discovered or heard of, go naked, as their mothers bore them, men and women alike. A few of the women, however, cover a single place with a leaf of a plant or piece of cotton which they weave for the purpose. They have no iron or steel or arms and are not capable of

This icon will direct you to interactive activities and study materials on the *Voyages* website: www.cengage.com/history/hansen/voyages1e

418

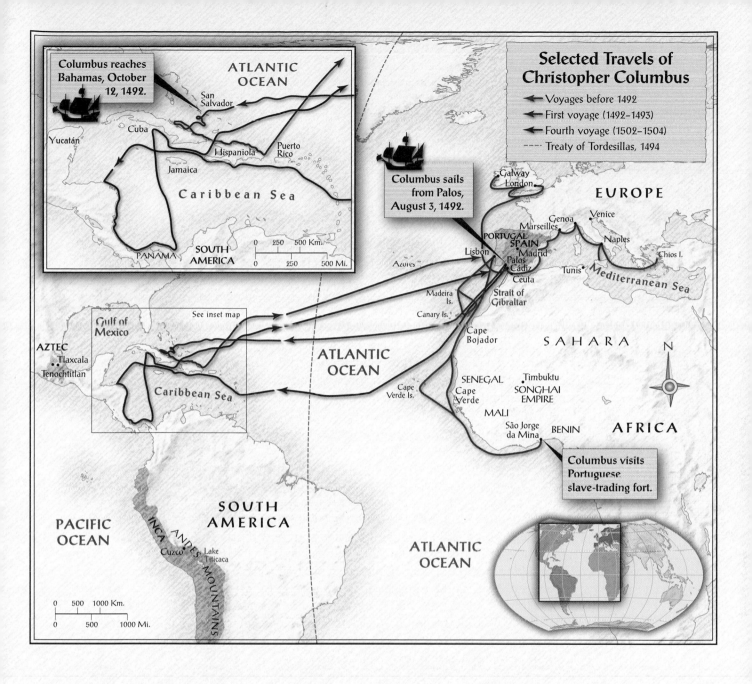

Selected Travels of Christopher Columbus

→ Voyages before 1492
→ First voyage (1492–1493)
→ Fourth voyage (1502–1504)
---- Treaty of Tordesillas, 1494

Columbus reaches Bahamas, October 12, 1492.

Columbus sails from Palos, August 3, 1492.

Columbus visits Portuguese slave-trading fort.

Inset map labels:
ATLANTIC OCEAN
San Salvador
Cuba
Yucatán
Hispaniola
Puerto Rico
Jamaica
Caribbean Sea
PANAMA
SOUTH AMERICA
0 250 500 Km.
0 250 500 Mi.

Main map labels:
EUROPE
Galway
London
Genoa
Venice
Marseilles
Naples
PORTUGAL SPAIN
Lisbon
Madrid
Palos
Cádiz
Ceuta
Chios I.
Tunis
Mediterranean Sea
Azores
Madeira Is.
Strait of Gibraltar
Canary Is.
Cape Bojador
SAHARA
SENEGAL
Cape Verde
Timbuktu
SONGHAI EMPIRE
Cape Verde Is.
MALI
São Jorge da Mina
BENIN
AFRICA
N
ATLANTIC OCEAN
See inset map
Gulf of Mexico
AZTEC
Tlaxcala
Tenochtitlan
Caribbean Sea
SOUTH AMERICA
PACIFIC OCEAN
INCA
ANDES MOUNTAINS
Cuzco
Lake Titicaca
ATLANTIC OCEAN
0 500 1000 Km.
0 500 1000 Mi.

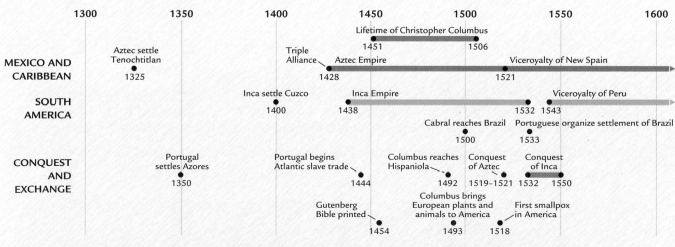

	1300	1350	1400	1450	1500	1550	1600
				Lifetime of Christopher Columbus 1451–1506			
MEXICO AND CARIBBEAN	Aztec settle Tenochtitlan 1325		Triple Alliance — Aztec Empire 1428		Viceroyalty of New Spain 1521		→
SOUTH AMERICA		Inca settle Cuzco 1400	Inca Empire 1438		1532	Viceroyalty of Peru 1543	→
				Cabral reaches Brazil 1500	Portuguese organize settlement of Brazil 1533		
CONQUEST AND EXCHANGE		Portugal settles Azores 1350	Portugal begins Atlantic slave trade 1444	Columbus reaches Hispaniola 1492	Conquest of Aztec 1519–1521	Conquest of Inca 1532 1550	
			Gutenberg Bible printed 1454	Columbus brings European plants and animals to America 1493	First smallpox in America 1518		

using them, not because they are not strong and well built but because they are amazingly timid. . . .

I gave them a thousand pretty things that I had brought, in order to gain their love and incline them to become Christians.[1]

●**Christopher Columbus** (1451–1506) Visited European colonies in the Mediterranean, the Atlantic Ocean, and the west coast of Africa before voyaging to the island of Hispaniola in 1492. Made three subsequent voyages before being removed as viceroy in 1499.

At the time of his first voyage to the Americas, Columbus was in his early 40s. Born in Genoa, Italy, as a teenager he had sailed on wooden boats to the different settlements of Genoese and Venetian merchants in the Mediterranean. Later, in his 30s, he lived for three years in the Madeira Islands, a Portuguese possession off the African coast in the Atlantic, and visited the Portuguese slave-trading fort at Sao Jorge da Mina on the west coast of Africa. Madeira, the world's largest sugar producer in 1492, hired indigenous peoples from the nearby Canary Islands and African slaves to work on its plantations. While in the Canary Islands, Columbus heard that one could sail west, and, assuming he could reach Asia by doing so, he persuaded the rulers of Spain to finance a trial voyage across the Atlantic in search of the Indies, the source of so many valuable spices. After the first voyage in 1492, he made three more trips to the Americas before his death in 1506.

Unlike the Viking voyages to Newfoundland (see Chapter 10) and unlike the Ming voyages to East Africa (see Chapter 14), the Spanish and Portuguese voyages had far-reaching consequences. After 1300, while the Aztec in Mexico and the Inca in Peru were creating powerful expansionist empires, on the opposite side of the Atlantic Europeans were learning about geography as part of their humanistic studies. Spanish and Portuguese explorers traveled farther and farther, first to the islands of the Mediterranean and the Atlantic, then to the west coast of Africa, and finally to the Americas, claiming each place they landed as colonies for the monarchs of Spain and Portugal. The Europeans transported plants, animals, and people (often against their will) to entirely new environments on the other side of the Atlantic. Within one hundred years of Columbus's first voyage, millions of Amerindians (the death toll reached 95 percent in some areas) had perished, victims of European diseases that no one understood.

Focus Questions

 How did the Aztec form their empire? How did the Inca form theirs? How did each hold their empire together, and what was each empire's major weakness?

 How did humanist scholarship encourage oceanic exploration? What motivated the Portuguese, particularly Prince Henry the Navigator, to explore West Africa?

How did the Spanish and the Portuguese establish their empires in the Americas so quickly?

 What was the Columbian exchange? Which elements of the exchange had the greatest impact on the Americas? On Afro-Eurasia?

The Aztec Empire of Mexico, 1325–1519

Starting sometime around 1325, the Aztec, a people based in western Mexico, moved into central Mexico to Tenochtitlan (some 30 miles, or 50 km, northeast of modern-day Mexico City), a site near the ancient city of Teotihuacan (see Chapter 5). The Aztec were one of many Nahua (NAH-wah) peoples who spoke the Nahuatl (NAH-waht) language. Like the Maya, the Nahua peoples had a complex calendrical system combining both lunar and solar calculations, built large stone monuments, and played a ritual ball game. The Aztec believed in a pantheon of gods headed by the sun that demanded blood sacrifices from their devotees. To sustain these gods, they continually went to war, gradually conquering many of the city-states in central Mexico to form the **Aztec Empire**.

The Aztec Settlement of Tenochtitlan

The Toltec, the most powerful successors to the Maya, collapsed in the 1200s (see Chapter 5). Though each people tells the story of its past differently, disparate accounts agree that around this time various groups migrated to central Mexico. The heart of this area is the Valley of Mexico, 10,000 feet (3,000 m) above sea level and surrounded by volcanoes. The Valley of Mexico contains many shallow lakes and much fertile land.

The first Nahua groups to arrive obtained the best land in the Valley of Mexico. Those who came twenty years later settled nearby, and the final group, who claimed their homeland was in a place called Aztlan, literally "heron-land," arrived last. It is not clear whether Aztlan was a genuine or a legendary place, but linguistic analysis of the Nahuatl language indicates that its speakers originated somewhere in the southwest United States or northern Mexico. *Aztlan* is the origin of the modern word *Aztec,* a term that no one at the time used but that this text will use despite its imperfections. The Aztlan migrants referred to themselves as "Mexica" (meh-SHE-kah), the origin of the word *Mexico.*

By the 1300s, some fifty city-states, called **altepetl**, occupied central Mexico, each with its own leader, or "speaker," and its own government. Each altepetl had a palace for its ruler, a pyramid-shaped temple, and a market. The Aztec migrated to the region around the historic urban center of Teotihuacan, a large city with many lakes. Since this region was already home to several rival altepetl, the Aztec were forced to settle in a swampland called **Tenochtitlan** (teh-noch-TIT-lan).

Traditional accounts say the Aztec people arrived at Tenochtitlan in 1325, a date confirmed by archaeological excavation. The Aztec gradually reclaimed large areas of the swamps and on the drier, more stable areas erected stone buildings

• Aztec Empire
An empire based in Tenochtitlan (modern-day Mexico City). Founded in 1325, the dynasty formed the Triple Alliance and began to expand its territory in 1428. At its peak it included 450 separate altepetl city-states in modern-day Mexico and Guatemala and ruled over a population of four to six million.

• altepetl The 450 city-states of the Aztec Empire. Each altepetl had its own leader, or "speaker," its own government, a palace for its ruler, a pyramid-shaped temple, and a market.

• Tenochtitlan
Capital city of the Aztec, which they reclaimed from swampland. Housed a population of some 200,000 people.

MAP 15.1
The Aztec Empire
Starting from their capital at Tenochtitlan (modern Mexico City), the Aztec conquered different neighboring peoples living between the Gulf of Mexico and the Pacific Ocean. Aztec rulers required the conquered peoples to pay taxes and submit tribute but gave few benefits in return. When Cortés landed on the coast of Mexico, he quickly found allies among the conquered peoples, particularly the Tlaxcalans.

(CL) Interactive Map

held together with mortar. They planted flowers everywhere and walked on planks or traveled by canoe from one reclaimed area to another.

At its height, Tenochtitlan contained 60,000 dwellings, home to perhaps 200,000 people in an area of 5 square miles (13 sq km). The central marketplace offered cooked and uncooked food, slaves, tobacco products, and luxury goods made from gold, silver, and feathers. Consumers used cotton cloaks, cacao beans, and feather quills filled with gold dust as media of exchange, since the Aztec had no coins.

Nahua Religion and Writing System

The most important Nahua deity, the sun, controlled agriculture, and crops—primarily corn, beans, and peppers—were the main source of food. Engaged in a constant struggle with the forces of dark, the sun needed regular offerings of "precious water," the Nahuatl term for human blood. Ranking just under the sun-god were the gods of rain and agriculture. In addition, each altepetl had several deities associated with its native place. The Aztec believed that their patron god was Huitzilopochtli (wheat-zeel-oh-POSHT-lee), the hummingbird of the south, whom they worshiped along with the god of rain, Tlaloc. A third important god was Quetzalcoatl (kate-zahl-CO-ah-tal), a creator god who was credited with devising the Nahuatl writing system.

The Nahua wrote on bark paper or deerskin covered with a thin white layer of limestone plaster. Their writing system functioned quite differently from Mayan. Nahuatl texts combine pictures with rebus writing, which uses images to represent something with the same sound; in English, for example, a picture of an eye functions as a rebus for the word *I*.

The Nahua writing system served as a trigger to memory; people who had been trained to tell a certain story could look at a Nahua manuscript and be reminded

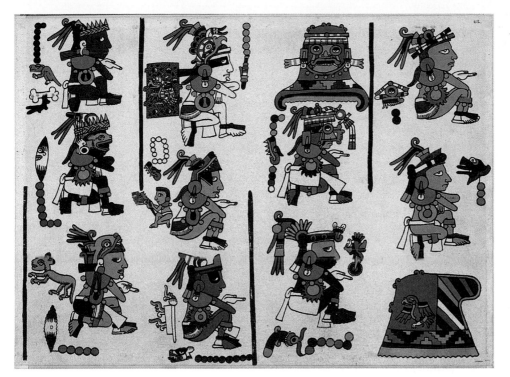

of the details. But if one did not know the original story beforehand, it was impossible to make it out.

Nahua Society

The Nahua peoples treated certain human beings like gods. The leader of the Aztec, their Great Speaker, was carried in a feathered chair. His advisers never looked at the Great Speaker or addressed him directly: a screen always separated them from him. The Great Speaker was in charge of all external matters, including war, the receipt of gifts, and relations with other altepetl. A group of nobles, priests, and successful warriors chose the new Great Speaker, and although they treated him as their ritual superior, they could depose him if they did not approve of his rule.

The second-highest leader, a man called the Female Snake, took charge of all internal affairs. Usually a close relative of the Great Speaker, he consulted with him frequently. All the top officials came from the royal family and had large private estates.

Most of the Nahuas were commoners, each of whom belonged to a "big house," a group who believed they were descended from a common ancestor. The Aztec capital contained some twenty big-house groups, and more lived in other regions. They had their own lands, and some had schools for warriors. The lowest-ranking people in Nahua society were slaves, often the original residents of the Valley of Mexico.

Ordinary people and slaves farmed the land and generated the surplus that underpinned the expansion of the Aztec altepetl. The Nahua prepared the soil and planted seeds by hand, often planting bean and pepper seeds in the same hole as corn seeds. Because they had no draft animals, metal tools, or wheels, everything had to be carried and cultivated by hand.

Corn ripened in only fifty days, providing sufficient food for a family as well as a surplus. Grinding corn was exclusively women's work; for fear that they might antagonize the gods, men were forbidden to help. Ordinary people were required to pay tribute to their Aztec overlords by contributing a share of the crop, performing labor service for a certain time, paying other goods, and most onerous of all, providing victims for human sacrifice.

The Military and the Conquests of the Aztec

If successful in battle, warriors could rise in Aztec society to a high position. They then received lands of their own and were not required to pay taxes on them. Conversely, the best human sacrifice one could offer to the gods, the Nahua believed, was a warrior taken captive in battle. In their system of thirteen heavens and eight underworlds, the highest heaven, the Paradise of the Sun God, was for men who had killed the enemy in battle and for women who had died in childbirth, a type of battle in its own right.

The Aztec troops fitted their clubs, spears, and darts with blades made from obsidian, a volcanic glass that was sharp and easy to work but dulled easily. They protected themselves with thick cotton armor. The Aztec also hired as mercenaries mountain peoples who used bows and arrows. Hand-to-hand combat was considered the most honorable form of warfare.

In 1428, the Aztec formed the Triple Alliance with two other peoples and launched a series of conquests that led to the creation of an empire. By 1500, they had conquered 450 altepetl in modern Mexico, extending all the way to Guatemala, and ruled over a subject population estimated between four and six million who lived in an area of 8,000 square miles (20,810 sq km).[2]

The Aztec conquered other peoples not simply to gain the wealth of subject peoples but also to feed their own deities. Conducting mass sacrifices at their temples, the Aztec killed tens of thousands of victims at a time and displayed their skulls on racks for all to see.

The Aztec empire, though large and with a beautiful capital, had one major weakness. Once the Aztec conquered a given people, they demanded tribute and took sacrificial victims from them, yet they did nothing to incorporate them further into their empire.

● The Inca Empire, 1400–1532

● Inca Empire
Founded in 1438 by Pachakuti (d. 1471), who launched a series of conquests outward from the capital at Cuzco. At its peak, the empire ruled over a population of ten to twelve million.

The **Inca Empire,** 2,500 miles (4,000 km) to the south in the highlands of the Andes, was structured differently. Each time the Inca conquered a new group, they integrated them into the empire, requiring them to perform labor and military service and resettling some groups to minimize the chances of revolt. Like the Aztec, the Inca worshiped deities that demanded human sacrifices, but never as many as in Mexico. Although the Inca successfully integrated subject peoples into their empire, they did not have an orderly system of succession. Each time their ruler died, everyone who hoped to succeed him plunged into full-time conflict until a new leader emerged victorious.

Inca Religion and Andean Society

The ordinary people of the Andes lived in kin groups called **ayllu** (aye-YOU) that worked the land in several adjacent ecological zones so they could maximize their yield should the crops in one zone fail. (See the feature "World History in Today's World: Miss Bolivia Speaks Out.") Most ayllu were divided into smaller subgroups, and men tended to marry women from another subgroup. All the people in a given ayllu recognized one person as a common ancestor. Ordinary people believed that, in addition to their ancestors, hundreds of spirits (*wak'a*) inhabited places in the landscape such as streams, caves, rocks, and hills.

●**ayllu** Andean kin groups of the Inca Empire that worked the land in several adjacent ecological zones so they could maximize their yield should the crops in one zone fail.

The Inca believed that some deities ranked far above these local spirits. The most important deities were the Creator (Wiraqocha), the Creator's child the Sun (Inti), and the Thunder (Inti-Illapa) gods.

By 1500, the sun-god had become the most important deity, probably because the Inca ruler, the Sapa Inca, or "Unique Inca," claimed descent from him. The priest of the sun-god was the highest-ranking priest in Inca society and the second most powerful person in the Inca Empire.

Both the Sapa Inca and the sun-god priest belonged to the aristocracy, which was divided into three tiers: the close relatives of the ruler and previous rulers, more distant relatives, and then the leaders of the groups who had been conquered by the Inca. Although most Inca traced their ancestry through their father's line, the ruler's mother's family played a central role in court politics because the ruler took his wives from his mother's family.

The Inca had no orderly system of succession. Each time the Inca ruler died, all contestants for the position from among his male kin launched an all-out war until a single man emerged victorious, much like the system of tanistry prevalent among the Mongols (see Chapter 14). The new ruler was then installed in an elaborate coronation honoring the sun-god. During his reign the Sapa Inca lived as a deity among his subjects, eating special foods and wearing unusual clothing. Even so, he had to keep the support of the aristocracy, who could easily overthrow him at any time.

Like the ayllu ancestors, the ruler was believed to continue to live even after death. The Inca mummified the bodies of deceased rulers and other high-ranking family members and then placed the mummies in houses around the main square of Cuzco, their capital city high in the Andes at an elevation of 11,300 feet (3,450 m). One Spanish observer described their interaction with these mummies:

> Most of the people of Cuzco served the dead, I have heard it said, who they daily brought out to the main square, setting them down in a ring, each one according to his age, and there the male and female attendants ate and drank. . . . The mummies toasted each other and the living, and the living toasted the dead.[3]

He did not explain how the living communicated with the dead, but it seems likely that priests intervened.

The Inca organized the worship of all the local spirits, ancestors of the rulers, and deities into a complex ritual calendar specifying which one was to be worshiped on a given day. Of 332 shrines in Cuzco, 31 received human sacrifices. These usually occurred in times of hardship, like an epidemic, or during unusual astronomical events like eclipses. In many cases, believers sacrificed a young boy and a young girl, a symbolic married couple, in the hope of pleasing the god involved and ending the suffering. Occasionally larger sacrifices occurred, such as when a ruler died, but the largest number of sacrificial victims killed at a single time was four thousand (as opposed to eighty thousand for the Aztec).

Miss Bolivia Speaks Out

Not all Bolivians are "poor people and very short people and Indian people," Miss Bolivia in the 2004 Miss Universe contest explained. "I'm from the other side of the country, from the east, where it's not cold. It's very hot, and we're tall, and we are white and can speak English."

Controversy immediately erupted because Gabriela Oviedo had dared to say out loud what many people only think. The divisions between the indigenous peoples and the descendents of Europeans run deep throughout Latin America, and nowhere deeper than in Bolivia, where fully 62 percent of the population of 8.8 million is Amerindian, members of thirty-six different groups.

Many of the indigenous peoples of Bolivia live on less than two dollars a day and have no electricity or gas in their homes. Bolivia's average national income is the lowest in Latin America, even though the country has both natural gas and oil reserves. Miss Bolivia lives in the city of Santa Cruz, whose prosperity is fueled by the export of large natural gas reserves, and many of her fellow citizens support further economic globalization, while most Amerindian groups remain vehemently opposed.

In December 2005, Evo Morales became the first Amerindian to be elected president of a Latin American nation since the mid-1800s. Before being elected, Morales raised the coca plant (from which cocaine is processed), played the trumpet, laid bricks, and worked as a union organizer. He staunchly defends the right of Bolivia's farmers to raise coca, which he maintains is a "sacred leaf" to the indigenous peoples of Bolivia.

Some indigenous leaders advocate nationalization of the natural gas industry and urge the government to buy out the foreign exporters. Threatening to secede, they propose forming a new Inca nation composed of the indigenous peoples who live in western Bolivia and the indigenous Aymara-speaking peoples of Peru and Chile. In this new Inca state, they suggest, all decisions would be made by councils called ayllus, a term drawn from the Inca Empire. Though illegal, discrimination against Amerindians persists; Bolivia's indigenous peoples gained the right to vote and to attend school only in 1952.

The Inca Expansion   As the Aztec believed their history began with their occupation of Tenochtitlan, the Incas traced their beginnings to their settlement in Cuzco. Archaeological evidence suggests that the Inca moved to Cuzco sometime around 1400. Although oral accounts conflict, most accept the date of 1438 as the year Pachakuti (patch-ah-KOO-tee) (d. 1471), the first great Inca ruler, seized the throne from his brother in a coup and launched the military campaigns outward from Cuzco. The Inca conquered neighboring lands because they desired the goods produced in each ecological zone: the herds of llamas and alpaca, crops like grain and potatoes, and the gold, feathers, shells, and minerals from the jungle lowlands and the shore.

Much of Inca warfare consisted of storming enemy forts with a large infantry, often after cutting off access to food and water. For several days enemy forces traded insults and sang hostile songs such as this: "We will drink from the skull of the traitor, we will adorn ourselves with a necklace of his teeth, we play the melody of the pinkullu [a musical instrument resembling a flute] with flutes made from his bones, we will beat the drum made from his skin, and thus we will dance." Attackers in quilted cotton launched arrows, stones from slingshots, and stone spears,

🌐 **MAP 15.2**

The Inca Empire In 1438, the Inca ruler Pachakuti took power in the capital at Cuzco and led his armies to conquer large chunks of territory along the Andes Mountains. Two north-south trunk routes, with subsidiary east-west routes, formed a system of over 25,000 miles (40,000 km) of roads. By 1532, the Inca ruled ten to twelve million people in an empire of 1,500 square miles (4,000 sq km).

Interactive Map

and in hand-to-hand combat used spears and clubs, some topped with stone or with bronze stars.

Like other Andean peoples (see Chapter 5), the Inca knew how to extract metallic ore from rocks and how to heat different metals to form alloys. They made bronze by combining copper with tin, as did most other Bronze Age peoples, and by combining copper with arsenic. But the Inca did not develop their metallurgical expertise beyond making club heads, decorative masks, and ear spools for the nobility.

At its height, the Inca army could field as many as 100,000 men in a single battle, most of the rank-and-file drawn from subject peoples who were required to serve in the army. Although soldiers fought only seasonally and returned home at harvesttime, the rate of Inca expansion was breathtaking. Starting from a single location, Cuzco, the Inca conquered large chunks of southern, central, and coastal Peru, Ecuador, the eastern lowlands of Peru and Bolivia, and the mountains of Argentina and Chile (see Map 15.2). By 1532, they ruled over an area of 1,500 square miles (4,000 sq km) with a population estimated at ten to twelve million inhabitants.

Inca Rule of Subject Populations Unique among the Andean peoples, the Inca incorporated each conquered land and its occupants into their kingdom. They resettled thousands of people, forcing them to move to regions far from their original homes. The Inca also brought many images of subjects' ancestral deities to Cuzco, holding the images hostage so that their devotees would not rise up against their Inca overlords.

The Inca, like the Mongols, encouraged different peoples to submit to them by treating those who surrendered gently. They allowed local leaders to continue to serve but required everyone to swear loyalty to the Inca ruler, to grant him all rights to their lands, and to perform labor service as the Inca state required.

Inca officials also delegated power to indigenous leaders. Those of high birth could serve in the Inca government as long as they learned Quechua (keh-chew-ah), the language of the Inca. Each official was in charge of a certain number of households: top officials supervised ten thousand households, while the lowest functionaries watched over ten. Inca officials registered the population in a census and

THE TEN STAGES OF INCA LIFE ACCORDING TO GUAMÁN POMA

In 1613, Felipe Guamán Poma de Ayala (FAY-leep gua-MAHN POH-mah duh AIE-ah-lah) wrote an illustrated letter of over one thousand pages to the king of Spain. The Spaniards, he charged, had violated Christian teachings (he himself was a convert), and he asked the Spanish king to return the former Inca Empire to local leaders. The child of a Spanish father and an Inca mother, he used the two languages of Spanish and Quechua. One part of his letter, which was discovered and published only in the 1900s, describes the Inca labor system. Since Inca officials were most concerned with an individual's ability to perform labor service, they placed those best able to work, the middle-aged, in the highest

This woman is too old to work. The writing above her head says "blind people," "lame," "dumb," and "always sick."

The fifth girl represents the category of "very beautiful girls of marriageable age" and is standing up, bigger than any of the other women or girls.

(Royal Library Copenhagen)

This infant girl represents the tenth road. The Inca did not name their children before they reached the age of 2, since too many died before that age.

categories. Those less able to work, the elderly, came next, with young children and infants ranking last. Guamán Poma diagrammed the ten stages, or "roads," of life for both men and women; each drawing has a title at the top, and some have additional captions as well.

The ten "roads" for women begin with a middle-aged woman at the peak of her productivity who is weaving, and this is followed by three frames showing successively older women. Then the order shifts to a young girl, with the final five frames showing younger and younger girls. The men's roads follow roughly the same order, starting in middle age, followed by old age, and then progressing from adolescence to newborns.

Guamán Poma's drawings allot equal space for men and women and depict them as the same size, suggesting that the labor they contributed was equally important to the Inca state.

In the first stage for men, a proud warrior stands up straight, his weapon in his left hand and the head of his captive in the right.

The boy of 18 or 20 in the fifth box is poised to carry a message, possibly a quipu set of tied ropes.

(Royal Library Copenhagen)

QUESTIONS FOR ANALYSIS

What do Guamán Poma's illustrations indicate about Inca conceptions of gender?

How did men and women contribute to the labor service system?

● **quipu**   Inca system of record keeping that used knots on strings to record the population in a census and divide people into groups of 10, 50, 100, 500, 1,000, 5,000, and 10,000.

(CL) **Primary Source: Chronicles**
Learn how the Incas used the mysterious knotted ropes called quipu as record-keeping devices that helped them govern a vast and prosperous empire.

assigned each person to groups of 10, 50, 100, 500, 1,000, 5,000, and 10,000. Each year they recorded the number of people in each group not with a written script but by using a system of knotted strings, called **quipu** (key-POOH). Each town had a knot keeper who maintained and interpreted the knot records, which were updated annually to record changes in the population.

To fulfill the Inca's main service tax, male household heads between 25 and 50 had to perform two to three months' labor each year. Once assigned a task, a man could get as much help as he liked from his children or wife, a practice that favored families with many children (See the feature "Visual Evidence: The Ten Stages of Inca Life According to Guamán Poma.")

The Inca did not treat all subject peoples alike. From some resettled peoples they exacted months of labor, and many subject groups who possessed a specific artistic skill, such as carving stones or making spears, performed that skill for the state. Others did far less. For example, many Inca looked down on a people they called Uru, literally meaning "worm," who lived on the southern edge of Lake Titicaca. The Uru were supposed to catch fish, gather grasses, and weave textiles, but they performed no other labor service. An even more despised group was required each year to submit a single basket filled with lice, not because the Inca wanted the lice, but because they hoped to teach this group the nature of their tax obligations.

Each household also contributed certain goods, such as blankets, textiles, and tools, that were kept in thousands of storehouses throughout the empire. One Spaniard described a storehouse in Cuzco that particularly impressed him: "There is a house in which are kept more than 100,000 dried birds, for from their feathers articles of clothing are made." This system functioned so well that the corn and potatoes in the storehouses could support an army for months.

One lasting product of the Inca labor system was their magnificent highways, which included over 25,000 miles (40,000 km) of roads (see Map 15.2). While some of these routes predated the Inca conquest, the Inca linked them together into an overall system with two main trunk roads running north-south that were linked by twenty different

■ **Keeping Records with Knots**   The Inca kept all their records by using knotted strings, called quipu, attaching subsidiary cords, sometimes in several tiers, to a main cord. Different types of knots represented different numeric units; skipped knots indicated a zero; the color of the string indicated the item being counted.   (The Granger Collection)

east-west routes. Since the Inca did not have the wheel, most of the traffic was by foot, and llamas could carry small loads only short distances each day. With no surveying instruments, the Inca constructed these roads across deserts, yawning chasms, and mountains over 16,000 feet (5,000 m) high. Individual messengers working in shifts could move at an estimated rate of 150 miles (240 km) per day, but troops moved much more slowly, covering perhaps 7 to 9 miles (12–15 km) per day.

Despite its extent, the Inca Empire appeared stronger than it was. Many of the subject peoples resented their heavy labor obligations, and each time an Inca ruler died, the ensuing succession disputes threatened to tear the empire apart.

Intellectual and Geographic Exploration in Europe, 1300–1500

Between 1300 and 1500, as the Aztec and Inca were expanding their empires over-land in the Americas, Portuguese and Spanish ships colonized lands farther and farther away, ultimately reaching the Americas. In the years after the Black Death (see Chapter 13), European scholars extended their fields of study to include many new topics. They found that the traditional Greek and Latin sources they revered often contradicted each other, and they struggled to make sense of these differences. Meanwhile, new printing technology made books more available and affordable, enabling people like Christopher Columbus to read and compare many different books.

During the same period, European navigators between 1350 and 1492 began to venture into previously unexplored waters and sailed past the Strait of Gibraltar into the Atlantic. Portuguese and Spanish voyagers founded colonies on the Canary Islands, which were inhabited by an indigenous Stone Age people, and on the uninhabited Madeira Islands. Columbus's own trips to the Americas extended the expeditions of earlier explorers.

The Rise of Humanism

Since the founding of universities in Europe around 1200 (see Chapter 13), students had read Greek and Latin texts and the Bible. Instructors like Peter Abelard used scholastic approaches to study the authors of the past. The main goal of instruction was to reconcile the many differences among ancient authorities to form a logical system of thought.

Around 1350, a group of Italian scholars opposed to scholasticism pioneered a new intellectual movement called **humanism.** Humanists claimed expertise in the humanities, a broad field of study including the traditional liberal arts (see Chapter 13) as well as newer subjects like language, history, literature, and philosophy. The humanists studied many of the same texts that the scholastics had, but they tried to impart a more general understanding of them to their students in the hope that students would improve morally and be able to help others do the same.

Once of the earliest humanist writers was the Italian poet Petrarch (1304–1374). Scholasticism was misguided, Petrarch felt, because it was too abstract. It did not

humanism Intellectual movement begun around 1350 in Italy by scholars who opposed scholasticism. Humanists claimed expertise in the humanities, which included traditional liberal arts as well as fields of study like language, history, literature, and philosophy.

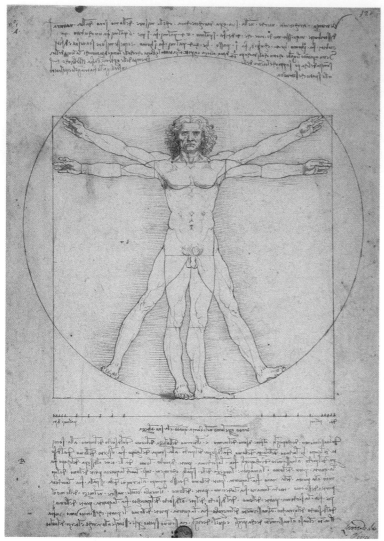

■ **The Art of Humanism** In 1487, the scientist, artist, and engineer Leonardo da Vinci portrayed man, not God, as the center of the universe. Above and below the ink drawing, the left-handed Da Vinci wrote notes in mirror writing to explain that his drawing illustrated a text about proportions by the Roman architect Vitruvius (ca. 75–ca. 15 B.C.E.). Unlike earlier artists, da Vinci personally dissected corpses so that he could portray the structure of human muscles as accurately as possible. (Accademia, Venice, Italy/Cameraphoto/Art Resource, NY)

teach people how to live and how to obtain salvation. Petrarch searched for previously unknown Latin texts that could serve as literary models and also as moral treatises. Although he composed much poetry in Latin, he is remembered for the poetry he composed in Italian, one of several European vernacular languages that came into written use in the fourteenth and fifteenth centuries.

The ideals of humanism do not lend themselves to easy summary. In 1487, a Venetian woman named Cassandra Fedele (fay-DAY-lay) (1465–1558) addressed the students and faculty of the University of Padua in a public oration that set out her own understanding of humanism. Having studied Greek and Latin with a tutor, Fedele urged her audience to devote themselves to studying Cicero, Plato, and Aristotle because, she maintained, while wealth and physical strength cannot last, "those things which are produced by virtue and intelligence are useful to those who follow." She continued: "And how much more humane, praiseworthy and noble do those states and princes become who support and cultivate these studies! Certainly for this reason this part of philosophy has laid claim for itself to the name of 'humanity,' since those who are rough by nature become by these studies more civil and mild-mannered." She eloquently expressed the major tenet of humanism: studying the humanities made students, whether from noble or low-born families, more refined and better people.[4]

Rather than treat Latin translations as flawless, the humanists checked them against texts in the original languages, including the Greek of the Bible. When they did, they found that many of the most difficult-to-understand passages were corrupted by translation errors. One product of humanist scholarship was multilingual editions of the Bible that printed the Latin, Greek, Hebrew, and Aramaic texts on the same page so that scholars could compare them.

Historians call this period of humanist revival the Renaissance, which means "rebirth," to contrast it with the earlier centuries, but many continuities linked the intellectual advances of the twelfth and thirteenth centuries with those of the humanist era.

Europe's First Books Printed with Movable Type

The introduction of printing in Europe contributed greatly to the humanist movement because movable type made books cheaper, enabling scholars to more easily compare different versions of the same text. Johannes Gutenberg (ca. 1400–1468) printed the first European book, a Bible, using movable type sometime before 1454. This was not the first book in the world made using movable type; we have seen that the Chinese knew about movable type as early as the eleventh century and that the world's earliest surviving book using movable type was made in Korea in 1403 (see Chapter 12). We should remember, too, that Gutenberg could not have printed the Bible if paper, a Chinese invention, had not come into widespread use in Europe between 1250 and 1350 (see Chapter 13).

Movable type, however unsuited to Chinese with its thousands of characters, functioned beautifully for alphabetic languages like Latin. Gutenberg made several crucial innovations: a mold with rows in which different letters could be placed, an oil-based ink, and the type itself. Close analysis of Gutenberg's earliest books shows variation among individual letters, suggesting that he may have made hundreds of the same letter by hand, maybe even from wood, and did not cast them from a metal mold as is often supposed.

Within fifty years of its introduction, printing had transformed the European book. Although European readers had once prized illuminated manuscripts prepared by hand, with beautiful illustrations and exquisite lettering, now typesetters streamlined texts so that they could be printed more easily. Some of the most popular books described the marvels from around the world and included the first Latin translation in 1409 of the Greek geographer Ptolemy (see Chapter 7) and the travel account of Marco Polo (see Chapter 13). Columbus's personal library included copies of both books, and he carefully wrote long notes in the margins of the passages that interested him.

Early European Exploration in the Mediterranean and the Atlantic, 1350–1440

Widely read travel accounts whetted the appetite for trade and exploration. European merchants, primarily from the Italian city-states of Venice and Genoa, maintained settlements in certain locations far from Europe, such as Constantinople, the island of Cyprus, and other smaller islands in the Mediterranean (see Map 15.3). These communities, which existed primarily for the convenience of the merchants, had walled enclosures called *factories* that held warehouses, a place for ships to refit, and houses for short- and long-term stays.

The government of Venice appointed an official, the rector, to serve every two years in each of the city's various settlements. In deciding disputes, he could choose whether to apply local or Venetian law. The primary support the Venetians offered to their colonies was naval protection for the merchant fleet.

Starting around 1350, European navigators began to sail past the Strait of Gibraltar into the Atlantic Ocean. In 1350, two Italian explorers wrote the first book about the Canary Islands and their non-Christian inhabitants. The Europeans captured some of these Canary Islanders and sold them in the slave markets of Europe, where they were much in demand. Also around 1350, the Portuguese reached the Azores, which lie one-third of the distance from Europe to the Americas. After 1350, cartographers began to show the various Atlantic islands off the coast of Africa on their maps.

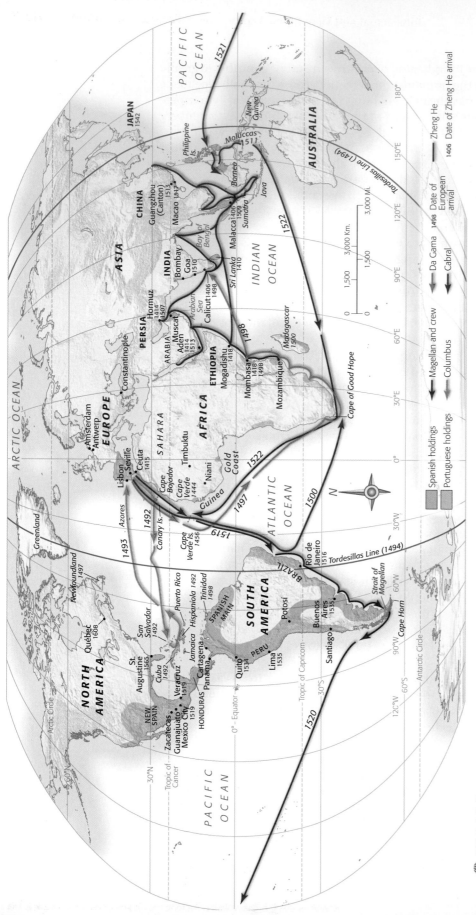

MAP 15.3

The Age of Maritime Expansion, 1400–1600 Between 1400 and 1600, maritime explorers pioneered three major new routes: (1) across the Atlantic Ocean from Europe to the Americas, (2) across the Pacific from the Americas to Asia, and (3) south along the west coast of Africa to the Cape of Good Hope. Once the Portuguese Vasco da Gama rounded the Cape in 1498, he connected with the well-traveled hajj route linking East Africa with China that Zheng He's ships had taken in the early 1400s.

 Interactive Map

One motivation for exploring these unknown islands was religious. As the Catholic rulers of Spain and Portugal regained different Islamic cities in Iberia during the Reconquista of the thirteenth and fourteenth centuries, they hoped to expand Christian territory into North Africa. At the time, Portugal was separate from Spain, which itself contained several distinct kingdoms. In 1415, a Portuguese prince named Henry, now known as **Henry the Navigator** (1394–1460), led a force of several thousand men that captured the Moroccan fortress of Ceuta (say-OO-tuh). Using the rhetoric of the Crusades and armed with an order from the pope, his goal was to convert the inhabitants to Christianity.

Henry tried to take the Canary Islands for Christianity in 1424, but the inhabitants, armed only with stone tools, repelled the invaders; nevertheless, the Portuguese continued to capture and enslave Canary islanders on a regular basis. The Portuguese occupied the island of Madeira, and in 1454 they established plantations there, which soon exported large amounts of sugar.

Many navigators were afraid to venture past the Madeira Islands because of the dreaded torrid zone. Greek and Roman geographers had posited that all the peoples of the known world lived in the northern temperate zone, which was bordered by an uninhabitable frigid zone to the north and a torrid zone to the south, whose scorching heat made it impossible to cross. Following the revival of interest in Greek and Roman geography in the twelfth century, all informed people realized, as the ancients had, that the globe was round. (The American writer Washington Irving invented the myth that everyone before Columbus thought the world was flat.)

Portuguese exploration along the west coast of Africa forced people to reconsider the existence of a torrid zone. Many Europeans had assumed that Cape Bojador (see Map 15.3), just south of the Canary Islands in modern Morocco, marked the beginning of the impenetrable torrid zone. But in 1434 the Portuguese successfully sailed past the Cape. An Arabic-speaking courtier sent by Henry to learn about the region's geography returned to his monarch after seven months to report that no torrid zone existed.

• Henry the Navigator (1394–1460) Portuguese prince who supported Portuguese explorations across the Mediterranean to the Moroccan city of Ceuta, across the Atlantic to the Canary and Madeira Islands, and along the West African coast past Cape Bojador (in modern Mauritania).

Portuguese Exploration of Africa and the Slave Trade After 1444

If there were no torrid zone, Henry realized, the Portuguese could transport slaves from the west coast of Africa and sell them in Europe. Portuguese vessels had already brought back thirty-eight African slaves from West Africa. In 1444, Henry dispatched six caravels to bring back slaves from the Arguin bank, south of Cape Bojador in modern-day Mauritania. The caravel was a small sailing ship, usually about 75 feet (23 m) long, that had two or three masts with square sails. Its main advantage was that it could sail close to the wind.

In 1444, Henry staged a huge public reception of the slaves for his subjects. The ships' captains presented one slave each to a church and to a Franciscan convent to demonstrate their intention to convert the slaves to Christianity. An eyewitness description captures the scene:

> These people, assembled together on that open space, were an astonishing sight to behold. Among them were some who were quite white-skinned, handsome and of good appearance; others were less white, seeming more like brown men; others still were as black as Ethiopians, so deformed of face and body that, to those who stared at them, it almost seemed that they were looking at spirits from the lowest hemisphere. But what heart, however hardened it might be, could not be pierced by a feeling of pity at the sight of that company?[5]

One could easily assume that this description is an early critique of slavery, but, in fact, the author, like many of his contemporaries, accepted the need for slavery. These Europeans saw the trade in slaves as a Christian act: the Africans, as non-Christians, were doomed to suffer in the afterlife, but, if they converted, they could attain salvation. From its very beginnings, the European slave trade combined the profit motive with a missionary impulse.

Within ten years the Portuguese slave traders had reached agreements with two rulers in northern Senegal to trade horses for slaves each year. The price of a horse varied from nine to fourteen slaves. Horses did not live long in Africa's tropical climate, but because rulers liked them as a symbol of power and a war tool, the demand never flagged. By the time of Henry's death in 1460, Portuguese ships had transported about 1,000 slaves a year, fewer than the 4,300 slaves who crossed the Sahara overland each year at the time. After 1460, the oceanic trade continued to grow because the Portuguese deliberately hoped to bypass the Sahara caravans, which they did not control.

Many of the African slaves worked on sugar plantations, either in the Canary Islands or on Madeira. Portugal and the Spanish kingdom of Castile, which ruled central Spain, signed the Treaty of Alcaçovas in 1479 in which they agreed that the Atlantic islands belonged to Castile while the Azores, Madeira, the Cape Verde islands, and any still-to-be-discovered islands beyond the Canaries belonged to Portugal. This treaty recognized the Portuguese right to continue their explorations along the African coast, and, in 1487, a Portuguese ship commanded by Bartholomew Dias rounded the Cape of Good Hope at Africa's southern tip. The Portuguese became convinced that the quickest way to Asia and the riches of the spice trade was around Africa, as Chapter 16 will show.

The Iberian Conquest of Mexico, Peru, and Brazil, 1492–1580

Columbus's landfall in the Caribbean had immediate and long-lasting consequences. Representatives of the Spanish and Portuguese crowns conquered most of Mexico and Latin America with breathtaking speed. In 1517, the Spanish landed for the first time on the Aztec mainland; by 1540, they controlled all of Mexico, Central America, and the northern sections of South America. Portugal controlled Brazil by 1550. By 1580, Spain had subdued the peoples of the southern regions of South America. Given that the residents of the Canary Islands, armed only with stone tools, managed to repel all attempts to conquer them for 150 years, how did the Spanish and Portuguese move into the Americas and conquer two sophisticated empires so quickly?

The subject peoples of the Aztec, who had not been incorporated into the empire, welcomed the Spanish as an ally who might help them overthrow their overlords. Moreover, the Spanish arrived in Peru just after the installation of a new Sapa Inca, whose opponents still hoped to wrest power from him. The Europeans had other advantages, like guns and horses, which the Amerindians lacked. Finally, the Europeans were completely unaware of their most powerful weapon: the disease pools of Europe.

Columbus's First Voyage to the Americas, 1492

In 1479, Isabella (1451–1504) ascended to the throne of Castile and married Ferdinand of Aragon, unifying the two major kingdoms of Spain. Throughout the 1480s, Columbus approached both the Spanish and the Portuguese monarchs to request funds for a voyage to the Indies by sailing west from the Canary Islands.

In keeping with the scholastic and humanist traditions, Columbus cited several authorities in support of the new route he proposed. One passage in the Bible (II Esdras 6:42) stated that the world was six parts land, one part water. Columbus interpreted this to mean that the distance from the Iberian Peninsula to the western edge of Asia in Japan was only 2,700 miles (4,445 km). In actuality, the distance is over 6,000 miles (10,000 km), and the world is about 70 percent water and 30 percent land, but no one at the time knew this.

In rejecting his proposal, the scholars advising the Portuguese and Spanish monarchs agreed on its main flaws: the world, they thought, was bigger than Columbus realized. Moreover, no ship carrying its own provisions could sail all the way to Japan because the men on board would die of starvation before reaching Asia. These scholars were correct about the distance from Iberia to Japan, but they did not realize that any ship crossing the Atlantic would be able to stop in the Americas and obtain food.

Several developments occurred in 1492 that prompted Isabella and Ferdinand to overturn their earlier decision. Granada, the last Muslim outpost, fell in 1492, and all of Spain came under Catholic rule. In that same year the rulers of Aragon and Castile expelled all Jews from Spain, a measure that had been enacted by France and England centuries earlier. Delighted with these developments, Ferdinand and Isabella decided to fund Columbus, primarily because they did not want the Portuguese to do so, and also because he was asking for only a small amount of money, enough to host a foreign prince for a week.

Isabella and Ferdinand gave Columbus two titles: *admiral of the ocean sea* and *viceroy*. An admiral commanded a fleet, but *viceroy* was a new title indicating a representative of the monarch who would govern any lands to which he sailed. Columbus was entitled to one-tenth of any precious metals or spices he found, with the remaining nine-tenths going to Isabella and Ferdinand. No provision was made for his men.

Columbus departed with three ships from Granada on August 3, 1492, and on October 12 of the same year arrived in Hispaniola, a Caribbean island occupied by the modern nations of Haiti and the Dominican Republic. Although Europeans knew about Islamic astrolabes and sextants, Columbus did not use them. He sailed primarily by dead reckoning: he used a compass to stay on a westerly course and, with the help of a clock, estimated his speed and so the approximate distance he traveled in a day. Columbus was not certain where he had arrived, but he suspected that he was in Japan.

His first encounter with the people on the island was peaceful: "In order to win their friendship," Columbus wrote in his logbook, "I gave some of them red caps and glass beads which they hung round their necks, and also other trifles. These things pleased them greatly and they became marvelously friendly to us." The two sides exchanged gifts and tried to make sense of each other's languages. The island's residents spoke **Arawak,** a language used over a large region spanning modern Venezuela to Florida. "They are the color of Canary Islanders (neither black nor white)," Columbus noted, an indication that he thought of the Arawak as potential slaves.

CL) **Primary Source: The Agreement with Columbus of April 17 and April 30, 1492** *Read the contract signed by Columbus and his royal patrons, and see what riches he hoped to gain from his expedition.*

• **Arawak** General name for a language of families spoken in the 1500s over a large region spanning modern Venezuela to Florida. The term also includes all the Arawak-speaking peoples, including those Columbus met on Hispaniola in 1492.

A Comparison of Columbus's and Zheng He's Voyages

Many people have wondered why the Spanish and the Portuguese, and not the Chinese of the Ming dynasty, established the first overseas empires. The Chinese, who first set off in 1405, had almost a century's head start on the Europeans (see Chapter 14). Their biggest ships extended a full 200 feet (61 m) in length, while Columbus's ships were two-fifths of that length. The full fleet of 317 Chinese treasure ships carried 28,000 men; the doctors on board outnumbered Columbus's entire crew.

Yet the size of the treasure ships did not give the Chinese an advantage, because they were too big to take into unknown waters. One of Columbus's original

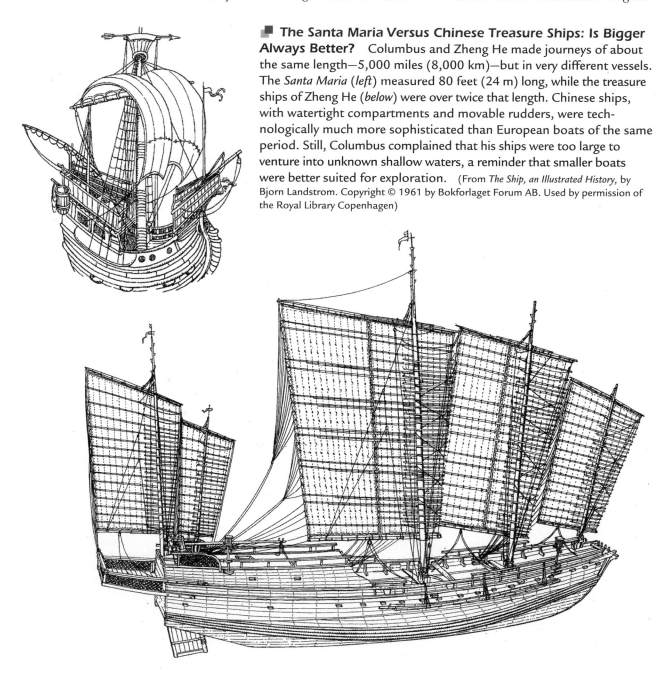

■ **The Santa Maria Versus Chinese Treasure Ships: Is Bigger Always Better?** Columbus and Zheng He made journeys of about the same length—5,000 miles (8,000 km)—but in very different vessels. The *Santa Maria* (*left*) measured 80 feet (24 m) long, while the treasure ships of Zheng He (*below*) were over twice that length. Chinese ships, with watertight compartments and movable rudders, were technologically much more sophisticated than European boats of the same period. Still, Columbus complained that his ships were too large to venture into unknown shallow waters, a reminder that smaller boats were better suited for exploration. (From *The Ship, an Illustrated History,* by Bjorn Landstrom. Copyright © 1961 by Bokforlaget Forum AB. Used by permission of the Royal Library Copenhagen)

three ships ran aground during the first voyage, and he complained that his ships—only 80 feet (24 m) long—were too large for successful exploration.

China was richer than either Spain or Portugal. It was arguably the richest country in the world in the early fifteenth century, while Spain and Portugal were far smaller. Yet their small size gave both the Portuguese and the Spanish powerful motivation to seek new lands.

Columbus's voyages differed from the Chinese voyages led by Admiral Zheng He in another critical sense. The navigators on the Chinese treasure ships knew each destination because they followed the best-traveled oceanic route in the world before 1500. Muslim pilgrims from East Africa traveled up the East African coast to reach Mecca, and Chinese pilgrims sailed around Southeast Asia and India to reach the Arabian peninsula. The Zheng He voyages simply linked the two hajj routes together. In contrast, when Columbus and other later explorers set off, they were consciously exploring, looking for new places to colonize. Columbus's voyages were genuine voyages of exploration because he was going where no one else (or at least no one else that anyone remembered) had gone before him.

The Ming dynasty governed a huge empire, and there is no indication that the Yongle emperor (r. 1403–1424) wanted to make it bigger by using the voyages. He simply hoped that the various nations of the world would acknowledge him as the rightful ruler of the Chinese. The Chinese had no concept of a "colony"—no colonies comparable to the Madeira or Canary Islands or even to the factories built by European merchants on different Mediterranean islands. Rulers of earlier Chinese dynasties had sometimes conquered other peoples, but always in contiguous neighboring lands, never overseas.

The Ming government ordered an end to the voyages in 1433 because they brought no financial benefit to the Chinese. In contrast, the Spanish and Portuguese voyages brought their countries immediate returns in gold and slaves and the promise of long-term profits if settlers could establish enterprises such as sugar plantations.

Spanish Exploration After Columbus's First Voyage, 1493–1517

From the beginning Columbus did not exercise tight control over his ships. When he first reached the Americas, the ship *Niña* set off on its own to search for gold, and Columbus had no choice but to welcome it back. The *Santa Maria* had already run aground and been dismantled to make a fort, and Columbus needed both remaining ships to return home. With only two ships, he was forced to leave thirty-nine men behind in the fort, but when he returned on his second voyage in 1493, he found that all had been killed, presumably in disputes with the Arawak over women. Relations between the Arawak and the Spanish were never again as harmonious as they had been during the first voyage.

Once the Spanish realized that Columbus had discovered a new landmass, they negotiated the **Treaty of Tordesillas** (tor-duh-SEE-yuhs) with the Portuguese in 1494, while Columbus was away on his second voyage. The treaty established a dividing line: all territory 1,185 miles (1,910 km) west of the line belonged to Castile, while all the islands to the east were reserved for Portugal. Lands already ruled by a Christian monarch were unaffected by the agreement. Although the pope, himself a Spaniard, supported the treaty, no other European power accepted its terms. Portugal gained Africa, the route to India, and, although no one knew it at the time, Brazil, which both the Spanish Vicente Pinzon and the Portuguese Pedro Álvares Cabral (1467/68–1520) reached six years later in 1500.

● **Treaty of Tordesillas** Treaty signed by the Portuguese and the Spanish in 1494 that established a dividing line: all territory 1,185 miles (1,910 km) west of the line belonged to Castile, while all the islands to the east were reserved for Portugal.

This treaty made the peoples of the Americas subjects of Ferdinand and Isabella. When Columbus returned from the second voyage with five hundred slaves on board, Isabella freed all of them on the grounds that her subjects could not be enslaved. Only non-Spanish subjects, like those of African rulers, could.

Columbus never solved the problem of how to compensate his men. When recruiting sailors in Spain he spoke of great riches, but the agreement he had signed with Ferdinand and Isabella left no share of wealth for his men. On his first voyage, his men expected to sail with him to Asia and return, but on subsequent voyages many joined him expressly so that they could settle in the Americas, where they hoped to make fortunes. In 1497, the settlers revolted against Columbus, and he agreed to allow them to use Indians as agricultural laborers. Because Columbus was unpopular with the settlers, in 1499 the Crown removed him from office and replaced him with a new viceroy.

● **encomienda system**
(Literally "entrusted.")
System established in
1503 by the Spanish in
the hope of clarifying
arrangements with the
colonists and of ending
the abuse of indigenous
peoples of the Americas.

In 1503 the Spanish established the **encomienda system** in the hope of clarifying arrangements with the colonists and of ending the abuse of American indigenous peoples. Under this system, the Spanish monarchs "entrusted" (the literal meaning of *encomienda*) a specified number of Amerindians to a Spanish settler, who gained the right to extract labor, gold, or other goods from them in exchange for teaching them about Christianity. The monarchs took as their model the governmental structure used to administer lands newly recovered from Muslim kingdoms in the Reconquista. Although designed to protect the indigenous peoples, the encomienda system often resulted in further exploitation.

Spanish and Portuguese navigators continued to land in new places after 1503. The Spanish crossed 120 miles (193 km) from Cuba to the Yucatán Peninsula in 1508–1509 and reached Florida in 1510. In 1513, Vasco Núñez de Balboa (bal-BOH-uh) crossed through Panama to see the Pacific, and by 1522 the Portuguese navigator Magellan had circumnavigated the globe, although he died before his ship returned home.

The Conquest of Mexico, 1517–1540

● **conquistadors**
Literally "conquerors,"
the term for the Spaniards who conquered
Mexico, Peru, and
Central America in the
1500s. Many came from
families of middling
social influence and
made their fortunes in
the Americas.

Hernán Cortés (kor-TEZ), the Spaniard who led the conquest of Mexico, came first to Hispaniola in 1506 and moved to Cuba in 1509. Like many of the other Spanish **conquistadors** ("conquerors"), he came from a family of middling social influence and made his fortune in the Americas. After rumors reached Cuba from the Maya peoples of the Yucatán about a larger, richer empire to the north, Cortés sought to launch an expedition. Within two weeks he had recruited 530 men to travel with him.

● **Malinché** Nahua
noblewoman who
served as translator for
and adviser to Cortés.
Trilingual in Spanish,
Nahuatl, and Mayan,
she played a crucial role
in the Spanish conquest
of Mexico because she
commanded the respect
of the Nahua peoples.

When Cortés landed in the Yucatán in early 1519, he immediately met a woman who helped him penetrate the language barrier separating the Spanish- and the Nahua-speakers: a Nahua noblewoman named **Malinché** (mah-lin-HAY) who had grown up among the Maya and could speak both the Nahuatl and Mayan languages. Given to Cortés as a gift, Malinché learned Spanish quickly. The Spaniards called her Dona Marina. As adviser to Cortés, she played a crucial role in the Spanish conquest of Mexico, partially because she commanded the respect of the Nahua peoples.

Cortés landed on the coast of Mexico on April 20, 1519, and slightly over two years later the Aztec had surrendered their capital and their empire to him. Yet this outcome had been far from certain. The Spanish had only 1,500 men.

The encounter between the Nahua and the Spaniards is unusual because we have surviving sources from both sides—the European colonizers and the

■ **Cortés's Interpreter, Malinché**   This image dates to the 1500s and shows what Cortés's army looked like when it first landed in Mexico. The Spaniards, with their heavy armor and horse, contrast sharply with the local peoples, who use bands tied around their foreheads to bear the weight of food in containers as well as to carry a small child (*far left*). The army was a mixed force: Malinché, who was Cortés's mistress and interpreter, stands at the far right, with the bearded Cortés on her left. (Bibliothèque nationale de France/Snark/Art Resource, NY)

indigenous peoples. One of Cortés's foot soldiers, Bernal Díaz del Castillo, wrote the most detailed account from the Spanish point of view. On the Nahua side, a Franciscan missionary named Fray Bernardino de Sahagún (FRAY burr-NARD-ee-noh duh sah-hah-GWUN) compiled the ***Florentine Codex*** in the 1550s on the basis of interviews he and his research assistants conducted and recorded in an alphabet for Nahuatl developed by Spanish missionaries. This account is not the same as a first-person contemporary account, yet, since Sahagún and his team systematically crosschecked what their informants reported, it is the best Nahuatl-language account we have.

The *Florentine Codex* records the response of the reigning Great Speaker Moctezuma (also spelled Montezuma) to the first envoy from the Spanish:

> It especially made him faint when he heard how the guns went off at the Spaniards' command, sounding like thunder. . . . And when it went off, something

● ***Florentine Codex***
The main source in Nahuatl about the events of the Spanish conquest. Compiled by a Franciscan missionary named Fray Bernardino de Sahagún in the 1550s on the basis of interviews he and his research assistants conducted and recorded.

like a ball came out from inside, and fire went showering and spitting out. . . . And if they shot at a hill, it seemed to crumble and come apart. . . . Their war gear was all iron. They clothed their bodies in iron, they put iron on their heads, their swords were iron. . . .

And their deer that carried them were as tall as the roof.[6]

The Spaniards' "deer" were horses, an animal not native to the Americas, whose size greatly impressed the Aztec.

On their way to Tenochtitlan, the Spaniards fought a major battle lasting nearly three weeks with the people of Tlaxcala (tlash-CAH-lah). After their defeat the Tlaxcalans became the Spaniards' most important allies against their own hated Aztec overlords. When, in November 1519, the Spaniards first arrived at the capital city of Tenochtitlan, the Great Speaker Moctezuma allowed them to come in unharmed. The Spaniards could not believe how beautiful the city was. Bernal Díaz described this event:

> Gazing on such wonderful sights, we did not know what to say, or whether what appeared before us was real, for on one side, on the land, there were great cities, and in the lake ever so many more, and the lake itself was crowded with canoes, and in the Causeway were many bridges at intervals, and in front of us stood the great City of Mexico.

For one week the Spaniards and the Aztec coexisted uneasily, until the Spanish placed Moctezuma under house arrest. Then, in the spring of 1520, while Cortés was away, one of his subordinates ordered his men to massacre the city's inhabitants, and prolonged battles resulted. The Spaniards killed Moctezuma and, after suffering hundreds of casualties, retreated to Tlaxcala, the city of their allies. At this point, it seemed that the Aztec would win.

But by then smallpox had reached the Americas. The native peoples of America had little or no resistance to European smallpox, measles, malaria, sexually transmitted diseases, or even the common cold. In December 1518, one-third of Hispaniola's population died; in 1519, disease ravaged Puerto Rico, Jamaica, and Cuba; and in the spring of 1520, smallpox crossed into the Yucatán, arriving in Tenochtitlan by October. Moctezuma's successor died of smallpox in early December, and the mass deaths threw the entire city into disarray.

Even so the Spaniards had great difficulty conquering the Aztec. They laid siege to Tenochtitlan for eighty days of sustained fighting before the city surrendered in August of 1521. Spanish guns and cannon were not decisive. Some 100,000 troops and a portable fleet of boats supplied by the Tlaxcalans enabled the Spaniards to win.

In 1524, twelve Franciscan friars arrived in Mexico, where they were welcomed by Cortés. The Franciscans became the most important missionary order among the Nahuatl speakers. They searched for parallels between native beliefs and Christian teachings at the same time that they suppressed practices, like human sacrifice and polygamy, that they saw as un-Christian. (See the feature "Movement of Ideas: *The Sacrifice of Isaac:* A Sixteenth-Century Nahuatl Play.") The Spanish gradually imposed a more regular administration over Mexico under the governance of a viceroy.

The Spanish Conquest of Peru, 1532–1550

The order of events in the Spanish conquest of Peru differed from that in Mexico, where Cortés had arrived before smallpox. The smallpox virus traveled overland from Mexico and, in 1528, caused an epidemic in which many Inca, including the Inca Sapa, died, four years before the first Spaniards arrived in Peru. War among the contenders to the throne broke out. In November 1532, when the Spanish forces, led by Francisco Pizarro (pih-ZAHR-oh) (1475–1541), arrived, they happened upon the moment of greatest instability in the Inca kingdom: when the newly enthroned Sapa Inca had not yet completely subdued his main rival. Atahualpa (ah-tuh-WAHL-puh; also spelled Atawallpa) had become ruler only after defeating his older half-brother, whom he still held in captivity. Atahualpa had taken severe counter-measures against his brother's supporters, many of whom sided immediately with the Spaniards.

When Pizarro and his 168 men arrived at Cajamarca, an important city in the Peruvian highlands where Atahualpa was living, Atahualpa initially received the Spanish peacefully. Then, on their second day in Cajamarca, the Spanish staged a crisis: a Dominican missionary gave a prayer book to Atahualpa, and an interpreter explained that the Spanish wanted to spread the teachings of God. Atahualpa threw the book down on the ground, and the Spanish charged out from behind the stone buildings where they had been hiding. Their guns, armor, and horses gave them an initial advantage. An estimated seven thousand Inca, yet not a single Spaniard, died in the ensuing carnage.

Pizarro himself captured Atahualpa, who offered to pay an enormous ransom for his release: he promised to fill a room 2,600 cubic feet (74 cubic m) half with gold and half with silver. By April, the Inca had amassed the metal for the ransom, which the Spaniards melted down and divided among Pizarro's troops. Those with horses received 90 pounds (41 kg), equivalent today to perhaps $500,000, and those on foot half that amount. Then the Spanish reneged on their agreement and killed Atahualpa.

It took twenty years for the Spanish to gain control of Peru. With the support of those who opposed Atahualpa, they installed a puppet Sapa Inca and played off different Inca groups against each other. Since the Inca maintained no standing army, their warriors had to return home for the harvest while their Spanish opponents did not.

As the Spanish conquered different sections of Inca territory, they imposed the encomienda system. In 1551, they named the first viceroy for Peru and gradually established a more stable administration. The first census, taken in the 1570s, showed that half the population had died from European disease, with the toll in some places reaching as high as 95 percent of the population. The Amerindians who lived at high altitudes suffered much fewer losses than those living on the coast.

The Portuguese Settlement of Brazil, 1500–1580

In 1500, Pedro Álvares Cabral (kah-BRAHL) (1467/68–1520) landed in Brazil. Although the Portuguese claimed Brazil following Cabral's voyage, few of them came to this resource-poor country. Most Portuguese sought their wealth in Asia, as discussed in the next chapter. In 1533 the Portuguese monarch John III (r. 1521–1557) made a systematic effort to encourage the settlement of Brazil by dividing it into fifteen slices, each occupying 160 miles (260 km) of the coastline and extending inland indefinitely. He granted these territories to Portuguese nobles, many of them his courtiers.

John III also authorized the Jesuits, a new order of Catholic priests founded in 1540, to preach in Brazil. Many Jesuits traveled to the interior, converted the

The Sacrifice of Isaac: A Sixteenth-Century Nahuatl Play

The members of the Catholic orders who lived in Mexico used different approaches to teach the Nahua peoples about Christianity. In addition to printing bilingual catechisms in Spanish and Nahuatl, they sponsored the composition of plays in Nahuatl on religious themes. Since these plays were not published but only circulated in handwritten manuscripts, very few survive. The short play *The Sacrifice of Isaac* recounts the story from the Hebrew Bible of Abraham and Isaac (see pages 52 and 244), which addresses a topic of great interest to the Nahua peoples: human sacrifice.

God the Father appears in the play to ask Abraham to sacrifice his son Isaac, but he later sends an angel to instruct Abraham to offer a lamb instead. Abraham, his first wife, and Isaac all embody obedience, a virtue prized both by the an-

cient Hebrews and the Nahua peoples. Abraham's slave Hagar and her son Ishmael urge Isaac to disobey his father; both still worship the sun (not God), a sure clue to the audience that they are evil.

Corresponding faithfully to the version in the Hebrew Bible, the play shows an obedient Isaac offering himself for sacrifice until the moment the angel instructs Abraham to free him and sacrifice a lamb instead. The lively quality of the Nahuatl language suggests that it was written sometime after the Spanish conquest, probably by a native speaker who converted to Christianity.

Source: Marilyn Ekdahl Ravicz, *Early Colonial Religious Drama in Mexico: From Tzompantli to Golgotha* (Washington, D.C.: The Catholic University of America Press, 1970), pp. 83–97. The first selection is from pp. 87–90; the second, pp. 95–96.

The Devil, Ishmael, and Hagar Trick Isaac

(A demon enters, dressed either as an angel or as an old man.)

DEMON: What are you doing, young man? For I see your affliction is very great.

ISHMAEL: Most certainly my affliction is great! But how is it that you know if I have pain? Who told you this?

DEMON: Do you not see that I am a messenger from heaven? I was sent here from there in order to tell you what you are to do here on earth.

ISHMAEL: Then I wait to hear your command.

DEMON: Hear then why it is that you are troubled. Do I astound you? Truly it is because of the beloved child, Isaac! Because he is a person of a good life, and because he always has confidence in the commands of his father. So you contrive and wish with all your energy that he not be obedient to his father and mother. Most assuredly I can tell you what you must do to accomplish this.

ISHMAEL: Oh how you comfort me when I hear your advice. Nor do I merit your aid. You are most truly a dweller in heaven and my protector!

DEMON: Open your heart wide to my command! Look now—his father and mother have invited many others to a banquet; they are relaxing and greatly enjoying themselves. Now is the time to give Isaac bad advice so that he might forget his father and his mother and go with you to amuse himself in some other place. And if he should obey you, they will certainly punish their son for this, however well they love him.

ISHMAEL: I shall do just as you command.

DEMON: Then, indeed, I am going to return to heaven. For I came only to console you and tell you what you must do. . . .

(Hagar the slave and her son Ishmael enter.)

444

HAGAR: Now while the great lord Abraham once again entertains many for the sake of his son whom he so greatly loves, we are only servants. He values us but little. And you, my son, merit nothing, are worthy of nothing! Oh that I might placate myself through you, and that you might calm all my torment upon earth! But so it is; your birth and its reward are eternal tears.

(Here they both weep—also the son.)

ISHMAEL: Oh you sun! You who are so high! Warm us even here with your great splendor as well as in every part of the world, and—in the way which you are able—prosper all the peoples of the earth! And to us, yes, even to us two poor ones—who merit nothing and who are worthy of nothing! Know now, oh my mother, what I shall do: later, when they are all feasting, perhaps I shall be able to lead Isaac away with some deceit, so that we might go to divert ourselves in some other quarter. With this action he will violate the precept of his father, who will not then love him with all of his heart.

Hagar: What you are thinking is very good. Do it in that way.

Abraham and Isaac on the Mountain

ABRAHAM: Now hear me, my beloved son! Truly this is what the almighty God has commanded me in order that His loving and divine precept might be fulfilled; and so that He might see whether we—the inhabitants of the earth—love Him and execute His Divine Will. For He is the Lord of the living and of the dead. Now with great humility, accept death! For assuredly He says this: "Truly I shall be able to raise the dead back to life, I who am the Life Eternal." Then let His will be done in every part of the earth.

(Here Abraham weeps. The Music of the "Misericordia" is heard.)

ISAAC: Do not weep, my beloved and honored father! For truly I accept death with great happiness. May the precious will of God be done as He has commanded you. . . .

ANGEL: Abraham! Abraham!

(Here an angel appears and seizes Abraham's hand so that he is unable to kill his son.)

ABRAHAM: Who are you, you who speak to me?

ANGEL: Now know the following by the authority and word of God. For He has seen how much you love Him; that you fulfill His divine precept; that you do not infringe it; that you brought your cherished son—he whom you love so much—here to the peak of the mountain; and that you have come to offer him here as a burnt sacrifice to God the almighty Father. Now truly for all this, by His loving Will, I have come to tell you to desist, for your cherished son Isaac does not have to die.

Abraham: May His adored will be done as He wishes it. Come here, oh my beloved son! Truly you have now been saved by death by His hand.

(Here he [Abraham or Isaac] unties the cloth with which he was blindfolded, and loosens the ropes with which his hands were bound.)

ANGEL: Then understand this: as a substitute for your beloved son, you shall prepare a lamb as God wishes it. Go, for I shall accompany you and leave you at your house.

QUESTIONS FOR ANALYSIS

▶ What information does the author include to make the audience think Ishmael is bad and Isaac good?

▶ What does the text propose as an appropriate substitute for human sacrifice?

indigenous peoples, and then resettled them in villages. The settlers searched for gold throughout the sixteenth century but never found significant amounts.

Instead the Portuguese began to build sugar plantations with the guidance of technicians brought from the Canary Islands. Since so many of the indigenous Amerindians had died, the plantation owners imported slaves from Africa, who had learned how to cultivate sugar in the Canary Islands and the Madeiras.

In 1580 Philip II succeeded to the throne of both Spain and Portugal, and the two countries remained under a single king until 1640. The Portuguese and Spanish empires had evolved parallel structures independently. The highest colonial official, the viceroy, presided over a royal colony and governed in concert with an advisory council who could appeal any decisions to the king.

The social structure in the colonies was basically the same throughout Latin America. At the top of society were those born in Europe, who served as military leaders, royal officials, or high church figures. Below them were creoles, those with two European parents but born in the Americas. Those of mixed descent (mestizos in Spanish-speaking regions, memlucos in Brazil) ranked even lower, with only Amerindians and African slaves below them. By 1600, 100,000 Africans lived in Brazil, many working in the hundreds of sugar mills all over the colony.

The Columbian Exchange

● **Columbian exchange** All the plants, animals, goods, and diseases that crossed the Atlantic, and sometimes the Pacific, after 1492.

The term **Columbian exchange** refers to all the plants, animals, goods, and diseases that crossed the Atlantic, and sometimes the Pacific, after 1492. At the same time that European diseases like smallpox devastated the peoples living in America, European animals like the horse, cow, and sheep came to the Americas and flourished. In the other direction came plant foods indigenous to the Americas like tomatoes, potatoes, peanuts, and chili peppers.

Of all the European imports, smallpox had the most devastating effect on the Americas. It did not strike until 1518, probably because no Spaniard who came to the Americas before suffered from an active outbreak. Only someone suffering an outbreak can transmit smallpox, which is contagious for about a month: after two weeks of incubation, fever and vomiting strike; the ill person's skin then breaks out with the pox, small pustules that dry up after about ten days. Either the victim dies during those ten days or survives, typically with a pock-marked face and body.

One Nahuatl description captures the extent of the suffering:

> Sores erupted on our faces, our breasts, our bellies. . . . The sick were so utterly helpless that they could only lie on their beds like corpses, unable to move their limbs or even their heads. . . . If they did move their bodies, they screamed with pain.[7]

Although no plants or animals had an effect as immediate as smallpox, the long-term effects of the Columbian exchange in plants and animals indelibly altered the landscape, diets, and population histories of both the Americas and Europe. When Columbus landed on Hispaniola, he immediately realized how different the plants were: "All the trees were as different from ours as day from night, and so the fruits, the herbage, the rocks, and all things." He also remarked on the absence of livestock: "I saw neither sheep nor goats nor any other beast."[8]

On his second voyage in 1493, Columbus carried cuttings of European plants, including wheat, melons, sugar cane, and other fruits and vegetables. He also brought pigs, horses, chickens, sheep, goats, and cattle. More like wild boars than modern hogs, pigs were the first to adapt to the Americas, eating wild grasses, reproducing in large numbers, and moving into many areas emptied of humans by the depredations of smallpox.

While smallpox traveled from Europe to the Americas, there is evidence that syphilis traveled in the other direction. The first well-documented outbreaks of syphilis in Europe occurred around 1495, and one physician claimed that Columbus's men brought it to Madrid soon after 1492 but that he did not recognize it until many years later. It is also possible that diseases resembling syphilis, often labeled "leprosy," existed in Europe before this time but that the modern form of syphilis only arose after 1492. No European skeletons with signs of syphilis before 1500 have been found, but an Amerindian skeleton with syphilis has, suggesting that the disease did indeed move from the Americas to Europe. Causing genuine pain, syphilis could be passed to the next generation and was fatal for about one-quarter of those who contracted it, but it did not cause mass deaths.

Assessing the loss of Amerindian life due to smallpox and the other European diseases has caused much debate among historians because no population statistics exist for the Americas before 1492. Different historians have come up with estimates for the regions with the heaviest populations—Mexico, between four and six million, and Peru, between ten and twelve million—but even these numbers are controversial. Figures for the population of the entire Americas can be little more than guesswork. The first reliable figures for Amerindian populations came with Spanish colonization. In 1568, Spanish authorities counted 970,000 non-Spanish living in Mexico and 1.2 million living in Peru.[9] For the entire period of European colonization in all parts of the Americas, guesses at the total death toll from European diseases, based on controversial estimates of precontact populations, range from a low of 10 million to a high of over 100 million.

By 1600, two extremely successful agricultural enterprises had spread through the Americas. One was sugar, and the other was cattle raising. The Spaniards who landed in the Americas had long experience with cattle. They knew how to lasso, to lead cattle to grass, and to round up cattle and bring them in for slaughter. The Americas contained huge expanses of grasslands in Venezuela and Colombia, from Mexico north to Canada, and in Argentina and Uruguay. In each case the Spaniards began on the coastal edge of a grassland and followed their rapidly multiplying herds of cattle to the interior.

As European food crops transformed the diet of those living in the Americas, so too did American food crops transform the eating habits of people in Afro-Eurasia. The climate of Latin America closely resembled that of Africa, and American food crops moved into West Africa, particularly modern Nigeria, where even today people eat corn, peanuts, squash, manioc (cassava), and sweet potatoes.

Two crops in particular played an important role throughout Afro-Eurasia: corn and potatoes (including sweet potatoes). Both produced higher yields than wheat and grew in less desirable fields, such as on the slopes of hills. Although few people anywhere in the world preferred corn or potatoes to their original wheat-based or rice-based diet, if the main crop failed, hungry people gratefully ate the American transplants. By the eighteenth century corn and potatoes had reached as far as India and China, and the population in both places increased markedly.

Chapter Review

KEY TERMS

Christopher Columbus (418)

Aztec Empire (421)

altepetl (421)

Tenochtitlan (421)

Inca Empire (424)

ayllu (425)

quipu (430)

humanism (431)

Henry the Navigator (435)

Arawak (437)

Treaty of Tordesillas (439)

encomienda system (440)

conquistadors (440)

Malinché (440)

Florentine Codex (441)

Columbian exchange (446)

CL Download the MP3 audio file of the Chapter Review and listen to it on the go.

Unlike the Viking voyages to Newfoundland and the Chinese expeditions to East Africa, Columbus's landfall in 1492 had lasting consequences. The major difference was that the arrival of the Spaniards and the Portuguese initiated the Columbian exchange, an unprecedented transfer of diseases, plants, and animals from one continent to another. The mass deaths of the Amerindians preceded the large-scale movement of Europeans and Africans to the Americas. The migrations in the first hundred years after Columbus's arrival in Hispaniola produced the mixed composition of the population of the Americas today. As we will see in the next chapter, the arrival of the Europeans had a very different impact on Asia.

How did the Aztec form their empire? How did the Inca form theirs? How did each hold their empire together, and what was each empire's major weakness?

The Aztec, based in modern Mexico, demanded much from their subject peoples, including payments of grain and other goods, a certain number of days of work each year, and sacrificial victims to provide the gods with precious "water," but they gave little in return. Living in their own communities, the subject peoples had little reason to be loyal to the Aztec and every reason to ally with any power against them.

The Inca Empire of the Andes was organized differently. Once the Inca conquered a locality, they incorporated its residents in their empire, sometimes even relocating them. Their weakness was that whenever the Sapa Inca died or became weak, all those desiring to succeed him engaged in a free-for-all struggle, which created great instability in the empire. When one leader emerged victorious, he took severe measures against all his rivals, who would readily ally with any enemy of the new Sapa Inca if doing so gave them a chance to reassert themselves.

How did humanist scholarship encourage oceanic exploration? What motivated the Portuguese, particularly Prince Henry the Navigator, to explore West Africa?

Benefiting from the lowered cost of printed books, the humanists emphasized the rigorous re-examination of the classics, preferably in the original Latin and Greek, including geographical works. Christopher Columbus owned copies of Ptolemy's geography and Marco Polo's travel account. Although ancient geographers posited the existence of a torrid zone that could not be crossed because it was scorchingly hot, Portuguese navigators, many sponsored by Prince Henry the Navigator, made their way down the coast of West Africa and realized that the zone did not exist. Hoping to make Portugal a wealthy slave-trading state, the Portuguese rulers professed a desire to convert the Africans they captured and brought to Europe as slaves.

How did the Spanish and the Portuguese establish their empires in the Americas so quickly?

The Spanish tapped the resentment of the subject peoples, including both the Tlaxcalans in Mexico and the Inca supporters of the unsuccessful brother of Atahualpa, against their rulers. European horses and guns frightened the Amerindians, but the most powerful European weapon was invisible: European smallpox and other diseases to which Amerindians had no resistance. The mass deaths made it possible for the Spanish and Portuguese to gain control over modern-day Mexico, Central America, and South America within one hundred years after Columbus's 1492 arrival in Hispaniola.

 **WEB RESOURCES**

Pronunciation Guide

Interactive Maps

MAP 15.1 The Aztec Empire

MAP 15.2 The Inca Empire

MAP 15.3 The Age of Maritime Expansion, 1400–1600

Primary Sources

Chapter Objectives

ACE Multiple-Choice Quiz

Flashcards

 ## What was the Columbian exchange? Which elements of the exchange had the greatest impact on the Americas? On Afro-Eurasia?

Of all the plants, animals, and microbes going between the Americas and Afro-Eurasia after 1492, disease had the greatest impact. The death toll from smallpox ranged between 50 and 90 percent, and estimates suggest that at least ten million Amerindians died in the years after the first outbreak of smallpox in 1518. American food crops traveling in the other direction, particularly corn and potatoes, spread throughout Afro-Eurasia and enabled many to survive famines.

For Further Reference

Coe, Michael. *Mexico*. London: Thames and Hudson, 1984.

Cohen, J. M., trans. *The Four Voyages of Christopher Columbus*. New York: Penguin, 1969.

D'Altroy, Terence. *The Incas*. Malden, Mass.: Blackwell Publishing, 2002.

Flint, Valerie I. J. *The Imaginative Landscape of Christopher Columbus*. Princeton: Princeton University Press, 1992.

Grafton, Anthony, et al. *New Worlds, Ancient Texts: The Power of Tradition and the Shock of Discovery*. Cambridge: The Belknap Press of Harvard University Press, 1992.

Lockhart, James. *The Nahuas After the Conquest: A Social and Cultural History of the Indians of Central Mexico, Sixteenth Through Eighteenth Centuries*. Stanford: Stanford University Press, 1992.

Lockhart, James, and Stuart Schwartz. *Early Latin America: A History of Colonial Spanish America and Brazil*. New York: Cambridge University Press, 1983.

Russell, Peter. *Prince Henry "the Navigator": A Life*. New Haven: Yale University Press, 2000.

Schwartz, Stuart B. *The Iberian Mediterranean and Atlantic Traditions in the Formation of Columbus as a Colonizer*.

Minneapolis: The Associates of the James Ford Bell Library, University of Minnesota, 1986.

Schwartz, Stuart B. *Victors and Vanquished: Spanish and Nahua Views of the Conquest of Mexico*. New York: Bedford/St. Martin's, 2000.

Smith, Michael E. *The Aztecs*. Malden, Mass.: Blackwell Publishing, 1996.

Websites

Foundation for the Advancement of Mesoamerican Studies, Inc. (http://www.famsi.org/research/pohl/pohl-aztec6.html).   Detailed description of the daily life of the Aztecs.

National Humanities Center: American Beginnings (http://nationalhumanitiescenter.org/pds/amerbegin/). Extensive collection of primary documents on European exploration and the first encounters between the Europeans and the Amerindians.

The Roots of the City (http://www.mexicocity.com.mx/history1.html). Excellent information about Tenochtitlan.

CHAPTER

16

Maritime Expansion in Afro-Eurasia, 1500–1700

The Italian priest **Matteo Ricci** (1552–1610) knew more about China than any other European of his time. Though frustrated by the small number of converts he made to Christianity during his two decades as a missionary, Ricci (REE-chee) described Chinese political and social life in positive terms. Though Ricci was sometimes less complimentary, in the following passage his idealized view of China was meant as a criticism of his own society. Ricci was correct in his assessment that China was more populous, more prosperous, and more stable than Europe in the first decade of the seventeenth century:

MATTEO RICCI (LEFT) AND ANOTHER MISSIONARY

(Private Collection/The Bridgeman Art Library)

It seems to be quite remarkable . . . that in a kingdom of almost limitless expanse and innumerable population, and abounding in copious supplies of every description, though they have a well-equipped army and navy that could easily conquer the neighboring nations, neither the King nor his people ever think of waging a war of aggression. . . . In this respect they are much different from the people of Europe, who are frequently discontent with their own governments and covetous of what others enjoy. . . .

Another remarkable fact and . . . marking a difference from the West, is that the entire kingdom is administered by . . . Philosophers. The responsibility for orderly management of the entire realm is wholly and completely committed to their charge and care. . . . Fighting and violence among the people are practically unheard of. . . . On the contrary, one who will not fight and restrains himself from returning a blow is praised for his prudence and bravery.[1]

CL This icon will direct you to interactive activities and study materials on the *Voyages* website: www.cengage.com/history/hansen/voyages1e

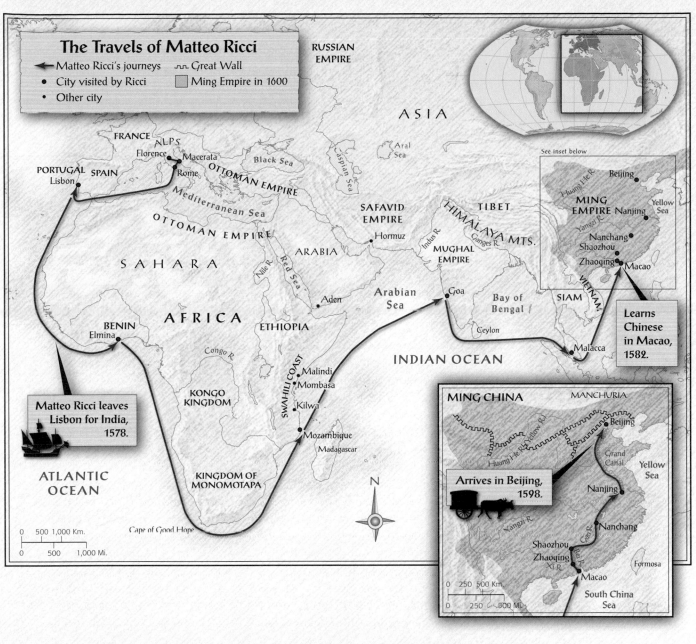

The Travels of Matteo Ricci

→ Matteo Ricci's journeys   ⌐⌐ Great Wall
• City visited by Ricci   ▨ Ming Empire in 1600
• Other city

RUSSIAN EMPIRE

ASIA

Aral Sea

See inset below

MING EMPIRE
Beijing
Huang He R.
Nanjing
Yellow Sea
Nanchang
Shaozhou
Zhaoqing   Macao

FRANCE
ALPS
Florence   Macerata
Rome
PORTUGAL   SPAIN
Lisbon
Black Sea
OTTOMAN EMPIRE
Caspian Sea

Mediterranean Sea

OTTOMAN EMPIRE

SAFAVID EMPIRE
Hormuz

TIBET
HIMALAYA MTS.
MUGHAL EMPIRE
Indus R.   Ganges R.

SAHARA
Nile R.   Red Sea
ARABIA
Arabian Sea
Goa
Bay of Bengal
Ceylon
INDIAN OCEAN
SIAM
VIETNAM
Malacca

Learns Chinese in Macao, 1582.

AFRICA
Aden
ETHIOPIA

BENIN
Elmina
Congo R.
KONGO KINGDOM
SWAHILI COAST
Malindi
Mombasa
Kilwa
Mozambique
Madagascar

Matteo Ricci leaves Lisbon for India, 1578.

ATLANTIC OCEAN

KINGDOM OF MONOMOTAPA
Cape of Good Hope

N

0   500   1,000 Km.
0   500   1,000 Mi.

MING CHINA
MANCHURIA
Huang He R.   Yellow R.
Beijing
Grand Canal
Yellow Sea
Nanjing
Arrives in Beijing, 1598.
Yangzi R.
Nanchang
Shaozhou
Zhaoqing   Gan R.
Xi R.   Macao
Formosa
South China Sea

0   250   500 Km.
0   250   500 Mi.

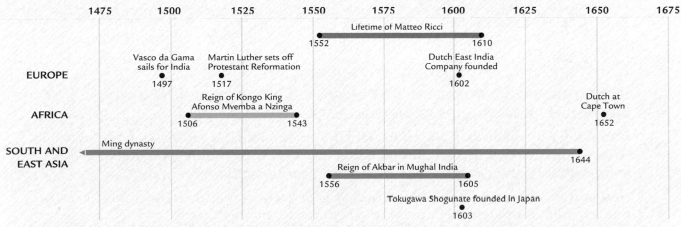

	1475	1500	1525	1550	1575	1600	1625	1650	1675

Lifetime of Matteo Ricci
1552 — 1610

EUROPE

Vasco da Gama sails for India
1497

Martin Luther sets off Protestant Reformation
1517

Dutch East India Company founded
1602

AFRICA

Reign of Kongo King Afonso Mvemba a Nzinga
1506 — 1543

Dutch at Cape Town
1652

SOUTH AND EAST ASIA

Ming dynasty
◄————————————————————————— 1644

Reign of Akbar in Mughal India
1556 — 1605

Tokugawa Shogunate founded in Japan
1603

● **Matteo Ricci** (1552–1610) Italian Jesuit missionary who traveled to China in the sixteenth century. Tried unsuccessfully to reconcile Christianity with Confucianism and convert Ming scholar-officials.

(CL) **Primary Source:**
Journals: Matteo Ricci
This story about Jesuit missionaries in China provides an interesting look at the link between religion and politics in the early seventeenth century.

From Ricci's point of view, all that China lacked was religious truth. He understood that to communicate his Christian ideas he had to conform to the expectations of the "Philosophers," the scholar-officials who staffed the enormous imperial bureaucracy of Ming China. To this end, he learned Mandarin Chinese, studied Confucian texts, and dressed in silk garments to show a social status "equal of a Magistrate."

Italian by birth, Ricci joined the Jesuits, a Catholic religious order dedicated to "conversion of the Infidels." Because it was the Portuguese who pioneered the direct oceanic route from Europe to Asia, Ricci traveled from Rome to Lisbon to learn Portuguese and prepare for his mission. He then spent four years in India before traveling to China, where he lived from 1582 until his death in 1610. Meanwhile, other Jesuits were traveling to Japan, Brazil, Quebec, West Africa, and the Mississippi River Valley. The Jesuits were taking advantage of the new maritime connections established in the sixteenth century by the navigators who pioneered direct routes from Europe to the Americas, West Africa, the Indian Ocean, and East Asia.

While European mariners were a new presence in the Indian Ocean, they traveled on routes that had long been used by Asian and African merchants. In fact, the new maritime routes from Europe to Africa, the Indian Ocean, and East Asia first developed by Portuguese sailors were far less revolutionary than the connections between Europe, Africa, and the Americas that followed from the voyages of Christopher Columbus (see Chapter 15). The dominant powers in Asia remained land-based empires, such as Mughal (MOO-gahl) India and Ming China, rather than European overseas colonies. As Matteo Ricci's story shows, Europeans who traveled the maritime routes often operated on the margins of powerful Asian empires.

Still, the creation of more direct and sustained networks accelerated commercial and cultural interaction between Europe, Africa, and South and East Asia in the sixteenth and early seventeenth centuries, especially after the Dutch displaced the Portuguese as the main European players in the Indian Ocean. Following the maritime trade routes to China, Matteo Ricci became a key figure in the beginning of an ongoing "great encounter" between Europe and China.[2] Between 1400 and 1600, new and deepening economic linkages developed in the Indian Ocean, even as the Asian empires, such as India and China, became larger and more ambitious. In both Europe and Asia, major cultural and intellectual developments accompanied new encounters and connections.

Focus Questions

 What changes and continuities were associated with Portuguese and Dutch involvement in the Indian Ocean trade?

 What were the main political characteristics of the major South Asian and East Asian states? How was their development influenced by the new maritime connections of the sixteenth and early seventeenth centuries?

 How did religious and intellectual traditions of Eurasia change during this period, and what were the effects of encounters between them?

Maritime Trade Connections: Europe, the Indian Ocean, and Africa, 1500–1660

Unlike the Atlantic, the Indian Ocean had long served to connect rather than divide, facilitating trade between East Africa, the Persian Gulf, India, Southeast Asia, and China. The Portuguese added a new element to this network when their ships appeared in Indian Ocean waters in the early 1500s. Though their intention was to create an empire like that being constructed by Spain in the Americas, their political and military ambitions went largely unmet. The Dutch followed the Portuguese, bringing with them innovations in naval technology and business organization that stimulated the older oceanic trade networks while also building new ones.

Africa was connected to both the Atlantic and Indian Ocean systems. In East Africa the Portuguese merely inserted themselves into an existing commercial network along the East African coast. In West Africa, however, an entirely new oceanic trade began: the Atlantic slave trade.

Portugal's Entry into the Indian Ocean, 1498–1600

Henry the Navigator's exploration of the coasts and currents of the Atlantic Ocean culminated in 1488 when Bartholomew Dias and his crew rounded the southern tip of Africa at the Cape of Good Hope (see Chapter 15). These journeys had both economic and religious motives: in seeking an oceanic trade link with Asia, the Portuguese were trying to outflank Muslim intermediaries who controlled the land routes through western Asia and North Africa.

In 1497 the Portuguese explorer **Vasco da Gama** (1460–1524) sailed for India. The trip was not an easy one. After reaching the Cape of Good Hope, most of the crew wanted to return home and nearly mutinied. Sailing up the East African coast, da Gama hired a local pilot who used Arabic-language charts and navigational guides to guide the Portuguese from Africa to western India. One of these books boasted of the superiority of Arab knowledge: "We possess scientific books that give stellar altitudes. . . . [Europeans] have no science and no books, only the compass. . . . They admit we have a better knowledge of the sea and navigation and the wisdom of the stars." The Portuguese were sailing into well-charted waters, the same ones visited by Zheng He one hundred years earlier (see Chapter 15).

When they reached India, the Portuguese anchored their ships in well-established, cosmopolitan ports. India was at the center of the world's most extensive maritime trading system. In the western Indian Ocean, merchants transported East African gold, ivory, slaves, and timber to markets in southern Arabia, the Persian Gulf, and western India. Among the many goods exported from India along the same routes was highly valuable cotton cloth, often dyed by Indian craftsman specifically to appeal to customers in distant markets across the ocean.

On the east coast of India another set of maritime networks connected the Bay of Bengal and the markets of island and mainland Southeast Asia with Ming China. Muslim-ruled Malacca (mah-LAK-eh), which controlled trade through the straits between Sumatra and the Malaya Peninsula, had a population of over fifteen thousand traders from all over the Indian Ocean world. Here silk and sugar joined the long list of traded commodities. Cinnamon from the fabled "spice islands" was particularly precious. Whoever controlled the narrow straits at Malacca would profit handsomely from all this commercial activity.

● **Vasco da Gama** (1460–1524) Portuguese explorer who in 1497–1498 led the first European naval expedition to reach India by sailing around the Cape of Good Hope, laying the foundation for the Portuguese presence in the Indian Ocean in the century.

Economically, the Portuguese had almost nothing to offer: the first Indian king with whom they negotiated was insulted by the poor quality of their gifts. But what the Portuguese lacked in trade resources they made up for with military technology. Their ship-mounted cannon allowed them not only to blow their competitors out of the water but also to destroy the coastal defenses of political authorities at strategic points around the Indian Ocean. Seizing important trading centers from East Africa to Malacca, the Portuguese controlled a huge area after 1582. Their aggressive behavior earned them a widespread reputation as rough, greedy, and uncivilized.

In some cases the Portuguese redirected trade to profit themselves at the expense of previous merchant groups. For example, one of the main sources of gold for the Indian Ocean was the kingdom of Monomotapa in the interior of south-central Africa. For centuries the gold trade had been dominated by Swahili (swah-HEE-lee) merchants, African Muslims who lived on the coast. The Swahili town of Kilwa was ideally suited for this trade, since it was the furthest point south that mariners from India, Persia, and Arabia could safely reach and return in the same year using the monsoon winds. The Portuguese used their cannon to destroy the sea walls of Kilwa and tried to divert the gold southward through their settlement at Mozambique. The fact that they did so while flying militant crusader crosses on their sails did not endear them to local Muslim merchants and rulers.

But the degree of disruption the Portuguese caused at Kilwa was exceptional. More often they simply inserted themselves into existing commercial networks and used military force to extort payments from Asian and African rulers and traders. "What they set up was not an empire," argues one historian, "but a vast protection racket." Portuguese officials required that all ships trading in the ocean purchase a license, and if an Indian Ocean captain was found trading without one he risked Portuguese cannon fire; according to this historian, "the Portuguese were selling protection from violence which they themselves had created."[3]

Thailand (or Siam as it was then known) is a good barometer of both the extent and limitations of Portuguese power. Siam was a rising kingdom in the 1500s, struggling to establish its independence from Burma. The Portuguese were welcomed as trading partners and military allies. Access to European cannon and local adaptation of Portuguese styles of military fortification helped Siamese leaders centralize power and establish their independence. Siam later remained open to the Dutch and French and benefited greatly from the expansion of Indian Ocean trade. There were limits on European influence, however. Popular culture remained rooted in Thai adaptations of Hinduism and Buddhism. Asian traders, including Japanese, Chinese, and Malays, far outnumbered European ones. And trade with China, not with Europe, was central to Thailand's commercial life.

The biggest gap between Portuguese ambition and achievement was in religion. They made few converts to Christianity, while Islam continued to spread. The Portuguese did form an alliance with the Christian king of Ethiopia to help secure access to the Red Sea. In fact, in 1542 Cristovão da Gama, son of the navigator, died while leading Portuguese forces against a Muslim enemy of the Ethiopian king. But the Portuguese/Ethiopian alliance did not last. Members of the Orthodox branch of Christianity, the Ethiopians rejected Catholic teachings of the missionaries from Portugal. In the sixteenth century these African Christians were surrounded by expanding Muslim states. Here in the Red Sea region, as in South and Southeast Asia and all across the Indian Ocean world, it was Islam rather than Christianity that proved most attractive to new converts.

By the early seventeenth century the Portuguese position in the Indian Ocean was growing tenuous. Other powers, both European and Asian, were now using ship-based cannon and challenging Portuguese fortifications. In 1622, for example, the British allied themselves with Safavid Iran (see Chapter 17) to take the strategic port of Hormuz, at the mouth of the Persian Gulf, from the Portuguese, and in 1631 a local uprising drove the Portuguese from their strategic East African fortification of Fort Jesus. But the most potent challenge to Portuguese commercial profit came from Dutch merchants, who were, by the early seventeenth century, developing both more efficient business systems and more advanced shipping technologies.

Fort Jesus, Mombasa Still standing on the Kenyan coast today, Fort Jesus was built by the Portuguese in 1593. The fort was built not only to protect Portuguese trade interests in the Indian Ocean, but also to assert the Christian conquest of the Swahili-speaking Muslims of Mombasa. The Swahili word for a jail, *gereza*, derives from the Portuguese word for a church, *igreja*, indicating how the residents of Mombasa themselves saw Fort Jesus.
(© Adriane Van Zandbergen/ Alamy)

The Dutch East India Company, 1600–1660

Early Dutch trading ventures in Europe and the Atlantic were often very profitable, but merchants could be financially ruined if violent storms sank their ships or if pirates stole their cargo. To spread the risk they developed joint-stock companies, a new form of business enterprise based on the sale of shares to multiple owners. In addition to helping investors avoid bankruptcy if a single venture failed, the joint-stock system allowed men and women of small means to buy a few shares and reap a modest profit with little risk.

The development of joint-stock companies put the Dutch at the forefront of early modern commercial capitalism. The development of financial institutions

■ **A Portrait of a Dutch Merchant**
Although Dutch merchants were among the most successful traders in the seventeenth-century world, the austerity of their clothing reflected their Calvinist religious beliefs. Here a ship-owner and his family are shown with the trading vessels that provided them with great wealth. (Musée des Beaux-Arts, Valenciennes, France/Erich Lessing/Art Resource, NY)

such as banks, stock exchanges, and insurance companies increased the efficiency with which capital could be accumulated and invested. Rather than simply look for a single big windfall that would allow them to retire in comfort, investors now looked for more modest but regular gain through shrewd reinvestment of their profits. This dynamic of using profit for reinvestment and further profit was at the core of the new capitalist ethos associated with the bourgeoisie, the rising social group in Amsterdam and other urban areas of western Europe in the seventeenth century. The bourgeoisie based their social and economic power, and their political ambitions, on ownership of property rather than inherited titles.

Dutch culture reflected the rise of this commercially dynamic bourgeoisie. In many cultures trade was a low-status activity, it being assumed that a merchant could only be rich if he had made someone else poor. Seeking higher social status for their families, successful merchants in cultures as diverse as Spain and China would often use their assets to educate their sons to be "gentlemen" (in Spain) or members of the "literati" (in China). In Holland, by contrast, the leading citizens were all involved in trade, and commerce was seen as a noble calling.

• Dutch East India Company Founded in 1602 in Amsterdam, a merchant company chartered to exercise a monopoly on all Dutch trade in Asia. The company was the effective ruler of Dutch colonial possessions in the East Indies.

The greatest of the joint-stock companies, and the largest commercial enterprise of the seventeenth century, was the **Dutch East India Company,** founded by a group of Amsterdam merchants in 1602. The government of the Netherlands granted a charter to the company giving it a monopoly on Dutch trade with Asia. As a "chartered company," the Dutch East India Company was also granted administrative and military responsibilities overseen from their headquarters in Batavia in what became the Dutch East Indies (today's Indonesia). In the coming centuries other European powers would copy the Dutch model and use chartered companies of their own to extend their national interests.

Dutch capitalism was not based on free-market principles. The Dutch East India Company was a heavily armed corporate entity that maintained its monopoly through force. "Trade cannot be maintained without war," said one governor of the East India Company, "nor war without trade."[4] The Dutch thus repeated the Portuguese pattern of using military force in the Indian Ocean to secure commercial profit, while at the same time introducing modern business and administrative techniques that made them more efficient and effective.

The Portuguese were no match for Dutch competition. In addition to their commercial innovations, the Dutch had made major advances in ship design and construction. In 1641 they took Malacca, the strategic choke point for Southeast Asian trade, from the Portuguese. They became a power in South Asia after they took the island of Sri Lanka (south of India) in 1658. The Dutch presence in Africa was focused on the settlement of Cape Town, established at the far southern tip of the continent in 1652. The fort at Cape Town was built to supply passing Dutch ships with water, meat, brandy, and fruit. At the other end of this vast oceanic expanse, ships of the Dutch East India Company made annual calls at the Japanese port of Nagasaki.

The Dutch East India Company made huge profits, especially from the spice trade. Sometimes they violently intervened in local affairs to increase production, as on the Bandas Islands, where they removed most of the local population and replaced them with slaves drawn from East Africa, Japan, and India to grow nutmeg. The estimated rate of profit ranged from several hundred to several thousand percent. Investors back in Holland were delighted.

The Dutch were lucky that at this time the entire Indian Ocean economy was being stimulated by the introduction of large quantities of American silver being mined by the Spanish in South America and shipped across the Pacific. In fact, the increased supply of silver into China and the Indian Ocean trade networks in the late sixteenth and early seventeenth centuries probably had a greater effect on those economies than the activities of European merchants. Still, the Dutch, with their efficient business organization and shipping infrastructure, were in an ideal position to profit from this development.

Origins of the Atlantic Slave Trade, 1483–1660

When their ships first ventured south in the fifteenth century, the Portuguese had regarded Africa primarily as a source of gold to finance their Asian trade. Almost immediately, however, slaves became part of European-African commerce (see Chapter 15). During the sixteenth century the foundation was laid for what became the largest movement of people to that point in human history: the forced migration of Africans across the Atlantic Ocean.

The lucrative and expanding market for sugar played a central role in the process. The Portuguese brought knowledge of slave-produced sugar from the Mediterranean to the Atlantic and first used African slaves to grow sugar on islands off the West African coast. By the early seventeenth century sugar plantations in Brazil and the Caribbean were generating huge profits (see Chapter 19). Looking to supply labor for expanding sugar plantations, Portuguese merchants found that they could purchase slaves in the markets of West Africa.

The **Kongo kingdom** was one of many African societies that were destabilized by the Atlantic slave trade. When the Portuguese arrived at the capital city of Mbanza Kongo in 1483, they found a prosperous, well-organized kingdom with extensive markets in cloth and iron goods. The Kongo king and aristocracy were quite interested in Portuguese technology. Firearms, though of limited military use in a forest environment, made a large impact when used for ceremonial purposes. The stone buildings that the Europeans constructed amid the mud-brick and thatch structures of the capital city aroused curiosity as well. (See the feature "Visual Evidence: An Ivory Mask from Benin, West Africa.")

● **Kongo kingdom** West-central African kingdom whose king converted to Christianity in the early sixteenth century and established diplomatic relations with the Portuguese. Became an early source of slaves for the new Atlantic slave trade.

AN IVORY MASK FROM BENIN, WEST AFRICA

The kingdom of Benin already had a long history of political and cultural achievement before the arrival of the first Europeans in the sixteenth century. Descendents of Oduduwa (oh-doo-doo-wah), ancestor of all Yoruba kings, Benin's rulers, the *obas,* were associated with great spiritual powers. Starting in the fourteenth century Beninese artists, organized into a guild by the king, began producing magnificent brass sculptures of royalty. Using a sophisticated "lost wax" technique, they made a beeswax model, covered it with bronze, molded it with clay, and then fired the sculpture, melting the wax and allowing the metal to flow into the open cavity. Their achievement was not only technical but also artistic. The Benin bronzes are known for their naturalism, a quality that made them highly attractive to European collectors. In fact, in 1897 the British colonial government looted over a thousand of these invaluable pieces, and the fight to return them to West Africa continues.

The bronze used in these sculptures was imported from the Mediterranean and was therefore extremely expensive. More often than lost-wax casting, Beninese artists carved masks and wall decorations directly from wood and ivory, sometimes incorporating cowrie shells imported from the Indian Ocean. This ivory mask, made around 1520, depicts Idia (ee-DEE-ah), the Queen Mother of Oba Esigie (eh-see-GEE-ay). Like the Benin bronzes, this ivory mask conveys a powerful sense of the individuality of its subject. The Portuguese were present in West Africa by this time and had allied with King Esigie and helped him fight off an enemy invasion. Their role in West African politics was still quite marginal, however, as indicated by the minor representation of European figures at the top.

A century and a half after this mask was made, a Dutch visitor was impressed with the capital city:

> The houses in this town stand in good order, one close and evenly placed with its neighbor, just as the houses in Holland stand. . . . The king's court is very great. It is built around many square-shaped yards. These yards have surrounding galleries where guards are always placed. I myself went into the court far enough to pass through four great yards like this, and yet wherever I looked I could still see gate after gate which opened into other yards.*

Earlier, in the sixteenth century, the pepper trade was so profitable that Benin's *obas* (kings) had closed the slave market. By the time the Dutch visitor came to Benin in 1688, however, slavery had become a major item of commerce, as elsewhere in West Africa. Nevertheless, Benin's artistic tradition continues until today.

---

*Olfert Dapper, *Description of Benin* (Madison: University of Wisconsin Press, 1998), p. 40.

QUESTION FOR ANALYSIS

 From the way they are represented on this mask, what might we infer about the extent of Portuguese influence on the artists of Benin?

In Benin, as in many African societies, the Queen Mother was a pivotal figure in the king's council, and he often relied on her to gain a consensus of opinion among clan leaders.

The Queen Mother had a special role in representing the interests and opinions of women.

The oba of Benin, King Esigie, is said to have worn this mask on his hip at a commemoration ceremony for Queen Idia.

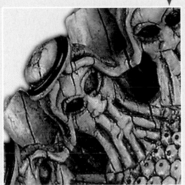

The figures on top represent the Portuguese who allied with King Esigie and helped him thwart an enemy invasion. These Portuguese figures resemble the mudfish often found in Beninese sculptures. Like mudfish, the Portuguese could travel both in the water and on land.

(© Trustees of the British Museum)

459

Portuguese missionaries in Kongo found a royal family and aristocracy open to the message of Christianity. A baptized Christian, King Afonso Mvemba a Nzinga (uh-fahn-so mm-VEM-bah ah nn-ZING-ah) (r. 1506–1543), renamed his capital San Salvador, sent his son Enrique to study in Lisbon, and exchanged diplomatic envoys with both Portugal and the Vatican. It seemed that this would be an alliance of equals. Afonso, aided by the Portuguese, undertook wars of conquest that added additional territory to the Kongo kingdom.

Afonso's wars also had the side effect of stimulating the slave trade. In West Africa, as in many parts of the world, captives taken during war were in a precarious position. War captives might simply be killed, but more often they were exchanged, redeemed for a ransom, or kept as dependent workers. Into this traditional system came the new labor demands of the Atlantic plantation system. As demand for slaves increased, so did the supply.

King Afonso complained to his "brother king" in Portugal that some of the European Christians had lost interest in spreading the faith and were enslaving and exporting Afonso's own subjects:

> In our Kingdoms there is another great inconvenience which is of little service to God, and this is that many of our people, keenly desirous as they are of the wares and things of your Kingdoms, which are brought here by your people, and in order to satisfy their voracious appetite, seize many of our people, freed and exempt men . . . and so great, Sir, is the corruption and licentiousness that our country is being completely depopulated. . . . That is why we beg of your Highness to help and assist us in this matter . . . because it is our will that in these Kingdoms there should not be any trade of slaves nor outlet for them.[5]

Foreign goods and foreign traders had distorted the traditional market in slaves, which had previously been a byproduct of warfare, into an economic activity in its own right. Afonso's complaints fell on deaf ears.

As sugar production surged, the demand for slaves increased decade by decade. Not all parts of Africa were affected. On the east coast, Swahili merchants continued to participate in the Indian Ocean trade without engaging in the rising slave trade of the Atlantic. Most Central Africans had as yet little or no connection to the commercial and cultural influences of either the Atlantic or Indian Ocean networks. Yet over time the rise of the Atlantic slave trade would fundamentally alter the terms of Africans' interactions with the wider world (see Chapter 19).

The Politics of Empire in Southern and Eastern Asia, 1500–1660

In the course of Matteo Ricci's long journey he came in contact with a great variety of cultural and political systems. The largest and most powerful were Mughal India and Ming China.

Mughal India was a young and rising state in sixteenth-century South Asia with an economy stimulated by internal trade and expanding Indian Ocean commerce. Great political skill was needed to keep the vast Mughal realms at peace, however. The prosperity of South Asia depended on the extent to which India's Muslim rulers could maintain a stable political structure in the midst of great religious and ethnic diversity.

In the sixteenth century Ming China was the most populous and most productive society in the world. As we saw in the introduction to this chapter, Matteo Ricci was impressed with the order and good governance maintained by the Chinese emperors and their extensive official networks. But even while the Ming Dynasty earned Ricci's admiration in the early seventeenth century, it was about to begin a downward spiral that would end in 1644 in loss of power and a change of dynasty.

Since political leaders in the neighboring East Asian states of Vietnam and Korea had long emulated Chinese systems and philosophies of statecraft, Ming officials recognized these states as "civilized." Japan, while also influenced by China in many ways, was by Ming standards disordered and militaristic in this period, though it did achieve a more stable political system in the seventeenth century.

The Rise of Mughal India, 1526–1627

During Matteo Ricci's four-year stay in western India, the **Mughal dynasty,** the dominant power in South Asia, was at the height of its glory under its greatest leader, **Emperor Akbar** (r. 1556–1605). Building on the military achievements of his grandfather, who had swept into northern India from Afghanistan in the early sixteenth century, Akbar's armies controlled most of the Indian subcontinent. Ruling 100 million subjects from his northern capital of Delhi, the "Great Mughal" was one of the most powerful men in the world.

The Mughal state was well positioned to take advantage of expanding Indian Ocean trade. It licensed imperial mints that struck hundreds of millions of gold, silver, and copper coins of uniform value and trusted purity. The influx of silver from the Americas starting in the sixteenth century stimulated market exchanges. Dyed cotton textiles were a major export, along with sugar, pepper, diamonds, and other luxury goods.

Agriculture was the ultimate basis of Mughal wealth and power, providing 90 percent of the tax income that paid for Mughal armies and the ceremonial pomp of the court at Delhi. By insisting that taxes be paid in currency, Mughal officials forced villagers into the money economy, selling surplus produce for the coins needed to pay their taxes. State investment in roads helped traders move goods to market. The Mughals also supported movement of populations into previously underutilized lands by granting tax-exempt status to new settlements. The eastern half of Bengal (today's Bangladesh) was transformed from a lightly populated land of tropical forests into a densely populated rice-producing region.

The tax collection system also had political implications. In many parts of India a pre-Mughal aristocracy was used to collecting and retaining revenue from local production. The Mughals intruded on their prerogatives by sending tax clerks out to the provinces, surveying the lands, and diverting much of the revenue to Delhi. But they also confirmed the old aristocracy's rights to 10 percent of the local revenue and thus assured their loyalty.

Finding ways to bring such existing Indian authorities into Mughal structures of governance was the principal political challenge faced by Akbar and his successors. People may be conquered by the sword, but more stable forms of administration are usually necessary if conquest is to turn into long-term rule. In this case, the challenge was that the Islamic faith of the Mughal rulers differed from the Hindu beliefs of most of their subjects.

●**Mughal dynasty** (1526–1857) During the height of their power in the sixteenth and seventeenth centuries, Mughal emperors controlled most of the Indian subcontinent from their capital at Delhi.

●**Emperor Akbar** (r. 1556–1605) The most powerful of the Mughal emperors, Akbar pursued a policy of toleration toward the Hindu majority and presided over a cosmopolitan court.

Conflict at Ayodhya

Peace and harmony have not always characterized relations between Muslims and Hindus in India. While the nation has a secular constitution, some Hindu nationalists feel that it is and should be a Hindu nation. The large Muslim minority has felt threatened by the growth of this Hindu nationalism in recent years.

A flashpoint of conflict is the town of Ayodhya in northern India. According to legend, it was the birthplace of the Hindu god Rama and the site of a great Hindu temple. Hindu nationalists claim that the temple was torn down by an early Mughal ruler and replaced with a mosque. After Indian independence in 1947, Muslims were offended after some Hindu statues were smuggled in; to avoid conflict, the government fenced off the site and strictly limited access to the mosque. Then in 1992 a group of militant Hindu nationalists tore down the fence and destroyed the mosque. Thousands were killed in the rioting that followed.

One of the groups involved in the destruction of the mosque, the Bharatiya Janata Party (BJP),

was the leader of a coalition of parties that won the 1998 national elections. Though the BJP had promised to rebuild the Temple of Rama, it took no action and kept the site closed off. In 2002 the conflict escalated once again when a train carrying Hindu activists returning to western India from Ayodhya was set on fire, allegedly by Muslims, resulting in fifty deaths. In the retaliatory violence that followed over one thousand people, mainly Muslim, were killed.

Although nationalists continue to agitate and raise funds for a rebuilt temple, archaeologists have turned up no firm evidence that a temple to Rama ever stood on the site. Partially for that reason, a stone-cutting project begun in anticipation of building a new temple was halted in 2007 because of lack of donations. Still, the Ayodhya controversy continues to strain the tradition of peaceful religious coexistence established by Akbar, as well as the tradition of secular government enshrined in India's constitution.

Primary Source:
Akbarnama
These selections from the history of the house of Akbar offer a glimpse inside the policies and religious outlook of the Mughal emperor.

● **Nur Jahan** (1577–1645) Mughal empress who dominated politics during the reign of her husband Jahangir. By patronizing the arts and architecture and by favoring Persian styles, she had a lasting cultural influence on north India.

Akbar's policy was one of toleration and inclusion. He canceled the special tax that Islamic law allows Muslim rulers to collect from nonbelievers and granted Hindu communities the right to follow their own social and legal customs. Hindu *maharajahs* were incorporated into the Mughal administrative system at the imperial and regional levels just as rural aristocrats were at the local level. For their part, the Hindu population was accustomed to a social system in which people paid little attention to matters outside their own caste groups. Thus the ruling Muslims were simply another caste with their own rituals and beliefs. (See the feature "World History in Today's World: Conflict at Ayodhya.")

Akbar's policy of religious tolerance was continued by his successor Jahangir (r. 1605–1627) and his remarkable wife **Nur Jahan** (1577–1645). When Jahangir was faced with regional rebellions, Nur Jahan (noor ja-HAN), an intelligent and skilled politician, took charge and kept Mughal power intact. Since women were secluded in the *zezana,* or women's quarters, she could not appear at court in person. Instead she issued government decrees through trusted family members. She took a special interest in women's affairs, such as by donating land and dowries for orphan girls. Originally from Iran, Nur Jahan had a great cultural influence through her patronage of Persian-influenced art and architecture. She built many of the most beautiful mosques and gardens in north India.

Nur Jahan was also interested in commerce and owned a fleet of ships that took religious pilgrims and trade goods to Mecca. Even more than Akbar, her policies facilitated both domestic and foreign trade. Though she dictated policy from behind the closed doors of the zezana, Nur Jahan's favorable attitude toward trade and entrepreneurship had a strong influence on the wider world. Indian merchants, sailors, bankers, and shipbuilders were important participants in Indian Ocean markets, and the cosmopolitan ports of Mughal India teemed with visitors from Europe, Africa, Arabia, and Southeast Asia (see Map 16.1). But there was little Chinese presence in the Indian Ocean, and no followthrough to the fifteenth-century voyages of Zheng He (see Chapter 15). Unlike the Mughal rulers of India, the leaders of Ming China saw maritime trade more as a threat than as an opportunity.

The Apogee and Decline of Ming China, 1500–1644

By 1500 the **Ming dynasty** in China was at the height of its power and prestige. In 1368 the Ming had replaced the Mongol Yuan dynasty, and the early Ming rulers were highly conscious of the need to restore Confucian virtue after years of what they saw as "barbarian" rule. Like earlier Chinese dynasties, the Ming defined their country as the "Middle Kingdom" and called the emperor the "Son of Heaven." China was at the center of the world, and the emperor ruled with the "Mandate of Heaven."

The emperor's residence in the Forbidden City in Beijing (bay-JING), constructed during the early Ming period and still standing today, was at the center of a Confucian social order based on strict hierarchical relationships. The emperor stood at the top of the social hierarchy, and everyone owed him unquestioning obedience. For his part, the emperor was expected to emulate the benevolent behavior of the greatest Confucian sages, seeking the best interests of those dependent on him. The junior official owed obeisance to the senior one, the younger brother to the older one, the wife to the husband, and so on throughout society.

Hierarchy governed foreign relations as well. Ming officials respected those societies that had most successfully emulated Chinese political, intellectual, and cultural models, such as Korea and Vietnam. Japan and the societies of Inner Asia were usually thought of as "inner barbarians," peoples touched by Chinese civilization but still uncouth. All the rest of the world's peoples were regarded as "outer barbarians." From a Ming standpoint, the only conceivable relationship between any of these other kingdoms and China was a tributary one. Foreign kings were expected to send annual missions bearing tribute in acknowledgement of China's pre-eminent position.

Confucians believed that if such stable hierarchies of obeisance and benevolence were maintained, then the people would prosper. And in the early sixteenth century peace and prosperity were the norm in Ming China. The network of canals and irrigation works on which so much of the empire's trade and agriculture depended were refurbished and extended. Most important for trade and governance was the Grand Canal connecting the political and military capital Beijing with the productive Yangzi River Valley and fertile rice-producing regions further south. Public granaries were maintained as a hedge against famine. New food crops, including high-yield strains of rice from Southeast Asia and crops like maize, peanuts, and potatoes from the Americas, improved the health of the population, which had reached about 120 million people by the time of Matteo Ricci's arrival in 1582.

The **examination system,** based on the Confucian classics, helped ensure that the extensive Ming bureaucracy was staffed by competent officials at the local, county, and imperial levels. Years of study and tremendous powers of recall were

● **Ming dynasty** (1368–1644) Chinese imperial dynasty in power during the travels of Matteo Ricci. At its height during the fifteenth century, by 1610 the Ming dynasty was showing signs of the troubles that would lead to its overthrow.

● **examination system** Chinese system for choosing officials for positions in the Ming imperial bureaucracy. Candidates needed to pass one or more examinations that increased in difficulty for higher positions.

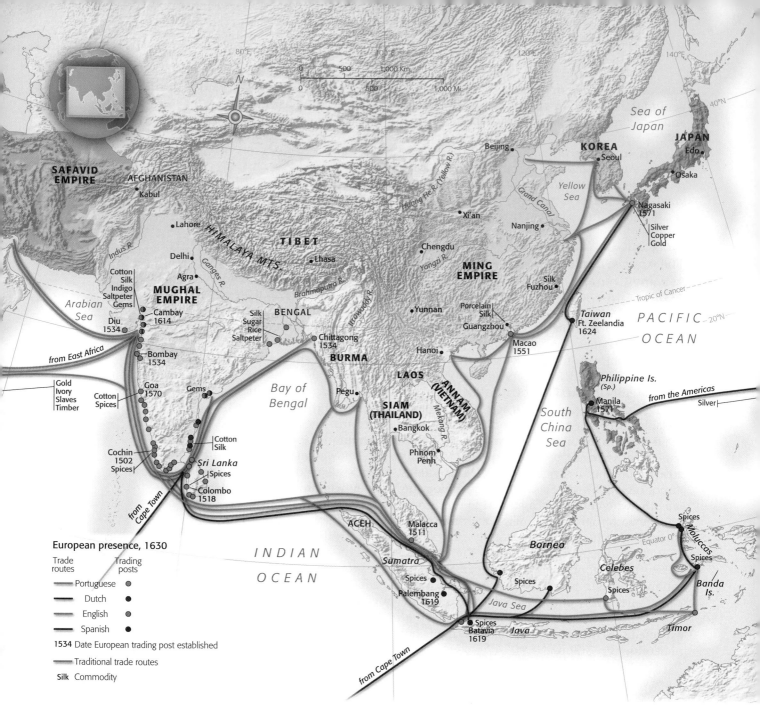

Map labels (north to south, west to east):

SAFAVID EMPIRE
AFGHANISTAN
Kabul
Lahore
TIBET
HIMALAYA MTS.
Indus R.
Delhi
Agra
MUGHAL EMPIRE
Ganges R.
Cotton Silk Indigo Saltpeter Gems
Arabian Sea
Cambay 1614
Diu 1534
Bombay 1534
Goa 1570
from East Africa
Gold Ivory Slaves Timber
Cotton Spices
Gems
Brahmaputra R.
BENGAL
Silk Sugar Rice Saltpeter
Chittagong 1534
BURMA
Irrawaddy R.
Cochin 1502
Spices
Sri Lanka
Spices
Colombo 1518
from Cape Town

Beijing
Seoul
KOREA
Sea of Japan
JAPAN
Edo
Osaka
Nagasaki 1571
Silver Copper Gold
Huang He R. (Yellow R.)
Grand Canal
Yellow Sea
Xi'an
Nanjing
Chengdu
Lhasa
Yangzi R.
MING EMPIRE
Yunnan
Silk Fuzhou
Porcelain Silk
Guangzhou
Macao 1551
Hanoi
Taiwan Ft. Zeelandia 1624
Tropic of Cancer
PACIFIC OCEAN
20°N
Philippine Is. (Sp.)
Manila 1571
from the Americas
Silver
South China Sea
Pegu
LAOS
SIAM (THAILAND)
ANNAM (VIETNAM)
Bangkok
Mekong R.
Phnom Penh
Bay of Bengal
INDIAN OCEAN
ACEH
Malacca 1511
Sumatra
Spices
Palembang 1619
Borneo
Celebes
Spices
Spices
Equator 0°
Moluccas
Spices
Spices
Banda Is.
Timor
Java Sea
Spices
Batavia 1619
Java
from Cape Town

European presence, 1630

Trade routes	Trading posts
Portuguese	●
Dutch	●
English	●
Spanish	●

1534 Date European trading post established

Traditional trade routes

Silk Commodity

CL Interactive Map

🌐 MAP 16.1

Maritime Trade in the Eastern Indian Ocean and East Asia

By 1630 the Dutch had overtaken the Portuguese in Indian Ocean trade, the French and English were becoming more active, and Spanish silver from American mines was stimulating trade across South, Southeast, and East Asia. Dutch ships passed through Cape Town in South Africa bearing Asian and African cargo, such as valuable spices, for European markets. Still, the dominant powers in Asia remained land-based empires such as the Mughal Empire in India and the Ming Empire in China. Traditional trade routes controlled by local sailors and merchants—between Japan and China, between the South China Sea and the Bay of Bengal, and between western India, the Persian Gulf, and East Africa—were also growing in volume in the seventeenth century.

necessary to succeed on the highest and most difficult levels of the civil service examination. With a hierarchy of well-educated officials supervised by dynamic emperors, the early Ming efficiently carried out such basic tasks of government as the collection of taxes and maintenance of public order.

The elaborate and expensive Ming bureaucracy required an efficient system of tax collections. In 1571 Ming officials decided that only payments in silver would be acceptable, generating a surge in global demand for silver. While Japan was the traditional source of silver for China, its mines could not keep up with demand. But at that time massive new silver discoveries in the Americas, combined with technological advances that increased the yield of silver from ore, made huge quantities of silver available to China (see Chapter 17). The Spanish city of Manila in the Philippines became the destination for the Manila Galleons, an annual shipment of silver from Mexico. Thus, silver was central to an emerging trans-Pacific trade, which was from the beginning connected to the Indian Ocean network. In the late sixteenth century this flow of silver between the Americas and Asia was helping to lay the foundation of a global economy.

Ming officials saw the development of these more intensive commercial networks as a mixed blessing. On the one hand, the flow of silver was essential to the functioning of the Chinese economy and the taxation it made possible. On the other hand, Ming officials regarded the sea with suspicion. It was unpredictable and difficult to control, the realm of "pirates" like the Japanese and Portuguese. Unlike the Mughal rulers of India, therefore, Ming officials tried to limit and control seaborne commerce. Their efforts met only limited success because the momentum of foreign trade driven by the demand for silver had become too powerful.

In this emerging world economy, reliance on foreign silver supplies made the Ming economy vulnerable to distant economic shocks. While the influx of silver stimulated Chinese economic growth, it also caused inflation. Rising prices caused distress to people less well poised to benefit from commercial expansion. Even more

■ **The Destitute of Ming China**   While acknowledging the power of the Ming dynasty and other great kingdoms and empires of the past, we might also remember that even amidst wealth and luxury, poverty was the fate of many. These scenes of the poor of Suzhou were painted in 1516 by the artist Zhou Chen as "a warning and admonition to the world." (The Cleveland Museum of Art [1964.94])

severe was the effect of declining silver supplies on the world market after 1620. By that date economic contraction was contributing to an accelerating crisis in Ming governance.

The decline of the Ming is associated with the **Wanli Emperor** (r. 1573–1620), whose apathetic attitude toward his duties did much to undermine the achievements of his predecessors. Within the walls of the Forbidden City personalities and petty jealousies became more important as the influence of uneducated court eunuchs rose at the expense of scholar-officials. Without imperial oversight, corruption increased: gifts could determine the outcome of court cases, grain intended for famine relief was sold on the market, and irrigation works went untended. Bandits vexed merchants on the roads, and local peasant uprisings became more common. When Matteo Ricci was finally granted permission to enter the Forbidden City and performed the ritual *kowtow,* prostrating himself with his forehead on the ground, he did so before a vacant Dragon Throne. The Wanli Emperor was inaccessible, remaining deep in the recesses of the Forbidden City.

Matteo Ricci, in his tribute to Ming governance cited in the chapter opening, appears to have failed to notice the decay that was setting in below the impressive façade of the Wanli Emperor's court. In 1644 northern invaders from Manchuria breached the walls of Beijing and drove the Ming from power (see Chapter 20).

• **Wanli Emperor** (r. 1573–1620) Ming emperor at the time of Matteo Ricci's mission to China. Vain and extravagant, he hastened the decline of the Ming dynasty through lack of attention to policy and the promotion of incompetent officials.

Tradition and Innovation: Korea, Vietnam, and Japan, 1500–1650

The societies most strongly connected to Chinese civilization in the early modern period were Korea, Vietnam, and, more loosely, Japan. The Chosŏn (choh-SAN) dynasty of Korea, who closely followed the Ming imperial model, established one of the world's most stable political systems, ruling the Korean peninsula from 1392 until the early twentieth century. The capital at Seoul (sole) was home to a Confucian academy that trained young men for examinations that led to social prominence and political power.

While early modern Korea was not as commercially dynamic as Ming China, it did benefit from a remarkable series of innovations undertaken by the **Emperor Sejong** (r. 1418–1450). Before his time, learning to read and write required years of training in the complexities of Chinese script. Then in 1446, Sejong (SAY-jung) brought together a group of scholars to devise a new phonetic script based on the Korean language. This distinctive *han'gul* (HAHN-goor) writing system, still in use today, enabled many more Koreans to read and write. Emperor Sejong supported projects to write the history of the country in the new Korean script and also to translate key Buddhist texts. He also patronized printers who were developing a more efficient technology to produce large books more cheaply. Korea became one of the world's most literate societies.

The Vietnamese were also strongly influenced by China, but their leaders, having repulsed fifteenth-century Ming armies, were protective of their political independence. In 1428 the general who took power in Vietnam after defeating a Ming army gave his name to the new **Lê dynasty.** One story relates that General Lê (lee) sent a gift of cattle to his retreating Ming counterpart, as if to say that the invasion would not stop Vietnam from pursuing positive relations with China. Indeed, Lê monarchs closely copied Chinese imperial models. Confucianism rose in importance in traditionally Buddhist Vietnam as scholar-officials gained influence at court. Military expeditions expanded the size and strength of the Vietnamese state, and

• **Emperor Sejong** (r. 1418–1450) Korean emperor of the Chosŏn dynasty, credited with the creation of the *han'gul* script for the Korean language.

• **Lê dynasty** (1428–1788) The longest-ruling Vietnamese dynasty. Drawing on Confucian principles, its rulers increased the size and strength of the Vietnamese state and promoted agricultural productivity.

agrarian reforms led to greater equality in landholding and greater productivity in agriculture.

Japan lay further outside the orbit of Chinese civilization than either Korea or Vietnam. Unlike in Ming China, political power was decentralized during Japan's Ashikaga (ah-shee-KAH-gah) Shogunate (1336–1568), and the Japanese emperor, unlike his Chinese, Korean and Vietnamese counterparts, was a ritual figure with no real authority. The greatest political power was the *shogun,* a supreme military ruler who acted independently of the imperial court. But the Ashikaga shoguns themselves had little control over the *daimyo* (DIE-mee-oh), barons who ruled their own rural domains. As each daimyo had an army of *samurai* (SAH-moo-rye) military retainers, incessant warfare spread chaos through the islands.

Ashikaga Japan was a land of contrasts. While the daimyo lords engaged in violent competition for land and power, they also acted as benefactors of Buddhist monasteries, which promoted spiritual reflection. The samurai warriors, with their strict *bushido* code of honor and loyalty, were also practitioners of the Zen school of Buddhism, with its emphasis on mental discipline and acute awareness. Flower arranging and the intricate refinement of the tea ceremony were also highly developed, peaceful counterpoints to the ceaseless military competition of the daimyo.

In the late sixteenth century several Japanese lords aspired to replace the Ashikaga family; the most ambitious was **Toyotomi Hideyoshi** (r. 1585–1598), whose plans included not only the consolidation of power on the Japanese islands but also conquest of the mainland. In 1592, as Matteo Ricci was journeying in southern China, Hideyoshi's forces attacked Korea with an army of 200,000 soldiers. A statue of Admiral Yi in central Seoul still commemorates his use of heavily fortified "turtle ships," armed with multiple cannon and wooden planks shielding their decks, to defend Korea against the Japanese attack.

● **Toyotomi Hideyoshi** (r. 1585–1598)　A *daimyo* (baron) who aspired to unify Japan under his own rule. His attempts to conquer Korea and China failed, and members of the competing Tokugawa family became shoguns and unified the islands.

In a power struggle following Hideyoshi's death, the Tokugawa (TOH-koo-GAH-wah) clan emerged victorious. After 1603, the **Tokugawa Shogunate** centralized power by restraining independence of the daimyo, forcing them to spend half the year in the shogun's new capital of Edo (today's Tokyo). Compared with the highly centralized imperial model of Korea, which persisted even after the fall of the Ming, political power in Japan was still diffuse, with many regional barons controlling their own domains. But the Tokugawa system brought a long-term stability that made possible economic and demographic growth. In the seventeenth century, as market exchanges became central to the Japanese economy (see Chapter 20), Japanese cities such as Osaka and Nagasaki emerged as vibrant commercial centers.

Despite this increased unity, some daimyo formed diplomatic and trade alliances with Christian missionaries, undercutting the centralizing ambitions of the Tokugawa court at Edo. As a result, Jesuit missionaries attracted many converts, and the shoguns became deeply suspicious of both European and Japanese Christians. After 1614 they outlawed the foreign faith; hundreds of Japanese Christians were killed, some by crucifixion, when they refused to recant their faith. Apart from an annual Dutch trade mission confined to an island in the port of Nagasaki, no Christians were allowed to enter the country. Japanese trade with China and Korea, however, continued to flourish.

● Eurasian Intellectual and Religious Encounters, 1500–1620

In the early modern Afro-Eurasian world, increased maritime trade networks also led to increased cultural interactions. Intellectual ferment in this period was often associated with new religious ideas. In western Europe the Protestant Reformation divided Christians over basic matters of faith. Matteo Ricci himself was a representative of the Catholic Reformation, which sought to re-energize Roman Catholicism. In Mughal India, many people converted to Islam and the new faith of Sikhism was founded, while the emperor himself promoted his own "Divine Faith" to reconcile diverse religious traditions. In China, Matteo Ricci attempted to convince Ming scholar-officials that Christianity was compatible with the oldest and purest versions of Confucianism.

Challenges to Catholicism, 1517–1620

While Renaissance humanism had led to significant artistic and intellectual achievement in western Europe (see Chapter 15), it coincided with increasing corruption in the Catholic Church. For example, popes and bishops raised money for prestigious building projects, such as Saint Peter's Basilica in Rome, by selling "indulgences," certificates that, according to church authorities, had the power to liberate souls from purgatory and allow them to enter into heaven. Thus the cultural richness of the Roman Church was underwritten by practices that some European Christians viewed as mere corruption and worldliness.

One of these, a cleric named **Martin Luther** (1483–1546), was infuriated. Surely, he argued, salvation could not be purchased; only God could determine the spiritual condition of a human soul. Luther made his challenge public in 1517 and refused to stand down when brought before church and civil authorities. Excommunicated by the church, he began to lead his own religious services, and the Protestant Reformation was under way. The Christian church, already divided since the eleventh century between its Eastern Orthodox and Roman Catholic branches, was now divided within western Europe itself (see Map 16.2).

As a significant minority of sixteenth-century western Europeans left Catholicism, they developed a variety of alternative church structures, rituals, and beliefs. Lutherans, as the followers of Martin Luther were called, downgraded the importance of intermediaries between the individual and God and therefore challenged the whole edifice of the Catholic priestly hierarchy. Taking advantage of increased literacy and the wider availability of printed Bibles after the fifteenth-century development of movable-type printing, Luther argued that individuals should read their own Bibles and not rely on priests to interpret God's word for them. He translated the Bible into the German language, making the scriptures available for the first time to the many who could read German but not Latin. In the seventeenth century the Protestant Reformation led to significant political violence as some leaders of western European states defended the reformers while others took up arms to defend Roman Catholicism (see Chapter 17).

There were no Protestants in Matteo Ricci's hometown in central Italy, where the pope held both civil and religious authority. In secure Catholic areas like this the inquisition, a church bureaucracy devoted to the suppression of heresy, was always on guard to squelch "heretical" ideas such as those of Martin Luther. But even here the impact of the Reformation was profound, for the Catholic Church was shaken out of its complacency and launched a response known as the **Catholic Reformation,** or Counter-Reformation.

A major focus of the Catholic Reformation was more rigorous training of priests to avoid the abuses that had left the church open to Protestant criticism. As a member of the Jesuit order, or Society of Jesus, Ricci was especially trained in the debating skills needed to fend off Protestant theological challenges. The Jesuits were one of several new Catholic orders developed to confront the Protestant challenge and, especially in the Jesuit case, to take advantage of the new maritime routes to spread their faith around the world.

Another challenge to Catholic belief that developed during Ricci's lifetime was the "new science" associated with his fellow Italian the great scientist **Galileo Galilei** (1564–1642). Catholic theologians had reconciled faith and reason by incorporating classical Greek thinkers, especially Aristotle, into church teachings. The work of Galileo (gal-uh-LAY-oh) struck at the heart of that intellectual system by challenging the authority of Aristotle. Carefully measuring the acceleration of balls rolled down inclined planes, he overturned Aristotle's law of inertia by arguing that a body in motion would stay in motion unless acted upon by some external force, an insight that would later prove essential to new understandings of planetary motion. Pointing his telescope toward the heavens, Galileo discovered things the church could not explain: spots on the sun, craters on the moon, and other indications that the heavens were not a place of absolute, unchanging perfection.

Galileo became convinced of the validity of the heliocentric theory first proposed in 1543 by the Polish astronomer Nicolaus Copernicus, which placed the sun rather than the earth at the center of the solar system. Further support for the Copernican system was offered by the German mathematician Johannes Kepler, who argued that elliptical rather than circular orbits best explained planetary motion,

CL Primary Source:
Table Talk
Read Martin Luther in his own words, speaking out forcefully and candidly—and sometimes with humor—against Catholic institutions.

● **Catholic Reformation**
Reform movement in the Catholic Church, also called the Counter-Reformation, that developed in response to the Protestant Reformation. The church clarified church doctrines and instituted a program for better training of priests.

CL Primary Source:
Letter to the Grand Duchess Christina
Read Galileo's passionate defense of his scientific research against those who would condemn it as un-Christian.

● **Galileo Galilei**
(1564–1642) Italian scientist who provided evidence to support the heliocentric theory, challenging church doctrine and the authority of Aristotle. He was forced to recant his position by the inquisition, but his theories were vindicated during the Scientific Revolution.

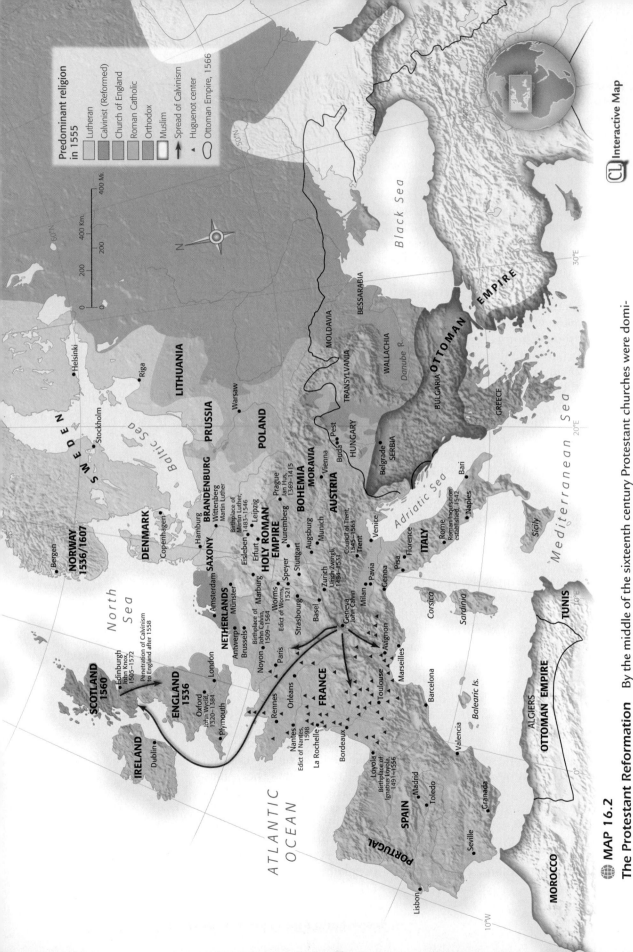

Predominant religion in 1555
- Lutheran
- Calvinist (Reformed)
- Church of England
- Roman Catholic
- Orthodox
- Muslim

↑ Spread of Calvinism
▲ Huguenot center
⬭ Ottoman Empire, 1566

Interactive Map

● **MAP 16.2**

The Protestant Reformation By the middle of the sixteenth century Protestant churches were dominant in England, Scotland, the Netherlands, Switzerland, and Scandinavia. German principalities were divided between Protestants and Catholics. Catholicism remained dominant across most of southern Europe, though Protestants formed a significant minority in France. The religious landscape was especially complex in southeastern Europe, where, under Ottoman authority, there were substantial communities of Catholics, Protestants, Orthodox Christians, and Muslims.

a theory contrary to both classical tradition and church teachings. Church authorities saw the "new science" as a direct challenge to Christianity; the heliocentric theory, they argued, contradicted the book of Genesis by displacing the earth from its central place in God's creation. The church put Galileo on trial and forced him to recant his support for the heliocentric theory.

The ferment of the new ideas arising from the Protestant Reformation and the "new science" helped sharpen Matteo Ricci's intellectual training and prepare him for his travels. In India he took part in lively religious and philosophical debates that were valuable preparation for his missionary work in China.

Islam, Sikhism, and Akbar's "Divine Faith," 1500–1605

The Mughal capital of Delhi was a cosmopolitan place. In addition to bringing Hindus and Muslims together, Akbar attracted to his court scholars, artists, and officials from Iran, Afghanistan, and Central Asia. Mughal India proved a fertile environment for artistic growth as Persian, Turkish, and Indian influences flowed together. The Taj Mahal, a "love poem in marble" built by Akbar's grandson as a memorial to his wife, is the best-known example of the Persian-influenced architecture inspired by Nur Jahan and other Mughal leaders.

Akbar was keenly interested in religion, and he routinely invited leaders from various religious traditions to debate at his court. In 1579, the year after Ricci arrived at Goa, a diplomatic embassy arrived from the Great Mughal requesting that Catholic missionaries come to Delhi. "We hope for nothing less than the conversion of all India," wrote Ricci. Two missionaries went to Delhi, bringing a richly produced, lavishly illustrated, and very costly Bible as a gift for the emperor. Although the emperor did not convert, his interest in the Jesuit mission was characteristic of his open-minded exploration of diverse faiths.

During this time Sufism was also attracting new converts. In addition to obeying the Muslim laws of submission, Sufis were often loyal to personal religious leaders who claimed to have special means of approaching God. The mystical Sufis often used rhythmic motion and special chants to create a meditative state in which they could feel God's presence. Some Muslim scholars, especially those who stressed the more legalistic aspects of

■ **Akbar with Representatives of Various Religions at His Court**   For years, the Mughal Emperor Akbar hosted weekly conversations among scholars and priests of numerous religions, including the Jesuits seen here on the left. Akbar sponsored the translation of varied religious texts, including the Christian Bible, into Persian, even though he himself was illiterate. When criticized by some Muslim scholars for his patronage of Hindu arts and his openness to other religious traditions, Akbar is said to have replied, "God loves beauty."   (The Chester Beatty Library, Dublin)

Islam, looked with suspicion on the more emotional Sufi forms of religious devotion. Akbar brought both the legal scholars and the Sufi mystics to his court and listened intently to their debates.

Akbar also brought Jews, Hindus, and representatives of other faiths to Delhi. Having encountered so many different spiritual traditions, he announced his own adherence to a "Divine Faith" that he said both included and transcended them all:

> O God, in every temple I see people that seek Thee; in every language I hear spoken, people praise Thee; if it be a mosque, people murmur in prayer; if it be a Christian church they ring the bell for love of Thee . . . it is Thou whom I seek from temple to temple.[6]

Akbar extended to the new faith of Sikhism the same tolerance he had granted more established religions. While Akbar's "Divine Faith" never spread beyond the Mughal court and disappeared after his own death, Sikhism grew into a successful new faith community. The first Sikh (sick) spiritual leader (*guru*) was Nanak (1469–1539). Through conversations with a wide range of religious thinkers, Nanak became convinced that Hinduism, despite its outward appearance of polytheism, had at its core a belief in a single God, and that this made Hinduism and Islam compatible. His reconciliation of the two faiths emphasized the equality of all believers, and he rejected the Hindu caste system.

Although Nanak emphasized peace and harmony, the Sikh community developed a formidable military tradition when a later Mughal emperor canceled Akbar's policy of tolerance and had their guru beheaded (see Chapter 20). The dead leader's son reorganized the Sikhs into an "army of the pure" with distinctive dress and appearance: unshaved beards, uncut hair beneath a turban, and a military style of dress with a sword prominently displayed. Ironically, Nanak's attempt to reconcile Hinduism and Islam led to the formation of a separatist religious community.

Hinduism was also undergoing important changes and reforms in the early modern period. The epic story of the *Ramayana,* formerly read only by priests trained in the ancient Sanskrit language, was retold in 1575 by a prominent poet using the commonly spoken Hindi language, making this story of the ancient king, a manifestation of the god Vishnu, more accessible. This development was part of a broader development of new forms of Hindu devotion that de-emphasized the role of Brahmin priests. The new version of the *Ramayana* was an achievement parallel to the translation of the Bible into languages like English and German and to the new availability of Buddhist texts in the Korean *han'gul* script. In all of these cases religious inquiry was not limited to kings and philosophers but could be found at all levels of society.

Ricci in China: Catholicism Meets Neo-Confucianism, 1582–1610

Ming China was less religiously diverse than Mughal India, with Buddhism as the empire's majority faith. In fact, when Ricci first arrived in Ming China, he adopted the dress of a Buddhist priest, with a shaved head, a beard, and flowing robes. Soon he came to understand, however, that affiliating himself with Buddhism would not carry much weight with the most prominent people in Chinese society, the scholar-officials who manifested the power of the emperor. Many of these *literati* looked down on the poorly educated Buddhist clergy. Ricci subsequently changed his appearance and habits to appeal to this prestigious class of individuals. His plan was to convert China through its leading Confucian scholars, from the top down.

Confucian scholars emphasized education as the main route to self-cultivation. While most of the emperor's subjects remained nonliterate peasant cultivators, young children from more privileged households were taught to read from a young age, often by memorizing a list of one thousand different characters that taught Confucian virtues like hard work and respect for elders and teachers. After they had mastered such basics, boys had to memorize the classic texts of Confucianism, collections of poems, and histories of past times that usually focused on the virtues of ancient sages.

In theory, any young man could take the annual examinations and, if successful, become an imperial official. In reality, the cost of private tutors meant that children of the elite held an advantage. Still, the Ming system was based on merit: wealth and status could not purchase high office, and even the privileged had to undergo years of intensive study.

Though women were barred from taking the examinations, the Ming emphasis on education did contribute to the spread of female literacy. Foreign observers noted how many girls were able to read and write. However, education for girls reinforced Confucian views of gender. Rather than reading histories of sages and virtuous officials, girls usually read stories about women who submitted to their parents when they were young, obeyed their husbands once they were married, and listened to their sons when they became widowed. Singled out for special praise were widows who demonstrated eternal loyalty to their husbands by declining to be remarried. Chinese girls were thereby indoctrinated into the Confucian ideal of strict gender hierarchy.

Matteo Ricci paid careful attention to debates between advocates of various schools of Confucianism as he built up an argument for the compatibility of Confucianism and Christianity. At this time the Neo-Confucian philosophy of Wang Yangming (1472–1529) was especially influential. While other Confucians had emphasized close observation of the external world as the path of the sage, Wang stressed self-reflection, arguing that "everybody, from the infant in swaddling clothes to the old, is in full possession of . . . innate knowledge." Ricci accused Wang's Neo-Confucian followers of distorting Confucianism. By returning to the original works of the ancient sages, Ricci said, the Chinese literati would discover that one could convert to Christianity while retaining the ethical and philosophical traditions of Confucius.

Once his language skills were sufficiently developed, Ricci took advantage of a favorite Ming pastime to share his views. Scholar-officials would often invite interesting speakers to a banquet and, after dinner, hold philosophical debates. For many in the audience Ricci's well-known ability to instantly memorize and repeat long lists of information, and even repeat them backwards, would have been of greater interest than his views on Confucian philosophy and Christian theology. It was a highly relevant skill in a society where difficult exams were the main path to power and status. But while his hosts might have been entertained by his arguments, few were persuaded by them.

Ricci also impressed his hosts with examples of European art and technology, especially printed books, paintings, clocks, and maps. Lavishly illustrated and beautifully bound books contrasted with the austerity of Chinese woodblock prints. Chinese artists adapted European techniques of landscape painting, and Ming astronomers were impressed by European telescopes and the precision with

Christianity in China

Are Christianity and Confucianism compatible? Matteo Ricci thought so, though other Jesuits disagreed. How did Chinese officials and intellectuals address this question?

At first, Ming toleration of Christianity continued during the Qing dynasty (see Chapter 20), as an edict of the Emperor Kangxi in 1692 proclaimed: "The Europeans . . . commit no crimes, and their doctrine has nothing in common with that of the false sects in the empire, nor has it any tendency to excite sedition." The emperor ordered that Christian churches be protected and open to worshipers. In 1715, however, the church reversed Ricci's policy by declaring that Confucian rites were incompatible with Christianity. Emperor Kangxi was furious: "To judge from this proclamation, their religion is no different from other small, bigoted sects of Buddhism." In 1721 he banned Christians from preaching in his empire.

Earlier, in the seventeenth century, Confucian intellectuals had given assessments of the Catholic faith, examples of which are given below.

Source: Jacques Gernet, *China and the Christian Impact: A Conflict of Cultures,* (New York: Cambridge University Press, 1986), pp. 39–40, 53, 82, 107, 108, 120, 159, 161.

Chinese Commentaries on Christianity

1) [The Jesuits] are extremely intelligent. Their studies concern astronomy, the calendar, medicine and mathematics; their customs are compounded of loyalty, good faith, constancy and integrity; their skill is wonderful. Truly they have the means to win minds. . . . The only trouble is that it is a pity that they speak of a Master of Heaven, an incorrect and distasteful term which leads them into nonsense. . . . Our Confucianism has never held that Heaven had a mother or a bodily form, and it has never spoken of events that are supposed to have occurred before and after his birth. Is it not true that herein lies the difference between our Confucianism and their doctrine?

2) Compared with the contents of the Buddhist books, what [the Christians] say is straightforward and full of substance. The principal idea comes down to respecting the Master of Heaven, leading a life that conforms with morality, controlling one's desires and studying with zeal. . . . Nevertheless . . . what they say about paradise and hell appears to differ barely at all from what the Buddhists maintain and they go even further than the latter when it comes to extravagance and nonsense.

3) [The Jesuits] openly take issue with the false ideas of Buddhism. . . . Meanwhile, where they do take issue with Confucianism, they do not dare to open their mouths wide for they wish to use the cap and gown of the literate elite to introduce their doctrine even into Court, so as to spread their poison more effectively.

4) The superiority of Western teaching lies in their calculations; their inferiority lies in their veneration of a Master of Heaven of a kind to upset men's minds. . . . When they require people to consider the Master of Heaven as their closest relative and to abandon their fathers and mothers and place their sovereign [king] in second place, giving the direction of the state to those who spread the doctrine of the Master of Heaven, this entails an unprecedented infringement on the most constant rules. How could their doctrine possibly be admissible in China?

5) [The Ming emperor] sacrifices to Heaven and to Earth; the princes sacrifice to the mountains and rivers within the domains; holders of high office sacrifice to the ancestral temple of the founder of their lineage; gentlemen and ordinary individuals sacrifice to the tables of their own [immediate] ancestors. . . . In this way . . . there is an order in the sacrifices that cannot be upset. To suggest that each person should revere a single Master of Heaven and represent Heaven by means of statues before which one prays each day . . . is it not to profane Heaven by making unseemly requests?

6) In their kingdom they recognize two sovereigns. One is the political sovereign [the king] the other is the doctrinal sovereign [the pope]. . . . The former reigns by right of succession and passes on his responsibilities to his descendents. He nevertheless depends upon the doctrinal sovereign, to whom he must offer gifts and tokens of tribute. . . . It comes down to having two suns in the sky, two masters in a single kingdom. . . . What audacity it is on the part of these calamitous Barbarians who would like to upset the [political and moral] unity of China by introducing the Barbarian concept of the two sovereigns!

7) We Confucians follow a level and unified path. Confucius used to say . . . "To study realities of the most humble kind in order to raise oneself to the comprehension of the highest matters, what is that if not 'serving heaven?'" . . . To abandon all this in order to rally to this Jesus who died nailed to a cross . . . to prostrate oneself before him and pray with zeal, imploring his supernatural aid, that would be madness. And to go so far as to enter darkened halls, wash oneself with holy water and wear amulets about one's person, all that resembles the vicious practices of witchcraft.

8) In the case of Jesus there is not a single [miracle] that is comparable [to those of the ancient sages]. Healing the sick and raising the dead are things that can be done by great magicians, not actions worthy of one who is supposed to have created Heaven, Earth and the Ten Thousand Beings. If one considers those to be exploits, how is it that he did not arrange for people never to be sick again and never to die? That *would* have increased his merit.

9) Our father is the one who engendered us, our mother the one who raised us. Filial piety consists solely in loving our parents. . . . Even when one of our parents behaves in a tyrannical fashion, we must try to reason with him or her. Even if a sovereign behaves in an unjust way, we must try to get him to return to human sentiments. How could one justify criticizing one's parents or resisting one's sovereign on the grounds of filial piety toward the Master of Heaven?

QUESTIONS FOR ANALYSIS

▶ In which documents is Christianity judged to be incompatible with China's social and political traditions? How is that incompatibility described?

▶ Matteo Ricci was critical toward Buddhism. In these documents, where and how do Chinese authors equate Christianity with Buddhism?

▶ Do these critiques seem to be based on a deep or superficial understanding of seventeenth-century Christianity?

which the Jesuits could predict such events as eclipses. Late-sixteenth-century European clocks, while not very reliable by later standards, were much more accurate than the water clocks used by the Chinese. And Ricci's world map, locating the "western barbarians" for the first time in relation to the "Middle Kingdom," was such a success that Chinese artisans were employed to print reproductions.

For Ricci, however, mnemonic tricks, maps, and clocks were only a means to convert his audience to Christianity. Criticizing both Buddhism and Neo-Confucianism, Ricci emphasized those aspects of the Western tradition that appealed most to Confucian intellectuals: its moral and ethical dimensions rather than its character as a revealed religion. For example, after learning that Chinese scholars were usually upset to hear about the suffering and death of Jesus, he largely avoided that central aspect of Christianity. (See the feature "Movement of Ideas: Christianity in China.")

Ricci's most influential work published in Chinese was *The True Meaning of the Lord of Heaven*. Composed with the aid of the small number of Chinese Christian converts, it is a dialogue between a "Chinese Scholar" and a "Western Scholar." In the following passage Ricci criticizes Buddhism and argues for the compatibility of Confucianism and Christianity:

> *Chinese Scholar:* The Buddha taught that the visible world emerges from "voidness" and made "voidness" the end of all effort. The Confucians say: "In the processes of *Yi* there exists the Supreme Ultimate" and therefore make "existence" the basic principle [of all things] and "sincerity" the subject of the study of self-cultivation. I wonder who, in your revered view, is correct?

> *Western Scholar:* The "voidness" taught by the Buddha [is] totally at variance with the doctrine concerning the Lord of Heaven [i.e., Christianity], and it is therefore abundantly clear that [it does] not merit esteem. When it comes to the "existence" and "sincerity" of the Confucians, however . . . they would seem to be close to the truth.[7]

Such arguments did not convince many, but at least the Jesuits in China, unlike their brethren in Japan, were accepted as representatives of a legitimate school of philosophy.

Some Jesuits and Vatican officials felt that *The True Meaning of the Lord of Heaven* and other attempts by Ricci to reconcile Christianity and Confucianism went too far. For example, Ricci argued that veneration of ancestors was compatible with Christianity and the biblical command to "honor your father and your mother." Less flexible church authorities felt that Chinese ancestor rites were pagan and should be rejected. Ricci knew that such a rigid interpretation of cultural practice would limit the appeal of Christianity among potential converts, who would be ostracized by family and friends if they abandoned their household shrines. Although Matteo Ricci made no more than a handful of converts, he played an important role in world history as the first major figure in the ongoing "great encounter" between Europe and China.

Chapter Review

Download the MP3 audio file of the Chapter Review and listen to it on the go.

The new maritime route from Europe to Asia that took Matteo Ricci from Europe through the Indian Ocean to Ming China, while not as revolutionary as the one that connected Europe with the Americas, stimulated important new economic, political, and cultural connections across early modern Afro-Eurasia. Among the important outcomes were the beginnings of the Atlantic slave trade, increased interaction between the great land-based Asian empires and European states, and competition among European states for dominance in Asian trade.

 What changes and continuities were associated with Portuguese and Dutch involvement in the Indian Ocean trade?

Even as the Portuguese and Dutch intruded on the Indian Ocean, there was significant continuity with earlier patterns of trade. While the Portuguese did manage to control strategic coastal locations, they did not create an overarching imperial structure for the Indian Ocean. In West Africa they had a significant effect on the Kongo kingdom and helped lay the foundations of the Atlantic slave trade, and they displaced some Swahili rulers along the Indian Ocean coast and became involved in the Christian kingdom of Ethiopia. But most Africans remained unaffected by such Portuguese initiatives. During the seventeenth century, the Dutch East India Company brought deeper changes, especially in commerce. Significant quantities of goods, such as Indian textiles, Chinese porcelain, and Southeast Asian spices, were now carried to Europe, often purchased with American silver. In fact, the huge inflow of silver was a greater stimulus to the Asian economies ringing the Indian Ocean than European merchant activity itself.

While the Dutch were a formidable new military presence, their direct influence, like that of the Portuguese, was limited to the few islands and coastal fortifications under their control. African and Asian rulers were still the key to politics in places like the Swahili city-states of East Africa, the Persian Gulf and Bay of Bengal, and mainland Southeast Asia.

KEY TERMS

Matteo Ricci (450)
Vasco da Gama (453)
Dutch East India Company (456)
Kongo kingdom (457)
Mughal dynasty (461)
Emperor Akbar (461)
Nur Jahan (462)
Ming dynasty (463)
examination system (463)
Wanli Emperor (466)
Emperor Sejong (466)
Lê dynasty (466)
Toyotomi Hideyoshi (467)
Tokugawa Shogunate (468)
Martin Luther (468)
Catholic Reformation (469)
Galileo Galilei (469)

What were the main political characteristics of the major South Asian and East Asian states? How was their development influenced by the new maritime connections of the sixteenth and early seventeenth centuries?

The dominant political players in East and South Asia were land-based empires with leaders who paid little attention to maritime affairs. Ming China, the most populous and most powerful, had ended its state-sponsored oceanic voyages even while benefiting from the increased tempo of maritime trade. Agriculture was the principal foundation on which the complex Ming imperial bureaucracy rested. By the time of Matteo Ricci's arrival in Beijing late in the sixteenth century, however, political and economic crises were about to undermine the Ming dynasty, and in 1644 the Forbidden City fell to northern invaders.

Korea, Vietnam, and Japan derived at least part of their political culture from China. The Korean state modeled its imperial system most closely on Ming China, and Vietnam, even after fending off a Ming military incursion, emulated the Chinese imperial system and sent tribute to the Forbidden City. Sixteenth-century Japan, by contrast, was a disordered land with little central authority. In the seventeenth century, the Tokugawa Shogunate consolidated power and brought greater stability that produced a surge in commercial activity and artistic innovation.

Like Ming China, Mughal India benefited from increased Indian Ocean commerce even as its wealth and power were primarily derived from taxation on agriculture. Under Akbar, India possessed military might, economic productivity, and cultural creativity. With a Muslim ruling class, a Hindu majority, and a royal court that looked to Persia, Turkey, and Central Asia for artistic stimulation, the artistic and administrative achievements of the Mughal Empire reflected the culture of tolerance promoted by Akbar.

 How did religious and intellectual traditions of Eurasia change during this period, and what were the effects of encounters between them?

Akbar's exploration of various religious traditions was characteristic of a Eurasian intellectual climate in which cultural encounters were becoming more frequent. His open-minded attitude was not universal, however. In western Europe differences between Protestants and Catholics increasingly led to violence and warfare (see Chapter 17), and in India Akbar's policy of tolerance would be reversed by his successors. Most Chinese literati were ethnocentric in their belief that Chinese traditions such as Confucianism gave them all the guidance they needed, and Ricci gained few converts. European clocks, paintings, telescopes, and maps impressed them, but mostly as novelties. Nevertheless, Ricci was usually received in a respectful manner and helped lay the foundations for ongoing encounters between China and Europe.

For Further Reference

Brook, Timothy. *The Confusions of Pleasure: Commerce and Culture in Ming China*. Berkeley: University of California Press, 1998.

Chaudhuri, K. N. *Asia Before Europe: Economy and Civilization of the Indian Ocean from the Rise of Islam to 1750*. Cambridge: Cambridge University Press, 1990.

Dale, Stephen Frederick. *Indian Merchants and Eurasian Trade, 1600–1750*. Cambridge: Cambridge University Press, 1994.

Hilton, Anne. *The Kingdom of Kongo*. Oxford: Clarendon Press, 1985.

Pearson, Michael. *The Indian Ocean*. New York: Routledge, 2007.

Richards, John. *The Mughal Empire*. New York: Cambridge University Press, 1996.

Spence, Jonathan. *The Memory Palace of Matteo Ricci*. New York: Viking Penguin, 1984.

Subrahmanyam, Sanjay. *The Portuguese Empire in Asia, 1500–1700*. New York: Longman, 1993.

Websites

Jesuit History
(http://www.sjweb.info/jesuits/jeshistory.cfm). A website of historical material on the Society of Jesus, maintained by the Catholic religious order.

WEB RESOURCES

Pronunciation Guide

Interactive Maps

MAP 16.1 Maritime Trade in the Eastern Indian Ocean and East Asia

MAP 16.2 The Protestant Reformation

Primary Sources

Chapter Objectives

ACE Multiple-Choice Quiz

Flashcards

Portuguese and Dutch Colonial History
(http://www.colonialvoyage.com/). Links to historical materials and contemporary legacies of Portuguese and Dutch colonialism.

World History Matters
(http://worldhistorymatters.org/). A useful portal to primary sources on world history, including Asian empires, organized chronologically and geographically, with a dedicated section on women in world history.

NOTES

Chapter 1

1. James C. Chatters, *Ancient Encounters: Kennewick Man and the First Americans* (New York: Simon and Schuster, 2001), pp. 20–21.
2. John Noble Wilford, "In Ancient Skulls from Ethiopia, Familiar Faces," *New York Times,* June 12, 2003, pp. A1, A8.
3. John Noble Wilford, "Report Reignites Feud over 'Little People' as Separate Species," *New York Times,* August 22, 2006, p. F2.
4. Thomas D. Dillehay, *The Settlement of the Americas: A New Prehistory* (New York: Basic Books, 2000), p. 167.
5. E. James Dixon, *Bones, Boats, and Bison* (Albuquerque: University of New Mexico Press, 1999), pp. 87 (Table 3.1), 100 (Table 4.1), 111–115 (Table 5.1).
6. Tom Koppel, *Lost World: Rewriting Prehistory—How New Science Is Tracing America's Ice Age Mariners* (New York: Atria Books, 2003), p. 110.
7. William H. Stiebing, *Ancient Near Eastern History and Culture* (New York: Longman, 2003), p. 13.

Chapter 2

1. Benjamin R. Foster, *The Epic of Gilgamesh* (New York: W. W. Norton, 2001), pp. 8–9 (Enkidu's encounter with Shamhat); 6–7 (description of Uruk); 11 (Enkidu's dream).
2. Martha T. Roth, *Law Collections from Mesopotamia and Asia Major* (Atlanta, Ga.: Scholars Press, 1997), pp. 76–81 (false accusation of murder); 121 (eye-for-an-eye clause).
3. Samuel Noah Kramer, *History Begins at Sumer: Thirty-nine Firsts in Recorded History* (Philadelphia: University of Pennsylvania Press, 1981), p. 58.
4. This book uses the chronology given in Douglas J. Brewer and Emily Teeter, *Egypt and the Egyptians* (New York: Cambridge University Press, 1999).
5. Anthony P. Sakovich, "Counting the Stones: How Many Blocks Comprise Khufu's Pyramid?" *KMT: A Modern Journal of Ancient Egypt* 13, no. 3 (Fall 2002): 53–57.
6. William H. Stiebing, Jr., *Ancient Near Eastern History and Culture* (New York: Longman, 2003), p. 127.
7. J. Pritchard, *Ancient Near Eastern Texts Relating to the Old Testament* (Princeton: Princeton University Press, 1955), p. 34.
8. Ann Hyland, "Chariots and Cavalry," in *The Seventy Great Inventions of the Ancient World,* ed. Brian M. Fagan (London: Thames & Hudson, 2004), p. 196.
9. Lionel Casson, *Travel in the Ancient World* (Baltimore: Johns Hopkins University Press, 1994), p. 39; for a recent critique of the nature of the text and its date, see also Benjamin Sass, "Wenamun and His Levant—1075 BC or 925 BC?" *Ägypten und Levante* 12 (2001): 247–255.
10. William G. Dever, *Did God Have a Wife? Archaeology and Folk Religion in Ancient Israel* (Grand Rapids, Mich.: William B. Eerdmans, 2005), p. 13.
11. Ibid., pp. 64–69.
12. Stiebing, p. 240.
13. William G. Dever, *What Did the Biblical Writers Know and When Did They Know It? What Archaeology Can Tell Us About the Reality of Ancient Israel* (Grand Rapids, Mich.: William B. Eerdmans , 2001), p. 127.
14. Ibid., p. 118.

Chapter 3

1. "13th Major Rock Edict," in *Aśoka and the Decline of the Mauryas,* ed. Romila Thapar (Delhi: Oxford University Press, 1973), Appendix 5, pp. 255–256. Translation slightly modified.
2. Jonathan Mark Kenoyer, "Uncovering the Keys to the Lost Indus Cities," *Scientific American* 289, no.1 (July 2003): 67–75.
3. Jonathan Mark Kenoyer, *Ancient Cities of the Indus Valley Civilization* (Karachi: Oxford University Press, 1998), pp. 63 (the great bath); 70–71 (the writing system).
4. J. P. Mallory and D. Q. Adams, *Encyclopedia of Indo-European Culture* (Chicago: Fitzroy Dearborn Publishers, 1997), p. 306.
5. Richard H. Davis, "Introduction: A Brief History of Religions in India," in *Religions of Asia in Practice: An Anthology,* ed. Donald S. Lopez, Jr. (Princeton: Princeton University Press, 2002), pp. 19–30.
6. Wendy Doniger O'Flaherty, *The Rig Veda* (New York: Penguin Books, 1981), pp. 235, "Human Diversity: A Hymn to Soma" (about different occupations); 31, "The Hymn of Man."
7. J. W. McCrindle, *Ancient India as Described by Megasthenes and Arrian* (London: Trübner, 1877), pp. 68 (city's size); 87 (tasks of government officials and those who take care of foreigners); 40 (the philosophers); 105 (the Buddhists); 44 (caste rules about marriage); 43 (rank of government officials).
8. "11th Major Rock Edict," in *Aśoka and the Decline of the Mauryas,* Appendix 5, pp. 254–255 (gift of dharma); 256 (sending of envoys); 253 (meetings); 252 (officers of dharma); 253 (officials reporting to him).

Chapter 4

1. Martin Kern, *The Stele Inscriptions of Ch'in Shih-huang: Text and Ritual in Early Chinese Imperial Representation* (New Haven: American Oriental Society, 2000), pp. 18–23.
2. *The Analects of Confucius,* trans. Simon Leys (New York: W. W. Norton, 1997), p. 50.
3. *Chuang Tzu: Basic Writings,* trans. Burton Watson (New York: Columbia University Press, 1964), pp. 41 (Perfect Man); 45 (butterfly); 115 (talking skull).
4. *Tao Te Ching: The Classic Book of Integrity and the Way,* trans. Victor Mair (New York: Bantam Books, 1990), p. 54.
5. Kern, pp. 19–20 (superb and shining); 13 (way of filial piety); 17 (creating regulations).
6. Denis Twitchett and Michael Loewe, eds., *The Cambridge History of China,* vol. 1, *The Ch'in and Han Empires*

221 B.C.– A.D. 220 (New York: Cambridge University Press, 1986), p. 61.

7. A. F. P. Hulsewé, *Remnants of Ch'in Law: An Annotated Translation of the Ch'in Legal and Administrative Rules of the Third Century B.C., Discovered in Yün-meng Prefecture, Hu-pei Province, in 1975* (Leiden: E. J. Brill, 1985), p. 205.
8. Hugh Scogin, "Between Heaven and Man: Contract and the State in Han Dynasty China," *Southern California Law Review* 63, no. 5 (1990): 1386.
9. Nancy Lee Swann, *Pan Chao: Foremost Woman Scholar of China* (New York: American Historical Association, 1932), pp. 84–85.

Chapter 5

1. http://www.pbs.org/wgbh/nova/maya/copa_transcript .html#08. For David Stuart's latest views about this text, see David Stuart, "The Beginnings of the Copán Dynasty: A Review of the Hieroglyphic and Historical Evidence," in *Understanding Early Classic Copán,* ed. Ellen E. Bell et al. (Philadelphia: University of Pennsylvania Museum of Archaeology and Anthropology, 2004), pp. 215–248; David Stuart, "'The Arrival of Strangers': Teotihuacan and Tollan in Classic Maya History," in *Mesoamerica's Classic Heritage: From Teotihuacan to the Aztecs,* ed. David Carrasco (Boulder: University Press of Colorado, 2000), pp. 465–513. To date, Professor Stuart has not published a full translation of this difficult text.
2. Scholars today use the word *Maya* to refer to the people and *Mayan* for the language they spoke.
3. Michael D. Coe, *The Maya,* 6th ed. (New York: Thames and Hudson, 1999), p. 196.
4. John Flenley and Paul Bahn, *The Enigmas of Easter Island: Island on the Edge* (New York: Oxford University Press, 2002), pp. 104 (the number of moai); 125–127 (van Tilburg's experiments).
5. K. R. Howe, *The Quest for Origins: Who First Discovered and Settled the Pacific Islands* (Honolulu: University of Hawai'i Press, 2003), p. 180.

Chapter 6

1. Herodotus, *The Histories,* trans. Aubrey De Sélincourt, further rev. ed. (New York: Penguin Books, 1954, 1996), pp. 188–189, Book III: passage 82 ("Constitutional Debate"); 57, I: 137 (truth-telling); 140, I: 57 (Zoroastrian burial practices); 399, VII: 83 (the Immortals); 193, III: 96 (melting of silver); 193, III: 97 (Ethiopian payments); 1, I: 0 (purpose of the book); 228–229, IV: 42 (circumnavigation of Africa by the Phoenicians with place names updated); 363, VI: 116 (casualties at Marathon); 402 403, VII: 99 (Artemisia as a commander).
2. M. Aperghis, "Population—Production—Taxation—Coinage: A Model for the Seleukid Economy," in *Hellenistic Economies,* ed. Z. H. Archibald et al. (London: Routledge, 2001), pp. 69–102, 77 (population estimate). Reference supplied by Christopher Tuplin (University of Liverpool).
3. Lionel Casson, *Travel in the Ancient World* (Baltimore: Johns Hopkins University Press, 1974), pp. 53–54;

estimates speed of the couriers and translates Herodotus VIII: 98.
4. Richard N. Frye, *The Heritage of Persia* (New York: World Publishing Company, 1963), p. 85.
5. Josef Wiesehöfer, *Ancient Persia from 550 BC to 650 AD,* trans. Azizeh Azodi (New York: I. B. Tauris, 2001), pp. 63, citing Herodotus III: 89 (about the differences among three Achaemenid rulers); 69 (order from Persepolis); 197 (Ammianus Marcellinus about the Parthian cavalry); 165 (Shapur I's inscription).
6. M. Cary and E. H. Warmington, *The Ancient Explorers* (London: Methuen, 1929), pp. 47–48.
7. Aeschylus, *The Persians,* trans. Anthony J. Podlecki (Englewood Cliffs: Prentice-Hall, 1970), pp. 49–50; l. 251–255.
8. Email, dated June 23, 2005, from Kevin van Bladel, University of Southern California, summarizing the unpublished research of Shaul Shaked.

Chapter 7

1. Polybius, *The Rise of the Roman Empire,* trans. Ian Scott-Kilvert (New York: Penguin Books, 1979), pp. 41–43 (the importance of the Roman empire); 221–222 (Polybius's trip to the Alps); 227–228 (difficult conditions in the Alps); 427–428 (composition of Hannibal's army); 271 (appearance of the army); 332–333 (punishment in camp); 528–529 (meeting with Scipio Aemilianus).
2. Plutarch, *Roman Lives: A Selection of Eight Roman Lives,* trans. Robin Waterfield (New York: Oxford University Press, 1999), pp. 83, 115.
3. "Slavery," in *The Oxford Companion to Classical Civilization,* ed. Simon Hornblower and Antony Sparforth (New York: Oxford University Press, 1998), p. 671.
4. "Population, Roman," in *The Oxford Companion,* pp. 561–562.
5. Betty Radice, *The Letters of the Younger Pliny* (New York: Penguin, 1963), pp. 166–168 (about Pompeii); 126–127 (about his wife).
6. "Population, Roman," in *The Oxford Companion,* pp. 561–562.
7. Morton Smith, *Jesus the Magician* (New York: Harper and Row, 1978), p. 45. Chapter 4 of this book, "What the Outsiders Said—Evidence Outside the Gospels," provides an excellent introduction to non-gospel sources about Jesus. Only one nonchurch source from the first century refers to Jesus: the Jewish historian Josephus, writing sometime in 90 C.E., mentions "the brother of Jesus, the so-called Christ, James was his name." In addition to the sources discussed by Morton Smith, some scholars believe that the gospel of Thomas contains earlier versions of Jesus' sayings than those recorded in the canonical gospels, while others contend that they are later.
8. *Documents of the Christian Church,* ed. Henry Bettenson (New York: Oxford University Press, 1966), p. 35.
9. *Egeria: Diary of a Pilgrimage,* trans. George E. Gingras (New York: Newman Press, 1970), pp. 75–76.
10. Peter Brown, *Augustine of Hippo: A Biography* (London: Faber and Faber Limited, 2000), p. 430.

Chapter 8

1. Huili, *Da Ci'en si sanzang fashi zhuan* (Beijing: Zhonghua shuju, 2000), p. 20. In doing my translation, I consulted *A Biography of the Tripitaka Master of the Great Ci'en Monastery of the Great Tang Dynasty,* trans. Li Rongxi (San Francisco: Numata Center for Buddhist Translation and Research, 1995), pp. 31–32, which contains a full description of the meeting.
2. Richard H. Davis, "Introduction: A Brief History of Religions in India," in *Religions of Asia in Practice: An Anthology,* ed. Donald S. Lopez, Jr. (Princeton: Princeton University Press, 2002), p. 5.
3. Robert Kaplan, *The Nothing That Is: A Natural History of Zero* (New York: Oxford University Press, 1999), p. 41.
4. *A Biography of the Tripitaka Master,* p. 58.
5. *Si-yu-ki: Buddhist Records of the Western World Translated from the Chinese of Hiuen Tsiang (A.D. 629),* trans. Samuel Beal (Delhi: Motilal Banarsidass, 1981; reprint of 1882 original), p. 82.
6. Anthony Reid, "Introduction: A Time and a Place," in *Southeast Asia in the Early Modern Era: Trade, Power, and Belief* (Ithaca: Cornell University Press, 1993), p. 3.
7. Valerie Hansen, *The Open Empire: A History of China to 1600* (New York: W.W. Norton, 2000), p. 159.
8. *Lives of the Nuns: Biographies of Chinese Buddhist Nuns from the Fourth to Sixth Centuries: A Translation of the Pi-ch'iu-ni chuan, compiled by Shih Pao-ch'ang,* trans. Kathryn Ann Tsai (Honolulu: University of Hawaii Press, 1994), pp. 20–21.
9. Hansen, p. 182.
10. Ilyon, *Samguk Yusa: The Legends and History of the Three Kingdoms of Ancient Korea,* trans. Tae-Hung Ha and Grafton K. Mintz (Seoul: Yonsei University Press, 1972), p. 188.

Chapter 9

1. Nabia Abbott, *Two Queens of Baghdad: Mother and Wife of Harun al-Rashid* (London: Al Saqi Books, 1986, reprint of 1946 original), p. 26; citing Jahiz (pseud.), *Kitab al-Mahasin wa Al-Addad,* ed. van Vloten (Leiden: E. J. Brill, 1898), pp. 232–233.
2. Charles Issawi, "The Area and Population of the Arab Empire: An Essay in Speculation," in *The Islamic Middle East, 700–1900: Studies in Economic and Social History,* ed. A. L. Udovitch (Princeton: Darwin Press, 1981), pp. 375–396; estimated population on p. 392.
3. Jacob Lassner, *The Topography of Baghdad in the Early Middle Ages* (Detroit: Wayne State University Press, 1970), p. 127, citing the Islamic writer Ya'qubi.
4. Lunde, Paul, and Caroline Stone, trans., *The Meadows of Gold: The Abbasids by Mas'udi* (New York: Kegan Paul International, 1989), p. 388. See an alternate translation in Dmitri Gutas, *Greek Thought, Arabic Culture: The Graeco-Arabic Translation Movement in Baghdad and Early Abbāsid Society (2nd–4th/8th–10th centuries)* (New York: Routledge, 1998), p. 30.
5. Richard W. Bulliet, *Conversion to Islam in the Medieval Period: An Essay in Quantitative History* (Cambridge, Mass.: Harvard University Press, 1979), p. 44, graph 5.
6. G. S. P. Freeman-Grenville, *The East African Coast: Select Documents from the First to the Earlier Nineteenth Century* (Oxford: Clarendon Press, 1962), excerpt # 5, "Buzurg Ibn Shahriyar of Ramhormuz: A Tenth-Century Slaving Adventure," pp. 9–13.
7. Abbott, pp. 89–90. Compare *The History of al-Tabari,* Vol. XXX: *The Abbasid Caliphate in Equilibrium,* trans. and annotated by C. E. Bosworth (Albany: State University of New York Press, 1989), p. 42; romanizations changed for consistency.
8. *The Abbasid Caliphate in Equilibrium,* p. 45; also translated in Abbott, p. 92.
9. *The Travels of Ibn Jubayr,* trans. R. J. C. Broadhurst (London: Jonathan Cape, 1952): number of pilgrims, p. 191; prayers and weeping, 180; riot and plunder, 184; bazaar goods, 184–185; road from Baghdad to Mecca, 216; palace of the caliph, 236; Frankish captives, 313.

Chapter 10

1. Magnus Magnusson and Hermann Palsson, trans., *The Vinland Sagas: The Norse Discovery of America* (New York: Penguin Books, 1965), pp. 97–98.
2. Warren Treadgold, *A History of the Byzantine State and Society* (Stanford: Stanford University Press, 1997), pp. 196, 297.
3. Katherine Fischer Drew, *The Laws of the Salian Franks* (Philadelphia: University of Pennsylvania Press, 1991), p. 127.
4. http://www.fordham.edu/halsall/source/gregtours1.html. "The Incident of the Vase at Soissons," in *Readings in European History,* ed. J. H. Robinson (Boston: Ginn, 1905), pp. 51–55.
5. Patrick J. Geary, *Before France and Germany: The Creation and Transformation of the Merovingian World* (New York: Oxford University Press, 1988), p. 115.
6. Ibid., p. 130.
7. R. W. Southern, *Western Society and the Church in the Middle Ages* (Harmondsworth: Penguin, 1970), p. 65.
8. Paul Edward Dutton, *Charlemagne's Courtier: The Complete Einhard* (Orchard Park, N.Y.: Broadview Press, 1998), II: 25.
9. Magnusson and Palsson: Warlock songs, pp. 82–83; a ghost's instructions on burial, 89–90; a former slave proposes to Gudrid, 80; Erik the Red and his father leaving Norway, 49; first encounter with Skraelings, 65; Skraeling catapult, 99; Skraeling life, 102–103; reasons for leaving the Americas, 100.
10. James E. Montgomery, "Ibn Fadlan and the Rusiyyah," *Journal of Arabic and Islamic* Studies 3 (2000): 10.
11. Serge A. Zenkovsky, *Medieval Russia's Epics, Chronicles, and Tales* (New York: E. P. Dutton, 1974), pp. 67–68.

Chapter 11

1. Because of differences in the calendars, Islamic years often straddle two Western years. Although most sources give the year in both the Islamic calendar and the Western, this chapter, like Chapter 9, will give only the Western equivalent.

2. H. A. R. Gibb, trans., *The Travels of Ibn Battuta* A.D. *1325–1354*, 4 vols. (London: Hakluyt Society, 1958–1994): departure from Tangier, I: 8; Mali griots, IV: 962; Taghaza and trading salt, IV: 947; inheritance in Mali, IV: 951; power of queens, IV: 963; Muslim practice, IV: 951; caravan leader and religious law, IV: 952; what was good, IV: 966; his divorce, I: 18; Ghazza, IV: 918; Damascus, I: 144; Mogadishu, II: 376; Kilwa, II: 379–380; Chinese ships, IV: 813–814.

3. David Lee Schoenbrun, *A Green Place, A Good Place: Agrarian Change, Gender, and Social Identity in the Great Lakes Region to the 15th Century* (Portsmouth, N.H.: Heinemann, 1998), p. 40.

4. Jan Vansina, *Paths in the Rainforest: Toward a History of Political Tradition in Equatorial Africa* (Madison: University of Wisconsin Press, 1990), pp. 31, 33.

5. Al-Bakri's *The Book of Routes and Realms,* as translated in *Corpus of Early Arabic Sources for West African History,* ed. N. Levtzion and J. F. P. Hopkins (New York: Cambridge University Press, 1981): Sijilmasa, pp. 65–66; Ghana, pp. 79–81.

6. Patricia and Fredrick McKissack, *The Royal Kingdoms of Ghana, Mali, and Songhay: Life in Medieval Africa* (New York: Henry Holt, 1994), p. 34.

7. D. T. Niane, *Sundiata: An Epic of Old Mali,* trans. G. D. Pickett (London: Longman, 1965).

8. D. T. Niane, "Mali and the Second Mandingo Expansion," in *General History of Africa* (California: Heinemann and UNESCO, 1984), p. 148, n. 62.

9. Ralph A. Austen, "The Trans-Saharan Slave Trade: A Tentative Census," in *The Uncommon Market: Essays in the Economic History of the Atlantic Slave Trade,* ed. Henry A. Gemery and Jan S. Hogendorn (New York: Academic Press, 1979), pp. 23–69; tables on pp. 31, 66.

10. Andrew M. Watson, "Back to Gold—and Silver," *Economic History Review* 20.1 (1967): 1–34, estimate in 30–31, n. 1.

11. Ross E. Dunn, *The Adventures of Ibn Battuta, a Muslim Traveler of the 14th Century* (Berkeley: University of California Press, 2005), p. 45.

12. J. N. Mattock, "Ibn Battuta's Use of Ibn Jubayr's Rihla," in *Proceedings of the Ninth Congress of the Union Européenne des arabisants et Islamisants,* ed. Rudolph Peters (Leiden: E. J. Brill, 1981), pp. 209–218, estimate on p. 211.

13. Michael W. Dols, *The Black Death in the Middle East* (Princeton: Princeton University Press, 1977), p. 215.

14. Peter Garlake, *Great Zimbabwe Described and Explained* (Harare: Zimbabwe Publishing House, 1982), p. 14.

15. P. S. Garlake, *Great Zimbabwe* (New York: Stein and Day, 1973): size of Elliptical Building, p. 27; estimate of number of laborers, 195; excavated horde, 131.

Chapter 12

1. Stephen Owen, "The Snares of Memory," in *Remembrances: The Experience of the Past in Classical Chinese Literature* (Cambridge: Harvard University Press, 1986): cartloads of books, p. 89; thirty years of calamity, 97; pawning clothes, 82; drinking game, 85; sacrificial vessels, 90.

2. *Women Writers of Traditional China: An Anthology of Poetry and Criticism,* ed. Kang-i Sun Chang and Haun Saussy (Stanford, Calif.: Stanford University Press, 1999), p. 98.

3. Valerie Hansen, *The Open Empire: A History of China to 1600* (New York: W. W. Norton, 2000), p. 266.

4. Tsien Tsuen-hsuin, *Chemistry and Chemical Technology, Part I: Paper and Printing,* vol. V:1 of *Science and Civilisation in China,* ed. Joseph Needham (New York: Cambridge University Press, 1985), pp. 201–202.

5. Patricia Buckley Ebrey, "The Women in Liu Kezhuang's Family," *Modern China* 10.4 (1984): 415–400, citation on 437.

6. Peter K. Bol, "The Sung Examination System and the Shih," *Asia Major,* 3d ser., 3.2 (1990): 149–171, statistic on 152.

7. Hansen, p. 295.

8. Ibid., p. 294.

9. Ellen Neskar, "Shrines to Local Former Worthies," in *Religions of China in Practice,* ed. Donald S. Lopez (Princeton: Princeton University Press, 1996).

10. Joseph Needham with Wang Ling, *Mathematics and the Sciences of the Heavens and the Earth,* vol. 3 of *Science and Civilisation in China,* ed. Joseph Needham (New York: Cambridge University Press, 1959), caption to fig. 226 facing p. 548.

11. Frederick Hirth and W. W. Rockhill, *Chau Ju-kua: His Work on the Chinese and Arab Trade in the Twelfth and Thirteenth Centuries, Entitled Chu-fan-chï* (St. Petersburg: Imperial Academy of Sciences, 1911): Vietnam, p. 46; Korea, 167; where the sun rises, 170; cedar planks, 171; Madagascar, 149.

Chapter 13

1. *The Letters of Abelard and Heloise,* trans. Betty Radice, rev. M. T. Clanchy (New York: Penguin Books, 2003), p. 3.

2. R. I. Moore, *The First European Revolution, c. 970–1215* (Oxford: Blackwell, 2000), p. 30, citing J. C. Russell.

3. Claudia Opitz, "Life in the Late Middle Ages," in *Silence of the Middle Ages,* ed. Chistiane Klapisch-Zuber, vol. 2 of *A History of Women in the West* (Cambridge, Mass.: Belknap Press of Harvard University Press, 1992), p. 296.

4. A. J. Minnis and A. B. Scott, *Medieval Literary Theory and Criticism, c. 1100–c. 1375* (Oxford: Clarendon Press, 1988), p. 99.

5. M. T. Clancy, *From Memory to Written Record,* 2d ed. (Oxford: Blackwell, 1993), pp. 120–121.

6. Joseph H. Lynch, *The Medieval Church: A Brief History* (London: Longman, 1992): inerrancy of the Roman Church, p. 146; Cistercians, 201; Franciscan followers, 232.

7. Robert the Monk's account, http://www.fordham.edu/halsall/source/urban2-5vers.html.

8. Francesco Gabrieli, *Arab Historians of the Crusades,* trans. E. J. Costello (London: Routledge and Kegan Paul, 1969), p. 100.

9. Thomas F. Madden, ed., *The Crusades: The Essential Readings* (Oxford: Blackwell, 2002), p. 109, n. 4; citing Robert of Clari, *The Conquest of Constantinople,* trans. Edgar Holmes McNeal (New York: Columbia University Press, 1936), p. 112.

10. Barbara H. Rosenwein, *A Short History of the Middle Ages* (Peterborough, Ont.: Broadview Press, 2002), p. 168.
11. Paul Freedman, "Spices and Late-Medieval European Ideas of Scarcity and Value," *Speculum* 80.4 (2005): 1209–1227.
12. Samuel K. Cohn, Jr., "The Black Death: End of a Paradigm," *American Historical Review* 107.3 (June 2002): 703–738: Avignon death statistics, p. 727; numbers of manuals, 707–708.

Chapter 14

1. Peter Jackson, trans., *The Mission of Friar William of Rubruck: His Journey to the Court of the Great Khan Möngke 1253–1255* (London: The Hakluyt Society, 1990): travel companions, pp. 70–71; division of labor, 90–91; khumis and open-air sleeping, 99; intense cold, 136; pick of horses, 140; description of Möngke, 178; drunk interpreter, 180; Hetum I's comments on William, Appendix V, 282; hunger, 141. Some changes made to avoid the use of brackets.
2. Joseph Fletcher, "The Mongols: Ecological and Social Perspectives," *Harvard Journal of Asiatic Studies* 46, no. 1 (1986): 1–56, explanation of tanistry on 17.
3. Ata-Malik Juvaini, *Genghis Khan: The History of the World Conqueror,* trans. J. A. Boyle (Seattle: University of Washington Press, 1958), p. 107.
4. André Wegener Sleeswyk, "The Liao and the Displacement of Ships in the Ming Dynasty," *The Mariner's Mirror* 81 (1996): 3–13.
5. Fei Xin, *Xingcha Shenglan: The Overall Survey of the Star Raft,* trans. J. V. G. Mills, rev. and ed. Roderich Ptak (Wiesbaden: Harrassowitz, 1996): size of ships and commodities at Mogadishu, p. 102.

Chapter 15

1. J. M. Cohen, trans., *The Four Voyages of Christopher Columbus* (New York: Penguin, 1969): description of Hispaniola, pp. 117–118; giving trifles, 35.
2. Michael E. Smith, *The Aztecs* (Malden, Mass.: Blackwell Publishing, 1996), p. 62, says four to six million.
3. Terence d'Altroy, *The Incas* (Malden, Mass.: Blackwell Publishing, 2002): mummies in Cuzco, p. 97 (citing Pedro Pizarro); human sacrifice statistics, 172; Inca insults, 226–227; population of the Inca empire, 48; storehouse of dried birds, 281.

4. Cassandra Fedele, "Oration to the University of Padua (1487)," in *The Renaissance in Europe: An Anthology,* ed. Peter Elmer et al. (New Haven: Yale University Press, in association with the Open University, 2000), pp. 52–56.
5. Peter Russell, *Prince Henry "the Navigator": A Life* (New Haven: Yale University Press, 2000), pp. 242–243, n. 8, citing *Crónica dos Feitos na Conquista de Guiné,* II:145–148.
6. Stuart B. Schwartz, *Victors and Vanquished: Spanish and Nahua Views of the Conquest of Mexico* (New York: Bedford/St. Martin's, 2000): Spanish weapons and armor, p. 97; description of Tenochtitlan, 133.
7. Michael Wood, *Conquistadors* (Berkeley: University of California Press, 2000), p. 81, citing the *Florentine Codex.*
8. Alfred W. Crosby, *The Columbian Exchange: Biological and Cultural Consequences of 1492* (Westport, Conn.: Greenwood Press, 1972), p. 4, n.2, citing Christopher Columbus, *Journals and Other Documents on the Life and Voyages of Christopher Columbus,* trans. Samuel Eliot Morison (New York: The Heritage Press, 1963), pp. 72–73, 84.
9. Smith, p. 61; Noble David Cook, *Demographic Collapse: Indian Peru, 1520–1620* (Cambridge: Cambridge University Press, 1981), p. 94.

Chapter 16

1. *The Diary of Matthew Ricci,* in Matthew Ricci, *China in the Sixteenth Century,* trans. Louis Gallagher (New York: Random House, 1942, 1970), pp. 54–55.
2. E. Mungello, *The Great Encounter of China and the West, 1500–1800,* 2d ed. (Lanham, Md.: Rowman and Littlefield, 2005).
3. Michael Pearson, *The Indian Ocean* (London: Routledge, 2003), p. 121.
4. James D. Tracy, *The Political Economy of Merchant Empires* (New York: Cambridge University Press, 1991), p. 1.
5. Cited in John Reader, *Africa: A Biography of the Continent* (New York: Vintage, 1999), pp. 374–375.
6. Steven Warshaw and C. David Bromwell with A. J. Tudisco, *India Emerges* (Berkeley: Diablo Press, 1974), p. 60.
7. Matteo Ricci, *The True Meaning of the Lord of Heaven,* trans. Douglas Lancashire and Peter Hu Kuo-chen, S.J. (Paris: Institut Ricci–Centre d'études chinoises, 1985), p. 99.

TEXT CREDITS

INDEX

Beijing, 379(map), 412; malaria in, 92; European merchants in, 380; Mongol conquest of, 394; Forbidden City in, 463

Belgium, 364

Belize, 117

Benedictine monks, 279

Benedict of Nursia, 279

Benedict XVI, Pope, 377

Bengal, 461

Benin, 458

Berber language, 250

Beringia land bridge, 13, 16, 20–21, 114

Bhagavad Gita, 70

Bhakti devotionalism, 214–215, 218, 222

Bharatiya Janata Party (India), 462

Bias, Bartholomew, 436

Bible, 171, 366, 437; Books of Tobit, 150–151; Hebrew Bible, 51–56, 203; human sacrifice in, 444–445; New Testament, 203, 248; translated into German, 469, 472; translated into Persian, 471(illus.)

Bipedalism, 6–7

Bi Sheng, 341–342 and illus.

Bishops, 200, 271; appointment of, 372; North African, 203, 204; councils of, 275, 372; Germanic peoples and, 278; monasteries and, 279; Great Schism and, 296

Black Death, 318. *See also* Plague; in Europe, 380–381

Black Sea region: Greek settlers in, 159(map); plague in, 318; European merchants in, 379

Blombos Cave (South Africa), 10–11

Blood rituals, in Maya, 126. *See also* Human sacrifice

Boats: *See also* Canoes; North American migration and, 16; Viking, 284 and illus.

Bodhisattvas, 212, 220, 230; images of, 219(illus.), 221(illus.), 229(illus.)

Bohemia, 254

Bolivia, 134; Amerindians in, 426

Bologna, University of, 366, 367, 370

Bombs and bombing, 332

Bone-rank system, 233, 234

Bonnichsen, Robson, 20

Book of Routes and Realms (al-Bakri), 247, 308

Book of the Dead (Egypt), 45

Books: *See also* Libraries; in Baghdad, 251–252; on travel to Mecca, 262–263; education boom, in China, 341–342 and illus., 344; in Korea, 342(illus.), 352, 433, 466; movable type and, 342(illus.), 352, 433; in Europe, 366; European, in China, 473

Borobudur, Buddhist monument at, 217, 220, 221(illus.)

Bourgeoisie, Dutch, 456

Bows and arrows (archers): Clovis people, 18; Hyksos, 46; Qin Chinese, 90; crossbows, 90, 364, 406; Mississippian, 132; Parthian, 170; Islamic, 248; Ghana, 308; Mali, 310; gunpowder used with, 332; English longbow, 382; Mongol, 392(illus.), 393 and illus., 406; Aztec Mexico, 424

Boycotts, by guilds, 367, 370

Brahmin priests, 69, 73, 77, 472; animal sacrifice and, 68, 82; Hinduism and, 212, 213, 214; ritual offerings made by, 216, 218; in Southeast Asia, 218

Brain size, of hominids, 7, 13

Brazil: Portuguese in, 436, 439, 443, 446; sugar and slavery in, 446, 457

Breadfruit, 138

Brihadeshwara Temple, 215(illus.)

Britain (England): Roman empire and, 191, 192; Viking settlements in, 283; Norman invasion of, 285; Industrial Revolution in, 337; farming in, 359; primogeniture in, 364; water mills in, 360; universities in, 370; Jews expelled from, 377; feudal society in, 380; Hundred Years' War and, 381–382; monarchy in, 382–383; Safavid Iran and, 455; West Africa colonies and, 458; Indian Ocean trade and, 464(map); Protestantism in, 470(map)

Bronze, 32, 36; Benin, 458; Chinese, 90, 92, 94–95 and illus.; Andean region, 134–135; Hittite, 50, 306; Chinese coins, 336, 347, 351; Inca, 427

Broquière, Bertrandon de la, 408

Bubonic plague, 381; in Byzantium, 271, 272, 273

Buddha (Siddhartha Gautama), 171; First Sermon of, 80–81; life of, 71–72; sculptures of, 73 and illus.; teachings of, 60, 72–73, 79

Buddhism, 476; rise of, 71–75; in India, 77; Ashoka and, 60, 62, 76, 79, 82–83, 210; stupa (monuments), 73, 74–75 and illus., 82, 220, 221(illus.); and Hinduism, in Southeast Asia, 217–219, 454; Lesser Vehicle (Hinayana), 212; Greater Vehicle (Mahayana), 211, 212, 228; chakravartin ideal ruler and, 79, 210, 222, 223, 224–225, 228; in China, 222–230, 240, 345, 346, 472; in Korea, 232 and illus., 233, 472; no-self doctrine in, 224; pilgrims, 217, 220, 233; Theravada, 212, 214; Zen, in Japan, 353, 467; in Vietnam, 352; in Mongolian Empire, 398, 401

Buddhist missionaries, 211, 213; in China, 223–224

Buddhist monks and monasteries: in India, 71, 72–73, 74, 82, 212, 213, 214; in China, 223, 224, 225, 229,

230, 347; in Japan, 234, 235; in Java, 220; in Korea, 231, 232; in Srivijaya, 217; travels of (Xuanzang), 208–210; in Vietnam, 352

Buddhist nuns, 73, 223, 347

Buddhist texts, 208, 210, 213, 347; in Japan, 353; woodblock printing of, 229(illus.), 352

Building. *See* Architecture and building; Housing; *specific building types*

Bukhara, 394, 403

Bulgaria, 296

Bulgars, 292–293, 403

Bureaucracy, 370, 469. *See also* Administration; Civil service examinations; Han China, 106, 107; Islamic caliphate, 252, 254; Song China, 331–332; Ottoman, 405; China, 463, 465

Burhan al-Din, 318

Burials: *See also* Tombs; early humans and, 9; Natufian, 22; at Catahoyuk, 25; in Mesoamerican pyramids, 122; in Southeast Asia, 218; North American mound builders, 131, 132; cremation, 9, 218, 286; Scandinavian, 286–287; Russian, 294–295

Burma, 454. *See* Myanmar (Burma)

Bursa, 405

Bushido code, 467

Business: *See also* East India companies; Dutch, 453, 455

Buyids, 260

Byzantine Empire, 205, 271–276. *See also* Constantinople; Constantine and, 199; Islam and, 245, 248, 249(illus.); plague in, 271, 272, 273, 274, 381; religion and state in, 274–276; Justinian and Roman legacy in, 271–272, 274; Carolingians and, 280; Kievan Rus and, 291(map), 293, 296; decline of, 276, 279; Russia and, 292; Seljuk Turks and, 374; Crusades and, 376; Ottoman conquest of, 405, 406–409

Cabot, John, 434(map)

Cabral, Pedro Álvares, 439, 443

Cacao, 125

Caesar (Rome), 184

Cahokia, 132

Cairo, 302, 314; Islamic caliphate in, 317, 318

Cajamarca, 443

Calendar: Olmec, 118–119; Maya, 125; Islamic, 244; Inca, 425

Calicut, 325, 412

Caliph, 241, 244

Caliphate: *See also* Abbasid caliphate; armies of, 171; roadbuilding in, 257, 258(illus.), 265; Umayyad, 240, 241, 248–249, 255(map); in Cairo, 317, 318

Calvinism, 470(map); Dutch, 456(illus.)